Programming with Constraints

Programming with Constraints:
An Introduction

Kim Marriott and Peter J. Stuckey

The MIT Press
Cambridge, Massachusetts
London, England

This book was set in Computer Modern by the authors using LaTeX and was printed and bound in the United States of America.

Library of Congress Cataloging-in-Publication Data

Marriott, Kim.
  Programming with constraints: an introduction / Kim Marriott and Peter J. Stuckey.
    p.   cm.
  Includes bibliographical references and index.
  ISBN 0-262-13341-5 (hardcover: alk. paper)
  1. Logic programming. 2. Constraint programming (Computer science).
I. Stuckey, Peter J. II. Title.
QA76.63.M37 1998
005.13—dc21   97-40549
                                                                                CIP

To Cole and Maria

Contents

Preface   **xi**

Introduction   **1**

    Notes 6

I   **Constraints**   **9**

1 **Constraints**   **11**

    1.1   Constraints and Valuations 11

    1.2   Modelling with Constraints 15

    1.3   Constraint Satisfaction 18

    1.4   Tree Constraints 22

    1.5   Other Constraint Domains 27

    1.6   Properties of Constraint Solvers 33

    1.7   (*) Determined Variables and Local Propagation 35

    1.8   Summary 41

    1.9   Exercises 42

    1.10 Practical Exercises 43

    1.11 Notes 47

2 **Simplification, Optimization and**

    Implication   **51**

    2.1   Constraint Simplification 51

    2.2   Projection 53

    2.3   Constraint Simplifiers 57

    2.4   Optimization 61

    2.5   The Simplex Algorithm 63

    2.6   (*) Canonical Form Simplifiers 72

    2.7   (*) Implication and Equivalence 75

    2.8   Summary 78

    2.9   Exercises 79

    2.10 Practical Exercises 80

    2.11 Notes 83

3   Finite Constraint Domains   **85**
   3.1   Constraint Satisfaction Problems   86
   3.2   A Simple Backtracking Solver   88
   3.3   Node and Arc Consistency   91
   3.4   Bounds Consistency   97
   3.5   Generalized Consistency   109
   3.6   Optimization for Arithmetic CSPs   114
   3.7   Summary   120
   3.8   Exercises   122
   3.9   Practical Exercises   123
   3.10 Notes   127

II   Constraint Logic Programming   **131**

4   Constraint Logic Programs   **133**
   4.1   User-Defined Constraints   133
   4.2   Programming with Rules   137
   4.3   Evaluation   140
   4.4   Derivation Trees and Finite Failure   143
   4.5   Goal Evaluation   146
   4.6   Simplified Derivation Trees   149
   4.7   The CLP Scheme   151
   4.8   (*) Independence from Rule Ordering and Literal Selection   153
   4.9   Summary   158
   4.10 Exercises   158
   4.11 Practical Exercises   160
   4.12 Notes   164

5   Simple Modelling   **167**
   5.1   Simple Modelling   167
   5.2   Modelling Choice   169
   5.3   Iteration   174
   5.4   Optimization   179
   5.5   Summary   181
   5.6   Practical Exercises   181
   5.7   Notes   184

6   Using Data Structures   **185**
   6.1   Records   186
   6.2   Lists   188
   6.3   Association Lists   193
   6.4   Binary Trees   198
   6.5   Hierarchical Modelling   201
   6.6   Tree Layout   203

6.7   Summary 208
6.8   Practical Exercises 208
6.9   Notes 211

7   Controlling Search   213
7.1   Estimating the Efficiency of a CLP Program 213
7.2   Controlling Search: An Example 217
7.3   Rule Ordering 220
7.4   Literal Ordering 220
7.5   Adding Redundant Constraints 223
7.6   Minimization 227
7.7   Identifying Deterministic Subgoals 230
7.8   An Extended Example: Bridge Building 235
7.9   Summary 246
7.10 Exercises 247
7.11 Practical Exercises 248
7.12 Notes 250

8   Modelling with Finite Domain Constraints   251
8.1   Domains and Labelling 252
8.2   Complex Constraints 256
8.3   Labelling 258
8.4   Different Problem Modellings 266
8.5   An Extended Example: Scheduling 272
8.6   (*) Arc Consistency 281
8.7   (*) Reified Constraints 284
8.8   Summary 285
8.9   Practical Exercises 286
8.10 Notes 291

9   Advanced Programming Techniques   293
9.1   Extending the Constraint Solver 293
9.2   Combined Symbolic and Arithmetic Reasoning 298
9.3   Programming Optimization 301
9.4   Higher-order Predicates 307
9.5   Negation 309
9.6   CLP Languages with Dynamic Scheduling 313
9.7   (*) Meta Programming 320
9.8   (*) Library Predicates 324
9.9   Summary 342
9.10 Practical Exercises 343
9.11 Notes 346

10 CLP Systems   349
10.1 Simple Backtracking Goal Evaluation 349

10.2   Incremental Constraint Solving 352
10.3   Efficient Saving and Restoring of the Constraint Store 358
10.4   Implementing If-Then-Else, Once and Negation 361
10.5   Optimization 366
10.6   Other Incremental Constraint Solvers 369
10.7   (*) Incremental Real Arithmetic Solving 376
10.8   Summary 385
10.9   Exercises 385
10.10 Notes 387

III   Other Constraint Programming Languages   389

11 Constraint Databases   391

11.1   Modelling with Constraint Databases 391
11.2   Bottom Up Evaluation 395
11.3   Bottom-Up versus Top-Down 405
11.4   Mimicking Top-Down Evaluation Bottom-Up 407
11.5   (*) Improving Termination 412
11.6   (*) Relationship with Relational Databases 416
11.7   Summary 421
11.8   Exercises 422
11.9   Practical Exercises 422
11.10 Notes 423

12 Other Constraint Programming Languages   425

12.1   The CLP Paradigm 425
12.2   Concurrent Constraint Programming Languages 427
12.3   Constraint Handling Rules 430
12.4   Functional Languages 433
12.5   Term Rewriting 436
12.6   Imperative Programming Languages 439
12.7   Constraint Solving Toolkits 440
12.8   Mathematical Languages 443
12.9   Notes 447

References   449

Index   459

Preface

This book has its roots in lecture notes which we prepared for a course on constraint logic programming given at both Monash University and the University of Melbourne for fourth year level students. The rapidly growing interest in constraint programming and, in particular, constraint logic programming, suggested that a course, which treated the area in some depth, should be offered. However, no adequate text was available. There are several good texts covering some aspects of such a course such as Tsang's *Foundations of Constraint Satisfaction*, Van Hentenryck's *Constraint Satisfaction in Logic Programming* (for constraint logic programming techniques for finite domains), and Sterling and Shapiro's *The Art of Prolog* (for logic programming techniques). However, a comprehensive introductory text covering constraint programming, one of the most interesting programming language paradigms ever invented, did not exist.

We hope that the present book provides such an introduction to the discipline of constraint programming and, in particular, constraint logic programming languages. It is self-contained, providing the necessary background material from artificial intelligence, logic programming, operations research and mathematical programming.

The book covers a wide spectrum of topics, from constraint solving techniques to programming methodologies for constraint programming languages. The chapters are organized into three parts:

1. **Constraints**. In this part, we discuss particular constraint domains and constraint solving techniques as well as other operations on constraints such as simplification, optimization and implication. Arithmetic, tree and finite domain constraint solving are discussed in some detail. Constraint satisfaction problems and generic constraint solving techniques are also introduced.

2. **Constraint Logic Programming**. Here, we introduce constraint logic programming languages and the way in which they can be used to build user-defined constraints. We then continue by examining techniques for modelling constraint problems using constraint logic programs. Example programs are taken from real-world applications of constraint programming and include financial modelling, circuit analysis, engineering design and job scheduling. Then we explore efficiency issues and how to write more efficient programs. Next we look at several advanced programming techniques that are used in constraint logic programming for extending or modifying the underlying solver and execution mechanism. Finally we discuss in some detail how practical CLP systems are implemented.

3. **Other Constraint Programming Languages**. In this part, we introduce other approaches to constraint programming. These include: constraint databases, which are similar to constraint logic programs, except that a bottom-up execution mechanism is used; concurrent constraint programming languages, which extend constraint logic programming languages by allowing parallel execution of procedures and asynchronous communication between procedures by way of constraint entailment; constraint toolkits, which provide constraint-solving within an object-oriented language; mathematical constraints languages, which are languages used by mathematicians to reason about constraints; constraint functional programming languages which combine constraint programming with functional programming; and constraint imperative languages which combine constraint programming techniques with object oriented languages.

How to Use This Book

The book has been designed to allow its use in a variety of courses at the undergraduate or postgraduate level. The first and second parts contain both core and supplementary chapters, the latter covering more esoteric or advanced material. The core chapters in the first two parts can be used to introduce constraint programming as part of an undergraduate course in modern programming language paradigms. Covering all the material in the first two parts provides a short postgraduate course in constraint programming. A longer course can also cover some of the material in the third part.

Some sections of the book are annotated with a (*). This indicates that the material is not core to the book and can be omitted if desired. Exercises and practical exercises that are annotated (*) are either more challenging or go beyond the material within the chapter.

An outline of the organization of the book is illustrated in Figure A. Core chapters are aligned in a column under the introduction. An arrow between two chapters indicates a dependency.

Programs are presented in a manner that is independent of any actual constraint logic programming language. This is because there is, as yet, no agreed syntax for these. When teaching from this book we have made use of the $CLP(\mathcal{R})$ and ECLiPSe constraint logic programming systems, which are both freely available for research and teaching purposes, as well as SICStus Prolog. Details of how to obtain these constraint logic programming systems is contained in the practical exercises sections of Chapters 1 and 3. Information about how to use each of these systems is given in the practical exercises sections of Chapters 1, 2, 3, 4, 8 and 9. The book is also designed for easy use with other constraint logic programming systems such as Prolog IV, clp(fd), and others.

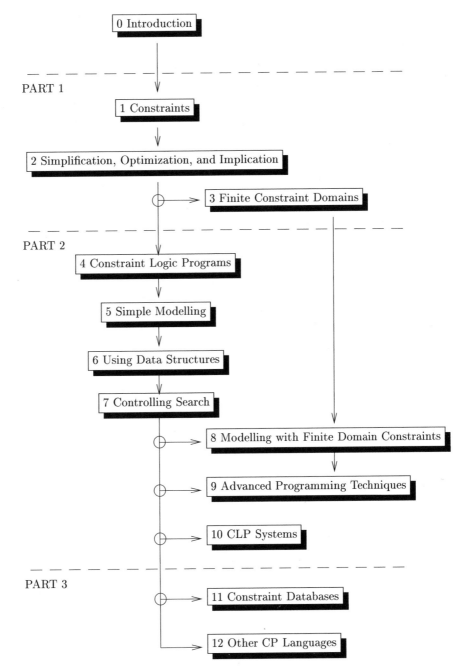

Figure A: Chapter dependencies.

Acknowledgements

Numerous people helped us by reviewing drafts of the book: John Crossley, Michael Maher and Rosemary Marriott provided invaluable help by reading and rereading successive drafts of the book, while Natashia Boland, Alan Borning, Graham Farr, Volker Gaede, Joxan Jaffar, Jimmy Lee, Steve Murphy, Harald Søndergaard, Mark Wallace and Roland Yap provided advice about specific topics and chapters. Of course, we are responsible for all remaining errors.

Harald Søndergaard provided many of the notes and references for Chapter 1 and we are grateful to Gert Smolka for permission to include the Oz program on page 435 and to Jean-François Puget for permission to include the ILOG SOLVER program on page 441. We would also like to thank Bob Prior of MIT Press for his encouragement and support and Deborah Cantor-Adams for her careful proofreading of the final manuscript.

Our partners, to whom this book is dedicated, have also contributed in many ways to this book, both directly and indirectly. Nicole Beyer provided valuable advice about graphic design and layout, while María García de la Banda carefully proofread several drafts. Most importantly, however, they helped each of us to keep the writing of this book in perspective.

Kim Marriott
Peter Stuckey

Programming with Constraints

Introduction

Constraint programming is one of the most exciting developments in programming languages of the last decade. Based on a strong theoretical foundation, it is attracting widespread commercial interest and is now becoming the method of choice for modelling many types of optimization problems, in particular, those involving heterogeneous constraints and combinatorial search. Not surprisingly, therefore, constraint programming has recently been identified by the ACM (Association for Computing Machinery) as one of the strategic directions in computing research.

The reason for this interest in constraint programming is simple. Early programming languages, such as FORTRAN-66, closely reflected the underlying physical architecture of the computer. Since then, the major direction of programming language design has been to give the programmer freedom to define objects and procedures which correspond to entities and operations in the application domain. Object oriented languages, in particular, provide good mechanisms for declaring program components which capture the behaviour of entities in a particular problem domain. However, traditional programming languages, including object oriented languages, provide little support for specifying *relationships* or *constraints* among programmer-defined entities. It is the role of the programmer to explicitly maintain these relationships, and to find objects which satisfy them.

For instance, consider Ohm's Law,

$$V = I \times R,$$

which describes the relationship between voltage V, current I and resistance R in a resistor. In a traditional programming language, the programmer cannot use this relationship directly, instead it must be encoded into statements which compute a value for one of the variables given values for the other two variables. Thus, I can be computed from V and R using the assignment

```
I := V / R.
```

But if the value of R must be determined from the other two, a different assignment statement is needed:

```
R := V / I.
```

Requiring the programmer to explicitly maintain relationships between objects in the program is reasonable for applications in which the relationships are simple and static. However, for many applications, the crux of the problem is to model the relationships and find objects that satisfy them. For this reason, since the late 1960's, there has been interest in programming languages which allow the programmer simply to state relationships between objects. It is the role of the underlying implementation to ensure that these relationships or "constraints" are maintained. Such languages are called *constraint programming* languages.

The first pioneering constraint programming languages were only partly successful. They involved augmenting a traditional language with constraints solved by simple ad hoc techniques. These languages primarily depended on "local" propagation for constraint solving. Local propagation works by using a constraint to assign a value to an unknown variable given known values for the other variables in the constraint. For instance, Ohm's Law can be used to compute a value for R, I or V, given the other two variables have known values. The problem with local propagation is that it is a relatively weak constraint solving method. For example, it cannot be used to solve simultaneous equations such as $X = Y - Z$ and $X = 2 \times Y + Z$. Owing partly to a reliance on local propagation these early languages had two major weaknesses: the constraint solving facilities were not powerful enough and the languages were not sufficiently expressive. This meant that the languages were not general-purpose, but rather primarily application oriented.

In the last decade there has been renewed interest in constraint programming languages. More recent constraint programming languages have overcome the difficulties of the early languages. They provide constraints which are thoroughly integrated into the programming language, allowing the programmer to state problems at a very high level, while their underlying execution mechanism uses powerful incremental constraint solvers. The new generation of constraint programming languages are true programming languages which are suited for a wide variety of applications.

As a simple example of an application using a modern constraint programming language, imagine that you are buying a house and want to investigate various options for repaying your loan. At each repayment interval, the amount of interest that is accrued is $P \times I$ where P is the amount borrowed (or principal) and I is the interest rate. The accrued interest is added to the current principle to obtain a new principal NP. If any repayment R is made this is subtracted. This behaviour is encapsulated in the equational constraint

$$NP = P + P \times I - R.$$

A multiple period loan (mortgage) that lasts for T time periods can be described by repeatedly applying this calculation, once for every time period, until there are no periods remaining. The final amount owing is called the balance B. This behaviour is encapsulated in the following constraint program:

```
mortgage(P, T, I, R, B) :-
    T = 0,
    B = P.
mortgage(P, T, I, R, B) :-
    T ≥ 1,
    NT = T - 1,
    NP = P + P * I - R,
    mortgage(NP, NT, I, R, B).
```

The user-defined constraint `mortgage` defines the relationship between the initial principal P, time of loan T, interest rate I, repayment amount R and final balance B. The first rule (the first 3 lines) handles the case when no time periods remain. In this case the balance is simply the current principal. The second rule (the last 5 lines) handles the case in which the number of periods remaining is greater than or equal to one. In this case a new time (NT) of one less is calculated. Then the change to the principal is calculated. The remainder of the loan is determined by considering it to be a new loan with the new amount owing for one less time period.

An equivalent program may seem easy to write in a traditional language such as C. The advantage of this program is, because all the statements are made up of constraints, it is extremely versatile. Program execution is initiated by giving a goal which the system then rewrites to constraints. For example, consider borrowing $1000 for 10 years at an interest rate of 10% and repaying $150 per year. This is expressed by the goal

```
mortgage(1000, 10, 10/100, 150, B).
```

Given this goal, the answer returned by the program is $B = 203.129$, indicating that the balance remaining will be $203.13.

The same program can be used in many other ways. For example, given the repayment is $150 and at the end of the loan the remaining balance should be 0, we may wish to ask "how much can be borrowed in a 10 year loan at 10% with repayments of $150 ?" This question is expressed by the goal

```
mortgage(P, 10, 10/100, 150, 0).
```

The answer given is $P = 921.685$. A more complex query is to ask for the relationship between the initial principal, repayment and balance in a 10 year loan at 10%. This is done with the goal:

```
mortgage(P, 10, 10/100, R, B).
```

The answer is the constraint, $P = 0.3855 * B + 6.1446 * R$, relating the variables P, R and B.

In all of these cases the *same* program has been used to solve the given problem. This contrasts with a conventional programming language in which a different program would be required to answer each of these queries. Indeed, writing a program to answer the last query would be quite difficult. Constraint programming has allowed us to specify the problem very naturally, and at a high level, in terms of arithmetic constraints. It is the job of the underlying language implementation to solve these constraints, rather than the job of the programmer.

This example program illustrates how constraint programming can be naturally used to model complex applications. For this reason constraint programming has been used in many diverse areas. The engineering disciplines are one area in which constraint programming has been applied with notable success. Many engineering problems are extremely well suited to constraint programming since they often involve hierarchical composition of complex systems, mathematical or Boolean models, and—especially in the case of diagnosis and design—deep rule-based reasoning. Another major area has been options trading and financial planning, where applications usually take the form of expert systems involving mathematical models. More exotic applications have included restriction site mapping in genetics and generation of test data for communications protocols.

Arguably, however, the most important application of the new constraint programming languages is for tackling difficult multi-faceted combinatorial problems, such as those encountered in job scheduling, timetabling and routing. These kinds of problems are very difficult to express and solve in conventional programming languages. This is because they require searching through a possibly exponentially sized solution space in order to find a good or optimal solution to the problem. To obtain reasonable efficiency, the constraints must be used to prune the search space.

There are two traditional approaches to solving difficult combinatorial problems: either hand-craft an algorithm which will solve the exact problem in a traditional programming language, or else model the problem using an off-the-shelf solver for a particular class of arithmetic constraints. The drawback of a hand-crafted solver is that it is expensive and it is not easy to modify when the problem changes. The drawback of an off-the-shelf solver is that it is unlikely to be sufficiently expressive for constraints in the application domain to be expressed naturally and flexible enough to allow domain-specific heuristics to be used in the solver. Modern constraint programming languages overcome these problems by providing a programming language built on top of a sophisticated constraint solver. This means that a programmer can code domain-specific methods in the programming language, while generic solving techniques are provided by the language implementation.

As a simple example, consider the crypto-arithmetic problem:

$$
\begin{array}{ccccc}
 & S & E & N & D \\
+ & & M & O & R & E \\
\hline
= & M & O & N & E & Y \\
\end{array}
$$

where each letter represents a different digit and the arithmetic equation holds. This is modelled by the following constraint program:

```
smm(S,E,N,D,M,O,R,Y) :-
    [S,E,N,D,M,O,R,Y] :: [0..9],
    constrain([S,E,N,D,M,O,R,Y]),
    labeling([S,E,N,D,M,O,R,Y]).

constrain([S,E,N,D,M,O,R,Y]) :-
    S ≠ 0, M ≠ 0,
    alldifferent_neq([S,E,N,D,M,O,R,Y]),
                1000*S + 100*E + 10*N + D
    +           1000*M + 100*O + 10*R + E
    = 10000*M + 1000*O + 100*N + 10*E + Y.
```

In the program, each of the variables S, E, N, D, M, O, R and Y is declared to range over the values [0..9] while the other constraints in the problem are defined by the user-defined constraint constrain. The underlying solver for such integer constraints is very fast, employing sophisticated propagation techniques. The price of this speed is that the solver is incomplete, and so may return an answer *unknown* indicating that it does not know if there is a solution or not. In this example, the programmer has called an auxiliary function, labeling, which extends the underlying solver by using search to try different values in the range [0..9] for each variable. This means that the program is guaranteed to find a solution when it exists. In this case, labeling is a library function provided by the system, but a strength of the CLP approach is that the programmer can define their own problem-specific solver extension. Given the goal smm(S,E,N,D,M,O,R,Y), the program will quickly determine that $S = 9$, $E = 5$, $N = 6$, $D = 7$, $M = 1$, $O = 0$, $R = 8$ and $Y = 2$.

The first modern constraint programming languages were extensions of logic programming languages. These languages were called *constraint logic programming languages* and extended logic programming languages such as Prolog by replacing unification with a test for constraint satisfaction using a dedicated solver. They arose from research in Europe and Australia in the late 1980's. Both programs given above are examples of constraint logic programs. Different solvers and different application domains led to different languages which share a common evaluation mechanism.

Inspired by the success of constraint logic programming, several other classes of constraint programming languages have recently been suggested. These include: concurrent constraint languages which use constraint entailment to extend constraint logic programming languages by providing asynchronous communication between "agents," constraint query languages for databases which extend relational databases by allowing tuples that contain "constrained variables," constraint functional programming languages, constraint imperative programming languages, and object oriented constraint solving toolkits.

Constraint logic programming languages are, however, the archetypal constraint programming languages. They are, in a sense, the minimal and purest constraint programming languages since, essentially, the only operation a programmer can perform is to define new "user-defined" constraints in terms of the primitive constraints supported by the underlying solver. For this reason, an understanding of constraint logic programming is relevant to any constraint programming language.

A striking feature of constraint programming is its multi-disciplinary nature. It embraces facets of mathematics, traditional computer science and artificial intelligence. Constraint programming draws on work in constraint solving algorithms from operations research, numerical computing and on constraint solving techniques used in constraint satisfaction problems, an important area of artificial intelligence. It also draws on techniques from programming language design and implementation, from automated reasoning, as well as from database theory and implementation.

The present book provides an introduction to the exciting new discipline of constraint programming and, in particular, constraint logic programming languages. It is self-contained and covers the necessary background material from artificial intelligence, logic programming, operations research and mathematical programming.

Notes

Sutherland's SKETCHPAD [133] was one of the first computer systems to employ constraints. A constraint-based graphic editor, it employed relaxation and numerical techniques to solve arithmetic constraints modelling the relations between graphical objects.

Earlier constraint programming languages were suggested by, among others, Steele [123] and Borning [14]. These languages allowed the user to describe the behaviour of systems using static collections of constraints. In Steele's language CONSTRAINTS simple macro definitions of constraints were allowed, while in the Thinglab system [14] constraints were constructed through a graphical interface. In essence, these languages were domain specific modelling languages without the computational power of true programming languages.

Constraint logic programming (CLP) languages arose from research at three different locations. In Melbourne, Joxan Jaffar and Jean-Louis Lassez gave a semantic foundation [69] and, with others, developed the language CLP($\mathcal{R}$) [75], while in Marseilles Alain Colmerauer and his group developed an extension of Prolog called Prolog-III [35] and in Munich, at the European Computer-Industry Research Center (ECRC), a team headed by Mehmet Dincbas developed the language CHIP [44] and employed it to solve many different types of combinatorial problems.

Concurrent constraint languages originate from work on concurrent logic programming languages. Maher [90] and Saraswat [115] generalized the ideas behind these languages to the context of constraints. Kanellakis [77] introduced constraint query languages, while Darlington was the first to study constraint functional programming languages [39]. One popular constraint programming language, Oz, developed by Smolka and his research group, extends concurrent constraint programming to also allow functions [121, 120]. Kaleidoscope, developed by Borning, Freeman-

Benson and others, is the first constraint imperative programming language [49]. There are now several object oriented constraint solving toolkits. One of the first was an object oriented Lisp based toolkit called PECOS [105] which was the precursor to the commercially available C++ based ILOG SOLVER [106]. Further references for these different paradigms can be found at the end of Chapters 11 and 12.

Constraint programming is now a fertile research area, with two main international conferences: *Principles and Practice of Constraint Programming (CP)*, proceedings of which are published by Springer-Verlag in the Lecture Notes in Computer Science Series; and *Practical Applications of Constraint Technology (PACT)*, proceedings of which are published by The Practical Application Company. There are also numerous international workshops devoted to specific applications and classes of languages, together with sessions at the major international conferences on programming languages. One journal, *Constraints*, published by Kluwer Academic is exclusively devoted to constraints and constraint programming. Many other journals, in particular *The Journal of Logic Programming* and *Artificial Intelligence*, also publish papers on constraint programming. Information about constraint programming is available on the internet starting from the Constraints Archive at `http://www.cirl.uoregon.edu/constraints/` and through the news group `comp.constraints`.

I Constraints

1   Constraints

Constraint programming is built upon constraints and constraint solving. Therefore, some knowledge of different constraint domains and algorithms for constraint manipulation is needed to fully understand the constraint programming paradigm.

In the first part of this book we introduce the three most important types of constraints in constraint programming: arithmetic constraints, tree constraints and finite domain constraints. We also investigate three fundamental operations involving constraints. The most important operation is to determine if a constraint is satisfiable. The second operation, simplification, rewrites a constraint in a form which makes its information more apparent. The third operation, optimization, finds a solution which is "best" according to some criterion.

In this chapter we introduce constraints and study the most basic question we can ask about a system of constraints—is it "satisfiable," that is to say, does the system have a solution? Constraints are a mathematical formalization of relationships which can hold between objects. For example "next to" or "father of" are constraints which hold between objects in the real world. We will be chiefly concerned with more idealized constraints between mathematical objects, such as numbers. Real world constraints and objects can be modelled by these idealized mathematical constraints. Building such models is the job of the constraint programmer.

1.1   Constraints and Valuations

The statement $X = Y + 2$ is an example of a *constraint*. X and Y are *variables*, that is they are *place-holders* for values, presumably in this case numbers. It stipulates a relation which must hold between any values with which we choose to replace X and Y, namely, the first must be two greater than the second. The statement $X = Y + 2$ is not simply true or false. Its status depends on the values we substitute for X and Y. However, when we have a statement involving variables, one question we can meaningfully ask is whether *any* substitution will yield truth. In the case of $X = Y + 2$ the answer is clearly *yes* (take $X = 3$ and $Y = 1$, for example), but in other cases the answer will be *no*, witness $X = X + 2$. Occasionally the answer may even be *don't know*!

Throughout this book we shall use strings which start with an upper case letter or an underscore "_" to name variables. For example: $X, Y, CI, T_A, List, \_X, \_List$ are all variables.

Constraints occur in all sorts of everyday reasoning. Consider the following constraint which describes a simple loan. Let P be the principal of the loan (the amount to be borrowed), let I be the interest rate of the loan (so $I \times P$ is the amount of interest to be paid), and let B be the final balance of the loan (the amount owed at the end). Then the constraint

$$B = P + I \times P$$

describes the relationship forced to hold between these variables in a simple loan. For example, if the principal P is \$1000 and the interest rate I is 12% (that is 12/100), then the balance must be \$1120. The constraint imposes a value on the balance given the principal and interest rate, but it also works in other ways. Suppose the balance B is \$2100 and the principal P is \$2000, then the interest rate I must be 5% or 5/100, because it is the only number that satisfies the relationship

$$2100 = 2000 + I \times 2000.$$

The legitimate forms of constraint and their meaning is specified by a *constraint domain*. Constraints are written in a language made up of constants like 0 and 1, functions like $+$ and $\times$, and constraint relations like equality ($=$) and less-than-or-equal-to ($\leq$).

The constraint domain specifies the "syntax" of the constraints. That is, it specifies the rules for creating constraints in the domain. It details the allowed constants, functions and constraint relations as well as how many arguments each function and constraint relation is required to have and how the arguments are placed. For instance, both $+$ and $\leq$ require two arguments and are written between their arguments.

The constraint domain also determines the values that variables can take. For example, the constraint $X \times X \leq 1/2$ means quite different things depending on whether X can take integer values, real values, or complex values.

Finally, the constraint domain determines the meaning of all of these symbols. It determines what will be the result of applying a function to its arguments and whether a constraint relation holds for given arguments. For example, for arithmetic the application of the $+$ function in the expression $3 + 4$ evaluates to 7, and the constraint $1 \leq 2$ holds while it is not the case that $2 \leq 1$ holds.

Given a constraint domain $\mathcal{D}$ the simplest form of constraint we can define is a *primitive constraint*. A primitive constraint consists of a constraint relation symbol from $\mathcal{D}$ together with the appropriate number of arguments. These are constructed from the constants and functions of $\mathcal{D}$ and variables. Most constraint relations are binary, that is they require two arguments.

For example, in the constraint domain of real numbers, which we call *Real*, variables take real number values. We shall use *Real* as the default constraint domain throughout most of the text. The set of function symbols for this constraint domain is $+, \times, -$ and $/$, while the set of constants is all the floating point numbers. The constraint relation symbols are $=, <, \leq, >, \geq$, all of which take two arguments. $X > 3$ and $X + Y \times Y - 3 \times Z = 5$ are examples of primitive constraints.

More complicated constraints can be built from primitive constraints by using the conjunctive connective $\wedge$ which stands for "and". Consider a second year of the loan. The balance after two years, $B2$, is related to the balance after the first year, B, and the interest rate I, as follows: $B2 = B + I \times B$. Hence the entire two year loan is described by:

$$B = P + I \times P \ \wedge \ B2 = B + I \times B.$$

We can use the constraint to calculate values of interest. For example, if the initial principal is \$1000, and the interest rate is 12%, then the balance after two years, $B2$, is \$1254.40. In general, constraints are just sequences of primitive constraints, joined by conjunction.

Definition 1.1

A *constraint* is of the form $c_1 \wedge \cdots \wedge c_n$ where $n \geq 0$ and $c_1, \ldots, c_n$ are primitive constraints. The symbol $\wedge$ denotes *and*, so a constraint $c_1 \wedge \cdots \wedge c_n$ holds whenever all of the primitive constraints $c_1, \ldots, c_n$ hold.

There are two distinct constraints *true* and *false*. The constraint *true* always holds, while *false* never holds. The empty conjunction of constraints (when $n = 0$) is written as *true*.

The *conjunction* of two constraints C_1 and C_2, written $C_1 \wedge C_2$ is defined to be

$$c_1 \wedge \cdots \wedge c_n \wedge c'_1 \wedge \cdots \wedge c'_m$$

where C_1 is $c_1 \wedge \cdots \wedge c_n$ and C_2 is $c'_1 \wedge \cdots \wedge c'_m$.

Given a constraint, we can determine values of variables for which the constraint holds. By replacing variables by their values, the constraint can be simplified to a variable-free constraint which may then be seen to be either true or false. For example, consider the constraint

$$B = P + I \times P \wedge \ B2 = B + I \times B.$$

The assignment of values to variables

$$\{P \mapsto 1000, I \mapsto 20/100, B \mapsto 1200, B2 \mapsto 1440\}$$

makes the constraint take the form

$$1200 = 1000 + 20/100 \times 1000 \wedge 1440 = 1200 + 20/100 \times 1200$$

which after some simplification can be seen to be true. The assignment

$$\{P \mapsto 0, I \mapsto 1, B \mapsto 1, B2 \mapsto 1\}$$

leaves the constraint in the form

$$1 = 0 + 1 \times 0 \wedge 1 = 1 + 1 \times 1$$

which is false.

Definition 1.2

A *valuation* θ for a set V of variables is an assignment of values from the constraint domain to the variables in V. Suppose $V = \{X_1, \ldots, X_n\}$ then θ may be written $\{X_1 \mapsto d_1, \ldots, X_n \mapsto d_n\}$ indicating that each X_i is assigned the value d_i.

An expression e over variables V is given a value $\theta(e)$ under the valuation θ over variables V. $\theta(e)$ is obtained by replacing each variable by its corresponding value and calculating the value of the resulting variable free expression. Let $vars(e)$ denote the set of variables occurring in an expression e. Similarly, let $vars(C)$ denote the set of variables occurring in a constraint C. If θ is a valuation for $V \supseteq vars(C)$, then it is a *solution* of C if $\theta(C)$ holds in the constraint domain.

A constraint C is *satisfiable* if it has a solution. Otherwise it is *unsatisfiable*.

For example, the value of the expression $P + I \times P$ under the valuation $\{P \mapsto 1000, I \mapsto 20/100\}$ is 1200. The valuation $\{X \mapsto 7\}$ is a solution of the constraint $X \geq 4$. Similarly $\{X \mapsto 5, Y \mapsto 7\}$ is a solution of $X \geq 4$, but $\{X \mapsto 0\}$ is not a solution. This constraint, since it has solutions, is satisfiable. In contrast, the constraint

$$X \leq 3 \wedge X = Y \wedge Y \geq 4$$

has no solutions—it is unsatisfiable.

We shall consider constraints as pieces of syntax, that is strings of symbols. Thus, for example, $X = Y$ and $Y = X$ are different constraints. We consider a constraint to be a sequence of primitive constraints, so bracketing is not required. For example, $(X = 0 \wedge Y = 1) \wedge Z = 2$ and $X = 0 \wedge (Y = 1 \wedge Z = 2)$ represent the same constraint. The order of constraints, however, does matter. For example, $X = 0 \wedge Y = 1$ is not the same constraint as $Y = 1 \wedge X = 0$. But even though these two constraints are different, clearly they represent the same information. Similarly $X = Y$ and $Y = X$ represent the same information. The following definition captures what it means for two constraints to contain the same information.

Definition 1.3

Two constraints C_1 and C_2 are *equivalent*, written $C_1 \leftrightarrow C_2$, if they have the same set of solutions.

The reason we consider constraints to be sequences of primitive constraints is because the order of the primitive constraints will prove to be important for some of the constraint manipulation algorithms we shall define later. Many algorithms, however, produce the same result, independent of the order and the number of occurrences of each primitive constraint. That is, in these algorithms constraints are treated as sets of primitive constraints. We shall find it useful to have a function which takes a constraint and returns the set of primitive constraints in the constraint:

Definition 1.4
The function *primitives* takes a constraint $c_1 \wedge \cdots \wedge c_n$ and returns the set of primitive constraints $\{c_1, \ldots, c_n\}$. That is to say,

$$primitives(c_1 \wedge \cdots \wedge c_n) = \{c_1, \ldots, c_n\}.$$

Clearly, if $primitives(C_1) = primitives(C_2)$ then $C_1 \leftrightarrow C_2$.

For example, $primitives(X = 0 \wedge Y = 1 \wedge X = 0)$ and $primitives(Y = 1 \wedge Y = 1 \wedge X = 0)$ are both $\{X = 0, Y = 1\}$. Not all equivalent constraints contain the same set of primitive constraints. For instance, $X \geq 0 \wedge Y = X + 2$ is equivalent to $X = Y - 2 \wedge Y \geq 2$.

Satisfiability and equivalence are some of the most basic questions we can ask about constraints and we shall return to these in Section 1.3 and Chapter 2 respectively. We first investigate why constraints are useful.

1.2 Modelling with Constraints

Constraints are used to model the behaviour of systems of objects in the real world by capturing an idealised view of the interaction among the objects. It is the job of the constraint programmer to simplify a real world situation into a system of constraints about idealised objects, and use this system of constraints to better understand the behaviour of the real world. The trick is to abstract at the right level—too much abstraction and the constraints lose the essence of the real world problem, too little abstraction and the constraints are too difficult to understand. The laws of physics are a well-known example of this type of modelling.

As an example, we shall now look at how electric circuits can be modelled by constraints. Ohm's Law,

$$V = I \times R$$

describes the relationship among voltage V, current I and resistance R in a resistor. Kirchhoff's Voltage Law (KVL) states that the sum of the voltages around any loop in a circuit must equate to zero. Dually Kirchhoff's Current Law (KCL) states that the sum of currents entering a junction in a circuit must equate to zero.

Consider the electric circuit shown in Figure 1.1. Using the above laws we can model the behaviour of the circuit. The following list gives the primitive constraints derived from the circuit together with their justification:

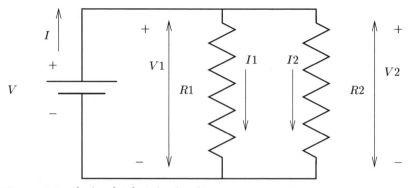

Figure 1.1   A simple electric circuit.

$$V_1 = I_1 \times R_1 \qquad \text{Ohm's Law for resistor 1,}$$
$$V_2 = I_2 \times R_2 \qquad \text{Ohm's Law for resistor 2,}$$
$$V - V_1 = 0 \qquad \text{KVL around the loop } (V, R_1),$$
$$V - V_2 = 0 \qquad \text{KVL around the loop } (V, R_2),$$
$$V_1 - V_2 = 0 \qquad \text{KVL around the loop } (R_1, R_2),$$
$$I - I_1 - I_2 = 0 \qquad \text{KCL at the top junction,}$$
$$-I + I_1 + I_2 = 0 \quad \text{KCL at the bottom junction.}$$

The conjunction of these primitive constraints models the behaviour of the complete circuit. Note that the same constraint information is repeated in some parts of the description, for example, $I - I_1 - I_2 = 0$ and $-I + I_1 + I_2 = 0$ are equivalent.

Given the constraint describing the circuit, we can investigate the circuit's behaviour under various conditions. Suppose the battery is 10V and the resistors $R_1 = 10\Omega$ and $R_2 = 5\Omega$. Then the constraint

$$V = 10 \wedge R_1 = 10 \wedge R_2 = 5 \wedge$$
$$V_1 = I_1 \times R_1 \wedge V_2 = I_2 \times R_2 \wedge$$
$$V - V_1 = 0 \wedge V - V_2 = 0 \wedge V_1 - V_2 = 0 \wedge$$
$$I - I_1 - I_2 = 0 \wedge -I + I_1 + I_2 = 0$$

describes the circuit. This constraint has the single solution

$$\{V \mapsto 10, R_1 \mapsto 10, R_2 \mapsto 5, V_1 \mapsto 10, V_2 \mapsto 10, I_1 \mapsto 1, I_2 \mapsto 2, I \mapsto 3\}.$$

Thus, if we are interested in the current, I, drawn from the battery in this situation, we find it is 3A.

Similarly, we can determine the behaviour when I_1 is known to be 5A, V is known to be 10V and R_2 is known to be 10Ω. In this case there is again a single solution

$$\{V \mapsto 10, R_1 \mapsto 2, R_2 \mapsto 10, V_1 \mapsto 10, V_2 \mapsto 10, I_1 \mapsto 5, I_2 \mapsto 1, I \mapsto 6\}.$$

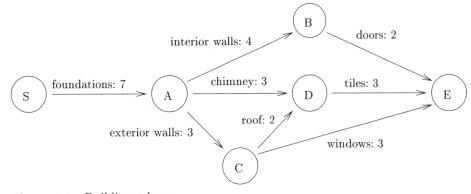

Figure 1.2 Building a house.

If we ask for the behaviour when V is 10V, R_1 is 5Ω, I is 1A and knowing only that the resistance of R_2 is some positive value, that is, $R_2 \geq 0$, we find there are no solutions, since the constraint

$$V = 10 \wedge R_1 = 5 \wedge I = 1 \wedge R_2 \geq 0 \wedge$$
$$V_1 = I_1 \times R_1 \wedge V_2 = I_2 \times R_2 \wedge$$
$$V - V_1 = 0 \wedge V - V_2 = 0 \wedge V_1 - V_2 = 0 \wedge$$
$$I - I_1 - I_2 = 0 \wedge \, - I + I_1 + I_2 = 0$$

describes an impossible situation, and so is unsatisfiable.

Information can be extracted from constraints even when there is more than one solution. Suppose we have that $R_1 = 10\Omega$ and $R_2 = 5\Omega$. In every solution to

$$R_1 = 10 \wedge R_2 = 5 \wedge$$
$$V_1 = I_1 \times R_1 \wedge V_2 = I_2 \times R_2 \wedge$$
$$V - V_1 = 0 \wedge V - V_2 = 0 \wedge V_1 - V_2 = 0 \wedge$$
$$I - I_1 - I_2 = 0 \wedge \, - I + I_1 + I_2 = 0$$

we find that the relationship $3 \times V = 10 \times I$ holds. We will later discuss how to obtain such information.

Constraints are not only useful for modelling physical systems. They may also be used to naturally model other types of systems, for example those occurring in project management. Consider building a house. This project can be broken down into smaller tasks such as: laying foundations, building interior and exterior walls, building the chimney and roof, fitting doors and windows and tiling the roof. Natural restrictions apply to the ordering of these tasks. For example, the roof must be built before it can be tiled. If each task is assigned a duration we can represent the relationships by the graph shown in Figure 1.2 where each arc represents a task, labelled by its name and duration in days, and the nodes represent stages in the project.

To reach a particular stage in the project we need to have completed all the tasks that point to that stage. This means for each such task we must have reached the stage required to begin the task at least a number of days before equal to the duration of the task. If we associate a variable T_s with the time for the earliest arrival at stage s in the project, we can write primitive constraints corresponding to each arc in Figure 1.2 that reflect this information as follows:

$$
\begin{array}{ll}
\text{start} & T_S \geq 0, \\
\text{foundation} & T_A \geq T_S + 7, \\
\text{interior walls} & T_B \geq T_A + 4, \\
\text{exterior walls} & T_C \geq T_A + 3, \\
\text{chimney} & T_D \geq T_A + 3, \\
\text{roof} & T_D \geq T_C + 2, \\
\text{doors} & T_E \geq T_B + 2, \\
\text{tiles} & T_E \geq T_D + 3, \\
\text{windows} & T_E \geq T_C + 3.
\end{array}
$$

A solution of the constraint obtained by conjoining the above primitive constraints represents a possible time-line for the project, that is, a time when each of the stages of the project may be reached. For example

$$\{T_S \mapsto 0, T_A \mapsto 7, T_B \mapsto 11, T_C \mapsto 10, T_D \mapsto 12, T_E \mapsto 15\}$$

is a solution.

Now imagine we are the house builder and that we have promised to have the house ready in two weeks. Unfortunately for us, the constraint above conjoined with the primitive constraint $T_E \leq 14$ yields an unsatisfiable constraint. Thus it is impossible to finish within two weeks, and we had better inform the people paying for the house.

1.3 Constraint Satisfaction

As we have seen, given a constraint, the natural question to ask is: "What are the solutions of the constraint?" Since there may be many solutions to a constraint, this question is usually modified to either the *solution problem* "Give me a solution to the constraint if one exists" or the *satisfaction problem* "Does the constraint have a solution?"

These two questions are closely related. In a sense, the satisfaction problem is more basic since an answer to the solution problem also answers the satisfaction problem. We now examine methods for answering the satisfaction problem. An algorithm for determining the satisfaction of a constraint is called a *constraint solver*. We shall see that algorithms for determining constraint satisfaction often construct a solution as a by-product and so can also be used to give a solution.

The obvious way to answer the satisfaction (and solution) question is to enumerate the valuations for the constraint and test whether any is a solution. One rather large drawback of this approach is that there may be an infinite number of valuations to test. Consider the constraint $X > Y$, where X and Y are natural numbers. Checking each possible valuation in the following order never actually finds a solution to the constraint although one exists.

$$\{X \mapsto 1, Y \mapsto 1\} \quad false$$
$$\{X \mapsto 1, Y \mapsto 2\} \quad false$$
$$\{X \mapsto 1, Y \mapsto 3\} \quad false$$
$$\vdots$$

For the natural numbers, it is possible to enumerate all possible solutions in an order that is guaranteed to find a solution in finite time if one exists. For example,

$$\{X \mapsto 1, Y \mapsto 1\} \quad false$$
$$\{X \mapsto 1, Y \mapsto 2\} \quad false$$
$$\{X \mapsto 2, Y \mapsto 1\} \quad true$$
$$\{X \mapsto 1, Y \mapsto 3\} \quad false$$
$$\{X \mapsto 2, Y \mapsto 2\} \quad true$$
$$\{X \mapsto 3, Y \mapsto 1\} \quad true$$
$$\{X \mapsto 1, Y \mapsto 4\} \quad false$$
$$\vdots$$

this sequence finds a solution at the third attempt and could stop at that stage. However, there is no way to determine in finite time that a given constraint is unsatisfiable. For real number constraints there is no way to enumerate all the possible solutions. Hence no method based on considering all valuations is possible. For constraint domains which have only a finite number of values, we will see in Chapter 3 that enumeration approaches are important.

The problem with enumeration methods is that they only use the constraints in a passive manner, to test the result of applying a valuation, rather than using them to help construct a valuation which is a solution. Of course the way in which the constraints are used depends very much on the type of constraint, therefore, details of how the constraint solver works are usually quite specific to the constraint domain.

One constraint domain that has been intensively studied, is the so called "linear" arithmetic constraints. They are defined as follows. A *linear expression* is of the form $a_1 x_1 + a_2 x_2 + \cdots + a_n x_n$ where each $a_i, 1 \le i \le n$ is a number and each $x_i, 1 \le i \le n$ is a variable. A *linear equation* is of the form $e_1 = e_2$ where e_1 and e_2 are linear expressions. Similarly a *linear inequality* is of the form $e_1 \le e_2$, $e_1 < e_2$, $e_1 \ge e_2$ or $e_1 > e_2$ where e_1 and e_2 are linear expressions. A *linear constraint* is a conjunction of linear equations and inequalities.

One general technique used by many constraint solvers is to repeatedly rewrite a constraint into an equivalent constraint until a constraint in "solved" form is obtained. A *solved form* constraint has the property that it is clear whether it is satisfiable or not. For historical reasons such solvers are called *normalising* solvers.

We now give an example of a normalising constraint solver for testing satisfiability of conjunctions of linear real equations. The solver uses *Gauss-Jordan elimination*, which you probably met in high school. The principal step in Gauss-Jordan elimination is to take an equation c, rewrite it into the form $x = e$ where x is a variable and e is a linear expression not involving x, and replace every other occurrence of x by e. Consider the following conjunction of equations:

$$\begin{aligned}
1 + X &= 2Y + Z \wedge \\
Z - X &= 3 \wedge \\
X + Y &= 5 + Z.
\end{aligned}$$

Selecting the first equation, we can rewrite it into the form $X = 2Y + Z - 1$. Replacing every other occurrence of X we obtain

$$\begin{aligned}
X &= 2Y + Z - 1 \wedge \\
Z - 2Y - Z + 1 &= 3 \wedge \\
2Y + Z - 1 + Y &= 5 + Z.
\end{aligned}$$

Examining the second equation, it simplifies to $-2Y = 2$, so we can rewrite it to $Y = -1$. Replacing Y everywhere else by -1, we obtain

$$\begin{aligned}
X &= Z - 3 \wedge \\
Y &= -1 \wedge \\
-2 + Z - 1 - 1 &= 5 + Z.
\end{aligned}$$

The final equation simplifies to $-4 = 5$, which is an unsatisfiable equation. As this final system of equations is equivalent to the initial system we have determined that the original constraint is unsatisfiable.

If we ignore the last equation the resulting system is $X = Z - 3 \wedge Y = -1$. This is clearly satisfiable since we can choose an arbitrary value for Z (say 4) and then calculate values for Y and X using the equations. The reader may verify that $\{X \mapsto 1, Y \mapsto -1, Z \mapsto 4\}$ is a solution of $1 + X = 2Y + Z \wedge Z - X = 3$.

In general, a conjunction of equations is in *solved form* if it has the form

$$x_1 = e_1 \wedge x_2 = e_2 \wedge \cdots \wedge x_n = e_n,$$

where each of the variables $x_1, \ldots, x_n$ (the *non-parameters*) is distinct and none of them appear in any of the expressions $e_1, \ldots, e_n$. For a large class of constraint domains, including linear real equations, if the variables occurring in $e_1, \ldots, e_n$ (the *parameters*) are each assigned an arbitrary value by valuation θ, then the constraint can be satisfied by assigning to each x_i the value of the expression e_i under θ.

```
r is a real number;
x is a variable;
e is a linear arithmetic expression;
c is an equation;
C, C_0 and S are conjunctions of equations.


gauss_jordan_solve(C)
    if gauss_jordan(C) ≡ false then return false
    else return true
    endif

gauss_jordan(C)
    S := true
    while C is not the empty conjunction true
        let C be of the form c ∧ C_0
        C := C_0
        if c can be written in a form without variables then
            if c can be written as 0 = r where r ≠ 0 then
                return false
            endif
        else
            write c in the form x = e where e does not involve x
            substitute e for x throughout C and S
            S := S ∧ x = e
        endif
    endwhile
    return S
```

Figure 1.3   Gauss-Jordan elimination.

The Gauss-Jordan elimination algorithm has two sets of equations: C, the unsolved equations and S, the solved form equations. At each step the constraint $C \wedge S$ is equivalent to the initial constraint. The algorithm works by repeatedly selecting an equation c from C. If c has no variables it is tested for satisfiability. Otherwise it can be rewritten into the form $x = e$ and used to eliminate x from the remaining equations in C and S. The equation $x = e$ is then added to S.

Note that in this and subsequent algorithms we consider an empty conjunction to be the same as *true*. We use the symbol $\equiv$ to denote syntactic equivalence, that is, $x \equiv y$ holds if x and y are syntactically identical.

Algorithm 1.1: Gauss-Jordan elimination
INPUT: A conjunction of linear real arithmetic equations C.
OUTPUT: Returns *true* if C is satisfiable, otherwise *false*.
METHOD: The algorithm is shown in Figure 1.3. $\square$

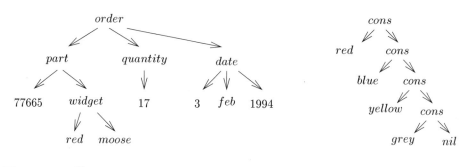

Figure 1.4   Two trees.

1.4   Tree Constraints

Until now, the only constraints we have considered have been arithmetic constraints over the real numbers. However, arithmetic constraints are only one sort of constraint. In this section we introduce another important constraint domain, the domain of *tree constraints* which we shall call *Tree*. Tree constraints allow us to model data structures commonly used in programming, such as records, lists and trees.

Definition 1.5

A *tree constructor* is a string of characters beginning with a lower case letter. A *constant* is a tree constructor or a number.

A *tree* is defined recursively as follows. A constant is a tree, and a tree constructor together with an ordered list of $n \geq 1$ trees, which are called its *children*, is a tree.

Trees are usually drawn with a tree constructor above its children which are displayed in left-to-right order. Arcs are drawn from the tree constructor to each of its children. Figure 1.4 shows some examples of trees. Note that, in the context of trees, numbers such as 17 and 3 are simply constants.

Trees are important because they allow information to be packaged in a structured way. The left tree in Figure 1.4 can be thought of as representing an order for a company. In this case the order is for part number #77665, called a red moose widget, the quantity required is 17 and the date of the order is the 3rd of February 1994. The right tree is a representation of the list $[red, blue, yellow, grey]$. The *cons* tree constructor is the means of connecting the elements of the list together. The constant *nil* signals the end of the list, or rather, stands for the empty list. Trees allow us to express many data structures that are common in programming, such as records, lists and binary trees.

Consider the following C data structure definition for the binary tree data structure:

```
struct tnode {
    struct tnode *left;
    data item;
    struct tnode *right; };
```

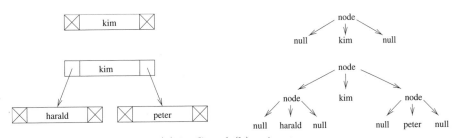

Figure 1.5   Binary trees (a) in C and (b) using trees.

Diagrams of a C binary tree data structure containing the item "kim," and a C binary tree data structure containing the items "harald", "kim" and "peter" are shown in Figure 1.5 (a). A crossed-out pointer box indicates a null pointer. Corresponding trees are shown in Figure 1.5 (b). Note that *null, kim, peter* and *harald* are all constant trees (with no children), and each tree with the constructor, *node*, has exactly 3 children.

The above definition of trees allows for infinite trees. For example, we can build an infinite tree using a tree constructor f with a single child which has the same form. This gives an infinite chain of f's. However, we will restrict attention to finite trees.

Definition 1.6
A constant a has *height* 1. A tree built from tree constructor f and child trees $t_1, \ldots t_n$ has height equal to one more than the maximum of the heights of the subtrees $t_1, \ldots, t_n$.
A tree is *finite* if it has finite height. Otherwise it is *infinite*.

The bottom tree in Figure 1.5 (b) is of height 2, while the left tree in Figure 1.4 is of height 4. We can write finite trees textually by appropriate bracketing. We first write the tree constructor, then within parentheses a comma separated list of its child trees. For example, the bottom tree of Figure 1.5 (b) can be written

$$node(node(null, harald, null), kim, node(null, peter, null)),$$

the left tree of Figure 1.4 can be written

$$order(part(77665, widget(red, moose)), quantity(17), date(3, feb, 1994)),$$

and the right tree can be written

$$cons(red, cons(blue, cons(yellow, cons(grey, nil)))).$$

In the tree constraint domain, *Tree*, variables take finite trees as values. Constraints in the tree domain are equalities between *terms*, which are trees with some subtrees replaced by variables. Note that variables replace entire trees and not tree constructors.

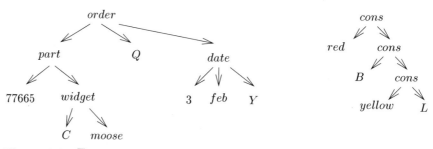

Figure 1.6   Two terms.

Definition 1.7

A *term* is defined recursively as follows: it is either a constant, or a variable, or a tree constructor together with an ordered list of $n \geq 1$ terms.

A *term equation* is of the form $s = t$ where s and t are terms. A valuation θ is a solution of term equation $s = t$ if $\theta(s)$ is syntactically identical to $\theta(t)$.

A *tree constraint* is a conjunction of term equations.

Two example terms are shown in Figure 1.6. The terms are written as

$$order(part(77665, widget(C, moose)), Q, date(3, feb, Y))$$

and

$$cons(red, cons(B, cons(yellow, L)))$$

respectively. In the tree constraint domain, the primitive constraints are term equations. Term equations are useful for constructing and accessing data stored in records or trees. The following constraint in effect builds the binary tree T containing "kim," "peter" and "harald" from the binary trees for "harald" and "peter":

$$K = node(H, kim, P) \wedge H = node(null, harald, null) \wedge P = node(null, peter, null).$$

It has a single solution

$$\{K \mapsto node(node(null, harald, null), kim, node(null, peter, null)),$$
$$H \mapsto node(null, harald, null), \ P \mapsto node(null, peter, null)\}.$$

Note that the terms K and $node(H, kim, P)$ under the valuation are both identical to

$$node(node(null, harald, null), kim, node(null, peter, null)),$$

and so the term equation is satisfied. Consider the constraint

$$Order = order(part(77665, widget(red, moose)), quantity(17), date(3, feb, 1994)) \wedge$$
$$Order = order(X, Y, date(Z, Month, U)).$$

The only solution ensures that the variable *Month* takes the value *feb*, in some sense accessing the "month" field of the order. As a final example, the following constraint has the effect of extracting the first element H and the remainder T of the list represented by the right tree in Figure 1.4:

$$List = cons(red, cons(blue, cons(yellow, cons(grey, nil)))) \land List = cons(H, T).$$

The only solution to the constraint is

$$\{List \mapsto cons(red, cons(blue, cons(yellow, cons(grey, nil)))),$$
$$H \mapsto red,\ T \mapsto cons(blue, cons(yellow, cons(grey, nil)))\}.$$

In later chapters we shall see that tree constraints provide constraint logic programming languages with the full power of the usual recursive and non-recursive data structures used in traditional programming languages.

The most important question, of course, is how we determine whether a conjunction of term equations is satisfiable. The constraint solver for tree constraints described below is also a normalising solver that repeatedly eliminates variables from the term equations until a solved form is reached.

Algorithm 1.2: Tree constraint solver
INPUT: A conjunction of term equations.
OUTPUT: Returns *true* if they are satisfiable, otherwise *false*.
METHOD: The algorithm is shown in Figure 1.7. Cases are tried in order, so that the first condition that is satisfied by the equation will determine the case to be used. □

The algorithm works by selecting a term equation from the constraint to be solved, C, and either replacing it with an equivalent tree constraint or discovering unsatisfiability. If the term equation is of the form $x = t$ where x is a variable and t a term, then x is replaced everywhere by t and the equation is added to the solved form constraint S.

We can justify the correctness of the algorithm as follows. The constraint $C \land S$ has the same solutions after each iteration of the algorithm. For case (1), observe that any equation of the form $x = x$ is always satisfied whatever value is assigned to x, so it can be removed. For case (2), no tree which has root labelled f can ever be identical to a tree with root labelled g if the tree constructors are different ($f \not\equiv g$) or the number of children is different ($n \neq m$). For case (3), if two trees with the same tree constructor f and the same number of children n are to be equal then each of their corresponding subtrees must be equal. Case (4) simply swaps the two sides of the equation; any solution for $x = t$ is also a solution for $t = x$ and vice versa. Case (5) is a little more subtle to justify. Suppose there is a solution to the equation $x = t$. Then x is assigned a tree of, say, height h. Now t contains x but it is not just the variable x, so x must occur as an argument to some tree constructor. Thus t under the valuation is a tree of height $h+1$ or greater. But therefore it cannot

---

x is a variable;
s, t, s_i, t_j are terms;
c is a term equation;
C, C_0 and S are conjunctions of equations.

tree_solve(C)
   if unify(C) $\equiv$ *false* **then return** *false*
   else return *true*
   endif

unify(C)
   $S := true$
   while C is not the empty conjunction
     let C be of the form $c \wedge C_0$
     cases
     (1) c is of the form $x = x$:
        $C := C_0$
     (2) c is of the form $f(s_1, \ldots, s_n) = g(t_1, \ldots, t_m)$
       where $f \not\equiv g$ or $n \neq m$:
       return *false*
     (3) c is of the form $f(s_1, \ldots, s_n) = f(t_1, \ldots, t_n)$:
       $C := (s_1 = t_1 \wedge \cdots \wedge s_n = t_n) \wedge C_0$
     (4) c is of the form $t = x$ where t is not a variable:
       $C := (x = t) \wedge C_0$
     (5) c is of the form $x = t$ and t contains x:
       return *false*
     (6) c is of the form $x = t$:
       substitute t for x throughout C_0 and S
       $C := C_0$
       $S := S \wedge c$
     endcases
   endwhile
   return S

Figure 1.7   A tree constraint solver.

be equal to the tree assigned to x, and so we have a contradiction. Hence there is no solution to $x = t$. Finally, case (6) is correct by the principle of substitutivity of equals for equals, since it simply incorporates the constraint information from c into C and S. Thus, we have proved the algorithm is correct. Proof of termination is left as an exercise.

Let us trace the execution of unify on a simple tree constraint

$$cons(Y, nil) = cons(X, Z) \wedge Y = cons(a, T).$$

The following table shows the values of C and S at the start of each iteration of the **while** loop in unify. We use underlining to show which primitive constraint gets processed in each iteration.

	C	S
Initially,	$cons(Y, nil) = cons(X, Z) \wedge Y = cons(a, T)$	*true.*
Using rule (3),	$\underline{Y = X} \wedge nil = Z \wedge Y = cons(a, T)$	*true.*
Using rule (6),	$\underline{nil = Z} \wedge X = cons(a, T)$	$Y = X.$
Using rule (4),	$\underline{Z = nil} \wedge X = cons(a, T)$	$Y = X.$
Using rule (6),	$\underline{X = cons(a, T)}$	$Y = X \wedge Z = nil.$
Using rule (6),	*true* $Y = cons(a, T) \wedge Z = nil \wedge X = cons(a, T).$	

The resulting solved form is clearly satisfiable. By assigning any tree to T, for example *nil*, we can calculate assignments for each of the other variables that satisfy the equations. Thus

$$\{X \mapsto cons(a, nil), Z \mapsto nil, Y \mapsto cons(a, nil), T \mapsto nil\}$$

is a solution of the final constraint and therefore of the initial constraint. An example of an unsatisfiable constraint is $cons(X, Z) = cons(Z, nil) \wedge X = a$. The algorithm unify proceeds as follows:

	C	S
Initially	$cons(X, Z) = cons(Z, nil) \wedge X = a$	*true,*
Using rule (3)	$\underline{X = Z} \wedge Z = nil \wedge X = a$	*true,*
Using rule (6)	$\underline{Z = nil} \wedge Z = a$	$X = Z,$
Using rule (6)	$\underline{nil = a}$	$X = nil \wedge Z = nil,$
false using rule (2).		

Notice the strong similarity between unify and gauss_jordan. Both algorithms rewrite constraints to solved form. In addition, in both solvers the key step in obtaining the solved form is to eliminate a variable.

1.5   Other Constraint Domains

Numerous other constraint domains are of interest. Many of these have been closely studied in mathematics, for example Booleans, sets, sequences and groups. Here we take a look at Boolean constraints, sequence constraints and, as our last example of a constraint domain in this chapter, symbolic constraints for an application (planning) in artificial intelligence.

1.5.1   Boolean Constraints

Boolean primitive constraints are made up of Boolean variables, which may take the value *true* (represented by 1) or *false* (represented by 0), and Boolean operations such as conjunction (&), disjunction ($\vee$), exclusive-or ($\oplus$), implication ($\rightarrow$) and bi-implication ($\leftrightarrow$). Note that we deliberately use a different symbol for Boolean con-

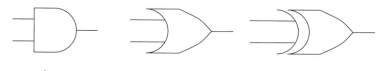

and gate   or gate   exclusive or gate

Figure 1.8 Gates for logic circuits.

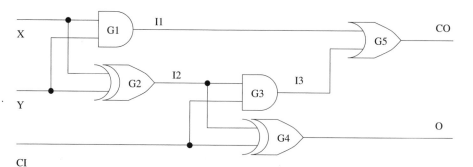

CI

Figure 1.9 A full adder logic circuit.

junction (& as opposed to $\wedge$) to differentiate primitive constraints from constraints. The meaning of each of these functions on Booleans is given by the following truth tables, where, for example, $0 \to 1$ is 1 but $1 \to 0$ is 0:

$\neg$		&	0	1	$\vee$	0	1	$\oplus$	0	1	$\to$	0	1	$\leftrightarrow$	0	1
0	1	0	0	0	0	0	1	0	0	1	0	1	1	0	1	0
1	0	1	0	1	1	1	1	1	1	0	1	0	1	1	0	1

One important application of Boolean constraints is for modelling logic circuits. A full adder is a circuit which takes three binary inputs X, Y and CI and gives two outputs O and CO. X and Y are the bits to be added, CI is the input carry bit, O is the output bit and CO is the output carry bit. The results of the full adder satisfy the arithmetic equation $O + 2 \times CO = X + Y + CI$. Different gate types are shown in Figure 1.8, and the circuit implementing a full adder is shown in Figure 1.9.

Each gate in the diagram is modelled by a Boolean primitive constraint as shown in the table below. The conjunction of these constraints models the entire circuit.

$$
\begin{aligned}
I1 &\leftrightarrow X \,\&\, Y & \text{And gate } G1, \\
I2 &\leftrightarrow X \oplus Y & \text{Xor gate } G2, \\
I3 &\leftrightarrow I2 \,\&\, CI & \text{And gate } G3, \\
O &\leftrightarrow I2 \oplus CI & \text{Xor gate } G4, \\
CO &\leftrightarrow I1 \vee I3 & \text{Or gate } G5.
\end{aligned}
$$

For example, the above conjunction, conjoined with the information that $X \leftrightarrow 1 \wedge Y \leftrightarrow 0 \wedge CI \leftrightarrow 1$ has the single solution

$$\{X \mapsto 1, Y \mapsto 0, CI \mapsto 1, I1 \mapsto 0, I2 \mapsto 1, I3 \mapsto 1, O \mapsto 0, CO \mapsto 1\}.$$

This shows that the output of the circuit for input $X = 1$, $Y = 0$, and $CI = 1$ is $O = 0$ and $CO = 1$ as expected. In other words, $0 + 2 \times 1 = 1 + 0 + 1$.

A more interesting problem is to consider fault analysis of the adder. We associate with each gate Gi a variable F_i which is 1 if the gate is faulty and 0 if it is not. The behaviour of the adder is then given by the conjunction of the following primitive constraints:

$$\neg F_1 \rightarrow (I1 \leftrightarrow X \,\&\, Y) \qquad \text{And gate } G1 \text{ works if not faulty,}$$
$$\neg F_2 \rightarrow (I2 \leftrightarrow X \oplus Y) \qquad \text{Xor gate } G2 \text{ works if not faulty,}$$
$$\neg F_3 \rightarrow (I3 \leftrightarrow I2 \,\&\, CI) \qquad \text{And gate } G3 \text{ works if not faulty,}$$
$$\neg F_4 \rightarrow (O \leftrightarrow I2 \oplus CI) \qquad \text{Xor gate } G4 \text{ works if not faulty,}$$
$$\neg F_5 \rightarrow (CO \leftrightarrow I1 \vee I3) \qquad \text{Or gate } G5 \text{ works if not faulty.}$$

The following constraint enforces the reasonable hypothesis that at most one gate is faulty in the adder:

$$\neg(F_1 \,\&\, F_2) \wedge \neg(F_1 \,\&\, F_3) \wedge \neg(F_1 \,\&\, F_4) \wedge \neg(F_1 \,\&\, F_5) \wedge \neg(F_2 \,\&\, F_3) \wedge$$
$$\neg(F_2 \,\&\, F_4) \wedge \neg(F_2 \,\&\, F_5) \wedge \neg(F_3 \,\&\, F_4) \wedge \neg(F_3 \,\&\, F_5) \wedge \neg(F_4 \,\&\, F_5).$$

Suppose we conjoin this constraint information with some observed faulty behaviour of the gate. Say that, with inputs $X = 0$, $Y = 0$ and $CI = 1$, the outputs were $O = 0$ and $CO = 1$. Then, the only solution is

$$\{F_1 \mapsto 0, F_2 \mapsto 1, F_3 \mapsto 0, F_4 \mapsto 0, F_5 \mapsto 0\}.$$

So we know, if we assume that only one gate is faulty, it must be the second gate, $G2$.

There are many different approaches to solving Boolean constraints. Unfortunately the problem of deciding whether a Boolean constraint is satisfiable (SAT) is the most famous of the so-called NP-complete problems, a large and important class of intrinsically difficult problems. So far, all algorithms for solving SAT have a worst-case running time which is exponential in the size of the constraint. Moreover, it is impossible to do better, unless *every* NP-complete problem has a polynomial-time solution, something most computer scientists believe to be impossible. Nonetheless, here we give a polynomial-time solver for Boolean constraints!

```
C is a Boolean formula;
ε is a number between 0 and 1;
i, m and n are integers.


bool_solve(C)
    let m be the number of primitive constraints in C
    (assume m > 1)
    n := ⌈ln(ε)/ ln(1 − (1 − 1/m)^m)⌉
    for i := 1 to n do
        generate a random valuation φ over the variables in C
        if φ satisfies C then return true endif
    endfor
    return unknown
```

Figure 1.10   Probabilistic Boolean solver.

Algorithm 1.3: Incomplete Boolean solver

INPUT: A Boolean constraint C, and ϵ, a number between 0 and 1, indicating the degree of incompleteness.

OUTPUT: *true* or *unknown*, indicating either that C is satisfiable or that C may or may not be satisfiable.

METHOD: The algorithm is shown in Figure 1.10. □

The price we pay for having a polynomial time algorithm is that the solver is not complete. That is, it sometimes returns the answer *unknown*. Later we shall see that solvers that do not always completely answer the satisfiability problem may still be useful.

The Boolean solver is an example of a *probabilistic* algorithm. One parameter of the algorithm is a number, ϵ, between 0 and 1, indicating the degree of incompleteness we are willing to tolerate. The larger the value of ϵ, the smaller the chance of a useful answer. The algorithm repeatedly guesses a random valuation, and, relying on an assumption that the input constraint is "random," utilises the fact that satisfiability of a random Boolean constraint is much more likely than unsatisfiability. Figure 1.11 shows some examples of n as a function of ϵ and m. Notice how the algorithm is particularly well suited for large constraints, since the number of iterations remains almost constant as the size grows, although, the larger the constraint, the more work is required to check that a valuation is a solution.

If the constraints given to this solver are in a particular form called *conjunctive normal form* (CNF), we can get a better measure of the incompleteness of the solver. In this case, the probability that the solver returns *unknown* is exactly ϵ.

A Boolean constraint is in conjunctive normal form if it is either 0 or 1 or a conjunction of primitive constraints each of the form $L_1 \vee \cdots \vee L_n$ where each L_i is of the form x or $\neg x$ and x is a Boolean variable. For example, the constraint $A \vee \neg B \wedge \neg A \vee B$ is in CNF. Any Boolean constraint can be written into an equivalent Boolean constraint in CNF (see Exercise 2.6a). The CNF constraint above is equivalent to $A \leftrightarrow B$.

m	5	50	500	5000	50000
ϵ					
0.1	6	6	6	6	6
0.01	12	11	11	11	11
0.001	18	16	16	16	16
0.0001	24	21	21	21	21

Figure 1.11   Values for n in terms of ϵ and m.

1.5.2   Sequence Constraints

Sequence constraints are another type of constraint. One important application of sequence constraints is in genetics. DNA, that is, deoxyribonucleic acid, is the material which forms the chromosomes of all known life. DNA consists of two long sequences of the molecules adenine (A), thymine (T), cytosine (C) and guanine (G), called *bases*, organized in a double helix shape. The bases in each strand are always paired together in the same way, adenine with thymine and cytosine with guanine. Thus, each strand uniquely determines the other.

Much research in genetics is devoted to taking a strand from an organism's DNA and finding the ordering of the bases in the strand. This is called *mapping* the DNA. Mapping allows a geneticist to decode the message contained in the organism's chromosomes. A large international effort (the Human GENOME project) is currently devoted to mapping and decoding the DNA of humans.

However, chromosomes are very long—for humans the chromosome's DNA strand may contain several billion bases. To map a chromosome, one of the DNA strands is broken into small manageable pieces which can be mapped individually. These pieces are known as *clones*, because once they have been extracted, they are inserted into a host chromosome and copied many times (or "cloned"). Different clones that are from the same section of chromosome are called *contigs* (from contiguous).

An important problem in genetics is, therefore, the reconstruction of an original chromosome from its contigs. Contigs may overlap, so the problem is to find the minimal length sequence which the contigs may yield when overlaid.

For example, imagine that we have the three contigs

        A-A-A-A-T-C-G,
        A-T-C-G-G-G-C,
        G-C-C-A-T-T.

These can be combined to give the overall sequence A-A-A-A-T-C-G-G-G-C-C-A-T-T as follows:

        A-A-A-A-T-C-G
            A-T-C-G-G-G-C
                    G-C-C-A-T-T.

How the contigs can be overlaid to give this particular sequence is expressed by the sequence constraint:

$$T = UC_1 :: O_{12} :: UC_2 :: O_{23} :: UC_3 \land$$
$$C_1 = UC_1 :: O_{12} \land C_2 = O_{12} :: UC_2 :: O_{23} \land C_3 = O_{23} :: UC_3 \land$$
$$O_{12} \neq \epsilon \land O_{23} \neq \epsilon \land$$
$$C_1 = a\text{-}a\text{-}a\text{-}a\text{-}t\text{-}c\text{-}g \land C_2 = a\text{-}t\text{-}c\text{-}g\text{-}g\text{-}g\text{-}c \land C_3 = g\text{-}c\text{-}c\text{-}a\text{-}t\text{-}t.$$

We use :: to denote sequence concatenation. T is the total or overall sequence, C_1, C_2 and C_3 are the contigs, UC_i is the non-overlapped portion of contig C_i and O_{ij} is the overlap between contigs C_i and C_j. As one would expect, the only solution to these constraints requires T to be *a-a-a-a-t-c-g-g-g-c-c-a-t-t*.

It may be possible to overlay the contigs in some other way. For instance, another possible overlapping is given by:

$$T = UC_3 :: O_{32} :: UC_2 :: O_{21} :: UC_1 \land$$
$$C_3 = UC_3 :: O_{32} \land C_2 = O_{32} :: UC_2 :: O_{21} \land C_1 = O_{21} :: UC_1 \land$$
$$O_{32} \neq \epsilon \land O_{21} \neq \epsilon \land$$
$$C_1 = a\text{-}a\text{-}a\text{-}a\text{-}t\text{-}c\text{-}g \land C_2 = a\text{-}t\text{-}c\text{-}g\text{-}g\text{-}g\text{-}c \land C_3 = g\text{-}c\text{-}c\text{-}a\text{-}t\text{-}t.$$

However, in this case the constraints are unsatisfiable. There are another 4 ways we might overlay the contigs, corresponding to the other left-to-right orderings of the contigs, but in all cases these lead to unsatisfiable constraints.

1.5.3   Blocks World Constraints

Not all constraint domains are taken from mathematics. The *blocks world* is a well-studied artificial intelligence example of knowledge representation and planning. The blocks world (for our example) consists of a large floor space and a set of coloured objects: cubes, spheres and square pyramids.

A constraint domain for reasoning about the blocks world takes values from the set of available objects together with their position. For example, we might have two cubes, one yellow (yc) and one green (gc), a red sphere (rs), two pyramids, one green (gp) and one red (rp), as the set of possible objects. Primitive constraints on objects can force two references to be to the same object, for example $X = Y$, or restrict the colour, for example $red(X)$, or the shape, for example $sphere(Y)$. Others constrain the relative stacking position of the objects: $on(X, Y)$ requires that object X is on top of object Y, and $floor(X)$ requires that X is on the floor. These primitive constraints are allowed together with their negations, for example $X \neq Y$ (X and Y are different objects), *not_green*(X) (X is not green), and *not_on*(X, Y) (object X is not on Y).

The physical laws of the blocks world limit how objects may be placed. For example, an object must be on exactly one other object or the floor, a sphere cannot be placed on any object but the floor, and no object can be placed on a

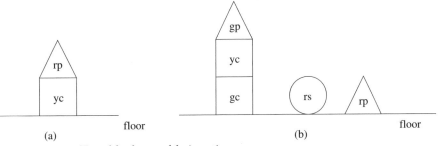

Figure 1.12   Two blocks world situations.

sphere or pyramid. A valuation (or situation) in the blocks world is a legitimate placement of each of the objects in the world. It assigns to each variable both an object and a position in the world. For simplicity, we will represent the position of the object simply by the object it is on.

The following constraint requires a red object to be on something:

$$red(X) \wedge on(X, Y).$$

A solution $\{X \mapsto rp \ on \ yc, Y \mapsto yc \ on \ floor\}$ is illustrated in Figure 1.12 (a). The following constraint requires a yellow object to be off the floor, a pyramid to be on an object which is not green, and two red objects to be on the floor:

$$yellow(X) \wedge on(X, Y) \wedge pyramid(Z) \wedge on(Z, T) \wedge not\_green(T) \wedge$$
$$red(U) \wedge red(V) \wedge floor(U) \wedge floor(V) \wedge U \neq V.$$

For our example world, the unique solution (apart from swapping U and V)

$$\{X \mapsto yc \ on \ gc, Y \mapsto gc \ on \ floor, Z \mapsto gp \ on \ yc, T \mapsto yc \ on \ gc,$$
$$U \mapsto rs \ on \ floor, V \mapsto rp \ on \ floor\}$$

is illustrated in Figure 1.12 (b).

1.6   Properties of Constraint Solvers

Except for bool_solve, all of the solvers we have examined so far are complete in the sense that they are able to determine for every constraint whether it is satisfiable (*true*) or unsatisfiable (*false*). In general, solvers may not have this property either because a complete algorithm is considered too expensive (as in the case of the Booleans) or a complete solver is unknown or cannot exist. For example, it is impossible to give an algorithm to determine whether a conjunction of nonlinear integer constraints has a solution. Thus, no complete solver for the domain of integers exists. In the case of nonlinear constraints over the reals, in theory it is decidable if a constraint is satisfiable or not, but the inherent complexity of doing so is highly exponential. Therefore, we cannot expect a complete solver to answer all satisfiability questions within a reasonable amount of time.

For these reasons we allow a solver to be *incomplete* and to answer some satisfaction questions with *unknown*, indicating that the solver cannot determine whether the constraint is satisfiable or unsatisfiable. Thus a solver can be formalised as follows:

Definition 1.8

A *constraint solver*, *solv*, for a constraint domain $\mathcal{D}$ takes as input any constraint C in $\mathcal{D}$ and returns *true*, *false* or *unknown*. Whenever $solv(C)$ returns *true* the constraint C must be satisfiable, and whenever $solv(C)$ returns *false* the constraint C must be unsatisfiable.

The constraint solver must answer the satisfiability question correctly or else return *unknown*. Note that the definition allows a constraint solver to be very weak. For example, the function which always returns *unknown* regardless of its input is a constraint solver for any domain (albeit not a very useful one).

Apart from being correct, there are a number of desirable properties we might expect our constraint solver to satisfy. The first relates to the textual form of the constraint. A constraint solver should give the same answers for a conjunction of primitive constraints regardless of their order, or the number of times a primitive constraint is repeated. In other words, the result of the constraint solver should depend only on the set of primitive constraints, *primitives(C)*, of the input constraint C.

The next desirable property a constraint solver should satisfy reflects our understanding of the meaning of conjunction. If C_1 is an unsatisfiable constraint, then any conjunction of C_1 with another constraint C_2 must also be unsatisfiable. A constraint solver should reflect this behaviour.

Finally, we would like the result of the constraint solver not to depend on the exact names of the variables, because the variables just represent place-holders. For example, $X \geq Y \wedge Y \geq 2$ and $U \geq V \wedge V \geq 2$ should not be distinguished. To define rigorously what we mean by a solver being independent of variable names, we introduce renamings and variants.

Definition 1.9

A *renaming* is a mapping from variables to variables in which no two variables are mapped to the same variable. We shall write a renaming ρ as the set

$$\{x_1 \mapsto y_1, \ldots x_n \mapsto y_n\}.$$

The result of *applying* ρ to a constraint C, written $\rho(C)$, is the constraint obtained by replacing each variable x in C by $\rho(x)$. A constraint C is a *variant* of constraint C' if there is a renaming ρ such that $\rho(C) \equiv C'$.

For example, $\rho_1 = \{X \mapsto U, Y \mapsto V\}$ is a renaming. $\rho_2 = \{X \mapsto Z, Y \mapsto Z\}$ is not a renaming since both X and Y are mapped to Z. Applying ρ_1 to $X \geq Y \wedge Y \geq 2$ gives $U \geq V \wedge V \geq 2$. Thus, $X \geq Y \wedge Y \geq 2$ is a variant of $U \geq V \wedge V \geq 2$ and vice versa.

Idealized constraint solvers almost always satisfy the set based, monotonic and variable name independent conditions which are defined below. In practice, however, some constraint solvers may occasionally treat constraints unfairly, that is, process some primitive constraints indefinitely while ignoring other primitive constraints. Such a constraint solver will not satisfy these conditions.

Definition 1.10
A constraint solver *solv* for constraint domain $\mathcal{D}$ is *well-behaved* if for any constraints C_1 and C_2 from $\mathcal{D}$:

set based: $solv(C_1) = solv(C_2)$ whenever $primitives(C_1) = primitives(C_2)$.

monotonic: If $solv(C_1) = false$ then $solv(C_1 \wedge C_2) = false$.

variable name independent: If C_1 is a variant of C_2 then $solv(C_1) = solv(C_2)$.

Except for bool_solve, the solvers we have examined so far are well-behaved. The reason that the Boolean solver is not well-behaved is that, because of its probabilistic nature, bool_solve(C) may not give the same answer even for the same constraint. For the remainder of this text, unless specifically noted otherwise, we shall assume that all solvers are well-behaved. As we have previously discussed, the strongest condition we can ask of a constraint solver, completeness, is not always achievable.

Definition 1.11
A constraint solver *solv* for constraint domain $\mathcal{D}$ is *complete* if for each constraint C in $\mathcal{D}$, $solv(C)$ is either *true* or *false*. A solver which is not complete is said to be *incomplete*.

For example, gauss_jordan_solve is a complete constraint solver for the domain of linear real equations and tree_solve is a complete constraint solver for tree constraint domains. Clearly bool_solve is an incomplete solver. Complete solvers are the most desirable because they answer all questions. It is not too difficult to show that every complete solver is well-behaved. (See Exercise 1.10.)

1.7 (*) Determined Variables and Local Propagation

In previous sections we have seen a variety of constraint solvers. However, all of these were applicable to only one constraint domain. Here we present a general constraint solving algorithm that can be used with almost any type of constraints. This generality comes with a price—the solver is usually incomplete.

The algorithm is based on repeatedly detecting variables whose value is fixed by the constraint and eliminating these variables from the constraint. A core step in the algorithm is therefore determining variables which are fixed by a constraint to take a single value. We say such variables are determined by the constraint.

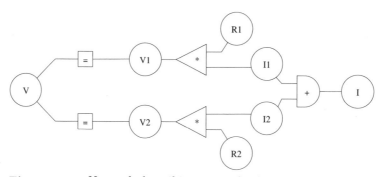

Figure 1.13   Network describing a simple electric circuit.

Definition 1.12

Let e be an expression containing no variables. A variable x is *determined* by C to have value e if every solution of C is also a solution of $x = e$.

For example, X is determined by $X = Y + 2Z - 2 \land Y = 1 - 2Z$ to have value -1 and X is determined by $2 = X \times X \land X \geq 0$ to have value $\sqrt{2}$.

Detecting determined values and simplifying the resulting constraints provides a general approach to solving constraints from any constraint domain. The idea arises from viewing constraints as a vehicle for "data-flow" propagation of values of variables. Consider the constraint describing the simple circuit shown in Figure 1.1:

$$V = V1 \land V = V2 \land V1 = I1 \times R1 \land V2 = I2 \times R2 \land I = I1 + I2.$$

This constraint can be represented by a network of operations shown in Figure 1.13. Each variable is shown in a circle and each operation is shown in another shape. An equality node, labelled with "=", ensures that the nodes it connects have the same value. Addition and multiplication nodes ensure that the result of applying the operation to the values of nodes connected to the incoming arcs (that is, those entering the flat side of the node) is equal to the value of the node on the outgoing arc (that is, the one leaving the non-flat side).

Now consider the additional constraint $V = 10 \land R1 = 5 \land R2 = 10$. This constraint corresponds to setting the values $V = 10$, $R1 = 5$ and $R2 = 10$. The corresponding network is shown at the top of Figure 1.14. Consider the operation of the network when these values are set. The value of the variable node for V can be propagated through the topmost equality node to set the value of $V1$ to 10. The resulting network is shown at the bottom of Figure 1.14. Then propagation through the topmost multiplication node can set $I1$ to 2 so as to satisfy $V1 = R1 \times I1$.

Propagation of the known values continues as follows. Propagation through the lower equality node sets $V2$ to 10, and then propagation through the other multiplication node sets $I2$ to 1. Finally, the addition node sets I to 3. At this point every variable has a determined value, and we can read the following solution from the network:

$$\{V \mapsto 10, R1 \mapsto 5, R2 \mapsto 10, V1 \mapsto 10, I1 \mapsto 2, V2 \mapsto 10, I2 \mapsto 1, I \mapsto 3\}.$$

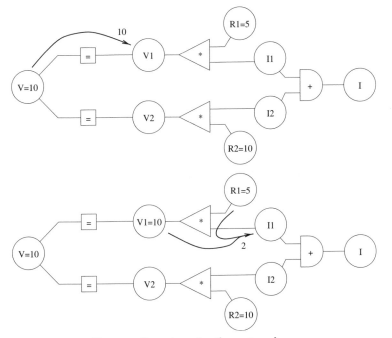

Figure 1.14   Propagation steps in the network.

The local propagation solver will return *true*.

As another example, imagine the additional constraint was instead $I1 = 2 \wedge V1 = 10$. In this case local propagation proceeds as follows. The topmost multiplication node determines that $R1 = 5$, the top equality node determines $V = 10$, and then the remaining equality node sets $V2 = 10$. No further information is available. Because not every variable is determined, local propagation cannot determine whether the constraint conjoined with the additional information $I1 = 2 \wedge V1 = 10$ is satisfiable or not, and will return *unknown*.

We now describe a general algorithm to perform local propagation. Local propagation can be thought of as manipulating two objects: a set of currently determined variables with their values and a constraint. We can represent the set of determined variables with their values using a solved form constraint containing these determined variables.

Definition 1.13
A constraint is in *determined solved form* if it has the form

$$x_1 = e_1 \wedge x_2 = e_2 \wedge \cdots \wedge x_n = e_n$$

where each x_i is a distinct variable and each e_i is a variable free expression.

The basic idea of local propagation is to repeatedly look at the primitive constraints in the constraint being solved and determine which other variables are constrained to take a single value, then to add this information to the determined solved form.

For example, if X is determined to be 3 then the constraint $X = Y + 2 \land Y + 1 + X = Z$ determines that Y must take value 1. Then with $X = 3 \land Y = 1$ the constraint determines that $Z = 5$.

Detecting when a variable is determined allows us to eliminate the variable. Unfortunately computing which variables are determined by an arbitrary constraint is at least as hard as determining whether the constraint is satisfiable. One key idea behind local propagation is that it is the interaction between arbitrary conjunctions of primitive constraints which is difficult to understand. In the execution of the local propagation algorithm, at each step we only determine which variables are determined by some single primitive constraint in the conjunction. Clearly this is much easier.

The generic algorithm relies on two domain specific functions, each of which takes a primitive constraint c. The first function, $satisfiable(c)$, is a solver for primitive constraints and returns *unknown*, *true* or *false*. Like all solvers, if it returns *true*, c must be satisfiable, and if it returns *false*, c must be unsatisfiable. The second function, $determines(c)$, takes a primitive constraint and returns a determined solved form,

$$x_1 = e_1 \land x_2 = e_2 \land \cdots \land x_n = e_n,$$

where for each i, c determines that x_i takes value e_i.

The local propagation algorithm works by repeatedly selecting a primitive constraint. If the primitive constraint is definitely unsatisfiable, the algorithm returns *false* since the original constraint is also unsatisfiable. Otherwise, the algorithm finds which variables this primitive constraint determines, eliminates them from the constraint and adds them to the determined solved form. If, at any stage, a constraint contains no variables and is satisfiable, it can be removed. This process continues until no further step can be taken. If the final constraint is *true*, the original system is definitely satisfiable. Otherwise the algorithm returns *unknown*.

Algorithm 1.4: Local propagation solver
INPUT: A constraint C.
OUTPUT: Returns *true* if C is shown to be satisfiable, *false* if C is shown to be unsatisfiable, otherwise *unknown*.
METHOD: The algorithm is shown in Figure 1.15. $\square$

As an example of the execution of local_propagation_solve, consider the Boolean constraint

$$X \leftrightarrow Y \land \neg Y \land \neg Y \rightarrow X.$$

Initially C is this constraint and S is *true*. C_0 is set to C, and each primitive constraint in C_0 is examined in turn. We assume that the primitive constraints are processed in textual order. The first constraint selected is $X \leftrightarrow Y$, so c is set to this and C_0 is set to $\neg Y \land \neg Y \rightarrow X$. Processing of $X \leftrightarrow Y$ leaves S and C unchanged

```
x is a variable;
e is an expression not involving variables;
c is a primitive constraint;
C, C₀, C₁ are constraints;
S is a constraint in determined solved form.


local_propagation_solve(C)
    S := true
    repeat
        C₀ := C
        while C₀ is not the empty conjunction
            let C₀ be of the form c ∧ C₁
            C₀ := C₁
            if satisfiable(c) ≡ false then
                return false
            elseif satisfiable(c) ≡ true and vars(c) ≡ ∅ then
                C := C with primitive constraint c removed
            endif
            S := S ∧ determines(c)
            for each constraint (x = e) ∈ determines(c) do
                replace x by e in C and C₀
            endfor
        endwhile
    until S and C are unchanged
    if C is the empty conjunction then
        return true
    else
        return unknown
    endif
```

Figure 1.15   Local propagation solver.

as $satisfiable(X \leftrightarrow Y)$ returns $true$ but $X \leftrightarrow Y$ does not determine any variables. Next c is set to $\neg Y$ and C_0 becomes $\neg Y \rightarrow X$. Now, $\neg Y$ is satisfiable and also determines that Y is assigned 0. Thus S becomes $Y = 0$, C becomes

$$X \leftrightarrow 0 \wedge \neg 0 \wedge \neg 0 \rightarrow X$$

and C_0 becomes $\neg 0 \rightarrow X$ as Y is replaced by 0. Next $\neg 0 \rightarrow X$ is processed. This is satisfiable and determines that X is assigned 1. Thus S becomes $Y = 0 \wedge X = 1$ and C becomes

$$1 \leftrightarrow 0 \wedge \neg 0 \wedge \neg 0 \rightarrow 1.$$

The iteration finished because all primitive constraints have been processed. In the next iteration of the **repeat** loop, C_0 is set to $1 \leftrightarrow 0 \wedge \neg 0 \wedge \neg 0 \rightarrow 1$ and then $1 \leftrightarrow 0$ is processed. This is unsatisfiable, so the algorithm returns $false$, indicating that the original constraint is unsatisfiable.

As another example of the algorithm's operation, again consider the simple circuit show in Figure 1.1 together with specific values for the voltage of the battery and the resistance of the resistors. The initial constraint C describing it is

$$V = V1 \wedge V = V2 \wedge V1 = I1 \times R1 \wedge V2 = I2 \times R2 \wedge I = I1 + I2 \wedge$$
$$V = 10 \wedge R1 = 5 \wedge R2 = 10.$$

In the first iteration of the **repeat** loop, if primitive constraints are processed in textual order, processing of the first five primitive constraints

$$V = V1, \ V = V2, \ V1 = I1 \times R1, \ V2 = I2 \times R2, \ I = I1 + I2$$

leaves S and C unchanged as each is satisfiable and does not determine the value of a variable. Processing of

$$V = 10 \wedge R1 = 5 \wedge R2 = 10$$

leads to the elimination of V, $R1$ and $R2$. Thus S becomes

$$V = 10 \wedge R1 = 5 \wedge R2 = 10$$

and C becomes

$$10 = V1 \wedge 10 = V2 \wedge V1 = I1 \times 5 \wedge V2 = I2 \times 10 \wedge I = I1 + I2 \wedge 10 = 10 \wedge 5 = 5 \wedge 10 = 10.$$

In the next iteration, processing of $10 = V1$ and $10 = V2$ causes S to become

$$V = 10 \wedge R1 = 5 \wedge R2 = 10 \wedge V1 = 10 \wedge V2 = 10$$

and C becomes

$$10 = 10 \wedge 10 = 10 \wedge 10 = I1 \times 5 \wedge 10 = I2 \times 10 \wedge I = I1 + I2 \wedge 10 = 10 \wedge 5 = 5 \wedge 10 = 10.$$

Now processing of $10 = I1 \times 5$ and $10 = I2 \times 10$ leads to S becoming

$$V = 10 \wedge R1 = 5 \wedge R2 = 10 \wedge V1 = 10 \wedge V2 = 10 \wedge I1 = 2 \wedge I2 = 1$$

and C becomes

$$10 = 10 \wedge 10 = 10 \wedge 10 = 2 \times 5 \wedge 10 = 1 \times 10 \wedge I = 2 + 1 \wedge 10 = 10 \wedge 5 = 5 \wedge 10 = 10.$$

Processing of $I = 2 + 1$ eliminates I and causes S to become

$$V = 10 \wedge R1 = 5 \wedge R2 = 10 \wedge V1 = 10 \wedge V2 = 10 \wedge I1 = 2 \wedge I2 = 1 \wedge I = 3$$

and C becomes

$$10 = 10 \wedge 10 = 10 \wedge 10 = 2 \times 5 \wedge 10 = 1 \times 10 \wedge 3 = 2 + 1 \wedge 10 = 10 \wedge 5 = 5 \wedge 10 = 10.$$

Subsequent processing will remove all of the primitive constraints in C. Finally, the

algorithm will return *true* since each primitive constraint is satisfiable and contains
no variables.

Local propagation solvers are simple to implement and quite good at handling
some kinds of constraints. However, they are usually not complete. One reason is
that they are weak at solving constraints with cyclic dependencies. For example,
consider the constraint

$$X = Y + Z \wedge X = T - Y \wedge T = 5 \wedge Z = 7.$$

A local propagation solver will detect the determined variables $T = 5$ and $Z = 7$. However the constraint determines the variables X and Y to be 6 and -1
respectively. This will not be found by local propagation because it cannot be
determined by looking at the primitive constraints one at a time. Local propagation
behaves as above for the unsatisfiable constraint

$$X = Y + Z \wedge X = T - Y \wedge T = 5 \wedge Z = 7 \wedge Y \geq 2,$$

determining that $T = 5$ and $Z = 7$ but not that $X = 6$ and $Y = -1$.

Another weakness of local propagation solvers is their handling of non-equality
primitive constraints. Usually this is very weak because the *determines(c)* relation
for non-equality primitive constraints c is almost always empty.

In Chapter 3 we will investigate more powerful propagation based approaches to
constraint solving, which are used to solve constraints over finite domains.

1.8 Summary

Constraints are powerful tools for modelling many real-world problems. In this
book, a constraint is considered to be a conjunction of primitive constraints. A
constraint can be understood only in the context of a constraint domain, such as
Boolean values, trees or real numbers, which dictates the meaning of the function
and relation symbols and the values that variables in the constraint can range over.

One of the most fundamental questions we can ask about a constraint is whether
it is satisfiable, and, if so, what a solution looks like. A constraint solver answers
such questions. Ideally, a constraint solver is complete, that is always answer *true*
or *false*, but a constraint solver may also be incomplete, sometimes returning
unknown. Even incomplete solvers should be well-behaved in the sense that they
should be monotonic, set-based and variable name independent.

In this chapter we gave examples of complete constraint solvers for linear real
equality constraints, finite-tree constraints, and an incomplete solver for Boolean
constraints. We also examined some other constraint domains: the blocks worlds and
sequence constraints. Finally we presented local propagation, a general approach
to constraint solving for any domain.

1.9   Exercises

1.1. Model an electric circuit similar to the one in Figure 1.1, except the resistors R_1 and R_2 should be serially connected. Investigate the behaviour of the resulting circuit under the constraints given in Section 1.2.

1.2. Determine the result of applying gauss_jordan to the following constraints:

(a) $X = 3 \wedge Y = 2 - X \wedge Z = 3 + X + Y$,

(b) $Y = 2 - X \wedge Z = 3 + X + Y \wedge Z = 4$.

1.3. Give a term equation which will force the use of rules (1) and (5) in unify.

1.4. Using unify, determine which of the following term equations are satisfiable:

(a) $p(X, X, Y) = p(f(U), Y, f(V))$,

(b) $p(X, X, Y) = p(f(U), Y, a)$,

(c) $p(f(X, Y), g(Y), X) = p(U, g(g(V)), a)$,

(d) $p(a, X, f(g(Y))) = p(Z, h(Z, W), f(W))$,

(e) $p(f(X, Y), f(X, Z), Z) = p(f(U, a), f(V, V), f(U, a))$.

1.5. (*) A common way to prove that an algorithm terminates for all inputs is to come up with a *bound function* for one or more of the variables. A bound function returns non-negative integers. If one can show that the bound function applied to (some of) the algorithm's variables yields *strictly decreasing* values in successive iterations, then the algorithm must eventually halt.

The objective here is to argue that unify terminates for all input. In a first attempt to give a bound function, we may choose to let the function return the number of symbols in the constraint C. But unfortunately, not all rules in unify decrease the total number of symbols in the equation set. For example, application of rule (6) typically *increases* it!

Show that unify nevertheless must terminate. [Hint: There is something (in a sense more important) which rule (6) *does* decrease.]

1.6. Try out bool_solve in an attempt to show that

$$(\neg U \vee V) \wedge (U \vee \neg V) \wedge (X \vee Y) \wedge (Y \vee Z) \wedge (Z \vee X)$$

is satisfiable. Choose ϵ to be 0.1 and generate random truth assignments ϕ by throwing a coin (tail = 1, head = 0), once per variable.

1.7. Huey, Dewey and Louie are being questioned by their uncle. These are the statements they make:

Huey: "Dewey and Louie had equal share in it; if one is guilty, so is the other."

Dewey: "If Huey is guilty, then so am I."

Louie: "Dewey and I are not both guilty."

Their uncle, knowing that they are cub scouts, realises that they cannot tell a lie. Has he got sufficient information to decide who (if any) are guilty? Model the problem as Boolean constraints, and decide.

1.8. In the context of the example blocks world used in Section 1.5, count the number of solutions to the following blocks world problems:

    (a) $red(X) \wedge floor(Y) \wedge on(Y, X)$,

    (b) $green(X) \wedge on(X, Y) \wedge floor(Y)$,

    (c) $green(X) \wedge pyramid(Y) \wedge yellow(Z) \wedge on(X, Z)$.

1.9. (*) Give an algorithm for a (possibly incomplete) solver for a constraint domain of sets. The only constant of the domain is $\emptyset$ representing the empty set. The constraint relations are $\subseteq, \subset, \neq, =$ with the usual meaning. Although always returning *unknown* is correct, try to make your constraint solver as strong as possible (that is, answering *true* or *false* in as many cases as possible).

1.10. (*) Prove the following: if *solv* is a complete constraint solver, then *solv* is well-behaved.

1.11. (*) Determine the answers for local_propagation_solve applied to the problems in Question 1.2.

1.12. (*) Use local propagation to determine the satisfiability of $X = 2Y \wedge Y = 1 \wedge Z = X \times X \wedge Y \leq Z$.

1.13. (*) Find conditions that ensure that local_propagation_solve is well-behaved.

1.10 Practical Exercises

This book is designed for use with real constraint logic programming languages. Many of these are available free for research and educational purposes. One widely used constraint programming language is $CLP(\mathcal{R})$, a constraint programming language for a constraint domain that combines tree constraints with real arithmetic constraints using a floating point representation of real numbers. It is available for most architectures including the majority of Unix architectures, Linux, DOS and OS/2. It can be obtained by sending an email request to Joxan Jaffar (`joxan@iscs.nus.sg`).

$CLP(\mathcal{R})$ includes a constraint solver which handles real arithmetic constraints and tree constraints. $CLP(\mathcal{R})$ is usually executed by typing the command `clpr` from the command shell. The $CLP(\mathcal{R})$ system presents a prompt to the user.

```
1 ?-
```

Constraints can be typed in at the prompt and $CLP(\mathcal{R})$ will invoke its constraint solver, and give one of three answers: *** Yes corresponding to *true*, *** No corresponding to *false*, and *** Maybe corresponding to *unknown*. If the result is not *** No the system also returns a representation of the constraints (an equivalent constraint to that which was typed in).

Constraints are represented using the following conventions: * is used for multiplication, linear expressions need explicit multiplication symbols, that is $2Y$ must be written as 2 * Y, conjunction ($\wedge$) is represented using a comma ",", $\geq$ and $\leq$ are represented by ">=" and "<=" respectively, and finally a full stop (or period) "." is used to terminate the constraint. To interrupt execution the user can type *control-C*, that is type "c" while holding down the control key. To quit from $CLP(\mathcal{R})$ the user can type *control-D*, that is type "d" while holding down the control key.

For example, the constraint $1 + X = 2Y + Z \wedge Z - X = 3$ is typed as shown in the following *emphasized text* after the prompt

```
1 ?- 1 + X = 2 * Y + Z, Z - X = 3.
```

This results in the system returning the answer

```
Y = -1
X = Z - 3


*** Yes
```

The last line *** Yes indicates that the constraint solver has determined that the constraints are satisfiable. Similarly, typing the following *emphasized text*

```
2 ?- 1 + X = 2 * Y + Z, Z - X = 3, X + Y = 5 + Z.
```

results in the system returning the answer

```
*** No
```

indicating that the constraint solver has determined the constraints are unsatisfiable. Finally, typing the following constraint

```
3 ?- X * X <= -1.
```

results in the system returning the answer

```
X * X <= -1


*** Maybe
```

indicating the solver cannot determine satisfiability or unsatisfiability.

Term equations are typed exactly as they appear in the text. For example

```
4 ?- cons(Y,nil) = cons(X,Z), Y = cons(a,T).
```

results in the system returning

```
X = Y
Z = nil
Y = cons(a, T)


*** Yes
```

indicating the constraint is satisfiable.

Prolog is a constraint logic programming language over the domain of tree constraints. However many recent Prolog systems include other constraint solving facilities. SICStus Prolog release 3 includes libraries for real arithmetic constraint solving. It provides solvers which use two different representations of numbers: infinite precision rational numbers, and floating point numbers. SICStus is widely used and available from the Swedish Institute of Computer Science (see `http://www.sics.se/isl/sicstus.html`).

SICStus Prolog is usually executed by typing the command `sicstus` from the command shell. The system presents a prompt to the user.

```
| ?-
```

In order to use the arithmetic constraint solving facilities one needs to load one of the constraint solving libraries either by typing:

```
| ?- use_module(library(clpq)).
```

to load the rational number solver, or

```
| ?- use_module(library(clpr)).
```

to load the floating point solver.

Constraints can be typed in at the prompt and SICStus Prolog will use the loaded constraint solver to determine satisfiability of the constraint. It will either return `no` if the solver determines the constraint to be unsatisfiable or return a representation of the constraints which is equivalent to the typed constraint. Both arithmetic solvers are incomplete. If the solver cannot determine whether the constraint is satisfiable or not, the answer returned by the system starts with a term of the form `nonlin`:t, indicating the result *unknown*.

Constraints are represented using almost the same notational conventions as $CLP(\mathcal{R})$ above, except $\leq$ is written as "=<" rather than "<=", a $\neq$ primitive constraint is supported written as "=/=", and importantly all primitive constraints or conjunctions of primitive constraints must be enclosed between braces "{" and "}". Term equations are typed exactly as they appear in the text, as for $CLP(\mathcal{R})$. Interrupting execution and quitting from SICStus Prolog is the same as for $CLP(\mathcal{R})$.

For example, using the rational constraint solver the constraint $1 + X = 2Y + Z \wedge Z - X = 3$ is typed as shown in the following *emphasized text* after the prompt

```
| ?- {1 + X = 2 * Y + Z, Z - X = 3}.
```

This results in the system returning the answer

```
Y = -1,
{Z = 3+X} ?
```

The question mark indicates the system is waiting for input, for the purposes of this chapter just type Enter or Return in response. The answer `yes` will then be displayed. Since the answer does not begin with `nonlin:` this indicates the constraint solver has determined that the constraint is satisfiable.

If the floating point constraint solver is used the answer is slightly different because the numbers are represented differently. For the constraint above the system returns the answer

```
Y = -1.0,
{Z = 3.0+X} ?
```

Using the rational constraint solver typing the following *emphasized text*

```
| ?- {1 + X = 2 * Y + Z, Z - X = 3, X + Y = 5 + Z}.
```

results in the system returning the answer

```
no
```

indicating that the constraint solver has determined the constraint is unsatisfiable. Finally, typing the following constraint

```
| ?- {X * X =< -1}.
```

results in the system returning the answer

```
nonlin:{1+X^2=<0} ?
```

indicating that the solver cannot determine satisfiability or unsatisfiability.

P1.1. Use $CLP(\mathcal{R})$ or SICStus Prolog to determine the satisfiability of the constraints

(a) $X = 3 \land Y = 2 - X \land Z = 3 + X + Y$,

(b) $Y = 2 - X \land Z = 3 + X + Y \land Z = 4$.

Compare the constraint output by the system with your answer to Question 1.2.

P1.2. Write down what you expect as an answer to the following two constraints, then try them using $CLP(\mathcal{R})$ or SICStus Prolog.

(a) $X = 3 \land Y = 0 \land Z = X/Y$,

(b) $X = 0 \land Y = 0 \land Z = X/Y$.

P1.3. Use $CLP(\mathcal{R})$ or SICStus Prolog to determine the satisfiability of the constraints.

(a) $p(X, X, Y) = p(f(U), Y, f(V))$

(b) $p(X, X, Y) = p(f(U), Y, a)$

(c) $p(f(X, Y), g(Y), X) = p(U, g(g(V)), a)$

(d) $p(a, X, f(g(Y))) = p(Z, h(Z, W), f(W))$

Compare the constraint output by the system with your answer to Question 1.4.

P1.4. Use $CLP(\mathcal{R})$ or SICStus Prolog to determine the voltage V and current I in the circuit shown in Figure 1.1 when the resistor values are $R_1 = 4$ and $R_2 = 3$ and the current $I_1 = 3$.

P1.5. Write a constraint that describes the house building project of Figure 1.2 with the additional constraint that stages B and D of the project are reached at the same time. Use $CLP(\mathcal{R})$ or SICStus Prolog to determine the earliest completion time of the house with this new constraint. [Hint: Type in the constraints and see what the system says.]

P1.6. (*) Try the term constraint $X = f(X)$ in $CLP(\mathcal{R})$ or SICStus Prolog. How does the system respond? Try the missing constraint from Question 1.4, that is $p(f(X,Y), f(X,Z), Z) = p(f(U,a), f(V,V), f(U,a))$. Execute unify by hand on the constraint $X = f(X)$ but ignoring case (5) (thus using (6)). What does unify answer? Now imagine displaying the tree which results. For efficiency the $CLP(\mathcal{R})$ system does not perform the check in case (5). Can you explain its behaviour on these two constraints?

P1.7. (*) Sometimes the $CLP(\mathcal{R})$ or SICStus Prolog system answers `*** Maybe` or `nonlin:t` indicating an *unknown* answer. Try the following constraints:

(a) $X \times Y = Z$,

(b) $X \times Y = Z \land Z = 2$,

(c) $X \times Y = Z \land Y = 2$,

(d) $X \times Y = Z \land X = 2$,

(e) $X \times Y = Z \land Y = 0$.

Can you give a rule for determining when the solver answers *unknown*?

1.11 Notes

The concept of constraint solving has a long history in mathematics. Finding solutions to equations over the integers is one of the oldest mathematical problems and the Babylonians are known to have solved a variety of equations with two variables. Several Greek mathematicians studied equation solving, most notably Diophantus, who wrote his *Arithmetica* around the year 250. Diophantus solved many specific equational problems, but it is unlikely that he or any of his contemporaries knew and applied general solving methods. According to Struik [127], the first general solution in integers to equations of the form $aX + bY = c$ is due to the Indian mathematician Brahmagupta from the seventh century. (Such equations are today referred to as "Diophantine" although Diophantus, unlike Brahmagupta, allowed rational solutions and disallowed negative solutions.) In the ninth century, the Persian astronomer al-Khwarizmi wrote an influential treatise on equation solving, *Hisab al jabr wal muqabala*. The term "algebra" originated from the title which, until the nineteenth century, meant nothing but "equational reasoning." Incidentally, the term "algorithm" is also derived from al-Khwarizmi's latinised name.

Until the sixteenth century, constraint solving was dealt with only through cumbersome verbal descriptions of problems and methods. The use of symbols such as '+', '−', and '=' (or symbols resembling those) made reasoning much easier, and the next step forward was taken by Viète who, in the late sixteenth century, began to use letters for constants and variables. This allowed many practical and theoretical breakthroughs, including Descartes's application of algebra to problems in geometry.

By the end of the eighteenth century, solving linear equations by variable elimination was a standard technique, even though a precise algorithm had not been published. Gauss used variants (often called *Gaussian elimination*) of the Gauss-Jordan elimination method as early as 1809, but the method given in Section 1.3 is usually attributed to an 1829 paper by Gauss [54]. However, Schrijver [116] suggests that the Gauss-Jordan elimination method was not spelled out in detail before Clasen did so in 1888.

The algebra of propositional logic is due to Boole [13]. Many methods for solving Boolean constraints are known. The probabilistic algorithm used for the Boolean solver in Section 1.5.1 is related to one suggested by Wu and Tang [145]. For other automated approaches to Boolean constraint solving see [22, 93, 9].

In the late twentieth century, Frege extended Boole's work by developing what would, later, be known as predicate logic. Terms, or trees, in the sense of Section 1.4, and tree constraint solving is the cornerstone of most automated deduction. The tree constraint solver given in Section 1.4 is essentially due to Herbrand [65]. Independently, a rather different algorithm was given by Robinson, as part of the so-called resolution approach to automated theorem proving [112].

Apart from mathematics, the two areas that have had the greatest impact on a modern theory of constraints and their use in automated problem solving are Operations Research (OR) and Artificial Intelligence (AI). OR is concerned with building mathematical *models* of real world situations in order to allow the experimental analysis of problems, typically by computer. Much of the motivation for building computers came from OR and its wartime applications. Since most real-world problems include some notion of "constraints," many of the techniques developed in OR (linear programming, integer programming and so on) involve constraint solving.

AI is an umbrella term for a number of automated problem-solving techniques, which goes back to the sixties. We shall have more to say about the influence of AI after we have discussed other constraint operations in the next chapter. The blocks world was suggested by Sacerdoti [114] as an interesting "plan-formation" problem. For an overview of the state-of-the-art in constraint-based diagnosis, planning, scheduling, language understanding, machine vision, and other areas, see Freuder and Mackworth [50].

Sequences have a long history in computer science and are more commonly referred to as strings. The overlaying of contigs can be seen as a slightly more complicated instance of the standard problem of string matching, that is looking for one instance of a string in another. Well known algorithms for string matching like Knuth-Morris-Pratt [80] and Boyer-Moore [17] can be adapted to solve the problem. Solving more complicated constraints over sequences is considerably more difficult. The first complete constraint solver for sequence constraints is due to Makanin [91], while a more efficient solver results from the work of Jaffar [68].

Local propagation has been developed independently by a number of researchers to solve arithmetic and Boolean constraints. The term is generally attributed to Sussman and Steele [132], who used local propagation to solve constraints in the early constraint language CONSTRAINTS. Sutherland used it even earlier in SKETCHPAD [133] where it was called the "One Pass Method." Roth [113] used local propagation to solve satisfiability of Boolean constraints for test pattern generation for digital circuits.

2   Simplification, Optimization and Implication

In the preceding chapter, we studied various constraint domains and investigated how to determine satisfiability of constraints in these domains. In this chapter we look at other operations on constraints that are also of interest to the constraint programmer.

The first operation we study is simplification. This operation takes a system of constraints and simplifies it, so that information implicit in the original system becomes apparent. An important case of simplification is projection, that is simplifying constraints in terms of the variables that are of interest. In general this is a difficult and expensive operation. Simplification is important in constraint programming because of the need to present the answer constraints generated by a constraint program in a form which is understandable to the user.

Next, we examine optimization. In many constraint programming problems we would like to find the "best" answer where answers are ranked by some "objective function." Such problems are called optimization problems. We describe the simplex algorithm for solving linear real arithmetic optimization problems, that is a problem with a linear arithmetic constraint and a linear objective function, and show how it may also be used to efficiently determine satisfiability of a linear arithmetic constraint.

We conclude by investigating constraint implication, that is, whether one constraint has solutions which are a subset of the solutions of another constraint, and equivalence, that is, whether two constraints have exactly the same set of solutions. These operations are of interest for constraint databases and concurrent constraint programming.

2.1   Constraint Simplification

Although a large and complicated constraint may model some system or problem accurately it may be very difficult to understand. Sometimes the apparent complexity of the constraint is misleading and the same information can be expressed more succinctly. Simplification is the process of replacing a constraint by an equivalent constraint which has a "simpler" form.

The following list of arithmetic constraints are all equivalent. This is because changing the order of the primitive constraints, inverting a primitive constraint, substituting one variable for another by using an equation, performing simple arithmetic simplification or adding a "redundant" constraint do not change the set of solutions of a constraint.

$$X \geq 3 \wedge 2 = Y + X$$
$$\leftrightarrow \quad 3 \leq X \wedge X = 2 - Y$$
$$\leftrightarrow \quad X = 2 - Y \wedge 3 \leq X$$
$$\leftrightarrow \quad X = 2 - Y \wedge 3 \leq 2 - Y$$
$$\leftrightarrow \quad X = 2 - Y \wedge Y \leq -1$$
$$\leftrightarrow \quad X = 2 - Y \wedge Y \leq -1 \wedge Y \leq 2.$$

The most obvious method of constraint simplification is to simplify the individual primitive constraints. For example, $0 \leq 3$ can be simplified to *true*, as can $(X + 1)^2 \geq X^2 + 2X$. Primitive constraints may have much simpler equivalent forms, for example $X - 2 + 2Y + 3 \geq 2X - Z - 4$ is equivalent to $X - 2Y - Z \leq 5$. Similarly the primitive term constraint $succ(succ(succ(X))) = succ(succ(Y))$ is equivalent to $succ(X) = Y$.

An important kind of simplification is to remove from a constraint C those primitive constraints which do not affect the meaning of C. In order to determine whether removing a (not necessarily primitive) constraint C_2 from $C_1 \wedge C_2$ will leave the meaning unchanged, we introduce the concept of "redundancy."

Definition 2.1

One constraint C_1 *implies* another C_2, written $C_1 \rightarrow C_2$, if the solutions of C_1 are a subset of the solutions of C_2. Alternatively, we say that constraint C_2 is *redundant* with respect to constraint C_1, if $C_1 \rightarrow C_2$.

A constraint C of the form $c_1 \wedge \cdots \wedge c_n$, where $c_1, \ldots, c_n$ are primitive constraints, is *redundancy-free*, if no c_i is redundant with respect to the remaining primitive constraints. That is, it is not the case that

$$(c_1 \wedge \cdots \wedge c_{i-1} \wedge c_{i+1} \wedge \cdots \wedge c_n) \rightarrow c_i.$$

For example, $X \geq 3$ is redundant with respect to $X \geq 4$. Therefore, we may simplify the constraint $X \geq 4 \wedge X \geq 3$ to give the equivalent constraint $X \geq 4$. Similarly, $Y \leq X + 2 \wedge Y \geq 4 \rightarrow X \geq 1$. Thus, $Y \leq X + 2 \wedge Y \geq 4 \wedge X \geq 1$ can be simplified to $Y \leq X + 2 \wedge Y \geq 4$. In the tree constraint domain,

$$cons(X, X) = cons(Z, nil) \rightarrow Z = nil.$$

Thus, $cons(X, X) = cons(Z, nil) \wedge Z = nil$ can be simplified to $cons(X, X) = cons(Z, nil)$.

It follows that $C_1 \rightarrow C_2$ if C_1 and $C_1 \wedge C_2$ are equivalent. Furthermore, every constraint is implied by the unsatisfiable constraint, *false*.

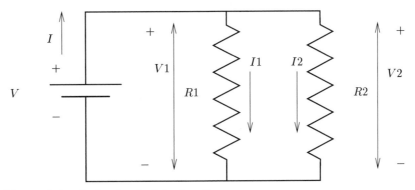

Figure 2.1 A simple electric circuit.

Normalising constraint solvers work by transforming one constraint to an equivalent constraint. They can also be seen as constraint simplifiers since the normal form is usually simpler than the original and some redundant information is removed. Consider the operation of **unify** on the constraint

$$cons(X, X) = cons(Z, nil) \wedge Y = succ(X) \wedge succ(Z) = Y \wedge Z = nil :$$

C	S
$cons(X, X) = cons(Z, nil) \wedge Y = succ(X) \wedge succ(Z) = Y \wedge Z = nil$	$true$
$X = Z \wedge X = nil \wedge Y = succ(X) \wedge succ(Z) = Y \wedge Z = nil$	$true$
$Z = nil \wedge Y = succ(Z) \wedge succ(Z) = Y \wedge Z = nil$	$X = Z$
$Y = succ(nil) \wedge succ(nil) = Y \wedge nil = nil$	$X = nil \wedge Z = nil$
$succ(nil) = succ(nil) \wedge nil = nil$	$X = nil \wedge Z = nil \wedge Y = succ(nil)$
$nil = nil \wedge nil = nil$	$X = nil \wedge Z = nil \wedge Y = succ(nil)$
$nil = nil$	$X = nil \wedge Z = nil \wedge Y = succ(nil)$
$true$	$X = nil \wedge Z = nil \wedge Y = succ(nil)$

The resulting constraint, $X = nil \wedge Z = nil \wedge Y = succ(nil)$, is far simpler than the original constraint even though it is equivalent.

2.2 Projection

The usefulness of constraint simplification is even more apparent when we are only interested in some of the variables appearing in the constraint. For example, take the constraints modelling the circuit in Figure 2.1 together with the knowledge that $R1 = 5$ and $R2 = 10$. This gives the constraint:

$$R1 = 5 \wedge R2 = 10 \wedge V1 = I1 \times R1 \wedge V2 = I2 \times R2 \wedge$$
$$V - V1 = 0 \wedge V - V2 = 0 \wedge V1 - V2 = 0 \wedge$$
$$I - I1 - I2 = 0 \wedge -I + I1 + I2 = 0.$$

If we are only interested in the relationship between the overall current I and overall voltage V in the circuit, we would like to simplify the constraint so that the simplification only involves the *variables of interest*, namely V and I. As we saw in Section 1.2, the resulting simplification should be $3 \times V = 10 \times I$.

A more interesting example of constraint simplification involves reasoning about arbitrary resistance values. Imagine that we add the constraint $V = I \times R$ to the constraint describing the circuit, reflecting our belief that the overall current and voltage are related as if by a single resistor. If we only want to know the relationship between the effective resistance value R and the resistance values $R1$ and $R2$ of the components, then we would like to know the effect of these constraints restricted to only the variables $R, R1$ and $R2$. This is simply:

$$R = (R1 \times R2)/(R1 + R2)$$

which is, of course, the rule for describing the effect of resistors wired in parallel.

Restricting consideration of a constraint to some of the variables in the constraint means that we examine the solutions of the constraint, but ignore the values assigned to variables that are not of interest. This leads to the following definitions:

Definition 2.2
If θ is a valuation of the form $\{x_1 \mapsto d_1, \ldots, x_m \mapsto d_m\}$ then α is an *extension* of θ if it is of the form $\{x_1 \mapsto d_1, \ldots, x_m \mapsto d_m, x_{m+1} \mapsto d_{m+1}, \ldots, x_n \mapsto d_n\}$.
θ is a *partial solution* of C if there exists an extension of θ which is a solution of C.

For example $\{X \mapsto 3, Y \mapsto 4\}$ is an extension of $\{Y \mapsto 4\}$. Since $\{X \mapsto 3, Y \mapsto 4\}$ is a solution of $X \leq Y$, $\{Y \mapsto 4\}$ is a partial solution of $X \leq Y$.

Definition 2.3
The *projection* of a constraint C_1 on to variable set V, where $V \subseteq vars(C_1)$ is a constraint C_2 involving only variables in V such that:

(a) if θ is a solution of C_1, then it is a solution of C_2; and

(b) if θ is a valuation over V which is a solution of C_2, then it is a partial solution of C_1.

Projection formalises our informal notion of simplifying a constraint with respect to the particular variables of interest. It allows us to extract information about the interaction among these variables of interest from a large complex constraint.

For example, the projection of the constraint

$$X \geq Y \wedge Y \geq Z \wedge Z \geq T \wedge T \geq 0$$

on to the variable X is the constraint $X \geq 0$. This is because:
(a) Every solution θ of $X \geq Y \wedge Y \geq Z \wedge Z \geq T \wedge T \geq 0$ is a solution of $X \geq 0$. This follows since the original constraint implies that $X \geq Y \geq Z \geq T \geq 0$.
(b) Every solution of $X \geq 0$, say $\{X \mapsto n\}$ where $n \geq 0$, can be extended to a solution of $X \geq Y \wedge Y \geq Z \wedge Z \geq T \wedge T \geq 0$. One such extension is simply, $\{X \mapsto n, Y \mapsto n, Z \mapsto n, T \mapsto n\}$.

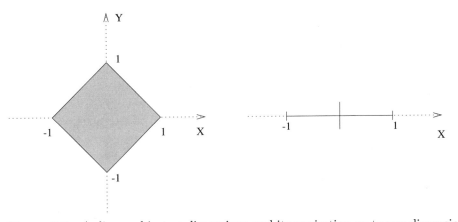

Figure 2.2 A diamond in two dimensions and its projection on to one dimension.

As another example, the projection of

$$cons(Y, Y) = cons(X, Z) \wedge succ(Z) = succ(T)$$

on to the variables $\{X, T\}$ is the constraint $X = T$. This is because:
(a) Every solution θ to $cons(Y, Y) = cons(X, Z) \wedge succ(Z) = succ(T)$ is a solution
of $X = T$. This follows since the original constraint implies that $X = Y = Z = T$.
(b) Every solution to $X = T$, say $\{X \mapsto t, T \mapsto t\}$ where t is any tree, can be
extended to a solution to $cons(Y, Y) = cons(X, Z) \wedge succ(Z) = succ(T)$. The
extension is simply, $\{X \mapsto t, Y \mapsto t, Z \mapsto t, T \mapsto t\}$.

In the case of arithmetic constraints we can give an interesting geometric interpretation of projection. A constraint on $n + m$ variables defines a region in $n + m$ dimensional space. If we project this constraint on to the subspace spanned by m of the variables, the resulting constraint defines the *shadow* of the region in $n + m$ dimensional space in m dimensional space. This is easiest to visualise (and draw!) in the case where we project a 2-dimensional object on to one dimension.

The following constraint on variables X and Y defines the diamond shape shown in Figure 2.2,

$$X + Y \leq 1 \wedge X - Y \leq 1 \wedge -X + Y \leq 1 \wedge -X - Y \leq 1.$$

The shadow of the diamond on the X axis is the line segment shown in Figure 2.2, geometrically illustrating that the projection of this constraint on to the variable X is the constraint $-1 \leq X \wedge X \leq 1$.

Fourier's algorithm for variable elimination can be used to project a conjunction of linear real inequalities on to a set of variables of interest. At each step, Fourier elimination is used to *eliminate* a variable which is not of interest from the current constraint. This step is repeated until all variables which are not of interest are eliminated. We restrict our presentation to non-strict linear inequalities ($\leq$ and $\geq$), however it is straightforward to extend Fourier's algorithm to strict inequalities ($>$ and $<$) (see Exercise 2.2).

Consider a constraint, C, composed of linear inequalities which we regard as a set of linear inequalities. That is to say, we are really dealing with $primitives(C)$. Elimination of a variable y from C proceeds as follows. First, C is partitioned into three subsets: C^0, those inequalities which do not involve y; C^+, those inequalities which are equivalent to an inequality of the form $y \leq t$, where t does not involve y; and C^-, those inequalities which are equivalent to an inequality of the form $t \leq y$, where again t does not involve y. Then, for each pair of the form $t_1 \leq y$ in C^- and $y \leq t_2$ in C^+, we form a new inequality $t_1 \leq t_2$. This set of new inequalities together with C^0 is the projection of the original constraint C on to the original variables except for y.

For example, consider the inequalities representing the diamond in Figure 2.2. We wish to project on to the variable set $\{X\}$, thus we must eliminate Y from the inequalities. The inequalities are partitioned as follows:

$$C^0 = \{\},$$
$$C^- = \{X - 1 \leq Y, \ -1 - X \leq Y\},$$
$$C^+ = \{Y \leq 1 - X, \ Y \leq 1 + X\}.$$

We now pair each inequality in C^- with each in C^+:

$$\begin{array}{llll}
X - 1 \leq Y & \text{together with} & Y \leq 1 - X & \text{gives} \quad X \leq 1, \\
X - 1 \leq Y & \text{together with} & Y \leq 1 + X & \text{gives} \quad 0 \leq 2, \\
-1 - X \leq Y & \text{together with} & Y \leq 1 - X & \text{gives} \quad 0 \leq 2, \text{ and} \\
-1 - X \leq Y & \text{together with} & Y \leq 1 + X & \text{gives} \quad -1 \leq X.
\end{array}$$

Thus, after simplification, we discover that the projection of the original constraint on to the variable set $\{X\}$ is $X \leq 1 \wedge -1 \leq X$.

Algorithm 2.1: Fourier elimination
INPUT: A set of linear inequalities, C, and a set of variables, V.
OUTPUT: A set of linear inequalities, which is the projection of C on to V.
METHOD: The algorithm is given in Figure 2.3. □

It is easy to extend the Fourier elimination algorithm to handle linear equations as well as linear inequalities. All we need to do is rewrite an equality $t = t'$ into the equivalent inequalities $t \leq t'$ and $t' \leq t$.

As another example of a projection algorithm, we now consider Boolean constraints. There is a simple method for eliminating a variable x from a Boolean constraint C. It relies on the observation that C is equivalent to the formula $(x \wedge C_x) \vee (\neg x \wedge C_{\neg x})$ where C_x is obtained from C by replacing all occurrences of x by 1 and $C_{\neg x}$ is obtained from C by replacing all occurrences of x by 0. It follows that the projection of C on to $vars(C) - \{x\}$ is just $C_x \vee C_{\neg x}$.

For example, we can eliminate the variable Y from the constraint C,

$$(\neg X \vee Y) \wedge (\neg X \vee Z) \wedge (X \vee \neg Y \vee \neg Z),$$

```
y is a variable;
t, t₁ and t₂ are linear arithmetic terms not including y;
C, C⁰, C⁺ and C⁻ are sets of linear inequalities;
V is a set of variables.


fourier_simplify(C, V)
    while vars(C) − V is not empty
        choose y ∈ vars(C) − V
        C := fourier_eliminate(C,y)
    endwhile
    return C

fourier_eliminate(C, y)
    let C⁰ be those inequalities in C not involving y
    let C⁺ be those inequalities in C which can be written t ≤ y
    let C⁻ be those inequalities in C which can be written y ≤ t
    for each t₁ ≤ y ∈ C⁺
        for each y ≤ t₂ ∈ C⁻
            C⁰ := C⁰ ∪ {t₁ ≤ t₂}
        endfor
    endfor
    return C⁰
```

Figure 2.3   Linear inequality simplifier.

as follows. C_Y is simply

$$(\neg X \lor 1) \land (\neg X \lor Z) \land (X \lor \neg 1 \lor \neg Z),$$

which is simplified to

$$(\neg X \lor Z) \land (X \lor \neg Z).$$

$C_{\neg Y}$ is

$$(\neg X \lor 0) \land (\neg X \lor Z) \land (X \lor \neg 0 \lor \neg Z),$$

which is simplified to $\neg X$. Now the projection of C on to $\{X, Z\}$ is $C_Y \lor C_{\neg Y}$ which is therefore

$$((\neg X \lor Z) \land (X \lor \neg Z)) \lor \neg X.$$

2.3   Constraint Simplifiers

In the preceding section we have seen algorithms which can be used to simplify a constraint by projecting the constraint on to the variables of interest. Unfortunately, it is not possible to do this in all constraint domains. The problem is, there may be a constraint C_1 in the domain which involves variables V (among others) but for which there is no constraint C_2 in the domain which is the projection of C_1 on to V.

For example, consider the domain of tree constraints and the constraint $X = succ(Y)$. Some sample solutions of this constraint are

$$\{X \mapsto succ(0), Y \mapsto 0\},$$
$$\{X \mapsto succ(succ(0)), Y \mapsto succ(0)\},$$
$$\{X \mapsto succ(succ(succ(0))), Y \mapsto succ(succ(0))\}.$$

The projection of $X = succ(Y)$ on to X must therefore have solutions

$$\{X \mapsto succ(0)\},$$
$$\{X \mapsto succ(succ(0))\},$$
$$\{X \mapsto succ(succ(succ(0)))\},$$

but it cannot have $\{X \mapsto 0\}$ as a solution. From the definition of projection, the projection of $X = succ(Y)$ on to X must be a constraint only involving the variable X. But there is no tree constraint involving only the single variable X which has $\{X \mapsto succ(0)\}$ and $\{X \mapsto succ(succ(0))\}$ as solutions and does not have $\{X \mapsto 0\}$ as a solution.

To avoid this problem, we must generalize our notion of simplification with respect to a set of variables in order to allow the simplification to contain extra "local" variables. In general, a constraint simplifier takes a constraint and a set of variables and returns a constraint that has the same solutions as the original with respect to the variables of interest.

Definition 2.4
Constraints C_1 and C_2 are *equivalent* with respect to the set of variables $\{x_1, \ldots, x_n\}$ if:
(a) for each solution $\{x_1 \mapsto d_1, \ldots, x_n \mapsto d_n, \ldots\}$ of C_1, $\{x_1 \mapsto d_1, \ldots, x_n \mapsto d_n\}$ is a partial solution of C_2; and
(b) for each solution $\{x_1 \mapsto d_1, \ldots, x_n \mapsto d_n, \ldots\}$ of C_2, $\{x_1 \mapsto d_1, \ldots, x_n \mapsto d_n\}$ is a partial solution of C_1.

Definition 2.5
A *simplifier*, *simpl*, for constraint domain $\mathcal{D}$ takes a constraint C_1 in $\mathcal{D}$ and a set V of *variables of interest* and returns a constraint C_2 in $\mathcal{D}$, such that C_1 and C_2 are equivalent with respect to V.

Clearly the algorithms given in the last section for Boolean constraint projection and Fourier elimination can be used to simplify Boolean constraints and linear arithmetic inequalities. In the case of tree constraints, the preceding example shows that there is no algorithm for projection. However, the following algorithm is a constraint simplifier for tree constraints.

```
x is a variable;
t is a term;
C, C₁, C₂ and S are tree constraints;
V is a set of variables.


tree_simplify(C, V)
    C₁ := unify(C)
    if C₁ ≡ false then return false endif
    S := true
    while C₁ is of the form x = t ∧ C₂
        C₁ := C₂
        if x ∈ V then
            if t is a variable and t ∉ V then
                substitute x for t in C₁ and S
            else
                S := S ∧ x = t
            endif
        endif
    endwhile
    return S
```

Figure 2.4   Tree constraint simplifier.

Algorithm 2.2: Tree constraint simplifier

INPUT: Conjunction of term equations C and set V of variables.

OUTPUT: Conjunction of term equations S.

METHOD: The algorithm is shown in Figure 2.4. □

Consider the use of **tree_simplify** to simplify the constraint

$$h(f(X, Y), Z, g(T)) = h(f(g(T), X), f(X, X), g(U))$$

in terms of the variables of interest Y and T. As a first step, the solved form, C_1, of the original constraint is computed to be

$$Z = f(g(U), g(U)) \wedge X = g(U) \wedge Y = g(U) \wedge T = U.$$

Now each primitive constraint in C_1 is examined. The first two equations, $Z = f(g(U), g(U))$ and $X = g(U)$, are discarded since Z and X are not in the variables of interest. The third equation, $Y = g(U)$ is placed into S as Y is of interest and $g(U)$ is not a variable. The fourth equation, $T = U$, is used to eliminate the variable U, which is not of interest, from S and C_1, replacing it by the variable T, which is of interest. Thus, S becomes $Y = g(T)$, which is the constraint returned by the algorithm.

In this example, **tree_simplify** has managed to return a constraint which is the projection of the original constraint on to the variables of interest. However, as we have seen it is not always possible to return the exact projection. In this case the answer will contain extra "local" variables. For example, if **tree_simplify** is applied to the constraint $X = succ(Y)$ with variable of interest X, the original constraint is returned as the answer.

The preceding definition of constraint simplifier is not very demanding. For instance, the identity function is always a constraint simplifier, that is to say, a simplifier which always returns the input constraint meets the specification. However, in practice we usually wish the simplification algorithm to remove as many variables which are not of interest as possible, and we would like the form of the constraint to be as simple as possible.

It is difficult to quantify what simple means in some respects since there is a tradeoff between different aspects of simplicity. Whether one form of a constraint is to be considered simpler than another form is not a straightforward question to answer. In some cases the result of a simplifier may not appear simpler to a human than the original constraint. For example, the result of applying tree_simplify to the constraint $X = f(X_1, X_1) \wedge X_1 = f(X_2, X_2) \wedge \cdots \wedge X_{n-1} = f(X_n, X_n)$ for the set of variables $\{X\}$ is exponentially larger than the original constraint. However, although it is larger it involves only one equation instead of n.

Individuals may argue which of many textual forms of a constraint is the simplest, but there are some guiding principles for constraint simplifiers. For some constraint domains, for example, the linear real inequalities and Boolean constraints, we have seen that we can use projection to simplify a constraint so that it only relates the variables of interest. Such simplifiers are said to be "projecting":

projecting: $vars(simpl(C, V)) \subseteq V$.

Even in the case in which no projecting simplifier exists for a constraint domain, it is desirable that the constraint simplifier does not introduce unnecessary extra variables in the simplified constraint:

weakly projecting: $|vars(simpl(C_1, V)) - V| \leq |vars(C_2) - V|$ for all constraints C_2 such that C_1 and C_2 are equivalent with respect to V. $|S|$ is defined to be the number of elements in the set S.

The tree constraint simplifier tree_simplify is weakly projecting but not projecting.

Projecting and weakly projecting simplifiers are very powerful. In effect, they give a complete solver for a constraint domain. This is because we can test if a constraint is satisfiable by projecting it on to the empty variable set. The resulting constraint cannot contain variables and so must be equivalent to either *true*, indicating the original constraint is satisfiable, or *false*, indicating the original constraint is unsatisfiable.

Redundant constraint information does not usually help in understanding a constraint, hence it is desirable that simplified constraints are redundancy-free.

redundancy-free: $simpl(C, V)$ is redundancy-free.

The tree constraint simplifier tree_simplify described above is redundancy-free. The Fourier elimination simplifier in Figure 2.3 is not redundancy-free, in fact it produces highly redundant constraints if used in the form described.

2.4 Optimization

Sometimes we are not only interested in the satisfiability of a constraint but also wish to find a solution to the constraint. In this case, we rarely desire any arbitrary solution, but instead want a solution that is "best." Finding a "best" solution to a constraint is called an *optimization problem*. This requires some way of specifying which solutions are better than others. The usual way of doing this is by giving an *objective function* that maps each solution to a real value. By convention, we will assume that the aim is to minimize the objective function f. Of course, we can also maximize an objective function, f, just by minimizing $-f$.

Definition 2.6
An *optimization problem*, written (C, f), consists of a constraint C and an *objective function* f which is an expression over the variables in C and which evaluates to a real number.
A valuation, θ, is *preferred* to valuation, θ', if the value of the objective function f under θ is less than the value under θ'. In other words, $\theta(f) < \theta'(f)$.
An *optimal solution*, θ, of (C, f) is a solution of C such that there is no other solution of C which is preferred to θ.

The optimization problem (C, f) in which C is the constraint $X + Y \geq 4$ and f is the objective function $X^2 + Y^2$ is illustrated in Figure 2.5. The shaded polygon in the figure represents the set of solutions to the constraint. The semi-circles across the polygon are contours for the objective function $X^2 + Y^2$ with the value of the objective function written next to the contour line. For instance, some solutions of C are $\{X \mapsto 0, Y \mapsto 4\}, \{X \mapsto 3, Y \mapsto 3\}$ and $\{X \mapsto 2, Y \mapsto 2\}$. Applied to f they give $16, 18$ and 8, respectively. From this diagram it is easy to see that the optimal solution is $\{X \mapsto 2, Y \mapsto 2\}$.

Optimization problems do not necessarily have a single optimal solution. For example, consider the above constraint $X + Y \geq 4$ together with the objective function $X + Y$. Any solution of the constraint $X + Y = 4$ is an optimal solution to this optimization problem.

On the other hand, an optimization problem may not have an optimal solution at all. There are two possible reasons for this. The first possibility is that the constraint has no solution, for instance consider the optimization problem $(X \geq 0 \wedge X \leq -2, X)$. The second possible reason is that every solution has a solution which is preferred to it. For instance, consider an arbitrary solution to $(X \leq 0, X)$ of the form $\{X \mapsto r\}$ where r is a negative number. The solution $\{X \mapsto r - 1\}$ is preferable. Since this is the case for any solution, there is no optimal solution.

Optimization problems are not only important in arithmetic constraint domains. Recall the blocks world of Section 1.5. We might wish to minimize the number of objects on the floor while satisfying the constraint

$$red(X) \wedge red(Y) \wedge X \neq Y \wedge pyramid(Z) \wedge yellow(X) \wedge floor(X).$$

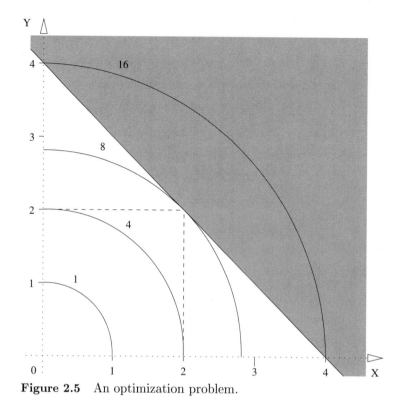

Figure 2.5   An optimization problem.

As a more practical example of the use of optimization, consider the example of building a house from Section 1.2. Suppose we wish to know the earliest time in which the house can be completed. The optimization problem is described by the constraint, C_H,

$$T_S \geq 0 \wedge T_A \geq T_S + 7 \wedge T_B \geq T_A + 4 \wedge T_C \geq T_A + 3 \wedge$$
$$T_D \geq T_A + 3 \wedge T_D \geq T_C + 2 \wedge T_E \geq T_B + 2 \wedge T_E \geq T_D + 3 \wedge T_E \geq T_C + 3$$

together with the objective function T_E. An optimal solution is

$$\{T_S \mapsto 0, T_A \mapsto 7, T_B \mapsto 11, T_C \mapsto 10, T_D \mapsto 12, T_E \mapsto 15\}.$$

Suppose that a building inspector is required to be on site during the period from stage B to stage E. Then minimizing the duration of the stay of the building inspector corresponds to minimizing the objective function $T_E - T_B$. An optimal solution of this problem is

$$\{T_S \mapsto 0, T_A \mapsto 7, T_B \mapsto 13, T_C \mapsto 10, T_D \mapsto 12, T_E \mapsto 15\}.$$

Another optimal solution is

$$\{T_S \mapsto 0, T_A \mapsto 10, T_B \mapsto 19, T_C \mapsto 14, T_D \mapsto 18, T_E \mapsto 21\}.$$

Optimization is quite closely related to simplification. If we consider the constraint C_H defining the house project problem above, and project the constraint on to the variable T_E the resulting constraint is (after redundancy elimination)

$$\text{fourier\_simplify}(C_H, \{T_E\}) = T_E \geq 15.$$

Clearly the minimum completion time is 15 days, and this can be read directly from the simplified constraint. If we require an optimal solution, this may be computed by conjoining $T_E = 15$ with C_H since any solution to this constraint is an optimal solution to the original problem.

The problem of minimizing the building inspector's stay can be answered in the same way. We first add a new variable S, equal to the length of the building inspector's stay, and then use fourier_simplify to project on to this variable:

$$\text{fourier\_simplify}(S = T_E - T_B \wedge C_H, \{S\}) = S \geq 2.$$

Again the minimum stay length is clear from the simplified constraint. Thus we can use fourier_simplify to answer optimization problems over linear arithmetic constraints with a linear objective function. In general however, it is extremely expensive to do so. A better algorithm is given in the next section.

2.5   The Simplex Algorithm

One of the algorithms most widely used in practice is Dantzig's simplex algorithm. This algorithm answers optimization problems for linear real arithmetic constraints in which the objective function is a linear real arithmetic expression. It is much more efficient than using fourier_simplify and in practice usually has polynomial cost.

To understand how the simplex algorithm works, it is useful to view the optimization problem from a geometric perspective. Consider the problem of minimizing $X - Y$ subject to the constraints $1 \leq X \wedge X \leq 3 \wedge 0 \leq Y \wedge 2Y - X \leq 3$. The problem is shown in Figure 2.6. The shaded polygon in the figure represents the set of solutions to the constraint. The dashed lines across the polygon are contours for the objective function $X - Y$ with the value of the objective function written next to the contour line. From this diagram it is easy to see that the minimum value for the objective function is -1 which occurs at the upper left hand vertex of the polygon. Now, consider the same constraint with the objective function $Y + X$. In this case the minimum value, 1, for the objective function occurs at the bottom left hand vertex of the polygon.

More generally, it can be seen from this diagram, that, for any linear objective function, there is a vertex of the polygon which gives the minimum value to this

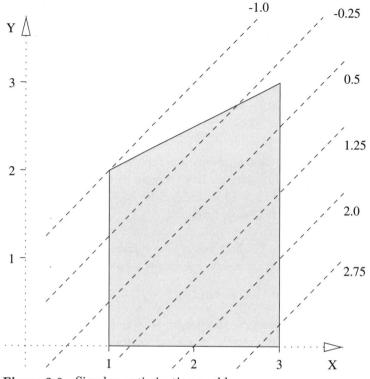

Figure 2.6   Simplex optimization problem.

objective function. Of course, if the contours of the objective function are parallel to one of the faces of the polygon, then this minimum value may occur along one face of the polygon, but, regardless of this, we still know that the minimum value of the objective function will occur at one of the polygon's vertices. This observation continues to hold true whenever we have linear real arithmetic constraints and a linear objective function. Thus to find the solution to a linear programming problem, we need only look at the vertices of the polygon containing the solutions to the constraint. The simplex method is simply a systematic procedure for searching through the vertices of the solution space of the optimization problem to find the vertex which minimizes the objective function.

We now give a presentation of the simplex algorithm which follows the format of the closely related Gauss-Jordan algorithm.

Definition 2.7
An optimization problem (C, f) is in *simplex form* if constraint C has the form $C_E \wedge C_I$ where C_E is a conjunction of linear arithmetic equations and C_I is $\bigwedge \{x \geq 0 \mid x \in vars(C)\}$ and f is a linear expression over the variables in C.

The following is an optimization problem in simplex form:

minimize $3X + 2Y - Z + 1$ subject to

$$
\begin{array}{rcrcrcrcrl}
X & + & Y & & & & & = & 3 & \wedge \\
-X & - & 3Y & + & 2Z & + & T & = & 1 & \wedge \\
& & X \geq 0 \wedge Y \geq 0 & \wedge & Z \geq 0 \wedge T \geq 0. & & & & &
\end{array}
\qquad (P1)
$$

It is not difficult to rewrite an arbitrary optimization problem over linear real equations and inequalities into an equivalent simplex form. Each variable x which is not constrained to be non-negative can be replaced by $x^+ - x^-$, where x^+ and x^- are two new variables that are constrained to be non-negative. Each inequality of the form $e \leq r$ where e is a linear real expression and r is a number can be replaced with $e + s = r$ where s is a new non-negative *slack* variable. For example, minimizing $X + 2Y$ subject to $X - 2Y \leq 5 \wedge -3X + 5Y = 4 \wedge Y \geq 0$ is written in simplex form as

minimize $X^+ - X^- + 2Y$ subject to

$$
\begin{array}{rcrcrcrcrl}
X^+ & - & X^- & - & 2Y & + & S & = & 5 & \wedge \\
-3X^+ & + & 3X^- & + & 5Y & & & = & 4 & \wedge \\
& & X^+ \geq 0 \wedge X^- \geq 0 & \wedge & Y \geq 0 \wedge S \geq 0. & & & & &
\end{array}
$$

The simplex method works by taking an optimization problem in "basic feasible solved" form and repeatedly applying an operation called "pivoting" to obtain a new basic feasible solved form.

Definition 2.8
A simplex form optimization problem is in *basic feasible solved form* if the equations are of the form $x_0 = b + a_1 x_1 + \ldots + a_n x_n$ where the variable x_0 does not occur in any other equation or in the objective function and the constant b is non-negative. The variable x_0 is said to be *basic* and the other variables are *parameters*.
A problem in basic feasible solved form has a corresponding *basic feasible solution* which is obtained by setting each parametric variable to 0 and each basic variable to the value of the constant on the right hand side of its equation.

For instance, the following constraint is in basic feasible solved form and is equivalent to the problem (P1) above.

minimize $10 - Y - Z$ subject to

$$
\begin{array}{rcrcrcrl}
X & = & 3 & - & Y & & & \wedge \\
T & = & 4 & + & 2Y & - & 2Z & \wedge \\
& & X \geq 0 \wedge Y \geq 0 & \wedge & Z \geq 0 \wedge T \geq 0. & & &
\end{array}
$$

X and T are basic variables and Y and Z are parameters. The basic feasible solution corresponding to this basic feasible solved form is $\{X \mapsto 3, Y \mapsto 0, Z \mapsto 0, T \mapsto 4\}$. The value of the objective function with this solution is 10.

The simplex algorithm finds the optimum by repeatedly looking for an "adjacent" basic feasible solved form whose basic feasible solution decreases the value of the objective function. When no such adjacent basic feasible solved form can be found, the optimum has been found. By adjacent we mean that the new basic feasible solved form can be reached by performing a single pivot.

For instance, in our example increasing Y or Z from 0 will decrease the value of the objective function. We arbitrarily choose to increase Y. We must be careful since we cannot increase the value of Y indefinitely as this may cause the constant value associated with some other basic variable to become negative. We must examine the equations to determine the maximum value we can choose for Y, while still maintaining basic feasible solved form. The first equation $X = 3 - Y$ allows Y to take at most a value of 3, since if Y becomes larger than this, X will become negative. The second equation $T = 4 + 2Y - 2Z$ does not restrict Y, since increasing Y will simply increase T. In general, we choose the most restrictive equation, and use it to eliminate Y. In the case of ties, we arbitrarily break the tie. In this example we choose $Y = 3 - X$. We replace Y everywhere by $3 - X$ and obtain

minimize $7 + X - Z$ subject to

$$
\begin{array}{rcccccc}
Y & = & 3 & - & X & & \wedge \\
T & = & 10 & - & 2X & - & 2Z \quad \wedge \\
\end{array}
$$
$$X \geq 0 \wedge Y \geq 0 \wedge Z \geq 0 \wedge T \geq 0.$$

This step is called *pivoting*, as we have moved X out of the set of basic variables and replaced it by Y. The variable selected to enter the set of basic variables, Y, is called the *entry variable*, while the variable selected to leave the set of basic variables, X, is called the *exit variable*.

We continue this process. Increasing the value of Z will also decrease the value of the objective. Note that while decreasing X will also decrease the objective function value, since X is constrained to be non-negative, it already takes its minimum value of 0 in the associated basic feasible solution. We choose Z as the entry variable and T as the exit variable and use the second equation to substitute for Z obtaining:

minimize $2 + 2X + 0.5T$ subject to

$$
\begin{array}{rcccccc}
Y & = & 3 & - & X & & \wedge \\
Z & = & 5 & - & X & - & 0.5T \quad \wedge \\
\end{array}
$$
$$X \geq 0 \wedge Y \geq 0 \wedge Z \geq 0 \wedge T \geq 0.$$

The objective value is 2 and clearly neither increasing the value of X nor that of T will improve this. Thus this is the optimum value.

In general, the simplex algorithm is described as follows. We are given a problem in basic feasible solved form in which the variables $x_1, \ldots, x_n$ are basic and the variables $y_1, \ldots, y_m$ are parameters.

minimize $e + \sum_{j=1}^{m} d_j y_j$ subject to

$$\bigwedge_{i=1}^{n} (x_i \;=\; b_i + \sum_{j=1}^{m} a_{ij} y_j) \;\wedge$$
$$\bigwedge_{i=1}^{n} (x_i \geq 0) \;\wedge\; \bigwedge_{j=1}^{m} (y_j \geq 0).$$

Select an entry variable y_J such that $d_J < 0$. Pivoting on such a variable can only decrease the value of the objective function. If no such variable exists, the optimum has been reached. Now determine the exit variable x_I. We must choose this variable so that it maintains basic feasible solved form by ensuring that the new b_i's are still positive after pivoting. This is achieved by choosing an x_I so that $-b_I / a_{IJ}$ is a minimum element of the set

$$\{-b_i / a_{iJ} \,|\, a_{iJ} < 0 \text{ and } 1 \leq i \leq n\}.$$

If there is no i for which $a_{iJ} < 0$ then we can stop since the optimization problem is unbounded, and so it does not have a minimum. This is because we can choose y_J to take an arbitrarily large value, and so make the objective function arbitrarily small. Otherwise we choose x_I and now pivot x_I out and replace it with y_J to obtain the new basic feasible solution form. We continue this process until either an optimum is reached or we discover that the problem is unbounded.

Algorithm 2.3: Simplex optimization.
INPUT: An optimization problem $(C_E \wedge C_I, f)$ in basic feasible solved form.
OUTPUT: Either *false* indicating that $(C_E \wedge C_I, f)$ does not have an optimal solution or else an optimal solution to $(C_E \wedge C_I, f)$.
METHOD: Call the algorithm shown in Figure 2.7 with simplex_opt(C_E, f), and let $\langle F, C', f' \rangle$ be the result. If F is *false*, output *false*; otherwise output the basic feasible solution corresponding to C'. $\square$

At this point it is instructive to go back and revisit the geometric example, shown in Figure 2.6. We can rewrite the constraints from this example into simplex form as follows:

$$
\begin{array}{rcrcrcrcl}
X & & & - & S_2 & & & = & 1 & \wedge \\
X & & & & & + & S_3 & = & 3 & \wedge \\
-X & + & 2Y & + & S_1 & & & = & 3 & \wedge
\end{array}
$$
$$X \geq 0 \wedge Y \geq 0 \wedge S_1 \geq 0 \wedge S_2 \geq 0 \wedge S_3 \geq 0.$$

Each of the vertices of the feasible region corresponds to a basic feasible solved form equivalent (with respect to the original variables) to the original constraints. For example, the upper right hand side vertex corresponds to the solved form

C is a conjunction of equations;
i, I, j, J, n, m are integers;
a_{ij}, b_i, e, d_i are real constants;
f, t are linear expressions;
$c_1, \ldots, c_n$ are equations;
x_i, y_j are variables.

simplex_opt(C,f)
    let C be of the form $c_1 \wedge \cdots \wedge c_n$
    for each $i \in \{1, \ldots, n\}$
    let c_i be of the form $x_i = b_i + \sum_{j=1}^{m} a_{ij} y_j$
    endfor
    let f be of the form $e + \sum_{j=1}^{m} d_j y_j$
    % Choose variable y_J to become basic
    if for all $j \in \{1, \ldots, m\}$ $d_j \geq 0$ **then**
        return $\langle true, C, f \rangle$
    endif
    choose $J \in \{1, \ldots, m\}$ such that $d_J < 0$
    % Choose variable x_I to become non-basic
    if for all $i \in \{1, \ldots, n\}$ $a_{iJ} \geq 0$ **then**
        return $\langle false, C, f \rangle$
    endif
    choose $I \in \{1, \ldots, n\}$ such that
        $-b_I/a_{IJ} = \min\{-b_i/a_{iJ} | a_{iJ} < 0 \text{ and } 1 \leq i \leq n\}$
    $t := (x_I - b_I - \sum_{j=1, j \neq J}^{m} a_{Ij} y_j)/a_{IJ}$
    $c_I := (y_J = t)$
    replace y_J by t in f
    for each $i \in \{1, \ldots, n\}$
        if $i \neq I$ **then** replace y_J by t in c_i **endif**
    endfor
    return simplex_opt($\bigwedge_{i=1}^{n} c_i$,f).

Figure 2.7   Simplex optimization.

minimize $0 + 0.5S_1 - 0.5S_3$ subject to

$$
\begin{array}{rcrcrcl}
Y & = & 3 & - & 0.5S_1 & - & 0.5S_3 \qquad \wedge \\
S_2 & = & 2 & & & - & S_3 \qquad \wedge \\
X & = & 3 & & & - & S_3 \qquad \wedge \\
\end{array}
$$
$$X \geq 0 \wedge Y \geq 0 \wedge S_1 \geq 0 \wedge S_2 \geq 0 \wedge S_3 \geq 0.$$

The corresponding basic feasible solution is

$$X = 3 \wedge Y = 3 \wedge S_2 = 2 \wedge S_1 = 0 \wedge S_3 = 0.$$

Now consider the operation of the simplex optimization algorithm when we start from this basic feasible solved form. The variable S_3 will be selected as the entry variable, since this is the only variable with a negative coefficient in the objective function. S_3 appears in all three constraints with a negative coefficient so the algorithm will examine the "$-b_i/a_{iJ}$" value for each constraint c_i where a_{iJ} is the coefficient of S_3 in the constraint. These values are, respectively, $(-3/-0.5) = 6$, $(-2/-1) = 2$, and $(-3/-1) = 3$, so the basic variable, S_2, of the second constraint is chosen as the exit variable. After pivoting, the new basic feasible solved form is

minimize $-1 + 0.5S_1 + 0.5S_2$ subject to

$$
\begin{aligned}
Y &= 2 &-& 0.5S_1 &+& 0.5S_2 && \wedge \\
S_3 &= 2 && &-& S_2 && \wedge \\
X &= 1 && &+& S_2 && \wedge
\end{aligned}
$$
$$X \geq 0 \wedge Y \geq 0 \wedge S_1 \geq 0 \wedge S_2 \geq 0 \wedge S_3 \geq 0.$$

Examination of the objective function reveals that no variable has a negative coefficient, therefore a minimum has been reached. The algorithm will return the corresponding basic feasible solution which is:

$$Y = 2 \wedge S_3 = 2 \wedge X = 1 \wedge S_1 = 0 \wedge S_2 = 0.$$

Examination of this solution reveals that, as the reader would expect, it corresponds to the upper left hand vertex of the original solution space.

  This example illustrates that the simplex optimization algorithm moves from one vertex to another vertex of the solution space in a direction which decreases the objective function. This process continues until the minimum is found.

  However, we have neglected to answer one rather important question, namely, how do we obtain the first basic feasible solved form? Actually, this is not as difficult as it may first appear. We can do this by solving an optimization problem for which we can trivially find an initial basic feasible solved form and which has the property that its optimal solution occurs at an initial basic feasible solved form for the original problem. More exactly, consider the optimization problem over the variables $x_1, \ldots, x_m$:

minimize $e + \sum_{j=1}^{m} d_j x_j$ subject to

$$
\bigwedge_{i=1}^{n} \left(\sum_{j=1}^{m} a_{ij} x_j = b_i \right) \wedge
$$
$$
\bigwedge_{j=1}^{m} (x_j \geq 0).
$$

We assume that the constraints have been rewritten so that for each $1 \leq i \leq n$, $b_i \geq 0$. This is always possible by negating both sides.

  The *first phase problem* is obtained by adding *artificial variables*, $z_1, \ldots, z_n$, to get the problem in basic feasible solved form. The problem becomes:

minimize $\sum_{i=1}^{n} (b_i - \sum_{j=1}^{m} a_{ij} x_j)$ subject to

$$
\bigwedge_{i=1}^{n} \left(z_i = b_i - \sum_{j=1}^{m} a_{ij} x_j \right) \wedge
$$
$$
\bigwedge_{j=1}^{m} (x_j \geq 0) \wedge \bigwedge_{i=1}^{n} (z_i \geq 0).
$$

The key idea is that we wish to minimize $\sum_{i=1}^{n} z_i$. An optimal solution to this problem where each z_i is 0 corresponds to a solution to the original constraints, since in this case the constraints with artificial variables are equivalent to the original constraints.

The optimization of the first phase problem can end in three ways.

(a) The optimal value of the objective function is > 0. In this case the original problem is unsatisfiable, since there are no solutions in which all of the artificial variables are 0.

(b) The optimal value of the objective function is 0 and all artificial variables are parametric. In this case, after removal of the artificial variables, we have a basic feasible solved form for the original problem.

(c) The optimal value of the objective function is 0 but not all artificial variables are parametric. Consider such a non-parametric artificial variable z. It must occur in an equation of form

$$z = 0 + \sum_{i=1}^{n} d_i' z_i + \sum_{j=1}^{m} a_j' x_j.$$

The first possibility is that all variables in the equation are artificial, that is all of the a_j' are 0. In this case we can delete the equation. This occurs when one of the original constraints is redundant. Otherwise, one of the original variables x_J, say, has a non-zero coefficient a_J'. We can use this equation to pivot z out of the basic variables and replace it by x_J. This maintains basic feasible solved form because the constant in the equation is 0. We can continue this process until all artificial variables become parameters.

Perhaps it is time for an example to clarify this. Consider the original problem:

minimize $3X + 2Y - Z + 1$ subject to

$$\begin{array}{rcrcrcrcrc}
X & + & Y & & & & & = & 3 & \wedge \\
-X & - & 3Y & + & 2Z & + & T & = & 1 & \wedge \\
\end{array}$$
$$X \geq 0 \wedge Y \geq 0 \wedge Z \geq 0 \wedge T \geq 0.$$

Adding two artificial variables we obtain the first phase problem:

minimize $A_1 + A_2$ subject to

$$\begin{array}{rcrcrcrcrcrc}
A_1 & = & 3 & - & X & - & Y & & & & & \wedge \\
A_2 & = & 1 & + & X & + & 3Y & - & 2Z & - & T & \wedge \\
\end{array}$$
$$X \geq 0 \wedge Y \geq 0 \wedge Z \geq 0 \wedge T \geq 0 \wedge A_1 \geq 0 \wedge A_2 \geq 0.$$

To put it into basic feasible solved form, we rewrite the objective function in terms of the parametric variables (by substituting for the artificial variables), giving the new objective

$$4 + 2Y - 2Z - T.$$

The simplex algorithm is now used to solve this problem. We must first choose Z or T as the new entry variable as they have negative coefficients in the objective. Arbitrarily we choose T. The exit variable is therefore A_2. After pivoting we obtain:

minimize $3 - X - Y + A_2$ subject to

$$
\begin{aligned}
A_1 &= 3 - X - Y && \wedge \\
T &= 1 + X + 3Y - 2Z - A_2 && \wedge \\
&X \geq 0 \wedge Y \geq 0 \wedge Z \geq 0 \wedge T \geq 0 \wedge A_1 \geq 0 \wedge A_2 \geq 0.
\end{aligned}
$$

In the next step we can choose either X or Y as the entry variable. Say we choose X. The exit variable must therefore be A_1. This gives:

minimize $A_1 + A_2$ subject to

$$
\begin{aligned}
X &= 3 - Y - A_1 && \wedge \\
T &= 4 + 2Y - 2Z - A_1 - A_2 && \wedge \\
&X \geq 0 \wedge Y \geq 0 \wedge Z \geq 0 \wedge T \geq 0 \wedge A_1 \geq 0 \wedge A_2 \geq 0.
\end{aligned}
$$

We have reached the optimal value and constructed a basic feasible solution form for the original problem since

$$
\begin{aligned}
X + Y &= 3 && \wedge \\
-X - 3Y + 2Z + T &= 1
\end{aligned}
$$

is equivalent to

$$
\begin{aligned}
X &= 3 - Y && \wedge \\
T &= 4 + 2Y - 2Z.
\end{aligned}
$$

The optimization problem can now be solved by starting from the above basic feasible solution although we must remember to first eliminate the basic variables from the original objective function. This gives:

minimize $10 - Y - Z$ subject to

$$
\begin{aligned}
X &= 3 - Y && \wedge \\
T &= 4 + 2Y - 2Z && \wedge \\
&X \geq 0 \wedge Y \geq 0 \wedge Z \geq 0 \wedge T \geq 0.
\end{aligned}
$$

Of course, finding a basic feasible solution of the original constraint is exactly a constraint satisfaction problem—thus the first phase of the simplex method provides an efficient constraint solver for linear inequalities. The algorithm is:

Algorithm 2.4: Simplex solver.
INPUT: A constraint $C_E \wedge C_I$ in simplex form.
OUTPUT: *true* if $C_E \wedge C_I$ is satisfiable and *false* if it is unsatisfiable.
METHOD: Return the result of simplex_solve(C_E) using the algorithm in Figure 2.8.
□

C, C' are conjunction of equations;
i, j, m are integers;
a_{ij}, b_i, e, d'_j, a'_i are real constants;
f, f', f_i are linear expressions;
c_i, c'_i are equations;
x_i are variables, z_i are new variables ;
$flag$ is either $true$ or $false$.

simplex_solve(C)
    let C be of the form $c_1 \wedge \cdots \wedge c_n$
    for each $i \in \{1, \ldots, n\}$
        let c_i be of the form $b_i = \sum_{j=1}^{m} a_{ij} x_j$ where $b_i \geq 0$
        $f_i := b_i - \sum_{j=1}^{m} a_{ij} x_j$
        $c'_i := (z_i = f_i)$
    endfor
    $f := \sum_{i=1}^{n} f_i$
    $\langle flag, C', f' \rangle := $ simplex_opt($\bigwedge_{i=1}^{n} c'_i, f$)
    let f' be of the form $e + \sum_{j=1}^{n} d'_j z_j + \sum_{i=1}^{m} a'_i x_i$
    if $e \equiv 0$ **then**
        return $true$
    else return $false$
    endif

Figure 2.8 Simplex solver.

No discussion of the simplex algorithm is complete without considering the problem of cycling. A basic feasible solution is *degenerate* if some of the basic variables take the value 0. If this is the case, we can perform a pivot which does not decrease the value of the objective function and which does not change the corresponding basic feasible solution. However, in such a case there is a danger of pivoting back to the original problem. This is called cycling. In practice it does not occur very often, and there are simple methods to avoid it. One of these is Bland's anti-cycling rule. This approach numbers the variables and, when selecting a variable to enter the basis, chooses the lowest possible numbered variable. Similarly when selecting a variable to exit the basis, and a tie occurs, it chooses the lowest numbered basic variable to break the tie.

2.6 (*) Canonical Form Simplifiers

When we discussed simplifiers previously we gave a number of properties which are desirable in a simplifier. Another desirable property for a simplifier to have is that it returns constraints which are in a *canonical form*. Such simplifiers are useful because they make it easy to determine if two constraints are equivalent since they will simplify equivalent constraints to exactly the same syntactic form.

Definition 2.9

A simplifier, *simpl*, is a *canonical form* simplifier if $simpl(C_1, V) \equiv simpl(C_2, V)$ whenever constraints C_1 and C_2 are equivalent with respect to the variables V. The *canonical form* of a constraint C is $simpl(C, vars(C))$.

One might hope that simplifiers based on solved form solvers, such as the tree constraint simplifier tree_simplify, are canonical as these simplify the constraints to a solved form. However, tree_simplify is not canonical. To see this, consider the constraint C_1 which is $X = Y \wedge Z = f(X)$ and the constraint C_2 which is $Y = X \wedge Z = f(X)$. Clearly, C_1 and C_2 are equivalent with respect to the variable set $\{X, Y, Z\}$. However, tree_simplify$(C_1, \{X, Y, Z\})$ is $X = Y \wedge Z = f(Y)$ while tree_simplify$(C_2, \{X, Y, Z\})$ is C_2.

This example illustrates one of the issues to be considered when designing a canonical form simplifier. It must take into account the name of variables since, for instance, it cannot treat $X = Y$ and $Y = X$ identically as one must be rewritten to the other. Another issue is the need for a standard way to write expressions. For instance, $3 \times X + Y/2$ and $(6/2) \times X + 0.5 \times Y$ must be rewritten to the same form.

As an example of a canonical form simplifier, we give one for linear equations. It is a modification of the Gauss-Jordan algorithm which ensures that variables are eliminated in a particular way. We take variable names into account by assuming that there is an ordering on variable names which allows us to determine the least variable in a set of variables in a constraint. In the examples we will use lexicographic ordering. For instance, X_1, X_2 and A have the relative ordering $A < X_1 < X_2$. The canonical form of a linear expression t is $b_0 + b_1 x_1 + \cdots b_n x_n$ where each b_i is a constant and $x_1 < x_2 < \cdots < x_n$. We assume within the algorithm that all linear expressions are maintained in canonical form.

Algorithm 2.5: Gauss-Jordan canonical form simplifier.
INPUT: A conjunction of linear arithmetic equations C and a set of variables V.
OUTPUT: A conjunction of linear arithmetic equations S in canonical form.
METHOD: The algorithm is shown in Figure 2.9. $\square$

For example, the execution of gauss_jordan_simplify$(C, \{X, Z, T\})$ where C is the constraint $1 + X = 2Y + Z \wedge Z = 3 + X \wedge T - Y = 2$ is detailed in the following table. It gives C and S and the substitution used in each elimination step.

Substitution	C	S
	$1 + X = 2Y + Z \wedge Z = 3 + X \wedge T - Y = 2$	*true*
$Y = 0.5 + 0.5X - 0.5Z$	$Z = 3 + X \wedge -0.5 + T - 0.5X + 0.5Z = 2$	*true*
$X = -3 + Z$	$1 + T = 2$	$X = -3 + Z$
$T = 1$	*true*	$X = -3 + Z \wedge T = 1$
sorting S		$X = -3 + Z \wedge T = 1$

```
r₁, r₂ are real constants;
x is a variable;
e is a linear arithmetic expression;
c is an equation;
C, C₁ and S are conjunctions of equations.


gauss_jordan_simplify(C,V)
    S := true
    while C is not the empty conjunction
        let C be of the form c ∧ C₁
        C := C₁
        if c is of the form r₁ = r₂ then
            if r₁ ≢ r₂ then
                return false
            endif
        else
            if c can be written in the form y = e where
                e does not involve x and y ∉ V then
                let x be this variable (y)
            else
                let x be the least variable in V such that
                    c can be written in the form x = e where e does not involve x
            endif
            substitute e for x throughout C and S
            if x ∈ V then
                S := S ∧ (x = e)
            endif
        endif
    endwhile
    sort S on the variables appearing on the left hand sides
    return S
```

Figure 2.9   Gauss-Jordan canonical form simplifier.

Producing a canonical form simplifier for a constraint domain which does not always allow a variable to be eliminated is slightly more complicated, since we may need to rename variables. For example, consider the tree constraint domain. If the variable of interest is X and we simplify $X = succ(Z)$ and $X = succ(Y)$ using the non-canonical tree constraint simplifier we will obtain $X = succ(Z)$ and $X = succ(Y)$. This is because we cannot eliminate Z or Y. However, $X = succ(Z)$ and $X = succ(Y)$ are equivalent with respect to the variable X and so a canonical form simplifier must return the same result if either is simplified with respect to X. We can solve this problem by eliminating as many of the variables as possible, and then systematically renaming those remaining variables which are not of interest. Thus, a canonical form simplifier for trees might simplify both $X = succ(Z)$ and $X = succ(Y)$ to $X = succ(W)$ if X is the variable of interest. See Exercise 2.7.

2.7 (*) **Implication and Equivalence**

Another important question involving constraints is that of implication. Given two constraints C_1 and C_2, this is the problem of determining whether $C_1 \rightarrow C_2$. That is to say, determining if every solution of C_1 is also a solution of C_2. We have already met with a use of implication for simplification, namely redundancy removal, but implication also has other uses.

Suppose we wish to model the actions of an air-conditioning system whose temperature control is set to some desired temperature T. We can model the temperature at time period X_{i+2} in terms of the temperature at the previous two time periods, X_i and X_{i+1}, and the temperature D_{i+2} which reflects the outside influence on the temperature by using the formula:

$$X_{i+2} = X_{i+1} + 3/4 \times (T - X_{i+1}) + 1/2 \times (T - X_i) + D_{i+2}.$$

Apart from D_{i+2} and X_{i+1} the remaining terms model the effect of the air-conditioning system which is trying to change the temperature to T.

Suppose the temperature control T is set to 10 and this is the initial temperature of the room, that is to say $X_0 = 10$. Then $X_0 = 10 \wedge C_1$ models the room temperature over the next 10 time periods where C_1 is

$$
\begin{aligned}
X_1 &= X_0 + D_1 \wedge \\
X_2 &= X_1 + 3/4 \times (10 - X_1) + 1/2 \times (10 - X_0) + D_2 \wedge \\
&\vdots \\
X_{10} &= X_9 + 3/4 \times (10 - X_9) + 1/2 \times (10 - X_8) + D_{10}.
\end{aligned}
$$

A graph of the change in room temperature over time is illustrated at the top of Figure 2.10, where the outside influence D_i is given by the graph illustrated at the bottom of Figure 2.10.

How can we judge how well the air-conditioning system works? One criterion might be that it is successful if the temperature always stays within two degrees of the set temperature, assuming that the outside effects never make a difference of more than one degree, that is $-1 \le D_i \wedge D_i \le 1$ for all $1 \le i \le 10$. Let C_2 be the constraint $X_0 = 10 \wedge C_1 \wedge \bigwedge_{i=1}^{10} (-1 \le D_i \wedge D_i \le 1)$. Then this question is formalised as the implication question:

$$C_2 \rightarrow 8 \le X_0 \wedge X_0 \le 12 \wedge \cdots \wedge 8 \le X_{10} \wedge X_{10} \le 12.$$

In this case the answer is no. However, the system does ensure that the temperature stays within three degrees of the set temperature (that is, between 7 and 13).

A more interesting question is whether the system reaches a stable state after 10 time periods. Suppose the system is switched on when the initial temperature X_0 is between 0 and 20 degrees. We can describe this situation using the constraint C_3

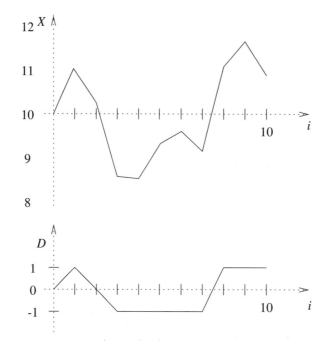

Figure 2.10   A graph of room temperature versus outside influence over time.

which is

$$0 \le X_0 \wedge X_0 \le 20 \wedge C_1 \wedge \bigwedge_{i=1}^{10}(-1 \le D_i \wedge D_i \le 1)$$

and we can ask if X_{10} is within three degrees of the set temperature, that is does

$$C_3 \to 7 \le X_{10} \wedge X_{10} \le 13.$$

In this case the answer is yes.

In both cases we are interested in determining whether an implication holds.

Definition 2.10
An *implication tester*, *impl*, takes two constraints C_1 and C_2 and returns *true*, *false* or *unknown*. Whenever $impl(C_1, C_2)$ returns *true* then $C_1 \to C_2$, while when it returns *false*, $C_1 \to C_2$ is not true.
An implication tester that always returns *true* or *false* is *complete*.

One important application of an implication tester is for simplification where it can be used to remove redundant primitive constraints. We will see later in Chapter 11 that determining if one constraint implies another is also important for deciding when a bottom-up evaluation of a constraint logic program can finish.

We shall now consider how we might implement an implication tester. The first point to note is that in any constraint domain, an arbitrary implication test can be simplified to a sequence of implication tests in which the second argument to the implication tester is always a primitive constraint. This is because if C_2 is $c_1 \wedge \cdots \wedge c_n$, then $C_1 \to C_2$ if and only if $C_1 \to c_i$ for each $i = 1, \ldots, n$.

The second point to note is that in many constraint domains (essentially those domains in which the primitive constraints are closed under negation), we can use a constraint solver to determine if $C_1 \to c$ where c is a primitive constraint. This is because $C_1 \to c$ holds if and only if $C_1 \wedge \neg c$ is unsatisfiable.

Consider the problem of the air-conditioning system. To determine whether $C_2 \to (7 \leq X_{10} \wedge X_{10} \leq 13)$, we decompose it into the two tests $C_2 \to 7 \leq X_{10}$ and $C_2 \to X_{10} \leq 13$. Each of these can be answered by using a complete solver. Since $solv(C_2 \wedge 7 > X_{10})$ returns $false$ we know that $C_2 \to 7 \leq X_{10}$. Similarly, since $solv(C_2 \wedge X_{10} > 13)$ also returns $false$ we know that $C_2 \to X_{10} \leq 13$. Thus $C_2 \to (7 \leq X_{10} \wedge X_{10} \leq 13)$.

Another operation over constraints which is closely related to implication is equivalence. Given two constraints C_1 and C_2, this is the problem of determining whether $C_1 \leftrightarrow C_2$. That is, determining if C_1 and C_2 have the same solutions.

Definition 2.11
An *equivalence tester*, *equiv*, takes two constraints C_1 and C_2 and returns $true$, $false$ or $unknown$. Whenever $equiv(C_1, C_2) = true$, $C_1 \leftrightarrow C_2$ holds and whenever $equiv(C_1, C_2) = false$, $C_1 \leftrightarrow C_2$ does not hold.
An equivalence tester *equiv* is *complete* if it always returns $true$ or $false$.

Given that we have an implication tester for a constraint domain, it is simple to build an equivalence tester for the domain since $C_1 \leftrightarrow C_2$ if and only if $C_1 \to C_2$ and $C_2 \to C_1$. Thus we can define an equivalence tester by

$$equiv(C_1, C_2) = impl(C_1, C_2) \wedge impl(C_2, C_1).$$

Conversely, given an equivalence tester it is also easy to build an implication tester since, using the definition of implication, $C_1 \to C_2$ if and only if $C_1 \leftrightarrow (C_1 \wedge C_2)$. Therefore,

$$impl(C_1, C_2) = equiv(C_1, C_1 \wedge C_2).$$

Thus, we can test if $Y = X - 1 \wedge X \geq 2$ is equivalent to $X = Y + 1 \wedge Y \geq 3$ by testing that

$$Y = X - 1 \wedge X \geq 2 \;\to\; X = Y + 1 \wedge Y \geq 3$$

and

$$X = Y + 1 \wedge Y \geq 3 \;\to\; Y = X - 1 \wedge X \geq 2.$$

Each of these implications can be tested using a constraint solver.

Since a canonical form simplifier can be used to determine equivalence, equivalence testing is closely related to canonical simplification More exactly, given a canonical simplifier *simpl*, we can test if two constraints C_1 and C_2 are equivalent, by simplifying both with respect to all variables of interest and checking if the result is syntactically identical. C_1 and C_2 are equivalent if and only if,

$$simpl(C_1, vars(C_1) \cup vars(C_2)) \equiv simpl(C_2, vars(C_1) \cup vars(C_2)).$$

For this reason, equivalence testers are often based on canonical form simplifiers.

Imagine we wish to determine if

$$Z - X = 3 \wedge T + Z - X = 4 \ \leftrightarrow \ T + Z - X = 4 \wedge 2T + Z - X = 5.$$

The canonical simplifier gauss_jordan_simplify applied to $Z - X = 3 \wedge T + Z - X = 4$ for the variables of interest $\{T, X, Z\}$ gives the answer $X = -3 + Z \wedge T = 1$. Similarly, gauss_jordan_simplify applied to $T + Z - X = 4 \wedge 2T + Z - X = 5$ with the same variables of interest gives the same result. Thus, $Z - X = 3 \wedge T + Z - X = 4$ is equivalent to $T + Z - X = 4 \wedge 2T + Z - X = 5$.

We have already seen that we can implement an implication tester in terms of an equivalence tester. Therefore a canonical simplifier can also be used to test implications. For example, imagine we wish to determine if $C_1 \rightarrow C_2$ where C_1 is

$$Z - X = 3 \wedge T + Z - X = 4$$

and C_2 is

$$X - Z + 2 = T.$$

The variables of interest, V, are $\{T, X, Z\}$. Since gauss_jordan_simplify(C_1, V) and gauss_jordan_simplify$(C_1 \wedge C_2, V)$ both return $X = -3 + Z \wedge T = 1$, the implication holds.

2.8   Summary

We have examined constraint simplification. This is needed in constraint programming languages because execution of a constraint program usually results in an "answer" constraint which must be simplified so as to make its meaning intelligible. Simplification is particularly important when we are not interested in all the variables in the constraints and only wish to understand the constraint in terms of the variables we are interested in. One desirable property of a simplifier is that it is projecting. That is, after simplification the constraint will only contain variables which are of interest. Unfortunately, for some constraint domains such as tree constraints, it is not possible to give a simplifier which is projecting. All we can hope for in such domains is a solver which is weakly projecting. We have given a simplifier for linear arithmetic inequalities which is projecting, and a simplifier for tree constraints which is weakly projecting.

Optimization is another important operation on constraints. This deals with the problem of finding a solution to a constraint which is the best in the sense that it minimizes some given objective function. We have studied the simplex algorithm which solves optimization problems for linear arithmetic constraints with a linear arithmetic objective function. A variant of the simplex algorithm can also be used to give an efficient complete constraint solver for linear arithmetic constraints.

Finally, we have investigated algorithms to determine if two constraints are equivalent or if one implies the other. Tests for equivalence and implication can be easily implemented if we have access to a constraint simplifier which is canonical.

2.9 Exercises

2.1. Recall the constraint describing the house project from Chapter 1:

$$T_S \geq 0 \wedge T_A \geq T_S + 7 \wedge T_B \geq T_A + 4 \wedge T_C \geq T_A + 3 \wedge$$
$$T_D \geq T_A + 3 \wedge T_D \geq T_C + 2 \wedge T_E \geq T_B + 2 \wedge T_E \geq T_D + 3 \wedge T_E \geq T_C + 3.$$

Use fourier_simplify to eliminate the variables T_S, T_B, T_C, T_A and T_D in turn.

2.2. Extend fourier_simplify to handle strict inequalities.

2.3. Using tree_simplify, simplify constraint $X = f(Y, U) \wedge U = Z \wedge Z = g(a, Y)$ in terms of variables X and Y.

2.4. Write an algorithm for Boolean simplification, based on the example in the text. Now consider the Boolean constraints describing the full adder from Chapter 1:

$$I_1 \leftrightarrow X \mathbin{\&} Y \qquad \text{And gate } G1$$
$$I_2 \leftrightarrow X \oplus Y \qquad \text{Xor gate } G2$$
$$I_3 \leftrightarrow I_2 \mathbin{\&} CI \qquad \text{And gate } G3$$
$$O \leftrightarrow I_2 \oplus CI \qquad \text{Xor gate } G4$$
$$CO \leftrightarrow I_1 \vee I_3 \qquad \text{Or gate } G5$$

Using your Boolean simplification algorithm, eliminate the internal variables I_1, I_2 and I_3.

2.5. In the text we saw how a projecting simplifier can be used to solve optimization functions. In the case of linear arithmetic constraints show how the simplex optimization algorithm can be used to project a set of constraints in simplex form on to a single variable.

2.6. (*) It is also possible to give an algorithm for Boolean simplification which is based on fourier_simplify. It relies on the Boolean constraints being written in conjunctive normal form. The idea is to eliminate a variable by combining those clauses in which the variable occurs positively with those in which the variable occurs negatively. The clauses in which the variable does not occur remain unchanged. This is the analogue of the Fourier elimination step.

For instance, we can eliminate the variable Y from

$$(\neg X \vee Y) \wedge (\neg X \vee Z) \wedge (X \vee \neg Y \vee \neg Z)$$

as follows. The set of clauses C^0 in which Y does not appear is $\{\neg X \vee Z\}$, the set of clauses C^+ in which Y appears positively is $\{\neg X \vee Y\}$, and the set of clauses C^- in which Y appears negatively is $\{\neg Y \vee \neg Z \vee X\}$. Combining C^+ with C^- we obtain the set $\{\neg X \vee \neg Z \vee X\}$. Thus, the projection of the original constraint on to the variables X and Z is

$$(\neg X \vee \neg Z \vee X) \wedge (\neg X \vee Z)$$

which is equivalent to $\neg X \vee Z$.

(a) Using the distribution and De Morgan's Laws for Boolean constraints:

  - $\neg\neg F = F$,
  - $\neg(F \vee G) = \neg F \wedge \neg G$,
  - $\neg(F \wedge G) = \neg F \vee \neg G$,
  - $F \vee (G \& H) = (F \vee G) \wedge (F \vee H)$;

write an algorithm which converts a Boolean constraint into a conjunctive normal form. For instance, the Boolean formula $X \leftrightarrow Y \& Z$ is equivalent to the conjunctive normal form constraint

$$(\neg X \vee Y) \wedge (\neg X \vee Z) \wedge (X \vee \neg Y \vee \neg Z).$$

(b) Write an algorithm for Boolean simplification based on the above example.

(c) Apply your algorithms to the Boolean constraints of Exercise 2.4. That is, rewrite these into conjunctive normal form, and then, using your Boolean simplification algorithm, eliminate the internal variables I_1, I_2 and I_3.

2.7. (*) Write a canonical simplifier for tree constraints based on tree_simplify.

2.8. (*) Write an implication tester for the linear arithmetic inequalities.

2.9. (*) Is the conjunctive normal form for Boolean constraints a canonical form? If not, suggest a canonical form for Boolean constraints which is based on conjunctive normal form.

2.10 Practical Exercises

We have already seen that CLP systems return a simplified form of the constraint which the user has typed. In addition, the language $CLP(\mathcal{R})$ has a library function, called dump for projecting and simplifying constraints and writing the result to standard output. The function dump takes a single argument which is a list of the variables of interest and works both for linear arithmetic constraints and for tree constraints.

For instance, to simplify constraint $X = f(Y, Z) \wedge Z = g(a, Y)$ in terms of the variables X and Y, we can type

```
1 ?- X = f(Y,Z), Z=g(a,Y), dump([X,Y]).
```

This leads to the output

```
X = f(Y,g(a,Y)).
```

which is the correct simplification.

As another example, we can type

```
2 ?- T = 3+Y, X = 2*Y+U, Z=3*U+Y, dump([X,T,Z]).
```

which gives

```
Z = 3*X-5*T+15.
```

demonstrating that $Z = 3X - 5T + 15$ is a simplification of

$$T = 3 + Y \wedge X = 2Y + U \wedge Z = 3U + Y$$

with respect to X, T and Z.

The SICStus Prolog real arithmetic constraint solving libraries also simplify constraints although they do not provide an explicit function for simplification (but see Section 28.7.1.1 of the SICStus Prolog v3 User's Manual [58]). For example, typing

```
| ?- {X + Y = Z + 2, 2*X + Y = Z}.
```

gives the answer

```
X = -2,
{Z=-4+Y} ?
```

The SICStus Prolog real arithmetic libraries also include an implementation of the simplex algorithm which can be used to answer optimization problems. The algorithm can be called using the library functions **inf** and **sup** (for infimum and supremum). The function **inf** takes two arguments, an expression to minimize and an expression to hold the minimum value. The behaviour of **sup** is analogous except that it attempts to maximize the expression.

For instance, to minimize $3X + 2Y - Z + 1$ subject to

$$X + Y = 3 \wedge - X - 3Y + 2Z + T = 1 \wedge X \geq 0 \wedge Y \geq 0 \wedge Z \geq 0 \wedge T \geq 0$$

we can type

```
| ?- {X + Y = 3, -X - 3*Y + 2*Z + T = 1, X >= 0, Y >= 0,
      Z >= 0, T >= 0}, inf(3*X + 2*Y - Z + 1, Inf).
```

The output is

```
     Inf = 2,
     Y=3-X,
     X>=0,
     X=<3,
     T>=0,
     Z=5-X-1/2*T,
     X+1/2*T=<5 ?
```

The result `Inf = 2` indicates that the minimum value is 2 while the remainder of the answer is a simplified form of the constraint.

Neither simplification in $CLP(\mathcal{R})$ nor in SICStus Prolog is canonical. For example, using $CLP(\mathcal{R})$ we obtain different simplifications depending on the order in which variables appear in the constraint. For instance,

```
     1 ?- 2*X + Y = Z, X - Y = W.
```

gives

```
     Y = -0.666667*W + 0.333333*Z
     X = 0.333333*W + 0.333333*Z
```

while

```
     2 ?- Z = 2*X - Y, W = X - Y.
```

gives

```
     X = W + Y
     Z = 2*W + Y.
```

P2.1. Use `dump` to verify your answer to Exercises 2.1 and 2.3 above.

P2.2. Use `dump` to simplify $X = f(Y, Z) \wedge Z = g(a, Y)$ in terms of X. What do you think the symbol starting with an underscore in the output represents?

P2.3. Use `sup` in SICStus Prolog to find the maximum value of the function

$$X1 + X2 + X3 + X4 + X5$$

subject to the constraints

$$3X1 + 2X2 + X3 = 1 \wedge$$
$$5X1 + X2 + X3 + X4 = 3 \wedge$$
$$2X1 + 5X2 + X3 + X5 = 4 \wedge$$
$$X1 \geq 0 \wedge X2 \geq 0 \wedge X3 \geq 0 \wedge X4 \geq 0 \wedge X5 \geq 0.$$

Can you also find values for $X1$, $X2$, $X3$, $X4$, $X5$, at which this maximum value occurs?

P2.4. You can use projection to find maximum and minimum values by examining the resulting expression by hand. Use `dump` in $CLP(\mathcal{R})$ to solve the previous problem.

2.11   Notes

Fourier elimination is sometimes referred to as Fourier-Motzkin elimination. The method goes back to a report by Fourier [48] from 1827. Motzkin is associated with the algorithm because he independently discovered the algorithm at a later date. Simplification algorithms used in constraint logic programming systems over linear real arithmetic constraints are based on Fourier elimination, see [73]. Strangely, most CLP systems employing tree constraints do not use a weakly projecting simplifier, such as tree_simplify, for simplifying tree constraints. Instead they simply return the equations resulting from unify of the form $x = t$ for each variable x of interest.

Techniques for solving optimization problems over the real and integer constraint domains have been extensively studied by mathematicians from the operations research community. For a comprehensive introduction to the main approaches see, for example, [116]. The simplex algorithm dates from 1951 and is due to Dantzig [37]. Schrijver [116] gives a detailed account of its history, pointing to forerunners of simplex used by, most notably, Fourier (1826) and de la Vallée Poussin (1910). The proper mathematical foundations for the algorithm were laid by Farkas (1895) and von Neumann (1947). Bland's anti-cycling rule was suggested in 1977 [12]. We describe the primal simplex algorithm, in a form close to Gauss-Jordan elimination. Modern constraint programming systems usually use a revised simplex algorithm [38] with explicit bounds handling (see for example [110]). This approach is well suited to incremental solving (see Chapter 10) and allows checks to be made on numerical stability. Recently interior point methods [144] have been developed for solving linear real arithmetic optimization problems. They are increasingly the method of choice for large problems, although they are not presently used in CLP systems because of difficulties with incremental use.

Efficient algorithms for determining equivalence or implication and for computing canonical forms have not been systematically studied for many constraint domains. However, these operations have been extensively studied in the case of Boolean constraints, in part because of the application of the operations to digital circuit design. See, for example, Brown [20] who describes several canonical forms. In particular, reduced ordered binary decision diagrams (ROBDDs) introduced by Bryant for circuit design applications have proved to be an efficient canonical representation of Boolean constraints [21]. Recently there has been increased interest in implication testing because of its application in concurrent constraint programming languages, which we discuss in Chapter 12. See, for instance, Podelski and Van Roy [102] who give an efficient algorithm for testing implication of tree constraints.

3   Finite Constraint Domains

In the previous two chapters we have looked at several constraint domains, including real arithmetic and trees. In this chapter, we investigate another important class of constraint domains:"finite constraint domains." These are constraint domains in which the possible values that a variable can take are restricted to a finite set. Boolean constraints and the blocks world are both examples of finite constraint domains. Another example of a finite constraint domain are integer constraints in which each variable x is constrained to lie within a finite range of integers.

Finite constraint domains are widely used in constraint programming. This is because they allow the programmer to naturally model constraint problems that involve choice, by letting the possible values of a variable correspond to different choices. Suppose we wish to colour a map of Australia as shown in Figure 3.1. It is made up of seven different states and territories[1] each of which may be coloured red, yellow or blue. Our colouring of the map should also satisfy the constraint that adjacent regions have different colours. This is an example of a finite domain problem, since the colours of each region come from the finite set $\{red, yellow, blue\}$.

In this chapter we will examine methods for solving constraints over finite constraint domains. Many real life problems, notably scheduling, routing and timetabling, are simple to express using finite constraint domains since, essentially, they involve choosing amongst a finite number of possibilities. Finding solutions to these problems is of great commercial importance to many businesses. For example, deciding how air crews should be allocated to aircraft flights is a crucial part of any airline business. A good solution reduces the expenses of the airline by minimizing the number of air crew needed and the number of flights on which the air crew must travel as passengers so as to be available at the source of their next flight.

Given the importance of finite constraint domains, it is not surprising that several research communities have developed methods for solving problems in finite constraint domains. Here we cover arc and node consistency techniques, developed by the artificial intelligence community to solve constraint satisfaction problems (a general type of finite constraint domain problem), bounds propagation techniques developed by the constraint programming community and integer programming techniques developed by the operations research community.

---

1. For the interested, non-Australian reader, these are: New South Wales, Northern Territory, Queensland, South Australia, Tasmania, Victoria and Western Australia.

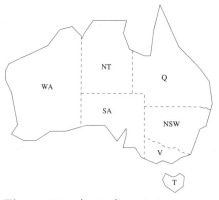

Figure 3.1   Australian states.

3.1   Constraint Satisfaction Problems

In the artificial intelligence community, satisfaction of constraint problems over finite domains has been studied under the name "constraint satisfaction problems."

Definition 3.1

A *constraint satisfaction problem*, or *CSP* for short, consists of a constraint C over variables $x_1, \ldots, x_n$ and a *domain* D that maps each variable x_i to a finite set of values, written $D(x_i)$, which it is allowed to take. The CSP is understood to represent the constraint $C \wedge x_1 \in D(x_1) \wedge \cdots \wedge x_n \in D(x_n)$.

Example 3.1

The *map colouring problem* is an archetypal CSP Problem. The problem is to colour the different regions in a particular map with a limited number of colours, subject to the conditions that no two adjacent regions have the same colour. For instance, consider the map of Australia in Figure 3.1 and the colours *red*, *yellow* and *blue*. With each region we associate a variable, WA, NT, SA, Q, NSW, V and T, which will be assigned the colour used to fill that region. Thus each variable has the domain $\{red, yellow, blue\}$. The following constraint captures that adjacent regions may not be filled with the same colour:

$$WA \neq NT \wedge WA \neq SA \wedge NT \neq SA \wedge NT \neq Q \wedge SA \neq Q \wedge$$
$$SA \neq NSW \wedge SA \neq V \wedge Q \neq NSW \wedge NSW \neq V.$$

The user is encouraged to verify that there is in fact a solution.

Example 3.2

Another well-known example of a CSP is the *N-queens problem*. This is the problem of placing N queens on a chess board of a size $N \times N$ so that no queen can capture another queen. Consider the 4-*queens* problem. We can formalise this as a CSP by associating with the ith queen two variables, R_i and C_i, which are, respectively, its

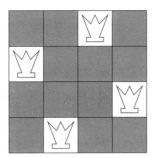

Figure 3.2   Example 4-queens solution.

row and column position on the board. The domain of each variable is $\{1, 2, 3, 4\}$. The constraint

$$R_1 \neq R_2 \wedge R_1 \neq R_3 \wedge R_1 \neq R_4 \wedge R_2 \neq R_3 \wedge R_2 \neq R_4 \wedge R_3 \neq R_4,$$

ensures that no two queens can be in the same row, the constraint

$$C_1 \neq C_2 \wedge C_1 \neq C_3 \wedge C_1 \neq C_4 \wedge C_2 \neq C_3 \wedge C_2 \neq C_4 \wedge C_3 \neq C_4,$$

ensures that no two queens can be in the same column, and the constraints

$$C_1 - R_1 \neq C_2 - R_2 \wedge C_1 - R_1 \neq C_3 - R_3 \wedge C_1 - R_1 \neq C_4 - R_4 \wedge$$
$$C_2 - R_2 \neq C_3 - R_3 \wedge C_2 - R_2 \neq C_4 - R_4 \wedge C_3 - R_3 \neq C_4 - R_4,$$

and

$$C_1 + R_1 \neq C_2 + R_2 \wedge C_1 + R_1 \neq C_3 + R_3 \wedge C_1 + R_1 \neq C_4 + R_4 \wedge$$
$$C_2 + R_2 \neq C_3 + R_3 \wedge C_2 + R_2 \neq C_4 + R_4 \wedge C_3 + R_3 \neq C_4 + R_4,$$

enforce that no two queens are on the same diagonal. One solution to the 4-queens problem is shown in Figure 3.2.

Since each variable has a finite domain, we can represent each of the primitive constraints in a CSP by its finite set of solutions over the values in the variable domains.

Example 3.3

The old-fashioned marriage problem (or, less floridly, the bipartite matching problem) aims to pair off a set of males and females, so that each pair likes each other. The problem is made up of a set of males and females, together with a constraint relation *likes* which describes friendships between males and females. A solution pairs each female with a different male whom they like. A sample problem consists of a set of males $\{kim, peter, bernd\}$, the set of females $\{nicole, maria, erika\}$ and

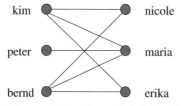

Figure 3.3   The old-fashioned marriage problem.

the relation *likes* defined as the set of pairs

$$\{(kim, nicole), (kim, maria), (kim, erika), (peter, maria),$$
$$(bernd, nicole), (bernd, maria), (bernd, erika)\}.$$

A diagram of the *likes* relation is given in Figure 3.3.

The problem can be described using a constraint that uses three variables X_{nicole}, X_{maria}, X_{erika} which represent the males chosen to match *nicole*, *maria* and *erika*, respectively. Each variable has domain $\{kim, peter, bernd\}$ and the constraint is

$$likes(X_{nicole}, nicole) \ \wedge \ likes(X_{maria}, maria) \ \wedge \ likes(X_{erika}, erika) \ \wedge$$
$$X_{nicole} \neq X_{maria} \wedge X_{nicole} \neq X_{erika} \wedge X_{maria} \neq X_{erika}.$$

One solution to the problem is $\{X_{nicole} \mapsto kim, X_{maria} \mapsto peter, X_{erika} \mapsto bernd\}$.

Much research has been devoted to the *binary CSP*s. These are CSPs in which the primitive constraints have at most two variables. The map colouring problem and old-fashioned marriage problem are both examples of binary CSPs.

One pleasing feature of a binary CSP is that it can be represented by an undirected graph. Each variable is represented by a node; a unary constraint on variable v is represented by an arc, labelled with the name of the constraint, from the node representing v to itself; and a binary constraint on variables u and v is represented by an arc, labelled with the name of the constraint, between the node corresponding to u and the node corresponding to v. The graph representing the CSP in Example 3.1 is shown in Figure 3.4.

More generally, we can represent non-binary CSPs using multi-graphs. However, it is beyond the scope of this text to pursue this.

3.2   A Simple Backtracking Solver

It is always possible to determine satisfiability of a CSP by a brute force search through all combinations of different values, since the number of such combinations is finite. However, this can be prohibitively expensive. But, any complete solver for CSP problems will, almost certainly, be exponential since solving CSPs is NP-hard. Thus, it is very unlikely that there is a polynomial algorithm to determine satisfiability of an arbitrary CSP. In this section we shall describe a complete solver

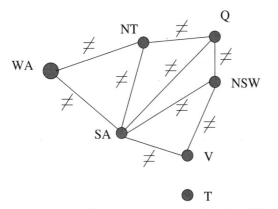

Figure 3.4 Graph of the map colouring CSP.

for CSPs which has exponential time complexity. In later sections we shall study various incomplete solvers which have polynomial time complexity.

One of the simplest techniques for determining satisfiability of an arbitrary CSP is *chronological backtracking*. The idea is to determine satisfiability of a CSP by choosing a variable, and then for each value in its domain, determining satisfiability of the constraint which results by replacing the variable with that value. This is done by calling the backtracking algorithm recursively. It makes use of a parametric function *satisfiable(c)* which takes a primitive constraint c that involves no variables and returns *true* or *false* indicating whether c is satisfiable or not.

Algorithm 3.1: Chronological backtracking solver
INPUT: A CSP with constraint C and domain D.
OUTPUT: Returns *true* if C is satisfiable, otherwise *false* .
METHOD: The algorithm is shown in Figure 3.5. □

Example 3.4
Consider the CSP consisting of the constraint $X < Y \wedge Y < Z$ and the variables X, Y, Z with domain $\{1, 2\}$. Execution proceeds by choosing a variable in the constraint, say X. The algorithm now iterates through the domain of X which is $\{1, 2\}$. First the domain value 1 is chosen and used to replace X in the original constraint giving $1 < Y \wedge Y < Z$. A call to partial_satisfiable determines that $1 < Y \wedge Y < Z$ is partially satisfiable in the sense that all primitive constraints without variables are satisfiable (in this case there are none so the test is trivial). Now a recursive call is made to the backtracking algorithm so as to determine satisfiability of the new constraint.

In this recursive call another variable, say Y, is chosen. The algorithm iterates through the domain values $\{1, 2\}$. First the domain value of 1 is chosen. Elimination of Y gives the constraint $1 < 1 \wedge 1 < Z$. This is not partially satisfiable, since $1 < 1$ is unsatisfiable. Therefore, in the next iteration the domain value 2 is chosen. Elimination of Y gives the constraint $1 < 2 \wedge 2 < Z$. This is partially satisfiable,

---

C and C_1 are constraints;
$c_1, \ldots, c_n$ are primitive constraints;
D a domain;
and x is a variable.

back_solve(C,D)
   if $vars(C) \equiv \emptyset$ **then**
      return partial_satisfiable(C)
   else
      choose $x \in vars(C)$
      for each value $d \in D(x)$ **do**
         let C_1 be obtained from C by replacing x by d
         if partial_satisfiable(C_1) **then**
            if back_solve(C_1,D) **then**
               return *true*
            endif
         endif
      endfor
      return *false*
   endif

partial_satisfiable(C)
   let C be of the form $c_1 \wedge \cdots \wedge c_n$
   for $i := 1$ to n **do**
      if $vars(c_i) \equiv \emptyset$ **then**
         if $satisfiable(c_i) \equiv false$ **then**
            return *false*
         endif
      endif
   endfor
   return *true*

Figure 3.5   Backtracking solver for CSPs.

so the backtracking algorithm is called with $1 < 2 \wedge 2 < Z$.

In this second recursive call the variable Z must be chosen. The recursive call now iterates through the domain values $\{1, 2\}$. First the domain value of 1 is chosen. Elimination of Z gives the constraint $1 < 2 \wedge 2 < 1$. This is not partially satisfiable, so in the next iteration the domain value 2 is chosen. Elimination of Z gives the constraint $1 < 2 \wedge 2 < 2$. Again this is not partially satisfiable, so the second recursive call returns with *false*, indicating that $1 < 2 \wedge 2 < Z$ is not satisfiable.

The first recursive call now returns *false*, since both domain values for Y have been tried and neither can satisfy the constraint $1 < Y \wedge Y < Z$. The original call now tries replacing X by the second domain value 2 giving rise to $2 < Y \wedge Y < Z$. This is partially satisfiable so the backtracking algorithm is called recursively to test for satisfiability. In this case, if Y is chosen for elimination, then both domain values lead to a constraint which is not partially satisfiable, so the recursive call returns *false*.

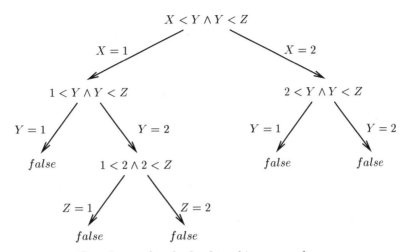

Figure 3.6 Search tree for the backtracking example.

The original call now returns *false* indicating that the original constraint is unsatisfiable. The search tree with recursive calls is shown in Figure 3.6.

As this example illustrates, the backtracking solver is expensive. Indeed, in the worst case it has exponential time complexity. This is to be expected since it is a complete solver. Note also that different choices of variables at different stages lead to different search trees. Good heuristics such as "choose the most constrained variable first" can lead to much smaller search trees. Nonetheless, the underlying worst case complexity remains the same.

3.3 Node and Arc Consistency

We now look at a variety of solvers for CSPs which have polynomial time worst case complexity, but are incomplete. These solvers are based on the observation that if the domain for any variable in the CSP is empty, then the CSP is unsatisfiable. The idea behind each of these solvers is to transform the CSP into an equivalent CSP but one in which the domains of the variables are decreased. If any of the domains become empty, then this CSP, and so the original CSP, are unsatisfiable. By equivalent, we mean that the constraints represented by the CSPs have the same set of solutions.

These solvers work by considering each primitive constraint in turn, and using information about the domain of each variable in the constraint to eliminate values from the domains of the other variables. The solvers are said to be "consistency based" since they propagate information about allowable domain values from one variable to another until the domains are "consistent" with the constraint.

We shall also see that consistency based solvers can be combined with backtracking search. This gives rise to complete solvers in which consistency tests are used to prune the domain of the variables at each step in the search.

It is useful to identify two special domains which may result after application of a consistency based solver. The first is a "false" domain which indicates that the original problem is unsatisfiable. The second is a "valuation" domain. In such a domain, the domain of each variable is a single value, and so the domain is essentially a valuation.

Definition 3.2
A domain is a *false domain* if some variable in the domain is mapped to the empty set.

A domain is a *valuation domain* if every variable in the domain is mapped to a singleton set.

Given a valuation domain we can straightforwardly determine whether a primitive constraint or constraint evaluates to *true* or *false* when each variable is assigned the value in its domain. We overload the parametric function *satisfiable* to do this. The function $satisfiable(C, D)$ takes a constraint C and a valuation domain D and returns *true* or *false* indicating whether C is satisfiable or not under this valuation.

For instance, consider the variables X, Y, Z. The domain D_1 in which $D_1(X) = D_1(Y) = \{1, 2\}$ and $D_1(Z) = \emptyset$ is a false domain. The domain D_2 in which $D_2(X) = \{1\}$, $D_2(Y) = \{2\}$ and $D_2(Z) = \{1\}$ is a valuation domain and $satisfiable(C, D_2)$ where C is the constraint $X < Y \wedge Y < Z$ is *false*.

The first propagation based solver we will look at is for binary CSPs. The solver is based on the following two notions of "consistency" which are based on the graph representation for binary CSPs.

Definition 3.3
A primitive constraint c is *node consistent* with domain D if either $|vars(c)| \neq 1$ or, if $vars(c) = \{x\}$, then for each $d \in D(x)$, $\{x \mapsto d\}$ is a solution of c.

A CSP with constraint $c_1 \wedge \cdots \wedge c_n$ and domain D is *node consistent* if each primitive constraint c_i is node consistent with D for $1 \leq i \leq n$.

Definition 3.4
A primitive constraint c is *arc consistent* with domain D if either $|vars(c)| \neq 2$ or, if $vars(c) = \{x, y\}$, then for each $d_x \in D(x)$, there is some $d_y \in D(y)$ such that $\{x \mapsto d_x, y \mapsto d_y\}$ is a solution of c and for each $d_y \in D(y)$, there is some $d_x \in D(x)$ such that $\{x \mapsto d_x, y \mapsto d_y\}$ is a solution of c.

A CSP with constraint $c_1 \wedge \cdots \wedge c_n$ and domain D is *arc consistent* if each primitive constraint c_i is arc consistent with D for $1 \leq i \leq n$.

For instance, the CSP in Example 3.1 is node and arc consistent. It is node consistent simply because there are no constraints involving only a single variable. Every disequation in the example is arc consistent since for every colour in the domain of the first variable in the disequality there is a colour not equal to that colour in the domain of the second variable, and vice versa. Thus all primitive constraints are arc consistent, so the CSP is arc consistent. Similarly, we can argue that the CSP in Example 3.2 is node and arc consistent.

If we modify the map colouring problem of Example 3.1 so as to allow only two colours, then it becomes unsatisfiable, since for example, there is no way to colour the three regions WA, NT and SA with two colours. However, it remains arc consistent, demonstrating that a binary CSP can be unsatisfiable even when it is node and arc consistent.

The CSP in Example 3.4 is node consistent, since it has no constraints that involve only a single variable. It is not arc consistent, however, because, for example, considering the constraint $X < Y$ and the value 1 for Y, there is no value in the domain of X, which is $\{1, 2\}$, that will satisfy the constraint.

An example of a CSP which is neither node nor arc consistent is the constraint

$$X < Y \land Y < Z \land Z \leq 2$$

with the domain D where $D(X) = D(Y) = D(Z) = \{1, 2, 3\}$. It is not node consistent because the value 3 for Z is not consistent with the primitive constraint $Z \leq 2$. It is not arc consistent using the same reasoning as in the previous paragraph.

It is straightforward to transform a CSP into an equivalent CSP which is node consistent—for each variable we intersect the solutions to the constraints involving only that variable with its original domain to give the new domain.

Algorithm 3.2: Node consistency
INPUT: A CSP with constraint C and domain D_1.
OUTPUT: Returns a domain D_2 such that the CSP with constraints C and domain D_2 is node consistent and is equivalent to the input CSP.
METHOD: The algorithm is shown in Figure 3.7. □

It is also easy to transform a CSP into an equivalent CSP which is arc consistent—for each variable x, the algorithm takes each binary constraint involving that variable and uses the domain of the other variable, y say, that appears in the constraint to restrict the domain of x. This process is repeated until the domain of no variable can be decreased. The algorithm given here is simple but it is quite inefficient. More efficient algorithms are referred to in the Notes section.

Algorithm 3.3: Arc consistency
INPUT: A CSP with constraint C and domain D_1.
OUTPUT: Returns a domain D_2 such that the CSP with constraints C and domain D_2 is arc consistent and is equivalent to the input CSP.
METHOD: The algorithm is shown in Figure 3.8. □

We can employ the arc and node consistency algorithms to give an incomplete solver for determining if a CSP is satisfiable as follows. Given a CSP, transform it to an equivalent node consistent CSP, then transform this to an equivalent arc consistent CSP with a new domain. If this domain is a false domain, the algorithm returns *false* since the original CSP must be unsatisfiable. If this

```
x is a variable;
C is a constraint;
D is a domain;
c₁, ... , cₙ are primitive constraints;
and d is a domain value.


node_consistent(C,D)
    let C be of form c₁ ∧ ··· ∧ cₙ
    for i := 1 to n do
        D := node_consistent_primitive(cᵢ,D)
    endfor
    return D

node_consistent_primitive(c,D)
    if |vars(c)| = 1 then
        let {x} = vars(c)
        D(x) := {d ∈ D(x) | {x ↦ d} is a solution of c}
    endif
    return D
```

Figure 3.7　Node consistency algorithm.

```
C is a constraint;
D and W are domains;
x, y are variables;
dₓ, d_y are domain values;
and c, c₁, ... , cₙ are primitive constraints.


arc_consistent(C,D)
    let C be of form c₁ ∧ ··· ∧ cₙ
    repeat
        W := D
        for i := 1 to n do
            D := arc_consistent_primitive(cᵢ,D)
        endfor
    until W ≡ D
    return D

arc_consistent_primitive(c,D)
    if |vars(c)| = 2 then
        let {x,y} = vars(c)
        D(x) := {dₓ ∈ D(x) | for some d_y ∈ D(y), {x ↦ dₓ, y ↦ d_y} is a solution of c}
        D(y) := {d_y ∈ D(y) | for some dₓ ∈ D(x), {x ↦ dₓ, y ↦ d_y} is a solution of c}
    endif
    return D
```

Figure 3.8　Arc consistency algorithm.

```
C is a constraint;
and D is a domain.


arc_solv(C,D)
    D := node_arc_consistent(C,D)
    if D is a false domain then
        return false
    elseif D is a valuation domain then
        return satisfiable(C, D)
    else
        return unknown
    endif

node_arc_consistent(C, D)
    D := node_consistent(C,D)
    D := arc_consistent(C,D)
    return D
```

Figure 3.9   Arc consistency solver.

domain is a valuation domain it returns the result of evaluating the constraint with that valuation. Otherwise it returns *unknown* since the CSP may or may not be satisfiable.

Although a constraint solver usually takes a single argument, a constraint, we relax this restriction for finite domain solvers, giving two arguments: a constraint and a domain. The two arguments can be extracted from a single constraint of the form $C \wedge x_1 \in D(x_1) \wedge \cdots \wedge x_n \in D(x_n)$ or some default domain D can be used which assigns some fixed finite set of values to all variables.

Algorithm 3.4: Incomplete node and arc consistency solver
INPUT: A CSP with constraint C and domain D.
OUTPUT: Returns *true*, *false* or *unknown*.
METHOD: The algorithm arc_solv is shown in Figure 3.9. □

For instance, consider the CSP for the constraint

$$X < Y \ \wedge \ Y < Z \ \wedge \ Z \leq 2,$$

with domain $D(X) = D(Y) = D(Z) = \{1, 2, 3\}$. Application of the node consistency algorithm will leave the domain of X and Y as $\{1, 2, 3\}$, but the domain of Z will become $\{1, 2\}$. Application of the arc consistency algorithm proceeds as follows. In the first iteration the constraint $X < Y$ is considered. The new domain of X is computed to be $\{1, 2\}$ from interaction of the constraint $X < Y$ and the domain $\{1, 2, 3\}$ for Y. The value of 3 is removed from the domain of X because there is no value in Y's domain which satisfies $3 < Y$. Similarly the new domain of Y is calculated to be $\{2, 3\}$. Examining the constraint $Y < Z$ the domain of Y is computed to be $\emptyset$ since there are no values lower than a value for Z. The domain of Z also becomes $\emptyset$. On the next iteration the domain of X will become the empty

```
C is a constraint;
D and D₁ are domains;
x is a variable;
and d is a domain value.


back_arc_solv(C,D)
    D := node_arc_consistent(C,D)
    if D is a false domain then
        return false
    elseif D is a valuation domain then
        if satisfiable(C, D) then
            return D
        else
            return false
        endif
    endif
    choose variable x such that |D(x)| ≥ 2
    for each d ∈ D(x)
        D₁ := back_arc_solv(C ∧ x = d,D)
        if D₁ ≢ false then
            return D₁
        endif
    endfor
    return false
```

Figure 3.10   Backtracking arc consistency solver.

set. The next iteration will not change the domains and the algorithm will return
that the original system is unsatisfiable.

The node and arc consistency algorithms can also be combined with the backtracking algorithm to give a complete solver. Initially the node consistency and arc
consistency algorithms are used to restrict the domains. Subsequently, whenever
the backtracking algorithm chooses a value for a variable, the node and arc consistency algorithm is used to restore the domains to node and arc consistency. If this
makes the domain false, then the resultant CSP is unsatisfiable and backtracking
to another domain value is required.

Algorithm 3.5: Complete node and arc consistency solver

INPUT: A CSP with constraint C and domain D.

OUTPUT: Returns *true* or *false*

METHOD: If the result of back_arc_solv(C, D) returns *false* then return *false*,
otherwise return *true*. The algorithm for back_arc_solv is shown in Figure 3.10.
□

3.4 Bounds Consistency

Arc and node consistency work well for pruning the domains in binary CSPs. However, they do not work well if the problem contains primitive constraints that involve more than two variables since such primitive constraints are ignored when performing consistency checks. We would, therefore, like to extend this technique to handle primitive constraints involving more than two variables.

Hyper-arc consistency extends the arc consistency condition to apply to every primitive constraint, regardless of the number of variables it contains.

Definition 3.5

A primitive constraint c is *hyper-arc consistent* with domain D if for each variable $x \in vars(c)$ and domain assignment $d \in D(x)$, there is an assignment to the remaining variables in c, say $x_1, x_2, \ldots, x_k$, such that $d_j \in D(x_j)$ for $1 \leq j \leq k$ and $\{x \mapsto d, x_2 \mapsto d_2, \ldots, x_k \mapsto d_k\}$ is a solution of c.

A CSP with constraint $c_1 \wedge \cdots \wedge c_n$ and domain D is *hyper-arc consistent* if each primitive constraint c_i is hyper-arc consistent with D for $1 \leq i \leq n$.

Hyper-arc consistency is a true generalization of node and arc consistency. In the case in which the primitive constraint has two variables, hyper-arc consistency is equivalent to arc consistency, and in the case when a primitive constraint has one variable, it is equivalent to node consistency.

Unfortunately, testing for hyper-arc consistency can be very expensive even for fairly simple primitive constraints which involve more than two variables. Consider the primitive constraint

$$X = 3Y + 5Z$$

with domain D where $D(X) = \{2, 3, 4, 5, 6, 7\}$, $D(Y) = \{0, 1, 2\}$ and $D(Z) = \{-1, 0, 1, 2\}$. Hyper-arc consistency applied to this primitive constraint must determine which possible values of X are legitimate. Take the first value, 2, for instance. It is consistent if there is a solution to $2 = 3Y + 5Z$ where $Y \in \{0, 1, 2\}$ and $Z \in \{-1, 0, 1, 2\}$. This is a non-trivial problem and is not simple to check. If values which are not hyper-arc consistent are removed the new domain is D_1 where $D_1(X) = \{3, 5, 6\}$, $D_1(Y) = \{0, 1, 2\}$ and $D_1(Z) = \{0, 1\}$.

For slightly more complex primitive constraints, such as

$$12X + 107Y - 17Z + 5T = 2$$

where the initial domains for all variables are $\{0, 1, \ldots, 1000\}$, we can see that the hyper-arc consistency check is very expensive. Indeed, in general, determining if an arbitrary primitive constraint is hyper-arc consistent is NP-hard and so is as expensive as determining if an arbitrary CSP is satisfiable. Thus, hyper-arc consistency is too expensive to use in an incomplete solver or to use at each step in a backtracking solver.

We therefore need some other consistency condition for primitive constraints involving more than two variables. Luckily, there is a large and useful class of CSPs for which there is a natural choice of a consistency condition which can be used with primitive constraints involving an arbitrary number of variables.

Definition 3.6
A CSP is *arithmetic* if each variable in the CSP ranges over a finite domain of integers and the primitive constraints are arithmetic constraints.

The 4-queens problem is an example of an arithmetic CSP. Arithmetic CSPs are, arguably, the most important class of CSPs since most problems of commercial interest can be naturally modelled using integer CSPs. Furthermore, it is possible to encode many non-arithmetic CSPs as arithmetic CSPs, simply by representing the domain values by integers. For instance, if we represent colours by integers, the map colouring problem becomes an arithmetic CSP.

The CSP solving methods discussed in the previous section can, of course, be used to solve arithmetic CSPs since they are simply a particular type of CSP. Indeed Examples 3.2 and 3.4 solve arithmetic CSPs. However, the restriction to integers and arithmetic constraints allows us to define a new type of consistency: bounds consistency. There are two ideas behind bounds consistency. The first is to approximate the domain of an integer variable using a lower and an upper bound. The second is to use real number consistency of primitive constraints rather than integer consistency.

Definition 3.7
A *range*, $[l..u]$, represents the set of integers $\{l, l+1, \ldots, u\}$ if $l \leq u$, otherwise it represents the empty set.

If D is a domain over the integers, $min_D(x)$ is the minimum element in $D(x)$ and $max_D(x)$ is the maximum element in $D(x)$.

Definition 3.8
An arithmetic primitive constraint c is *bounds consistent* with domain D if for each variable $x \in vars(c)$, there is:

- an assignment of *real* numbers, say $d_1, d_2, \ldots, d_k$, to the remaining variables in c, say $x_1, x_2, \ldots, x_k$, such that $min_D(x_j) \leq d_j \leq max_D(x_j)$ for each d_j and

$$\{x \mapsto min_D(x), x_1 \mapsto d_1, \ldots, x_k \mapsto d_k\}$$

is a solution of c and

- another assignment of *real* numbers, say $d'_1, d'_2, \ldots, d'_k$, to $x_1, x_2, \ldots, x_k$ such that $min_D(x_j) \leq d'_j \leq max_D(x_j)$ for each d'_j and

$$\{x \mapsto max_D(x), x_1 \mapsto d'_1, \ldots, x_k \mapsto d'_k\}$$

is a solution of c.

An arithmetic CSP with constraint $c_1 \wedge \cdots \wedge c_n$ and domain D is *bounds consistent* if each primitive constraint c_i is bounds consistent with D for $1 \leq i \leq n$.

Since bounds consistency only depends on the upper and lower bounds of the domains of the variables, when testing for bounds consistency we need only consider domains that assign ranges to each variable. Therefore, in the following examples we will often use ranges to describe the domain of each variable.

Consider the constraint from the previous example, $X = 3Y + 5Z$, with domain D where

$$D(X) = [2..7], \quad D(Y) = [0..2], \quad D(Z) = [-1..2].$$

This constraint is not bounds consistent with D. To see this, consider $5Z = X - 3Y$ which is equivalent to the original constraint. If Z takes its maximum value 2, then the left hand side has value 10, but the maximum value of the right hand side expression $X - 3Y$ is $7 - 3 \times 0 = 7$. Hence the range for Z must be changed to obtain bounds consistency. The domain D_1 where

$$D_1(X) = [2..7], \quad D_1(Y) = [0..2], \quad D_1(Z) = [0..1],$$

however, is bounds consistent with the constraint.

Given a current range for each of the variables in a primitive constraint we can devise an efficient method for calculating a new range for each variable in the constraint which is bounds consistent with the constraint. We will refer to such methods as *propagation rules*.

Consider the simple constraint $X = Y + Z$. By writing the constraint in the three forms:

$$X = Y + Z, \quad Y = X - Z \quad \text{and} \quad Z = X - Y$$

and reasoning about the minimum and maximum values of the right hand sides, we can see that

$$
\begin{aligned}
X &\geq min_D(Y) + min_D(Z), & X &\leq max_D(Y) + max_D(Z), \\
Y &\geq min_D(X) - max_D(Z), & Y &\leq max_D(X) - min_D(Z), \\
Z &\geq min_D(X) - max_D(Y), & Z &\leq max_D(X) - min_D(Y).
\end{aligned}
$$

From these inequalities we can derive simple rules for ensuring bounds consistency which use the current domains of each variable to calculate the values of the right hand side expressions, and use these values to appropriately update the minimum and maximum values of each variable's domain. An algorithm implementing the propagation rules for the constraint $X = Y + Z$ is shown in Figure 3.11.

For example, given the domain

$$D(X) = [4..8], \quad D(Y) = [0..3], \quad D(Z) = [2..2]$$

D is a domain;
X, Y and Z are fixed variables;
X_{min}, X_{max}, d_X, Y_{min}, Y_{max}, d_Y, Z_{min}, Z_{max} and d_Z are domain values.

bounds_consistent_addition(D)
   $X_{min} :=$ maximum $\{min_D(X), min_D(Y) + min_D(Z)\}$
   $X_{max} :=$ minimum $\{max_D(X), max_D(Y) + max_D(Z)\}$
   $D(X) := \{d_X \in D(X) | X_{min} \leq d_X \leq X_{max}\}$
   $Y_{min} :=$ maximum $\{min_D(Y), min_D(X) - max_D(Z)\}$
   $Y_{max} :=$ minimum $\{max_D(Y), max_D(X) - min_D(Z)\}$
   $D(Y) := \{d_Y \in D(Y) | Y_{min} \leq d_Y \leq Y_{max}\}$
   $Z_{min} :=$ maximum $\{min_D(Z), min_D(X) - max_D(Y)\}$
   $Z_{max} :=$ minimum $\{max_D(Z), max_D(X) - min_D(Y)\}$
   $D(Z) := \{d_Z \in D(Z) | Z_{min} \leq d_Z \leq Z_{max}\}$
   return D

Figure 3.11   Propagation rules for the primitive constraint $X = Y + Z$.

we can determine that

$$2 \leq X \leq 5,$$
$$2 \leq Y \leq 6,$$
$$1 \leq Z \leq 8.$$

Therefore, we can update the domain to

$$D(X) = [4..5], \quad D(Y) = [2..3], \quad D(Z) = [2..2]$$

without removing any solutions to the constraint.

If we now update this new domain using the propagation rules we determine that

$$4 \leq X \leq 5,$$
$$2 \leq Y \leq 3,$$
$$1 \leq Z \leq 3.$$

The new domain satisfies all these constraints. Thus, $X = Y + Z$ is bounds consistent with the new domain. In fact, we need only apply these propagation rules once to any domain to obtain a domain which is bounds consistent with the constraint $X = Y + Z$.

We can also determine propagation rules for more complicated linear arithmetic constraints. For example, consider the constraint

$$4W + 3P + 2C \leq 9.$$

We can rewrite this into the three forms

$$W \leq \tfrac{9}{4} - \tfrac{3}{4}P - \tfrac{2}{4}C, \quad P \leq \tfrac{9}{3} - \tfrac{4}{3}W - \tfrac{2}{3}C, \quad C \leq \tfrac{9}{2} - 2W - \tfrac{3}{2}P$$

D is a domain;
W, P and C are fixed variables;
W_{max}, d_W, P_{max}, d_P, C_{max}, and d_C are domain values;

bounds_consistent_inequality(D)
     $W_{max} := \text{minimum } \{max_D(W), \lfloor \frac{9}{4} - \frac{3}{4}\,min_D(P) - \frac{2}{4}\,min_D(C) \rfloor\}$
     $D(W) := \{d_W \in D(W) | d_W \leq W_{max}\}$
     $P_{max} := \text{minimum } \{max_D(P), \lfloor \frac{9}{3} - \frac{4}{3}\,min_D(W) - \frac{2}{3}\,min_D(C) \rfloor\}$
     $D(P) := \{d_P \in D(P) | d_P \leq P_{max}\}$
     $C_{max} := \text{minimum } \{max_D(C), \lfloor \frac{9}{2} - 2\,min_D(W) - \frac{3}{2}\,min_D(P) \rfloor\}$
     $D(C) := \{d_P \in D(C) | d_C \leq C_{max}\}$
     return D

Figure 3.12   Propagation rules for $4W + 3P + 2C \leq 9$.

and so we obtain the inequalities

$$
\begin{aligned}
W &\leq \tfrac{9}{4} - \tfrac{3}{4}\,min_D(P) - \tfrac{2}{4}\,min_D(C), \\
P &\leq \tfrac{9}{3} - \tfrac{4}{3}\,min_D(W) - \tfrac{2}{3}\,min_D(C), \\
C &\leq \tfrac{9}{2} - 2\,min_D(W) - \tfrac{3}{2}\,min_D(P).
\end{aligned}
$$

From these inequalities we obtain the propagation rules shown in Figure 3.12. Note that the function $\lfloor F \rfloor$ takes a real number and rounds it down to the nearest integer.

Given the initial domain

$$D(W) = [0..9], \quad D(P) = [0..9], \quad D(C) = [0..9]$$

we can determine that $W \leq \frac{9}{4}$, $P \leq \frac{9}{3}$, and $C \leq \frac{9}{2}$. Using the propagation rules we update the domain to give

$$D(W) = [0..2], \quad D(P) = [0..3], \quad D(C) = [0..4].$$

Notice that $W \leq \frac{9}{4}$ means we can lower the upper bound for W to $\lfloor \frac{9}{4} \rfloor = 2$, since we know W takes integer values only. Similarly, $C \leq \frac{9}{2}$ means we can lower the upper bound for C to 4.

Example 3.5

Consider the *smuggler's knapsack problem*. A smuggler has a knapsack of limited capacity, say 9 units. He can smuggle in bottles of whiskey of size 4 units, bottles of perfume of size 3 units, and cartons of cigarettes of size 2 units. The profit from smuggling a bottle of whiskey, bottle of perfume or carton of cigarettes is 15 dollars, 10 dollars and 7 dollars respectively. If the smuggler will only take a trip if he makes a profit of 30 dollars or more, what can he take?

This problem can be modelled as an arithmetic non-binary CSP using three variables W, P and C whose values are the number of whiskey, perfume and cigarette items in the knapsack, respectively. An initial domain for each variable is

$[0..9]$. The capacity constraint is

$$4W + 3P + 2C \leq 9,$$

while the profit constraint is

$$15W + 10P + 7C \geq 30.$$

Using the propagation rules given above for the capacity constraint we update the domain to get

$$D(W) = [0..2], \quad D(P) = [0..3], \quad D(C) = [0..4].$$

Application of the propagation rules for the profit constraint does not change the domain.

Another interesting case is for the primitive linear disequation constraint $Y \neq Z$. In this case the requirement for bounds consistency is quite weak since as long as each variable has a domain of two or more possible values then the disequation is bounds consistent. However when one variable, say Z, has a fixed value, that is $min_D(Z) \equiv max_D(Z)$, then we have

$$Y \quad \neq \quad min_D(Z).$$

With bounds consistency, the only time this disequality can be inconsistent is when the current minimum or maximum of Y equals the (fixed) value of Z. In this case we can remove this value from the domain of Y and increase or decrease the respective bound.

For instance, given the domain $D(Y) = [2..3], D(Z) = [2..2]$ and primitive constraint $Y \neq Z$, the minimum value of Y is disallowed by the constraint. Therefore, the updated domain is $D(Y) = [3..3], D(Z) = [2..2]$ which is now bounds consistent. Note that a simple disequation constraint of the form $Y \neq d$, where d is some integer, is handled analogously to $Y \neq Z$.

We can also devise propagation rules for nonlinear constraints. Consider, for example, the constraint

$$X = \text{minimum}\{Y, Z\}$$

which holds whenever X takes the minimum of the values of Y and Z. The propagation rules for this constraint follow directly from the following inequalities

$$\begin{aligned}
Y &\geq min_D(X), \\
Z &\geq min_D(X), \\
X &\geq \text{minimum}\{min_D(Y), min_D(Z)\}, \\
X &\leq \text{minimum}\{max_D(Y), max_D(Z)\}.
\end{aligned}$$

The first inequality holds because Y cannot take a value less than the minimum value of X since otherwise the constraint could not be satisfied. Thus, Y's minimum is greater than that of X. The second inequality has an analogous justification. The final two inequalities hold because the value of X is one of the values of Y and Z and so it cannot be less than both of their possible values, and it cannot be greater than either of their possible values.

However, for some nonlinear constraints determining propagation rules is more difficult. Consider the deceptively simple multiplication constraint

$$X = Y \times Z.$$

Let us first consider the case when all the numbers are strictly positive. In this case propagation rules can be based on the inequalities

$$
\begin{aligned}
X &\geq\ min_D(Y) \times min_D(Z), \\
X &\leq\ max_D(Y) \times max_D(Z), \\
Y &\geq\ min_D(X)/max_D(Z), \\
Y &\leq\ max_D(X)/min_D(Z), \\
Z &\geq\ min_D(X)/max_D(Y), \\
Z &\leq\ max_D(X)/min_D(Y).
\end{aligned}
$$

For example, for the domain

$$D(X) = [1..4], \quad D(Y) = [1..2], \quad D(Z) = [1..4]$$

these inequalities give

$$X \geq 1,\ X \leq 8,\ Y \geq 1,\ Y \leq 4,\ Z \geq 1,\ Z \leq 4.$$

Thus, propagation rules based on these inequalities will not change the domain.

With the possibility of variables taking zero or negative values the propagation rules become much more complex. In general, we can only calculate the bounds for X by examining all combinations of the extreme positions of Y and Z. Thus,

$$
\begin{aligned}
X \geq\ \text{minimum}\quad & \{min_D(Y) \times min_D(Z), min_D(Y) \times max_D(Z), \\
& max_D(Y) \times min_D(Z), max_D(Y) \times max_D(Z)\}, \\
X \leq\ \text{maximum}\quad & \{min_D(Y) \times min_D(Z), min_D(Y) \times max_D(Z), \\
& max_D(Y) \times min_D(Z), max_D(Y) \times max_D(Z)\}.
\end{aligned}
$$

Given domain

$$D(X) = [4..8], \quad D(Y) = [0..3], \quad D(Z) = [-2..2]$$

we can determine that

$$
\begin{aligned}
X &\geq\ \text{minimum}\{0, 0, -6, 6\} = -6, \\
X &\leq\ \text{maximum}\{0, 0, -6, 6\} = 6.
\end{aligned}
$$

Propagation rules for the other variables are even more complex. This is because variables may take values very near zero.

Given $D(X) = [4..8]$ and $D(Z) = [-2..2]$, any non-zero value of Y, say d, is bounds consistent because the valuation $\{X \mapsto 4, Y \mapsto d, Z \mapsto (4/d)\}$ is a solution of $X = Y \times Z$ since $-2 \leq 4/d \leq 2$ for all d where $|d| \geq 2$. Hence, updating Y is complicated. As long as the domain of Z is such that $min_D(Z) < 0$ and $max_D(Z) > 0$, the valuations used in testing bounds consistency for Y can contain arbitrarily small positive and negative real values for Z. This means that the multiplication constraint is bounds consistent with any value of Y. Therefore, as long as $min_D(Z) < 0$ and $max_D(Z) > 0$, bounds consistency cannot be used to reduce the range of variable Y. When this is not the case, we can propagate, again by simply examining the four possibilities at the extremes of the ranges for X and Z using the inequalities

$$
\begin{aligned}
Y &\geq \text{minimum} \quad \{min_D(X)/min_D(Z), min_D(X)/max_D(Z), \\
&\qquad\qquad\quad max_D(X)/min_D(Z), max_D(X)/max_D(Z)\}, \\
Y &\leq \text{maximum} \quad \{min_D(X)/min_D(Z), min_D(X)/max_D(Z), \\
&\qquad\qquad\quad max_D(X)/min_D(Z), max_D(X)/max_D(Z)\}
\end{aligned}
$$

where division by zero yields $+\infty$ when dividing a positive number, $-\infty$ when dividing a negative number and $0/0$ is considered as $-\infty$ on the right of a $\geq$ and $+\infty$ on the right hand side of a $\leq$. Using the same reasoning, the inequalities for Z are, when $min_D(Y) \geq 0$ or $max_D(Y) \leq 0$,

$$
\begin{aligned}
Z &\geq \text{minimum} \quad \{min_D(X)/min_D(Y), min_D(X)/max_D(Y), \\
&\qquad\qquad\quad max_D(X)/min_D(Y), max_D(X)/max_D(Y)\}, \\
Z &\leq \text{maximum} \quad \{min_D(X)/min_D(Y), min_D(X)/max_D(Y), \\
&\qquad\qquad\quad max_D(X)/min_D(Y), max_D(X)/max_D(Y)\}.
\end{aligned}
$$

Another complication of the multiplication constraint is that, unlike the previous constraints we have examined, applying the propagation rules to a domain once does not guarantee that the resulting domain will be bounds consistent. This is because the conditions required for applying the propagation rules for Y and Z may not be satisfied initially, but may be satisfied after applying the propagation rules. Thus we may need to apply the same rules repeatedly to obtain a bounds consistent domain.

For instance, given the domain

$$D(X) = [4..8], \quad D(Y) = [-1..1], \quad D(Z) = [-4..-1]$$

we initially determine that no propagation is possible for Z. However for X and Y

we have that

$$
\begin{aligned}
X &\geq \text{minimum}\{4, -4, 1, -1\} = -4, \\
X &\leq \text{maximum}\{4, -1, 1, -1\} = 4, \\
Y &\geq \text{minimum}\{\tfrac{4}{-4}, \tfrac{8}{-4}, \tfrac{4}{-1}, \tfrac{8}{-1}\} = \text{minimum}\{-1, -2, -4, -8\} = -8, \\
Y &\leq \text{maximum}\{-1, -2, -4, -8\} = -1.
\end{aligned}
$$

Thus, after applying the corresponding propagation rules, the domain becomes

$$
D(X) = [4..4], \quad D(Y) = [-1..-1], \quad D(Z) = [-4..-1].
$$

Another propagation step is required to determine that $D(Z) = [-4..-4]$.

As we have seen from these examples, determining the propagation rules for a particular primitive constraint is quite tedious. For this reason, bounds consistency constraint solvers usually handle only a restricted class of primitive constraints. A typical restriction is that constraints must either be linear arithmetic equations or inequalities or a nonlinear constraint in a specific form such as $t_1 = t_2 \times t_3$, $t_1 \neq t_2$, $t_1 = \text{minimum}\{t_2, t_3\}$, where each t_i is either a variable or a constant and no variable occurs more than once in the primitive constraint.

More complex primitive constraints must be replaced by conjunctions of these legitimate primitive constraints. Unfortunately, because the consistency methods are incomplete, replacing a complex constraint by different but equivalent legitimate primitive constraints may not lead to equivalent behaviour.

Example 3.6

Consider the constraint $(X - 1)^2 = Y$. We could rewrite this to

$$
T_1 = X - 1 \wedge T_1 = T_2 \wedge Y = T_1 \times T_2
$$

or to

$$
U_1 = X \wedge U_2 = U_1 \times X \wedge U_2 - 2X + 1 = Y.
$$

If the initial domain is $D(X) = [2..5]$, $D(Y) = [-3..10]$ then, using the first rewriting, bounds consistency determines the domain

$$
D(X) = [2..5], \quad D(Y) = [1..10], \quad D(T_1) = [1..4], \quad D(T_2) = [1..4].
$$

Using the second rewriting, bounds consistency determines the domain

$$
D(X) = [2..5], \quad D(Y) = [-3..10], \quad D(U_1) = [2..5], \quad D(U_2) = [4..25].
$$

In this case, the second rewriting leads to less propagation than the first.

One potential problem, therefore, is that if the breakdown of complex constraints is handled automatically by the constraint solver, the user of the solver may not understand why it fails to detect some inconsistencies.

It is simple to give an algorithm which transforms an arithmetic CSP to an equivalent bounds consistent CSP. The algorithm uses the parametric function

```
C is an arithmetic constraint;
C₀ is a set of primitive constraints;
D and D₁ are domains;
c₁,...,cₙ are primitive constraints;
and x is a variable.


bounds_consistent(C,D)
    let C be of form c₁ ∧ ··· ∧ cₙ
    C₀ := {c₁,...,cₙ}
    while C₀ ≢ ∅ do
        choose c ∈ C₀
        C₀ := C₀ \ {c}
        D₁ := bounds_consistent_primitive(c, D)
        if D₁ is a false domain then return D₁ endif
        for i := 1 to n do
            if there exists x ∈ vars(cᵢ) such that D₁(x) ≠ D(x) then
                C₀ := C₀ ∪ {cᵢ}
            endif
        endfor
        D := D₁
    endwhile
    return D
```

Figure 3.13   Bounds consistency algorithm.

$bounds\_consistent\_primitive(c, D)$ which applies the propagation rules for primitive constraint c to the domain D and returns the new domain. Examples of this function for particular linear constraints have been given above. We assume that the original CSP has been transformed into a CSP containing only legitimate primitive constraints.

The algorithm works by repeatedly processing the *active set* of primitive constraints C_0. A primitive constraint is active if it may not be bounds consistent with the current domain D. The main **while** loop repeatedly selects a primitive constraint c from the active set and modifies the domain D to be bounds consistent with c. If this gives a false domain, the algorithm terminates, otherwise those constraints which might no longer be bounds consistent because of the changes made to D are added to the active set. The algorithm terminates when there are no primitive constraints in the active set since this means all of the primitive constraints are bounds consistent with the current domain.

Algorithm 3.6: Bounds consistency
INPUT: An arithmetic CSP with constraint C and domain D.
OUTPUT: $bounds\_consistent(C, D)$ returns a domain D_1 such that the CSP with constraints C and domain D_1 is bounds consistent and is equivalent to the input CSP.
METHOD: The algorithm is shown in Figure 3.13. □

For example, consider the constraint $X = Y + Z \land Y \neq Z$ and domain

$$D(X) = [4..8], \quad D(Y) = [0..3], \quad D(Z) = [2..2].$$

Execution of bounds_consistent proceeds as follows. Initially, C_0 is set to the set $\{X = Y + Z, Y \neq Z\}$. Now some c, say $X = Y + Z$, is removed from C_0. The procedure bounds_consistent_primitive evaluates the propagation rules for $X = Y + Z$ giving the updated domain

$$D(X) = [4..5], \quad D(Y) = [2..3], \quad D(Z) = [2..2].$$

Since the variable X has changed its range, the constraint $X = Y + Z$ is added to C_0 (although this is unnecessary since its propagation rules ensure bounds consistency with respect to itself). Now another primitive constraint, say $Y \neq Z$, is removed from C_0. The call to bounds_consistent_primitive removes the value 2 from the range of Y giving the updated domain

$$D(X) = [4..5], \quad D(Y) = [3..3], \quad D(Z) = [2..2].$$

The constraint $Y \neq Z$ is added to C_0 because Y's range has changed. Another constraint is removed from C_0, say $X = Y + Z$, and its propagation rules are applied yielding the domain

$$D(X) = [5..5], \quad D(Y) = [3..3], \quad D(Z) = [2..2].$$

Since the range of X has changed, $X = Y + Z$ is added to C_0. Further processing of the constraints, $X = Y + Z$ and $Y \neq Z$, in C_0 does not change the domain so the procedure terminates returning this domain which is bounds consistent with the constraint.

It is simple to define an incomplete constraint solver for arithmetic CSPs based on the bounds consistency algorithm.

Algorithm 3.7: Bounds consistency solver
INPUT: An arithmetic CSP with constraint C and domain D
OUTPUT: bounds_solv(C,D) returns *true*, *false* or *unknown* depending on the satisfiability of the constraint C with domain D.
METHOD: bounds_solv(C,D) is identical to arc_solv(C,D) (shown in Figure 3.9) except that the call to node_arc_consistent is replaced by a call to bounds_consistent.
□

Consider the execution of this solver on the constraint $X < Y \land Y < Z$ where each variable lies in the range $[1..4]$. Initially, we have $D(X) = D(Y) = D(Z) = [1..4]$. The call to bounds_consistent(C, D) sets C_0 to $\{X < Y, Y < Z\}$. Considering the primitive constraint $X < Y$, we obtain $D(X) = [1..3], D(Y) = [2..4]$ and $D(Z)$ is unchanged. This causes the constraint $X < Y$ to be replaced in C_0. Now considering $Y < Z$ we obtain $D(Y) = [2..3], D(Z) = [3..4]$, and $Y < Z$ is replaced in C_0. Reconsidering $X < Y$ we obtain $D(X) = [1..2]$ and $X < Y$ is replaced in

C_0. Processing $X < Y$ and $Y < Z$ causes no further change to D so the call to bounds_consistent returns

$$D(X) = [1..2], \quad D(Y) = [2..3], \quad D(Z) = [3..4].$$

Thus, bounds_solv returns *unknown*.

It is also straightforward to combine the bounds consistency algorithm with a backtracking search to produce a complete bounds consistency solver, analogous to the node and arc consistency based solver given in Algorithm 3.5.

Algorithm 3.8: Complete bounds consistency solver
INPUT: An arithmetic CSP with constraint C and domain D.
OUTPUT: Returns *true* or *false*.
METHOD: If the result of back_bounds_solv(C,D) returns *false* then return *false*, otherwise return *true*. back_bounds_solv(C,D) is identical to back_arc_solv(C,D) (shown in Figure 3.10) except that the call to node_arc_consistent is replaced by a call to bounds_consistent, and the recursive call to back_arc_solv is replaced by a call to back_bounds_solv. □

Using the complete bounds consistency solver on the problem above, after bounds_consistent returns

$$D(X) = [1..2], \quad D(Y) = [2..3], \quad D(Z) = [3..4]$$

the solver selects a variable, say Z, and tries different values in its domain. First, the complete bounds consistency solver calls itself recursively with the constraint $X < Y \wedge Y < Z \wedge Z = 3$ and the domain

$$D(X) = [1..2], \quad D(Y) = [2..3], \quad D(Z) = [3..4].$$

The procedure bounds_consistent is evaluated with this new constraint and domain. Examining $Z = 3$ gives $D(Z) = [3..3]$. Now examining $Y < Z$ gives $D(Y) = [2..2]$. Finally, examining $X < Y$ gives $D(X) = [1..1]$. No more propagation results, so the resulting domain is

$$D(X) = [1..1], \quad D(Y) = [2..2], \quad D(Z) = [3..3].$$

This is returned by bounds_consistent and, since this is a valuation domain which satisfies the constraint, the solver returns *true*.

Example 3.7
Consider the smuggler's knapsack problem from Example 3.5 which has constraint

$$4W + 3P + 2C \leq 9 \ \wedge \ 15W + 10P + 7C \geq 30$$

and initial domain

$$D(W) = [0..9], \quad D(P) = [0..9], \quad D(C) = [0..9].$$

Using the complete bounds propagation solver we begin by applying the bounds_consistent procedure to this problem. This gives the domain

$$D(W) = [0..2], \quad D(P) = [0..3], \quad D(C) = [0..4].$$

Then, choosing to branch on W, we first try adding $W = 0$. Applying bounds_consistent returns

$$D(W) = [0..0], \quad D(P) = [1..3], \quad D(C) = [0..3].$$

Now, choosing to branch on P, we add the constraint $P = 1$. Applying bounds consistency gives rise to the domain

$$D(W) = [0..0], \quad D(P) = [1..1], \quad D(C) = [3..3],$$

and so we have found a solution to the problem: $\{W \mapsto 0, P \mapsto 1, C \mapsto 3\}$. A diagram of the search tree is shown in Figure 3.14. The solver explores the left part of the tree until the first solution is found. Notice that if all solutions were required we could modify the solver to explore the entire tree, and return each solution (leaf nodes that are not *false*). Also note that the size of the search tree is significantly smaller than that obtained if the chronological backtracking solver given in Algorithm 3.1 is used.

3.5 Generalized Consistency

We have now seen three consistency-based approaches to solving CSPs, namely arc, node and bounds consistency. In this section we consider how these can be combined with each other and also with specialized consistency methods for "complex" primitive constraints.

It is straightforward to use different consistency methods in combination with one another, since they communicate through a common medium, the domain. In particular, we can combine arc and node consistency with bounds consistency. For constraints involving only two variables we can use the stronger arc consistency test to remove values, while, for constraints with more than two variables, we can use the weaker, but more efficiently computable, bounds consistency approach.

The reason for combining these approaches is that each is better in certain circumstances. Clearly, in the case that the primitive constraints have more than two variables, bounds consistency will force more domain pruning since arc and node consistency is satisfied by any domain. Conversely, with constraints involving only two variables, arc consistency may perform more domain pruning than bounds consistency. For instance, consider the constraint $X^2 = 1 - Y^2 \wedge X \neq 0 \wedge Y \neq 0$ with the domain $D(X) = D(Y) = \{-1, 0, 1\}$. The original domain is bounds consistent but not arc consistent. Application of the arc consistency algorithm will determine that the constraint is unsatisfiable.

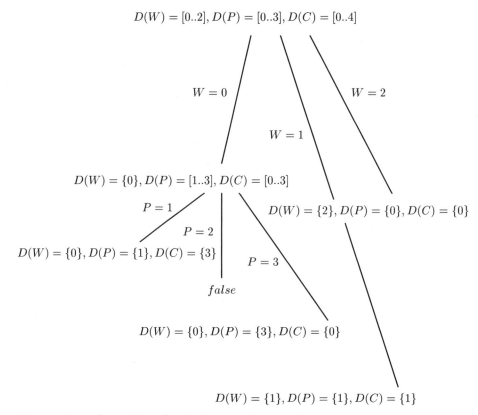

$D(W) = [0..2], D(P) = [0..3], D(C) = [0..4]$

$W = 0$

$W = 2$

$W = 1$

$D(W) = \{0\}, D(P) = [1..3], D(C) = [0..3]$

$P = 1$

$P = 2$

$D(W) = \{2\}, D(P) = \{0\}, D(C) = \{0\}$

$D(W) = \{0\}, D(P) = \{1\}, D(C) = \{3\}$

$P = 3$

$false$

$D(W) = \{0\}, D(P) = \{3\}, D(C) = \{0\}$

$D(W) = \{1\}, D(P) = \{1\}, D(C) = \{1\}$

Figure 3.14   Search tree for the knapsack example.

It is easy to modify the bounds consistency solver so as to also employ arc and node consistency. We simply replace the call to bounds_consistent_primitive by a procedure that uses node_consistent_primitive for primitive constraints with one variable, arc_consistent_primitive for primitive constraints with two variables and bounds_consistent_primitive for primitive constraints with more than two variables.

One weakness of consistency based approaches is that primitive constraints are examined in isolation from each other. Sometimes knowledge about other primitive constraints can dramatically improve domain pruning. For this reason it is common to provide "complex" primitive constraints which are understood as a conjunction of simpler primitive constraints but which have specialized propagation rules.

Consider a specialized "primitive" constraint $\texttt{alldifferent}(\{V_1, \dots, V_n\})$ which holds whenever each of the variables V_1 to V_n in its argument takes a different value. Instead of this constraint we could use a conjunction of disequality constraints. For example, the primitive constraint $\texttt{alldifferent}(\{X, Y, Z\})$ can be replaced by $X \neq Y \wedge X \neq Z \wedge Y \neq Z$. The disadvantage of using a conjunction of disequalities is that arc consistency methods for such a constraint are quite weak since the disequalities are considered in isolation. For instance, the constraint

$$X \neq Y \wedge X \neq Z \wedge Y \neq Z$$

---

c is a single **alldifferent** primitive constraint;
D is a domain;
V is a set of variables;
v is a variable;
d is a domain value;
r is a set of values;
and nv is an integer.

alldifferent_consistent_primitive(c,D)
    let c be of form **alldifferent**(V)
    while exists $v \in V$ with $D(v) = \{d\}$ for some d
        $V := V - \{v\}$
        for each $v' \in V$
            $D(v') := D(v') - \{d\}$
        endfor
    endwhile
    $nv := |V|$
    $r := \emptyset$
    for each $v \in V$
        $r := r \cup D(v)$
    endfor
    if $nv > |r|$ **then return** *false* **endif**
    return D

Figure 3.15 Consistency method for the **alldifferent** primitive constraint.

with domain

$$D(X) = \{1,2\}, \quad D(Y) = \{1,2\}, \quad D(Z) = \{1,2\}$$

has no solutions, since there are only two possible values for the three variables to take but arc consistency techniques cannot determine this.

Specialized propagation rules for the primitive constraint **alldifferent** can detect such situations, and so will find failure more often. An algorithm for updating the domains of variables involved in an **alldifferent** constraint is shown in Figure 3.15. Basically the algorithm works by removing the values of any fixed variables from the domains of other variables and checking that the number of unfixed variables, nv, does not exceed the total number of values left to variables which are not fixed, $|r|$.

For example, on the constraint **alldifferent**$(\{X,Y,Z\})$ and domain

$$D(X) = \{1,2\}, \quad D(Y) = \{1,2\}, \quad D(Z) = \{1,2\}$$

the consistency algorithm calculates $nv = 3$ and $r = \{1,2\}$. It therefore returns *false*.

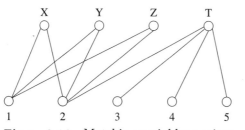

Figure 3.16   Matching variables against values.

Note that the algorithm is still not complete. For instance, consider the constraint `alldifferent`$(\{X, Y, Z, T\})$ with domain

$$D(X) = \{1, 2\}, \quad D(Y) = \{1, 2\}, \quad D(Z) = \{1, 2\}, \quad D(T) \doteq \{2, 3, 4, 5\}.$$

There is no assignment to X, Y and Z which satisfies the constraint, but this is hidden by the large domain of the variable T.

One way to write a more complete consistency checker for `alldifferent` is to recognize that the constraint essentially represents a maximal bipartite matching between variables and values in which each variable must be "matched" with a different value. For example, the constraint `alldifferent`$(\{X, Y, Z, T\})$ with the domain above can be represented by the bipartite matching problem shown in Figure 3.16. A maximal bipartite matching algorithm for this graph will determine a maximal matching size of 3 indicating that at most three variables can be matched and so the constraint is unsatisfiable. However, we defer a discussion of how to find a maximal bipartite matching until the notes at the end of this chapter.

Introducing new "complex" primitive constraints with specialized consistency methods can greatly improve efficiency for solving real-life problems. Another example of a complex primitive constraint which is useful in many practical applications is `cumulative`. This was introduced for solving scheduling and placement problems. The constraint

$$\texttt{cumulative}([S_1, \dots, S_m], [D_1, \dots, D_m], [R_1, \dots, R_m], L)$$

constrains the variables to satisfy a simple scheduling problem. There are m tasks to schedule whose start times are $S_1, \dots, S_m$ and durations are $D_1, \dots, D_m$, and which require $R_1, \dots, R_m$ units of a single resource. At most L units of the resource are available at any one time. Consistency methods for cumulative constraints are very complex since there are numerous possibilities for inferring new information depending on which of the variables are known. In the following example we illustrate only one simple case.

Example 3.8

Bernd is moving house again and must schedule the removal of his furniture. Only he and three of his friends are available for the move and the move must be completed in one hour. The following list details the items of furniture which must be moved, how long each takes to move and how many people are required. For example,

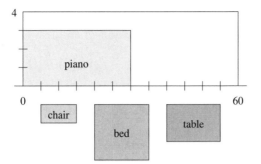

Figure 3.17 A `cumulative` constraint.

moving the piano requires 3 people and takes 30 minutes, while moving a chair requires 1 person and takes 10 minutes.

Item	Time required to move	No. of people required
piano	30	3
chair	10	1
bed	15	3
table	15	2

This problem can be modelled by the cumulative constraint

$$\texttt{cumulative}([S_p, S_c, S_b, S_t], [30, 10, 15, 15], [3, 1, 3, 2], 4)$$

where the variables S_p, S_c, S_b, S_t represent the start times for moving the piano, chair, bed and table, respectively. The initial domain for these variables is

$$D(S_p) = [0..30], \quad D(S_c) = [0..50], \quad D(S_b) = [0..45], \quad D(S_t) = [0..45]$$

which was obtained by computing the latest time that the furniture could be moved and still meet the one hour deadline.

With this initial domain the `cumulative` constraint consistency methods cannot determine any extra information about the variables. Now suppose Bernd decides to move the piano first. Then $S_p = 0$. The situation is displayed graphically in Figure 3.17. The remaining tasks (boxes) must be placed in the empty space so that they do not overlap. Clearly, the bed and table cannot be moved before the piano is moved so consistency can determine that $D(O_b) = [30..45]$ and $D(O_t) = [30..45]$.

Now suppose the furniture has to be moved within 50 minutes. Then reasoning about consistency reveals that no two of the piano, bed or table can be moved at the same time. Thus the minimum time required to move the furniture is 60 minutes. This demonstrates how specialized reasoning about consistency of the `cumulative` constraint can determine that the constraint is unsatisfiable without requiring exhaustive search through the possible time assignments for each task.

Our final example of a complex primitive constraint is the `element` constraint. The `element` constraint mimics the behaviour of an array. The constraint

$$element(I, [V_1, \ldots, V_m], X)$$

maintains the relationship that, if $I = i$, then $X = V_i$. We can understand this by thinking of the list $[V_1, \ldots, V_m]$ as an array v, and the constraint as stating that $X = v[I]$.

We can use this primitive to enforce ad-hoc functional relationships. For instance, suppose X must be equal to $I^2 - 3$ where the domain of I is [0..5]. This is described by the constraint `element(I, [-3, -2, 1, 6, 13, 22], X)`. Consistency techniques for `element` constraints can reduce the domain of I from information about X and vice versa. For example, given the above `element` constraint and a domain of X equal to [-20..20] consistency reasoning immediately reduces the domain of X to $\{-3, -2, 1, 6, 13\}$ and the domain of I to [0..4].

Example 3.9

The `element` constraint gives us another way of modelling the smuggler's knapsack problem of Example 3.5. Given the capacity constraints there can be at most five items in the knapsack. We can encode the type of each of these items as 1: no object, 2: whiskey, 3: perfume and 4: cigarettes. Each variable $O_i, 1 \leq i \leq 5$ represents the type of the ith object and has domain [1..4]. We then use `element` constraints to relate the type to a weight and profit for that element. The array of weights is [0, 4, 3, 2], and the array of profits is [0, 15, 10, 7]. The following model determines the total weight and total profit of the objects and ensures the constraints hold.

$$element(O_1, [0, 4, 3, 2], W_1) \ \wedge \ element(O_1, [0, 15, 10, 7], P_1) \ \wedge$$
$$element(O_2, [0, 4, 3, 2], W_2) \ \wedge \ element(O_2, [0, 15, 10, 7], P_2) \ \wedge$$
$$element(O_3, [0, 4, 3, 2], W_3) \ \wedge \ element(O_3, [0, 15, 10, 7], P_3) \ \wedge$$
$$element(O_4, [0, 4, 3, 2], W_4) \ \wedge \ element(O_4, [0, 15, 10, 7], P_4) \ \wedge$$
$$element(O_5, [0, 4, 3, 2], W_5) \ \wedge \ element(O_5, [0, 15, 10, 7], P_5) \ \wedge$$
$$W_1 + W_2 + W_3 + W_4 + W_5 \leq 9 \ \wedge \ P_1 + P_2 + P_3 + P_4 + P_5 \geq 30$$

For this problem the model using `element` is more complex than the original model and so is not as good. But for other problems modelling with `element` may be useful.

3.6 Optimization for Arithmetic CSPs

So far in this chapter we have considered constraint solvers for constraints over finite constraint domains, and in particular for arithmetic CSPs. While there are many problems in which finding any solution at all answers the problem, for many arithmetic CSPs the aim is not simply to find a solution but rather to find an

C is an arithmetic constraint;
D is a domain;
D_{val} is a valuation domain or *false*;
f is an arithmetic expression;
θ is a solution;
θ_{best} is either a solution or *false*.

retry_int_opt(C, D, f, θ_{best})
   $D_{val} :=$ int_solv(C, D)
   if $D_{val} \equiv false$ **then**
      return θ_{best}
   else
      let θ be the solution corresponding to D_{val}
      return retry_int_opt($C \wedge f < \theta(f)$, D, f, θ)
   endif

Figure 3.18 Integer optimizer based on retry.

optimal (or at least a good) solution. In this section we examine how to solve such integer optimization problems. We first show how to use the arithmetic CSP solvers described earlier in the chapter to find an optimal solution. Finally, we examine an approach from the operations research community which makes use of algorithms for linear arithmetic constraint solving over the real numbers.

The simplest approach to finding an optimal solution to an arithmetic CSP is to make use of a complete solver for these problems and use it iteratively to find better and better solutions to the problems. More exactly, we can use the solver to find any solution to the CSP, and then add a constraint to the problem which excludes solutions that are not better than this solution. The new CSP is solved recursively, giving rise to a solution which is closer to the optimum. This process can be repeated until the augmented CSP is unsatisfiable, in which case the optimal solution is the last solution found. At each stage we keep track of the best solution found so far, θ_{best}. Initially this is set to *false* indicating that no solutions have been found so far.

Algorithm 3.9: Integer optimizer based on retrying
INPUT: An arithmetic CSP with constraint C and domain D and an arithmetic expression f which is the objective function.
OUTPUT: An optimal solution θ or *false* if the CSP is unsatisfiable.
METHOD: The answer is the result of evaluating retry_int_opt(C, D, f, *false*). The algorithm is shown in Figure 3.18. It assumes that int_solv is an algorithm for arithmetic CSPs (such as `back_bounds_solv`) which returns either a valuation domain corresponding to a solution or *false* if the CSP is unsatisfiable. $\square$

Example 3.10
Consider the smuggler's knapsack problem from Example 3.5. Ideally the smuggler wishes to maximize the profit made on a journey. Thus the problem is more properly

viewed as an optimization problem in which the smuggler wishes to maximize his profit, $15W + 10P + 7C$, subject to the constraint

$$4W+3P+2C \leq 9 \ \wedge \ 15W+10P+7C \geq 30 \ \wedge \ W \in [0..9] \ \wedge \ P \in [0..9] \ \wedge \ C \in [0..9].$$

Couched as a minimization problem, the smuggler's aim is to minimize the loss, $-15W - 10P - 7C$, subject to

$$4W+3P+2C \leq 9 \ \wedge \ 15W+10P+7C \geq 30 \ \wedge \ W \in [0..9] \ \wedge \ P \in [0..9] \ \wedge \ C \in [0..9].$$

Execution of the integer optimization algorithm using retrying on this optimization problem proceeds as follows. First back_bounds_solv is called to solve the original CSP. As detailed in Example 3.7, this traverses the tree shown in Figure 3.14 in a depth-first left-to-right manner. The first solution found is the valuation domain $D(W) = \{0\}, D(P) = \{1\}, D(C) = \{3\}$ which corresponds to the solution $\{W \mapsto 0, P \mapsto 1, C \mapsto 3\}$. This has a loss of -31 (or profit of 31).

Now the problem obtained by adding the constraint $-15W - 10P - 7C < -31$ is solved. This causes exploration of a search tree similar to that shown in Figure 3.14. Initial propagation gives the same domain

$$D(W) = [0..2], \quad D(P) = [0..3], \quad D(C) = [0..4].$$

However, this time after choosing $W = 0$ propagation leads to a false domain, so $W = 1$ is tried. In this case propagation finds the valuation domain $D(W) = \{1\}, D(P) = \{1\}, D(C) = \{1\}$ which has loss -32.

Now the problem obtained by adding the constraint $-15W - 10P - 7C < -32$ is solved. Initial propagation gives the same domain as above but propagation after choosing $W = 0, W = 1$ and $W = 2$ gives false domains. Therefore, back_bounds_solv returns *false* for this problem.

The optimization algorithm therefore terminates, returning the previous best solution, $\{W \mapsto 1, P \mapsto 1, C \mapsto 1\}$, since this is the optimal solution. Overall there are 10 visits to nodes in the various search trees.

The problem with this approach to optimization is that, given a solver that uses backtracking to find a solution to the problem—as most complete solvers for arithmetic CSPs do, much of the search required to find a solution to the problem is essentially repeated when solving the new problem resulting from the tighter bound on the optimization variable. Instead, if we are using some form of consistency based solver with backtracking, we can interleave the process of finding an optimal solution with the search for the next solution. In this way, we only traverse the search tree once instead of many times.

Algorithm 3.10: Backtracking integer optimizer
INPUT: An arithmetic CSP with constraint C and domain D and an objective function f.
OUTPUT: An optimal solution θ or *false* if the CSP is unsatisfiable.
METHOD: The answer is the result of evaluating back_int_opt(C, D, f, *false*)

```
C is an arithmetic constraint;
D is a domain;
f is an arithmetic expression;
and θ_best is a solution or false.


back_int_opt(C, D, f, θ_best)
    D := int_consistent(C, D)
    if D is a false domain then return θ_best
    elseif D is a valuation domain then
        return the solution corresponding to D
    endif
    choose variable x ∈ vars(C) for which |D(x)| ≥ 2
    W := D(x)
    for each d ∈ W
        if θ_best ≢ false then
            c := f < θ_best(f)
        else
            c := true
        endif
        θ_best := back_int_opt(C ∧ c ∧ x = d, D, f, θ_best)
    endfor
    return θ_best
```

Figure 3.19   Backtracking integer optimizer.

The algorithm is shown in Figure 3.19. It assumes that $\mathsf{int\_consistent}(C,D)$ is a consistency based solver which returns a domain D_1 such that C with D has the same set of solutions as C with D_1. □

Example 3.11

Consider the optimization version of the smuggler's knapsack problem again. Execution of this optimization problem using the backtracking integer optimizer searches the tree shown in Figure 3.14 in a depth-first left-to-right manner. As before, the first solution found is $\{W \mapsto 0, P \mapsto 1, C \mapsto 3\}$, which has a loss of -31 (or profit of 31). θ_{best} is set to $\{W \mapsto 0, P \mapsto 1, C \mapsto 3\}$.

Backtracking returns to the node labelled $D(W) = \{0\}, D(P) = [1..3], D(C) = [0..4]$ and the new constraint c is set to $-15W - 10P - 7C < -31$ and added. Both $P = 2$ and $P = 3$ are tried. In each case propagation gives rise to a false domain. Note that $P = 3$ in the original search tree gave rise to a successful leaf $D(W) = \{0\}, D(P) = \{3\}, D(C) = \{0\}$. This now fails because its profit is 30.

Backtracking proceeds up to the node with domain $D(W) = [0..2], D(P) = [0..3], D(C) = [0..4]$ with θ_{best} still set to $\{W \mapsto 0, P \mapsto 1, C \mapsto 3\}$. Now $W = 1$ is tried. Propagation gives the valuation domain $D(W) = \{1\}, D(P) = \{1\}, D(C) = \{1\}$ which has loss -32. θ_{best} is set to $\{W \mapsto 1, P \mapsto 1, C \mapsto 1\}$ and $-15W - 10P - 7C < -32$ is added to the problem. Backtracking continues, trying $W = 2$ but propagation gives a false domain.

Therefore, since the entire search tree has been explored, the algorithm terminates returning the optimal solution $\{W \mapsto 1, P \mapsto 1, C \mapsto 1\}$. Overall the algorithm visits each node in the tree given in Figure 3.14 once, meaning that only 7 nodes are visited.

Both of these algorithms for integer optimization are naive in the sense that they only use the objective function to eliminate solutions which are not better than the best solution already discovered. In particular, they do not use the objective function to direct the search to that part of the solution space in which it is likely to find better solutions. This contrasts to optimization algorithms for the real numbers, such as the simplex algorithm (see Section 2.4), in which the objective function is used to direct the search. In a sense, this is made possible because it is relatively easy in linear arithmetic problems over the real numbers to move from one solution to another. When the linear arithmetic problem is over integers, directing the search is more difficult since it may be difficult to move from one solution to another. However, we can use a real optimizer which does employ directed search to guide the search for an optimal solution over the integers.

One of the oldest algorithms for solving integer optimization problems does this, making use of an optimizer working over the real numbers to direct the search. Consider an optimization problem (C, f) over the integers and an optimizer real_opt which can solve optimization problems over real numbers and which returns an optimal (that is, minimal) solution to a particular problem. Now, if real_opt(C, f) returns the solution θ then the optimal solution over the integers, θ', must satisfy $\theta'(f) \geq \theta(f)$ since, if θ' was preferable to θ, then θ could not be the optimal solution over the real numbers.

This observation leads to the branch and bound solver. To solve the optimization problem (C, f) over the integers, the optimizer real_opt is used to find an optimal solution over the real numbers. If the optimal solution found is *integral*, that is, assigns integers to all variables, we are finished since, from the above observation, this must be the optimal solution over the integers. If the optimal solution returned by real_opt is not integral, the branch and bound solver must search. This is done by choosing an variable x which takes a non-integral value, say d, in the optimal solution. The two optimization problems $(C \wedge x \leq \lfloor d \rfloor, f)$ and $(C \wedge x \geq \lceil d \rceil, f)$ are recursively evaluated. Note that $\lfloor d \rfloor$ is the d rounded down to the nearest integer, while $\lceil d \rceil$ is d rounded up to the nearest integer.

The optimal solution to the original problem must be the optimal solution to one of these problems since they eliminate no integer solutions. An additional improvement is made possible by noticing that the optimal value over the real numbers can be no worse than the optimal solution over the integers. Hence, if we have already found an integer solution θ_{best}, then any subproblem with optimal solution θ over the real numbers such that $\theta(f) \geq \theta_{best}(f)$ can be discarded since it can never lead to a better integer solution than the current best, θ_{best}.

The algorithm is called a "branch and bound" algorithm because it selects a variable x to branch on, and then investigates two problems in which this variable is further bounded.

---

d is a real value;
x is a variable;
f is an integer expression;
θ and θ_{best} are valuations or *false*;
C is an integer constraint.

bb_int_opt(C,f,θ_{best})
    $\theta := $ real_opt(C, f)
    if $\theta \equiv false$ **then return** θ_{best} **endif**
    if $\theta_{best} \not\equiv false$ and $\theta(f) > \theta_{best}(f)$ **then return** θ_{best} **endif**
    if θ is integral **then return** θ **endif**
    choose variable x such that $d = \theta(x)$ is not an integer
    $\theta_{best} := $ bb_int_opt($C \wedge x \leq \lfloor d \rfloor$, f, θ_{best})
    $\theta_{best} := $ bb_int_opt($C \wedge x \geq \lceil d \rceil$, f, θ_{best})
    return θ_{best}

Figure 3.20   Integer optimization using a real optimizer.

Algorithm 3.11: Branch and bound integer optimizer
INPUT: A linear arithmetic constraint C and objective function f.
OUTPUT: An optimal solution θ or *false* if no solution exists.
METHOD: The answer is the result of the call bb_int_opt($C, f, false$) The algorithm
is shown in Figure 3.20. It assumes that real_opt(C,f) is an optimizer for arithmetic
constraints that either returns *false* if the problem is unsatisfiable or an optimal
solution over the real numbers. □

Example 3.12
For example, consider maximising Y, that is minimising the expression f where f
is $-Y$, subject to the constraint C which is

$$Y \leq X \wedge Y \leq 8 - 2X \wedge X - Y + 1 = 3Z.$$

A diagram of the (X, Y) plane for this constraint is shown in Figure 3.21. The two
constraints on X and Y are shown by solid lines, while the constraint $X - Y + 1 = 3Z$
has the effect of eliminating all but the shaded possibilities for X and Y.

Initially θ_{best} is *false* and real_opt(C, f) returns the intersection point of the two
solid lines $\{X \mapsto \frac{8}{3}, Y \mapsto \frac{8}{3}, Z \mapsto \frac{1}{3}\}$. Splitting on X, the next call is

$$\text{bb\_int\_opt}(C \wedge X \leq 2, f, \theta_{best}).$$

The real optimizer returns $\{X \mapsto 2, Y \mapsto 2, Z \mapsto \frac{1}{3}\}$. Splitting on Z results in the
call

$$\text{bb\_int\_opt}(C \wedge X \leq 2 \wedge Z \leq 0, f, \theta_{best}).$$

The real optimizer fails, so this call immediately returns θ_{best} which is still set to *false*. The other half of the split for Z results in the call

$$\text{bb\_int\_opt}(C \wedge X \leq 2 \wedge Z \geq 1, f, \theta_{best}).$$

For this call the real optimizer returns θ_1 which is $\{X \mapsto 2, Y \mapsto 0, Z \mapsto 1\}$. This is returned as the answer and so θ_{best} is set to θ_1.

The remaining half of the split for X is examined by the call

$$\text{bb\_int\_opt}(C \wedge X \geq 3, f, \theta_{best}).$$

The real optimizer finds the optimal solution is $\{X \mapsto 3, Y \mapsto 2, Z \mapsto \frac{2}{3}\}$. Again we split on Z, first calling

$$\text{bb\_int\_opt}(C \wedge X \geq 3 \wedge Z \leq 0, f, \theta_{best}).$$

This immediately fails, so now we call

$$\text{bb\_int\_opt}(C \wedge X \geq 3 \wedge Z \geq 1, f, \theta_{best}).$$

The optimal solution over the reals is $\{X \mapsto \frac{10}{3}, Y \mapsto \frac{4}{3}, Z \mapsto 1\}$. Again we split on X. The first call is

$$\text{bb\_int\_opt}(C \wedge X \geq 3 \wedge Z \geq 1 \wedge X \leq 3, f, \theta_{best}).$$

The real optimizer returns θ_2 which is $\{X \mapsto 3, Y \mapsto 1, Z \mapsto 1\}$. As this is integral it is returned and θ_{best} set to θ_2.

The remaining call for the split on X is then

$$\text{bb\_int\_opt}(C \wedge X \geq 3 \wedge Z \geq 1 \wedge X \geq 4, f, \theta_{best}).$$

The optimal solution over the reals is θ_3 which is $\{X \mapsto 4, Y \mapsto 0, Z \mapsto \frac{5}{3}\}$. Since $\theta_3(f) > \theta_{best}(f)$ we cannot hope to find a solution in this part of the solution space which is better than that already found so the call returns the current θ_{best}.

3.7 Summary

Constraints in which variables range over finite domains form a well studied and useful class of constraint problems which are often called constraint satisfaction problems (CSPs) in the artificial intelligence literature. They are important because they can be used to model combinatorial problems, such as scheduling or timetabling, which have widespread commercial applications.

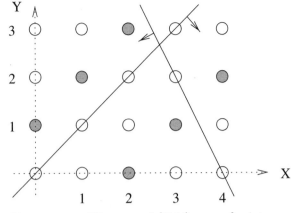

Figure 3.21 Diagram of (X,Y) space for integer optimization problem

We have considered two general techniques for solving finite domain problems:

- backtracking search, and
- consistency techniques.

Backtracking search gives rise to complete solvers with exponential worst-case cost, while consistency methods give rise to fast solvers which are, however, incomplete. We have examined three kinds of consistency: node and arc consistency, which arose from the artificial intelligence community, and bounds consistency, which arose from the constraint programming community. Completeness of consistency based approaches can be improved by combining different kinds of consistency and by providing specialized consistency techniques for complex primitive constraints such as `alldifferent`, `cumulative` and `element`. We have also detailed how backtracking can be combined with consistency techniques to give faster complete solvers for finite domain problems.

In many applications of finite domain constraints, such as scheduling, it is important to be able to find the best solution. We have shown how a complete constraint solver can be used as the basis for solving such optimization problems and have given two algorithms based on this idea. The first repeatedly solves a new problem, which only has solutions that are better than the current solution to the optimization problem. The second intermingles a backtracking search for all solutions to the problem with the search for an optimal solution. Finally, we have given an algorithm from the operations research community for solving such optimization problems. This approach, called branch and bound, makes use of a solver over the real numbers to direct the search towards an optimal solution over the integers.

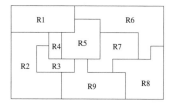

Figure 3.22 A map for colouring.

3.8   Exercises

3.1. For the map given in Figure 3.22 and the three colours $\{red, yellow, blue\}$ encode the map colouring problem for this map as a binary CSP. Give the constraint graph for this constraint problem and find a solution.

3.2. Another way to model the 4-queens problem is to assume that each queen must appear in a separate column. In this model the position of the queen in column i is given by a variable R_i which holds the row number in which the queen occurs. Using this idea give an encoding of the 4-queens problem that only uses binary constraints.

3.3. Consider the old-fashioned marriage problem in Example 3.3. Solve the problem using back_arc_solv.

3.4. Give a probabilistic solver for CSPs based on the Boolean constraint solver of Figure 1.10. Use it solve the old-fashioned marriage problem of Example 3.3.

3.5. Give propagation rules for the linear arithmetic constraint

$$a_1 x_1 + a_2 x_2 + \cdots + a_n x_n - b_1 y_1 - b_2 y_2 - \cdots - b_m y_m = d$$

and

$$a_1 x_1 + a_2 x_2 + \cdots + a_n x_n - b_1 y_1 - b_2 y_2 - \cdots - b_m y_m \le d$$

where the constants $a_1, \ldots, a_n$ and $b_1, \ldots, b_m$ are all positive.

3.6. (*) Prove that the propagation rules for the above example need only to be applied once to give a bounds consistent domain.

3.7. Give propagation rules for the primitive constraint $x = y \mod k$ where k is a fixed but unknown integer.

3.8. Give propagation rules for the primitive constraint $X = Y^2$ which will give more propagation information than using the rules for $X = Y \times Y$.

3.9. Give propagation rules for the Boolean primitive constraints: $X = Y \& Z$, $X = Y \vee Z$ and $X = \neg Y$. You should assume that every variable x appearing in a Boolean constraint has a domain $D(x) \subseteq \{0, 1\}$.

3.10. Compare the execution of arc_solv and bounds_solv on the CSP with constraint $X \ne 4 \wedge X \ne Y \wedge X \le Y + 2$ and domain $D(X) = [2..5]$, $D(Y) = [0..5]$.

3.11. Execute the complete bounds consistency solver on the constraint

$$X \neq Y \wedge Y \neq 1 \wedge X = Y \times Y \wedge Y \leq -1$$

with domain $D(X) = [-2..6]$, $D(Y) = [-4..4]$.

3.12. (*) Assume the propagation rules for the multiplication constraint $X = Y \times Z$ are changed to wait until either Y or Z has a fixed value (that is, either X or Y has a singleton domain) before determining any bounds for Y or Z. Argue whether bounds_solv ensures bounds consistency or not.

3.13. Consider solving the smuggler's knapsack problem using back_int_opt. Show the 4 different search trees of calls to back_int_opt (analogous to Figure 3.14) that result when the variables are selected in the order W, P, C or in the order C, P, W and when the domain values are tried in increasing order or in decreasing order.

3.14. Consider a modification of the smuggler's knapsack problem in which the capacity of the knapsack is increased to 17 units. Find the maximum profit and the items which give this profit using either retry_int_opt or back_int_opt.

3.9 Practical Exercises

There are a number of finite domain constraint solvers available as part of constraint logic programming languages. The ECLiPSe system, developed at ECRC, is (at the time of publication) available free for academic purposes. It is a PROLOG system which includes a library for finite domain constraint solving. It can be obtained by sending email to eclipse-request@doc.ic.ac.uk. See also the Eclipse WWW home pages at http://www.ecrc.de/eclipse/ and http://www-icparc.doc.ic.ac.uk/eclipse/. Using the ECLiPSe system as a finite domain constraint solver is similar to using $CLP(\mathcal{R})$ for real number constraint solving.

For example the ECLiPSe system presents a prompt to the user

[eclipse 1]:

To invoke the finite domain constraint solver the user types what is shown in *italics*.

[eclipse 1]: *use_module(library(fd)).*

Constraints are entered using the following conventions: * is used for multiplication, linear expressions need an explicit multiplication symbol, so $2Y$ must be written as 2 * Y, $\wedge$ is represented using "," and the operators $=, \geq, >, \leq, <$ and $\neq$ are represented by "#=", "#>=", "#>", "#<=", "#<" and "##" respectively, and finally a full stop "." is used to terminate the constraint. To interrupt execution the user can type *control-C*, that is type 'c' while holding down the control key.

The initial domain of the variables is specified using the following syntax. To set the variable X to have initial domain $\{1, 2, 3, 4\}$ either the form X :: [1,2,3,4] or

`X :: [1..4]` can be used. Multiple variables can be initialised to the same domain using the syntax of the following example: `[X,Y,Z] :: [1..4]`. If no initial domain is given for an integer variable it is assumed to be $[-10000000..10000000]$.

The constraint solver in ECLiPSe has approximately the same behaviour as the incomplete bounds consistency solver bounds_solv described in Algorithm 3.7. For example, if the following constraint is typed,

```
[eclipse 2]: [X,Y,Z] :: [1..4], X #< Y, Y #< Z.
```

the resulting answer is

```
X = X{[1, 2]}
Y = Y{[2, 3]}
Z = Z{[3, 4]}
Delayed goals:
      Z{[3, 4]} - Y{[2, 3]}#>=1
      Y{[2, 3]} - X{[1, 2]}#>=1
yes.
```

The initial part of the answer details the variables in the constraint and their current domains. The second part shows primitive constraints which are not guaranteed to be consistent with all valuations possible in the current domain. If any such constraints remain the solver has answered *unknown*. If there are none, the constraint solver has answered *true* as in the following examples:

```
[eclipse 3]: [X,Y,Z] :: [1..3], X #< Y, Y #< Z.
X = 1
Y = 2
Z = 3
```

and

```
[eclipse 4]: X :: [1,2], Y :: [3,4], X #< Y.
X = X{[1, 2]}
Y = Y{[3, 4]}
```

If the solver detects unsatisfiability then the result has the following form:

```
[eclipse 5]: [X,Y,Z] :: [1..3], X #< Y, Y #< Z, Z #<= 2.
no (more) solution.
```

A complete solver can be imitated using the inbuilt backtracking search of the ECLiPSe system. By appending the constraint to be solved with an expression of the form labeling(*Vars*) where *Vars* is the list of variables appearing in the constraint, the ECLiPSe system will work analogously to back_bounds_solv described in Algorithm 3.8. For example, evaluation of the constraint:

```
[eclipse 6]: [X,Y,Z] :: [1..4], X #< Y, Y #< Z, labeling([X,Y,Z]).
```

returns the answer

```
X = 1
Y = 2
Z = 3 More? (;)
```

The `More? (;)` prompts the user to ask if another solution is required. The user can type ";" or "y" to request another solution. In this case it is,

```
X = 1
Y = 2
Z = 4 More? (;)
```

Otherwise, evaluation finishes.

The SICStus Prolog v3 system also includes a library for finite domain constraints. How to obtain SICStus Prolog is discussed in the Practical Exercises section of Chapter 1. In order to make use of the finite domain constraint solving facilities of SICStus one needs to load the finite domain constraint solving library by typing:

```
| ?- use_module(library(clpfd))
```

Constraints are written using almost the same notation as that detailed above for ECLiPSe, except that the $\neq$ primitive constraint is written as "#\=" and the $\leq$ primitive constraint is written as "#=<." Be warned that #<= is legal SICStus code which means reverse implication. The initial domains of a variable can be specified by a declaration of the form `X in 1..4`. Multiple variables can be initialized to have the same domain using the library function `domain`, for example, the declaration

```
domain([X,Y,Z], 1, 4)
```

assigns the range [1..4] to each of the variables X, Y and Z.

The finite domain constraint solver in SICStus Prolog has again approximately the behaviour of the incomplete bounds consistency solver bounds_solv described in Algorithm 3.7. For example, if the following constraint is typed,

```
| ?- domain([X,Y,Z],1,4), X #< Y, Y #< Z.
```

the resulting output is

```
    X in 1..2,
    Y in 2..3,
    Z in 3..4 ?
```

The answer simply shows the current domains of the variables. Section 29.6 of the SICStus Prolog Users Manual [58] shows how to change the behaviour of the system to output any constraints which are not guaranteed to be consistent. However, if the domain is a valuation domain then the corresponding valuation satisfies the constraint. This is exemplified in the following evaluation.

```
| ?- domain([X,Y,Z],1,3), X #< Y, Y #< Z.
X = 1
Y = 2
Z = 3 ?
```

If the solver detects unsatisfiability then the result has the following form:

```
| ?- domain([X,Y,Z],1,3), X #< Y, Y #< Z, Z #<= 2.
no
```

A complete solver can be imitated using the inbuilt backtracking search of the SICStus Prolog system. By appending the constraint to be solved with an expression of the form labeling([], *Vars*) where *Vars* is the list of variables appearing in the constraint the system will work analogously to back_bounds_solv. For example, the constraint:

```
| ?- domain([X,Y,Z],1,4), X #< Y, Y #< Z, labeling([], [X,Y,Z]).
```

returns the answer

```
X = 1
Y = 2
Z = 3 ?
```

The "?" prompts the user, asking if another solution is required. Typing ";" requests the next solution, in this case

```
X = 1
Y = 2
Z = 4 ?
```

Otherwise, typing Enter/Return terminates evaluation of the constraint. In the example above, after typing ";" four times the system returns no indicating that there are no more solutions.

P3.1. Type in the constraints for the 4-*queens* problem, and see what answer the solver gives. Add the labeling goal and examine the answers now.

P3.2. Solve the old-fashioned marriage problem using ECLiPSe or SICStus Prolog.

P3.3. Find a solution to the smuggler's knapsack problem using a complete solver.

P3.4. Examine how your system executes the CSP with constraint

$$X \neq 4 \land X \neq Y \land X = Y + 2$$

and domain $D(X) = [2..5]$, $D(Y) = [0..5]$. Determine if the solver is closer to arc_solv or bounds_solv. Experiment with similar constraints to improve your understanding.

P3.5. Examine the execution of the following goals:

(a) $X = Y \times Y \wedge 0 \leq Y \wedge Y \leq 2$,

(b) $X = Y \times Y \wedge 0 \leq X \wedge X \leq 2$,

(c) $X = Y \times Y \wedge Y = 2$ and

(d) $X = Y \times Z \wedge Z = 1 \wedge Y \leq 2$.

Can you determine the propagation rules that your system uses for the constraint $X = Y \times Z$?

P3.6. (*) Using your answer to Exercise 3.9 above, translate the Boolean constraint defining the full adder in Figure 1.9 into an integer constraint. Giving each variable an initial domain of [0,1] see what the complete solver gives as solutions of the constraint.

P3.7. Describe how, by hand, to use the finite domain system to imitate the behaviour of the retry_int_opt algorithm. Try it out on the smuggler's knapsack example.

3.10   Notes

CSPs as introduced in Section 1.7 date back to work in artificial intelligence, picture processing and computer vision. See for example Montanari [94] and Waltz [141]. Stefik [124] built a system for planning gene-splicing experiments, using consistency based methods.

It follows from the NP-hardness of SAT, one of the most famous NP-hard problems [53] that solving arbitrary CSPs is NP-hard. SAT is essentially the problem of finding if a Boolean formula is satisfiable or not. Thus it can be seen as a particular type of CSP.

Node and arc consistency originate from Montanari [94]. An in depth coverage of constraint satisfaction problems and their solution is provided by Tsang's book "Foundations of Constraint Satisfaction"[134]. This also describes more efficient algorithms for transforming a CSP into an equivalent arc consistent CSP. The book "Constraint Satisfaction and Logic Programming" by Van Hentenryck [135] also provides a theoretical introduction to different consistency methods. Bounds consistency has been introduced under many different names by various authors, for example [138] call it interval consistency.

The consistency based approaches described in this chapter are related to the local propagation method described in Section 1.7. In this view of local propagation, it is seen as a technique for reducing the domain to a single value, whenever this is possible. However, local propagation is relatively weak compared to the methods described here.

The tradeoff between stronger consistency methods, which remove more values, and weaker consistency methods, which are faster to compute but remove less values, is complex, especially when the consistency methods are being employed in a complete backtracking solver. Since the optimal tradeoff may be problem specific, some finite domain solvers allow the user to define their own problem specific propagation rules for constraints. *Indexicals* introduced in [138] (see also [41]) are a language for defining propagation rules. Indexicals are of the form X in S where X is a finite domain variable and S is a expression denoting a set of values. For example,

$$X \text{ in } min(Y) + min(Z)..max(Y) + max(Z)$$

and

$$X \text{ in } dom(Y) + dom(Z)$$

are two indexicals defining the propagation rule for variable X and constraint $X = Y + Z$. The first implements bounds consistency, while the second implements arc consistency. A number of finite domain solvers are implemented by means of indexicals, for example clp(FD) [41] and SICStus Prolog [58].

The element constraint originated in the CHIP system [3], as does the cumulative constraint which is introduced in [2].

The alldifferent constraint is available in CHIP, ILOG Solver and SICStus Prolog. Implementations range from the simple consistency method illustrated in Figure 3.15 to methods based on maximal matching. Maximal bipartite matching algorithms are well studied, see for example [101]. Regin [111] gives an algorithm for maintaining hyper-arc consistency for alldifferent constraints. See also [107] for a discussion of alldifferent.

The branch and bound method for integer linear programming is due to Dakin. For detailed descriptions of branch and bound and other techniques to solve integer linear programming problems developed by the operations research community see, for example, Papadimitriou and Steiglitz [101] or Schrijver [116].

In this chapter we have concentrated on integer finite domain constraints. Another important class of finite domain constraints are those over floating point numbers. At first this seems paradoxical since floating point numbers are used to represent real numbers which clearly do not have a finite domain. However, in any particular implementation of floating point numbers, there are only a fixed number of floating point numbers. This means that the techniques described in this chapter are also applicable to solving arithmetic constraints over the floating point numbers. There are, however, a few provisos.

First, a floating point range, for instance $[1.14151, 1.14152]$, is meant to represent all the real numbers within this range, rather than just the floating point numbers in this range. This subtly alters the propagation rules. They need to round up or down to the "closest" floating point number, so as to ensure that no real solution is excluded. For example, the propagation rules for variable Y in primitive constraint $X = Y \times Z$ where $D(X) = [1..1]$, $D[Z] = [9..9]$ give $Y \leq 1/9$ and $Y \geq 1/9$. Since $1/9$ is not representable exactly as a floating point number, we need to take the nearest floating point number above, and below, respectively as defining the bounds for Y. So the propagation rules (for the case where everything is positive) are

$$Y \leq fp\_ceil(max_D(X)/min_D(Z))$$
$$Y \geq fp\_floor(max_D(X)/min_D(Z))$$

where $fp\_ceil(r)$ gives the least floating point number bigger than real number r, and $fp\_ceil(r)$ gives the largest floating point number less than real number r. In general, propagation rules similar to those in this chapter can be used for solving constraints over floating point numbers, as long as care is taken with the direction of rounding in all floating point computations.

Second, floating point ranges include many elements, for example the range [1..2] may include 2^{32} floating point numbers. Therefore arc consistency methods are inappropriate, and domains are almost always ranges. Furthermore, any technique based on enumerating all possible elements in the domain is not practical. Instead floating point solvers rely on splitting the domain into pieces. See the discussion (for integers) in Section 8.3.

The use of floating point intervals for constraint solving was suggested by Cleary [31] and independently by Hyvönen [67]. The first implementation in a CLP system was in BNR Prolog, and is discussed in [98, 99].

In this chapter we have not mentioned an important class of methods used for solving constraint satisfaction problems—stochastic search methods. These combine heuristics with a non-deterministic search to find a solution or optimal solution to a CSP. Typically the algorithms proceed from one valuation to another attempting to find a solution. There is a wide variety of such methods including simulated annealing, genetic algorithms and local search.

We have not explored such methods because their use within a CLP system— our eventual goal for solvers—is not straightforward and the subject of current research. Methods for making use of stochastic constraint solvers in CLP systems are discussed in [129, 84]. Two general purpose stochastic methods which have been used with CLP systems are GENET [134] and E-GENET [85]. These are both artificial neural networks which make use of min-conflict search and heuristic learning.

II Constraint Logic Programming

4   Constraint Logic Programs

In the first part of this book we examined various constraint domains, including real arithmetic constraints, tree constraints and finite domains, as well as three fundamental operations involving constraints—satisfaction, simplification and optimization. We have also seen how constraints can be used to model the behaviour of physical objects and processes.

In this part we introduce the constraint logic programming (CLP) paradigm. In this chapter we define constraint logic programs and their evaluation mechanism and in subsequent chapters we will investigate programming techniques. Finally we will examine the implementation of CLP systems.

Constraint logic programming languages are parametric in the choice of the underlying constraint domain and the solver and simplifier for that domain. In essence, constraint logic programming languages provide only one programming construct—"rules." Rules allow programmers to define their own constraints in terms of the underlying constraint domain of the CLP language. Somewhat surprisingly, this simple extension leads to a fully-fledged programming language based on constraints in which a program is simply a collection of rules.

Rules are used to evaluate "goals" given by the user. This is done by repeatedly using the rules to replace the definition of user-defined constraints in the goal until only primitive constraints are left. The resulting constraint is the "answer" to the goal. This process of rewriting is called a "derivation."

4.1   User-Defined Constraints

In most of the examples so far of modelling an object or process with a constraint, the constraint could be partitioned into two parts: a general description of the object or process being modelled, and specific information detailing the situation at hand. Since many questions use the same general constraint description, it is useful to have a mechanism which allows a constraint description to be reused in different problems. In general, we would like users, that is programmers, to be able to define their own problem specific constraints in terms of the underlying primitive constraints. *Rules* enable this.

Example 4.1

Consider the circuit described in Figure 2.1. If we are only interested in its behaviour with respect to the overall voltage V, overall current I and the two resistance values $R1$ and $R2$, then we can introduce the new constraint,

```
parallel_resistors(V, I, R1, R2),
```

which describes this behaviour. The new constraint is defined using a *rule* as follows.

```
parallel_resistors(V,I,R1,R2) :- V = I1*R1, V = I2*R2, I1+I2 = I.
```

The rule says that θ is a solution to `parallel_resistors(V, I, R1, R2)` if θ is a partial solution to the constraint

$$V = I1 \times R1 \wedge V = I2 \times R2 \wedge I1 + I2 = I.$$

Note that we shall use `typewriter` font for defining rules and programs and for referring to user-defined constraints in text. Constraints (from the constraint domain) are written in italics as usual. This means that we shall sometimes refer to the same variable, for example V using two different fonts V and `V`.

Now, rather than writing the conjunction of arithmetic constraints describing parallel resistors each time we need them, we can use this new constraint. For instance, suppose we are interested in the behaviour of two parallel resistors of values 10Ω and 5Ω. The constraint,

$$\texttt{parallel\_resistors}(V, I, R1, R2) \wedge R1 = 10 \wedge R2 = 5,$$

models this behaviour. Similarly, if we are studying such a circuit in which the voltage is 10V and the resistors are only known to have the same value, it can be described by

$$\texttt{parallel\_resistors}(10, I, R, R).$$

Intuitively, the meaning of the above statement can be understood by using the defining rule to replace an instance of `parallel_resistors` by the constraint on the right hand side of the rule. Thus the statement above represents the constraint

$$10 = I1 \times R \wedge 10 = I2 \times R \wedge I1 + I2 = I.$$

Rules enable the programmer to define new constraints which model the behaviour of a particular problem. We call these new constraints user-defined constraints.

Definition 4.1

A *user-defined constraint* is of the form $p(t_1, \ldots, t_n)$ where p is a n-ary *predicate* and $t_1, \ldots, t_n$ are expressions from the constraint domain. We shall use strings beginning with a lower case letter and made up of alphabetic characters and digits and the underscore "_" character to name predicates.

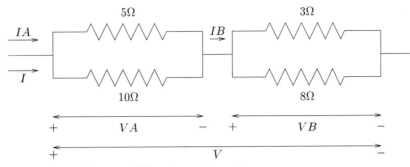

Figure 4.1 Two parallel resistors in series.

A *literal* is either a primitive constraint or a user-defined constraint.

A *goal*, G, is a sequence of literals. That is, G has the form $L_1, L_2, \ldots, L_m$, where $m \geq 0$ and each L_i is a literal. In the case $m = 0$, the goal is said to be *empty* and is represented by "□."

A *rule*, R, is of the form A :- B where A is a user-defined constraint and B is a goal. A is called the *head* of R and B is called the *body* of R.

A *fact*, is a rule with the empty goal as body, A :- □, and is simply written as A.

A *(constraint logic) program* is a sequence of rules.

The *definition* of a predicate p in a program P is the sequence of rules appearing in P which have a head involving predicate p.

In Example 4.1 above, `parallel_resistors` is a predicate, which is defined by a single rule:

```
parallel_resistors(V,I,R1,R2) :- V = I1*R1, V = I2*R2, I1+I2 = I.
```

The head of this rule is `parallel_resistors(V, I, R1, R2)` and the body is `V = I1*R1, V = I2*R2, I1+I2 = I`. Another example of a user-defined constraint is the literal `parallel_resistors(10, I, R, R)`.

Intuitively, rules in a constraint logic program can be viewed as "macro" definitions. However, we need to be careful when defining the mechanism of rewriting, in order to avoid problems with the scope of local names in the body of the rule.

Example 4.2

Consider the goal representing two parallel resistors in sequence as shown in Figure 4.1:

```
parallel_resistors(VA, IA, 10, 5),
parallel_resistors(VB, IB, 8, 3),
VA + VB = V, I = IB, I = IA.
```

Simply replacing each predicate by the body of its definition gives

```
VA = I1 * 10, VA = I2 * 5, IA = I1 + I2,
VB = I1 * 8, VB = I2 * 3, IB = I1 + I2,
VA + VB = V, I = IB, I = IA.
```

As this goal only involves primitive constraints, we can treat it as a constraint by replacing the commas by conjunction ($\wedge$). The resulting constraint has only one solution, namely,

$$\{V \mapsto 0, VA \mapsto 0, VB \mapsto 0, IA \mapsto 0, IB \mapsto 0, I \mapsto 0, I1 \mapsto 0, I2 \mapsto 0\}.$$

This is incorrect since it does not model the actual behaviour of the circuit in Figure 4.1. The problem arises because "macro" replacement has confused the two uses of the local variables $I1$ and $I2$.

The solution to this problem is to use new variables each time we use a rule to replace a user-defined constraint within a goal. To do this we make use of "renamings". Renamings were introduced in Section 1.6, but now we extend their definition from constraints to other syntactic objects.

Definition 4.2

A *syntactic object* is a constraint, user-defined constraint, rule or goal.

The result of *applying* a renaming ρ to a syntactic object o, written $\rho(o)$, is the expression obtained by replacing each variable x in o by $\rho(x)$.

A syntactic object o is a *variant* of syntactic object o' if there is a renaming ρ such that $\rho(o) \equiv o'$.

It is convenient to be able to use rules in which the arguments in the head of the rule are not distinct variables. For example, the parallel resistor definition can be simplified by writing it as

```
parallel_resistors(V, I1+I2, R1, R2) :- V = I1 * R1, V = I2 * R2.
```

To handle such definitions correctly we define the rewriting process as follows.

Definition 4.3

Let goal G be of the form

$$L_1, \ldots, L_{i-1}, L_i, L_{i+1}, \ldots, L_m$$

where L_i is the user-defined constraint $p(t_1, \ldots, t_n)$ and let rule R be of the form

$$p(s_1, \ldots, s_n) \text{ :- } B.$$

A *rewriting* of G at L_i by R using ρ is the goal

$$L_1, \ldots, L_{i-1}, t_1 = \rho(s_1), \ldots, t_n = \rho(s_n), \rho(B), L_{i+1}, \ldots, L_m$$

where ρ is a renaming chosen so that the variables in $\rho(R)$ do not appear in G.

Example 4.3

Consider the goal

```
    parallel_resistors(VA, IA, 10, 5),
    parallel_resistors(VB, IB, 8, 3),
    VA + VB = V, I = IB, I = IA.
```

from before. Rewriting the first user-defined constraint with the rule

```
parallel_resistors(V,I,R1,R2)  :-  V = I1*R1, V = I2*R2, I1+I2 = I.
```

and the renaming $\{V \mapsto V', I \mapsto I', R1 \mapsto R1', R2 \mapsto R2', I1 \mapsto I1', I2 \mapsto I2'\}$ gives

```
VA = V', IA = I', 10 = R1', 5 = R2',
V' = I1' * R1', V' = I2' * R2', I1' + I2' = I',
parallel_resistors(VB, IB, 8, 3),
VA + VB = V, I = IB, I = IA.
```

Rewriting the remaining user-defined constraint using the same rule and the renaming $\{V \mapsto V'', I \mapsto I'', R1 \mapsto R1'', R2 \mapsto R2'', I1 \mapsto I1'', I2 \mapsto I2''\}$ gives

```
VA = V', IA = I', 10 = R1', 5 = R2',
V' = I1' * R1', V' = I2' * R2', I1' + I2' = I',
VB = V'', IB = I'', 8 = R1'', 3 = R2'',
V'' = I1'' * R1'', V'' = I2'' * R2'', I1'' + I2'' = I'',
VA + VB = V, I = IB, I = IA.
```

Since this goal only involves primitive constraints we can consider it a constraint by replacing commas by $\wedge$. The overall behaviour of the circuit is the relationship between variables V and I. Simplifying the resulting constraint in terms of the variables V and I, gives the answer $V = (26/3) \times I$.

Using user-defined constraints we can write goals that naturally and concisely specify large, complicated constraints. The specified constraint can be found by repeatedly applying rewriting steps until the goal consists entirely of primitive constraints. This resulting constraint is the answer to the goal. However, the use of renamings in rewriting introduces many new variables which are almost certainly not of interest to the constraint programmer writing the goal. For this reason, after rewriting is finished, the resulting constraint should be simplified with respect to the variables in the original goal, as we have done in the previous examples.

4.2   Programming with Rules

User-defined constraints are more powerful than the example of the parallel resistor suggests. The definition of rules allows predicates to be defined in terms of other predicates. In particular, this allows a predicate to be defined *recursively* in terms of itself. It also allows a predicate to be defined by more than one rule. This enables us to model choice and case statements.

The following example illustrates how multiple rules can be used to capture different cases in the definition of a predicate. They can also be used to give a natural modelling of choice.

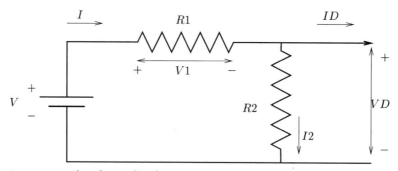

Figure 4.2 A voltage divider circuit.

Example 4.4

A voltage divider is used to create an output voltage satisfying some constraints from the available resistor and voltage cell components. Consider the problem of building a voltage divider circuit of the form shown in Figure 4.2. The constraint describing the circuit behaviour can be captured by the rule

```
voltage_divider(V, I, R1, R2, VD, ID) :-
    V1 = I * R1, VD = I2 * R2, V = V1 + VD, I = I2 + ID.
```

Suppose we wish to build a circuit which has divider voltage VD in the range 5.4V to 5.5V when the divider current ID is 0.1A. These conditions are simply expressed by the constraint $5.4 \leq VD \wedge VD \leq 5.5 \wedge ID = 0.1$. In addition, the circuit components must be chosen from those available in our laboratory. The cell must be 9V or 12V, and the resistors must be $5\Omega, 9\Omega$ or 14Ω.

We can use multiple rules to express the choice of the cell and the choice of the resistors. Each rule is considered to be one possible definition of the predicate, and the process of rewriting a goal chooses which rule to apply. The constraint that the cell must be 9V or 12V is expressed by the facts:

```
cell(9).
```
```
cell(12).
```

Similarly the constraint that resistors should be $5\Omega, 9\Omega$ or 14Ω is expressed as:

```
resistor(5).
```
```
resistor(9).
```
```
resistor(14).
```

The complete voltage divider problem is specified by the goal

```
    voltage_divider(V, I, R1, R2, VD, ID),
    5.4 ≤ VD, VD ≤ 5.5, ID = 0.1,
    cell(V), resistor(R1), resistor(R2).
```

One possible sequence of rewritings for this goal uses the rule for predicate `voltage_divider` to rewrite `voltage_divider(V, I, R1, R2, VD, ID)`, the first rule for predicate `cell` to rewrite `cell(V)` and (two copies of) the first rule for `resistor` to rewrite `resistor(R1)` and `resistor(R2)`. The resulting constraint (after replacing comma's by conjunction) is

$$V = V' \wedge I = I' \wedge R1 = R1' \wedge R2 = R2' \wedge VD = VD' \wedge ID = ID' \wedge$$
$$V1' = I' * R1' \wedge VD' = I2' * R2' \wedge V' = V1' + VD' \wedge I' = I2' + ID' \wedge$$
$$5.4 \leq VD \wedge VD \leq 5.5 \wedge ID = 0.1 \wedge V = 9 \wedge R1 = 5 \wedge R2 = 5.$$

Unfortunately, this is unsatisfiable and so it does not give a solution to the problem of designing the voltage divider.

Another possible sequence of rewritings for this goal, uses the rule for predicate `voltage_divider` to rewrite the `voltage_divider(V, I, R1, R2, VD, ID)`, the first rule for predicate `cell` to rewrite `cell(V)`, the first rule for `resistor` to rewrite `resistor(R1)` and the second rule for `resistor(R2)`. The resulting constraint is

$$V = V' \wedge I = I' \wedge R1 = R1' \wedge R2 = R2' \wedge VD = VD' \wedge ID = ID' \wedge$$
$$V1' = I' * R1' \wedge VD' = I2' * R2' \wedge V' = V1' + VD' \wedge I' = I2' + ID' \wedge$$
$$5.4 \leq VD \wedge VD \leq 5.5 \wedge ID = 0.1 \wedge V = 9 \wedge R1 = 5 \wedge R2 = 9.$$

This is satisfiable. Simplifying the constraint on to the variables we are interested in, namely the values for the components in the design V, $R1$ and $R2$, gives the constraint $V = 5 \wedge R1 = 5 \wedge R2 = 9$. From this we can see how to design the voltage divider using the available components.

Overall there are 18 different possible rewritings of the original goal, of which all but one is unsatisfiable. This illustrates why we may need to search through possible rewritings of the goal in order to find a solution.

Rules also allow us to define predicates recursively, that is in terms of themselves. This ability vastly increases the expressive power of constraint programs, and it is what makes CLP languages true programming languages rather than just constraint definition languages.

Consider the factorial function which is defined by

$$N! = \begin{cases} 1 & \text{if } N = 0 \\ N \times (N-1)! & \text{if } N \geq 1. \end{cases}$$

We can write a predicate `fac(N,F)` which is true if F is $N!$ by

```
fac(0,1).                           (R1)
fac(N, N * F)   :-   N ≥ 1, fac(N-1,F).   (R2)
```

Note that we have labelled each rule with a name in parentheses. This is solely for reference in the text and is not part of the program. Each rule captures a different case in the definition of the function. The rule $R1$ expresses the base case, while the rule $R2$ naturally expresses the recursive case.

We can use this predicate to compute the factorial function as follows. Imagine we wish to compute the factorial of 2. We start with the goal `fac(2,X)` and repeatedly rewrite it as follows:

$$fac(2, X)$$
$$\Downarrow R2$$
$$2 = N,\ X = N \times F,\ N \geq 1,\ fac(N - 1, F)$$
$$\Downarrow R2$$
$$2 = N,\ X = N \times F,\ N \geq 1,\ N - 1 = N',\ F = N' \times F',\ N' \geq 1,\ fac(N' - 1, F')$$
$$\Downarrow R1$$
$$2 = N,\ X = N \times F,\ N \geq 1,\ N - 1 = N',\ F = N' \times F',\ N' \geq 1,\ N' - 1 = 0,\ F' = 1.$$

In each step the rule used is written beside the arrow. We can simplify the final goal, treated as a constraint, with respect to the variable X and we obtain the expected answer, $X = 2$.

Now consider what would have happened if we had selected rule $R2$ instead of $R1$ in the last rewrite step. In this case we obtain the goal:

$$2 = N,\ X = N \times F,\ N \geq 1,\ N - 1 = N',\ F = N' \times F',\ N' \geq 1,$$
$$N' - 1 = N'', F' = N'' \times F'', N'' \geq 1, fac(N'' - 1, F'').$$

Although the conjunction of the primitive constraints appearing in the goal is unsatisfiable, we can still rewrite the predicate `fac`. In fact, by always choosing $R2$ we can go on rewriting forever. However, such a rewriting does not provide any more information as the conjunction of primitive constraints appearing in each goal will remain unsatisfiable since rewriting will only add constraints to an already unsatisfiable conjunction.

4.3 Evaluation

Examples in the last section suggest that, when rewriting a goal, we check that the primitive constraints already collected are satisfiable. If they are not, rewriting can stop, since further rewriting can only lead to an unsatisfiable constraint. We now give an evaluation method for constraint logic programs, formalising this idea.

The evaluation method is based on a *derivation*. At each step in the derivation a literal is processed. If the literal is a user-defined constraint, it is rewritten as before. If it is a primitive constraint it is collected in the *constraint store*. The new constraint store is then tested for satisfiability. If it is unsatisfiable, rewriting stops immediately. Otherwise, the process continues until there are no literals left. At each step in the derivation we therefore have the constraint store, which is a conjunction of primitive constraints, and the remaining goal, which is a sequence of literals. We call this a *state* of computation.

Definition 4.4
A *state* is a pair written $\langle G \mid C \rangle$ where G is a goal and C is a constraint. C is called the *constraint store*.

A *derivation step* from $\langle G_1 \mid C_1 \rangle$ to $\langle G_2 \mid C_2 \rangle$, written $\langle G_1 \mid C_1 \rangle \Rightarrow \langle G_2 \mid C_2 \rangle$, is defined as follows. Let G_1 be the sequence of literals

$$L_1, L_2, \ldots, L_m.$$

There are two cases.

1. L_1 is a primitive constraint. Then C_2 is $C_1 \wedge L_1$ and, if $solv(C_2) \equiv false$, G_2 is the empty goal; otherwise G_2 is $L_2, \ldots, L_m$.

2. L_1 is a user-defined constraint. Then C_2 is C_1 and G_2 is a rewriting of G_1 at L_1 by some rule R in the program using a renaming ρ such that the variables in $\rho(R)$ are different from those in C_1 and G_1. If there is no rule defining the predicate of L_1 then C_2 is $false$ and G_2 is the empty goal.

A *derivation* for state $\langle G_0 \mid C_0 \rangle$ is a sequence of states

$$\langle G_0 \mid C_0 \rangle \Rightarrow \langle G_1 \mid C_1 \rangle \Rightarrow \langle G_2 \mid C_2 \rangle \Rightarrow \ldots$$

such that for each $i \geq 0$ there is a derivation step from $\langle G_i \mid C_i \rangle$ to $\langle G_{i+1} \mid C_{i+1} \rangle$ and the renamed rules used in each derivation step do not contain variables which occur earlier in the derivation.
If G is a goal then a *derivation for G* is a derivation for the state $\langle G \mid true \rangle$.

The different choices of renaming that are possible in a derivation step essentially make no difference since the names of the variables are irrelevant to the constraint solver, which we assume is well-behaved. The different choices of rule that are possible in rewriting a user-defined constraint may, however, lead to different derivations.

Example 4.5
Recall the earlier definition of the factorial predicate. One derivation from the goal `fac(2,X)` is illustrated in Figure 4.3.

In each step, if a user-defined constraint is rewritten, the rule used is shown beside the arrow. No further derivation steps are possible because the goal has become empty. This corresponds to a complete rewriting. The final constraint store is an answer to the initial state. The intermediate variables are not of interest. Thus the answer we would really like is the final constraint store simplified with respect to the variables in the initial goal, in this case X. This is simply $X = 2$, which is thus an "answer" to `fac(2,X)`.

A derivation can continue until the goal becomes empty. A derivation that can no longer continue can be either successful or failed.

$$\langle fac(2, X) \mid true \rangle$$
$$\Downarrow R2$$
$$\langle 2 = N, X = N \times F, N \geq 1, fac(N - 1, F) \mid true \rangle$$
$$\Downarrow$$
$$\langle X = N \times F, N \geq 1, fac(N - 1, F) \mid 2 = N \rangle$$
$$\Downarrow$$
$$\langle N \geq 1, fac(N - 1, F) \mid 2 = N \wedge X = N \times F \rangle$$
$$\Downarrow$$
$$\langle fac(N - 1, F) \mid 2 = N \wedge X = N \times F \wedge N \geq 1 \rangle$$
$$\Downarrow R2$$
$$\langle N - 1 = N', F = N' \times F', N' \geq 1, fac(N' - 1, F') \mid 2 = N \wedge X = N \times F \wedge N \geq 1 \rangle$$
$$\Downarrow$$
$$\langle F = N' \times F', N' \geq 1, fac(N' - 1, F') \mid 2 = N \wedge X = N \times F \wedge N \geq 1 \wedge N - 1 = N' \rangle$$
$$\Downarrow$$
$$\langle N' \geq 1, fac(N' - 1, F') \mid 2 = N \wedge X = N \times F \wedge N \geq 1 \wedge N - 1 = N' \wedge F = N' \times F' \rangle$$
$$\Downarrow$$
$$\langle fac(N' - 1, F') \mid 2 = N \wedge X = N \times F \wedge N \geq 1 \wedge N - 1 = N' \wedge F = N' \times F' \wedge N' \geq 1 \rangle$$
$$\Downarrow R1$$
$$\langle N' - 1 = 0, F' = 1 \mid 2 = N \wedge X = N \times F \wedge N \geq 1 \wedge N - 1 = N' \wedge$$
$$F = N' \times F' \wedge N' \geq 1 \rangle$$
$$\Downarrow$$
$$\langle F' = 1 \mid 2 = N \wedge X = N \times F \wedge N \geq 1 \wedge N - 1 = N' \wedge F = N' \times F' \wedge$$
$$N' \geq 1 \wedge N' - 1 = 0 \rangle$$
$$\Downarrow$$
$$\langle \Box \mid 2 = N \wedge X = N \times F \wedge N \geq 1 \wedge N - 1 = N' \wedge F = N' \times F' \wedge$$
$$N' \geq 1 \wedge N' - 1 = 0 \wedge F' = 1 \rangle$$

Figure 4.3 A successful derivation for `fac(2,X)`.

Definition 4.5

A *success state* is a state $\langle G \mid C \rangle$ where G is the empty goal and $solv(C) \not\equiv false$.
A *fail state* is a state $\langle G \mid C \rangle$ where G is the empty goal and $solv(C) \equiv false$.
A derivation

$$\langle G_0 \mid C_0 \rangle \Rightarrow \cdots \Rightarrow \langle G_n \mid C_n \rangle$$

is *successful* if $\langle G_n \mid C_n \rangle$ is a success state. The constraint $simpl(C_n, vars(\langle G_0 \mid C_0 \rangle))$
is said to be an *answer* to the state $\langle G_0 \mid C_0 \rangle$.
If G is a goal, then an *answer* for G is an answer to the state $\langle G \mid true \rangle$.
A derivation

$$\langle G_0 \mid C_0 \rangle \Rightarrow \cdots \Rightarrow \langle G_n \mid C_n \rangle$$

is *failed* if $\langle G_n \mathbin{|} C_n \rangle$ is a fail state.

The derivation in Figure 4.3 is an example of a successful derivation. From the definition of a derivation step, failed derivations can occur in two ways. Either a primitive constraint is added to the current constraint store making it unsatisfiable or a user-defined constraint is selected which has no rules defining it. Below we give examples of both kinds of failed derivation.

Consider the factorial predicate. One failed derivation for the goal `fac(2,X)` is:

$$\langle fac(2, X) \mathbin{|} true \rangle$$
$$\Downarrow \ R1$$
$$\langle 2 = 0, X = 1 \mathbin{|} true \rangle$$
$$\Downarrow$$
$$\langle \square \mathbin{|} 2 = 0 \rangle$$

Now consider the goal `X = 2, nodefinition(X)` where `nodefinition` is a predicate without any defining rules. There is only one derivation for this goal and it is failed.

$$\langle X = 2, nodefinition(X) \mathbin{|} true \rangle$$
$$\Downarrow$$
$$\langle nodefinition(X) \mathbin{|} X = 2 \rangle$$
$$\Downarrow$$
$$\langle \square \mathbin{|} false \rangle$$

In practice the second type of failed derivation illustrated above rarely occurs. It is usually considered a programming error, much like calling a procedure without first defining it in a traditional programming language.

4.4   Derivation Trees and Finite Failure

Because there may be multiple derivations for a goal, evaluation of the goal may need to search to find a successful derivation. In order to do this, the CLP system explores a tree, called the *derivation tree*, which contains all the derivations for a particular goal. The derivation tree is a tree in which each path from the top of the tree is a derivation. Branches occur in the tree whenever there is a choice of rule to rewrite a user-defined constraint with.

Definition 4.6
A *derivation tree* for a goal G and program P is tree with states as nodes. It is constructed as follows. The root of the tree is the state $\langle G \mathbin{|} true \rangle$. The children of each state $\langle G_i \mathbin{|} C_i \rangle$ in the tree are those states which can be reached in a single derivation step from that state. A state which has two or more children is called a *choicepoint*.

It follows from this definition that, if the first literal in G_i is a primitive constraint, the node $\langle G_i \mid C_i \rangle$ has a single child. However, if the first literal is a user-defined constraint then there is a child for each rule in the definition of the literal. These children are ordered from left-to-right according to the relative ordering of the rules in the program.

A derivation tree represents all of the derivations from a goal. Different branches arise at choicepoints because there is a choice of rule with which to rewrite a user-defined constraint. A successful derivation is represented in a derivation tree by a path from the root to a success state. A failed derivation is represented in a derivation tree by a path from the root to a fail state. To help distinguish successful and failed derivations, we shall use "■" to represent the empty goal in a fail state and "□" to represent the empty goal in a success state.

Again recall the definition of the factorial predicate. The derivation tree for the goal `fac(2,X)` is shown in Figure 4.4. We have labelled arcs arising when a user-defined constraint is rewritten by the rule used in the rewriting. Note that states resulting from rewriting with rule $R1$ appear to the left of states resulting from rewriting $R2$, since $R1$ occurs before $R2$ in the program. The constraints in the derivation tree are:

$C_0 : true$

$C_1 : 2 = 0$

$C_2 : 2 = N$

$C_3 : 2 = N \wedge X = N \times F$

$C_4 : 2 = N \wedge X = N \times F \wedge N \geq 1$

$C_5 : 2 = N \wedge X = N \times F \wedge N \geq 1 \wedge N - 1 = 0$

$C_6 : 2 = N \wedge X = N \times F \wedge N \geq 1 \wedge N - 1 = N'$

$C_7 : 2 = N \wedge X = N \times F \wedge N \geq 1 \wedge N - 1 = N' \wedge F = N' \times F'$

$C_8 : 2 = N \wedge X = N \times F \wedge N \geq 1 \wedge N - 1 = N' \wedge F = N' \times F' \wedge N' \geq 1$

$C_9 : 2 = N \wedge X = N \times F \wedge N \geq 1 \wedge N - 1 = N' \wedge F = N' \times F' \wedge N' \geq 1 \wedge$
$\quad\quad N' - 1 = 0$

$C_{10} : 2 = N \wedge X = N \times F \wedge N \geq 1 \wedge N - 1 = N' \wedge F = N' \times F' \wedge N' \geq 1 \wedge$
$\quad\quad N' - 1 = 0 \wedge F' = 1$

$C_{11} : 2 = N \wedge X = N \times F \wedge N \geq 1 \wedge N - 1 = N' \wedge F = N' \times F' \wedge N' \geq 1 \wedge$
$\quad\quad N' - 1 = N''$

$C_{12} : 2 = N \wedge X = N \times F \wedge N \geq 1 \wedge N - 1 = N' \wedge F = N' \times F' \wedge N' \geq 1 \wedge$
$\quad\quad N' - 1 = N'' \wedge F' = N'' \times F''$

$C_{13} : 2 = N \wedge X = N \times F \wedge N \geq 1 \wedge N - 1 = N' \wedge F = N' \times F' \wedge N' \geq 1 \wedge$
$\quad\quad N' - 1 = N'' \wedge F' = N'' \times F'' \wedge N'' \geq 1$

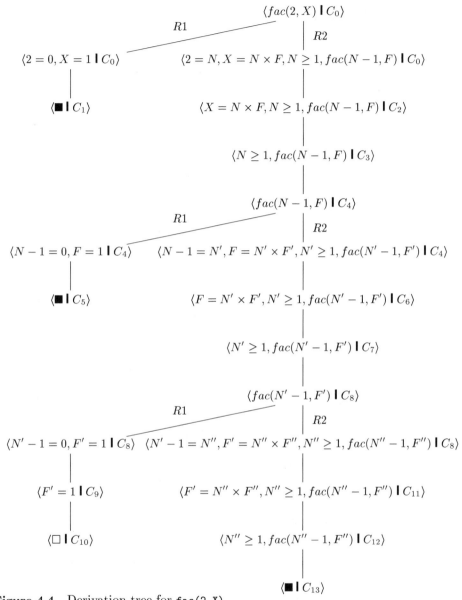

Figure 4.4 Derivation tree for `fac(2,X)`.

Examination of the derivation tree shows that the goal `fac(2,X)` has four derivations, one for each leaf node in the tree. Three are failed while one is the successful derivation shown in Figure 4.3.

It may be the case that all of the derivations for a particular goal are failed, in which case there are no answers to the goal.

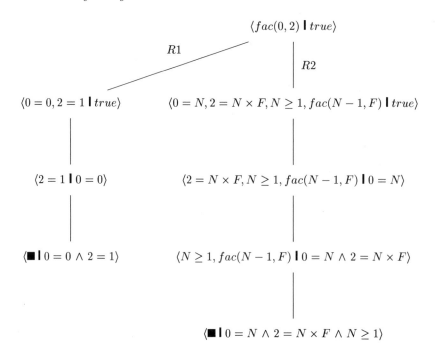

Figure 4.5   Derivation tree for `fac(0,2)`.

Definition 4.7
If a state or goal G has a finite derivation tree and all derivations in the tree are failed, G is said to *finitely fail*.

The derivation tree for the goal `fac(0,2)` is shown in Figure 4.5. Both derivations contained in the tree are failed so the goal has finitely failed.

A derivation tree is not necessarily finite. Infinite derivations may occur when the program is recursive. Consider the simple program:

```
stupid(X) :- stupid(X).          (S1)
stupid(1).                       (S2)
```

The top part of the derivation tree for goal `stupid(X)` is shown in Figure 4.6. The leftmost branch is infinite.

4.5   Goal Evaluation

CLP systems evaluate a goal by constructing the derivation tree for the goal and searching through it for successful derivations. Indeed, because evaluation is essentially a search through the derivation tree, the derivation tree is sometimes called the *search space*.

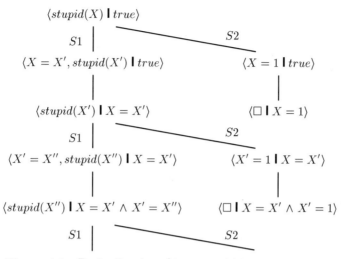

Figure 4.6   Derivation tree for `stupid(X)`.

Definition 4.8

A goal is *evaluated* by performing an in-order, that is depth-first left-to-right, traversal of the goal's derivation tree. Whenever a success state is encountered the system returns the corresponding answer to the user. The user is given the option either to halt the execution or to continue traversing the tree to find more answers. Execution halts either when the user stops the search for more answers or when the entire tree has been explored.

It is important to realise that the CLP system does not construct the entire derivation tree before traversing it to look for success states. This would be very inefficient, especially if only the first answer is required. Instead the CLP system constructs the tree as it is traversed. Exactly how this is done is discussed more fully in Chapter 10.

For example, the goal `fac(2,X)` is evaluated as follows. Essentially, the CLP system searches the derivation tree shown in Figure 4.4. Evaluation begins at the root of the tree $\langle fac(2, X) \mathbin{|} C_0\rangle$. This is a choicepoint as there is more than one rule in the definition of `fac`. The first rule in the definition, $R1$, is tried first. This leads to an exploration of the left branch in the tree. Using this rule, a derivation step is applied to $\langle fac(2, X) \mathbin{|} C_0\rangle$ giving $\langle 2 = 0, X = 1 \mathbin{|} C_0\rangle$. A further derivation step is applied giving the child $\langle \blacksquare \mathbin{|} C_1\rangle$. This is a fail state since the constraint C_1 is unsatisfiable. Evaluation, therefore, *backtracks* up the derivation tree to the closest state with unexplored children. In this case it is the root $\langle fac(2, X) \mathbin{|} C_0\rangle$. Now the system tries the second rule in the definition of `fac`, effectively exploring the right branch in the tree. Rewriting with this rule gives the state $\langle 2 = N, X = N \times F, N \geq 1, fac(N - 1, F) \mathbin{|} C_0\rangle$. Application of subsequent derivation steps produce the states

$$\langle X = N \times F, N \geq 1, fac(N - 1, F) \mid C_2 \rangle,$$
$$\langle N \geq 1, fac(N - 1, F) \mid C_3 \rangle \text{ and}$$
$$\langle fac(N - 1, F) \mid C_4 \rangle.$$

This state is another choicepoint. Evaluation will try the first rule, $R1$, first, leading to an exploration of the left branch. Similarly to above, this leads to a failed state so execution backtracks to this state. Now the second rule is tried, leading to an exploration of the right branch. Derivation steps produce the states

$$\langle N - 1 = N', F = N' \times F', N' \geq 1, fac(N' - 1, F') \mid C_4 \rangle,$$
$$\langle F = N' \times F', N' \geq 1, fac(N' - 1, F') \mid C_6 \rangle,$$
$$\langle N' \geq 1, fac(N' - 1, F') \mid C_7 \rangle \text{ and}$$
$$\langle fac(N' - 1, F') \mid C_8 \rangle$$

which are visited in turn.

Again evaluation has reached a choicepoint and again the first rule, $R1$, is tried. This leads to the exploration of the left branch which contains the following states $\langle N' - 1 = 0, F' = 1 \mid C_8 \rangle$, $\langle F' = 1 \mid C_9 \rangle$ and finally $\langle \Box \mid C_{10} \rangle$. Since $solv(C_{10})$ is *true* a success state has been reached. This reflects the fact that the path from the root of the tree to this state is a successful derivation. The CLP system returns the answer $simpl(C_{10}, \{X\})$, which is $X = 2$.

Since the derivation tree has not been fully explored, the system asks the user whether they wish to continue the search. If the user answers yes, the search continues, otherwise execution of the goal finishes. In this case, if the user asks for more answers the search backtracks up the tree to the first state with a remaining unexplored child. This is $\langle fac(N' - 1, F') \mid C_8 \rangle$. The second rule, $R2$, for `fac` is now tried, leading to an exploration of the right branch from this state. In turn, the states

$$\langle N' - 1 = N'', F' = N'' \times F'', N'' \geq 1, fac(N'' - 1, F'') \mid C_8 \rangle,$$
$$\langle F' = N'' \times F'', N'' \geq 1, fac(N'' - 1, F'') \mid C_{11} \rangle,$$
$$\langle N'' \geq 1, fac(N'' - 1, F'') \mid C_{12} \rangle \text{ and}$$
$$\langle \blacksquare \mid C_{13} \rangle$$

are created and visited. Since a failed state has been reached, the system attempts to backtrack. However, there are no states with unexplored children, so the system halts with the message that there are no more answers since the entire derivation tree has now been explored.

When evaluating a goal which is finitely failed a CLP system will return the answer *no* indicating that the goal has no answers. As an example, the derivation tree for the goal `fac(0,2)` is shown in Figure 4.5. Evaluation proceeds by visiting the state $\langle fac(0, 2) \mid true \rangle$ and proceeding down the left branch to states $\langle 0 = 0, 2 = 1 \mid true \rangle$, $\langle 2 = 1 \mid 0 = 0 \rangle$ and $\langle \blacksquare \mid 0 = 0 \wedge 2 = 1 \rangle$. Evaluation now backtracks to state $\langle fac(0, 2) \mid true \rangle$ and tries the right branch. The right branch also leads to a failed state, so, since the entire tree has been explored without finding any answers, the answer *no* is returned.

For goals with infinite derivation trees, evaluation may not terminate. Evaluation of the goal `stupid(X)` whose derivation tree is illustrated in Figure 4.6 never returns an answer, even though the goal has successful derivations. This is because the CLP system spends all of its time searching down the infinite leftmost branch and never finds a successful derivation.

We will return to the issue of non-termination and how to overcome it in Chapter 7. In this case it is simple to remove the problem by reversing the order of the two rules defining predicate `stupid` so that the fact comes first. The reordered program is

```
stupid(1).
stupid(X) :- stupid(X).
```

Evaluation of the goal with this program corresponds to searching the derivation tree in Figure 4.6 from right-to-left rather than left-to-right. First the state $\langle stupid(X) \mid true \rangle$ is visited, then $\langle X = 1 \mid true \rangle$, and then $\langle \Box \mid X = 1 \rangle$. The answer $X = 1$ is returned to the user. If the user asks for evaluation to continue, it backtracks up to state $\langle stupid(X) \mid true \rangle$, then visits $\langle X = X', stupid(X') \mid true \rangle$, $\langle stupid(X') \mid X = X' \rangle$, $\langle X' = 1 \mid X = X' \rangle$ and then $\langle \Box \mid X = X' \wedge X' = 1 \rangle$. The second answer, which is again $X = 1$, is returned to the user. This example illustrates how the user can obtain more than one answer to a goal. In fact this goal has an infinite number of answers all of which are equivalent.

4.6   Simplified Derivation Trees

Unfortunately, except for toy programs, derivation trees are too large and cumbersome to illustrate evaluation of a goal. Here we introduce a variant—"simplified derivation trees"—which provide a more compact representation for a derivation tree.

One key insight behind simplified derivation trees is that only the variables from the original goal and those appearing in the goal part of the state can be of interest in the remaining derivation. Therefore, the constraint can be simplified with respect to these variables. The second insight is that derivation steps in which a primitive constraint is successfully added to the constraint store are straightforward. The steps of real interest in a derivation and derivation tree occur when user-defined constraints are rewritten; in particular, we are interested in which rule in the definition is used for the rewriting.

Definition 4.9
A state $\langle G_0 \mid C_0 \rangle$ occurring in a derivation or derivation tree for goal G can be simplified in the following way. Let $V = vars(G)$ and $V_0 = vars(G_0)$. First, we compute $simpl(C_0, V \cup V_0)$. Call the result C_1. Second, for each variable $x \in V_0 - V$ which appears exactly once in C_1 in an equation of the form $x = t$, we replace

x everywhere in G_0 by t, obtaining the goal G_2. Finally, we simplify again in order to remove the substituted variables. That is to say, we compute C_2 as $simpl(C_1, V \cup vars(G_2))$. The *simplified state* is $\langle G_2 \mid C_2 \rangle$.

Consider the state $\langle fac(N' - 1, F') \mid C_0 \rangle$ where C_0 is

$$2 = N \wedge X = N \times F \wedge N \geq 1 \wedge N - 1 = N' \wedge F = N' \times F' \wedge N' \geq 1$$

which occurs in a derivation tree for the goal `fac(2, X)`. First, C_0 is simplified with respect to the variables $\{X, N', F'\}$ giving C_1:

$$N' = 1 \ \wedge \ X = 2 \times F'.$$

Then, G_2 is constructed by replacing N' by 1. This, if we take some liberty in simplifying expressions, gives $fac(0, F')$. Finally, C_2 is computed to be $simpl(C_1, \{X, F'\})$, which is $X = 2 \times F'$. Thus the simplified state is

$$\langle fac(0, F') \mid X = 2 \times F' \rangle.$$

Definition 4.10
A state in a derivation is *critical* if

- it is the first or last state; or
- the first literal in the state is a user-defined constraint.

A *simplified derivation* for goal G is obtained from a derivation for G by removing states which are not critical from the derivation and simplifying the remaining states in the derivation.

A *simplified derivation tree* for G is obtained by simplifying each of the derivations that form it.

For example, the simplified form of the derivation shown in Figure 4.3 is:

$$\langle fac(2, X) \mid true \rangle$$
$$\Downarrow \ R2$$
$$\langle fac(1, F) \mid X = 2 \times F \rangle$$
$$\Downarrow \ R2$$
$$\langle fac(0, F') \mid X = 2 \times F' \rangle$$
$$\Downarrow \ R1$$
$$\langle \square \mid X = 2 \rangle$$

The simplified form of a derivation is much smaller than the original derivation, yet essentially contains the same information. However, some dependencies between variables in different states can be lost. For instance, the connection between the variables F and F' in the above simplified derivation is not visible.

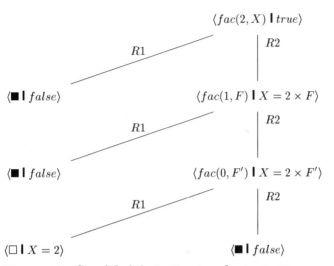

Figure 4.7 Simplified derivation tree for `fac(2,X)`.

The simplified form of the derivation tree shown in Figure 4.4 is shown in Figure 4.7. Note that in a simplified derivation tree the answer constraints for the original goal appear in the successful leaves of the derivation and failed derivation end in a state whose constraint is *false*.

4.7 The CLP Scheme

Although all the examples we have examined so far have used arithmetic constraints, the definitions for rules, derivations and evaluation do not depend on any particular constraint domain. Rather, they provide a scheme for creating languages which share the same evaluation mechanism.

This *constraint logic programming scheme* defines a family of languages. Given a particular constraint domain, constraint solver and constraint simplifier, the scheme defines a language for writing programs and a mechanism for evaluating goals and programs written in this language. The constraint domain details the primitive constraints in the language, while the solver and simplifier are used in the evaluation of goals.

For example, the tree constraint domain, $Tree$, together with the tree solver, tree_solve, and simplifier, tree_simplify, give rise to a constraint logic programming language, which we call $CLP(Tree)$. The following is an example of a $CLP(Tree)$ program. It defines the predicate `delete(X,Y,Z)` which deletes an element Y from list X to give list Z.

```
delete(cons(Y,X), Y, X).
delete(cons(A,X), Y, cons(A,Z)) :- delete(X, Y, Z).
```

Our reasons for requiring constraint solvers to be well-behaved become apparent in the context of the CLP scheme. The most important property is that the solver is variable name independent. This means that the behaviour of the solver, and so of the CLP system, is the same, regardless of which renamings are used in the derivation steps. The other properties ensure that goals which contain the same literals, but possibly in a different order, have the same answers. We investigate this further in the next section.

The importance of constraint simplification is illustrated by the size and complexity of the final constraint store for even simple goals. For instance, compare the final constraint store for the successful derivation for `fac(2,X)`

$$2 = N \wedge X = N \times F \wedge N \geq 1 \wedge N - 1 = N' \wedge F = N' \times F' \wedge N' \geq 1 \wedge$$
$$N' - 1 = 0 \wedge F' = 1$$

with the result simplified on to X, namely $X = 2$. Being able to simplify the answer with respect to the variables in the original goal by using a projecting or weakly projecting simplifier greatly improves intelligibility of the result, since many intermediate variables may be introduced in a derivation.

In the remainder of this book we shall make use of three CLP systems. The first is $CLP(Tree)$, the constraint logic programming language over tree constraints introduced above. This is, essentially, the pure component of the logic programming language, Prolog. Tree constraints are present in almost all CLP languages because they allow the programmer to build and access data structures—a necessity for modelling of more complex problems. We shall investigate the use of tree constraints for data structure manipulation in Chapter 6.

The second language is $CLP(\mathcal{R})$. This language results from combining the *Real* and *Tree* constraint domains in a straightforward and natural manner. Elements of the domain are trees (as for the *Tree* domain) with the addition that any arithmetic constant is also a tree (with no children). Thus, domain elements are trees which may have arithmetic constants as leaves. Real constants are available using the usual decimal representation and the usual arithmetic functions are provided for reals: +, -, * and /; as well as trigonometric functions, exponentiation, minimization and maximization : sin, cos, pow, min, and max. Primitive constraints for arithmetic terms are equality (=), inequality ($\leq$, $\geq$), and strict inequality (<, >). We will not make use of arithmetic disequality ($\neq$) although it is available in some implementations. For trees there are only two primitive constraints: equality (=) and disequality ($\neq$) between terms. Disequality is not available in all CLP systems, but later, in Chapter 9, we shall discuss how it can be implemented on top of a solver providing only equality.

The third language, $CLP(FD)$, combines tree constraints with finite domain constraints. Elements of the constraint domain are trees which may have integer constants as leaves. Finite domain variables either range over a finite domain of integers or a finite domain of arbitrary constants which are treated as names for integers. The usual mathematical constraints are provided for integer finite domain variables, that is equality (=), inequality ($\leq$, $\geq$)), strict inequality (<, >) and disequality ($\neq$). We shall also use complex constraints such as `element` and `cumulative`. The constraints over trees are the same as for $CLP(\mathcal{R})$, namely equality (=) and disequality ($\neq$). This means that complex data structures can be created and manipulated in the same way as in $CLP(Tree)$ and $CLP(\mathcal{R})$.

4.8   (*) Independence from Rule Ordering and Literal Selection

The answers for a goal are obtained from the successful derivations for a goal. One of the nice properties of constraint logic programs is that we can modify a program in a number of ways without altering the answers to a goal. This allows us to modify the program to improve its efficiency of execution without changing the answers—a subject we shall investigate in Chapter 7. In this section we demonstrate that the answers to a goal are independent of the order of rules in a program and the order of the literals in a goal or rule body.

It is easy to see that the answers to a goal are not effected by the order of the rules defining a predicate p. The only effect the ordering has is on the order of the children of a state in which p is rewritten. Clearly, the same set of derivations exist regardless of the order, although they may appear in different places in the tree.

However, although rule ordering does not change the answers themselves it may change the order in which the answers will be discovered or, indeed, if they will ever be discovered. This is illustrated by the `stupid` predicate. For the rules given on page 146, evaluation of the goal `stupid(X)` will fail to find any answers even though they exist in the derivation tree. However, if the rules are reordered as shown on page 149, evaluation will find an infinite number of answers.

Now let us consider the effect of the order in which literals are processed. In a derivation the literals in the goal are treated left-to-right. That is, the leftmost literal in the goal is either added to the constraint store, if it is a primitive constraint, or rewritten, if it is a user-defined constraint. We shall now show that the same answers are obtained even if the literals are processed in a different order. This means that a goal and program will give the same answers independent of the ordering of literals in the goal and in the rule bodies. This property is important because it means the CLP programmer can improve efficiency by reordering goals or bodies in a correct program with the knowledge that the answers will not change.

To make this discussion more precise, we first need to extend our notion of derivation so that we do not, necessarily, process the first literal in the goal. Instead, we allow any literal from the goal to be *selected* for processing.

Definition 4.11

A *selection derivation step* from $\langle G_1 \mid C_1 \rangle$ to $\langle G_2 \mid C_2 \rangle$, written $\langle G_1 \mid C_1 \rangle \Rightarrow \langle G_2 \mid C_2 \rangle$, is defined as follows. Let G_1 be the sequence of literals

$$L_1, \ldots, L_{i-1}, L_i, L_{i+1}, \ldots, L_m$$

and let L_i be the *selected literal*. There are two cases.

1. L_i is a primitive constraint. Then C_2 is $C_1 \wedge L_i$ and, if $solv(C_2) \equiv false$, G_2 is the empty goal; otherwise G_2 is $L_1, \ldots, L_{i-1}, L_{i+1}, \ldots, L_m$.

2. L_i is a user-defined constraint. Then C_2 is C_1 and G_2 is a rewriting of G_1 at L_i by some rule R in the program using a renaming ρ such that the variables in $\rho(R)$ are different from those in C_1 and G_1. If there is no rule defining the predicate of L_i then C_2 is $false$ and G_2 is the empty goal.

A *selection derivation* for state $\langle G_0 \mid C_0 \rangle$ is a sequence of states

$$\langle G_0 \mid C_0 \rangle \Rightarrow \langle G_1 \mid C_1 \rangle \Rightarrow \langle G_2 \mid C_2 \rangle \Rightarrow \ldots$$

such that for each $i \geq 0$ there is a selection derivation step from $\langle G_i \mid C_i \rangle$ to $\langle G_{i+1} \mid C_{i+1} \rangle$ and the renamed rules used in each selection derivation step do not contain variables which occur earlier in the derivation.

Derivations are a particular case of selection derivations in which the leftmost literal in the goal is always selected. However, other strategies for literal selection are possible. For instance, a derivation from the goal `fac(2,X)` in which the rightmost literal is selected is shown in Figure 4.8. The selected literal is underlined in each state.

Somewhat surprisingly, answers are independent of literal selection. To see why, consider Figure 4.8 again. The corresponding derivation in which the leftmost literal in the goal is always selected is shown in Figure 4.3. Both derivations are successful and give rise to the same answer $X = 2$. The point is that, regardless of the order in which literals are selected, if a derivation is successful then all literals will be selected. The only difference is the order of the primitive constraints in the constraint store. However, because the constraint solver is well-behaved, this cannot change the behaviour of the CLP system.

Independence from literal selection strategy depends on the constraint solver being well-behaved since, as we have seen, different literal selection strategies can lead to different orders of primitive constraints in the constraint store. If the solver is not set based, the solver might answer *false* for one constraint and *unknown* for the reordered constraint. One derivation will fail and the other succeed, and so the answers will be different.

$$\langle fac(2, X) \mid true \rangle$$
$$\Downarrow R2$$
$$\langle 2 = N, X = N \times F, N \geq 1, \underline{fac(N - 1, F)} \mid true \rangle$$
$$\Downarrow R2$$
$$\langle 2 = N, X = N \times F, N \geq 1, N - 1 = N', F = N' \times F', N' \geq 1, \underline{fac(N' - 1, F')} \mid true \rangle$$
$$\Downarrow R1$$
$$\langle 2 = N, X = N \times F, N \geq 1, N - 1 = N', F = N' \times F', N' \geq 1, N' - 1 = 0, \underline{F' = 1} \mid true \rangle$$
$$\Downarrow$$
$$\langle 2 = N, X = N \times F, N \geq 1, N - 1 = N', F = N' \times F', N' \geq 1, \underline{N' - 1 = 0} \mid F' = 1 \rangle$$
$$\Downarrow$$
$$\langle 2 = N, X = N \times F, N \geq 1, N - 1 = N', F = N' \times F', \underline{N' \geq 1} \mid F' = 1 \wedge N' - 1 = 0 \rangle$$
$$\Downarrow$$
$$\langle 2 = N, X = N \times F, N \geq 1, N - 1 = N', \underline{F = N' \times F'} \mid F' = 1 \wedge N' - 1 = 0 \wedge N' \geq 1 \rangle$$
$$\Downarrow$$
$$\langle 2 = N, X = N \times F, N \geq 1, \underline{N - 1 = N'} \mid F' = 1 \wedge N' - 1 = 0 \wedge N' \geq 1 \wedge F = N' \times F' \rangle$$
$$\Downarrow$$
$$\langle 2 = N, X = N \times F, \underline{N \geq 1} \mid F' = 1 \wedge N' - 1 = 0 \wedge N' \geq 1 \wedge F = N' \times F' \wedge N - 1 = N' \rangle$$
$$\Downarrow$$
$$\langle 2 = N, \underline{X = N \times F} \mid F' = 1 \wedge N' - 1 = 0 \wedge N' \geq 1 \wedge F = N' \times F' \wedge N - 1 = N' \wedge N \geq 1 \rangle$$
$$\Downarrow$$
$$\langle \underline{2 = N} \mid F' = 1 \wedge N' - 1 = 0 \wedge N' \geq 1 \wedge F = N' \times F' \wedge N - 1 = N' \wedge$$
$$N \geq 1 \wedge X = N \times F \rangle$$
$$\Downarrow$$
$$\langle \Box \mid F' = 1 \wedge N' - 1 = 0 \wedge N' \geq 1 \wedge F = N' \times F' \wedge N - 1 = N' \wedge N \geq 1 \wedge$$
$$X = N \times F \wedge 2 = N \rangle$$

Figure 4.8 A right-to-left derivation for `fac(2,X)`.

For example, imagine

$$solv(F \leq 0 \wedge 0 = 0 \wedge F = 1) = unknown$$

but

$$solv(0 = 0 \wedge F = 1 \wedge F \leq 0) = false.$$

Then the two derivations for the goal

```
F ≤ 0, fac(0,F)
```

illustrated below, using different literal selections give different answers.

$$\langle \underline{F \leq 0}, fac(0, F) \mathbin{\mathbf{I}} true \rangle \qquad \langle F \leq 0, \underline{fac(0, F)} \mathbin{\mathbf{I}} true \rangle$$

$$\Downarrow \qquad\qquad\qquad \Downarrow R1$$

$$\langle \underline{fac(0, F)} \mathbin{\mathbf{I}} F \leq 0 \rangle \qquad \langle F \leq 0, \underline{0 = 0}, F = 1 \mathbin{\mathbf{I}} true \rangle$$

$$\Downarrow R1 \qquad\qquad\qquad \Downarrow$$

$$\langle \underline{0 = 0}, F = 1 \mathbin{\mathbf{I}} F \leq 0 \rangle \qquad \langle F \leq 0, \underline{F = 1} \mathbin{\mathbf{I}} 0 = 0 \rangle$$

$$\Downarrow \qquad\qquad\qquad \Downarrow$$

$$\langle \underline{F = 1} \mathbin{\mathbf{I}} F \leq 0 \wedge 0 = 0 \rangle \qquad \langle \underline{F \leq 0} \mathbin{\mathbf{I}} 0 = 0 \wedge F = 1 \rangle$$

$$\Downarrow \qquad\qquad\qquad \Downarrow$$

$$\langle \square \mathbin{\mathbf{I}} F \leq 0 \wedge 0 = 0 \wedge F = 1 \rangle \qquad \langle \blacksquare \mathbin{\mathbf{I}} 0 = 0 \wedge F = 1 \wedge F \leq 0 \rangle$$

Similarly, if the solver is not monotonic, different answers can result, even if the solver is set based. Imagine

$$solv(F \leq 0 \wedge F = 1) = false$$

but

$$solv(F \leq 0 \wedge F = 1 \wedge 0 = 0) = unknown.$$

Therefore, since the solver is set based,

$$solv(F \leq 0 \wedge 0 = 0 \wedge F = 1) = unknown.$$

Then the two derivations for the goal

```
F ≤ 0, fac(0,F)
```

illustrated below, using different literal selections give different answers.

$$\langle \underline{F \leq 0}, fac(0, F) \mathbin{\mathbf{I}} true \rangle \qquad \langle \underline{F \leq 0}, fac(0, F) \mathbin{\mathbf{I}} true \rangle$$

$$\Downarrow \qquad\qquad\qquad \Downarrow$$

$$\langle \underline{fac(0, F)} \mathbin{\mathbf{I}} F \leq 0 \rangle \qquad \langle \underline{fac(0, F)} \mathbin{\mathbf{I}} F \leq 0 \rangle$$

$$\Downarrow R1 \qquad\qquad\qquad \Downarrow R1$$

$$\langle \underline{0 = 0}, F = 1 \mathbin{\mathbf{I}} F \leq 0 \rangle \qquad \langle 0 = 0, \underline{F = 1} \mathbin{\mathbf{I}} F \leq 0 \rangle$$

$$\Downarrow \qquad\qquad\qquad \Downarrow$$

$$\langle \underline{F = 1} \mathbin{\mathbf{I}} F \leq 0 \wedge 0 = 0 \rangle \qquad \langle \blacksquare \mathbin{\mathbf{I}} F \leq 0 \wedge F = 1 \rangle$$

$$\Downarrow$$

$$\langle \square \mathbin{\mathbf{I}} F \leq 0 \wedge 0 = 0 \wedge F = 1 \rangle$$

Independence from literal selection is one of the most important properties of constraint logic programs. It means that the program can be understood independently of the underlying control flow used in the implementation. One reason this is important is if the CLP system employs *dynamic scheduling* to choose the literal. Dynamic scheduling is provided by many CLP languages. It allows the programmer to specify run-time conditions under which the leftmost literal should not be selected. This is discussed in Chapter 9. Independence from literal selection allows the programmer to ignore the precise details about the order in which literals will be evaluated with dynamic scheduling since the same answers will result.

Given that the answers to a goal are independent from literal selection, it is natural to ask if finite failure is also independent from the literal selection.

Example 4.6

Consider the program

```
p   :-   p.
```

and the goal p, 1 = 2. With left-to-right literal selection this goal has a single infinite derivation, in which p is repeatedly rewritten to itself. With right-to-left literal selection, however, the goal has a single failed derivation, so the goal finitely fails. The derivation trees are shown below.

$$\langle \underline{p}, 1 = 2 \mid true\rangle \qquad \langle p, \underline{1 = 2} \mid true\rangle$$
$$| \qquad\qquad\qquad |$$
$$\langle \underline{p}, 1 = 2 \mid true\rangle \qquad \langle \blacksquare \mid 1 = 2\rangle$$
$$|$$
$$\langle \underline{p}, 1 = 2 \mid true\rangle$$
$$|$$
$$\vdots$$

This example clearly shows that finite failure is not independent of literal selection. Another, more realistic example is the goal fac(2,3). It is easy to verify that this goal is finitely failed with left-to-right literal selection but not for right-to-left.

The reason independence does not hold for finite failure is that in an infinite derivation a literal which will cause failure may never be selected. We can overcome this problem if we require that literal selection is *fair* in the sense that every literal occurring in an infinite derivation is eventually selected. So long as selection is fair, finite failure is independent of literal selection.

Unfortunately, always selecting the leftmost literal is not fair. For example, in the left derivation above, the literal $1 = 2$ is never selected. Therefore, since most CLP systems do not use a fair literal selection strategy, the programmer has to consider the order of literals when reasoning about finite failure.

4.9 Summary

In this chapter we have introduced the constraint logic programming scheme. This provides a generic way of creating a constraint logic programming language given a constraint domain and a solver and simplifier for that domain. We have seen that constraint logic programs are made up of rules. These let the programmer define predicates which are simply user-defined constraints or relations. Multiple rules allow a predicate to have more than one possible definition. This allows the programmer to encode relations defined by cases or relations in which there is a choice of possible definitions. Rules may also be recursive, which provides the power of a true programming language.

Given a constraint logic program, a goal can be asked. Evaluation of the goal is via a derivation. A derivation collects primitive constraints into a constraint store and rewrites user-defined constraints using rules. The derivation stops when either the constraint store is detected by the solver to be false or all user-defined constraints have been eliminated. In the second case, we have discovered a successful derivation and, by applying a simplifier to the constraint store, we can determine an answer to the goal.

In general, because there may be a choice of rules with which to rewrite a user-defined constraint, there may be more than one derivation and answer. The different derivations for a goal are grouped together in the goal's derivation tree. We have seen that the CLP system evaluates a goal by searching the goal's derivation tree using a depth-first left-to-right traversal. Whenever an answer is discovered, the system returns this to the user. The user can then ask for further exploration of the tree. If there are no answers to the goal and the derivation tree is finite, evaluation is said to finitely fail and the system returns "no." We also introduced a concise representation for derivations and derivation trees in which the states are simplified and non-critical states are removed.

Finally we have demonstrated that the answers of a goal and program are independent of the order of literals in the goal and rule bodies. This means that goals and bodies can be reordered without changing their answers, a property we will make use of later when we investigate how to make CLP programs more efficient.

4.10 Exercises

4.1. What does the following program compute?

```
p(0,0).
p(X,(X*X)+Y)  :-  p(X-1,Y).
```

Give the derivation tree and simplified derivation tree for the goal p(2,Y).

4.2. For the constraint logic program

```
p(X, Y + X)   :-   X ≥ 1, p(X - 1, Y).
p(0, 0).


q(X, Y + X)   :-   X ≥ 1, Y ≥ 0, q(X - 1, Y).
q(0, 0).
```

(a) Show the derivation tree for the goal p(X, 3) to a depth where no more than four uses of the recursive rule are made on any derivation.

(b) Show the derivation tree for the goal q(X, 3) to depth 4 (that is, four recursive calls).

(c) Suppose the domain of the program P is now Boolean. That is to say, interpret 0 to be *false*, 1 to be *true*, + to be ∨, − to be ⊕ and $X \geq Y$ to be $\neg(X \rightarrow Y)$ (see Section 1.5.1). Determine the set of all answers to the goal p(X,Y).

4.3. The evaluation of a goal depends on the constraint solver used. Give the derivation tree for the goal p(X,Y) for the program

```
p(X,Y)    :-   X = Y + 2, Y ≥ 0, q(X,Y).


q(X,Y)    :-   X ≤ 1, r(X, Y).
q(X,Y)    :-   X ≤ 3, r(X, Y).


r(2,0).
r(X,2).
```

using

(a) a complete real solver;

(b) a solver that uses **gauss_jordan_solve** to handle equations, but ignores the inequalities; and

(c) a solver that uses **gauss_jordan_solve** to handle equations but collects the inequalities and only checks an inequality is satisfiable when all of its variables have fixed values determined by **gauss_jordan_solve**.

4.4. Using the program on page 151, give the derivation tree for the goals

(a) delete(cons(a,cons(b,nil)), X, R) and

(b) delete(cons(a,cons(b,nil)), b, L).

4.11   Practical Exercises

Almost all of the example programs in this chapter use only real arithmetic constraints. The $CLP(\mathcal{R})$ system can be used to execute these programs. The syntax for $CLP(\mathcal{R})$ programs is basically that of the example programs. To read in rules to the system, you must *consult* the files in which the rules are written. This can be done in three ways. The first is to use the $CLP(\mathcal{R})$ library function, `consult`, which takes as a single argument the name of the file to be read in. The second is to type the list of filenames at the $CLP(\mathcal{R})$ command line, remembering to end the line with a period. Finally, you can also consult files by including their names as command line arguments to the initial `clpr` command. By default the $CLP(\mathcal{R})$ system will add a ".clpr" suffix to each filename.

For example, imagine that we have used a text editor to write the factorial program:

```
fac(0,1).
fac(N, N * F)   :-  N >= 1, fac(N-1,F).
```

in the file `fac.clpr`. We can read these rules into our $CLP(\mathcal{R})$ session by doing the following.

```
$ clpr

CLP(R) Version 1.2

1 ?- consult(fac).

** Yes
```

We could also have done the following:

```
1 ?- [fac].

** Yes
```

Or, we could have simply typed

```
$ clpr fac
```

Once we have read rules into the $CLP(\mathcal{R})$ system, it is useful to be able to display them. The list commands `ls(P)` and `ls` can be used to do this. The command `ls` lists all of the rules while `ls(P)` lists the rules defining predicate P.

To evaluate a goal, we just type the goal at the $CLP(\mathcal{R})$ prompt, remembering to terminate the goal with a full stop (or period).

For instance, in the following session we read in the factorial program, list the rules in the definition of `fac` and run a simple goal.

```
1 ?- [fac].

*** Yes

2 ?- ls(fac).

fac(0, 1).
fac(N, N * F):-
    N >= 1,
    fac(N - 1, F).

** Yes

3 ?- fac(X,Y).

Y = 1
X = 0

** Retry? y

Y = 1
X = 1

** Retry? y

Y = 2
X = 2

** Retry? n
```

Note that $CLP(\mathcal{R})$ finds one answer at a time to the goal `fac(X,Y)`. If the entire derivation tree has not yet been explored, the user is asked if they want to "retry" the goal, that is, to find another answer to the goal. Answering "y" or ";" indicates the search should continue, while answering "n" or Enter/Return indicates the search should halt.

Once we have read our rules from a file, we may discover an error in our program and modify the program in the file. To *reconsult*, that is re-read, the changed file we need to use the library function `reconsult` which takes as a single argument the file to be re-read. Alternatively we can backquote the name of the file in the consult list.

For example imagine that we have modified the file `fib` and wish to reconsult the file. We can either use the $CLP(\mathcal{R})$ command `reconsult(fac)` or the command `['fac]`. Much more information about using $CLP(\mathcal{R})$ is given in the $CLP(\mathcal{R})$ Programmers Manual included in the $CLP(\mathcal{R})$ distribution.

SICStus Prolog can also be used to execute arithmetic constraint programs using the real arithmetic constraint solving libraries. The syntax for rules requires that all arithmetic constraints and terms occur within braces { and }. This requires considerable modification of the programs from how they are written in the text.

The factorial program above would be written in a text file (say `fac.pl`) as follows:

```
:- use_module(library(clpr)).
fac(N, F) :- {N = 0, F = 1}.
fac(N, F1)  :-  {F1 = N*F, N >= 1, N1 = N-1}, fac(N1,F).
```

The first line ensures that the constraint solver (using floating points) is loaded. The first rule is equivalent to `fac(0,1)` but since 0 and 1 are arithmetic constants they must appear between braces, so new equations must be introduced. The second line similarly introduces the new variables `F1` and `N1` to represent the expressions `N*F` and `N-1`, and all constraints are within braces.

We can read these rules into our SICStus Prolog session by doing the following. By default the suffix ".pl" is added to a filename.

```
$ sicstus

SICStus 3 #5:
| ?- consult(fac).
```

≪ lots of messages about loading ≫

```
yes
```

We could also have done the following:

```
| ?- [fac].
```

≪ lots of messages ≫

```
yes
```

The listing command `listing` lists all of the rules of the program. The command `listing(P)` lists all of the rules defining predicate symbol P.

Given the file `fac.pl` is defined as above, the following SICStus Prolog session is analogous to that given above for $CLP(\mathcal{R})$.

```
| ?- [fac].
```

≪ lots of messages about loading ≫

```
yes
```

```
| ?- listing(fac).

fac(A, B) :-
    {A=0,B=1}.
fac(A, B) :-
    {B=A*C,A>=1,D=A-1},
    fac(D, C).

yes
| ?- fac(X,Y).

X = 0.0
Y = 1.0 ? ;

X = 1.0
Y = 1.0 ? ;

X = 2.0
Y = 2.0 ? <Return/Enter>
```

In SICStus Prolog to reconsult a file we simply consult it as above. Much more information about using SICStus Prolog is given in the SICStus Prolog User's Manual.

Be warned that legitimate Prolog programs can result when the braces {} are not added around arithmetic constraints. This can result in strange behaviour. Using the file `fac.clpr` rather than `fac.pl` the following session results.

```
| ?- ['fac.clpr'].

yes
| ?- listing(fac).

fac(0, 1).
fac(A, A*B) :-
    A>=1,
    fac(A-1, B).

yes
| ?- fac(X,Y).

X = 0
Y = 1 ? ;
{INSTANTIATION ERROR: _33>=1 - arg 1}
```

The error occurs because the `>=` predicate has a different meaning depending on whether it occurs inside or outside the braces. Notice how the program actually managed to give the correct first answer!

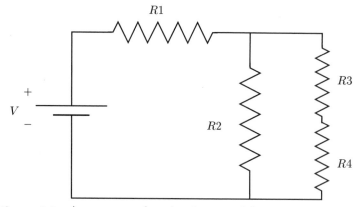

Figure 4.9   A more complex circuit to model.

P4.1. Write a rule describing the circuit shown in Figure 4.9. Use the program to find a set of available resistors and cells such that the total current is

(a) exactly 0.75 A,

(b) greater than 1.3 A.

P4.2. Write the program for computing factorial and use it to find all of the answers to the following goals:

(a) `fac(5,X)`.

(b) `fac(2,3)`.

(c) `fac(X,Y), X ≤ 3`.

Explain the behaviour of the last goal. What would have been a better way of writing it?

P4.3. Write rules defining a predicate `abs(X,A)` which holds if A is the absolute value of X.

P4.4. Write a rule defining the user-defined constraint `line(X,Y,G,C)` which holds if the point (X, Y) lies on a line with gradient G and which intercepts the y axis at C. Use your program to:

(a) Test whether the point $(2, 3)$ lies on the line $y = 4x + 2$.

(b) Find a line passing through the two points $(1, 2)$ and $(2, 4)$.

(c) Write a rule defining a predicate which determines the line passing between two points.

4.12   Notes

Constraint logic programming originated in the mid eighties as a combination of constraint programming and logic programming. It arose by generalising logic programming from tree constraints to other constraint domains. Jaffar *et al.* [70]

showed how the term equations of a logic programming system could be extended to equational constraints over arbitrary constraint domains, while maintaining the semantic results of logic programming. Colmerauer designed the first true constraint logic programming language PROLOG II [33], in which constraints were not only equations but, rather, were equations and *disequations* over rational trees. Jaffar and Stuckey [76] showed how the usual semantic results of logic programming could be obtained in the case of PROLOG II. Then Jaffar and Lassez [69] recognised that all these extensions were, in fact, *instances* of a more general scheme, the *constraint logic programming* scheme. It is from this paper that the term "constraint logic programming" originates.

Early work on constraint logic programming systems occurred independently at three locations: Colmerauer, at the Groupe d'Intelligence Artificielle in Marseilles, extended PROLOG II to PROLOG III [34, 35] which provided constraints over trees, strings, Booleans and real linear arithmetic; Jaffar *et al.* [74, 75], at Monash University, developed the language $CLP(\mathcal{R})$ which provided constraints over trees and real arithmetic; and Dincbas *et al.* [4], at ECRC, developed an extension to Prolog, called CHIP, which handled constraints over trees, finite domains, and finite ranges of integers.

Many good introductory articles and surveys of constraint logic programming are available. Cohen [32] gives a short introduction and an historical overview. Jaffar and Maher [71] give a more in-depth survey and include a wealth of references. The paper by Jaffar *et al.* [72] provides a good introduction to the semantics of constraint logic programs. In particular, it provides proofs for the various independence results concerning literal scheduling.

A large variety of problems have been solved successfully by using constraint logic programming languages over various constraint domains. Wallace [140] gives a number of examples of industrial applications of constraint logic programming. We now briefly discuss a few example applications.

The most significant industrial impact of constraint logic programming languages has been in solving management decision problems traditionally solved by operations research methods, for example cutting stock problems [42] and scheduling problems [43]. The book by Van Hentenryck [135] shows how a wide variety of problems can be solved in constraint logic programming over finite domains.

Another major application area has been electrical circuit analysis, synthesis and diagnosis [62, 56, 95, 118, 119]. There are also examples of problem solving in civil engineering [81]. Engineering applications tend to combine hierarchical composition of complex systems, mathematical or Boolean models, and—especially in the case of diagnosis and design—deep rule-based reasoning. Because of this, constraint logic programming has proved to be well suited for these problems.

Other areas of application include options trading [82, 66] and financial planning [10, 11, 19], where solutions often take the form of expert systems involving mathematical models. More exotic applications have included restriction site mapping in genetics [146] and generating test data for communications protocols [55].

5   Simple Modelling

In this chapter we investigate how to model simple constraint problems using a constraint logic programming language. Modelling is at the heart of constraint programming since it is by this process that the problem is specified in terms of constraints that can be handled by the underlying solver.

Novice CLP programmers often find their greatest difficulty is adjusting to the high level nature of CLP languages: the programmer can simply state the constraints and leave the constraint solving to the underlying system. This contrasts with traditional programming languages in which the programmer is responsible for solving the constraints and explicitly assigning values to all variables. The primary role of the constraint programmer is simply to model the problem, by translating the high level constraints of the problem to the lower level primitive constraints supported by the solver.

Clearly, before starting to model the problem, the programmer needs to know what are the primitive constraints available to them, since ultimately the problem must be described in terms of these primitives. In this and the following chapter we will employ an idealised CLP language, $CLP(\mathcal{R})$, which provides tree constraints as well as arithmetic constraints over the reals.

We shall now look at how to use $CLP(\mathcal{R})$ for modelling a variety of problems and explain the generic modelling techniques we have used. In the next chapter we will explore more complex modelling in which recursive data structures are used to create the constraints modelling the problem.

5.1   Simple Modelling

We have already seen examples of simple modelling in Chapters 1 and 3 in which a problem can be straightforwardly described by a conjunction of primitive constraints. Let us now discuss how such models can be developed.

The first step in modelling is to choose the variables that will be used to represent the parameters of the problem. In many cases this step is straightforward. In other cases there may be a number of different ways to define the problem and the choice may be crucial to the final performance of the model. We defer a discussion about different problem modelling until Section 8.4.

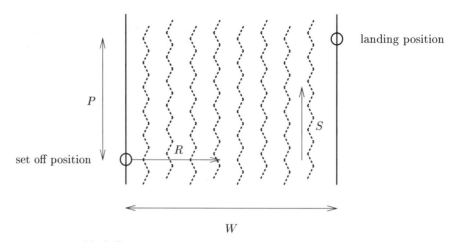

Figure 5.1   Modelling a river crossing.

For many problems, however, determining the variables of the problem is straightforward, and modelling is simply a matter of writing the constraints defining the problem in the right form.

Consider a traveller somewhere in the tropical rain forest of northern Australia. She wishes to paddle across a fast flowing river in an inflatable boat. It is important to cross the river as quickly as possible since it is full of crocodiles. There is a single small clearing on the other side of the river at which she must land. Where should she set off from her side of the river in order to reach the clearing in the least time?

We can refine this problem by observing that the quickest way to cross a river is to row directly across it, allowing the boat to drift downstream. The problem therefore becomes: how far upstream of this clearing should she set off from her side of the river?

What are the variables of the problem? Clearly the width, W, of the river is important as well as the speed, S, at which it flows. The rowing speed, R, of the traveller is also important and finally we need a variable, P, to represent the distance upstream—the desired answer. Let all measurements be in metres or metres/second. The problem with its variables is illustrated in Figure 5.1

When defining the constraints for the problem, we reason that in the time the traveller rows the width of the river, the boat floats downstream a distance given by the speed of flow by the time. We have discovered an auxiliary variable, T, the time to cross. We may not be interested in this variable but we need it to fully model the problem. Now we can write the constraints modelling the problem as a user-defined constraint `river(W, S, R, P)`. Note that, since we are not interested in the auxiliary variable T, it is not an argument of the user-defined constraint.

```
river(W, S, R, P) :- T = W/R, P = S*T.
```

We can use this model to answer the traveller's question. Suppose the traveller can row at 1.5 m/s and the river flows at speed 1 m/s and is 24 m wide. The goal:

```
S = 1, W = 24, R = 1.5, river(W, S, R, P).
```

gives the answer $P = 16 \wedge S = 1 \wedge W = 24 \wedge R = 1.5$ from which we can see the traveller needs to set off from 16 m upstream.

A feature of constraint programming is its flexibility. We can often use the same model of the problem to answer many different questions. Suppose the traveller is unsure of her precise rowing speed but knows it is somewhere between 1 and 1.3 m/s and that thick undergrowth on her side of the river prevents her setting off more than 20 m upstream. Can she make it? The goal

```
S = 1, W = 24, 1 ≤ R, R ≤ 1.3, P ≤ 20, river(W, S, R, P).
```

models this question. The reader is encouraged to determine if the intrepid traveller will survive the river crossing (see Exercise P5.1).

5.2 Modelling Choice

The underlying solver in a CLP language can only handle conjunctions of primitive constraints. However, problems often involve relationships which are not directly expressible as a conjunction of primitive constraints. Multiple rules in the definition of a predicate allow us to model these more complex relationships.

One form of information that cannot be expressed simply as a conjunction of primitive constraints are *relations*, that is to say tables of data. But by using multiple facts it is simple to represent a relation in a constraint logic program.

Consider a genealogical database describing a small family. The father(X, Y) relation holds when X is the father of Y. Similarly, the mother(X, Y) relation holds when X is the mother of Y. In addition, the relation age(X,Y) details the age Y of person X. The following program defines these relations for a not so fictional family (although the ages are fictional):

```
father(jim,edward).        mother(maggy,fi).      age(maggy,63).
father(jim,maggy).         mother(fi,lillian).    age(helen,37).
father(edward,peter).                             age(kitty,35).
father(edward,helen).                             age(fi,43).
father(edward,kitty).                             age(lillian,22).
father(bill,fi).                                  age(jim,85).
                                                  age(edward,60).
                                                  age(peter,33).
                                                  age(bill,65).
```

The goal `father(edward,X)` can be used to find the children of Edward. It gives the answers $X = peter$, $X = helen$ and $X = kitty$. Conversely, the goal `mother(X,fi)` can be used to find the mother of Fi. It has the answer $X = maggy$.

We can extend the simple program above by defining the predicates `parent`, `sibling`, `cousin` and `older` in terms of `father`, `mother` and `age`. The relation `parent(X,Y)` holds if X is a parent of Y, `sibling(X,Y)` holds if X and Y are siblings, `cousin(X,Y)` holds if X and Y are cousins and `older(X,Y)` holds if X is older than Y. They may be defined by:

```
parent(X,Y)    :-   father(X,Y).
parent(X,Y)    :-   mother(X,Y).
sibling(X,Y)   :-   parent(Z,X), parent(Z,Y), X ≠ Y.
cousin(X,Y)    :-   parent(Z,X), sibling(Z,T), parent(T,Y).
older(X,Y)     :-   AX ≥ AY, age(X,AX), age(Y,AY).
```

Notice how the `parent` predicate is defined with two rules. The first for the case the parent is the mother, the second for when the parent is the father.

For example the goal, `cousin(peter, X)`, has the single answer $X = fi$. We can also determine if Fi has a cousin who is older than she is using the goal

```
cousin(fi,Y), older(Y,fi).
```

This finitely fails, indicating that there are no older cousins.

Indeed, this example illustrates how constraint logic programs provide a powerful and high-level query language for databases. We shall return to this theme in Chapter 11.

Another more involved example is the interesting real life problem of modelling options trading. Options are contracts whose value depends upon the value of some underlying commodity such as company shares or frozen concentrated orange juice. We will concentrate on the two most common types of option: "call" and "put" options on company shares.

A *call* option gives the holder the right to buy a fixed number of shares for a fixed price, known as the *exercise* price. A *put* option gives the holder the right to sell a fixed number of shares for a fixed exercise price. Both call and put options have an expiry date, after which they cannot be used to buy or sell shares. Usually option contracts are for lots of 100 shares and like (almost) any other commodity may be bought or sold.

As an example, you might have had the good fortune to have bought for $200 a call option which gives you the right to buy 100 shares in a new software company, CLP Inc., at an exercise price of $300 with an expiry date of January 1st 2000. In order to understand the worth of this option consider the *pay off*, that is the profit or loss, associated with it as a function of the actual price of CLP Inc. shares on December 31st 1999. If share prices of CLP Inc. are only worth $2, then it is pointless to use the option, since you can buy 100 shares of CLP Inc. more cheaply without using it. Thus the pay off is a loss equal to the cost of purchasing the

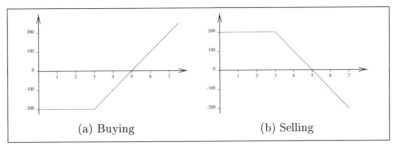

Figure 5.2 Payoff for a *call* option.

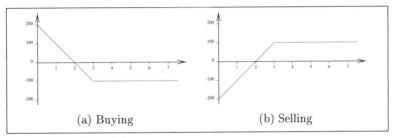

Figure 5.3 Payoff for a *put* option.

option, in other words −$200. However, if the company has done well and share prices have soared to $7, then you can use the option to buy 100 shares for $300 and immediately sell them for $700. After subtracting the cost of the option, the pay off is therefore $200 (being $700 − $300 − $200). Figure 5.2 (a) shows the graph of the pay off function for buying this call option.

We can also look at the cost of *selling* a call option. This is simply the negation of the cost of buying the call option. For instance, if Peter sold you the above call option and share prices were $2, then his pay off would be $200 since that is what you paid him for the option, and you have chosen not to use it. On the other hand, if share prices are $7, then he would make a loss of $200 since he made $200 from the original sale, but he must buy 100 shares for $700 and sell them to you for $300, giving a pay off of $200 + $300 − $700. Figure 5.2 (b) shows the pay off function for selling this call option.

We can also consider the pay off associated with a put option. Imagine that you have also bought a put option for $100 which gives you the right to sell 100 shares in CLP Inc. for $500. If the share price is $2, the pay off is $500 - $200 - $100 = $200. However, if share prices have risen to $7, the pay off is -$100, the initial purchase cost, since it is not worth using the option. The pay off for selling a put option is, of course, just the negation of the pay off for buying the option. Figure 5.3 shows the pay off functions for buying and selling this put option.

Options trading involves buying and selling complex combinations of options together with shares and bonds. Combining options allows traders to tailor their risk and return in almost arbitrary ways. For example, imagine that you believe

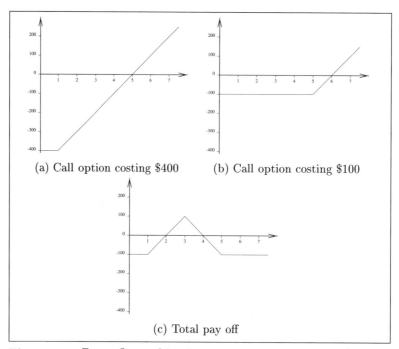

(a) Call option costing $400   (b) Call option costing $100

(c) Total pay off

Figure 5.4   Butterfly combination.

share prices for CLP Inc. will remain around $3. However, being a prudent options trader, you would like to ensure that if share prices for CLP Inc. do go dramatically up or down you do not lose too much money. This can be done by buying a call at a exercise cost greater than $300, say at $500, buying another call at an exercise cost less than $300, say at $100, and selling two calls for an exercise cost of $300. To understand this combination, called a *butterfly*, imagine that you bought the first call for $100, the second for $400 and sold each call for $200. The pay off for each of the calls bought is shown in Figure 5.4 (a) and (b), the pay off for each of the two calls sold is shown in Figure 5.2 (b), and the combination of all four options (obtained by summing them) is shown in Figure 5.4 (c). We can see that you will make money if share prices are between $2 and $4 and you can never lose more than $100.

In order to model such problems we need to model the pay off behaviour of an option. This is reasonably straightforward. The variables of interest are clear: C is the cost of the option, E is the exercise price, S is the share price, and P is the pay off of the option. We have chosen not to include the expiry date of the option since it does not influence the pay off until it is reached.

Each pay off function is a piecewise linear function. For instance, the function associated with buying the call option shown in Figure 5.2 (a) (where $C = 200$ and

$E = 300$) is

$$PayOff(S) = \begin{cases} -200, & \text{if } 0 \le S \le 3 \\ 100S - 500, & \text{if } S \ge 3. \end{cases}$$

More generally, the pay off for an arbitrary call option is given by the function which maps stock price S, cost C and exercise price E to pay off as follows:

$$PayOff(S, C, E) = \begin{cases} -C, & \text{if } 0 \le S \le E/100 \\ 100S - E - C, & \text{if } S \ge E/100. \end{cases}$$

This function is modelled by the user-defined constraint `buy_call_payoff(C,E,S,P)` defined below, where P is the pay off and S, C, E are defined as above.

```
buy_call_payoff(S, C, E, P) :- 0 ≤ S, S ≤ E / 100, P = -C.
buy_call_payoff(S, C, E, P) :- S ≥ E / 100, P = 100 * S - E - C.
```

Notice how each of the two cases in the function definition is modelled by a different rule. Together they completely define the behaviour of the pay off function. This exemplifies a standard modelling technique for representing a function by a constraint logic program. The idea is to model a function f taking n arguments by a predicate with $n+1$ arguments in which the last argument to the predicate is the value of the function.

If a call option is sold, the pay off function is simply $-PayOff(S, C, E)$. Because the relationship between buying and selling an option is so simple, we can model both possibilities simply through a parameter, B, which multiplies the pay off for buying the option by either 1 or -1.

The user-defined constraint, `call_option(B,C,E,S,P)`, models the profit for buying or selling a call option, where S, C, E, and P are as above and B is a parameter set to 1 if the call option is bought, and set to -1 if it is sold.

```
call_option(B,S,C,E,P) :- 0 ≤ S, S ≤ E / 100, P = -C * B.
call_option(B,S,C,E,P) :- S ≥ E / 100, P = (100 * S - E - C) * B.
```

Similarly, we can model a put option by means of the user-defined constraint, `put_option(B,S,C,E,P)` defined below. Again S is the current share price, C is the cost of the put option, E the exercise price, P is the pay off and B is a flag set to 1 if the put option is bought, and sent to -1 if it is sold.

```
put_option(B,S,C,E,P) :- 0 ≤ S, S ≤ E/100, P = (E - 100 * S - C) * B.
put_option(B,S,C,E,P) :- S ≥ E / 100, P = - C * B.
```

For instance, if we want to know the value of the call option shown in Figure 5.2 (a) when share prices are \$7, we simply evaluate the goal,

```
call_option(1, 7, 200, 300, P).
```

which gives the answer $P = \$200$.

We can also ask more interesting questions. For example, the following program models the collection of options in the "butterfly" shown earlier in Figure 5.4.

```
butterfly(S, P1 + 2*P2 + P3) :-
    Buy = 1, Sell = -1,
    call_option(Buy, S, 100, 500, P1),
    call_option(Sell, S, 200, 300, P2),
    call_option(Buy, S, 400, 100, P3).
```

A natural question to ask is: "For what values of the share price will we make a profit?" This is simply couched as the goal

$$P \geq 0, \texttt{butterfly(S,P)}.$$

The first answer found is $P = 100S - 200 \wedge 2 \leq S \wedge S \leq 3$, indicating that if S is between 2 and 3 we make a profit. If we ask the system to find another answer, we obtain $P = -100S + 400 \wedge 3 \leq S \wedge S \leq 4$, indicating that we also make a profit if S is between 3 and 4. If we ask for another answer, the system says no, indicating these are the only values of S which give a profit.

At this point the reader might want to think about how they would write a program in a traditional language to answer this query. It would not be very easy, and would certainly require more than a few lines of code. Nor could we perform this type of reasoning using a spreadsheet, since it requires a symbolic reasoning.

As can be seen even from this simple example, options trading is a rather complex matter and sophisticated mathematical modelling is required to make money out of it. CLP languages are ideal for this sort of modelling. This is because complex trading strategies, usually formulated as rules, require a combination of symbolic and numerical calculation. There is a need to search through the different ways of combining options, together with the use of well developed mathematical models for describing option behaviour. It is also important to have a flexible powerful language for such modelling so as to allow the investigation of hypothetical or "what-if" scenarios.

5.3   Iteration

Sometimes the most natural way of modelling a constraint problem is to use iteration over some parameter of the problem in order to guide the number and form of the primitive constraints in the model. For example, if we have N warehouses in a warehouse allocation problem, we may want to iterate from 1 to N and, at each stage, add the primitive constraints modelling the ith warehouse. The parameter i is used to control an iterative loop for collecting the constraints.

CLP languages do not directly provide iteration constructs, such as **for** or **while** loops, provided in more traditional languages. Instead iteration is programmed using recursive rules. We have already used such programming in the factorial program introduced in Section 4.2, in which we used a recursive rule to iterate over the number we wish to find the factorial of.

A program to compute mortgage repayments provides a more interesting example of the use of recursive rules. We wish to model the `mortgage` constraint that holds between the following parameters: P the principal or amount owed, T the number of periods in the mortgage, I the interest rate of the mortgage, R the repayment due each period of the mortgage and B the balance owing at the end.

For a single period mortgage the relationship is easy to write,

$$B = P + P \times I - R.$$

That is, the balance is given by the principal plus the interest on the principal minus the repayment. For a loan of three periods the relationship is also easy to write,

$$P_1 = P + P \times I - R \; \wedge$$
$$P_2 = P_1 + P_1 \times I - R \; \wedge$$
$$P_3 = P_2 + P_2 \times I - R \; \wedge$$
$$B = P_3.$$

The relationships between the principal after i periods, P_i, and the principal after $i+1$ periods, P_{i+1}, is straightforward. But how can we write a program that will, in effect, build these constraints for an arbitrary value of the parameter T?

The direct approach is to reason about the `mortgage` constraint recursively. Let us consider the relationship between the parameters P, T, I, R, and B. When the number of periods in the loan is 0 the relationship is easy. The balance B is just the principal P. Now consider mortgages of one or more periods. The key step is to see that a mortgage of $T \geq 1$ periods can be viewed in the following terms. In the first period the new amount owing is obtained by adding the interest (principal by interest rate) and then subtracting the repayment from the amount currently owing. The remaining periods simply form another mortgage for the new amount owing but for one less period.

This leads us to the program below where there is one rule for the case where $T = 0$ and another rule for where $T \geq 1$. The program is simple and concise:

```
mortgage(P,T,I,R,B) :-                    (M1)
    T = 0,
    B = P.
mortgage(P,T,I,R,B) :-                    (M2)
    T ≥ 1,
    NP = P + P * I - R,
    NT = T - 1,
    mortgage(NP,NT,I,R,B).
```

The (partially simplified) successful derivation for the goal `mortgage(P,3,I,R,B)` is:

$$\langle mortgage(P, 3, I, R, B) \mid true \rangle$$

$$\Downarrow M2$$

$$\langle mortgage(P_1, 2, I, R, B) \mid P_1 = P + P \times I - R \rangle$$

$$\Downarrow M2$$

$$\langle mortgage(P_2, 1, I, R, B) \mid P_1 = P + P \times I - R \wedge P_2 = P_1 + P_1 \times I - R \rangle$$

$$\Downarrow M2$$

$$\langle mortgage(P_3, 0, I, R, B) \mid \begin{array}{l} P_1 = P + P \times I - R \wedge P_2 = P_1 + P_1 \times I - R \wedge \\ P_3 = P_2 + P_2 \times I - R \end{array} \rangle$$

$$\Downarrow M1$$

$$\langle \Box \mid \begin{array}{l} P_1 = P + P \times I - R \wedge P_2 = P_1 + P_1 \times I - R \wedge \\ P_3 = P_2 + P_2 \times I - R \wedge B = P_3 \end{array} \rangle$$

Clearly it collects the constraints we desire. No other successful derivation is possible because of the constraints on T. In effect T is a variable controlling the number of times a copy of the constraint for a single period is added to the constraint store.

Describing a mortgage as a recursive relationship may be difficult for many readers. A trick which is sometimes useful for novice CLP programmers is to think about writing a procedure in a traditional language to compute one parameter given all of the other parameters. Given this procedural definition, we first remove all direct iteration constructs and replace them by recursive calls. Finally, we "translate" the tests and assignments into constraints, and obtain a constraint logic program which models the problem.

For instance, in this case imagine we compute the balance in terms of the other parameters. Given we know everything but the balance we can reason as follows. For each time period in the mortgage we recompute the amount owed by adding to the current amount owed the interest which is interest rate multiplied by the current amount owed and subtracting the repayment. After the last time period the amount owed is the balance. A pseudo-C function which returns the balance looks something like

```
float mortgage1(float P, int T, float I, float R)
{
    while ( T >= 1) {
        P = P + P * I - R;
        T = T - 1;
    }
    return P;
}
```

We first remove the **while** loop from this program to give the following recursive pseudo-C procedure:

```
float mortgage2(float P, int T, float I, float R)
{
    if (T >= 1) {
        P = P + P * I - R;
        T = T - 1;
        return mortgage2(P, T, I, R); }
    else
        return P;
}
```

To move from this procedural specification to a constraint program we need to be aware that *variables* in procedural languages can take multiple values over the course of computation. This is not true of constraint variables. For instance, the constraint $T = T - 1$ is simply equivalent to $false$. So a C statement such as

$$P = P + P * I - R$$

is actually relating two variables (as we have seen before), the principal before a time period, and the principal after. Therefore, in a constraint program we need to represent this using two distinct variables. We thus modify our program to

```
float mortgage3(float P, int T, float I, float R)
{
    if (T >= 1) {
        NP = P + P * I - R;
        NT = T - 1;
        return mortgage3(NP, NT, I, R); }
    else
        return P;
}
```

Finally, predicates as used in constraint logic programs do not return numbers. Instead of returning the answer using a function, we must modify the program so that the balance is passed by reference, and the procedure sets the balance rather than returning its value. We thus modify our program to

```
mortgage3(float P, int T, float I, float R, float *B)
{
    if (T >= 1) {
        NP = P + P * I - R;
        NT = T - 1;
        mortgage3(NP, NT, I, R, B); }
    else
        *B = P;
}
```

We can now translate this to CLP giving the `mortgage` program

```
mortgage(P,T,I,R,B)    :-   T ≥ 1,
                            NP = P + P * I - R,
                            NT = T - 1,
                            mortgage(NP,NT,I,R,B).
mortgage(P,T,I,R,B)    :-   T = 0, B = P.
```

Note that we have translated the **if** (C) S_1 **else** S_2 statement into two rules—one for the **if** branch and one for the **else** branch. When doing so we must be careful to add the branching condition C to the rule representing the **if** branch and the negation of the branching condition to the rule representing the **else** branch. Note that in this case the negation of the branching condition is actually $T < 1$. However, given our implicit assumption that T is a non-negative integer, this is equivalent to $T = 0$.

The program we arrived at has the rules in the opposite order to the original CLP program. This will modify the order of branches in the search tree. We discuss why the program should be written in the original way in Section 7.3.

At this point it is worthwhile comparing the CLP and the pseudo-C programs. All are simple and concise and all compute the remaining balance from the other parameters with roughly the same efficiency. However, the CLP program for computing mortgage repayments is considerably more versatile than the versions written in pseudo-C. This is because the CLP program states constraints between the arithmetic variables, rather than specifying assignments to the variables. Thus it can be used to compute a number of different functions.

For instance, given the interest rate is 10% and we can repay \$150 per year we may wish to find out how much can be borrowed in a 3 year loan so that we owe nothing at the end. This question is expressed by the goal

```
    mortgage(P, 3, 10/100, 150, 0).
```

The simplified successful derivation is

$$\langle mortgage(P, 3, 10/100, 150, 0) \,|\, true \rangle$$
$$\Downarrow M2$$
$$\langle mortgage(P_1, 2, 10/100, 150, 0) \,|\, P_1 = 1.1 * P - 150 \rangle$$
$$\Downarrow M2$$
$$\langle mortgage(P_2, 1, 10/100, 150, 0) \,|\, P_2 = 1.21 * P - 315 \rangle$$
$$\Downarrow M2$$
$$\langle mortgage(P_3, 0, 10/100, 150, 0) \,|\, P_3 = 1.331 * P - 496.5 \rangle$$
$$\Downarrow M1$$
$$\langle \square \,|\, P = 373.028 \rangle$$

This has answer $P = 373.028$.

A more complex query is to ask for the relationship between the initial principal, repayment and balance in a 10 month loan at 10%. This is done with the goal:

```
mortgage(P, 10, 10/100, R, B).
```

The answer is a constraint relating the variables P, R and B. It is

$$P = 0.385543 * B + 6.14457 * R.$$

Writing a C program to answer this query would not be straightforward.

5.4 Optimization

All of the examples we have seen so far model satisfaction problems. That is, they model problems in which we are interested in finding if there is a solution to the problem and, if so, returning one. However, in many problems we are interested in finding the "best" solution to a problem. This can be couched as an optimization problem. Suppose we are given a function which evaluates the merit of a particular solution by returning a real value. By convention, the lower the value the better the solution is. In an optimization problem we wish to find the answer to a goal which minimizes the value of this function.

Most CLP systems provide the capacity for finding the minimal or maximal solutions to a goal. Unfortunately, there is, as yet, no clear acceptance of the precise syntax and behaviour of these built-ins. In this book we will use the notation $minimize(G, E)$.

Definition 5.1
A *minimization literal* is of the form $minimize(G, E)$ where G is a goal and E is an arithmetic expression. The answers to the literal $minimize(G, E)$ are the answers to goal G which minimize the expression E.

As an example of its use, consider the program

```
p(X,Y)   :-   X=1.
p(X,Y)   :-   Y=1.
```

and the goal

```
    X ≥ 0, Y ≥ 0, minimize(p(X,Y), X+Y).
```

Evaluation will return the answers $X = 1 \land Y = 0$ and $X = 0 \land Y = 1$.

A minimization literal need not return an assignment to all variables in the minimization expression. For instance, the goal

```
    X ≥ 0, X ≥ Y, minimize(true, X-Y)
```

has the answer $X \geq 0 \land X = Y$.

As a slightly more realistic example, consider the options trading example from

Section 5.2. The following goal can be used to find the maximum profit possible for the butterfly combination:

```
minimize( butterfly(S,P), -P).
```

This will return the answer $S = 3 \wedge P = 100$ indicating that the maximum profit is \$100.

A precise definition of the operational behaviour of optimization built-ins is quite complex. The definition for $minimize(G, E)$ is, unfortunately, no exception.

Definition 5.2

A valuation θ is a *solution* of a state or goal if it is a solution of some answer to the state or goal.

We extend the definition of a derivation step from $\langle G_1 \mid C_1 \rangle$ to $\langle G_2 \mid C_2 \rangle$ by allowing a *minimization derivation step* in which a minimization subgoal is rewritten. Let G_1 be of the form

$$L_1, L_2, \ldots, L_m$$

where L_1 is $minimize(G, E)$. There are two cases.

1. There is at least one solution ϕ of $\langle G \mid C_1 \rangle$ with $\phi(E) = m$, and for all other solutions θ of $\langle G \mid C_1 \rangle$, $m \le \theta(E)$. Then C_2 is $C_1 \wedge E = m$ and G_2 is $G, L_2, \ldots, L_m$.

2. If evaluation can detect that $\langle G \mid C_1 \rangle$ has no solutions or has an unbounded minimum, then C_2 is *false* and G_2 is the empty goal.

This definition captures the following intuition. Suppose we encounter a minimization goal $minimize(G, E)$ when the current constraint is C_1. We first find the minimum value m that E can take in any answer to the state $\langle G \mid C_1 \rangle$. Now the answers to $minimize(G, E)$ are simply the answers to the state $\langle G \mid C_1 \wedge E = m \rangle$, that is to say, the answers to G in which E takes the minimum value m.

If $\langle G \mid C_1 \rangle$ has a finite derivation tree and has no minimal solutions, either because $\langle G \mid C_1 \rangle$ finitely fails or because it has an unbounded minimum, then the original state is rewritten to a fail state. Be warned that if $\langle G \mid C_1 \rangle$ has an infinite derivation tree, evaluation of the minimization literal may not terminate.

Optimization need not be used only in the goal. We can also use it in rules, allowing us to define more complex user-defined constraints.

A *straddle* option involves buying a call and a put option at the same exercise price. Its behaviour can be modelled as

```
straddle(S, C, E, P)   :-   Buy = 1, C = C1 + C2, P = P1 + P2,
                            call_option(Buy, S, C1, E, P1),
                            put_option(Buy, S, C2, E, P2).
```

The following rule defines the best profit that can be made from a straddle.

```
best_straddle(C, E, P) :- minimize(straddle(S, C, E, P), -P).
```

5.5 Summary

Modelling in a CLP language is quite different to programming in a traditional programming language and requires an ability to reason about a problem in terms of constraints. At first, this may seem both difficult and unintuitive. However, because the resulting program uses constraints rather than Boolean tests and assignments, it is considerably more flexible than a program written in a conventional language, and may be used to answer a wide variety of questions.

We have seen how predicates with multiple rule definitions allow us to model choice, conditional statements and fixed tables of data (that is, relations). Recursion allows us to model more complex problems in which the number of constraints and their form depends on the input parameters of the problem. Thus recursion provides the functionality of the more standard iteration constructs of traditional programming languages. For the novice programmer, recursion is often the largest stumbling block. Knowledge of a functional language may help, but the best way to learn is by programming.

With experience, a constraint programmer is able to immediately define their problem in constraint terms. The most important words of advice are—practice, practice, and then practice some more.

5.6 Practical Exercises

Unfortunately, the $CLP(\mathcal{R})$ system does not provide any minimization constructs, while both SICStus Prolog and ECLiPSe provide minimization but only for finite domain constraints. Therefore, none of the examples of minimization given in this chapter are directly executable. The use of minimization in both SICStus Prolog and ECLiPSe requires minimization literals minimize(G, E) to be used in such a way that any answer to the goal G fixes E to a particular value. Only one minimal answer is returned. In Chapter 9 we show how to implement minimization as defined in this chapter using the library functions of these languages.

P5.1. Try the goal corresponding to the second question about crossing the river in Section 5.1. Can you explain the answer? Note that the faster the rowing speed of the traveller the better the chance of crossing the river. Can you give a different goal which can give a useful answer to the second question?

P5.2. Actually in the wet season there are no crocodiles and the traveller does not need to travel directly across the river. She may set out at an angle θ to the direction straight across (this could be negative if she sets off heading downstream). This is illustrated in Figure 5.5. Give a model of the river crossing constraint which takes into account this new freedom. Using this model, determine how wide the river must be if she rows at 1.5 m/s at an angle of $\pi/6$ upstream, the river flows at 1 m/s and she lands 20 m downstream from the setting off point.

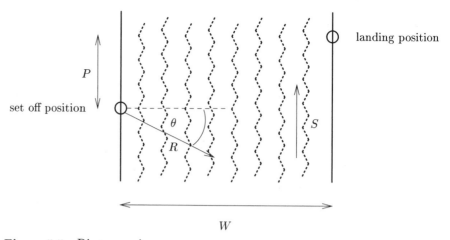

Figure 5.5   River crossing.

P5.3. A spring with force constant k exerts a force of kx if compressed by distance x. It exerts no force if it is not compressed. Write a program defining the relationship between a force constant, compression distance and exerted force for a spring.

A spring holder is shown in Figure 5.6 where the length of the springs are $L1$ and $L2$ and the width of the spring holder is L. Given that the spring constants are $K1$ and $K2$ respectively, define a predicate `stable` so that the user-defined constraint `stable(L, L1, K1, L2, K2, W, X)` holds when X is any distance from the left wall of the placement of the left hand side of an object of width W so that the object will be stable, that is, the force on it from both springs will be the same.

Find where an object of width 10 cm will be stable if the left spring is 10 cm long and has spring constant 1 N/cm and the right spring is 6 cm long and has spring constant 2 N/cm, assuming the gap is 20 cm wide. Find where an object of width 2 cm will be stable, in the same circumstances.

P5.4. A butterfly combination of options involves a call of cost $C1$ at exercise price $E1$, and another call of cost $C3$ at a higher exercise price $E3$, as well as selling two calls for $C2$ each at exercise price $E2$ between the other two exercise prices. A butterfly combination is only sensible if it can make a profit. Write a program to determine which butterfly combinations are sensible. Test the following combinations:

  (a) $C1 = 100 \wedge E1 = 4 \wedge C2 = 200 \wedge E2 = 6 \wedge C3 = 300 \wedge E3 = 8$,
  (b) $C1 = 100 \wedge E1 = 3 \wedge C2 = 200 \wedge E2 = 7 \wedge C3 = 300 \wedge E3 = 8$,
  (c) $C1 = 100 \wedge E1 = 1 \wedge C2 = 300 \wedge E2 = 5 \wedge C3 = 100 \wedge E3 = 6$.

P5.5. Write a predicate using `minimize` to determine the maximum loss for a butterfly combination defined as in the previous question. Find the maximum loss for each of the combinations in the previous question.

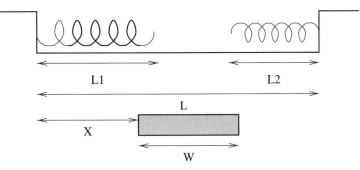

Figure 5.6   A spring holder.

P5.6. Write rules which define the following family relationships:

  (a) X is a grandparent of Y,

  (b) X is an uncle of Y.

P5.7. The relation `flight(S,E,D)` details the flights from a start city S to an end city E with distance D.

```
flight(melbourne, sydney, 1000).
flight(melbourne, perth, 4000).
flight(perth, singapore, 5000).
flight(sydney, singapore, 8500).
flight(melbourne, cairns, 4000).
flight(sydney, cairns, 3200).
flight(cairns, singapore, 4900).
flight(singapore, london, 10000).
flight(perth, bahrain, 8000).
flight(bahrain, london, 6500).
```

Write a program defining the predicate `path(S, E, D)` which gives the distance D travelled from start city S to end city E using the flights described above. For example, given the goal

```
path(melbourne, singapore, D).
```

it should return answers $D = 9500$, $D = 9000$ and $D = 9900$ corresponding to flying via Sydney, Perth or Cairns respectively.

P5.8. Write a predicate `shortest_path(S, E, D)`, using `minimize`, that finds the shortest possible distance D that can be covered travelling from start city S to end city E using the flights described in Exercise P5.7.

P5.9. On the first day of Christmas, traditionally one gives one's true love one object, on the second day $1 + 2$ objects, on the third day $1 + 2 + 3$ objects. Write a program to define the predicate `gifts(N, T)` where T is the total number of gifts given in the first N days of Christmas.

P5.10. In the drinking game **CLP** one must drink one glass every time a number is reached which is divisible by 7 or divisible by 5, unless the previous drink was taken less than 8 numbers ago.

Write a predicate `divides(N,D)` which holds if D exactly divides N assuming both are positive integers. (Note this is trivial with integer arithmetic constraints, but not so for reals).

Write a predicate `drinks(N, C)` that counts the number of drinks C that are taken in counting from 1 to N.

5.7   Notes

Modelling of real-world problems using constraints is not a new activity. Mathematicians have been doing this since the very beginning of mathematics. Any introductory operations research text discusses modelling using arithmetic constraints.

The programming language $CLP(\mathcal{R})$ used in this chapter is essentially the CLP language developed by Jaffar and his students. One of the first CLP languages, it was introduced in [61, 69] and is described more fully in [75].

Using facts to represent tables and simple rules for querying these tables is a well-known programming technique from the logic programming community, where it is called (for obvious reasons) "database programming." For further examples, the reader is referred to any introduction to Prolog, for instance [125]. The relationship between CLP and databases will be explored more fully in Chapter 11.

The options trading modelling example is based on work of Lassez *et al* [82] who have developed a sophisticated expert system in $CLP(\mathcal{R})$ for reasoning about options trading. The example programs given here merely provide a brief introduction to the way the expert system works. Their system is considerably more powerful and employs nonlinear numerical modelling as well as rules modelling the strategies of option traders.

Translating iteration into recursion is a well known method for writing iterative programs in either logic or functional programming languages. The program for computing mortgage repayments is taken from [61].

Minimization primitives were first included in the constraint logic programming language CHIP [4]. Although we give only one minimization primitive, usually a number are provided by a CLP system which correspond to different implementations of the minimization search. Unfortunately, most implemented minimization primitives do not agree with the definition given here since they will only ever return a single answer. For more about this see the discussion in Chapter 10.

6   Using Data Structures

In the last chapter we investigated ways in which to model constraint problems in a constraint logic programming language. In this chapter we continue our investigation by examining how tree constraints can be used to provide data structures which allow the programmer to model more complex problems. Problems such as analysis and design of circuits or tree layout in which traversal of a (usually recursive) data structure is necessary to construct the constraints of the particular problem instance.

Example 6.1

Finite element modelling is a common technique used to approximate a continuous object by a grid of discrete points. As long as the points are sufficiently close together, they provide a good model for the original object. For instance, we can model the temperatures on a rectangular sheet of metal by using an $n \times m$ grid which details the temperature of the plate at each of the points on the grid. Such a finite element model allows us to approximate what happens in the actual sheet of metal. If the temperature of the sheet is in a steady-state, the temperature at every interior point on the sheet of metal is equal to the average of its four orthogonal neighbour points. Given information about the temperature of each point on the boundary of the plate, all of the (approximate) steady-state temperatures at the interior points can be determined.

We can model a particular instance of this problem quite simply using only arithmetic equations. For example, for a 3×4 grid with variables corresponding to the positions shown below:

$$
\begin{array}{cccc}
T11 & T12 & T13 & T14 \\
T21 & T22 & T23 & T24 \\
T31 & T32 & T33 & T34
\end{array}
$$

The steady state temperature constraints are simply

$$T22 = (T12 + T21 + T23 + T32)/4 \wedge T23 = (T13 + T22 + T24 + T33)/4.$$

However, generating these arithmetic equations by hand for larger grids, such as the 6×7 grid shown in Figure 6.1, is tedious and error prone. The key question is how can we build a program which allows us to model a plate using a grid of arbitrary size? In order to do so, we must be able to represent an arbitrary sized grid of variables and build a program which iterates over this grid to set up the

T = 100C

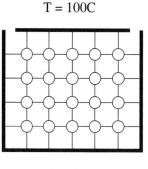

T = 0C

Figure 6.1   A 6×7 finite element description of a metal plate.

primitive constraints. In this chapter we shall investigate how to do this.

We will discover that tree constraints give us the ability to build and access data structures in a simple manner. Terms can be used to succinctly define almost all data structures that a user may require. Including, for example, records, lists, trees and stacks. In particular, seemingly complex recursive data structures are easy to define and program with. Because of the importance of data structures, almost all CLP languages provide tree constraints, and so the programming techniques discussed in this chapter are important tools in the constraint programmer's work box.

6.1   Records

The simplest type of data structure is the record. This simply packages together a fixed number of items of information, usually of a different type. We saw examples of how to use tree constraints to define record data structures in Section 1.4.

As an example, consider how we might represent complex numbers. A complex number $X + iY$ can be considered as an ordered pair of numbers, X and Y. This is easily represented using a term $c(X, Y)$ where c is a binary tree constructor. This is analogous to defining a record whose first field is the real component and whose second field is the imaginary component of the complex number.

Using this representation we can simply define predicates, c_add and c_mult, to perform addition and multiplication of complex numbers respectively.

```
c_add(c(R1,I1),c(R2,I2),c(R3,I3)) :-
     R3 = R1 + R2, I3 = I1 + I2.
c_mult(c(R1,I1),c(R2,I2),c(R3,I3)) :-
     R3 = R1*R2 - I1*I2, I3 = R1*I2 + R2*I1.
```

$$\langle C1 = c(1,3), C2 = c(2,Y), c\_add(C1, C2, C3) \mid true \rangle$$
$$\Downarrow$$
$$\langle C2 = c(2,Y), c\_add(C1, C2, C3) \mid C1 = c(1,3) \rangle$$
$$\Downarrow$$
$$\langle c\_add(C1, C2, C3) \mid C1 = c(1,3) \wedge C2 = c(2,Y) \rangle$$
$$\Downarrow$$
$$\langle C1 = c(R1, I1), C2 = c(R2, I2), C3 = c(R3, I3), R3 = R1 + R2, I3 = I1 + I2 \mid$$
$$C1 = c(1,3) \wedge C2 = c(2,Y) \rangle$$
$$\Downarrow$$
$$\langle C2 = c(R2, I2), C3 = c(R3, I3), R3 = R1 + R2, I3 = I1 + I2 \mid$$
$$C1 = c(1,3) \wedge C2 = c(2,Y) \wedge R1 = 1 \wedge I1 = 3 \rangle$$
$$\Downarrow$$
$$\langle C3 = c(R3, I3), R3 = R1 + R2, I3 = I1 + I2 \mid$$
$$C1 = c(1,3) \wedge C2 = c(2,Y) \wedge R1 = 1 \wedge I1 = 3 \wedge R2 = 2 \wedge I2 = Y \rangle$$
$$\Downarrow$$
$$\langle R3 = R1 + R2, I3 = I1 + I2 \mid C1 = c(1,3) \wedge C2 = c(2,Y) \wedge R1 = 1 \wedge$$
$$I1 = 3 \wedge R2 = 2 \wedge I2 = Y \wedge C3 = c(R3, I3) \rangle$$
$$\Downarrow$$
$$\langle I3 = I1 + I2 \mid C1 = c(1,3) \wedge C2 = c(2,Y) \wedge R1 = 1 \wedge$$
$$I1 = 3 \wedge R2 = 2 \wedge I2 = Y \wedge C3 = c(3, I3) \wedge R3 = 3 \rangle$$
$$\Downarrow$$
$$\langle \Box \mid C1 = c(1,3) \wedge C2 = c(2,Y) \wedge R1 = 1 \wedge$$
$$I1 = 3 \wedge R2 = 2 \wedge I2 = Y \wedge C3 = c(3, 3 + Y) \wedge R3 = 3 \wedge I3 = 3 + Y \rangle$$

Figure 6.2   Derivation for a complex addition goal.

Let us examine how the predicate for addition works by using it to add the complex numbers $1 + 3i$ and $2 + Yi$ where Y is unknown. This is achieved by evaluating the goal

```
C1 = c(1,3), C2 = c(2, Y), c_add(C1, C2, C3).
```

The derivation is shown in Figure 6.2, where the constraint store is shown in solved form.

Initally, the derivation adds $C1 = c(1,3)$ and $C2 = c(2,Y)$ to the constraint store, effectively constructing the parameters for the call to c_add. Now the call to c_add is evaluated.

The equation $C1 = c(R1, I1)$ has the effect of setting $R1$ to 1 and $I1$ to 3 since the equation $C1 = c(1,3)$ is in the constraint store. Similarly, the equation $C2 = c(R2, I2)$ sets $R2$ to 2 and forces $I2$ to take the same value as Y since the equation $C2 = c(2,Y)$ is in the store. Thus, these two equations which are implicit in the head of the rule are used to access the data in the record.

The third equation, $C3 = c(R3, I3)$, in effect builds the term $c(R3, I3)$. Evaluation of the equation $R3 = R1 + R2$ effectively sets $R3$ (or equivalently the first element of the record $C3$) to 3, and finally the equation $I3 = I1 + I2$ sets $I3$ to $3 + Y$. Thus, these equations are used to build a new record representing the result of the addition.

Simplifying the final constraint in terms of Y and $C3$ we see the resulting relationship clearly: $C3 = c(3, 3 + Y)$.

In general, programming with records requires us to use term equations both to access data in the record and to build a new record. If $T1$ and $T2$ are items, we can use the equation $R = c(T1, T2)$ to construct a new record R containing these items. Conversely, the same equation allows us to access the items in the record if R is fixed. Of course, as we have seen in the above example, not all information in a record needs to be fixed since records can contain variables as well as fixed data.

CLP languages also provide a feature which simplifies access to items in a record. An unnamed variable, written as an underscore "_", sometimes called an *anonymous variable* can be used as a place holder for items in the record which we are not interested in. Rather than having to give a name to a variable we do not wish to refer to again, CLP languages allow this special notation. The underscore is understood to be a variable with a different name from all other variables. It is important to realise that each occurrence of an underscore denotes a distinct new variable. For instance, we can use the constraint $R = c(T1, \_)$ to ensure that the variable $T1$ refers to the first item in R. Similarly, we can access the second item using the constraint $R = c(\_, T2)$.

6.2   Lists

Records allow us to group a fixed number of objects together. The standard data structure in CLP languages for collecting a variable number of similar objects is the list. Since lists are such an important data structure, CLP languages provide a special notation for dealing with them concisely. In the examples of Section 1.4 we used the tree constructors *cons* and *nil*. However, rather than use *cons* as the list constructor and *nil* to represent an empty list, CLP languages use "." as the list constructor and "[]" to represent an empty list. Note that "." is treated like any other binary tree constructor.

Special notation is also available to represent both lists and partially constructed lists. The expression $[X_1, X_2, \ldots, X_n]$ represents a fixed size list containing the n elements $X_1, \ldots, X_n$ while $[X_1, X_2, \ldots, X_n | Y]$ represents a list whose first n elements are $X_1, \ldots, X_n$ and whose remaining elements form the list Y. The various notations are summarized in Figure 6.3.

There are two standard equations for manipulating lists. The first equation, $L = [\,]$, constrains L to be an empty list. The second equation, $L = [F|R]$, constrains L to be a non-empty list with F as the first element and R the list of remaining elements. This equation can be used to break a list L into its first element F and remainder R, or to construct a list L from an element F and a list R. From the constraint viewpoint, these actions are equivalent.

Notation	Term with "."	Representation with *cons/nil*
[]	[]	*nil*
$[X\|Y]$	$X.Y$	$cons(X, Y)$
$[X_1, X_2, \ldots, X_n]$	$X_1.X_2.\cdots.X_n.[]$	$cons(X_1, cons(X_2, \cdots cons(X_n, nil)\cdots))$
$[X_1, X_2, \ldots, X_n\|Y]$	$X_1.X_2.\cdots.X_n.Y$	$cons(X_1, cons(X_2, \cdots cons(X_n, Y)\cdots))$

Figure 6.3   List notation

The key to programming with lists is to reason recursively about the list. Either the list is empty and the operation of interest should be straightforward, or it is non-empty and can be broken into a first element and a remaining shorter list which is dealt with recursively.

Example 6.2

Lists allow us to represent sequences. A rather important constraint on sequences that we may wish to model is that of concatenation. Suppose we wish to define a user-defined constraint `append(L1, L2, L3)` which holds if $L3$ is $L1$ concatenated with $L2$.

Let us consider the problem of concatenation. If $L1$ is an empty list then $L3$ is simply equal to $L2$. Otherwise $L1$ is of the form $[F|R]$ where F is the first element and R is the rest. Can we relate F and R to the problem at hand? Yes! Suppose we were to append $L2$ to the end of R, obtaining the list Z. Z is almost the answer but it is missing the element F which must be placed in front of Z to obtain the result. We can model this reasoning using the program

```
append([],Y,Y).                            (A1)
append([F|R], Y, [F|Z])  :-  append(R,Y,Z).  (A2)
```

Consider the execution of the goal `append([a],[b,c],L)`. The (single) successful derivation is shown in Figure 6.4, where the constraint store is shown in solved form.

The first step in the successful derivation is to rewrite the initial goal using the second rule, $A2$, in the definition of `append`. Rewriting with this rule sets F to the first element and R to the remainder of the list $[a]$. That is, F is set to a and R to the empty list $[\,]$. Y is set to the second list $[b, c]$ and the final list L is constrained to be a followed by Z. Now the base case, $A1$, is used to process the remaining call to `append`. The first constraint, $R = [\,]$, checks that the end of the list has been reached. Subsequent constraints, $Y = Y'$ and $Z = Y'$, in effect equate Y and Z. This forces L to become equal to $[a, b, c]$, which is the answer.

One rather nice feature of the `append` program is its flexibility. Not only can it be used to concatenate lists together, it can also be use to test whether one list is the prefix of another, or even to enumerate all the lists which can be concatenated together to give a fixed list. For example, the goal

```
append([1,2],_,[1,2,3]).
```

can be used to confirm that $[1, 2]$ is a prefix of the list $[1, 2, 3]$. On the other hand

$$\langle append([a],[b,c],L) \mathbin{\textbf{I}} true \rangle$$
$$\Downarrow A2$$
$$\langle [a] = [F|R], [b,c] = Y, L = [F|Z], append(R,Y,Z) \mathbin{\textbf{I}} true \rangle$$
$$\Downarrow$$
$$\langle [b,c] = Y, L = [F|Z], append(R,Y,Z) \mathbin{\textbf{I}} F = a \wedge R = [] \rangle$$
$$\Downarrow$$
$$\langle L = [F|Z], append(R,Y,Z) \mathbin{\textbf{I}} F = a \wedge R = [] \wedge Y = [b,c] \rangle$$
$$\Downarrow$$
$$\langle append(R,Y,Z) \mathbin{\textbf{I}} F = a \wedge R = [] \wedge Y = [b,c] \wedge L = [a|Z] \rangle$$
$$\Downarrow A1$$
$$\langle R = [], Y = Y', Z = Y' \mathbin{\textbf{I}} F = a \wedge R = [] \wedge Y = [b,c] \wedge L = [a|Z] \rangle$$
$$\Downarrow$$
$$\langle Y = Y', Z = Y' \mathbin{\textbf{I}} F = a \wedge R = [] \wedge Y = [b,c] \wedge L = [a|Z] \rangle$$
$$\Downarrow$$
$$\langle Z = Y' \mathbin{\textbf{I}} F = a \wedge R = [] \wedge Y = [b,c] \wedge L = [a|Z] \wedge Y' = [b,c] \rangle$$
$$\Downarrow$$
$$\langle \square \mathbin{\textbf{I}} F = a \wedge R = [] \wedge Y = [b,c] \wedge L = [a,b,c] \wedge Y' = [b,c] \wedge Z = [b,c] \rangle$$

Figure 6.4   Derivation for `append([a],[b,c],L)`

the goal

        `append(X,Y,[1,2]).`

will return the answers

$$X = [] \wedge Y = [1,2],$$
$$X = [1] \wedge Y = [2], \text{ and}$$
$$X = [1,2] \wedge Y = [].$$

As another example of a simple list manipulation program, consider how we might model the `alldifferent` constraint introduced in Section 3.5.

Example 6.3
The user-defined constraint `alldifferent_neq([`$V_1, \ldots, V_n$`])` is intended to hold if each of the elements in the list, V_1 to V_n, is different. We can define this in terms of the primitive constraint $\neq$ as follows:

```
alldifferent_neq([]).
alldifferent_neq([Y|Ys]) :- not_member(Y,Ys), alldifferent_neq(Ys).

not_member(_, []).
not_member(X, [Y|Ys]) :- X ≠ Y, not_member(X, Ys).
```

Like many list manipulation predicates, `alldifferent_neq` has two rules. The first is the base case for when the list is empty and the second is a recursive rule for a non-empty list. The base case is simple: every item in an empty list is (vacuously) different. The recursive case is a little more complex: all items in the list $[Y|Ys]$ are different if Y does not equal any item in the list Ys and all items in Ys are different.

We use the auxiliary predicate **not_member** to check that Y does not equal any element of the list Ys. It also consists of two rules: a base case for the empty list and a recursive rule for the non-empty list. The base case states that every element is not a member of the empty list. The recursive case states that X is not a member of the list $[Y|Ys]$ if it does not equal Y and it is not a member of the list Ys.

Usually **alldifferent_neq** will be applied to a list of variables, to ensure that none of them can take the same value. The goal **alldifferent_neq([A,B,C])**, for example, has the single answer $A \neq B \wedge A \neq C \wedge B \neq C$.

By using lists we can build models composed of complex structured data. A data structure of interest in many mathematical and engineering applications is the matrix. For instance, the matrix is the standard way to represent rectangular grids used in finite modelling. One simple representation of a matrix is as a list of lists. We can now return to the motivating example given at the beginning of this chapter and give a program that models a plate using an arbitrary sized grid of temperatures.

Example 6.4

The following program ensures that every interior point of the grid has a value equal to the average of its four neighbours. It uses case based reasoning similar to **append** except that the two cases are whether the list has three or more elements or exactly two elements. The predicate **rows** iterates through the rows in the matrix, selecting each three adjacent rows in the matrix and passing these as arguments to **cols**. The predicate **cols** iterates through the points in these rows, constraining the middle point M of a square of nine points in the matrix to equal the average of its orthogonal neighbours.

```
rows([_, _]).                                             (RW1)
rows([R1,R2,R3|Rs]) :- cols(R1, R2, R3), rows([R2,R3|Rs]).  (RW2)

cols([_, _], [_, _], [_, _]).                            (CL1)
cols([TL,T,TR|Ts], [ML,M,MR|Ms], [BL,B,BR|Bs]) :-        (CL2)
    M = (T + ML + MR + B) / 4,
    cols([T,TR|Ts], [M,MR|Ms], [B,BR|Bs]).
```

The metal plate shown in Figure 6.1 can be represented by the following list of lists, which we abbreviate to *plate*:

```
[[0,   100,   100,   100,   100,   100,    0],
 [0,    -,     -,     -,     -,     -,     0],
 [0,    -,     -,     -,     -,     -,     0],
 [0,    -,     -,     -,     -,     -,     0],
 [0,    -,     -,     -,     -,     -,     0],
 [0,    0,     0,     0,     0,     0,     0]].
```

In our query we specify the temperatures of the points on the outside edges, but the temperature of each interior point is a distinct unknown variable which we indicate by using the underscore. Evaluation of the goal

$$P = plate, \ \texttt{rows(P)}$$

results in the answer

$$P = \begin{matrix} [[0.00, & 100.00, & 100.00, & 100.00, & 100.00, & 100.00, & 0.00] \\ [0.00, & 46.61, & 62.48, & 66.43, & 62.48, & 46.61, & 0.00] \\ [0.00, & 23.97, & 36.87, & 40.76, & 36.87, & 23.97, & 0.00] \\ [0.00, & 12.39, & 20.27, & 22.88, & 20.27, & 12.39, & 0.00] \\ [0.00, & 5.34, & 8.95, & 10.19, & 8.95, & 5.34, & 0.00] \\ [0.00, & 0.00, & 0.00, & 0.00, & 0.00, & 0.00, & 0.00]]. \end{matrix}$$

Now let us examine the way in which the program works. On selection of the user-defined constraint `rows(P)`, evaluation of the first rule, $RW1$, fails because it constrains P to have exactly two rows. Execution of the rule $RW2$ proceeds by setting $R1$ to the first row in P, $R2$ to the second row, $R3$ to the third row and Rs to the remaining (4th to 6th) rows. Then `cols(R1, R2, R3)` is called. Initially the rule $(CL1)$ is tried, but this fails since it constrains $R1$, $R2$, and $R3$ to be lists of only two elements. Next rule $CL2$ is tried. In effect, this rule sets the variables $TL, T, TR, ML, M, MR, BL, B, BR$ to be the nine element grid comprising the first three elements of each of the rows $R1$, $R2$ and $R3$.

$$\begin{array}{lll} R1 = [& \boxed{\begin{matrix} TL & T & TR \\ ML & M & MR \\ BL & B & BR \end{matrix}} & \begin{matrix} |Ts] \\ |Ms] \\ |Bs] \end{matrix} \end{array}$$

The variables Ts, Ms and Bs refer to the remaining elements in the top, middle and bottom of the three rows. Now the constraint $M = (T + ML + MR + B)/4$ is added to the constraint store, enforcing that the middle point is the average of its orthogonal neighbours. Next the recursive call to `cols` is passed the top, middle and bottom rows minus their first elements. When matching with the rule $CL2$ the grid is shifted one place to the right. When there are only two elements left in each of the three lists the original `cols(R1, R2, R3)` call finishes. Next `rows` is called with the first row of the plate removed, in effect moving the computation down one row. Eventually, when there are only two rows left, evaluation finishes.

Both of the last two programs illustrate an important constraint programming technique. Not only can we make use of data structures to store fixed values, we can also use them to store variables to represent data that is presently unknown.

6.3 Association Lists

Lists allow the constraint programmer to represent and manipulate collections of objects. We can store any kind of object in a list, ranging from simple objects such as numbers to more complex objects such as records. Lists of records are often useful since they provide a way of accessing information by associating it with a key.

Consider a simple phone record with two parts: a name and phone number. We can encode this record as the tree made from the binary constructor p whose first argument is the name of the person and whose second argument is the phone number. For example, the collection of phone numbers

peter	5551616
kim	5559282
nicole	5559282

can be represented by the list of records below, abbreviated by *phonelist*:

$$[p(peter, 5551616), p(kim, 5559282), p(nicole, 5559282)]$$

The phone list gives a simple example of an *association list* data structure. For each name there is an associated phone number, and each phone number is associated with one or more names. The most basic operation on an association list is to find the information, in this case the telephone number, corresponding to a key, in this case a name.

The member(X, L) predicate defined in the program below constrains X to be a member of the list L. It can be used to find information in an association list, for example to look up the phone number corresponding to a name.

```
member(X, [X | _]).                    (E1)
member(X, [_ | R])   :-   member(X, R).   (E2)
```

The first rule holds when X is the first element of the list L. The second rule holds when X is not the first element of L but is a member of the rest of the list.

The goal member(p(kim, N),*phonelist*) finds the phone number, N, of *kim*. The (partially) simplified derivation tree is shown in Figure 6.5. Notice how information can flow is in both directions. The term $p(kim, N)$ causes failure when equated to the term $p(peter, 5551616)$. Conversely when the term $p(kim, 5559282)$ is equated with $p(kim, N)$ then N is constrained to be 5559282.

We have already seen how to look up information in an association list. The predicate lookup uses member to find the correct entry in the list. This is captured

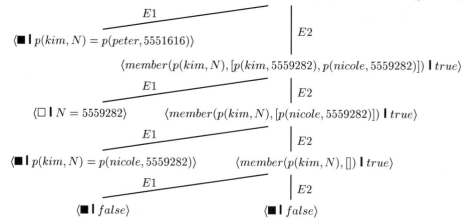

Figure 6.5   Simplified derivation tree for `member(p(kim, N)`, *phonelist*).

in the rule:

```
lookup(AList, Key, Info) :- member(p(Key, Info), AList).
```

Note that `lookup` can also be used to find all keys matching some information. For example, the goal `lookup(`*phonelist*`, Key, 5559282)` has the answers $Key = kim$ and $Key = nicole$.

Apart from looking up information in an association list, there are four other operations involving association lists that we may be interested in.

The first of these is determining if an association list is empty or building an empty association list. The same rule can be used for both tasks, since from a constraint viewpoint they are the same. It simply states that an empty association list is the empty list:

```
empty_alist([]).
```

The second operation is to add a new record, consisting of a key and associated information, to an association list:

```
addkey(AList0,Key,Info,AList) :- AList = [p(Key,Info)|AList0].
```

The predicate `addkey` simply adds another record to the start of the list *AList0* to obtain the new association list *AList*. It assumes the key is not already in the list.

The third operation is to delete a record with a specific key from the association list:

```
delkey([], _, []).
delkey([p(Key,Info)|AList], Key, AList).
delkey([p(Key0,Info0)|AList0], Key, [p(Key0,Info0)|AList]) :-
    Key ≠ Key0, delkey(AList0, Key, AList).
```

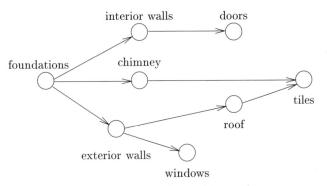

Figure 6.6   Job precedence for building a house.

The predicate `delkey` searches for the entry of the form $p(Key, \_)$ and deletes it from *AList*0 obtaining *AList*. If the key is not found in the association list the new association list is set to the original list.

The final operation is to update the information about a key:

```
modkey(AList0, Key, Info, AList) :-
    delkey(AList0, Key, AList1),
    addkey(AList1, Key, Info, AList).
```

The predicate `modkey` first deletes an element from the list and then inserts the new information.

Note that since each of the last three operations changes the association list, the predicates need two association lists as arguments—the list before the action, and the list after.

The association list data structure is useful for a variety of interesting tasks. As another example of its application, consider the project management problem of building a house from Chapter 1 and imagine that we wish to find all tasks which must be completed before a certain task can begin.

The immediate precedence relation is represented as a graph. For each task the graph contains arcs to those tasks that must be completed before this task can be started. For example, see the graph for house construction shown in Figure 6.6.

The first question is how to represent such a graph using the list and record data structures. The most obvious representation is to use a record to represent each arc in the graph. That is, to use a record of the form $arc(n_1, n_2)$ to represent an arc from node n_1 to n_2. A graph is then represented as list of arcs and, possibly, a list of nodes.

Unfortunately, this representation is not very suitable for our task since it requires multiple look ups to find all arcs from a node. A representation which is more suitable for this task is a variant of the *adjacency list*—the standard computer representation for sparse graphs. We can represent the graph as a list of records, each of which has two components. The first component is the name of a node, say n_1, in the graph and the second component is a list of those nodes who are at the start of an arc ending at n_1. That is, the second component is a list of those nodes n_2 for which there is an arc in the graph from n_2 to n_1.

Thus a node corresponding to a particular task t is represented by the pair $p(t, list\_of\_tasks)$ where $list\_of\_tasks$ comprises those tasks for which there is an arc to t. The entire graph can be represented using a list of these pairs. It forms an association list between tasks and their list of immediate predecessor tasks.

For example, the graph for the house (shown in Figure 6.6) can be represented by the following data structure, which we will abbreviate by *house*:

```
[p(foundations,[]), p(int_walls,[foundations]),
 p(chimney,[foundations]), p(ext_walls,[foundations]),
 p(roof,[ext_walls]), p(windows, [ext_walls]),
 p(tiles, [chimney, roof]), p(doors, [int_walls])].
```

Using this data structure it is relatively straightforward to find all tasks which must be completed before a given task can start.

Example 6.5
Suppose we wish to find all tasks that need to be completed before, for instance, the `tiles` task can begin. Clearly both `roof` and `chimney` need to be completed. However, before `roof` can be begun, its immediate predecessors must be completed, in this case `ext_walls`. Again `ext_walls` cannot begin before `foundations` is finished.

More generally, in order to find those tasks which must be completed before a given task T can start, we reason recursively as follows. If $T_1, \ldots T_n$ are the immediate predecessors of task T, and $L_1, \ldots, L_n$ are lists of all of the predecessors of $T_1, \ldots, T_n$ respectively, then the list of all predecessors of T is simply the concatenation of the lists $L_1, \ldots, L_n$. This reasoning is succinctly captured in the following program:

```
predecessors(N, AList, Pre) :-
    lookup(AList, N, NImPre),
    list_predecessors(NImPre, AList, ListOfPre),
    list_append([NImPre | ListOfPre], Pre).

list_predecessors([], _, []).
list_predecessors([N|Ns], AList, [NPre|NsPres]) :-
    predecessors(N, AList, NPre),
    list_predecessors(Ns, AList, NsPres).

list_append([], []).
list_append([L|Ls], All) :-
    list_append(Ls, AppendedLs),
    append(L, AppendedLs, All).
```

The predicate `predecessors` works by first finding the immediate predecessors of N using the `lookup` predicate to find the record for N in the association list *AList*. Then `list_predecessors` recursively constructs a list, each of whose elements is a list of all predecessors of one of the immediate predecessors of N. Finally, all of these lists, together with the list of immediate predecessors of N are appended together using `list_append`.

For example, the goal

$$\text{predecessors(tiles, } house \text{, Pre)}$$

returns the answer

        Pre = [chimney, roof, foundations, ext_walls, foundations].

Notice that the answer contains two copies of the `foundations` task because it can be reached on two paths (of precedence) from `tiles`. To avoid this duplication in the answer (which also required duplication of computation because two goals of the form `predecessors(foundations, `*house*`, Pre)` were executed) we need to keep track of which predecessors have already been discovered in the current computation. The above formulation does not allow us to access the information we have currently found when determining a new predecessor.

One approach to overcome this is to use an extra argument to `predecessors` to *accumulate* the predecessors we have already found. The meaning of the goal `predecessors(N, AList, Initial, Final)` is that if *Initial* is the list of tasks which we have already examined in the computation, then *Final* should be the initial list together with those tasks from which there is a path to task N not passing through a member of the list *Initial*

```
predecessors(N, AList, Pre0, Pre) :-
    lookup(AList, N, NImPre),
    cumul_predecessors(NImPre, AList, Pre0, Pre).

cumul_predecessors([], _, Pre, Pre).
cumul_predecessors([N|Ns], AList, Pre0, Pre) :-
    member(N, Pre0),
    cumul_predecessors(Ns, AList, Pre0, Pre).
cumul_predecessors([N|Ns], AList, Pre0, Pre) :-
    not_member(N, Pre0),
    predecessors(N, AList, [N|Pre0], Pre1),
    cumul_predecessors(Ns, AList, Pre1, Pre).
```

In `cumul_predecessors` if the first element of the list, N, is a member of the predecessors already visited, *Pre0*, then it can be ignored and the remainder of the tasks in the list *Ns* can be examined. Otherwise, if N is a not a member of the list, it is added to the list $[N|Pre0]$ and examined using `predecessors`. The resulting new list of predecessors *Pre1* (which will include N) is then used when examining the remainder *Ns* of the tasks.

Notice that the program no longer needs to explicitly use `append`, since new predecessors are collected one by one in the *initial* argument as they are discovered. Using this program the goal

$$\text{predecessors(tiles, } house\text{, [], Pre)}$$

returns the answer

$$\text{Pre = [ext\_walls, roof, foundations, chimney]}$$

This second program is preferable to the first. It is more succinct and it is also more efficient since the number of steps in the successful derivation is less.

6.4   Binary Trees

Lists are just one example of a recursive data structure. Another important example of a recursive data structure is binary trees.

We can define binary trees using tree constraints quite easily. We let the constant *null* represent the empty tree, and use a term of the form $node(t_1, i, t_2)$ to represent a non-null tree in which t_1 and t_2 are the left and right sub-trees, respectively, and i is the information stored at the root of the tree. For instance, the term

$$node(node(null, harald, null), kim, node(null, peter, null)),$$

which we shall abbreviate to *hkp*, is illustrated in Figure 1.5 (b) in Chapter 1.

Programs for dealing with tree data structures generally follow the recursive structure of the data structure itself. For example, as we have seen, list manipulation predicates often have a rule for the empty list and a rule for a non-empty list which processes the first element of the list and then calls the predicate recursively with the remaining elements in the list.

Most programs for manipulating binary trees also follow this pattern. They have a rule for the empty tree *null* and a recursive rule (or rules) for a non-empty tree $node(t_1, i, t_2)$. This structure will be apparent in almost all of our example programs which deal with binary trees.

As our first example of binary tree manipulation, consider how to write a program which performs an in-order traversal of a tree. The following predicate, `traverse`, does so. It returns a list containing the elements in the tree in the order in which they were encountered.

```
traverse(null, []).
traverse(node(T1,I,T2), L) :-
    traverse(T1, L1),
    traverse(T2, L2),
    append(L1, [I|L2], L).
```

The first rule is for the empty tree, *null*. Clearly, the list of items in an empty tree is empty. The second rule is for a non-empty tree of the form $node(t_1, i, t_2)$. The list of items visited in an in-order traversal of a tree of this form is the list obtained by traversing the left subtree, followed by i, followed by the list obtained by traversing the right subtree.

For instance, the goal `traverse(`*hkp*`, L)` gives the single answer

$$L = [harald, kim, peter].$$

Suppose we have a total order on our data items, expressed by a predicate `less_than(X, Y)` which succeeds if X is less than Y. A *binary search tree* is a particular type of binary tree in which for each sub-tree of the form $node(t_1, i, t_2)$ all of the items in tree t_1 are less than or equal to i, and all of the items in tree t_2 are greater than or equal to i. If `less_than` is defined by

```
less_than(harald, kim).
less_than(harald, peter).
less_than(kim, peter).
```

then the tree *hkp* is an example of a binary search tree.

Binary search trees are useful because they allow data items to be quickly accessed by their value. A goal of the form `find(T, E)` will determine if item E is in the binary search tree T using the following program:

```
find(node(_TL, I, _TR), E) :- E = I.                   (F1)
find(node(TL, I, _TR), E) :- less_than(E, I), find(TL, E). (F2)
find(node(_TL, I, TR), E) :- less_than(I, E), find(TR, E). (F3)
```

Note that some of the variable names begin with an underscore "_." By convention this indicates that these variables appear only once in the rule. Here the tests $E = I$, `less_than(E, I)`, and `less_than(I, E)` are used to determine if the desired item is equal to that stored in the root of the tree, less than it or greater than it. In the latter two cases this determines which subtree of the root should be examined for the item. The `find` predicate is analogous to the `member` predicate for lists.

The goal `find(`*hkp*`, peter)` has the following successful (simplified) derivation:

$$\langle find(node(node(null, harald, null), kim, node(null, peter, null)), peter) \mathbin{\textbf{I}} true \rangle$$
$$\Downarrow F3$$
$$\langle less\_than(kim, peter), find(node(null, peter, null), peter) \mathbin{\textbf{I}} true \rangle$$
$$\Downarrow$$
$$\langle find(node(null, peter, null), peter) \mathbin{\textbf{I}} true \rangle$$
$$\Downarrow F1$$
$$\langle \Box \mathbin{\textbf{I}} true \rangle$$

It is quite easy to modify `find` so as to give a new predicate which takes a binary search tree and a data item and returns the new binary search tree which results from inserting the data item into the tree. If the item is already in the tree, the tree is left unchanged.

```
insert_bst(null, E, node(null,E,null)).
insert_bst(node(TL, I, TR), E, node(TL, I, TR)) :-
    E = I.
insert_bst(node(TL, I, TR), E, node(NTL, I, TR)) :-
    less_than(E, I), insert_bst(TL, E, NTL).
insert_bst(node(TL, I, TR), E, node(TL, I, NTR)) :-
    less_than(I, E), insert_bst(TR, E, NTR).
```

Using this predicate we can build a binary search tree, by inserting elements one by one into an initially empty tree.

Just as we can use lists to implement association lists, we can also use binary search trees. The advantage of the binary search tree implementation is that the time taken to find an item in a binary search tree is on average logarithmic in the size of the tree while the average time taken to find an element in the list representation of an association list is linear.

We will store the association list as a tree with each item in the tree being an association pair $p(key, info)$. Since we wish to access items in the tree by their key value, the ordering on the items must only depend on the key. Given the predicate key_less_than which compares two keys, the predicate to compare nodes in the tree is therefore

```
less_than(p(Key1, _), p(Key2, _)) :- key_less_than(Key1, Key2).
```

Given the above predicates for binary search tree manipulation, it is easy to implement the standard operations on association lists. The predicate to look up the information associated with a particular key simply calls **find** to search the tree for the item with that key value:

```
lookup(AList, Key, Info) :-
    find(AList, p(Key, Info)).
```

The empty association list is just the empty tree:

```
empty_alist(null).
```

while the predicate insert_bst can be used to add a new association pair to the tree:

```
addkey(Key, Info, AList0, AList) :-
    insert_bst(AList0, p(Key, Info), AList).
```

To implement the **delkey** procedure for an association list defined using binary search trees we need a method for deleting an item from a binary search tree. Because of the nature of binary search trees this is somewhat complicated and is left as an exercise for the reader.

Example 6.6

Recall the association list for phone numbers. Consider how we can store this in a binary search tree. The first issue is how to order the keys. One possibility is to exhaustively detail the ordering between the names in the list using facts but this is quite tedious. A better technique is to map non-numeric keys into a unique number and then use $\leq$ to compare these numbers. For instance we can order the keys using

```
number(peter, 3).
number(kim, 1).
number(nicole, 2).

key_less_than(K1,K2) :-
    N1 ≤ N2,
    number(K1,N1),
    number(K2,N2).
```

As an example, the goal

```
    empty_alist(L0),
    addkey(L0,peter,5551616,L1),
    lookup(L1,peter,Number).
```

will build the binary search tree $L1$ with the single item $p(peter, 5551616)$ and then determine the phone number of *peter*.

Data structures add considerable power and flexibility to the CLP paradigm, allowing it to be used as a general purpose programming language as well as a powerful modelling language. In the remainder of this chapter, we describe two non-trivial modelling applications which make use of sophisticated data structures to represent the problem and which traverse these data structures to generate the primitive constraints that model the problem.

6.5 Hierarchical Modelling

Constraint logic programs allow us to model a problem's structure by directly using user-defined constraints for each important concept. Many engineering problems are based on the analysis of complex objects made from simpler sub-components. Thus they are naturally hierarchical in structure. Such problems can be readily modelled using a hierarchy of rules in which concepts in each level of the hierarchy are defined in terms of concepts lower in the hierarchy.

As an example, consider the analysis of steady-state RLC electrical circuits, that is to say, circuits consisting of resistors (R), inductors (L) and capacitors (C). At the lowest level of the problem, individual (sinusoidal) voltages and currents can be represented by a complex number which is understood as a vector whose amplitude is the size of the voltage or current, and whose direction gives the phase of the voltage or current. Individual circuit components form the next layer in the hierarchy. Their behaviour in terms of voltage, current and circuit values is easily modelled in terms of complex numbers. Finally, more complicated circuits can be modelled by describing them in terms of series and parallel connections of circuit components.

In order to use the hierarchical modelling we need to make decisions about how the various levels of the hierarchy are modelled. We have already seen on page 186 how to model complex numbers in terms of real numbers by using a record construct of the form $c(x, y)$ to model $x + iy$.

At the level of the individual circuit components, the important information is the type of the component and the components value. We could represent this as a pair, for example $p(resistor, 100)$, but since we will only be interested in the component's value once the type of component is known, a simpler representation is to use the component type as a tree constructor. Thus we use $resistor(R)$ to represent a resistor with resistance R, $inductor(L)$ to represent an inductor with inductance L and $capacitor(C)$ to represent a capacitor with capacitance C. The advantage of this representation is that case-by-case handling of the different components is easy.

At the highest level of the hierarchy, we need to represent complex circuits made from individual components connected in parallel or in series. Complex circuits can be modelled using a representation similar to that for individual circuit components. We let the tree $series(C_1, C_2)$ represent the circuit obtained by placing circuit C_1 in series with circuit C_2. Similarly, $parallel(C_1, C_2)$ represents a circuit obtained by placing circuit C_1 in parallel with circuit C_2. Note that the data structure for representing circuits is recursive since we can connect arbitrary circuits or components in parallel or in series to create a more complex circuit.

The following program analyses the steady state behaviour of RLC circuits with sinusoidal frequency W.

```
resistor(R, V, I, _W)  :- c_mult(I, c(R,0), V).
inductor(L, V, I, W)   :- c_mult(c(0,W*L), I, V).
capacitor(C, V, I, W)  :- c_mult(c(0,W*C), V, I).

circuit(resistor(R), V, I, W)  :- resistor(R, V, I, W).
circuit(inductor(L), V, I, W)  :- inductor(L, V, I, W).
circuit(capacitor(C), V, I, W) :- capacitor(C, V, I, W).
circuit(series(C1, C2), V, I, W)  :-
    circuit(C1, V1, I, W),
    circuit(C2, V2, I, W),
    c_add(V1, V2, V).
circuit(parallel(C1, C2), V, I, W)  :-
    circuit(C1, V, I1, W),
    circuit(C2, V, I2, W),
    c_add(I1, I2, I).
```

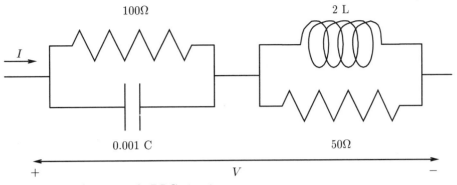

Figure 6.7   An example RLC circuit.

The behaviour of individual components is modelled using the user-defined constraints for complex numbers which specify the relationship between voltage and current for that component. The behaviour of circuits uses the component definitions for simple circuits of only one component, as well as simple recursive rules for more complex circuits. A series circuit, $series(C_1, C_2)$, implies the current through the two circuits is the same, and the voltage of the series circuit is the sum of the voltages over the individual circuits. A parallel circuit, $parallel(C_1, C_2)$, has the dual relation between voltage and current.

We can use this deceptively simple program to answer many goals. For example, we can analyze the behaviour of the circuit shown in Figure 6.7 when operating at 60 Hz by executing the goal

```
circuit(series(parallel(resistor(100),capacitor(0.001)),
            parallel(inductor(2),resistor(50))),
        V, I, 60).
```

The result is

```
I = c(_t23, _t24)
V = c(-1.53526*_t24 + 45.3063*_t23, 45.3063*_t24 + 1.53526*_t23)
```

where the relationship between voltage V and current I is shown in terms of the real and imaginary parts of the current ($\_t23, \_t24$).

6.6   Tree Layout

Trees are used in a wide variety of applications and are best understood if they are displayed pictorially. However, as anyone who has ever tried to write LaTeX code to display a tree knows, this is not that easy.

Our next example application is to write a program which computes a good layout for a tree. The program must take an arbitrary binary tree and compute (x, y) coordinates for each node which is where that node will be drawn. The layout must be aesthetically pleasing and should be no wider than necessary. As an example of what constitutes good layout consider the following term representing a binary tree:

```
node(node(node(node(null,kangaroo,null),
            marsupial,
            node(null,koala,null)
        ),
        mammal,
        node(null,
            monotreme,
            node(null,platypus,null)
        )
    ),
    animal,
    node(node(node(null,cockatoo,null),
            parrot,
            node(null,lorikeet,null)
        ),
        bird,
        node(null,
            raptor,
            node(null,eagle,null)
        )
    )
).
```

How would we like to display this tree? Reasonable requirements are that:

- Nodes of the tree on the same level are aligned horizontally.
- Different levels are spaced at equal intervals.
- There is a minimum gap between adjacent nodes on the same level.
- A parent node lies above and midway between its children.
- The width of the tree is minimized.

The basic idea behind the program is straightforward. The main predicate `layout_constraints` defines the constraints on the layout. It first builds an association list which associates each node in the input tree with a record $c(X,Y)$. The record will store the position of that node in the layout. Initially the coordinates are variables. Next it traverses the tree and adds layout constraints between nodes in which one is the parent of the other. Then it traverses the tree and adds layout constraints between nodes which are on the same level. Then the root is placed at the desired location. The overall goal is to build a layout which minimizes the width. The high level program is therefore:

```
layout_constraints(T,AL,W) :-
    traverse(T, L),
    build_assoc_list(L, AL),
    parent_constraints(T, AL),
    height(T, D),
    sideways_constraints(T, 1, D, AL),
    place_root(T, AL),
    width_exp(T, AL, W).
```

```
tree_layout(T, AL) :- minimize(layout_constraints(T,AL,W), W).
```

The predicate `traverse` was defined earlier in Section 6.4. It returns a list of the elements in a tree. The procedure to build the association list containing the node's coordinates is a straightforward list traversal. It associates a structure containing two new variables to each node of the binary tree.

```
build_assoc_list([], []).
build_assoc_list([N|Ns], [p(N,c(_,_))|AL]) :- build_assoc_list(Ns, AL).
```

The predicate to set up the constraints arising between the coordinates of each internal node and its children is relatively simple. It traverses the original tree and for each node N with children it looks up the coordinates of N and those of the children. It then adds the constraints that the y-coordinate of each child is 10 below that of its parent and that the parent's x-coordinate is midway between that of the children. The only complication is that several cases must be considered because of the different possible tree structures.

```
parent_constraints(null, _).
parent_constraints(node(null,_,null), _).
parent_constraints(node(null, N, node(T1,N2,T2)), AL) :-
    lookup(AL, N, c(XN,YN)),
    lookup(AL, N2, c(XN2,YN2)),
    XN2 = XN, YN2 = YN - 10,
    parent_constraints(node(T1,N2,T2), AL).
parent_constraints(node(node(T1,N2,T2), N,null ), AL) :-
    lookup(AL, N, c(XN,YN)),
    lookup(AL, N2, c(XN2,YN2)),
    XN2 = XN, YN2 = YN - 10,
    parent_constraints(node(T1,N2,T2), AL).
parent_constraints(node(node(T1,N1,T2), N, node(T3,N2,T4)), AL) :-
    lookup(AL, N, c(XN,YN)),
    lookup(AL, N1, c(XN1,YN1)),
    lookup(AL, N2, c(XN2,YN2)),
    XN1 + XN2 = 2 * XN, YN1 = YN - 10, YN2 = YN - 10,
    parent_constraints(node(T1,N1,T2), AL),
    parent_constraints(node(T3,N2,T4), AL).
```

There is a rule for each of the possible tree structures: an empty tree, a tree with no children, a tree with only a right child, only a left child, and a tree with two children. Note how the children are handled recursively.

Next we need to add the constraint that adjacent nodes are at least a certain distance apart. We do this by first computing the height of the tree using height (whose definition we leave as an exercise) and then calling the predicate sideways_constraints. This iterates through each level of the tree using level and by calling separate_list for each level to ensure adjacent nodes on this level are separated. The predicate level(T,N,L) returns a list L of items in tree T at level N. The predicate separate_list works by finding the x coordinate of the first element in the list and then calling sep_list with this and the remainder of the list. Predicate sep_list constrains the x coordinate of the first element FX in the list to be 10 more than the previous x coordinate PX. It then processes the remainder of the list with the previous x coordinate now set to FX.

```
sideways_constraints(_T, N, D, _AL) :-
    N > D.
sideways_constraints(T, N, D, AL) :-
    N ≤ D,
    level(T, N, L),
    separate_list(L, AL),
    sideways_constraints(T, N+1, D, AL).

level(null, _, []).
level(node(_, N, _), D, [N]) :- D = 1.
level(node(T1, _N, T2), D, L) :-
    D ≥ 1,
    level(T1, D-1, L1),
    level(T2, D-1, L2),
    append(L1, L2, L).

separate_list([F|R], AL) :-
    lookup(AL, F, c(FX,_FY)),
    sep_list(R, AL, FX).

sep_list([], _, _).
sep_list([N|Ns], AL, PX) :-
    lookup(AL, N, c(XN,_YN)),
    XN ≥ PX + 10,
    sep_list(Ns, AL, XN).
```

The predicate place_root fixes the position of the root of the tree. Its definition is left as an exercise.

Now we have to minimize the width of the tree. In fact we need to do more than this because this does not sufficiently restrict the positioning of nodes. Instead what

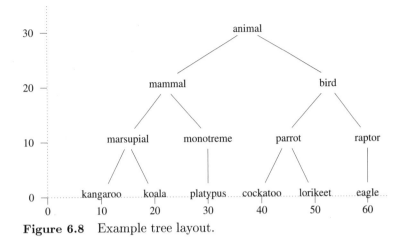

Figure 6.8   Example tree layout.

we can do is to minimize the sum of the distances between all pairs of children. To do this we recurse through the tree once more, summing the width of each subtree and returning the expression. The code is rather similar to `parent_constraints` and could in fact be combined with this phase albeit making it a little more complex.

```
width_exp(null, _, 0).
width_exp(node(null,_,null), _, 0).
width_exp(node(null, _N, node(T1,N2,T2)), AL, W) :-
    width_exp(node(T1,N2,T2), AL, W).
width_exp(node(node(T1,N2,T2), _N, null), AL, W) :-
    width_exp(node(T1,N2,T2), AL, W).
width_exp(node(node(T1,N1,T2), _N, node(T3,N2,T4)), AL, W) :-
    lookup(AL, N1, c(XN1,_YN1)),
    lookup(AL, N2, c(XN2,_YN2)),
    W = XN2 - XN1 + W1 + W2,
    width_exp(node(T1,N1,T2), AL, W1),
    width_exp(node(T3,N2,T4), AL, W2).
```

If we run this program with the tree given above and constrain the root to be at $(37.5, 30)$ we obtain the layout shown in Figure 6.8.

This program is relatively simple yet is remarkably flexible. With little effort it can be modified to take into account additional constraints on the node positions such that some nodes must be placed in a particular region or that nodes must be aligned vertically.

6.7   Summary

One of the most interesting features of CLP languages is that the same mechanism, constraints, provides both control and data structures. In this chapter we have seen that the tree constraint domain provides most of the usual data structures found in traditional languages—records, lists and trees—and that tree constraints provide a single uniform mechanism for building and accessing these data structures.

When programming with recursive data structures it is common for the program to reflect the structure of the data structure with recursive rules to process the recursive component of the data structure. One useful programming technique is the use of accumulators.

Association lists are another useful programming technique. They allow information to be accessed via a key. We have seen how association lists can be implemented as a list of records. An even better implementation of association lists makes use of binary search trees.

We have seen two larger examples illustrating the power of data structures for modelling. The first is for the analysis of electric circuits and uses a hierarchical representation of the circuit. The second computes a nice layout for binary trees. It makes extensive use of data structures to construct the layout constraints and the expression to minimize.

6.8   Practical Exercises

P6.1. We can also use multiple facts to represent association lists. For instance, the association list for phone numbers could be represented by the facts

```
phone_number(peter, 5551616).
phone_number(kim, 5559282).
phone_number(nicole, 5559282).
```

What are two advantages of using a list or tree to represent the association list? [Hint: consider why a multiple fact representation would not work for the tree layout example.]

P6.2. Use the circuit program from Section 6.5 to evaluate the circuit shown in Figure 2.1.

P6.3. Consider a metal plate modelled using a 9×9 grid. Suppose we know that the temperature at the centre of the plate is $50°C$ and at the point midway between the centre and the north sides, as well as the point midway between the centre and the east sides is $90°C$. Suppose we also know that exterior points on the same side have the same temperature. Use the program of Example 6.4 to find values for N, S, E, and W where these are the temperature of the exterior points on the north, south, east and west sides respectively. Note that the temperature of the corner points is irrelevant.

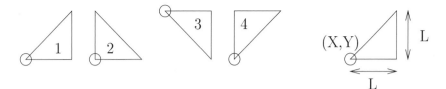

Figure 6.9 Four forms of right triangles.

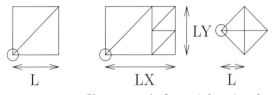

Figure 6.10 Shapes made from right triangles.

P6.4. Consider a domain of intervals where each element $[r_1, r_2]$ represents the set of points $\{X \mid r_1 \leq X \leq r_2\}$ on the real line. Addition of intervals I_1, I_2 is defined to be the smallest interval I containing the points $\{X_1 + X_2 \mid X_1 \in I_1, X_2 \in I_2\}$. Similarly for multiplication. Choose a representation of intervals. Write definitions for user-defined constraints to model interval addition `i_add(I1, I2, I3)` and multiplication `i_mult(I1, I2, I3)` using your representation.

P6.5. "Quarters" are right-angled triangles with both horizontal and vertical edges of equal length. Thus they take one of the four forms shown in Figure 6.9.

They can be represented using a record of the form `quarter(X,Y,L,T)` where (X, Y) are the coordinates of the leftmost point, and in the cases where there are multiple leftmost points (types 2, 4) the lowest such point, L is the length of the horizontal and vertical edges, and T is either 1, 2, 3 or 4 indicating the type of the quarter.

Write rules to define the predicate `intersect(Q1,Q2)` which succeeds if the two quarters $Q1$ and $Q2$ share a point in common and fails otherwise.

P6.6. Various shapes can be represented by lists of quarters, *quarter descriptions*, for example those shown in Figure 6.10.

Write rules that define three predicates which construct a quarter description for a square, rectangle and diamond respectively. For example, the predicate `square(X,Y,L,R)` should succeed if R is a quarter description of a square whose leftmost bottom point is (X, Y) and whose side length is L. For instance, evaluation of `square(0,0,1,R)` could give the answer

$$R = [quarter(0, 0, 1, 1), quarter(0, 0, 1, 4)].$$

Note that your predicate only has to produce one description, not all possible descriptions. Similarly define the predicates `rectangle(X,Y,LX,LY,R)` and `diamond(X,Y,L,R)`.

Extend the predicate `intersect(R1, R2)` to take two quarter descriptions. That is, it should succeed if $R1$ and $R2$ are quarter descriptions that intersect.

Write a definition for the predicate `area(R, A)` which calculates the area A of a quarter description R.

P6.7. In an options trading problem, we can represent an action to buy or sell a call option by the record *call(cost, exercise_price, buy_or_sell)*, where *cost* is the cost of the option, *exercise_price* is its exercise price, and *buy_or_sell* is 1 if buying and -1 for selling. A put option can be represented similarly as *put(cost, exercise_price, buy_or_sell)*. An option strategy is a list of options. Write a program for predicate *value(OS, S, P)* which calculates the pay off P for option strategy OS given the share price S.

P6.8. Write a predicate `build_bst(L, T)` which builds a binary search tree T from a list L of items. Your definition should make use of an accumulator by means of an auxiliary predicate `cumul_insert(L, T0, T)` which inserts each item in the list L into tree $T0$ obtaining tree T. The second argument of `cumul_insert_bst` is the tree built so far, while the third argument holds the final tree. Your program should work by iterating down the list of elements, using the second argument to accumulate the result of inserting each element into an initially empty tree until the list has been traversed.

P6.9. Write a predicate `height(T,D)` which computes the height of a binary tree. Note that the empty tree has height of 0.

P6.10. (*) Write a predicate `delete_bst(T0,I,T)` which deletes item I from the binary search tree $T0$ to give the new binary search tree T.

P6.11. The tree layout program is rather inefficient because every time we look up the coordinates of the node it takes time proportional to the size of the association list. A better approach is to build an augmented tree which is essentially the original tree but which directly stores the coordinates of each node at the node in the tree. The predicate `add_coords_to_nodes` does this:

```
add_coords_to_nodes( null, null).
add_coords_to_nodes( node(T1,N,T2), node(T3,p(N,c(X,Y)),T4)) :-
    add_coords_to_nodes( T1, T3),
    add_coords_to_nodes( T2, T4).
```

Modify the tree layout to work with the augmented tree rather than with an association list.

P6.12. Write predicates `put(Q0,I,Q)` and `get(Q0,I,Q)` which implement a queue. The call `put(Q0,I,Q)` should place item I at the tail of queue $Q0$ to give Q and the call `get(Q0,I,Q)` should return the item I at the head of queue $Q0$ and the remainder of the queue in Q. You should represent a queue simply as a list of elements.

P6.13. (*) Define `put` and `get` from the above exercise using the following data structure, called a *difference list*. We use the tree *queue*$([a_1, \ldots, a_n | T], T)$ to represent a queue with elements $[a_1, \ldots, a_n]$. The variable T provides fast access to the tail of the queue regardless of how long the queue is, so both `put(Q0,I,Q)` and `get(Q0,I,Q)` can take constant time.

P6.14. (*) Using the difference list $dl([a_1, \ldots, a_n | T], T)$ to represent the sequence $[a_1, \ldots, a_n]$ write a non-recursive predicate `append_dl` which returns the concatenation of two sequences. For instance, the goal

   `append_dl( dl([a,b|T1],T1), dl([c,d|T2],T2), dl(L,T3))`

should have the answer

$$L = [a, b, c, d | T3] \land T2 = T3 \land T1 = [c, d | T3].$$

6.9 Notes

The ability of syntactic trees to represent common data structures such as records, lists and trees and the use of term constraints to build and manipulate these data structures is the basis of the logic programming language Prolog. The programming techniques and representations described in this chapter for records, lists, association lists and binary trees originate from the earliest days of Prolog programming and are more fully described in Prolog programming texts such as that of Sterling and Shapiro [125].

The hierarchical modelling of circuits is taken from Heintze *et al* [62]. Tree layout is a well-studied special case of graph layout. The idea of couching binary tree layout as a linear programming optimization problem appears in Supowit and Reingold [131]. For more about tree and graph layout the interested reader is referred to the survey of Battisa *et al* [8].

7   Controlling Search

In the preceding chapters we have investigated how a programmer can model a constraint problem by using a CLP program. However constructing an initial model is often only the first part of the constraint programmer's task. In many cases, execution of the initial model may be too inefficient to solve the original problem and, in the extreme case, may not terminate. In such cases, a second phase of programming is required in which the programmer modifies the original program in order to improve its efficiency.

The size and shape of the derivation tree (also called the search space) is the primary factor in determining the efficiency of a CLP goal. If the derivation tree has an infinite derivation then the goal may not terminate, or if it is too large and the answers are not near the left part of the derivation tree, it may take too long to find a solution. In order to write efficient CLP programs the programmer therefore needs to understand the underlying search strategy and solver and the way they shape a goal's derivation tree.

In this chapter we look at how we can measure the efficiency of a CLP program. We describe several basic programming techniques—rule reordering, reordering of literals in a rule body and addition of extra constraints—which can be used to improve the efficiency of a CLP program by reducing its search space. We also describe standard CLP built-ins—if-then-else and once—which allow the programmer to tell the system not to search part of the derivation tree.

7.1   Estimating the Efficiency of a CLP Program

In Chapter 4 we saw that a CLP system evaluates a goal by searching the derivation tree for the goal. Reducing the size of the derivation tree is the main and most important strategy for improving the efficiency of CLP programs. The size and shape of a goal's derivation tree depends upon the order of literals in the program and goal and also upon the constraint solver. The order in which branches in the tree are searched depends on the order in which the rules for a predicate appear in the program. This means that when writing constraint logic programs the programmer needs to be aware that literals are evaluated left-to-right in goals and that rules are tried in textual order, as ignoring this may lead to inefficient programs, and even to that most inefficient of programs—one that is non-terminating. Conversely, using knowledge about the evaluation and the independence of the answers from literal ordering or rule ordering (discussed in Section 4.8) can allow a programmer to dramatically improve the performance of their programs.

In order to reason about the efficiency of a program, the programmer requires some way to estimate the cost of evaluating a goal. Unlike most programming languages, CLP languages are *non-deterministic*, that is, a goal can have more than one answer. As we have seen, their fundamental evaluation strategy is to explore the derivation tree from a goal in a depth-first manner. The overwhelming cost in goal evaluation is this search through the derivation tree to find the answers. Thus, the size of a goal's derivation tree (that is the number of states in the tree) is a rough measure of the cost of evaluating the goal. Although this measure does not take into account the cost of constraint solving or that we may only want to find the first answer, not all answers, it provides a rough guide when developing a program.

Another difference between CLP languages and most other languages is that CLP programs are very versatile and may be used to answer a wide variety of different queries. Therefore, when analyzing the efficiency of a program, it is important to consider the intended *mode of usage* of the user-defined constraints occurring in the program.

Definition 7.1
A *mode of usage* for a predicate p is a description of the way in which the arguments of calls to p will be constrained at the time when calls to p are evaluated.

Usually we shall specify a predicate's mode of usage by detailing which arguments to the predicate are *fixed* and which are *free*. An argument x is fixed in a particular call if, at the time of evaluation, the constraint store implies x can only take a single value. An argument x is free in a particular call if, at the time of evaluation, x can take any value in the constraint domain and still satisfy the constraint store. In the case of tree constraints we shall sometimes describe the type of term a variable is constrained to equal, for example a list or a list of fixed size. Other modes of usage are also possible, such as the argument is bounded above or the argument is bounded below.

Definition 7.2
A goal G *satisfies* a mode of usage for predicate p if, for every state in the derivation tree for G of form

$$\langle p(s_1, \dots, s_n), L_2, \dots, L_m \mid C \rangle,$$

the effect of the constraint store C on the arguments s_1, ..., s_n of p is correctly described by the mode of usage.

To make this discussion a little more concrete, consider the following program which sums the numbers in a list:

```
sumlist([], 0).
sumlist([N|L], N + S)   :-   sumlist(L, S).
```

One reasonable mode of usage for sumlist is that the first argument is fixed and that the second argument is free. The goals sumlist([1], S) and

    L=[1,2], S > Z, sumlist(L,S).

both satisfy this mode of usage while the goals sumlist(L, 2) and

    S > 3, sumlist(L,S), L=[1,2].

do not. To see that the goal sumlist([1], S) satisfies this mode of usage, consider Figure 7.1 which shows the derivation tree for this goal. The predicate sumlist is called in the states

$$\langle sumlist([1], S) \mathbin{\vert} true \rangle,$$
$$\langle sumlist(L', S') \mathbin{\vert} [1] = [N'|L'] \wedge S = N' + S' \rangle.$$

It is clear that in the first call, $sumlist([1], S)$, the first argument is fixed and the second is free. This is also true for the second call, $sumlist(L', S')$, since the associated constraint store constrains L' to be $[]$ while S' is still free to take any value (although S will be forced to be $1 + S'$).

An *intended mode of usage* for a program specifies a class of goals for which the program is designed. Any goal which satisfies the intended mode of usage is part of this class.

Efficiency of a program or predicate depends on its intended mode of usage. For a given mode of usage, the efficiency of predicate p is a measure of the size of the derivation trees for any state of the form

$$\langle p(s_1, \dots, s_n) \mathbin{\vert} C \rangle$$

for which the intended mode of usage describes the effect of C on the arguments $s_1, \dots, s_n$ of p.

For example, consider the efficiency of the sumlist program for the mode of usage in which the first argument is a list of fixed length. We must consider how the size of the derivation tree for sumlist(L,S) varies with the length of the list L. For the goal sumlist([],S), the size of the derivation tree is 6. For a goal with a list of length 1, we can see (from Figure 7.1) that the derivation tree has size $5 + 6 = 11$. The case when the first argument is a list with two elements gives a derivation tree of size $5 + 11 = 16$ and, in general, if the list has n elements, the derivation tree has size $5n + 6$. Thus, for this mode of usage, the size of the derivation tree is linear in the size of the initial goal.

As another example, consider sumlist for the mode of usage in which the first argument is free and the second argument is fixed. In this case the derivation tree is infinite, indicating that this is probably not a suitable mode of usage for this program.

Usually a program is designed to be as efficient as possible for one or two intended modes of usage. The programmer should, of course, add comments to the program to detail these modes. Standard practice is to add a procedure preface which explicitly

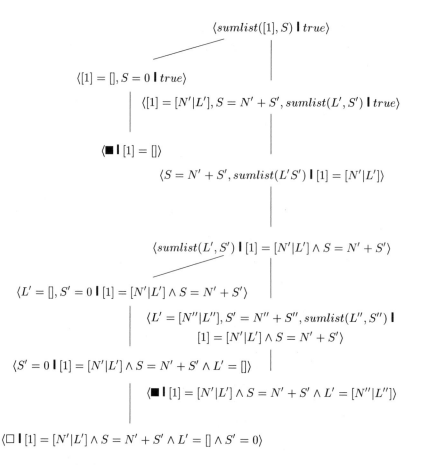

Figure 7.1   Derivation tree for `sumlist([1],S)`.

details the intended mode and to order the arguments so those arguments which are intended to be fixed are placed first and those arguments which are intended to be free are placed last. Thus the `sumlist` program should be written as:

```
% sumlist(L,S): S is the sum of the elements in the fixed size list L
sumlist([], 0).
sumlist([N|L], N + S) :- sumlist(L, S).
```

where % indicates that the rest of the line is a comment. In general, we will not include comments in our example programs since the surrounding text will describe the program and its intended modes of usage, but good CLP programmers will, naturally, include comments as part of their programs.

The reader should be aware, however, that the size of the derivation tree is only a coarse guide to program efficiency. Sometimes execution will only search the derivation tree until the first solution is found, in which case only the size of this part of the derivation tree is important. Furthermore, derivation tree size is not a good measure for comparing the efficiency of programs whose derivation trees are of the same order of magnitude in size. In this case, since a detailed theoretical comparison requires extensive knowledge of the underlying solver and its performance characteristics, empirical comparison of the programs is usually required. Because the derivation tree measure is coarse, we can also use the size of the simplified derivation tree as a measure of program efficiency. In this case we, in effect, count only the number of branches in the derivation tree and ignore constraint collection steps.

We now look at an example illustrating several techniques which may be used to improve the efficiency of a program.

7.2 Controlling Search: An Example

Imagine that we have been asked to write a program to compute

$$S = 0 + 1 + 2 + \cdots + N$$

for a given N. That is to say, we must write a program defining sum(N,S) which constrains N and S so that $S = 0 + 1 + 2 + \cdots + N$ and we want the program to work efficiently for goals of the form sum(N,S) where N is some fixed integer. This doesn't seem too difficult. We can reason recursively: the sum of the first N numbers is the sum S of the first $N - 1$ numbers plus N, and the sum of the first 0 numbers is 0. Our first attempt might be the following simple program:

```
sum(N, S + N)   :-   sum(N - 1, S).   (S1)
sum(0, 0).                            (S2)
```

Now consider what will happen if we type the goal sum(1,S) and ask our CLP system to evaluate it. We wait for a little while, then wait some more. Finally our system tells us that it has run out of stack space. What has gone wrong? To understand we need to look at the simplified derivation tree for the goal shown in Figure 7.2.

The problem is that the leftmost derivation in the tree is infinite. With a depth-first left-to-right search this is the first derivation which will be explored and, since the derivation is infinite, the system never gets a chance to find the successful derivation which is to the right.

After a little thought, we realise that we could reorder the two rules. In this way the successful derivation will be encountered first. The revised program is

```
sum(0, 0).                            (S3)
sum(N, N + S)   :-   sum(N - 1, S).   (S4)
```

Now when we type the goal sum(1,S), our system (quickly) informs us that the answer is $S = 1$.

Being experienced programmers, we decide that a little more testing is required. We type the goal sum(1,0). This is a new mode of usage in which both arguments

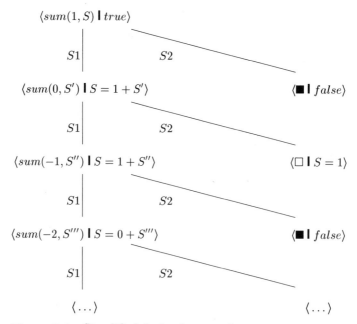

Figure 7.2 Simplified derivation tree for `sum(1,S)`.

are fixed. Unfortunately, instead of getting the desired answer of *no*, our system again complains that it has run out of stack space. What has gone wrong? The problem is that the goal `sum(1,0)` has an infinite derivation resulting from repeatedly choosing the second rule.

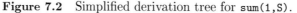

$$\langle sum(1,0) \mathbin{\text{\textbf{I}}} true \rangle$$
$$\Downarrow S4$$
$$\langle sum(0,-1) \mathbin{\text{\textbf{I}}} true \rangle$$
$$\Downarrow S4$$
$$\langle sum(-1,-1) \mathbin{\text{\textbf{I}}} true \rangle$$
$$\Downarrow S4$$
$$\langle sum(-2,0) \mathbin{\text{\textbf{I}}} true \rangle$$
$$\Downarrow S4$$
$$\langle sum(-3,2) \mathbin{\text{\textbf{I}}} true \rangle$$
$$\Downarrow$$
$$\vdots$$

How can we get rid of this unwanted derivation? Examining the simplified derivation reveals the problem. Our program was not intended to work when the first argument was negative. Therefore, the second rule is too general—it should only be used if N is greater than or equal to 1. If N is less than 1 it should fail. Thus we wish to add the constraint $N \geq 1$ to the second rule so as to prune the infinite derivation from the derivation tree. Our new program is now:

```
sum(0, 0).                                          (S5)
sum(N, N + S)   :-   sum(N - 1, S), N ≥ 1.          (S6)
```

The constraint $N \geq 1$ is redundant in the sense that any solution to the original program for sum will satisfy the constraint. But it makes this information explicit, allowing it to be used by the constraint solver earlier in the derivation tree to cause failure and so possibly reducing the size of the derivation tree.

We retry the goal sum(1,0). Unfortunately, again we get a message informing us that the system has run out of stack space. After scratching our heads, we examine the derivation that always uses the second rule and see what the problem is.

$$\langle sum(1,0) \mathbin{\mathbf{I}} true \rangle$$
$$\Downarrow S6$$
$$\langle sum(0,-1), 0 \geq 1 \mathbin{\mathbf{I}} true \rangle$$
$$\Downarrow S6$$
$$\langle sum(-1,-1), -1 \geq 1, 0 \geq 1 \mathbin{\mathbf{I}} true \rangle$$
$$\Downarrow S6$$
$$\langle sum(-2,0), -2 \geq 1, -1 \geq 1, 0 \geq 1 \mathbin{\mathbf{I}} true \rangle$$
$$\Downarrow S6$$
$$\langle sum(-3,2), -3 \geq 1, -2 \geq 1, -1 \geq 1, 0 \geq 1 \mathbin{\mathbf{I}} true \rangle$$
$$\Downarrow$$
$$\vdots$$

Because of the left-to-right processing of a goal, the constraints produced by the test we have just added are never reached, so that the infinite derivation still remains. To overcome this problem we need to reorder the literals in the second rule. Our revised program is

```
sum(0, 0).                                          (S7)
sum(N, N + S)   :-   N ≥ 1, sum(N - 1, S).          (S8)
```

We now test our program. As desired it returns *no* to the goal sum(1,0) and $S = 1$ to the goal sum(1,S). We have now written a program which meets the original specification since the derivation tree for sum(N,S) is finite and linear in the size of N for the mode of usage in which N is fixed.

It is worth recapitulating the three techniques which we used in the above example to make our program terminate. First, we used rule reordering. In general, this allows us to reorder finite derivations before infinite derivations. Second, we added a constraint to a rule. This allows us to prune derivations, infinite and otherwise, from the derivation tree. Third, we reordered the literals in a rule. This allows us to move constraints so that derivations are pruned earlier. These programming techniques are vital weapons in the armoury of the constraint programmer. We will now consider their use in more detail.

7.3 Rule Ordering

The guidelines for ordering the rules in a CLP program are quite simple. The most important is that base cases, that is rules without a (possibly indirect) recursive call, should be placed first in the definition of a recursive predicate. This helps to ensure termination since it means they will be tried before the recursive call. This guideline was exemplified in the sum example of the previous section in which the base case sum(0,0) had to be placed before the recursive rule.

The second guideline is that the rules should be ordered in order of their likelihood of leading to success. This means that on average the answers will be found in the leftmost part of the derivation tree. This rule is more of a heuristic and should be verified by empirical testing.

7.4 Literal Ordering

One of the most important questions facing the novice CLP programmer is how to order the literals in a rule body. Choosing the wrong order can lead to unnecessary search and, as we saw above, in the case of a recursive program, it can lead to non-termination. There are, however, a number of simple guidelines the programmer can use. All of them depend on the intended mode of usage.

The first guideline concerns primitive constraints. These should be placed at the first place in the rule body at which they might cause failure, but no earlier than this. Constraints which cannot cause failure should be put at the end of the rule. Placing the constraint at the first point at which it might cause failure ensures that failure is determined as early as possible, thus reducing the size of the derivation tree. By leaving the addition of constraints until they might cause failure, constraints are not added unnecessarily to the constraint store. This is good as it reduces the number of constraints in the store with the result the solver uses less space and may also run faster.

In the sum example we saw that we needed to reorder the body

$$\text{sum(N-1,S)}, \text{ N} \geq 1.$$

to

$$\text{N} \geq 1, \text{ sum(N-1,S)}.$$

since the constraint $N \geq 1$ can cause failure immediately for the intended mode of usage in which N is fixed.

The remaining guidelines concern user-defined constraints. These guidelines are more heuristic in nature, and are designed to ensure failure occurs as early as possible and that choices are left until as late as possible in the computation. This will tend to increase the work done before a choice is made, meaning that work is not duplicated in different derivations.

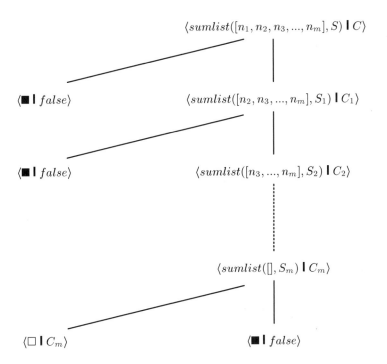

Figure 7.3 Simplified derivation tree for a call to `sumlist` with fixed first argument.

One useful guideline is to call "deterministic" predicates before "non-deterministic" predicates. A predicate is *deterministic* if it does not employ "deep" backtracking. That is, whenever a predicate definition contains multiple rules, all except one of those rules quickly leads to failure. More precisely:

Definition 7.3

A simplified derivation tree is *deterministic* if it is finite and each node in the tree has at most one child which is not a fail state.

A predicate p is *deterministic* for a particular mode of usage if, for any state of the form $\langle p(s_1, \ldots, s_n) \,|\, C\rangle$ satisfying that mode of usage, the states' simplified derivation tree is deterministic.

As an example, the predicate `sumlist` is deterministic for the mode of usage in which the first argument is fixed. To see this consider the simplified derivation tree shown in Figure 7.3 for a call to `sumlist` in which the first argument is a fixed list $[n_1, \ldots, n_m]$. Inspection of the tree reveals that it is finite and that each node has at most one child which is not a fail state. Thus `sumlist` is deterministic for this mode of usage.

The initial definition of the predicate `sum` using rules $S1$ and $S2$ is not deterministic for the mode of usage in which the first argument is fixed. This is because the simplified derivation tree in Figure 7.2 is not finite and also the node at the second choice point has two children which are not fail states. Similarly neither the reordered program ($S3$ and $S4$), nor the next modified version ($S5$ and $S6$) is deterministic. However, the final version of the program sum (*S7* and *S8*) is deterministic for this mode of usage.

Predicates which are used in a mode for which they are deterministic require little search to find an answer. It also follows from the definition that they have at most one answer. Therefore, they should be called before non-deterministic predicates. As an example, recall (part of) the genealogical database from Chapter 5:

```
father(jim,edward).          mother(maggy,fi).
father(jim,maggy).           mother(fi,lillian).
father(edward,peter).
father(edward,helen).
father(edward,kitty).
father(bill,fi).
```

The predicates father and mother are deterministic for the mode of usage in which the second argument is fixed since each person has exactly one father and mother. Note that this is not the case if the first argument is fixed since people can have more than one child.

Now imagine that we wish to define the grandfather(Z,X) relationship which holds if Z is the grandfather of X. One way to define it is:

```
grandfather(Z,X) :- father(Z,Y), father(Y,X).
grandfather(Z,X) :- father(Z,Y), mother(Y,X).
```

We wish to use the program to efficiently answer queries of the form "Who is the grandfather Z of a given person X?" That is, the intended mode of usage is that second argument of grandfather is fixed and the first is free. This means that in both the first and second rules, the first literal is non-deterministic since both of its arguments are free and the last literal is deterministic—for a fixed X there is only one mother or one father. Thus for increased efficiency, we may wish to swap the two literals in each of the rules since the second literal remains deterministic and this places the deterministic call before the non-deterministic. This gives the program:

```
grandfather(Z,X) :- father(Y,X), father(Z,Y).
grandfather(Z,X) :- mother(Y,X), father(Z,Y).
```

This program is much more efficient for the intended mode of usage than the original program, since reordering has made all literals deterministic. For instance, with the original program the goal grandfather(X,peter) generates a simplified derivation tree with 63 states, while, with the second program, the simplified derivation tree has only 23 states. The reader is encouraged to draw both trees.

However when using this guideline it is important to remember that moving a deterministic call too early may mean that it becomes non-deterministic. In general, it should only be moved to the first point at which it becomes deterministic. For instance, in the rule

```
grandfather(Z,X) :- father(Y,X), father(Z,Y).
```

The second user-defined constraint `father(Z,Y)` is deterministic at this point since, by the time it is reached, Y has a fixed value. But, we cannot move the user-defined constraint any earlier because it must follow the call `father(Y,X)` to be deterministic.

Generally, it is a good idea to place literals with a small number of answers before those with many answers, since this will reduce the size of the search tree. In particular, literals with a large number of answers should be placed last.

Imagine that we have already defined the predicate `parent(Y,X)` which holds if Y is the parent of X as follows:

```
parent(Y,X) :- father(Y,X).
parent(Y,X) :- mother(Y,X).
```

We can define the grandfather relationship by

```
grandfather(Z,X) :- father(Z,Y), parent(Y,X).
```

However for the mode of usage in which X is fixed, we are better off to reorder the two literals in the body, since `parent(Y,X)` has at most two answers for a fixed X, while `father(Z,Y)` has many answers for a free Z and Y. This gives us a program which is more efficient for this mode of usage:

```
grandfather(Z,X) :- parent(Y,X), father(Z,Y).
```

When considering the ordering of literals it is important to be aware that reordering can change the mode of usage of the reordered literals, so a call which was deterministic before reordering may become non-deterministic. Because of this, determining the best literal ordering is not always straightforward.

7.5 Adding Redundant Constraints

One useful technique for improving the efficiency of a CLP program is to add constraints which do not change the answers of a program, but which prune unsuccessful branches from the derivation tree earlier.

Definition 7.4
A constraint which can be removed from a rule in a program without changing the answers to any goal is said to be *redundant*.

There are two main types of redundant constraints which can be added to improve the performance of a CLP program.

The first type of redundant constraint is one that is redundant with respect to the answers of a rule's body. We call such constraints *answer redundant*. Given a rule

$$H :- L_1, \ldots, L_i, L_{i+1}, \ldots, L_n.$$

it can be useful to add a primitive constraint c to the rule giving

$$H :- L_1, \ldots, L_i, c, L_{i+1}, \ldots, L_n.$$

if, for some constraint store C satisfying the intended mode of usage of H, the state $\langle L_1, \ldots, L_i, c \mid C \rangle$ finitely fails while the state $\langle L_1, \ldots, L_i \mid C \rangle$ does not; and every answer to the original body, $L_1, \ldots, L_i, L_{i+1}, \ldots, L_n$, implies that c holds.

The constraint c is redundant since it does not change the answers of the rule for H but, since failure may occur earlier, adding it can make computation more efficient.

The constraint $N \geq 1$ added to the final $\mathtt{sum}$ program in Section 7.2, is an example of an answer redundant constraint. It is redundant because all answers to $\mathtt{sum(N\text{-}1,S)}$ imply $N \geq 1$ and, so, adding it does not change the answers. Moreover, adding this constraint is useful, since it can cause failure to occur earlier, as witnessed for the goal $\mathtt{sum(1,0)}$. Indeed, as we saw, adding this constraint drastically improves the performance of the program by pruning an infinite derivation.

As another example, imagine we now wish to extend the $\mathtt{sum}$ program to work efficiently for another mode of usage in which we use the program to answer queries of the form, "Is some fixed number S the sum of the first N numbers for some N?" Given the goal $\mathtt{sum(N,6)}$, the final $\mathtt{sum}$ program from Section 7.2 will correctly find that $N = 3$. The goal $\mathtt{sum(N,7)}$, however, will not terminate.

Consider the first four states in the simplified derivation for the goal $\mathtt{sum(N, 7)}$ resulting when the second rule is always selected.

$$\langle sum(N, 7) \mid true \rangle$$
$$\Downarrow S8$$
$$\langle sum(N', S') \mid N = N' + 1 \wedge S' = 6 - N' \wedge N' \geq 0 \rangle$$
$$\Downarrow S8$$
$$\langle sum(N'', S'') \mid N = N'' + 2 \wedge S'' = 4 - 2 * N'' \wedge N'' \geq 0 \rangle$$
$$\Downarrow S8$$
$$\langle sum(N''', S''') \mid N = N''' + 3 \wedge S''' = 1 - 3 * N''' \wedge N''' \geq 0 \rangle$$
$$\Downarrow S8$$
$$\langle sum(N'''', S'''') \mid N = N'''' + 4 \wedge S'''' = -3 - 4 * N'''' \wedge N'''' \geq 0 \rangle$$

None of these constraints is ever unsatisfiable and so the derivation is infinite. If we examine the constraint in the last state shown, clearly S'''' can only take negative values. But we know that no sum of numbers from 0 to n can be negative, so we know that this state should fail. The problem is that the program does not contain this extra information we know about the sum: that for every n the sum $0 + 1 + 2 + \cdots + n$ is greater than or equal to zero. We can modify the program to include this information by adding the answer redundant constraint $S \geq 0$:

sum(0,0). $(S9)$

sum(N, S+N)   :-   N $\geq$ 1, S $\geq$ 0, sum(N-1, S). $(S10)$

With this new program, execution of the goal sum(N,7) will now finite fail. The constraint store becomes unsatisfiable at the state corresponding to the last one shown above.

$$\langle sum(N, 7) \mathbin{|} true \rangle$$
$$\Downarrow S10$$
$$\langle sum(N', S') \mathbin{|} N = N' + 1 \wedge S' = 6 - N' \wedge N' \geq 0 \wedge N' \leq 6 \rangle$$
$$\Downarrow S10$$
$$\langle sum(N'', S'') \mathbin{|} N = N'' + 2 \wedge S'' = 4 - 2 * N'' \wedge N'' \geq 0 \wedge N'' \leq 2 \rangle$$
$$\Downarrow S10$$
$$\langle sum(N''', S''') \mathbin{|} N = N''' + 3 \wedge S''' = 1 - 3 * N''' \wedge N''' \geq 0 \wedge N''' \leq 1/3 \rangle$$
$$\Downarrow S10$$
$$\langle \blacksquare \mathbin{|} false \rangle$$

This program will answer goals in which the second argument S is fixed by constructing a derivation tree which is linear in S. This is because, at each stage in the derivation after the second state, there is an upper bound on the value of the first argument. Each application of the second rule will decrease the upper bound on the first argument until it conflicts with the constraint $N \geq 1$.

The second type of redundant constraints, "solver redundant" constraints, are useful to consider when the underlying solver is incomplete. A constraint is *solver redundant* if it is implied by the current constraint store. It may be useful to add a solver redundant constraint if it makes explicit information which is implied by the store but which the solver, because of incompleteness, is incapable of extracting.

Understanding the incompleteness of the underlying CLP solver is one of the more difficult tasks for the constraint programmer. Unfortunately such understanding is often necessary as incompleteness may mean a constraint does not prune the search as early as intended since the solver will be unable to determine that the constraint store is unsatisfiable. In such circumstances it is often useful to add another constraint which is redundant with regard to the constraints in the store but which causes failure.

Consider the factorial program from Chapter 4:

fac(0, 1). $(F1)$

fac(N, N*F)   :-   N $\geq$ 1, fac(N - 1, F). $(F2)$

If we execute the goal fac(N, 7), it will run forever for an analogous reason to the goal sum(N, 7) discussed above, namely the current program does not contain the information that all factorials are 1 or greater. Adding the answer redundant constraint $F \geq 1$, we obtain

```
fac(0, 1).                                      (F3)
fac(N, N*F)   :-   N ≥ 1, F ≥ 1, fac(N - 1, F).   (F4)
```

We might now expect that the goal `fac(N, 7)` will fail. Unfortunately, it does not. Let us examine the simplified derivation to see why.

$$\langle fac(N, 7) \mathbin{\textbf{I}} true \rangle$$
$$\Downarrow F4$$
$$\langle fac(N - 1, F') \mathbin{\textbf{I}} F' \geq 1 \wedge N \geq 1 \wedge 7 = N \times F' \rangle$$
$$\Downarrow F4$$
$$\langle fac(N - 2, F'') \mathbin{\textbf{I}} F'' \geq 1 \wedge N \geq 2 \wedge 7 = N \times (N - 1) \times F'' \rangle$$
$$\Downarrow F4$$
$$\langle fac(N - 3, F''') \mathbin{\textbf{I}} F''' \geq 1 \wedge N \geq 3 \wedge 7 = N \times (N - 1) \times (N - 2) \times F''' \rangle$$
$$\Downarrow F4$$
$$\langle fac(N - 4, F'''') \mathbin{\textbf{I}} F'''' \geq 1 \wedge N \geq 4 \wedge$$
$$7 = N \times (N - 1) \times (N - 2) \times (N - 3) \times F'''' \rangle$$
$$\Downarrow F4$$
$$\vdots$$

The constraint in the last state shown is unsatisfiable (since $F'''' \geq 1$ and $N \geq 4$ we have that $N \times (N - 1) \times (N - 2) \times (N - 3) \times F''''$ must be greater than 24). Unfortunately, solvers for real arithmetic constraints do not usually handle nonlinear constraints completely, so this unsatisfiability is not detected and the derivation is infinite.

However we can overcome the incompleteness of the constraint solver by adding the constraint that $N \leq F \times N$. This constraint is solver redundant since it is implied by the constraint $N \geq 1 \wedge F \geq 1$. We must take care when adding this constraint that we take proper account of the way in which the solver handles nonlinear constraints. For instance, the goal `1 = F * N, 2 = F * N` will succeed if different occurrences of the expression $F \times N$ are treated as different expressions by the incomplete solver. This is usually the case. Therefore, rather than use the expression `F * N` twice, we need to name the expression and use the name twice. The new program is:

```
fac(0, 1).                                          (F5)
fac(N, FN) :- FN = F*N, N ≥ 1, F ≥ 1, N ≤ FN, fac(N - 1, F). (F6)
```

The new variable FN names the expression $F \times N$. For this program the goal `fac(N, 7)` does fail, after 7 selections of a `fac` literal. The constraints after the 4th selection are still unsatisfiable (although the solver does not detect it). One effect of each derivation step is to increase a lower bound on N by one. From the first derivation step we have that $N \leq FN$ and $FN = 7$. Eventually, the effect of the derivation steps is to constrain $N \geq 8$ and so the derivation fails.

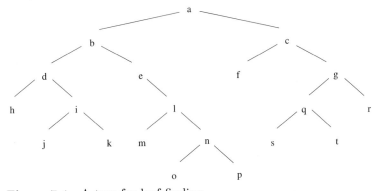

Figure 7.4 A tree for leaf finding.

7.6 Minimization

Much combinatorial search is hidden inside minimization literals. It is, therefore, important to ensure that the goal being minimized has the smallest possible search space.

One common mistake for the novice CLP programmer is to assume that the search space for `minimize(G,E)` for a particular mode of usage is simply that of G for that mode of usage. However, because of the implementation of minimization, the minimization subgoal will be evaluated using goals of the form

```
E < m, G.
```

where m is fixed. Thus it is important to ensure that the definition of G is also efficient for this mode of usage in which E is bounded above.

Consider a simple program which takes a binary tree and returns each leaf of the tree and its corresponding depth.

```
leaflevel(node(null, X, null), X, 0).                    (LL1)
leaflevel(node(TL, _, _), X, D+1) :- leaflevel(TL, X, D). (LL2)
leaflevel(node(_, _, TR), X, D+1) :- leaflevel(TR, X, D). (LL3)
```

The first rule succeeds when the tree is a leaf node and the remaining rules return the leaves of the left and right subtrees of a non-leaf node, appropriately increasing the depth. The goal `leaflevel(`t_a`, X, D)` where t_a is the term representation of the tree rooted at a shown in Figure 7.4 has the answers:

$$X = h \land D = 3, \quad X = j \land D = 4, \quad X = k \land D = 4,$$
$$X = m \land D = 4, \quad X = o \land D = 5, \quad X = p \land D = 5,$$
$$X = f \land D = 2, \quad X = s \land D = 4, \quad X = t \land D = 4,$$
$$X = r \land D = 3.$$

Suppose we wish to find the leaves at the minimum depth. The goal

```
minimize(leaflevel(t_a, X, D), D).
```

will answer this question. Unfortunately, evaluation of this goal will be rather inefficient for most implementations of minimization search.

To understand why, we first need to understand how `minimize` is usually implemented. Most implementations do not traverse the entire derivation tree of the minimization subgoal to find the minimum value of the objective function. Instead, they keep track of the minimum value found so far, and add a constraint to the constraint store which places this value as an upper bound on the objective function. With luck, this upper bound will substantially prune the derivation tree of the original subgoal. This is analogous to the techniques used in retry_int_opt and back_int_opt in Chapter 3 and will be discussed more fully in Section 10.5.

Now we can identify the problem with the current definition of `leaflevel`. Adding a constraint of the form $D < n$ in which n is fixed will not reduce the search space of the minimization subgoal `leaflevel(t, X, D)` since a constraint of this form can only cause failure when a leaf node is reached. Thus, evaluation of

```
minimize(leaflevel(t_a, X, D), D).
```

will be forced to traverse the entire tree shown in Figure 7.4. This is despite the fact that once a solution has been found in which $D = n$ then the tree does not need to be visited at depths greater than n.

To improve the efficiency of the minimization subgoal we need to modify the predicate `leaflevel` so that it is more efficient for calls in which the second argument is bounded above. Currently such information is not used by the `leaflevel` program to prune the derivation tree. To see exactly why, consider the goal

```
D < 3, leaflevel(t_a, X, D)
```

and its simplified derivation

$$\langle D < 3, leaflevel(t_a, X, D) \mathbin{|} true \rangle$$
$$\Downarrow$$
$$\langle leaflevel(t_a, X, D) \mathbin{|} D < 3 \rangle$$
$$\Downarrow LL2$$
$$\langle leaflevel(t_b, X, D-1) \mathbin{|} D < 3 \rangle$$
$$\Downarrow LL2$$
$$\langle leaflevel(t_d, X, D-2) \mathbin{|} D < 3 \rangle$$
$$\Downarrow LL3$$
$$\langle leaflevel(t_i, X, D-3) \mathbin{|} D < 3 \rangle$$
$$\Downarrow LL3$$
$$\langle leaflevel(t_k, X, D-4) \mathbin{|} D < 3 \rangle$$
$$\Downarrow LL1$$
$$\langle \blacksquare \mathbin{|} D < 3 \wedge D - 4 = 0 \rangle$$

where t_b, t_d, t_i, t_k are the subtrees of the tree illustrated in Figure 7.4, rooted at b, d, i and k respectively. We would like the derivation to fail before visiting i and k since any leaf in the subtree of t_d must occur at a depth greater than 3.

To do this we can modify the program by adding the answer redundant information that every leaf level is non-negative. Now an upper bound on depth can cause failure before a leaf is reached. The revised program is:

```
leaflevel(node(null,X,null),X,0).                              (LL4)
leaflevel(node(TL, _, _), X, D+1) :- D ≥ 0, leaflevel(TL, X, D).(LL5)
leaflevel(node(_, _, TR), X, D+1) :- D ≥ 0, leaflevel(TR, X, D).(LL6)
```

The corresponding derivation for the goal D < 3, leaflevel(t_a, X, D) is

$$\langle D < 3, leaflevel(t, X, D) \mathbin{\text{\textbar}} true \rangle$$
$$\Downarrow$$
$$\langle leaflevel(t_a, X, D) \mathbin{\text{\textbar}} D < 3 \rangle$$
$$\Downarrow LL5$$
$$\langle leaflevel(t_b, X, D-1) \mathbin{\text{\textbar}} D < 3 \wedge D \geq 1 \rangle$$
$$\Downarrow LL5$$
$$\langle leaflevel(t_d, X, D-2) \mathbin{\text{\textbar}} D < 3 \wedge D \geq 2 \rangle$$
$$\Downarrow LL6$$
$$\langle \blacksquare \mathbin{\text{\textbar}} D < 3 \wedge D \geq 3 \rangle$$

As required, the derivation fails before visiting nodes i and k.

Evaluation of the minimization subgoal minimize(leaflevel(t_a, X, D), D) with this revised program will be substantially faster than with the original program. A typical implementation of minimize will visit only half the nodes in the tree t_a since once leaf node h is found, subtrees below depth 3 will not be explored and once leaf node f is found, subtrees below depth 2 will not be explored.

It is not always possible for a minimization search to benefit from upper bounds placed on the objective function because of answers found previously. For example, imagine searching for the deepest leaf in the tree t_a using the goal

```
minimize(leaflevel(t_a, X, D), -D).
```

Knowing there is a leaf at depth 3 cannot save us from examining every node in the tree to see if it contains a deeper leaf. In other words, there is no more efficient way to write leaflevel for the mode of usage in which the depth is bounded from below. For this goal, the original formulation of leaflevel is arguably superior since it uses less constraints.

7.7   Identifying Deterministic Subgoals

We have identified a number of guidelines the programmer can follow for writing more efficient CLP programs. However, the default evaluation mechanism still uses depth-first search, which has substantial unnecessary overhead when evaluating deterministic calls. This is because evaluation of even a deterministic call can set up choicepoints to which subsequent execution may backtrack. This is expensive, both in terms of space and time, since the system needs to save information about each choicepoint. In the case of deterministic calls, this cost is unnecessary since, once a deterministic call has succeeded, there is no need to backtrack to a choicepoint within the call as trying other choices can only lead to failure.

We now look at two constructs—*if-then-else* and *once*—provided by many CLP languages which may be used by the programmer to identify pieces of code which are deterministic and so allow the system to evaluate these parts of the program more efficiently.

7.7.1   If-Then-Else

The conditional statement or *if-then-else* is the most common way of identifying deterministic subgoals.

Definition 7.5
An *if-then-else literal* is of the form $(G_{test} \; \text{->} \; G_{then} \; ; \; G_{else})$ where G_{test}, G_{then} and G_{else} are goals. It is read as "*if G_{test} then G_{then} else G_{else}.*"

Evaluation of a conditional literal $(G_{test} \; \text{->} \; G_{then} \; ; \; G_{else})$ is reasonably intuitive. First, the test subgoal G_{test} is evaluated to see if it succeeds. If it does, the *then* branch, G_{then}, is executed. Otherwise, if G_{test} finitely fails, the *else* branch, G_{else}, is executed. We extend the standard CLP evaluation mechanism by adding a derivation step for processing if-then-else literals:

Definition 7.6
An *if-then-else derivation step* is a derivation step $\langle G_1 \mid C_1 \rangle \Rightarrow \langle G_2 \mid C_2 \rangle$, in which an if-then-else literal is rewritten. Conceptually it is defined as follows (we shall explore the implementation further in Chapter 10). Let G_1 be the sequence of literals

$$L_1, L_2, \ldots, L_m$$

and let L_1 be of the form $(G_{test} \; \text{->} \; G_{then} \; ; \; G_{else})$. There are two cases.

1. The state $\langle G_{test} \mid C_1 \rangle$ succeeds and the leftmost successful derivation is

$$\langle G_{test} \mid C_1 \rangle \Rightarrow \cdots \Rightarrow \langle \square \mid C \rangle.$$

In this case, C_2 is C and G_2 is $G_{then}, L_2, \ldots, L_m$.

2. Evaluation of the state $\langle G_{test} \mid C_1 \rangle$ finitely fails. In this case, C_2 is C_1 and G_2 is $G_{else}, L_2, \ldots, L_m$.

Note that if evaluation of the test goal G_{test} does not terminate, the original goal $\langle G_1 \mid C_1 \rangle$ cannot be rewritten.

The *if-then-else* literal does not backtrack through different answers for the test goal G_{test}. It simply finds the first answer and commits to this. However, backtracking can occur inside goals G_{then} and G_{else}. The main benefit of *if-then-else* literals is that once the *then* branch is chosen, there is no need to backtrack to the *else* branch. Thus, there is no need for the system to set up a choicepoint.

As an example, let us define a predicate `abs(X,Y)` constraining Y to be the absolute value of X.

```
abs(X, Y) :- (X >= 0 -> Y = X ; Y = -X).
```

This has the natural reading: if $X \geq 0$ then the absolute value of X is X, else the absolute value of X is $-X$.

As an example of its evaluation, the goal `abs(4, A)` succeeds with the single answer $A = 4$ as expected. Execution starts by rewriting `abs(4,A)` to the state

$$\langle 4 = X, A = Y, (X \geq 0 \rightarrow Y = X \; ; \; Y = -X) \mid true \rangle.$$

The constraints $4 = X$ and $A = Y$ are added in turn to the constraint store giving

$$\langle (X \geq 0 \rightarrow Y = X \; ; \; Y = -X) \mid 4 = X \wedge A = Y \rangle.$$

The if-then-else literal is processed by first evaluating the state

$$\langle X \geq 0 \mid 4 = X \wedge A = Y \rangle.$$

This has a single successful derivation whose final constraint store is

$$4 = X \wedge A = Y \wedge X \geq 0.$$

Thus the state above is rewritten using the *then* branch of the if-then-else literal giving:

$$\langle Y = X \mid 4 = X \wedge A = Y \wedge X \geq 0 \rangle.$$

Finally, the constraint $Y = X$ is added to the constraint store, giving the answer.

Similar reasoning shows that the goal `abs(-4, A)` succeeds with answer $A = 4$ as expected.

To understand the advantage of if-then-else, consider how we would have had to write the `abs` program without it. This would have required two rules:

```
abs(X, X) :- X >= 0.
abs(X, -X) :- X < 0.
```

Evaluation of the goal `abs(4, A)` using this program will also succeed with the answer $A = 4$ as expected. However, unlike the definition using if-then-else, there will also be a choicepoint set up which, on subsequent failure, will cause the second rule in this definition of `abs` to be tried. This will of course fail. The advantage of the if-then-else definition is that is tells the CLP system that the definition for `abs` is deterministic in the sense that, if the test succeeds, there is no need to try the *then* branch since this will fail (once the implicit negation of the test is added).

Unfortunately, the programmer must be very careful when using if-then-else literals as their behaviour depends greatly on their mode of usage. One problem is that if the arguments to the test goal in an if-then-else literal are not fixed at the time of evaluation, answers may be lost.

The definition of `abs` using if-then-else works well for the mode of usage in which the first argument, X, is fixed. However, if X is not fixed then its behaviour is quite strange. For instance, the goal

```
abs(X, 2), X < 0.
```

fails, rather than giving the expected answer $X = -2$. This is because the test goal $X \geq 0$ succeeds, which commits the derivation to use the *then* part of the if-then-else subgoal $Y = X$. Later when we add $X < 0$ the derivation fails. This means that the order of the literals becomes important in reasoning with if-then-else literals since, for example, the goal

```
X < 0, abs(X, 2).
```

succeeds with answer $X = -2$.

Another potential problem with if-then-else is that only the *first* answer of the state $\langle G_{test} \mid C_1 \rangle$ is found and afterwards no other answers will be examined.

Suppose we wish to define a constraint between X and Y that holds if they are at least 4 apart or they are identical. We might use if-then-else to write this as:

```
far_or_equal(X, Y) :- (apart(X,Y,4) -> true ; X = Y).

apart(X,Y,D) :- X >= Y + D.
apart(X,Y,D) :- Y >= X + D.
```

Here, for the first time in a program, we use the primitive constraint `true`. Normally a *true* constraint adds nothing to the goal, so it is not used. But here we need to provide a goal G_{then} which does nothing. Therefore we use `true`. When it is processed it is simply removed from the goal.

The program states that either X and Y are at least 4 apart, or if this is not the case they are equal. The goal `far_or_equal(1, 6)` succeeds, and the goal `far_or_equal(1, 3)` fails as expected. They work correctly because the mode of usage ensures all variables in the test goal are fixed. The goal

```
far_or_equal(1, Y), Y = 6.
```

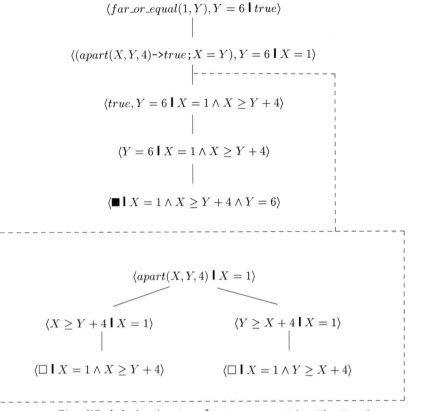

Figure 7.5   Simplified derivation tree for `far_or_equal(1, Y)`, `Y = 6`.

fails however. The derivation tree shown in Figure 7.5 illustrates why. At the state
in which the if-then-else literal is rewritten, the system first explores the derivation
tree for the goal $\langle apart(X, Y, 4) \mid X = 1 \rangle$. This tree is shown in the dashed box.
Execution of the test goal `apart(X,Y,4)` traverses this derivation tree until the
first answer, $X = 1 \wedge X \geq Y + 4$, is found. This gives the constraint store for the
subsequent execution of the then goal. But this answer is not compatible with the
constraint $Y = 6$, so the derivation eventually fails. However, if the other answer
to the test goal had been used the derivation would have succeeded.

Although if-then-else is dangerous to use when the mode of usage does not ensure
all the variables involved in the test are fixed, it can be very useful if all the variables
are fixed. In particular, once we test a constraint in which all of the variables are
fixed and it fails then we can be sure that the negation of the constraint holds, so
we do not need to test for this explicitly.

For example, we can redefine the `cumul_predecessors` predicate of Example 6.5
to avoid using `not_member` since its only purpose was to ensure that the `member`
constraint did not hold. The new code is:

```
cumul_predecessors_ift([], _, Pre, Pre).
cumul_predecessors_ift([N|Ns], AList, Pre0, Pre) :-
    (member(N, Pre0) ->
        Pre1 = Pre0
    ;
        predecessors(N, AList, [N|Pre0], Pre1)
    ),
    cumul_predecessors_ift(Ns, AList, Pre1, Pre).
```

If N has already been seen, that is, it is a member of $Pre0$, then the predecessors do not change so $Pre1 = Pre0$. Otherwise N is added to the accumulator and its predecessors are recursively added to obtain $Pre1$. Computation continues on the rest of the list Ns with the current accumulator $Pre1$. Correctness of this definition relies on N and $Pre0$ being fixed by the time member(N, Pre0) is evaluated.

7.7.2   Once

A construct closely related to if-then-else is once. This finds the first answer to a subgoal and commits to it.

Definition 7.7
A *once literal* is of the form $once(G)$ where G is a goal, called the *once subgoal*.

The operational behavior of a once literal is quite straightforward: find the first answer to the once subgoal. If the once subgoal finitely fails then fail.

Definition 7.8
A *once derivation step* is a derivation step $\langle G_1 \mid C_1 \rangle \Rightarrow \langle G_2 \mid C_2 \rangle$ in which a once subgoal is rewritten. Conceptually it is defined as follows (again we explore the implementation further in Chapter 10). Let G_1 be the sequence of literals

$$L_1, L_2, \ldots, L_m$$

and let L_1 be of the form $once(G)$. There are two cases.

1. The state $\langle G \mid C_1 \rangle$ succeeds and has the leftmost successful derivation

$$\langle G \mid C_1 \rangle \Rightarrow \cdots \Rightarrow \langle \Box \mid C \rangle.$$

In this case, C_2 is C and G_2 is $L_2, \ldots, L_m$.

2. The state $\langle G \mid C_1 \rangle$ finitely fails. In this case, C_2 is *false* and G_2 is ■.

The once operator is used when the programmer knows that each of the possible answers to some user-defined constraint are equivalent. Hence, once the first answer is found the other answers can be ignored.

Example 7.1

Consider the following definition for a predicate `intersect` which determines if two sets, which are represented by lists, intersect.

```
intersect(L1, L2) :- member(X,L1), member(X,L2).
```

Now consider the goal

```
intersect([a,b,e,g,h], [b,e,f,g,i]).
```

Part of the simplified derivation tree for this goal is shown in Figure 7.6. The total simplified derivation tree has 72 states. The first answer, *true*, is found after visiting 18 states. Exploration of the remaining part of the tree finds 2 more answers, both *true*.

Since all of the answers are equivalent, this definition of `intersect` can be improved by using a once literal.

```
intersect(L1, L2) :- once(member(X,L1), member(X,L2)).
```

The advantage of this formulation is that it tells the CLP system not to bother looking for alternate answers after finding the first answer. This can dramatically reduce the search space.

For example, using the original formulation of `intersect`, evaluation of the goal

```
intersect([a,b,e,g,h], [b,e,f,g,i]), 0 = 1.
```

searches a simplified derivation tree analogous to that partially illustrated in Figure 7.6, visiting a total of 72 states, before finite failing. With the improved formulation, only those (18) states in the derivation tree before the first answer are visited.

7.8 An Extended Example: Bridge Building

We conclude this chapter with an extended example that highlights many of the efficiency issues we have discussed. One of the strengths of CLP languages is in engineering analysis and design. We have already seen how arithmetic constraints and hierarchical definitions allow the natural and powerful modelling of complex systems. Design is facilitated by the built-in capacity for search. By first building a general program for analysis and then adding a component to search through designs, we can write simple yet powerful design programs. However, for this to be practical it is important that the design space is as small as possible. In this section we show how techniques for reducing the search space of a program can be used to develop a program for designing "spaghetti bridges."

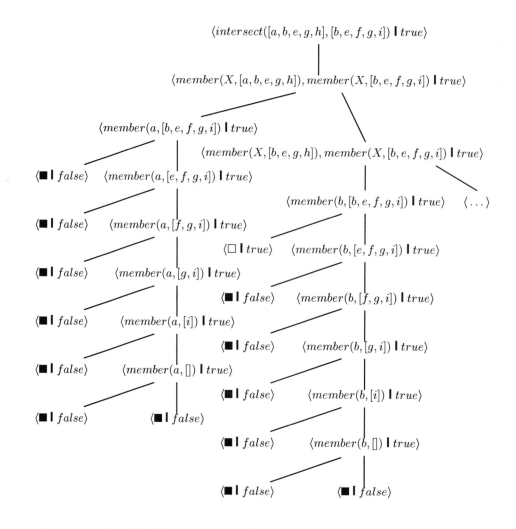

Figure 7.6 Simplified derivation tree for an intersection goal.

7.8.1 Analysis

Consider the problem of analysing a bridge made out of spaghetti. For simplicity we shall reduce the problem to two dimensions by ignoring the width of the bridge. The bridge is built out of spaghetti struts and joins, which have the following properties.

A strut can be stressed with an amount F of stretching force, parallel in direction to its length. A strut of length L cm can sustain any amount of stretching force F, but only $0.5 \times (6 - L)$ Newton (N) of compression force, that is negative stretching force. Implicitly this constrains each strut to be no longer than 6 cm. The total amount of spaghetti available to build struts is 20 cm.

Two fixed joins are available on each side of the gap to be spanned by the bridge. Other joins are floating joins, one of which must be placed in the center of the gap. For stability every floating join must be connected to at least three struts of

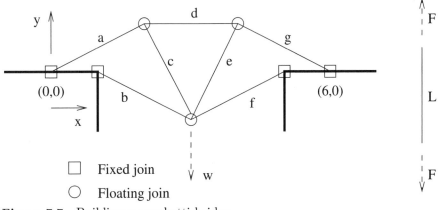

Figure 7.7 Building a spaghetti bridge.

spaghetti. An exception is the center join which only needs to be connected to two struts, since the weight hanging from the bridge acts as a third strut. A floating join can sustain any amount of compression force from any one strut, but only 2 N of stretching force. The vector sum of the forces at each floating join must equal zero. The bridge is adequate if it can support a weight of 2 N hanging from the center floating join. A sample bridge is shown in Figure 7.7.

To solve this problem we first need to decide how to represent a bridge. Let us use two lists, a list of floating joins and a list of struts which act as association lists detailing the data associated with struts and joins in a bridge. The centre join is represented by the term $cjoin(x, y, l)$ where (x, y) is the coordinates of the join and l is a list of the names of connected struts. Other floating joins are represented by $join(x, y, l)$. This representation allows us to test whether a join J is the centre join by simply using the constraint $J = cjoin(\_, \_, \_)$. A strut is represented by the term $strut(n, x_1, y_1, x_2, y_2)$ where n is the strut name, and the two endpoints are (x_1, y_1) and (x_2, y_2). The bridge shown in Figure 7.7 is represented by the list of joins, abbreviated to js,

```
[join(2,1,[a,c,d]), join(4,1,[d,e,g]), cjoin(3,-1,[b,c,e,f])]
```

and the list of struts, abbreviated to ss,

```
[    strut(a,0,0,2,1), strut(b,1,0,3,-1), strut(c,2,1,3,-1),
     strut(d,2,1,4,1), strut(e,3,-1,4,1), strut(f,3,-1,5,0),
     strut(g,4,1,6,0)]
```

Analysis of a bridge produces an association list detailing the forces on each strut. Records in the list are pairs of form $f(N, F)$ where N is the strut name and F the stretching force on the strut. A program which analyses a bridge design must simply collect the constraints on forces acting on each join and strut.

We begin by analyzing the forces in each strut. For each strut we must assert the maximum compression force constraint, and for the total group of struts we need to assert the total length constraint. The following program defines a predicate `struts_cons` which takes the list of struts and asserts the maximum compression constraints and calculates the total length of the struts.

```
struts_cons([], [], 0).
struts_cons([strut(N,X1,Y1,X2,Y2) | Ss], [f(N, F) | Fs], TL) :-
    L = √(X1-X2)*(X1-X2) + (Y1-Y2)*(Y1-Y2),
    F ≥ - 0.5 * (6 - L),
    TL = L + RL,
    struts_cons(Ss, Fs, RL).
```

This is a simple recursive program that adds constraints for each strut. The first argument is a list of strut information, as in the example above. The second argument is an association list relating the strut name to the force within the strut. The third argument is the total length of the struts in the list. The non-recursive rule is first, the usual rule ordering, so that the program is likely to work in more modes of usage (for example, the goal `struts_cons(Ss, Fs, TL)` will find answers before reaching an infinite derivation). The constraints in the recursive case are all placed before the recursive call in case they do not hold. The program is deterministic as long as either the first or second argument is a list of fixed length.

The goal `struts_cons(ss, Fs, TL)` succeeds with answer

$$Fs = [f(a, F_a), f(b, F_b), f(c, F_c), f(d, F_d), f(e, F_e), f(f, F_f), f(g, F_g)] \wedge$$
$$TL = 15.4164 \wedge$$
$$F_a \geq -1.88197 \wedge F_b \geq -1.88197 \wedge F_c \geq -1.88197 \wedge F_d \geq -2 \wedge$$
$$F_e \geq -1.88197 \wedge F_f \geq -1.88197 \wedge F_g \geq -1.88197$$

This shows the association list produced and the maximum compression constraints applied to each force associated to a strut, as well as the total length computation.

However this definition is not ideal for our purposes. This predicate will be required to evaluate partially specified designs, and, so as to ensure the design space is a small as possible, should fail as quickly as possible. The current definition does not always do this. Suppose the total length of the struts was limited to 5 cm, then the goal

$$TL \leq 5, \text{ struts\_cons}(ss, Fs, TL).$$

will fail. Unfortunately, the derivation will fail only after examining all of the struts. This is the same problem as occurred for the goal `sum(N,7)` in Section 7.5, although no infinite derivation is possible here.

We know that each strut is of length at least 0, so the total length of any group of struts is also at least 0. Any answer to `strut_cons` will reflect this, but the information is not available until the last strut is examined. By adding the answer redundant constraint that the remaining length RL must be at least 0, the derivation will fail earlier.

```
struts_cons([], [], 0).
struts_cons([strut(N,X1,Y1,X2,Y2) | Ss], [f(N, F) | Fs], TL) :-
    L = √(X1-X2)*(X1-X2) + (Y1-Y2)*(Y1-Y2),
    F ≥ - 0.5 * (6 - L),
    TL = L + RL,
    RL ≥ 0,
    struts_cons(Ss, Fs, RL).
```

The goal TL $\leq$ 5, strut_cons(*ss*, Fs, TL) now fails after examining the first three struts.

Now suppose we use the strut_cons program to analyse a partial design in which not all coordinates are known. Unfortunately, the constraint solver is incomplete for nonlinear constraints so it may not fail when we expect it to. For example, the goal

```
    Fa ≤ -4, struts_cons([strut(a,A,B,C,D)], [f(a,Fa)], TL).
```

asserts that the compression force in strut a is at least 4 N. Since the maximum compression force sustainable by any strut is 3 N, this goal should fail. However, it succeeds. This is because the incomplete solver does not determine that the length of the strut is at least 0. Adding the solver redundant constraint $L \geq 0$ will solve this problem. In fact we should probably add $L > 0$, which asserts that the length of every strut is greater than 0, since this is an implicit constraint on the design. The final code for strut_cons is therefore

```
struts_cons([], [], 0).
struts_cons([strut(N,X1,Y1,X2,Y2) | Ss], [f(N, F) | Fs], TL) :-
    L = √(X1-X2)*(X1-X2) + (Y1-Y2)*(Y1-Y2),
    L > 0,
    F ≥ - 0.5 * (6 - L),
    TL = L + RL,
    RL ≥ 0,
    struts_cons(Ss, Fs, RL).
```

With this definition, the goal above fails as desired.

Now let us examine how to model the constraints on a single join. We need to check that the join has enough incident struts, that the sum of the forces at the join equals zero and that no strut compresses the join more than 2 N. First, let us write a predicate to determine the sum of the forces in the x and y direction at a join.

```
sum_forces([], _, _, _, _, 0, 0).
sum_forces([N|Ns], X, Y, Ss, Fs, SFX, SFY) :-
    member(strut(N, X1, Y1, X2, Y2), Ss),
    whichend(X1,Y1,X2,Y2,X,Y,X0,Y0),
    member(f(N, F), Fs),
    F ≤ 2,
    L = √(X-X0)*(X-X0) + (Y-Y0)*(Y-Y0),
    FX = F * (X - X0) / L,
    SFX = FX + RFX,
    FY = F * (Y - Y0) / L,
    SFY = FY + RFY,
    sum_forces(Ns, X, Y, Ss, Fs, RFX, RFY).
```

```
whichend(X, Y, X0, Y0, X, Y, X0, Y0).
whichend(X0, Y0, X, Y, X, Y, X0, Y0).
```

The predicate `sum_forces(Ns, X, Y, Ss, Fs, SFX, SFY)` takes a list of strut
names, Ns, that are incident on the join at (X, Y), the list of struts, Ss, and
the force association list, Fs. It determines the sum of forces in the x direction,
SFX, and in the y direction, SFY. The base case is clear—the sum of the
forces in both directions is 0 for an empty list of struts. The recursive case first
looks up the information about the strut named N in the strut list. A call to
`whichend` determines which end of the strut $s(N, X1, Y1, X2, Y2)$ is connected to
the join (X, Y) (where $(X0, Y0)$ is the coordinate of the other end). Next, the force
information for the strut is looked up in the force list. A constraint enforcing the
stretching force to be no greater than 2 N is added (this implies the compression
force on the join is no greater than 2 N). Finally the proportion of the force in the
strut exerted in the x and y direction is calculated.

We can use the `sum_forces` predicate to build the constraints on each join. There
are two cases to consider. For the center join, the sum of forces must equal the
weight, W, in the y direction, and 0 in the x direction. For all other floating joins,
both sums must be zero. The following program places these constraints on the
joins.

```
joins_cons([], _Ss, _Fs, _W).
joins_cons([J|Js], Ss, Fs, W) :-
    one_join(J, Ss, Fs, W),
    joins_cons(Js, Ss, Fs, W).
```

```
one_join(cjoin(X, Y, Ns), Ss, Fs, W) :-
    Ns = [_,_|_],
    sum_forces(Ns, X, Y, Ss, Fs, 0, W).
one_join(join(X, Y, Ns), Ss, Fs, _W) :-
    Ns = [_,_,_| _],
    sum_forces(Ns, X, Y, Ss, Fs, 0, 0).
```

The predicate `joins_cons` checks each join J in the first argument using the predicate `one_join`. The first rule for `one_join` ensures that a center join has at least 2 incident struts by testing that the list Ns has at least two elements, and that the sum of the forces of struts incident at it adds up to W. The second rule ensures other floating joins have at least 3 incident struts (by testing that the list Ns has at least three elements) and the sum of forces incident at the join is zero.

The following goal tests whether the bridge design illustrated in Figure 7.7 satisfies the design constraints.

`TL` $\leq$ `20, W` $\geq$ `2, struts_cons(`*ss*`, Fs, TL), joins_cons(`*js*`, `*ss*`, Fs, W).`

The answer restricted to W is $2 \leq W \wedge W \leq 3.28328$ indicating the bridge satisfies the design constraints.

7.8.2   Design

Since we have written the analysis program with more complex modes of usage in mind, we can also use it for designing bridges. To avoid an explosion in the design search space, we need to add the analysis constraints *before* enumerating different designs, thus constraining the problem before generating possible solutions. This reduces the search space by ensuring that partial designs which do not satisfy the design constraints will be rejected as soon as possible.

Our aim is to design a bridge over a gap of width 4 cm, as shown in Figure 7.7, which can support the maximum possible weight hanging from the centre. However, simply running the goal

`TL` $\leq$ `20, minimize((struts_cons(Ss,Fs,TL),joins_cons(Js,Ss,Fs,W)),-W).`

will, unfortunately, not give an answer. There are three problems. First, not all implicit constraints about correct designs are modelled in `strut_cons` and `joins_cons`. For example, each strut must have both endpoints at either a fixed or floating join. Second, even if we added these implicit constraints, the evaluation is unlikely to find any correct designs before it finds an infinite derivation. Third, even if we found a suitable design, the constraints remaining are likely to be nonlinear (because of length calculations) and so it is unlikely that the minimization algorithm will be able to find an optimal solution. What can we do?

The `strut_cons` predicate is deterministic as long as the number of struts is fixed. The `joins_cons` predicate has one solution as long as the join list is fixed in length and a fixed list of distinct incident strut names is given for each join. It is not deterministic because of the search that occurs in the `member` and `whichend` literals. However, by using a once literal we can make it deterministic.

This suggests that we write a user-defined constraint to define suitable bridge topologies. This will fix the number of struts and joins, and ensure that implicit deign constraints, such as struts having endpoints at joins, are satisfied. Then we can apply the strut constraints and join constraints deterministically. Finally we can search for appropriate positions for the joins. The top-level goal will be of form

```
tpl(Js, Ss, Vs),
TL ≤ 20,
struts_cons(Ss,Fs,TL),
once(joins_cons(Js,Ss,Fs,W)),
minimize(position(Vs),-W).
```

The predicate `tpl(Js, Ss, Vs)` generates a topology for the bridge. *Js* is a list of the joins with variables for their coordinates, *Ss* is a list of the struts and their connections and *Vs* is the list of variables in the coordinates of the joins. To make it deterministic, the call to `joins_cons` is surrounded with `once`. The predicate `position(Vs)` searches through positions for the coordinate variables.

Unfortunately, automatic generation of meaningful bridge topologies is quite difficult. Even if we only consider the possible graphs for three floating joins there are 2^{15} possibilities. So if we are going to search through different topologies for our bridge we need to restrict this large search space very significantly. One reasonable solution to this problem is to involve the designer in this phase of design. Instead of generating different topologies automatically, a topology can be given by the user. In this way the design program is used interactively, with the user specifying the design topology, and the CLP system finding a good set of coordinates for a bridge that satisfies the given topology.

We shall now continue developing our bridge design program under the assumption that the designer has suggested the bridge has the same topology as the bridge in Figure 7.7. That is, the designer is interested in bridges with the same struts and connection. Since only the topology is decided, the position of the floating joins is not fixed. This can be achieved by defining the predicate `tpl` to be:

```
tpl([join(X1,Y1,[a,c,d]),join(X2,Y2,[d,e,g]),cjoin(X3,Y3,[b,c,e,f])],
    [strut(a,0,0,X1,Y1), strut(b,1,0,X3,Y3), strut(c,X1,Y1,X3,Y3),
    strut(d,X1,Y1,X2,Y2), strut(e,X3,Y3,X2,Y2), strut(f,X3,Y3,5,0),
    strut(g,X2,Y2,6,0)], [X1,Y1,X2,Y2,X3,Y3]) :- X3 = 3.
```

The call to `tpl(Js, Ss, Vs)` constrains the join list, *Js*, strut list, *Ss*, and list of coordinates, *Vs*, (which we shall make use of later). The coordinates of the floating joins are replaced by variables in both the join and strut list. The variables are collected in a list as the third argument. Note that, since we know that the centre join must be in the centre of the gap, we can set $X3 = 3$.

Assuming the constraint solver handles nonlinear constraints incompletely, the goal

```
tpl(Js,Ss,Vs), TL≤20, struts_cons(Ss,Fs,TL), joins_cons(Js,Ss,Fs,W).
```

will, unfortunately, fail to provide useful information since the constraints it sets up are nonlinear because of the length calculations. The answer to the goal is a large nonlinear constraint which is not particularly helpful in finding an actual solution.

We need to design a predicate `position` which will search for coordinate values. Once the coordinates are fixed, the nonlinear constraints become linear and therefore amenable to minimization. One simple restriction which greatly simplifies the search for coordinate values is to restrict the placement of floating joins to integral points, that is integers, in the range $[-2..6]$. This restriction makes the search space finite. It is important that we perform this non-deterministic search for coordinates *after* the analysis constraints have been added. In this way coordinates for the floating joins that do not satisfy the constraints are eliminated from consideration as soon as possible.

We can build a program to search through the designs as follows:

```
position([]).
position([V|Vs]) :-
    member(V, [6,5,4,3,2,1,0,-1,-2]),
    position(Vs).

bridge_constraints(W, Vs) :-
    tpl(Js, Ss, Vs),
    TL ≤ 20,
    struts_cons(Ss, Fs, TL),
    once(joins_cons(Js, Ss, Fs, W)).

design_goal(W, Vs) :-
    bridge_constraints(W, Vs),
    once(minimize(position(Vs), -W)).
```

The `position` predicate enumerates the 9 possible coordinate values for each variable in its list argument. (We will see more examples of this kind of "labelling" predicate in Section 8.3). The `bridge_constraints` predicate sets up the topology using `tpl`. It constrains the total length of struts to be less than 20 and adds the strut and join constraints. The `design_goal` predicate sets up the constraints and performs a minimization search over the different possible coordinate values. Since only the first answer is required, we use once.

The goal `design_goal(W, Vs)` results in the answer

$$W = 6.15663, \quad Vs = [2, 2, 5, 1, 3, 3].$$

showing that one of the strongest bridges based on the given design topology has joins at $(2, 2)$, $(5, 1)$ and $(3, 3)$.

Unfortunately, the above program is unable to make use of lower bounds on the weight to restrict the search inside the minimize literal, so evaluation of the minimization literal completely traverses the derivation tree of the minimization subgoal. However, since the weight that can be carried at the centre join is intimately connected to forces which rely on the nonlinear length calculations, it seems intrinsic to the problem that the entire design must be determined before an upper bound on the weight can be determined.

We can, however, take advantage of the restricted range of possible coordinate values, to add more redundant constraints. Since the joins are all positioned at integer coordinates, the length of each strut must be at least 1. By adding the answer redundant constraint $L \geq 1$ to `struts_cons` we get more information about the forces possible in each strut and so reduce the search space. We can also add constraints which linearly approximate the length calculation and so reduce the search space. The solver redundant linear constraint

$$X1 - X2 \leq L \wedge X2 - X1 \leq L \wedge Y1 - Y2 \leq L \wedge Y2 - Y1 \leq L,$$

which constrains the length of a strut to be longer than length spanned in both the horizontal and vertical directions, can be added to the definitions of `strut_cons` and `sum_forces`. Because it is linear the solver can use it to deduce information about strut lengths and so reduce the search space.

Restricting the solution to integral coordinates is rather severe. One way of finding better designs for the bridge is to perform a "local search" from the best integral solution. This search examines other coordinate values in the neighbourhood of the current best solution, in order to find a better solution. The search can continue until the new solution found is only slightly better than the previous one, in which case the search can halt. We can think of this local search as "perturbing" the coordinates of the current solution.

Given a best integral solution, we first search for the best bridge whose coordinates vary by 0, +0.5 or −0.5 from their value in the integral solution. We can then vary the coordinates in this solution by 0, +0.25 or −0.25, and so on, until the best perturbed design does not improve very much on the previous one. The following program does this.

```
perturbation([], [], _).
perturbation([V|Vs], [Val|Vals], D) :-
    perturb(V, Val, D),
    perturbation(Vs, Vals, D).

perturb(V, Val, D) :- V = Val - D.
perturb(V, Val, _D) :- V = Val.
perturb(V, Val, D) :- V = Val + D.

pert_goal(FW, FVs) :-
    design_goal(W,Vs),
    improve(Vs, W, FVs, FW, 0.5).

improve(Vs, W, FVs, FW, D) :-
    bridge_constraints(NW, NVs),
    NW >= W,
    once(minimize(perturbation(Vs, NVs, D), -NW)),
    ( NW < 1.01 * W ->
        FVs = NVs, FW = NW
    ;
        improve(NVs, NW, FVs, FW, D/2) ).
```

The program works as follows. The predicate `perturbation(Vs, Vals, D)` sets each variable in the list of variables Vs to be equal to its corresponding value in the list $Vals$, or D greater or less. This is the local search. The goal `pert_goal` finds an integral solution using `design_goal` and then uses `improve` with an initial perturbation length of 0.5 to search for a better solution. The predicate `improve(Vs, W, FVs, FW, D)` starts from an initial solution Vs which carries weight W, and finds a final solution FVs which carries weight FW starting with an initial perturbation D. After setting up a new copy of the bridge constraints on NVs and NW, and adding the constraint that the perturbed design must carry at least the same weight as the previous solution, the perturbation search is performed to find a new design. The resulting maximum weight NW is compared with the maximum weight of the previous design. If it fails to improve the previous design by at least 1%, the last design is returned. Otherwise another perturbation step is performed, with a halved perturbation length.

The goal `pert_goal(FW, FVs)` initially discovers a solution

$$W = 6.15663 \land Vs = [2, 2, 5, 1, 3, 3].$$

Perturbing this solution by 0.5 finds the solution

$$W = 6.3014 \land Vs = [2.5, 2.5, 4.5, 1.5, 3, 3.5]$$

Perturbing this solution by 0.25 finds the same solution. This is returned since it is less than 1% better than the previous solution. The perturbation search is essentially an implementation of a hill climbing approach where the step lengths are decreasing. Note that the search only finds a locally best design which may be far away from the best design.

The above designs are not symmetric. A reasonable requirement of the bridge design is that it be symmetric. That is to say, the two non center floating joins should be positioned at the same height and be horizontally symmetric with respect to the gap. By adding the constraints $Y1 = Y2$ and $X2 = 6 - X1$ to the rule for `tpl` we will only consider symmetric bridges. This reduces the search space considerably and actually leads to the program finding a better final solution.

Using the symmetry constraints the best integral solution found is

$$W = 6.15663 \land Vs = [2, 2, 4, 2, 3, 3].$$

Perturbing this by 0.5 finds the solution

$$W = 6.3014 \land Vs = [2.5, 2.5, 3.5, 2.5, 3, 3.5].$$

Perturbing this by 0.25 finds the solution

$$W = 6.62524 \land Vs = [2.25, 2.75, 3.75, 2.75, 3, 3.75],$$

and perturbing this by 0.125 finds the solution

$$W = 6.63839 \wedge Vs = [2.125, 2.625, 3.875, 2.625, 3, 3.75].$$

The last solution is less than 1% better than the previous solution so it is returned. The best bridge we have discovered therefore has joins at $(2.125, 2.625)$, $(3.875, 2.625)$ and $(3, 3.75)$. It improves on the best integral solution by approximately 7.5%.

7.9   Summary

In this chapter we have studied how constraint programmers can understand the efficiency of their programs and have described various techniques which can be used to improve efficiency.

Broadly speaking, efficiency is measured in terms of the size of a goal's derivation tree. Since the size of the derivation tree depends greatly on the type of goal being solved, efficiency depends on the intended mode of usage of a predicate. Understanding the shape of the derivation tree and the way in which it is explored is particularly important when writing recursive programs. By understanding the shape of the derivation tree for a given mode of usage, the programmer can ensure that a solution will be found before an infinite branch is reached. To fully understand the shape of the derivation tree, the programmer also needs to know for which types of constraints the underlying solver is incomplete.

Although the answers for the goal are independent of the order in which literals appear in goals, the size and shape of the derivation tree greatly depends on the order of rules in the program and order of literals in the rule bodies. We have examined how to order rules and literals in rule bodies so as to make programs more efficient. One guideline is that non-recursive rules should appear before recursive rules in a predicate definition. When ordering literals in a rule body, it is better to place constraints at the earliest point at which they may cause failure and to place user-defined constraints with fewer answers, in particular deterministic calls, earlier than those with many answers.

Another strategy we have investigated for improving efficiency is to add redundant constraints. These come in two flavours. Constraints which are redundant with respect to the "future" answers and constraints which are redundant with respect to the current constraint store. In the next chapter we shall see that adding redundant constraints is an important technique for improving the efficiency of CLP programs computing over finite domains.

We have also looked at two constructs—if-then-else and once—provided by many CLP systems to identify sub-computations which do not require backtracking. The programmer must be careful when using if-then-else as it is dangerous if the mode of usage does not ensure the test has, at most, one answer and the variables are fixed. However, if these conditions are met, it can be quite useful.

7.10 Exercises

7.1. What is the size of the derivation tree of the factorial program from Chapter 4 for goals in which the first argument to `fac` is fixed?

7.2. Give the simplified derivation trees for `grandfather(X,peter)` using the two different programs defining `grandfather`.

7.3. Consider the following program defining predicate `anc(Y,X)` which holds if Y is an ancestor of X.

```
anc(Z,X) :- anc(Y,X), parent(Z,Y).
anc(Y,X) :- parent(Y,X).
```

Modify the program by reordering rules and literals to make it more efficient for the mode of usage in which the second argument is given. Give simplified derivation trees for the goal `anc(X,peter)` for the original and the reordered program.

7.4. The following program

```
erk(X,Y)    :-  erk(X1,Y1), X1 = X - 1, Y = Y1 + 2.
erk(0, 0).
```

has several problems. For example, the goal `erk(5, Y)` does not terminate.

  (a) Modify the program by reordering rules and literals so that `erk(5, Y)` finds a first answer.

  (b) Change the program so that the derivation tree for `erk(5, Y)` is finite.

  (c) Change the program further so that the goal `erk(X, 11)` has a finite derivation tree.

  (d) Can you write an equivalent program which does not use recursion?

7.5. Consider the `member` predicate on page 193, and the following alternate code for `member`.

```
member(X, [Y|R]) :- (X = Y -> true ; member(X, R)).
```

Draw the derivation trees for the goals

```
member([p(kim,N),phonelist]).
```

and

```
member([p(P,5559282),phonelist]).
```

for both codes for `member`. Explain the limitations of the above version of `member`.

7.6. "Stupid sort" is a sorting algorithm that sorts a list by trying all possible permutations of the list and checking whether the permutation is ordered. The predicate `perm(L,P)` defined below produces answers P which are all possible permutations of the list L. The predicate `delete(L,X,R)` deletes element X from list L leaving the remaining elements, R. The predicate `sorted(L)` checks if the list L of numbers is sorted.

```
stupid_sort(L, P) :- perm(L, P), sorted(P).

perm([], []).
perm(L, [X|R]) :- delete(L, X, L1), perm(L1, R).

delete([X | Xs], X, Xs).
delete([X | Xs], Y, [X | R]) :- delete(Xs, Y, R).

sorted([]).
sorted([_]).
sorted([X,Y|L]) :- X ≤ Y, sorted([Y|L]).
```

Give the simplified derivation trees for the goals:

L = [2,6,2], P = [_,_,_], perm(L, P), sorted(P).

L = [2,6,2], P = [_,_,_], sorted(P), perm(L, P).

Compare the number of states. Both goals have two different derivations for the one answer. Using the derivation tree above, determine the number of states in the simplified derivation trees for the goal:

L = [2,6,2], P = [_,_,_], sorted(P), once(perm(L, P)).

7.7. Compare the execution of the goals (G_1 -> G_2 ; G_3) and (once(G_1) -> G_2 ; G_3) where G_1, G_2 and G_3 are arbitrary goals.

7.11   Practical Exercises

In $CLP(\mathcal{R})$ and SICStus Prolog pow(t_1, t_2) represents the expression $(t_1)^{(t_2)}$. For instance, $\sqrt{t}$ is pow(t, 0.5).

P7.1. Test your reordered anc program from Question 7.3 above and compare its speed with the original version.

P7.2. Write a version of anc which is efficient for the mode of usage in which the first argument is fixed. Compare the speed with the reordered version of anc from Question 7.3.

P7.3. Write a program for leaflevel_bst which determines the level of the leaves in a binary search tree in which the items are positive numbers. Ensure that the goal minimize(leaflevel_bst(T, X, N), X + N) will execute efficiently, that is it will not always search the entire tree to find the minimum. [Hint: think about the goal   X + N < m, leaflevel_bst(T, X, N).]

P7.4. Write a version of sumlist which uses if-then-else and is correct if the first argument is fixed. Give a goal for which the behaviour of the program is incorrect.

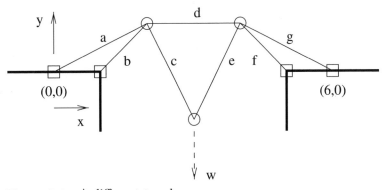

Figure 7.8   A different topology.

P7.5. Using the "stupid sort" program defined in Exercise 7.6 above, compare the execution time of the following goals to sort the list $[1, 6, 3, 4, 2, 6, 3, 2, 4]$:

```
L = [1,6,3,4,2,6,3,2,4], P = [_,_,_,_,_,_,_,_,_], perm(L,P), sorted(P).

L = [1,6,3,4,2,6,3,2,4], P = [_,_,_,_,_,_,_,_,_], sorted(P), perm(L,P).

L=[1,6,3,4,2,6,3,2,4],P=[_,_,_,_,_,_,_,_,_],sorted(P),once(perm(L,P)).
```

Compare the execution time when the constraint $0 = 1$ is appended on the end of the goal. This in effect searches for every solution and then fails.

P7.6. Write a predicate `strut_inter(S1,S2)` which holds if two struts (as defined in the bridge example) $S1$ and $S2$ intersect. Use it to write a predicate `not_strut_inter(S1,S2)` which holds if the two struts do not intersect. Determine the modes of usage for each predicate for which they will answer correctly.

P7.7. Write a rule for the `tpl` predicate for spaghetti bridges for the topology illustrated in Figure 7.8. Find the strongest bridge possible under this topology.

Choose a different topology of your own making, and see if you can create a stronger bridge than that found in Section 7.8.2

P7.8. (*) The local search used to find a better solution to the bridge could be improved. If the solution is improved by perturbing by distance D, it may be improved further by perturbing again by distance D. Only if perturbing by distance D fails to improve the solution enough should we halve the perturbation length. Halt the process when the perturbation length becomes less than 0.05. Implement this search and see if you can find a stronger bridge than that discovered in Section 7.8.2 with the same topology.

P7.9. (*) Improve the spaghetti bridge analysis program so it will take into account the weight of the spaghetti, 100 g per metre for struts, and 0.5 g for each floating join. Assume it acts through the midpoint of the strut or join.

7.12   Notes

The discussion of efficiency and techniques for ordering rules and user-defined constraints in rules originates from Prolog programming and is described in Prolog programming texts such as that of Sterling and Shapiro [125].

Modes of usage are important for constraint logic programming languages because the same program can work for multiple modes of usage (for example the `mortgage` program of the Introduction). For $CLP(Tree)$, that is Prolog, most arguments have a mode which is either fixed or free. For other constraint domains other modes of usage are more common. Arguments may be bounded from above, or below, or both, or constrained to be positive, or simply constrained in some unspecified way. In the modern logic programming language Mercury [122], modes of usage of predicates are explicitly defined by the programmer and checked by the compiler. This enables significantly more errors of usage to be discovered and allows the compiler to execute predicates more efficiently.

Guidelines for placing constraints in a rule and the use of answer redundant constraints were discussed by Marriott and Stuckey [92]. They also described how reordering and addition of redundant constraints could be automated.

If-then-else and once originated in Prolog, and their pitfalls are well known from Prolog folklore. In Prolog they are usually understood (and defined) using a more basic construct, the cut. We introduce the cut in Chapter 10 to explain the implementation of if-then-else and once. Naish's book [97] discusses in some detail, among many other things, modes of usage for Prolog and their interaction with if-then-else and cut.

Constraint logic programming has been used extensively for solving design problems. Some examples are: analog circuitry synthesis [118], transistor amplifier design [62], analysis and partial synthesis of truss structures [81], designing gear boxes [126] and other mechanical systems [130].

8   Modelling with Finite Domain Constraints

Many difficult and important problems which arise in management decision support, for instance scheduling and resource allocation, may be expressed as satisfaction or optimization problems involving constraints over variables with finite domains. CLP languages providing constraints over finite domains have proved ideal for tackling such problems and so these CLP languages have had the most industrial impact and are now used to solve many real-world industrial problems.

In this chapter, we investigate how to model and solve such problems efficiently using a CLP language whose constraints range over finite domains. We start with simple examples to illustrate the operation of the solver and its combination with backtracking. We then discuss labelling strategies. These ensure that, by the end of every derivation, each variable is constrained to take a single value. For such derivations the finite domain solver is complete. As a larger more realistic example, we solve a simple scheduling problem with resources.

A recurring theme of the chapter is the need to consider efficiency and, in particular, to control the size of the search space. We shall discuss different labelling strategies, complex constraints, show how to add redundant information to improve the search behaviour and demonstrate how different models of the same problem may have different efficiency.

Throughout this chapter we shall use the language $CLP(FD)$ introduced in Chapter 4. It combines finite domain constraints with tree constraints. Elements of the constraint domain are trees which may have integer constants as leaves. Finite domain variables range over either a finite domain of integers or a finite domain of arbitrary constants. In effect, however, all variables ranging over finite domains are treated as if they range over integers since the constants in each domain are mapped to integers. The usual mathematical constraints are provided for integer finite domain variables, that is to say, equality ($=$), inequality ($\leq, \geq$), strict inequality ($<, >$) and disequality ($\neq$). We will also discuss the use of complex primitive constraints such as element and cumulative. The constraints over trees are the same as those provided in $CLP(\mathcal{R})$, namely equality ($=$) and disequality ($\neq$). This means complex data structures can be created and manipulated in the same way as in $CLP(\mathcal{R})$.

The $CLP(FD)$ system uses unification to solve tree constraints and an incomplete bounds consistency based solver for finite domain constraints. We shall see that an awareness of the incompleteness of the solver and the way in which it handles different constraints is important when considering the efficiency of a program.

8.1   Domains and Labelling

In Chapter 5 we saw how we can use multiple facts to model a relation. As an example the `likes` relation shown in Figure 3.3 consists of the ordered pairs:

> { *(kim, maria)*, *(kim, nicole)*, *(kim, erika)*, *(peter, maria)*,
> *(bernd, nicole)*, *(bernd, maria)*, *(bernd, erika)* }.

It can be modelled by the simple program:

```
likes(kim, maria).
likes(kim, nicole).
likes(kim, erika).
likes(peter, maria).
likes(bernd, nicole).
likes(bernd, maria).
likes(bernd, erika).
```

Given this definition of the *likes* relation we can now solve the old-fashioned marriage problem of Example 3.3 using finite domain constraints. We can model the marriage problem by the goal:

> `[N,M,E] :: [kim, peter,bernd]`, $N \neq M$, $N \neq E$, $M \neq E$,
> `likes(N, nicole)`, `likes(M, maria)`, `likes(E, erika)`.

This will give the desired answers:

$$N = kim \wedge M = peter \wedge E = bernd \text{ and } N = bernd \wedge M = peter \wedge E = kim.$$

The initial literal in the goal, `[N,M,E] :: [kim, peter,bernd]`, is used to tell the $CLP(FD)$ system that variables N, M and E each have the domain $\{kim, peter, bernd\}$. The syntax for specifying the domains of variables is quite simple. For instance, to tell the system that variable X has the initial domain $\{1, 2, 3, 4\}$ a literal of the form `X :: [1,2,3,4]` or `X :: [1..4]` is used. Variables are assigned non-integer domains using the form `X :: [red, white, blue]`. Multiple variables can be initialised to the same domain using the syntax illustrated in the above example. If no initial domain is given for a finite domain variable it is usually assumed to be an integer with some large default range, for example $[-10000000..10000000]$.

As another example, we can model the smuggler's knapsack problem of Example 3.5 using the goal:

`[W,P,C] :: [0..9]`, $4*W + 3*P + 2*C \leq 9$, $15*W + 10*P + 7*C \geq 30$.

Now consider what happens when this goal is executed. The $CLP(FD)$ system will simply return *unknown*. This is because the consistency based finite domain solver is incomplete and, in this case, not powerful enough to determine that the constraint is satisfiable.

The reason CLP systems usually provide an incomplete solver for finite domain constraints is that complete solvers are expensive and so should not be employed every time a constraint is added to the constraint store. However, as in the above example, eventually the programmer will wish to know if the finite domain constraint is satisfiable and, if so, what the answer is. Fortunately most CLP systems also provide a complete backtracking constraint solver for finite domains. Because of the expense of the solver, it is not automatically used by the CLP system. Instead it must be explicitly called by the programmer, typically, after all of the constraints have been collected.

The complete constraint solver for finite domain constraints system is usually provided by the built-in predicate `labeling`.[1] The predicate `labeling(Vs)` takes a list of finite domain variables, Vs, and uses a backtracking search to find a solution for those variables. In Chapter 3 we gave a complete propagation based backtracking solver for finite domains. One of the strengths of the CLP approach is that such solvers can be easily programmed in CLP itself. We shall investigate how to program `labeling` in the next section. For the moment, however, we regard `labeling` as a black-box.

Execution of the goal

```
[W,P,C] :: [0..9],
4*W + 3*P + 2*C ≤ 9, 15*W + 10*P + 7*C ≥ 30,
labeling([W,P,C]).
```

finds the solutions

$$W = 0 \wedge P = 1 \wedge C = 3, \quad W = 0 \wedge P = 3 \wedge C = 0,$$
$$W = 1 \wedge P = 1 \wedge C = 1, \quad W = 2 \wedge P = 0 \wedge C = 0.$$

This goal illustrates the typical form of a constraint program over finite domains. First, the variables and their initial domains are defined. Then the constraints modelling the problem are given. Finally, a labelling predicate is used to invoke a complete solver. This is the so-called *constrain and generate* methodology: first the constraints are applied, then a solution is generated by labelling.

We can also use optimization constructs when modelling with $CLP(FD)$. For instance, the smuggler can determine his maximum profit by executing the goal

```
L = -15*W - 10*P - 7*C,
minimize(([W,P,C] :: [0..9],
          4*W + 3*P + 2*C ≤ 9, 15*W + 10*P + 7*C ≥ 30,
          labeling([W,P,C])),
         L).
```

This will give the answer $W = 1 \wedge P = 1 \wedge C = 1 \wedge L = -32$ corresponding to a profit of 32.

---

1. The American spelling of "labelling"

Some care must be taken when using `minimize` with finite domain constraints. For `minimize` to work correctly, execution of the minimization goal must ensure that the variables in the objective function take fixed values by the time the goal has executed and that a complete solver is employed when executing the goal. For this reason, it is usual for `labeling` to be a literal in the minimization goal.

The crypto-arithmetic problem from the introduction provides a slightly more complex example of modelling with $CLP(FD)$. The problem is to solve the arithmetic equation

$$
\begin{array}{ccccc}
  & S & E & N & D \\
+ &   & M & O & R & E \\
\hline
= & M & O & N & E & Y
\end{array}
$$

where each letter represents a different digit.

This is modelled by the following program.

```
smm(S,E,N,D,M,O,R,Y) :-
    [S,E,N,D,M,O,R,Y] :: [0..9],
    constrain([S,E,N,D,M,O,R,Y]),
    labeling([S,E,N,D,M,O,R,Y]).

constrain([S,E,N,D,M,O,R,Y]) :-
    S ≠ 0, M ≠ 0,
    alldifferent_neq([S,E,N,D,M,O,R,Y]),
              1000*S + 100*E + 10*N + D
    +         1000*M + 100*O + 10*R + E
    = 10000*M + 1000*O + 100*N + 10*E + Y.
```

The program works as follows. Each of the variables is declared to range over the values [0..9] while the constraints defined by the crypto-arithmetic problem are expressed by the user-defined constraint `constrain`. To ensure that a valuation is returned, the built-in `labeling` is called to make sure that each variable is set to one of the values in the range [0..9].

The `constrain` predicate ensures that neither S nor M take the value zero since they are digits that appear leftmost in a number. Each of the variables is forced to be different by the user-defined constraint `alldifferent_neq` from Example 6.3 which sets up disequation constraints between each pair of variables. Finally the arithmetic equation is represented by the last constraint.

The program executes the goal `smm(S,E,N,D,M,O,R,Y)` as follows. After the domain declarations the domain is

$$D(S) = [0..9], \quad D(E) = [0..9], \quad D(N) = [0..9], \quad D(D) = [0..9],$$
$$D(M) = [0..9], \quad D(O) = [0..9], \quad D(R) = [0..9], \quad D(Y) = [0..9].$$

Adding the constraints $S \neq 0$ and $M \neq 0$ narrows the domain so that $D(S) = [1..9]$ and $D(M) = [1..9]$. The `alldifferent_neq` predicate adds the disequalities

$S \neq E, S \neq N, S \neq D, \ldots, R \neq Y$ to the constraint store. As each of these constraints involves variables with no fixed value, no propagation occurs. Addition of the equation initiates propagation. For simplicity, we shall assume the constraint solver treats the final equation in its simpler (equivalent) linear form of

$$1000 * S + 91 * E + D + 10 * R = 9000 * M + 900 * O + 90 * N + Y.$$

One of the propagation rules for this constraint is based on the inequality that M is less than or equal to

$$\frac{1}{9} max_D(S) + \frac{91}{9000} max_D(E) + \frac{1}{9000} max_D(D) + \frac{1}{900} max_D(R)$$
$$- \frac{1}{10} min_D(O) - \frac{1}{100} min_D(N) - \frac{1}{9000} min_D(Y).$$

Given the current domains this implies that

$$M \leq \frac{9}{9} + \frac{91 * 9}{9000} + \frac{9}{9000} + \frac{9}{900} - \frac{0}{10} - \frac{0}{100} - \frac{0}{9000} = 1.102.$$

Thus $D(M)$ is updated to [1..1]. From propagation using the constraint $S \neq M$ we obtain $D(S) = [2..9]$. Next the propagation rule based on the inequality that S is greater than

$$9 \, min_D(M) + \frac{9}{10} min_D(O) + \frac{9}{100} min_D(N) + \frac{1}{1000} min_D(Y)$$
$$- \frac{91}{1000} max_D(E) - \frac{1}{1000} max_D(D) - \frac{1}{100} max_D(R)$$

is used with the current domain to infer that $S \geq 8.082$. Propagation therefore sets $D(S)$ to [9..9]. Now using the constraint $S \neq E$ we obtain that $D(E)$ is [0..8] and similarly we obtain that the domains of N, D, O, R, Y are also [0..8].

Propagation continues until the following domain is obtained:

$$D(S) = [9..9], \quad D(E) = [4..7], \quad D(N) = [5..8], \quad D(D) = [2..8],$$
$$D(M) = [1..1], \quad D(O) = [0..0], \quad D(R) = [2..8], \quad D(Y) = [2..8].$$

Notice that three of the variables already have fixed values and that every other variable has had its range of possible values decreased. Since this is not a valuation domain, the constraint solver cannot determine whether the constraint store is satisfiable or not and so returns *unknown*. In order to guarantee that a valid solution is found we must use `labeling`.

Essentially the action of the `labeling` built-in is to backtrack through each variable's initial domain setting the variable to each of the values from 0 to 9 in turn. The variables are tried in order of their appearance in the list passed to `labeling`. Thus, the first variable to be assigned a value is S. Trying the first value in the initial domain, 0, will cause failure since the constraint $S = 0$ is inconsistent with the current domain of S. So the next value, 1, is tried. This also causes failure. Subsequent values lead to failure until we try $S = 9$, which is consistent. Now `labeling` tries to find a value for E. First we add $E = 0$, which fails and we continue trying values for E until we try $E = 4$. Propagation reduces

$D(N)$ to [5..5] and $D(R)$ to [8..8] and then finds failure because variable D has no possible value. Removing the last choice $E = 4$, we now add $E = 5$ and propagation determines that $N = 6$, $R = 8$, $D = 7$ and $Y = 2$. Execution of `labeling` continues until (eventually) each of these values is selected and so we have found a solution to the problem. Since the resulting domain is a valuation domain, the underlying propagation based constraint solver will return the answer *true*, guaranteeing that this a valid answer.

This example demonstrates the power of the constraint solver to direct the search. In contrast, consider a *generate and test* methodology for solving the same problem. Generate and test is the reverse of the constrain and generate methodology. In generate and test, first possible solutions are generated and then tested to see if they satisfy the constraints. The generate and test methodology gives rise to the following program:

```
smm_gt(S,E,N,D,M,O,R,Y) :-
    [S,E,N,D,M,O,R,Y] :: [0..9],
    labeling([S,E,N,D,M,O,R,Y]),
    constrain([S,E,N,D,M,O,R,Y]).
```

In this program a unique value for each of the variables is first chosen by `labeling`, then the constraints of the problem are checked by `constrain`. For this program the solution is found after testing 95671082 choices, contrasting with the first program in which the solution was found after making only one choice, $E = 4$, that did not result in immediate failure.

In this chapter we shall often compare different programs for the same problem, by discussing the number of choices each makes. This is because for the same problem, the size of the derivation tree is roughly proportional to the number of choices in the tree. Thus comparing the number of choices provides a rough measure of the program's relative efficiency.

As this example demonstrates, constrain and generate is almost always preferable to generate and test. This is a simple consequence of the guideline we discussed in Section 7.4, namely that it is usually more efficient to call predicates with many possible answers after those with a few answers. Since labelling usually has a huge number of possible answers, it is better to delay calling `labeling` until last.

8.2   Complex Constraints

In Section 3.5 we saw consistency based solvers for finite domains often provide complex primitive constraints such as `alldifferent`, `cumulative` or `element`. When possible, the constraint programmer should make use of these complex primitive constraints. One reason is that they often allow a succinct description of the problem. A second, more important reason, is that they will, usually, lead to a more efficient program since the constraint solver provides specialized propagation

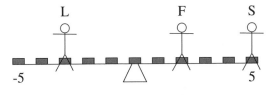

Figure 8.1   Balancing a seesaw.

rules for these constraints which will be more effective at domain pruning than those
for the equivalent "simple" primitive constraints.

For example, the old fashioned marriage problem above could be modelled by
the goal

```
[N,M,E] :: [kim, peter,bernd], alldifferent([N,M,E]),
likes(N, nicole), likes(M, maria), likes(E, erika).
```

in which the primitive constraints $N \neq M$, $N \neq E$, and $M \neq E$ have been replaced
by a call to the complex primitive constraint `alldifferent`.

Sometimes a degree of ingenuity is required in order to find a way of modelling a
problem by using complex primitive constraints. This effort is worthwhile provided
the constraint solver handles the complex constraint well.

Example 8.1

Suppose that Liz, Fi and Sarah are playing on a 10 foot long seesaw which has seats
placed uniformly one foot apart along the bar. The seesaw is shown in Figure 8.1.
They wish to position themselves on the seesaw so that it balances. They also wish
to be able to swing their arms freely, requiring that they are at least three feet
apart. The weights of Liz, Fi and Sarah are respectively 9, 8 and 4 stone.

To solve the problem, we need to assign seats to Liz, Fi and Sarah. If we number
the seats on the seesaw from -5 to 5, we can use the variables L, F and S to
represent the number of the seat of Liz, Fi and Sarah, respectively. The constraint
that the seesaw balances is simply that the moments of inertia sum to 0, that is:

$$9 \times L + 8 \times F + 4 \times S = 0.$$

The "at least 3 apart" constraint can be modelled with the user-defined constraint
`apart(X,Y,N)` which holds if integers X and Y are at least N apart. It is defined
by the two rules:

```
apart(X, Y, N) :- X ≥ Y + N.
apart(X, Y, N) :- Y ≥ X + N.
```

The complete problem is modelled by the goal

```
[L,F,S] :: [-5..5], 9 * L + 8 * F + 4 * S = 0,
apart(L,F,3), apart(L,S,3), apart(F,S,3),
labeling([L,F,S]).
```

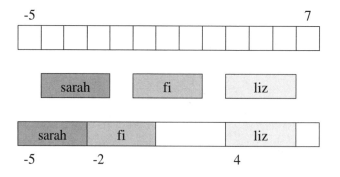

Figure 8.2   A cumulative constraint for apartness.

Notice that for efficiency, we have ordered the literals in the goal according to their degree of non-determinism. The deterministic literals `[L,F,S] :: [-5..5]` and `9 * L + 8 * F + 4 * S = 0` are first, while the literal with most possible answers, `labeling`, is last.

However, using the complex primitive constraint `cumulative` it is possible to give a model which is more efficient. The key is that the three apartness constraints can be modelled by a single cumulative constraint. If we think of a child as a box of width 3 to be placed in the range -5 to 7, then, if their boxes do not overlap, all children are at least three feet apart. Figure 8.2 shows how this is an instance of a cumulative constraint. Once *sarah* is placed at position -5, then no other box (child) can be placed in the range $[-5..-3]$. We can therefore model the problem using the goal

```
[L,F,S] :: [-5..5], 9 * L + 8 * F + 4 * S = 0,
cumulative([L,F,S],[3,3,3],[1,1,1],1),
labeling([L,F,S]).
```

Since the `cumulative` constraint is deterministic but the `apart` constraint is non-deterministic, this model is more efficient than our original model. Each call to `apart` gives rise to a binary choice in the derivation tree. This means the derivation tree of the original goal is considerably larger than that of the new goal.

8.3   Labelling

As we have seen, $CLP(FD)$ programs typically end with a call to a labelling predicate which uses a backtracking search to find a solution to the constraints. For many problems, most of the execution time occurs during the execution of this labelling predicate. Indeed, it is quite common for all of the search to occur during labelling. Thus for many $CLP(FD)$ programs, efficiency is synonymous with efficient labelling and the constraint programmer is well advised to consider strategies for labelling which reduce the search space and lead to finding a (first) solution faster.

Fortunately, labelling predicates may be readily programmed in $CLP(FD)$ itself, making it easy for the programmer to develop and experiment with different strategies. To facilitate such programming $CLP(FD)$ systems provide several built-in predicates which allow the programmer to access information about the current domain of a variable. We will make use of:

- dom(V,D) which returns the list of values D in the current domain of variable V,

- maxdomain(V,Max) which returns the maximum value Max in the current domain of variable V, and

- mindomain(V,Min) which returns the minimum value Min in the current domain of variable V.

Using dom(X,D) it is simple to write a recursive definition of labeling:

```
labeling([]).
labeling([V|Vs]) :-
    indomain(V),
    labeling(Vs).

indomain(V) :-
    dom(V,D),
    member(V,D).
```

The predicate labeling iterates through each variable V in the list of variables to be labelled, calling indomain(V) to set V to each of the remaining values in its domain. The predicate indomain(V) calls dom(V,D) to determine the values in the domain of V and then uses member to backtrack through these values. Note that this definition of labeling is marginally more efficient than that described in Section 8.1 since it only backtracks through the values in the current domain of a variable instead of the values in the original domain. To understand its definition consider execution of the goal smm(S,E,N,D,M,O,R,Y). Execution proceeds as described in Section 8.1 until the literal labeling([S,E,N,D,M,O,R,Y]) is called. This calls indomain(S) to backtrack through the values in the current domain of S. This immediately adds the equation $S = 9$, rather than trying $S = 0$, $S = 1, \ldots, S = 8$. This is because the current domain of S is [9..9] and so dom(S,D) will constrain D to be the list [9] and the call to member adds $S = 9$. Next indomain(E) is called. This is rewritten to member(E, [4, 5, 6, 7]) since $D(E) = [4..7]$. Execution of the literal member(E, [4, 5, 6, 7]) first adds $E = 4$ which fails, and then adds $E = 5$. Since the domains of the remaining variables are now all singletons, execution of the subsequent calls to indomain essentially does nothing.

There are two choices to be made when labelling: the order in which variables are labelled and the order in which the values for a particular variable are explored. We will investigate these in turn.

8.3.1   Choice of Variable

Altering the order in which variables are labelled can have dramatic effects on the size of the derivation tree. We have seen that a useful heuristic to minimize the amount of repeated work and the size of the derivation tree is to delay choice as long as possible, calling literals with many possible answers after those with fewer possible answers. This heuristic suggests that when labelling a list of variables, we should choose to label those variables with the smallest current domain first. A further motivation for this strategy is that, with luck, once these variables are assigned a value, propagation will trim the domains of the remaining variables.

In the smm program when the labelling predicate is reached the range domain is

$$D(S) = [9..9], \quad D(E) = [4..7], \quad D(N) = [5..8], \quad D(D) = [2..8],$$
$$D(M) = [1..1], \quad D(O) = [0..0], \quad D(R) = [2..8], \quad D(Y) = [2..8].$$

Since the variables S, M and O have singleton domains we should label these variables first (effectively doing nothing but remembering they are "dealt with"). Both E or N have domains with 4 elements, while the remaining variables have larger domains. Thus, a good strategy is to choose either E or N to label next.

We can program a labelling predicate that chooses the variable to label based on its domain size as follows:

```
labelingff([]).
labelingff(Vs) :-
    deleteff(Vs, V, Rest),
    indomain(V),
    labelingff(Rest).

deleteff([V0|Vs], V, Rest) :-
    get_domain_size(V0, S0),
    min_size(Vs, S0, V0, V, Rest).

min_size([], _, V, V, []).
min_size([V1|Vs], S0, V0, V, [V0|Rest]) :-
    get_domain_size(V1, S1),
    S1 < S0,
    min_size(Vs, S1, V1, V, Rest).
min_size([V1|Vs], S0, V0, V, [V1|Rest]) :-
    get_domain_size(V1, S1),
    S1 ≥ S0,
    min_size(Vs, S0, V0, V, Rest).

get_domain_size(V, S) :- dom(V, D), length(D, S).

length([], 0).
length([_|L], N) :- N = N1 + 1, length(L, N1).
```

At each stage the predicate `labelingff` selects the variable with the fewest elements in its current domain. The call `get_domain_size(V, S)` determines the current domain size of variable V using the built-in `dom(V,D)` and the user-defined constraint `length` which counts the number of elements in a list. We note that `get_domain_size` for range domains could also have been defined by the more efficient code:

```
get_domain_size(V, S) :-
       mindomain(V, Min), maxdomain(V, Max), S = Max - Min + 1.
```

However, this code does not give an accurate size if the domain is not a range.

The predicate `min_size(Vs, S0, V0, V, Rest)` iterates through the list of variables Vs looking for a variable which has a smaller domain than the variable $V0$ which has $S0$ elements in its domain. On return, V is set to the variable with smallest domain size amongst $V0$ and the Vs and the list of remaining variables is returned in *Rest*.

This labelling strategy can be significantly more efficient than the naive strategy of simply labelling the variables in order; so much so that `deleteff` is often provided as a built-in predicate. It is an example of a labelling based on the *first fail principle*.

"To succeed, try first where you are most likely to fail."

Choosing the variable with smallest domain limits the branching factor and potentially allows failure of the entire branch to be determined quickly, thus guiding the search to more profitable areas.

There are other factors that can be taken into account in applying the first fail principle. For example, we might assume that a variable involved in many constraints is more likely to cause failure when it is set to a value. Thus some $CLP(FD)$ systems provide a built-in predicate `deleteffc` which takes a list of variables and first selects the variables with smallest current domains, and then selects from these, the variable involved in the most constraints.

8.3.2 Choice of Domain Value

The second choice in labelling is the order in which to try the different domain values. Different choices will change the order in which solutions are found and the order in which branches in the derivation tree are explored. Using problem-specific knowledge, we may be able to select a value that is more likely to lead to a solution, helping us to find a (first) solution faster. Ordering of domain values is also important when evaluating optimization goals. In this case, it may mean that the optimum solution is found more quickly and other branches which cannot lead to a better solution are pruned.

The following example illustrates the importance of appropriately ordering the choice of domain values.

Example 8.2

Consider the *N-queens problem* introduced in Chapter 3. This is the problem of placing N queens on a chess board of a size $N \times N$ so that no queen can capture another queen. Another way of modelling this problem (different from that in Chapter 3) is to recognize that in any solution there is exactly one queen in every column. We associate with the ith column the variable R_i which represents the row number of the queen in that column. The following program models the N-queens problem using this representation.

```
goal(N, Queens) :-
     length(Queens, N),
     Queens :: [1..N],
     queens(Queens),
     labeling(Queens).
```

```
queens([]).
queens([X|Y]) :-
     safe(X,Y,1),
     queens(Y).
```

```
safe(_,[],_).
safe(X,[F|T],Nb) :-
     noattack(X,F,Nb),
     Newnb = Nb + 1,
     safe(X,T,Newnb).
```

```
noattack(X,Y,Nb) :- Y + Nb =/= X, X + Nb =/= Y, X =/= Y.
```

Evaluation of the literal goal(N, Queens) first uses the user-defined predicate length to constrain *Queens* to be a list of N distinct variables. These correspond to the row variables $R_1, \ldots, R_N$. Next each row variable is given an initial domain of 1 to N. The predicate queens ensures that no queen falls on the same row or diagonal as any other queen. It iterates through the list of queens calling safe to ensure that each queen X does not fall on the same row or diagonal as the remaining queens in the list Y. The predicate safe iterates through the queens in Y enforcing that each queen F in the list is not on the same row or diagonal as X. Finally the labelling occurs.

For large N it is well-known that solutions to the N-queens problems are more likely to be found by starting in the middle of the domain. Unfortunately, execution of the N-queens program using indomain in labelling will first try the smallest value in the domain, then the next smallest, and so on. We can program a better labelling strategy as follows.

```
indomain_middle(Var) :-
     make_list_of_values(Var, List),
     member(Var, List).
```

No. of queens	10–19	20–29	30–39	40–49	50–59	60–69	70–79	100–109
Straight	777.6	—	—	—	—	—	—	—
First fail	26.0	51.0	80.5	176	1331.3	189.6	1337.4	—
Middle out	28.5	47.7	43.1	50.7	79.2	73.6	81.5	106.7

Table 8.1 Empirical comparison of different labelling strategies.

```
make_list_of_values(Var, List) :-
    dom(Var, Domain),
    length(Domain, Size),
    N = Size div 2,
    halve_list(N, Domain, [], RFirst, Second),
    merge(Second, RFirst, List).

halve_list(0, L2, L1, L1, L2).
halve_list(N, [H|R], Li, L1, L2) :-
    N ≥ 1,
    N1 = N-1,
    halve_list(N1, R, [H|Li], L1, L2).

merge([], L, L).
merge([X|L1], L2, [X|L3]) :- merge(L2, L1, L3).
```

The program works by taking the current domain of a variable Var as a list and breaking it into two halves using halve_list. The predicate halve_list succeeds with $RFirst$ as the reverse of the first half of the list and $Second$ set to the remaining part. In the call,

```
        halve_list(3, [1,2,5,6,8,9,10], [], RFirst, Second).
```

succeeds with $Rfirst = [5, 2, 1]$ and $Second = [6, 8, 9, 10]$. The predicate merge then merges the two lists, interleaving the elements. In this example, the resulting list is $[6, 5, 8, 2, 9, 1, 10]$. Finally indomain_middle uses member to set Var to each of these values in turn.

To see the benefit of the middle ordering heuristic we can compare the different labellings empirically. Table 8.1 gives figures for the average number of choices required to find the first solution over different ranges for N, using straight labelling, the first fail principle, and the first fail principle with the middle ordering heuristic above. We use "—" to indicate greater than 10000.

Our results clearly demonstrate that the first fail principle is more efficient than straight labelling and that combining first fail with the middle out labelling heuristic reduces the search space even more. This example also illustrates the importance of empirical testing to compare different labelling strategies.

8.3.3   Domain Splitting

Labelling strategies, however, need only ensure that every variable is eventually constrained to take a single domain value (so that the incomplete solver will answer *true* or *false*). The strategies we have seen so far choose a variable and a value and assign the value to the variable, but other types of labelling strategies are also possible.

One useful strategy is to repeatedly reduce the domain of each variable, by splitting the current domain into two possibilities, for example the lower and upper halves. This approach to labelling is justified by the *principle of least commitment*. This states that when making a choice for some variable we should make the choice which "commits us as little as possible." The advantage is that, if we detect unsatisfiability after making a weak commitment, more of the search space is removed than if we detect unsatisfiability after a strong commitment. Setting a variable to a value commits the variable to a single value, which is very restrictive. Domain splitting is less restrictive. It only removes half of the remaining values in the variable's domain rather than all but one. The principle of least commitment, therefore, tells us to prefer domain splitting since the usual labelling approach leads to a stronger commitment. Of course the drawback is that less commitment may create less information for the incomplete solver to determine satisfiability or unsatisfiability.

The following program captures the domain splitting strategy. It repeatedly splits the domains of variables in half until they are singletons.

```
labelingsplit([]).
labelingsplit([V|Vs]) :-
    mindomain(V, Min),
    maxdomain(V, Max),
    (Min = Max ->
        labelingsplit(Vs)
    ;
        Mid = (Min + Max) div 2,
        labelsplit(V, Mid, Vs)
    ).
labelsplit(V, M, Vs):-
    V ≤ M,
    append(Vs, [V], NVs),
    labelingsplit(NVs).
labelsplit(V, M, Vs):-
    V ≥ M+1,
    append(Vs, [V], NVs),
    labelingsplit(NVs).
```

The predicate `labelingsplit` selects the first variable V and, using the built-ins `mindomain` and `maxdomain`, determines its minimum and maximum current domain values. If V's current domain is a singleton, then the domain is completely split and so labelingsplit calls itself recursively to split the domains of the remaining variables. Otherwise, the midpoint Mid of the range is determined and labelsplit forces the choice of either the higher or lower half of the values for V. V is placed on the end of the list of variables to be handled using append and domain splitting continues.

Example 8.3

Consider the seesaw problem of Example 8.1. The problem can be modelled by the goal

```
[L,F,S] :: [-5..5], 9 * L + 8 * F + 4 * S = 0,
cumulative([L,F,S],[3,3,3],[1,1,1],1),
labelingsplit([L,F,S]).
```

Initial propagation does nothing so when computation reaches the labelling the domain is

$$D(L) = [-5..5], \quad D(F) = [-5..5], \quad D(S) = [-5..5].$$

The first split is on the domain of L. This adds $L \leq 0$. This modifies the domain to

$$D(L) = [-5..0], \quad D(F) = [-2..5], \quad D(S) = [-5..5].$$

The next split is on the domain of F. This adds $F \leq 1$ and propagation modifies the domain to

$$D(L) = [-3.. - 2], \quad D(F) = [0..1], \quad D(S) = [3..5].$$

Now we split on S. This adds $S \leq 4$ which fails, and then tries $S \geq 5$ which also fails.

Execution backtracks to try the other split on F, $F \geq 2$. Consistency modifies the domain to

$$D(L) = [-5..0], \quad D(F) = [2..5], \quad D(S) = [-5..5].$$

Now the domain of S is split. This adds $S \leq 0$ which leaves the domain as

$$D(L) = [-4..0], \quad D(F) = [2..5], \quad D(S) = [-5..0].$$

Now the domain of L is split again (the second split for L in this branch). This adds $L \leq -2$ giving rise to

$$D(L) = [-4..-2], \quad D(F) = [3..5], \quad D(S) = [-5..0].$$

Finally the domain of F is split again. This adds $F \leq 4$ which fails, and then $F \geq 5$ which reduces the domain to

$$D(L) = [-4..-4], \quad D(F) = [5..5], \quad D(S) = [-1..-1].$$

This is a valuation domain so the domain is returned as the answer.

For the example above, domain splitting produces a larger derivation tree than ordinary labelling. This is because the problem is so small. However, when there are many variables and their domains are large, domain splitting can be far more efficient than labelling. In general, the domain splitting approach is better than regular labelling when the constraints involving the variables to be labelled can gain substantial consistency information from the split domain since, in this case, by using domain splitting we may be able to eliminate half of a variable's possible domain values by adding a single constraint.

8.4   Different Problem Modellings

An important issue that arises when solving problems over finite domains is that there is often more than one way to model the problem. Different models arise because other ways of viewing a problem lead to different formulations involving different variables and constraints. These models may have very different efficiency depending on the number of variables and types of constraints in the model.

Ideally, the constraint programmer wishes to find a model which can be efficiently evaluated by the solver in their CLP system. However, reasoning about efficiency is quite difficult. This is because of the incomplete nature of the constraint solver—in some models search will be pruned by the solver while in others it will not, even though the constraints are equivalent. If efficiency is an issue (as it usually is), it is worthwhile investigating different models of the problem empirically.

Example 8.4

Consider a simple assignment problem. A factory has four workers w_1, w_2, w_3 and w_4, and four products p_1, p_2, p_3 and p_4. The problem is to assign workers to products so that each worker is assigned to one product, and each product is assigned to one worker. The profit made by worker w_i working on product p_j is given in the table below.

	p_1	p_2	p_3	p_4
w_1	7	1	3	4
w_2	8	2	5	1
w_3	4	3	7	2
w_4	3	1	6	3

A solution to this assignment problem is acceptable if the total profit is at least 19.

A traditional approach to modelling this kind of problem comes from the operations research community. The problem is modelled by 16 Boolean variables B_{ij}, with each corresponding to the proposition "worker i is assigned to product j". Each Boolean is represented by an integer ranging between 0 and 1. Using Boolean variables we can model the problem with linear arithmetic constraints. The constraint c_{wi} which is $B_{i1} + B_{i2} + B_{i3} + B_{i4} = 1$ ensures that worker w_i is assigned to exactly one task. Similarly, the constraint c_{pj} which is $B_{1j} + B_{2j} + B_{3j} + B_{4j} = 1$ ensures that product p_j is assigned to exactly one worker. The total profit P is

$$P = 7 \times B_{11} + B_{12} + 3 \times B_{13} + 4 \times B_{14} + 8 \times B_{21} + 2 \times B_{22} + 5 \times B_{23} + B_{24} +$$
$$4 \times B_{31} + 3 \times B_{32} + 7 \times B_{33} + 2 \times B_{34} + 3 \times B_{41} + B_{42} + 6 \times B_{43} + 3 \times B_{44}.$$

Thus, the requirement for enough profit is simply the constraint $P \geq 19$.

Note that the conjunction of the four worker constraints $\wedge_{i=1}^{4} c_{wi}$ and the four product constraints $\wedge_{j=1}^{4} c_{pj}$ imply that the sum of all 16 variables is 4. It follows that any one of these primitive constraints is redundant and so can be eliminated from the model. Whether or not this is worthwhile depends on the underlying solver. With a propagation based solver, the extra constraint may lead to more propagated information and so it is better to include it.

Example 8.5

The following constraint models the simple assignment problem using Boolean variables:

```
[B11,B12,B13,B14,B21,B22,B23,B24,B31,B32,
 B33,B34,B41,B42,B43,B44] :: [0,1],
B11 + B12 + B13 + B14 = 1,
B21 + B22 + B23 + B24 = 1,
B31 + B32 + B33 + B34 = 1,
B41 + B42 + B43 + B44 = 1,
B11 + B21 + B31 + B41 = 1,
B12 + B22 + B32 + B42 = 1,
B13 + B23 + B33 + B43 = 1,
B14 + B24 + B34 + B44 = 1,
P =   7 * B11 + B12 + 3 * B13 + 4 * B14
    + 8 * B21 + 2 * B22 + 5 * B23 + B24
    + 4 * B31 + 3 * B32 + 7 * B33 + 2 * B34
    + 3 * B41 + B42 + 6 * B43 + 3 * B44,
P >= 19,
labeling([B11,B12,B13,B14,B21,B22,B23,B24,B31,B32,
          B33,B34,B41,B42,B43,B44]).
```

The goal above will find each of the four solutions to the problem using a total of 28 choices. That is, when executing the labelling predicate, there are 28 derivation steps in the tree in which there is a choice of a value for a variable.

This modelling approach arises from the operations research approach to solving integer constraints. They use a real linear constraint solver together with some kind of enumeration such as "branch and bound" (discussed in Section 3.6). Because of the choice of solver, there is no direct way to represent disequations ($X \neq Y$) and so Boolean variables are used. Given a constraint solver that handles disequations well, more natural models of the problem are possible.

We shall now model the problem by using four variables W_1, W_2, W_3 and W_4 which represent the four workers. If the ith worker works on product j then W_i takes value j. The assignment constraints are simply that each variable takes a different value. That is, $W_i \neq W_k$ for all $1 \leq i \neq k \leq 4$. We can use the complex primitive constraint `alldifferent` to model this.

Evaluating the total profit is more difficult. We need to know the profit generated by each worker (one working on each of the four products). This can be encoded using four arrays, one for each worker. The array $profit_i$ details the profit of worker i for each product with $profit_i[j]$ being the profit if product j is made by that worker. For instance,

$$profit_1[1] = 7, \quad profit_1[2] = 1, \quad profit_1[3] = 3, \quad profit_1[4] = 4.$$

The profit of worker i, WP_i, is found by looking up $profit_i$ for the value of W_i.

In Chapter 3 we introduced the `element` complex primitive constraint. It is used to mimic array lookup. We can use a `element` constraint to model each of the $profit_i$ arrays. For instance,

$$element(W_1, [7, 1, 3, 4], WP_1)$$

mimics the constraint that WP_1 is $profit_1[W_1]$.

Example 8.6

A second model for the simple assignment problem using worker variables is

```
[W1,W2,W3,W4] :: [1..4],
alldifferent([W1,W2,W3,W4]),
element(W1,[7,1,3,4],WP1),
element(W2,[8,2,5,1],WP2),
element(W3,[4,3,7,2],WP3),
element(W4,[3,1,6,3],WP4),
P = WP1 + WP2 + WP3 + WP4,
P ≥ 19,
labeling([W1,W2,W3,W4]).
```

Since only 14 choices are required to find all solutions to the problem, this model is more efficient than the first model. Arguably, this model is also simpler since there are 7 primitive constraints, as opposed to 10 in the first model, although five of these (the `alldifferent` and `element` constraints) are more complex.

The principal difference between these models occurs because of the different solver and primitive constraints with which the constraint programmer had to work. However, it is not only different solvers which lead to different models. We can just as easily model the assignment problem by using variables to represent the products and by selecting a worker for each product. This is analogous to the second model but swaps the role of worker and product.

Example 8.7
Therefore, a third model for the simple assignment problem using product variables is

```
[T1,T2,T3,T4] :: [1..4],
alldifferent([T1,T2,T3,T4]),
element(T1,[7,8,4,3],TP1),
element(T2,[1,2,3,1],TP2),
element(T3,[3,5,7,6],TP3),
element(T4,[4,1,2,3],TP4),
P = TP1 + TP2 + TP3 + TP4,
P ≥ 19,
labeling([T1,T2,T3,T4]).
```

Like the second model there are 7 primitive constraints. Somewhat surprisingly, however, this model is more efficient than the second since only 7 choices are required to find all solutions to the problem. Why is the derivation tree smaller in this model? The reason is that profit depends more on the product than on the worker. If we examine the profits for each product TP_1, TP_2, TP_3 and TP_4 we see that the initial domains are [3..8], [1..3], [3..7] and [1..4] respectively. The propagation rule for $P = TP_1 + TP_2 + TP_3 + TP_4$ based on the inequality

$$TP_1 \geq min_D(P) - max_D(TP_2) - max_D(TP_3) - max_D(TP_4)$$

determines that $TP_1 \geq 5$. The constraint $element(T_1, [7, 8, 4, 3], TP_1)$ therefore reduces the domain of T_1 to [1..2]. Similar reasoning also reduces the domain of T_3. This reduction to the domain of T_1 and T_3 before labelling starts leads to the improvement in search.

Determining the relative efficiency of different models is a difficult problem and one which relies upon an understanding of the underlying constraint solver. The best model will be the one in which information is propagated earliest. This often means that the more direct the mapping from the problem into the primitive constraints in the program, the better the model. Another guideline is that the fewer the variables the better, so long as propagation of information is similar. This is because it means there will be less variables to label. Given the difficulty of understanding interaction between the constraints and the solver it is often useful to empirically evaluate the different models.

In the above example the last two models are better since they model the problem more naturally as an assignment of one of four objects to each of four objects. The Boolean formulation is less natural, requiring more variables and more constraints. Since these constraints are quite complex, their propagation rules are slower to propagate information. Of course the choice of model also depends on the constraint solver. The first model is clearly the best choice when disequations and complex primitive constraints, such as `element`, are not available.

Efficiency is not the only criteria by which to compare models. Flexibility is also an important issue. It is unusual for an application to remain static. Often there will be a need to extend the program to model constraints which were not part of the problem's original formulation. Flexibility measures how easy it is to express these additional constraints in the model. Of course the flexibility of a model greatly depends on the form of these new constraints. A model may be flexible for one class of constraints but not for another.

As an example consider the three models for the assignment problem. Suppose we wish to add the requirement that we cannot have both "worker 1 assigned to product 1" and "worker 4 assigned to product 4." In the Boolean formulation this is easily expressed as the constraint $B_{11} + B_{44} \leq 1$. It is considerably more difficult to express this requirement in either of the other two models. In the second model, one approach would be to add Boolean variables B_{11} and B_{44} and define them in terms of W_1 and W_4 using `element` constraints:

```
[B11,B44] :: [0,1],
element(W1,[1,0,0,0],B11),
element(W4,[0,0,0,1],B44),
B11 + B44 ≤ 1.
```

The element constraints ensure that if $W_1 = 1$ then $B_{11} = 1$ and vice versa. A similar extension can also be made to the third model.

As another example, suppose a new requirement is that worker 3 must work on a product numbered greater than that which is worked on by worker 2. In the second model, this is simply the constraint $W_3 > W_2$. In the first model the requirement can be modelled by

$$B_{31} = 0 \wedge$$
$$B_{32} \leq B_{21} \wedge$$
$$B_{33} \leq B_{21} + B_{22} \wedge$$
$$B_{34} \leq B_{21} + B_{22} + B_{23} \wedge$$
$$B_{24} = 0.$$

Although this formulation is equivalent in terms of information propagation to $W_3 > W_2$, it is considerably more complex, which means there is more chance of an error in specifying it, and larger, meaning that there may be more overhead in propagating the information. It is much more difficult to see how the requirement could be added to the third model.

As we have seen, different models may behave very differently in terms of the amount of information they can infer and propagate. In addition, some constraints may be very difficult to express in one model, but easy in another. For these reasons it may be worthwhile to combine different models. Combining models is a particular example of adding solver redundant constraints as discussed in Section 7.5. The constraints in the second model are redundant, but they may give better solver behaviour.

In general, we can combine models by using relations which the original problem dictates must hold between the variables in each model. Given that the variables specify an answer to the problem, the values the variables take in one model will correspond to values the variables take in another model. For instance, in the different models for the assignment problem, B_{11} is 1 precisely when W_1 is 1, and W_3 is 2 precisely when T_2 is 3.

Because of the importance of combining models, many CLP systems provide complex primitive constraints which facilitate this process. We will assume that there is a primitive constraint $\text{iff}(var_1, val_1, var_2, val_2)$ which holds if $var_1 \equiv val_1$ implies that $var_2 = val_2$ and $var_2 \equiv val_2$ implies that $var_1 = var_2$.

For example, $\text{iff}(\text{W3, 2, T2, 3})$ constrains W_3 to be 2 exactly when T_2 is 3. Thus if T_2 becomes set to 3 then this constraint will set W_3 to 2. Conversely, suppose the domain of W_3 is reduced to [3..4], then since $W_3 \neq 2$, the constraint $T_2 \neq 3$ can be added.

Example 8.8

A goal which combines the second and third model is

```
[W1,W2,W3,W4] :: [1..4],
alldifferent([W1,W2,W3,W4]),
element(W1,[7,1,3,4],WP1),
element(W2,[8,2,5,1],WP2),
element(W3,[4,3,7,2],WP3),
element(W4,[3,1,6,3],WP4),
P = WP1 + WP2 + WP3 + WP4,
[T1,T2,T3,T4] :: [1..4],
alldifferent([T1,T2,T3,T4]),
element(T1,[7,8,4,3],TP1),
element(T2,[1,2,3,1],TP2),
element(T3,[3,5,7,6],TP3),
element(T4,[4,1,2,3],TP4),
P = TP1 + TP2 + TP3 + TP4,
P ≥ 19,
iff(W1,1,T1,1), iff(W1,2,T2,1), iff(W1,3,T3,1), iff(W1,4,T4,1),
iff(W2,1,T1,2), iff(W2,2,T2,2), iff(W2,3,T3,2), iff(W2,4,T4,2),
iff(W3,1,T1,3), iff(W3,2,T2,3), iff(W3,3,T3,3), iff(W3,4,T4,3),
iff(W4,1,T1,4), iff(W4,2,T2,4), iff(W4,3,T3,4), iff(W4,4,T4,4),
labeling([W1,W2,W3,W4]).
```

Note that we can choose to label either the variables of the second or those of the third model. It is unnecessary to label both because, if all of the W_i variables are fixed, we are guaranteed that all of the T_j variables are fixed by the iff constraints, and vice versa.

For this model only 5 choices are required to find all solutions to the problem. However, since there are 39 primitive constraints, we might expect execution to take longer overall because of the extra work in the propagation solver.

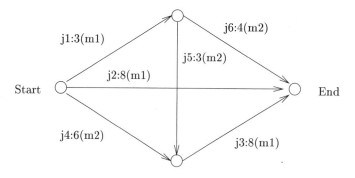

Figure 8.3   Tasks and precedences for scheduling problem.

8.5   An Extended Example: Scheduling

Combinatorial search problems such as those in the examples above are useful for illustrating the way in which a $CLP(FD)$ system works but they are not particularly realistic. We now investigate a more standard commercial problem, that of scheduling. In a scheduling problem we are given a list of tasks, each of which must be performed on one of a selection of machines, and a list of precedences between the tasks indicating which tasks must be completed before a particular task can begin. The aim is to find a schedule, that is to say, a start time for each task, so that the precedences are maintained and no more than one task is being performed on any machine at any given moment. This problem is most commonly couched as an optimization problem in which the aim is to minimize the overall time for completion of all of the tasks. However, we will first consider the simpler problem of determining whether it is possible to schedule the tasks given an upper bound on the total time available.

We shall model the scheduling problem using the following data structure. A task is a record of the form

$$task(name, duration, [names], machine)$$

where *name* is a constant identifying the task, *duration* is an integer detailing the number of minutes the task requires, the third argument is a list of task names which must be completed before this task can begin and *machine* is the machine on which the task must be performed. A problem description is simply a list of tasks.

Consider the specific problem illustrated in Figure 8.3 where tasks are represented by arcs in the graph. The label of an arc is of the form *name* : *duration(machine)*. Thus, $j3 : 8(m1)$ means that job $j3$ takes 8 minutes to complete and requires machine $m1$. The precedence constraints are given by "no task can start before all tasks ending at its start point are completed." This problem instance is represented by the following problem description, which we shall abbreviate to *problem*:

```
[task(j1, 3, [], m1), task(j2, 8, [], m1), task(j3, 8, [j4,j5], m1),
 task(j4, 6, [], m2), task(j5, 3, [j1], m2), task(j6, 4, [j1], m2)]
```

A relatively simple program to model the scheduling problem is as follows:

```
schedule(Data, End, Joblist) :-
    makejoblist(Data, Joblist, End),
    precedences(Data, Joblist),
    machines(Data, Joblist),
    labeltasks(Joblist).

makejoblist([],[],_).
makejoblist([task(N,D,_,_)|Ts], [job(N,D,TS)|Js], End) :-
    TS :: [0..1000],
    TS + D ≤ End,
    makejoblist(Ts, Js, End).

getjob(JL, N, D, TS) :- once(member(job(N,D,TS), JL)).

precedences([],_).
precedences([task(N,_,Pre,_)|Ts], Joblist) :-
    getjob(Joblist, N, _, TS),
    prectask(Pre, TS, Joblist),
    precedences(Ts, Joblist).

prectask([], _, _).
prectask([Name|Names], PostStart, Joblist) :-
    getjob(Joblist, Name, D, TS),
    TS + D ≤ PostStart,
    prectask(Names, PostStart, Joblist).

machines([], _).
machines([task(N,_,_,M)|Ts], Joblist) :-
    getjob(Joblist, N, D, TS),
    machtask(Ts, M, D, TS, Joblist),
    machines(Ts, Joblist).

machtask([], _, _, _, _).
machtask([task(SN,_,_,MO)|Ts], M, D, TS, Joblist) :-
    (M = MO ->
        getjob(Joblist, SN, SD, STS),
        exclude(D, TS, SD, STS)
    ; true ),
    machtask(Ts, M, D, TS, Joblist).

exclude(_D, TS, SD, STS) :- STS + SD ≤ TS.
exclude(D, TS, _SD, STS) :- TS + D ≤ STS.
```

```
labeltasks([]).
labeltasks([job(_,_,TS)|Js]) :-
    indomain(TS),
    labeltasks(Js).
```

Execution of the program proceeds as follows. First the predicate `makejoblist` is called. This builds a list that holds the task names with their duration and a variable which represents their start time. The start times are each constrained so that the task will begin after time zero and end before the time *End*.

The predicate `getjobs` is used to look up the joblist constructed by `makejoblist`. Given a task name it will find the corresponding duration and start time. The joblist is an association list between names and start times. Since a job only appears once in the joblist there is only ever one solution. Thus it is has been programmed using `once`.

The predicate `precedences` builds the precedence constraints for each task. The predicate `prectask` makes sure that the start time for a given task is after the end of each of the tasks in its precedence list.

The predicate `machines` sets up the exclusion constraints between jobs on the same machine. For each task on machine M, it finds every task later in the problem description that is also on machine M and makes sure (using `exclude`) that they are not performed simultaneously.

Finally, the call `labeltasks` labels the start time variables, ensuring that every start time takes a fixed value.

Executing the program on the test data *problem* using the goal

$$\text{End = 20, schedule}(\textit{problem}, \text{End, Joblist})$$

creates many constraints, most of which deal with the data structures. The result of `makejoblist` is to equate *Joblist* to a data structure of the form

$$[\text{job(j1, 3, } TS_1), \text{ job(j2, 8, } TS_2), \text{ job(j3, 8, } TS_3),$$
$$\text{job(j4, 6, } TS_4), \text{ job(j5, 3, } TS_5), \text{ job(j6, 4, } TS_6)]$$

where the variables are given initial domain [0..1000] and constrained by:

$$0 \leq TS_1, \quad TS_1 + 3 \leq 20, \quad 0 \leq TS_2, \quad TS_2 + 8 \leq 20,$$
$$0 \leq TS_3, \quad TS_3 + 8 \leq 20, \quad 0 \leq TS_4, \quad TS_4 + 6 \leq 20,$$
$$0 \leq TS_5, \quad TS_5 + 3 \leq 20, \quad 0 \leq TS_6, \quad TS_6 + 4 \leq 20.$$

At this point the propagation solver has computed the domain

$$D(TS_1) = [0..17], \quad D(TS_2) = [0..12], \quad D(TS_3) = [0..12],$$
$$D(TS_4) = [0..14], \quad D(TS_5) = [0..17], \quad D(TS_6) = [0..16].$$

The effect of the user-defined constraint `precedences` is to add the constraints

$$TS_1 + 3 \leq TS_5, \quad TS_1 + 3 \leq TS_6, \quad TS_4 + 6 \leq TS_3, \quad TS_5 + 3 \leq TS_3.$$

After these are added propagation gives rise to the domain

$$D(TS_1) = [0..6], \quad D(TS_2) = [0..12], \quad D(TS_3) = [6..12],$$
$$D(TS_4) = [0..6], \quad D(TS_5) = [3..9], \quad D(TS_6) = [3..16].$$

The effect of the predicate `machines` is to build choices of constraints that correspond to the requirement that no two tasks are executed on the same machine at the same time. The choices are

$$TS_2 + 8 \leq TS_1 \text{ or } TS_1 + 3 \leq TS_2,$$
$$TS_3 + 8 \leq TS_1 \text{ or } TS_1 + 3 \leq TS_3,$$
$$TS_3 + 8 \leq TS_2 \text{ or } TS_2 + 8 \leq TS_3,$$
$$TS_5 + 3 \leq TS_4 \text{ or } TS_4 + 6 \leq TS_5,$$
$$TS_6 + 4 \leq TS_4 \text{ or } TS_4 + 6 \leq TS_6,$$
$$TS_6 + 4 \leq TS_5 \text{ or } TS_5 + 3 \leq TS_6.$$

The first sequence of choices which leads to an answer is to choose the second choice in each pair, except for the fourth pair. This sequence of choices results in the propagation solver finding the domain:

$$D(TS_1) = [0..0], \quad D(TS_2) = [3..4], \quad D(TS_3) = [12..12],$$
$$D(TS_4) = [6..6], \quad D(TS_5) = [3..3], \quad D(TS_6) = [12..16].$$

The `labeltasks` predicate chooses the first element of each domain obtaining the final answer

$$D(TS_1) = [0..0], \quad D(TS_2) = [3..3], \quad D(TS_3) = [12..12],$$
$$D(TS_4) = [6..6], \quad D(TS_5) = [3..3], \quad D(TS_6) = [12..12].$$

The scheduling program again illustrates the typical form of a constraint satisfaction problem expressed in CLP using the constrain and generate methodology. First, the constraints of the problem are added to the store and, then, a labelling method is used to ensure a definite solution is found. The order in which constraints are added is important since it may affect efficiency. Since the basic time constraints and precedence constraints are deterministic they are added first. The machine exclusion constraints are not deterministic since these are modelled by choosing to place one task before or after another task on the same machine. This choice is made during execution, so, if a wrong choice is made, the other will be tried. Following the guidelines from Chapter 7 we, therefore, place the machine exclusion constraints after the basic time constraints and precedence constraints. This ensures that choices are made as late as possible, reducing both repeated computation and the size of the derivation tree.

For the scheduling problem, ideally, we wish to find a schedule with minimum total time. This is simply the answer to the goal

```
End :: [0..1000], schedule(problem, End, Joblist), indomain(End).
```

which minimizes the value of End. Thus the following goal will compute the schedule with minimum total time.

```
End :: [0..1000],
minimize((schedule(problem, End, Joblist), indomain(End)), End).
```

Executing this goal, a solution is found with $End = 19$ and

$$TS_1 = 0 \land TS_2 = 3 \land TS_3 = 11 \land TS_4 = 0 \land TS_5 = 6 \land TS_6 = 9.$$

This is a better solution than that found when solving the satisfiability problem since that solution required 20 minutes to complete the tasks.

8.5.1   Redundant Information

As is it stands, the simple scheduling program given above is not useful for solving larger scheduling problems because the search space rapidly becomes too large. In Section 7.5 we saw that adding redundant constraints to a program can sometimes reduce its search space. Here we investigate how the addition of answer redundant constraint information to the scheduling program can help reduce its search space.

The large search space arises because of the mutual exclusion constraints for machine usage. The problem is that the mutual exclusion information is represented in different rules, and so is only available once a rule has been chosen. If we can add constraints that are redundant with respect to all of the choices, we can reduce the search space by making information available before a choice is made.

Let us take a concrete example. Suppose that, for some task t_0, all of the tasks $[t_1, \ldots, t_n]$ have to be performed before t_0, and each of them must be performed on the same machine. The tasks $t_1, \ldots, t_n$ must take at least $D_1 + \cdots + D_n$ time to complete where D_i is the duration of task t_i since they must all be completed on the same machine. Furthermore, they cannot start before the minimum of their start times $TS_1, \ldots, TS_n$. Thus, t_0 cannot begin before the sum of the minimum start time of $t_1, \ldots, t_n$ together with the total duration of $D_1 + \cdots + D_n$. That is,

$$TS_0 \geq \text{minimum}(\{TS_1, \ldots, TS_n\}) + D_1 + \cdots + D_n.$$

This is an answer redundant constraint since the information is implicit in the current representation of the problem and so any answer to the problem must satisfy this constraint. However, if it is added, using a deterministic user-defined constraint, it may reduce the search space.

For example, note task j3 can begin only after j4 and j5 (and hence j1) have finished. Since both these tasks require m2 they cannot both be completed before 9 minutes, the sum of their durations after the earliest one begins. Thus we can add the information $TS_3 \geq \text{minimum}(\{TS_4, TS_5\}) + 9$, which can reduce the domain of TS_3 before adding any machine exclusion constraints.

```
schedule(Data, End, Machinelist, Joblist) :-
    makejoblist(Data, Joblist, End),
    precedences(Data, Joblist),
    makeemptylists(Machinelist, Emptys),
    extrainfo(Data,Joblist,Machinelist,Emptys,Joblist),
    machines(Data, Joblist),
    labeltasks(Joblist).

makeemptylists([],[]).
makeemptylists([_|L],[[]|R]) :- makeemptylists(L,R).

extrainfo(_, [], _, _, _).
extrainfo(Data, [job(N,_,TS)|Js], Machinelist, Emptys, Joblist) :-
    predecessors(N, Data, [], Pre),
    splittasks(Pre, Data, Machinelist, Emptys, Split),
    list_redundant(Split, Joblist, TS),
    extrainfo(Data, Js, Machinelist, Emptys, Joblist).

splittasks([], _, _, Split, Split).
splittasks([N|Ns], Data, Machines, Split0, Split) :-
    gettask(Data, N, task(_,_,_,M)),
    insert(Machines, M, N, Split0, Split1),
    splittasks(Ns, Data, Machines, Split1, Split).

insert([M|_], M, T, [L|Ls], [[T|L]|Ls]).
insert([M0|Ms], M, T, [L|Ls0], [L|Ls]) :-
    M0 ≠ M,
    insert(Ms, M, T, Ls0, Ls).

list_redundant([], _, _).
list_redundant([L|Ls], Joblist, TS) :-
    redundant(L, Joblist, TS, 0, []),
    list_redundant(Ls, Joblist, TS).

redundant([], _, TS, TotalD, ListTS) :-
    TS ≥ minimum(ListTS) + TotalD.
redundant([N|Ns], Joblist, TS, TotalD0, ListTS) :-
    getjob(Joblist, N, DN, TSN),
    TotalD = TotalD0 + DN,
    redundant(Ns, Joblist, TS, TotalD, [TSN|ListTS]).

gettask(Data, N, T) :-
    T = task(N, _, _, _),
    once(member(T, Data)).

lookup(Data, N, P) :- member(task(N,_,P,_), Data).
```

The above program calculates the list of predecessors for each task using the definition of **predecessors** from Chapter 5 (where **lookup** is re-defined as shown in the program above). Then **splittasks** splits the list of predecessors into a list of lists, where each list corresponds to the tasks performed on one machine. Finally, `list_redundant` builds the redundant constraint for each such list using `redundant`.

Conversely, we could extend the original program to calculate the descendants of each task, and ensure that each task is started early enough so that all of its descendants on the same machine can be completed before *End*. If we use both methods we can expect to reduce the search space more substantially since they will interact with each other.

It may be useful to compute and add this redundant information more than once during the computation. In particular, after we have made a number of choices about which tasks on the same machine are before or after others, we increase the total number of tasks that must occur before a particular task. Thus, if we repeat the calculation we may get stronger constraints.

Suppose we have chosen that j5 should be executed after j6. This will cause us to add the constraint $TS_6 + 4 \leq TS_5$. We could now update the immediate predecessor list for j5 to include j6 and recalculate the redundant constraints. Now tasks j1, j4, j5, j6 must all be completed before j3 can begin. Since j4, j5 and j6 are all jobs for machine m2 with a total duration of 13, we know that j3 cannot begin before time 13 after the earliest of start time for one of j4, j5, j6. Therefore we can add the constraint

$$TS_3 \geq \text{minimum}(\{TS_4, TS_5, TS_6\}) + 13.$$

By maintaining lists of predecessors and updating them whenever we make a choice about the order of tasks on the same machine, we can add more information after each choice is made. For large scheduling problems this may drastically reduce the search space.

There is, however, a tradeoff between the extra computation required to generate the redundant constraints and the pruning of the search space these extra constraints produce. For some data, the redundant constraints may not reduce the search space at all. Indeed, this is the case for the data for *problem*. On the other hand, for some scheduling problems computing and adding the redundant constraints may mean an answer is found in minutes instead of requiring many hours.

One of the more difficult tasks of the constraint programmer is to understand the tradeoff between the cost of adding redundant constraints and the reduction in search space they cause. Understanding, usually gained through experimentation, allows the programmer to weigh the relative benefits and, so, to obtain an efficient solution to the particular problem they are interested in.

8.5.2   Using `cumulative` Constraints

Another way to model the scheduling problem is to use the complex primitive constraint `cumulative`. If available, this constraint provides a way to model the machine exclusion constraints without requiring multiple rules and, hence, choice. The stronger consistency information it can provide will reduce the search required for a solution. We can modify the above program to use the stronger, but more complex, cumulative constraint, as follows:

```
schedule(Data, End, Machinelist, Joblist) :-
    makejoblist(Data, Joblist, End),
    precedences(Data, Joblist),
    makeemptylists(Machinelist, Emptys),
    extrainfo(Data,Joblist,Machinelist,Emptys,Joblist),
    cumulative_machines(Data,Joblist,Machinelist,Emptys),
    labeltasks(Joblist).

cumulative_machines(Data, Joblist, Machinelist, Emptys) :-
    datatolist(Data, Names),
    splittasks(Names, Data, Machinelist, Emptys, Split),
    makecumulatives(Split, Joblist).

datatolist([],[]).
datatolist([task(N,_,_,_)|Ts],[N|Ns]) :-
    datatolist(Ts,Ns).

makecumulatives([], _).
makecumulatives([L|Ls], Joblist) :-
    makecumulative(L, Joblist, [], [], []),
    makecumulatives(Ls, Joblist).

makecumulative([], _, Ts, Ds, Rs) :-
    cumulative(Ts, Ds, Rs, 1).
makecumulative([N|Ns], Joblist, Ts, Ds, Rs) :-
    getjob(Joblist, N, DN, TSN),
    makecumulative(Ns, Joblist, [TSN|Ts], [DN|Ds], [1|Rs]).
```

The predicate cumulative_machines works by first building a list of all task names, *Names*, and then splitting the tasks into a list of lists of names, *Split*, one for each machine, using splittasks. Then the lists in *Split* are traversed one by one using makecumulative which collects a list of start times, Ts, durations, Ds, and resources, Rs, for the cumulative constraint which is added when the end of the list is reached. Note that the value of the available and required resource is always one since each task requires sole use of the single machine.

This formulation gains from the greater consistency reasoning available for cumulative and delaying the choice of ordering until labelling. For example, for the data of our example *problem* two cumulative constraints are set up

$$(m1) \quad \text{cumulative}([TS_1, TS_2, TS_3], [3, 8, 8], [1, 1, 1], 1)$$

$$(m2) \quad \text{cumulative}([TS_4, TS_5, TS_6], [6, 3, 4], [1, 1, 1], 1)$$

Suppose we have labelled TS_4 as 3. The second cumulative constraint will propagate the information that the range of TS_6 should be [9..16] since it cannot fit elsewhere (see Figure 8.4).

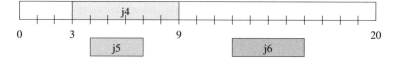

Figure 8.4   Propagation from a cumulative constraint.

After applying the cumulative constraints the resulting domain for the example problem is

$$D(TS_1) = [0..1], \quad D(TS_2) = [3..4], \quad D(TS_3) = [11..12],$$
$$D(TS_4) = [0..6], \quad D(TS_5) = [3..9], \quad D(TS_6) = [6..16].$$

Propagation using the cumulative constraints has solved most of the problem. The relative order of the tasks j1, j2 and j3 is already fixed, while the remaining domains are significantly reduced.

So far we have not discussed different labelling strategies for the scheduling problem. We have simply used the standard labelling predicate. The initial program only creates constraints of the form

$$TS_i + d \leq TS_j, \quad d \leq TS_i \text{ or } \quad TS_i \leq d$$

where d is a constant. The bounds propagation solver is actually complete for this class of constraints, so, by the time the initial program reaches the `labeltasks` predicate, setting each of the variables to its current lower bound must be a solution to the problem. The default labelling quickly finds this solution.

When we replace the machine exclusion constraints by `cumulative` constraints, the labelling method can have an impact on the amount of search required to find a solution. We should therefore consider writing a problem specific labelling strategy.

One possibility is to label the tasks in order of execution. That is, find the task with the earliest possible starting time, and attempt to set its start time to that time. If this fails, we remove the earliest starting time from the possible starting time of the chosen task and continue, looking for the task which now has the earliest possible start time. The reasoning behind this strategy is that placing the earliest task will increase the lower bounds on the other tasks. If it cannot lead to a solution we should discover this quickly. The following labelling predicate implements this strategy.

```
labeltasks([]).
labeltasks(Js) :-
    gettimes(Js, Ts),
    label_earliest(Ts).

gettimes([],[]).
gettimes([job(_,_,TS)|Js], [TS|Ts]) :- gettimes(Js, Ts).
```

```
label_earliest([]).
label_earliest([TS0|Ts]) :-
    mindomain(TS0, M0),
    find_min_start(Ts, TS0, M0, TS, M, RTs),
    rest_earliest(TS, M, [TS0|Ts], RTs).

rest_earliest(TS, M, _Ts, RTs) :-
    TS = M,
    label_earliest(RTs).
rest_earliest(TS, M, Ts, _RTs) :-
    TS ≠ M,
    label_earliest(Ts).

find_min_start([], TS, M, TS, M, []).
find_min_start([TS1|Ts], TS0, M0, TS, M, RTs) :-
    mindomain(TS1, M1),
    (M1 < M0 ->
        RTs = [TS0|RTs1],
        find_min_start(Ts, TS1, M1, TS, M, RTs1)
    ;
        RTs = [TS1|RTs1],
        find_min_start(Ts, TS0, M0, TS, M, RTs1)
    ).
```

The predicate `labeltasks` builds the list of start times, Ts, using `gettimes`. The predicate `label_earliest` does the real work. It searches for the start time with the smallest minimum by calling `find_min_start`. The call

```
find_min_start(Ts, TS0, M0, TS, M, RTs)
```

finds the variable TS with earliest start time M from the variables in $\{TS0\} \cup Ts$, while RTs is set to the remaining variables in this set. The variable $TS0$ is the current selection and $M0$ is the earliest time it can start. The call `rest_earliest` tries both choices of setting TS to M and labelling the remaining variables or removing M from the domain of TS and retrying the heuristic.

We could break ties in tasks with the same minimum by choosing the most tightly constrained task (an application of the first fail principle).

8.6 (*) Arc Consistency

In our description of our idealized system $CLP(FD)$ we have assumed that it uses a bounds propagation solver. However, as we saw in Section 3.5 arc consistency allows more values to be eliminated from the domains of variables occurring in binary constraints than does bounds consistency. For this reason many CLP systems also use arc consistency.

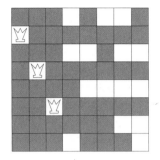

Figure 8.5   Example 8-queens partial solution.

Disequality constraints are a particular type of binary constraint on which arc consistency performs significantly better than bounds consistency. For example, consider the *8-queens* problem. The initial domain of each variable $R_1, \dots, R_8$ is [1..8]. Suppose that we are part way through labelling the variables and we have found the partial solution $\{R_1 \mapsto 2, R_2 \mapsto 4, R_3 \mapsto 6\}$.

A constraint solver based on bounds consistency determines the domains of the remaining variables (given the partial solution) to be

$$D(R_4) = [1..8], \quad D(R_5) = [3..5], \quad D(R_6) = [1..5],$$
$$D(R_7) = [1..7], \quad D(R_8) = [3..8].$$

An arc consistency based solver for the same constraints and partial solution will obtain the domain,

$$D(R_4) = \{1, 3, 8\}, \quad D(R_5) = \{3, 5\}, \quad D(R_6) = \{1, 5\},$$
$$D(R_7) = \{1, 3, 5, 7\}, \quad D(R_8) = \{3, 5, 7, 8\}.$$

The arc consistent domain values are shown as unshaded squares in Figure 8.5.

The reason that arc consistency is so much more effective at pruning the domains is that all of the constraints are of the form $C_i \neq C_j + d$ where d is a constant. Bounds propagation does not perform well on these constraints since a bounds propagation solver can only makes use of disequalities when they change a lower or upper bound. However, the constraints are all binary and therefore simple to handle using arc consistency. Because of the importance of disequations, most CLP systems use arc consistency when solving disequations. Note when using labelling methods that make use of the size of the domain, such as first fail labelling, arc consistency also gives much more accurate information about the possible values a variable can take.

Another advantage of arc consistency over bounds consistency is that arc consistency works well with arbitrary binary constraints while bounds consistency works only with arithmetic constraints. Some CLP systems allow the programmer to define their own binary relations and to direct the system to employ arc consistency to solve these relations. The programmer defines the binary relation as a user-defined constraint with multiple facts. The call to the relation in the goal is annotated with a `consistent` suffix to indicate that it should be evaluated by using arc consistency rather than the standard CLP evaluation mechanism. The `consistent` suffix can also be used with unary constraints, in which case node consistency is used. The programmer may even use it with relations that have greater arity than two. In this case the system will use hyper-arc consistency.

For example, recall the program to solve an instance of the old-fashioned marriage problem given in Section 8.1. The `likes` relation is still described by the simple program consisting of seven facts. However, instead of backtracking through the different rules we can use arc consistency to evaluate the `likes` relation. The following goal does this:

```
[N,M,E] :: [kim, peter,bernd], N ≠ M, N ≠ E, M ≠ E,
likes(N, nicole) consistent,
likes(M, maria) consistent,
likes(E, erika) consistent,
labeling([N,M,E]).
```

Note that we now need to call a labelling predicate since evaluation of `likes` will no longer ensure that N, M and E are assigned fixed values.

Using arc consistency to solve the disequalities and `likes` constraints gives rise to the domain

$$D(N) = \{kim, bernd\}, \quad D(M) = \{kim, bernd, peter\}, \quad D(E) = \{kim, bernd\}.$$

Evaluation of the labelling predicate will first set N to kim. Arc consistency will reduce the domain of the remaining variables to

$$D(M) = \{peter\}, \quad D(E) = \{bernd\},$$

so no other choices are required to find the first answer. If the system is asked for another answer, backtracking will immediately set N to $bernd$ and no other choices will be required to find the second answer. This contrasts with the original goal in which many more choices are required to find the two answers.

Providing arc consistency removes the need for the complex primitive constraint `element`. The constraint `element(I,[a₁, ... ,aₙ],V)` is essentially equivalent to the constraint `array(I,V) consistent` where the relation `array` is defined by

```
array(1,a₁).
array(2,a₂).
   ⋮
array(n,aₙ).
```

For instance, the constraint `element(W1,[7,1,3,4],WP1)` from the program for the second model for the simple assignment problem (Example 8.6) can be replaced by the literal, `profit_1(W1,WP1) consistent`, where `profit_1` is defined by

```
profit_1(1,7).
profit_1(2,1).
profit_1(3,3).
profit_1(4,4).
```

8.7   (*) Reified Constraints

Using the facilities we have discussed so far, efficient modelling of certain complex combinations of constraints can be difficult. Suppose we have 5 primitive constraints $\{c_1, c_2, c_3, c_4, c_5\}$ over the variables X and Y of which we want between two and three to hold in our solution. We can model this (abstractly) using a program of the form

$$
\begin{array}{llll}
\texttt{comb(X, Y)} & \texttt{:-} & c_1, \; c_2, \; \neg c_3, \; \neg c_4. \\
\texttt{comb(X, Y)} & \texttt{:-} & c_1, \; c_2, \; \neg c_3, \; \neg c_5. \\
\texttt{comb(X, Y)} & \texttt{:-} & c_1, \; c_2, \; \neg c_4, \; \neg c_5. \\
\texttt{comb(X, Y)} & \texttt{:-} & c_1, \; c_3, \; \neg c_2, \; \neg c_4. \\
\texttt{comb(X, Y)} & \texttt{:-} & c_1, \; c_3, \; \neg c_2, \; \neg c_5. \\
& \vdots
\end{array}
$$

This program is large and difficult to follow. A better way of modelling this requirement is to use "reified" constraints.

A *reified constraint* is of form $c \Leftrightarrow B$. It consists of a constraint c together with an attached Boolean variable B. The reified constraint $c \Leftrightarrow B$ does not require the constraint c to hold but only that the relationship between the implication of the constraint and the value of the Boolean variable B holds. The intention is that $B = 1$ when c holds in the current store and $B = 0$ if $\neg c$ holds.

Using reified constraints we can easily model the above combination by

$$
\begin{array}{l}
c_1 \Leftrightarrow \texttt{B1}, \; c_2 \Leftrightarrow \texttt{B2}, \; c_3 \Leftrightarrow \texttt{B3}, \; c_4 \Leftrightarrow \texttt{B4}, \; c_5 \Leftrightarrow \texttt{B5}, \\
\texttt{B = B1 + B2 + B3 + B4 + B5}, \\
\texttt{2} \leq \texttt{B, B} \leq \texttt{3}.
\end{array}
$$

Reified constraints are somewhat complex to implement since they require the solver to determine whether or not a constraint is implied by the current constraint store and whether or not its negation is implied. However, because of the usefulness of reified constraints, some finite domain constraint solvers provide them. Usually they are restricted so that only certain kinds of primitive constraints can be reified.

The main use of reified constraints is to program complex relationships between constraints without using choice.

For example, if we want to model the requirement that $X = 1$ or $X = 2$ but do not want to make a choice then the literal `either(X,1,2)` will do this where the predicate `either` is defined by

```
either(X,X1,X2) :-
    [B1,B2] :: [0..1],
    (X=X1 ⇔ B1), (X=X2 ⇔ B2),
    1 ≤ B1+B2.
```

Consider a call to `either(A,C,E)`. If at some later stage

$$D(A) = \{1,2\}, \quad D(C) = \{3,4\}, \quad D(E) = \{2,3\},$$

then since $A = C$ must be false, $A = E$ is true and the resulting domain is

$$D(A) = \{2\}, \quad D(C) = \{3,4\}, \quad D(E) = \{2\}.$$

One interesting application of reified constraints is to define the built-in `iff` which was introduced in Section 8.4 to facilitate combining different models of the same problem. We can define `iff` by

```
iff(X1,V1,X2,V2) :-
    B :: [0..1],
    (X1=V1 ⇔ B),
    (X2=V2 ⇔ B).
```

The literal `iff(X1,V1,X2,V2)` will hold if $X1$ has the value $V1$ exactly when $X2$ has the value $V2$.

8.8 Summary

Finite domain problems make up the largest class of real life problems tackled by CLP systems. Because of the weak and incomplete solving methods used for such problems, the constraint programmer often has to explicitly use a labelling phase in which a backtracking search tries different values for the variables. Because of this, the usual form of a CLP program solving a finite domain problem reflects the constrain and generate methodology. It consists of constraints which model the problem followed by a labelling phase which generates an answer to the problem.

Since labelling is expensive, the programmer needs to be aware of techniques for reducing the search space and of how constraints are handled by the particular solver being used. In this chapter we have seen a variety of techniques for reducing the search space.

One of the features of the CLP approach to solving constraints over finite domains is that the programmer can specialize the labelling method to take advantage of the structure of the particular problem. We have investigated different strategies for choosing which variable to label and in which order to explore the values in a variable's domain.

Another technique for reducing the search space is to use specialized complex primitive constraints. Often, these allow more concise modelling of a problem and may also improve the efficiency of a model since a complex constraint usually provides better propagation behaviour than does an equivalent conjunction of simpler primitive constraints.

A third technique for reducing the search space is to add redundant constraints. Sometimes it is useful to add solver redundant constraints. These are constraints which are redundant with respect to the constraints in the solver but which improve the propagation behaviour of the solver. It is also useful to add answer redundant constraints. These explicitly add information which is implicitly represented in the solutions to the program.

Another more fundamental way of changing the search space is by choosing a different model for the problem, that is to say, finding a different way of expressing the problem in terms of constraints. Factors influencing the efficiency and flexibility of a model are:

- ease of expression;
- strength of the constraint solver on the constraints;
- number of constraints;
- number of variables.

All of these factors need to be considered. For some problems adding redundant constraints and extra variables may be the best approach to solving the problem, because they significantly reduce the search space. For other problems which require few choices or for which the constraints are well-handled by the solver, the fewer the constraints the better.

Given the somewhat complicated runtime behaviour of $CLP(FD)$ systems, it is often difficult for even the most experienced constraint programmer to predict how a particular technique will affect the execution speed. For this reason, it is usually important to try a variety of approaches and to compare them empirically.

8.9   Practical Exercises

Most of the programs given in this chapter will execute almost unchanged under ECLiPSe, with the compiler directive :- `use_module(library(fd))`. How to obtain ECLiPSe is discussed in the Practical Exercises section of Chapter 3. Some translation of symbols is required to express constraint relations: replace = with #=, $\neq$ with ##, > with #>, < with #<, $\geq$ with #>= and $\leq$ with #<=. The `iff` constraint described in Section 8.4 is not available in ECLiPSe. Similarly the `minimum` function and `cumulative` constraint used in Sections 8.5.1 and 8.5.2 are not supported by ECLiPSe. All can be programmed using the extensible constraint library of ECLiPSe. The built-ins `dom`, `mindomain`, `maxdomain` and `indomain` are provided in ECLiPSe. ECLiPSe also provides for the declaration of (hyper-) arc consistency using the suffix `infers most` rather than `consistent` that we have used in the text. The library `propia` must be loaded. For more information see [104].

Similarly, most of the programs given in this chapter will run under SICStus Prolog with the compiler directive `:- use_module(library(clpfd))`. How to obtain SICStus Prolog is discussed in the Practical Exercises section of Chapter 1. Some translation of symbols is required to express constraint relations: replace = with `#=`, ≠ with `#\=`, > with `#>`, < with `#<`, ≥ with `#>=` and ≤ with `#=<`. The labelling predicate in SICStus takes two arguments, the first of which is a list of options. Ordinary labelling is provided by `labeling([], [`*Vars*`])`. Different options can be used to label the variable with the smallest domain first, to use domain splitting or even to use a labelling that minimizes a cost function. See the SICStus Prolog manual for details. The `iff` constraint described in Section 8.4 is not available in SICStus Prolog. The `minimum` function which takes a list of arguments is not available, though a binary minimum function `min` is. Both can be programmed using the extensible constraint library of SICStus. The complex constraint `alldifferent` is available in two versions named `all_different` and `all_distinct`, which implement the consistency methods of Figure 3.15 and [111] respectively. The built-ins `mindomain`, `maxdomain` have different names in SICStus, being called `fd_min` and `fd_max` respectively. The built-in `dom` is not available but can be programmed using the built-in `fd_dom`. Reified constraints are supported in the SICStus Prolog finite domain constraint solving library using the notation *constraint* `#<=>` *Boolean*.

Neither ECLiPSe nor SICStus provide `div`. However, the constraint `s = t div 2` can be replaced by `B :: [0,1], 2*s + B = t`.

P8.1. Write a program to three colour a map represented using a binary adjacency relation. Use it to colour the map in Figure 3.22.

P8.2. Write a program to solve the crypto-arithmetic problem $DONALD + GERALD = ROBERT$. Each letter represents a different digit.

P8.3. Write two programs based on different models, to find the maximum profit for the assignment problem assigning 4 workers to one of 6 tasks, with the profit matrix given below.

	p_1	p_2	p_3	p_4	p_5	p_6
w_1	7	4	3	6	5	4
w_2	3	2	3	2	3	1
w_3	7	5	6	4	4	2
w_4	4	2	1	3	3	1

Compare the number of choices made to find all solutions in which the total profit is greater than 16.

P8.4. A perfect number X is equal to the sum of the numbers less than X that divide it exactly. For example, $6 = 1 + 2 + 3$, so 6 is a perfect number. Write a $CLP(FD)$ program for `perfect(X)` that succeeds whenever X is a perfect number.

P8.5. Write a pizza ordering program in $CLP(FD)$. Pizza slice types are *vegetarian, margherita, bolognese, special, tropical, garlic, capricciosa*. Your program should output a pizza order, in terms of large (8 slice) and medium (6 slice) pizzas given the list of attendees. For example,

```
pizza([peter, thomas, roland, max], Q)
```

should return a list Q detailing the pizza order. Note that a pizza can be ordered with half of one type and half of another, and that all slices in the order must be eaten.

The preferences for various individuals are: Peter requires four or five pieces, one or two vegetarian, one bolognese, no special, and at least one garlic. Roland wants four or five pieces, no more than one of any type, except garlic. Thomas asks for three or four pieces, at least one vegetarian, and one bolognese, no special, margherita, capricciosa, and at most one garlic. David requires two or three pieces, no vegetarian or tropical, no more than two of any kind of slice. Tim requires three or four pieces, at least one bolognese, no garlic, vegetarian, tropical or capricciosa. Ashley wants exactly one garlic, one bolognese and one margherita. Sandy asks for no more than four pieces and only vegetarian, margherita or garlic will do.

P8.6. Consider the following logic puzzle. There are 5 houses, each of a different colour and inhabited by a person from a different country who has a different pet, drink and make of car.

(a) The English woman lives in the red house.

(b) The Spaniard owns the dog.

(c) Coffee is drunk in the green house.

(d) The Ukrainian drinks tea.

(e) The green house is immediately to the right of the ivory house.

(f) The BMW driver owns snails.

(g) The owner of the yellow house owns a Toyota.

(h) Milk is drunk in the middle house.

(i) The Norwegian lives in the first house on the left.

(j) The person who drives a Ford lives in the house next to the owner of the fox.

(k) The Toyota driver lives in the house next to the house where the horse is kept.

(l) The Honda owner drinks orange juice.

(m) The Japanese drives a Datsun.

(n) The Norwegian lives next to the blue house.

Write a $CLP(FD)$ program to find who owns the zebra and who drinks water.

P8.7. Boolean variables can be treated as integers over the range [0..1]. Write predicates not(X,Y), and(X,Y,Z), or(X,Y,Z), if(X,Y,Z) and iff(X,Y,Z) which

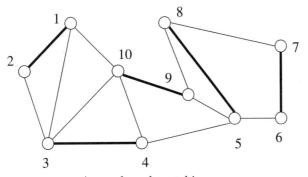

Figure 8.6   A graph and matching.

model the Boolean constraints $Y = \neg X$, $Z = X \& Y$, $Z = X \vee Y$, $Z = X \rightarrow Y$ and $Z = X \leftrightarrow Y$ respectively using integer constraints. For example, **and** can be defined by

```
and(X, Y, Z) :- Z ≤ X, Z ≤ Y, X + Y ≤ Z + 1.
```

Use these predicates to find a solution to the constraints of the fault analysis example in Section 1.5.1

P8.8. Give two different models for solving the matching problem for the graph shown in Figure 8.6. A matching is a set of edges from the graph so that every vertex is the endpoint of exactly one edge. In the figure, the thick edges give one matching for this graph. The first model should have variables representing edges and the second should have variables representing vertices.

P8.9. For N-queens not only is middle-out best for value ordering, but also for variable ordering. Thus, a better variable ordering strategy is to choose the variable with the smallest current domain, and in the case of a tie, to choose the variable closest to the center of the board. Write a labelling predicate which implements this strategy.

P8.10. Rewrite the N-queens program so that it makes use of the complex primitive constraint **alldifferent**. There should be three calls to **alldifferent**, one to ensure the queens are in different rows and two to ensure that they are in different diagonals.

P8.11. Often a problem is *symmetric*. Allowing symmetric answers to the same problem (answers which in some sense "encode" the same solution to the problem) increases the search space for the problem, and can mean considerable extra work. By recognising symmetric solutions and adding extra constraints to remove symmetric solutions, we can improve the search behaviour of a constraint program. As an example, consider the seesaw problem of Example 8.1. The two sides of the seesaw are identical. To avoid getting symmetric solutions such as

$$L = -4 \wedge F = 2 \wedge S = 5 \text{ and } L = 4 \wedge F = -2 \wedge S = -5$$

we can simply force one person to be on one side of the seesaw. For example, we can force Liz to be on the negative side of the seesaw (or in the centre) by adding the constraint $L \leq 0$. The resulting goal not only avoids finding symmetric solutions, but also finds the first solution faster because of more information.

Symmetries of reflection are not the only kinds of symmetry. Another possibility is circular symmetries. Consider the following *dinner party problem*. Four couples have been invited to dinner: Peter and Maria, Kim and Nicole, Bernd and Erika, and Hugh and Chiara. Each guest must be assigned a seat at a circular table. This is a very traditional dinner party, so members of the same couple are not allowed to sit next to each other and no guest is allowed to sit next to a guest of the same sex. Write a program which will find a seating arrangement. Your program should try to avoid unnecessary symmetry.

P8.12. Extend the first program for simple scheduling so that it allows more than a single machine of each type. A description of a scheduling problem instance now also details the number of machines of each type and the task details which type of machine it needs.

P8.13. Write a program to do the same thing as described in the previous question but using the `cumulative` constraint.

P8.14. (*) Rewrite the program for the second model for the simple assignment problem (Example 8.6) so that all calls to `element` are replaced by calls to arc consistent binary relations.

P8.15. (*) Using the reification facilities of the finite domain library for SICStus Prolog write a program for a user-defined constraint `posneg(L, P, Q)` that constrains exactly P of the elements of the list L to be strictly positive integers and N of the elements to be strictly negative integers.

The goal $C \leq$ `-3`, `posneg([1, B, 2, -1, C], 2, 2)` should infer that $B = 0$, and the goal $C \leq$ `1`, `posneg([1, B, 2, C], P, 0)` should infer that P is in the range $[2..4]$, C is in $[0..1]$ and that $B \geq 0$.

P8.16. (*) Reification of linear inequalities can be mimicked by translation. For example, the reified constraint $X \geq Y \Leftrightarrow B$ where the initial domains of X and Y are $[0..100]$ is equivalent to the constraint:

`B :: [0..1], X - Y ≥ 100 * B - 100, X - Y ≤ 101 * B - 1.`

Verify the behaviour of the translation when B takes the values 0 or 1, or X and Y both take values from the set $\{0, 100\}$.

Give a single rule defining a user-defined constraint that is equivalent to `apart(X,Y,3)` using mimicked reification, given that the initial domains of X and Y are both $[0..100]$. Can you extend this to mimic `apart(X,Y,N)` given that the initial domain of N is also $[0..100]$?

8.10   Notes

Constraint logic programming over finite domains was first implemented in the language CHIP [4] developed at ECRC. An excellent description of constraint logic programming for finite domains is given in the book "Constraint Satisfaction and Logic Programming" [135] by Van Hentenryck using the language CHIP.

Since CHIP, implementations of propagation solvers have improved, and one approach to implementing propagation solvers is described in [41] and provided in the CLP system clp(FD). The particular CLP(FD) language described in the chapter is roughly based on the ECLiPSe language's finite domain library. ECLiPSe is available from IC-PARC. See Chapter 3 for details. The latest version of CHIP is available from Cosytech.

The send-more-money and N-queens problems are classic constraint satisfaction problems. Task assignment and scheduling are also standard constraint satisfaction problems with considerable commercial application. The redundant constraints for job shop scheduling used in Section 8.5.1 are more general versions of constraints discussed by Van Hentenryck in [135] to solve a bridge scheduling problem. One of the original motivations for introducing cumulative constraints was, indeed, for representing resource constraints in scheduling problems.

The first fail principle was introduced in [60]. The use of a middle out search for the N-queens problem appears in an early CHIP demonstration program. Domain splitting also appears in early CHIP programs. It is, of course, closely related to the branch and bound technique for integer programming described in Chapter 3.

An excellent discussion of how to combine different problem modellings, and an example of the advantages that can be obtained, is given by Cheung *et al* [27].

Disjunctive scheduling problems are one area in which constraint logic programming can outperform even specialized programs written in a traditional language. Van Hentenryck [135] discusses a scheduling problem for building a five-segment bridge. Recently Caseau and Laburthe [23] showed how CLP techniques can be used to solve 10×10 job-shop scheduling problems efficiently. In [24] they also give an interesting discussion of cumulative scheduling with CLP.

Modelling disjunction or "or" without using choice has always been a concern of constraint programming, since it limits the size of the search tree. The *cardinality* constraint [136] was one of the first constraints used to model disjunctive combinations of constraints without using choice. Reified constraints arise from modelling techniques used in operations research (for example see [89]). Many constraint programming languages now support *reification* of (certain classes of) primitive constraint. For example the finite domain constraint solver in SICStus Prolog supports reified constraints and also provides special notation for combining constraints using reified disjunction and implication.

9 Advanced Programming Techniques

In the preceding chapters we have shown how the constraint programmer can use CLP to write programs which provide a high-level model of an application and which can be used to efficiently answer queries about the model. Sometimes, however, the underlying constraint solver or search mechanism of the CLP system may not be sufficiently powerful or expressive enough for the task at hand. One of the main strengths of CLP languages is that, as well as being modelling languages, they are also fully-fledged programming languages which can be used to extend the underlying constraint solver and to provide different search and minimization behaviour.

In this chapter, we look at several advanced programming techniques which the constraint programmer can employ to code sophisticated constraint solving and optimization algorithms within the CLP language itself. These include symbolic arithmetic reasoning using tree constraints, dynamic scheduling and meta-programming. Finally, we discuss the built-ins or library functions provided by most CLP languages since they are often used in conjunction with the techniques described in this chapter.

9.1 Extending the Constraint Solver

A CLP system provides a language for defining user-defined constraints and its evaluation mechanism a method for solving these user-defined constraints by rewriting them into primitive constraints which can be handled by the underlying solver. So, in a certain sense, all programming in a CLP language can be viewed as extending the underlying constraint solver.

However the majority of user-defined constraints are application specific and designed to work only for restricted modes of usage. This is in contrast to constraint solvers which support constraints that are applicable in many different contexts and which can be called in any mode of usage. Sometimes, however, it is useful for the programmer to define constraints which are sufficiently generic to be useful in many applications and whose implementation is robust enough to allow these constraints to be called with a variety of modes of usage. Such programming is said to extend the constraint solver. There is, of course, a continuum between application specific constraints and constraint solver extension so the difference is a question of degree rather than absolute.

In this section we will investigate three natural extensions of the real arithmetic solver of $CLP(\mathcal{R})$ which illustrate this style of programming. In each case we take a constraint domain which is not supported by the built-in solver, choose a representation for elements in the constraint domain and then write predicates which define the primitive constraints and functions over the domain in terms of the underlying solver.

The first, and simplest, extension of the solver is to allow complex numbers. Indeed, we have already seen how to do this in Section 6.5. We can represent the complex number $x + iy$ by the record $c(x, y)$. Equations over complex numbers are provided by term equality "=." As we saw earlier, addition and multiplication of complex numbers is defined by

```
c_add(c(R1,I1),c(R2,I2),c(R3,I3)) :-
    R3 = R1 + R2, I3 = I1 + I2.
c_mult(c(R1,I1),c(R2,I2),c(R3,I3)) :-
    R3 = R1*R2 - I1*I2, I3 = R1*I2 + R2*I1.
```

Using these definitions we can model a variety of applications by means of complex numbers.

A slightly more difficult example is to extend the solver to handle vectors. We can represent a vector $\langle x_1, \ldots, x_n \rangle$ by the list $[x_1, \ldots, x_n]$. With this representation it is straightforward to write predicates v_add, vs_mult, element and dotprod which, respectively, add two vectors, multiply a vector by a scalar, access the ith element in a vector and compute the dot product of two vectors. We give the code for vector addition and leave the code for the three other predicates as an exercise.

```
v_add([],[],[]).
v_add([X1|Y1], [X2|Y2], [X|Y])  :-  X = X1+X2, v_add(Y1,Y2,Y).
```

Again equations over vectors are provided for by term equality. An inequality relation over vectors is simply defined by

```
v_leq([],[]).
v_leq([X1|Y1], [X2|Y2])  :-  X1 ≤ X2, v_leq(Y1,Y2).
```

Our third example is to extend the solver to the sequence constraints domain described in Chapter 1. We can represent sequences using lists. As usual, equations over sequences are provided for by term equality. It is simple to write a function concat which concatenates a non-empty list of sequences to give a sequence and a predicate not_empty which holds if a sequence is non-empty.

```
not_empty([_|_]).
concat([S1],S1).
concat([S1,S2|Ss],S)  :-  append(S1,T,S), concat([S2|Ss],T).
```

The solution to a set of sequence constraints can be determined by using the `concat` predicate to find all possible concatenations through search and so we have a simple constraint solver for sequence constraints.

We can translate the contig problem discussed in Section 1.5.2 into a program over tree constraints. The problem is, given three sequences of chromosomes: a-t-c-g-g-g-c, a-a-a-a-t-c-g and g-c-c-a-t-t, find a relative order for which the sequences overlap to build a single sequence.

```
sequence_problem(T) :-
    contigs(Contigs),
    perm(Contigs, [C1, C2, C3]),
    not_empty(O12), not_empty(O23),
    concat([UC1,O12], C1),
    concat([O12,UC2,O23], C2),
    concat([O23,UC3], C3),
    concat([UC1,O12,UC2,O23,UC3], T).


contigs([[a,t,c,g,g,g,c], [a,a,a,a,t,c,g], [g,c,c,a,t,t]]).


delete([X | Xs], X, Xs).
delete([X | Xs], Y, [X | R]) :- delete(Xs, Y, R).


perm([], []).
perm(L, [X|R]) :- delete(L, X, L1), perm(L1, R).
```

The sequence constraint $X :: Y = Z$ is translated to the user-defined constraint `concat([X,Y],Z)`. Longer sequence concatenations, for example $T = UC1 :: O12 :: UC2 :: O23 :: UC3$ are also translated using `concat`. The constraint $X \neq \epsilon$, indicating X is not an empty sequence, is translated to `not_empty(X)`. The predicate `perm` generates all permutations of the first argument, by deleting some element from the list (using `delete`) and placing it in the front of a permutation of the remaining elements of the list. The `delete` predicate holds if the third argument is the list resulting from deleting the second argument from the first argument which is a list. The goal `sequence_problem(T)` finds the single answer

$$T = [a, a, a, a, t, c, g, g, g, c, c, a, t, t].$$

The goal works by first choosing a relative order of the contigs using `perm` and then checks the sequence constraints.

These examples also illustrate some of the limitations of programming constraint solver extensions in a CLP language. The first is that you cannot overload the function and primitive constraint names already used in the solver. Thus, we could not overload $\leq$ so that it also stood for vector inequality. Instead we had to introduce another name. The second limitation is that, in most CLP systems, it is not possible to directly define functions. Rather a function, such as addition, must be encoded as a relationship between its arguments and an extra argument which is the result of applying the function to these arguments. This has the consequence that complex expressions must be flattened into a sequence of predicate calls by introducing temporary variables. For example, the vector constraint $\vec{x} = \vec{y} + 2 \times \vec{z}$ must be written by the programmer as

```
vs_mult(2,Z,Temp), v_add(Y,Temp,X).
```

These restrictions mean that programming over a constraint domain which is an extension of the underlying solver is more cumbersome than one in which the constraint solver directly supports the domain.

A more important limitation is that, because of the standard evaluation mechanism employed by the CLP system to process the constraints in the extension, often the constraints can only be used in a restricted mode of usage. For other modes of usage, the extended solver may not be well-behaved or, even worse, may not terminate.

In the contig ordering program the order of literals was carefully chosen. If we delay the choice of the ordering of the contigs until after the sequence constraints, the program would not determine an answer. The problem arises because the `concat` predicate provides only a weak constraint solver for concatenation constraints. If the first or second argument to `concat` is not fixed, evaluation may give rise to an infinite derivation. A simpler example of the same behaviour can be seen when trying to solve the (unsatisfiable) sequence constraint problem of finding two sequences $L1$ and $L2$, where $L2$ is not empty, which give the empty list when concatenated. This can be expressed as the goal

```
not_empty(L2), concat([L1,L2], L), L=[].
```

The goal runs forever without finding an answer because evaluation of the second "constraint" gives rise to an infinite search for answers. In effect, it tries $L1 = [\,]$, then $L1 = [\_]$, $L1 = [\_,\_]$, and so on. None of which lead to an answer.

In Sections 9.6 and 9.7 we shall see techniques for modifying the default left-to-right evaluation mechanism of CLP languages. This ability allows us to program constraint solvers which are robust and which terminate in all modes of usage.

Another reason that we may wish to extend the underlying constraint solver is that the solver is not powerful enough to handle the constraints we wish to use, even if it is a solver for that constraint domain. This problem may arise, of course, whenever the underlying solver is incomplete.

For example, the $CLP(\mathcal{R})$ solver is incomplete for nonlinear arithmetic constraints. What can we do if our application requires us to solve nonlinear constraints? The answer is simple—write a solver in $CLP(\mathcal{R})$ for the particular nonlinear constraints we are interested in.

Imagine that we have a nonlinear arithmetic function f which has a single unknown variable x and we wish to solve $f(x) = 0$. For example, suppose $f(x)$ is $(x + 2)^3$. Evaluating the goal

```
(X + 2) * (X + 2) * (X + 2) = 0.
```

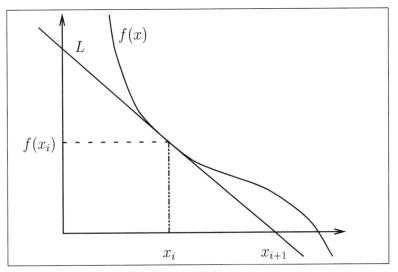

Figure 9.1 Newton-Raphson iteration.

with $CLP(\mathcal{R})$ will give the answer

```
0 = (X + 2) * (X + 2) * (X + 2)
*** Maybe
```

indicating that the $CLP(\mathcal{R})$ constraint solver cannot determine the satisfiability of the constraint since it is nonlinear.

However, there is no reason why we cannot program a more sophisticated constraint solver for nonlinears. CLP languages are true programming languages, and therefore it is possible to program any constraint solving algorithm in the language itself. Indeed, it is often very easy to write constraint solvers in a CLP language since the programmer can leverage from the underlying constraint solver.

To return to our example, given that the function f is differentiable, one of the simplest techniques for finding x such that $f(x) = 0$ is Newton-Raphson iteration. This starts from an initial guess at the solution x_0, and repeatedly computes a new guess, x_{i+1}, of the solution from the previous solution, x_i, as follows. The new solution is computed by approximating f by a line, L, which passes through the point $(x_i, f(x_i))$ and which has gradient $f'(x_i)$ where f' denotes the derivative of f. The value for x_{i+1} is simply the x-axis intercept of the line L. This is shown graphically in Figure 9.1. The process terminates when x_i is sufficiently close to a solution of $f(x) = 0$. That is, when $-\epsilon \leq f(x_i) \leq \epsilon$ for some given $\epsilon > 0$.

It is straightforward to write a program which uses Newton-Raphson iteration to solve this type of constraint. The program assumes that the relation $f(x) = y$ is defined by a predicate `f(x,y)` and $f'(x) = y$ is defined by a predicate `df(x,y)`.

Imagine that the function we wish to solve is $(X + 2)^3$. This has derivative, $3 * (X + 2)^2$. The program is simply

```
f(X, F)              :-   F = (X+2)*(X+2)*(X+2).
df(X,DF)             :-   DF = 3*(X+2)*(X+2).

solve_nr(E, X0, X0)  :-   f(X0,F0), -E ≤ F0, F0 ≤ E.
solve_nr(E, X0, X)   :-   f(X0, F0),
                          df(X0, DF0),
                          F0 = DF0 * X0 + C,
                          0 = DF0 * X1 + C,
                          solve_nr(E, X1, X).
```

The goal `solve_nr(E, X0, X)` finds a value for X which satisfies

$$-E \leq f(X) \leq E$$

by using Newton-Raphson iteration and starting from the initial guess $X0$. The first rule simply checks if the current guess is sufficiently close to the solution. If so the process terminates. Otherwise the second rule computes a new guess at the solution $X1$ as the point where the line L, defined by $y = DF0 \times x + C$, hits the x axis.

The intended mode of usage for `solve_nr` is that the second argument is fixed, so the nonlinear constraints encountered in `f` and `df` are effectively linear and are therefore completely handled by the solver. Subsequent solutions will converge toward the true zero.

Given the goal `solve_nr(0.0001,0.0,X)`, the first answer found is $X = -1.96532$. The second answer is $X = -1.97688$. The goal actually has an infinite sequence of answers that approach the actual answer -2. Since the first answer is an answer that meets the accuracy required, a sensible goal for usage of this program is instead `once(solve_nr(0.0001,0.0,X))`, which only has a single answer, $X = -1.96532$. For this mode of usage in which the first argument is also fixed, it is possible to write a deterministic version of the program that uses if-then-else.

As it is written, the predicate `solve_nr` has two defects. First, the function whose zero is to be found is hardwired into the predicate. Second, the programmer has had to explicitly provide the derivative, rather than letting the program itself compute it from the function. In the next section we develop a better version of the program which overcomes both shortcomings.

9.2 Combined Symbolic and Arithmetic Reasoning

A natural strength of CLP languages which provide tree constraints and arithmetic constraints, is the ability to combine symbolic and arithmetic reasoning. Tree constraints may be used for symbolic reasoning, while arithmetic constraints may be used for arithmetic reasoning. Combining both types of reasoning can lead to sophisticated and powerful programs.

In this section we will modify the above program for finding a zero for a nonlinear function so that the function and its derivative are not hardwired into it. We do this by adding a parameter which is the function whose zero is to be computed. We represent this function by a tree and the program can "symbolically" differentiate the function to find the derivative.

We can represent mathematical expressions over a variable x as follows. A number is represented by itself, the variable of interest is simply the constant x, and the trees $plus(t_1, t_2)$, $mult(t_1, t_2)$, and $power(t_1, t_2)$ represent the expressions $t_1 + t_2$, $t_1 \times t_2$, and $(t_1)^{(t_2)}$, respectively. Similarly, we use the trees $minus(t)$, $sine(t)$ and $cosine(t)$ to represent the expressions $-t$, $sin(t)$ and $cos(t)$ respectively.

For instance, the function over x defined by the expression $x^2 + 3x + 2$ may be represented by the tree $plus(power(x, 2), plus(mult(3, x), 2))$.

Given a tree representation for a function over x, we can write a predicate which returns the value of the function for a given value of x. The user-defined constraint `evaln(T, X, V)` does this, returning in V the value of the function represented by the tree T for the value of x given in X.

```
evaln(x,X,X).
evaln(N,_,N) :- arithmetic(N).
evaln(power(x,N),X,E) :- E = pow(X, N).
evaln(sine(x),X,E) :- E = sin(X).
evaln(cosine(x),X,E) :- E = cos(X).
evaln(minus(F),X,E) :- E = -EF, evaln(F,X,EF).
evaln(plus(F,G),X,E) :- E = EF + EG, evaln(F,X,EF), evaln(G,X,EG).
evaln(mult(F,G),X,E) :- E = EF * EG, evaln(F,X,EF), evaln(G,X,EG).
```

The program makes use of the library function `arithmetic(X)` which succeeds if X is determined by the solver to take a fixed arithmetic value. The predicate `evaln` recursively traverses the sub-expressions in tree T, evaluating each sub-expression for the given value of X, and then appropriately combines the results. For instance, `evaln(plus(power(x,2),plus(mult(3,x),2)),2,V)` returns the answer $V = 12$.

However, so long as the first argument is fixed, this program can be used in other modes of usage. The goal `evaln(T, X, V)` adds constraints which ensure that V is constrained with respect to X analogously to the way expression T is constrained with respect to x. For instance, the goal

```
evaln(plus(power(x,2),plus(mult(3,x),2)),X,F).
```

succeeds with a single answer which constrains F to be equal to $X^2 + 3X + 2$.

The main interest in having a symbolic representation of an arithmetic expression is that it allows us to manipulate the expression symbolically. One useful symbolic manipulation of an arithmetic expression over variable x is to differentiate it with respect to x.

Given the goal $deriv(F, DF)$, the following program takes the expression F over x and computes its derivative DF with respect to x. It is designed to work deterministically in the mode of usage where the first argument is fixed.

```
deriv(x,1).
deriv(N,0) :- arithmetic(N).
deriv(power(x,N),mult(N,power(x,N1))) :- N1=N-1.
deriv(sine(x),cosine(x)).
deriv(cosine(x),minus(sine(x))).
deriv(minus(F),minus(DF)) :- deriv(F,DF).
deriv(plus(F,G),plus(DF,DG)) :- deriv(F,DF), deriv(G,DG).
deriv(mult(F,G),plus(mult(DF,G),mult(DG,F))) :-
     deriv(F,DF), deriv(G,DG).
```

For instance, the goal `deriv(plus(power(x,2),plus(mult(3,x),2)),F)` succeeds with answer

$$F = plus(mult(2, power(x, 1)), plus(plus(mult(0, x), mult(1, 3)), 0))$$

which represents the expression $2x^1 + 0x + 1 \times 3 + 0$ or, equivalently, $2x + 3$.

The present program cannot handle all such expressions, for example it cannot differentiate $sin(cos(x))$, nor, as we have seen, does it perform simplification. It is left as an exercise to add these features.

Using these two rather simple user-defined constraints, we can now build an improved Newton-Raphson solver which makes use of symbolic reasoning to evaluate and differentiate the function whose zero we wish to find.

The program needs to be only slightly modified. We need arguments, say F and DF, to carry around the representations of the function and its derivative. These are used with `evaln` to determine values of the function and its derivative. The remainder of the program is the same. For the initial goal `dsolve` we use `deriv` to compute the derivative function. Thus the program is:

```
dsolve(E,F,X0,X) :- deriv(F,DF), solve_nr(E,F,DF,X0,X).

solve_nr(E,F,_DF,X0,X0) :- evaln(F,X0,F0), -E =< F0, F0 =< E.
solve_nr(E,F,DF,X0,X) :-
    evaln(F,X0,F0),
    evaln(DF,X0,DF0),
    F0 = DF0 * X0 + C,
    0 = DF0 * X1 + C,
    solve_nr(E,F,DF,X1,X).
```

For example given the function on x described by the expression $x^2 + 3x + 2$ we can determine a zero of the expression starting from $x = 5$ and within accuracy 0.00001 by the following goal:

```
dsolve(0.00001, plus(power(x,2), plus(mult(3,x), 2)), 5, X).
```

The answer is $X = -1$.

9.3   Programming Optimization

In the last two sections we have seen how to extend the underlying constraint solver by either supporting constraints over a new constraint domain or by building a solver which is more powerful than that provided by the CLP system for specialized forms of constraints. However, testing constraint satisfaction is only one of the facilities provided by a CLP system.

Another important function provided by the CLP system is optimization, that is, finding a solution which minimizes a particular expression. Just as a CLP programmer can extend the constraint solver, they can extend or modify the optimization facilities provided by their system. We now investigate how to do this by means of two examples.

The first example illustrates how to extend the minimization facilities provided by a real arithmetic constraint solver in order to handle integer constraints. The technique used is branch and bound. The second example shows how to develop a special purpose minimization predicate for a problem in which the programmer can make use of special properties of the problem to reduce the search space.

9.3.1   Branch and Bound

In Section 3.6 we gave a procedure for finding the optimal solution for an integer problem which is based on repeatedly solving the optimization problem over the real numbers. In essence the process is this. First, the optimal solution of the problem over the real numbers is found. If all values in this solution are integers, the problem is finished. Otherwise, there is a variable x whose value d in the optimal solution over the reals is not integral. Two new problems are generated with $x \leq \lfloor d \rfloor$ and $x \geq \lceil d \rceil$. Each of these is treated in turn using the method above. Eventually a solution containing only integer values will be discovered (assuming the solution space is bounded). The current best solution over the integers is threaded throughout the computation so that, if for any sub-problem the optimal solution over the reals is worse than the best current solution over the integers, the sub-problem is discarded since it can never yield a better solution over the integers.

This algorithm is straightforward to program in any CLP system providing real arithmetic optimization. We assume the optimization problem is defined by a predicate `problem(`*vars, f*`)` where *vars* is a list of the problem variables, and *f* is the optimization function. Since the optimization problem will be augmented with constraints placing upper and lower bounds on the variables, we need some structure in which to store information about these bounds. In the program below, we use a list of pairs of the form $b(lb, ub)$ where lb is either the constant u, indicating no lower bound (unbounded), or an integer, and ub is similarly defined. The nth element of the list of pairs gives the bounds for the nth element of the list *vars*.

The predicate `bounds` converts the bounds data structure in its second argument into constraints on the variables in the first argument. The predicate bounded_problem constructs the constraints for the problem with the added bounds, while new_bounds takes an optimal solution over the reals to the problem, Vs, and the current bounds, $Bnds$, and builds two new bounds structures, $BndsL$ and $BndsR$, by splitting the current bounds on the first non-integral value in the solution. If the solution is completely integral then $BndsL = BndsR$.

These are called by the branch-and-bound predicate bnb. This takes the current minimal integral solution, $CVals$, and the current minimal optimization function value, $CBest$, together with the current bounds structures, $Bnds$, which defines the subspace of the original problem's solutions to be explored. It returns the best integer solution found after this solution subspace has been explored, $BestVals$, together with the corresponding value, $Best$, of the optimization function.

The predicate bnb first finds an optimal solution over the reals to the bounded problem, which must be better than the current best integer solution. If none exists, then the current best solution is returned. Otherwise the solution, Vs, is used to split the current bounds structure, $Bnds$, into two parts. If the solution, Vs, is all integral, that is $BndsL = BndsR$, this solution is returned as the best. Otherwise the two sub-problems are investigated in turn.

```
bnb(CBest, CVals, Bnds, Best, BestVals) :-
    (minimize((F < CBest, bounded_problem(Vs, Bnds, F)), F) ->
        new_bounds(Vs, Bnds, BndsL, BndsR),
        (BndsL = BndsR -> Best = F, BestVals = Vs
        ;
            bnb(CBest, CVals, BndsL, LBest, LVals),
            bnb(LBest, LVals, BndsR, Best, BestVals)
        )
    ;
        Best = CBest, BestVals = CVals
    ).


new_bounds([], [], [], []).
new_bounds([V|Vs], [B|Bs], [BL|BLs], [BR|BRs]) :-
    (integer(V) ->
        BL = B, BR = B,
        new_bounds(Vs, Bs, BLs, BRs)
    ;
        B = b(L,U),
        VL = ⌊ V ⌋,
        VU = ⌈ V ⌉,
        BL = b(L,VL), BR = b(VU, U),
        BLs = Bs, BRs = Bs
    ).
```

```
bounded_problem(Vs, Bnds, F) :-
    bounds(Vs, Bnds),
    problem(Vs, F).

bounds([], []).
bounds([V|Vs], [b(L,U)|Bs]) :-
    (L = u -> true ; L ≤ V),
    (U = u -> true ; V ≤ U),
    bounds(Vs, Bs).
```

The program makes use of the library function `integer(X)` which succeeds whenever X is constrained to take an integral value, as well as the functions $\lfloor V \rfloor$ and $\lceil V \rceil$ which return the largest integer no greater than V and the smallest integer no less than V respectively.

Example 9.1

Consider the simple integer optimization problem which is to maximize Y subject to the constraints

$$2Y \le 3X - 3 \wedge X + Y \le 5.$$

We can encode this as the minimization problem

```
problem([X,Y], -Y) :- 2 * Y ≤ 3 * X - 3, X + Y ≤ 5.
```

Figure 9.2 shows the solution space of this problem, together with the various subspaces that are explored by the predicate.

The initial call is

```
bnb(CBest₁, CBestVals₁, [b(u,u), b(u,u)], Best₁, BestVals₁).
```

The solid lines correspond to the initial inequalities. Minimizing `bounded_problem` finds the optimal solution of the initial real problem is $X = 2.6 \wedge Y = 2.4$ (indicated by a small box). Execution of `new_bounds` finds that X is the first variable with a non-integer solution. It sets $BndsL$ to $[b(u, 2), b(u, u)]$ and $BndsR$ to $[b(3, u), b(u, u)]$, effectively splitting the solution space by using the constraints $X \le 2$ and $X \ge 3$. These inequalities are shown as dashed vertical lines in the diagram.

Computation continues with the call

```
bnb(CBest₁, CBestVals₁, [b(u,2), b(u,u)], Best₂, BestVals₂),
```

which investigates the left subspace of solutions. Minimizing `bounded_problem` finds the optimal solution $X = 2 \wedge Y = 1.5$. The call to `new_bounds` finds that Y is the first variable with a non-integer solution and sets $BndsL$ to $[b(u, 2), b(u, 1)]$ and $BndsR$ to $[b(u, 2), b(2, u)]$. The split of the solution space is shown by dashed horizontal lines in the diagram.

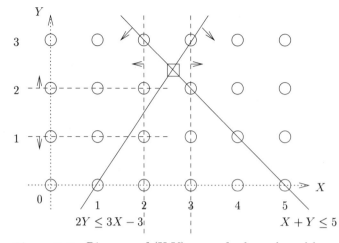

Figure 9.2   Diagram of (X,Y) space for branch and bound optimization.

Computation continues with the call

```
bnb(CBest₁, CBestVals₁, [b(u,2), b(u,1)], Best₃, BestVals₃).
```

The optimal solution found is $X = 2 \wedge Y = 1$. Since this solution is integer, **new_bounds** constructs $BndsL = BndsR = [b(u,2), b(u,1)]$ and so the call returns $Best_3 = 1$ and $BestVals_3 = [2, 1]$.

The next call is the second half of the split on Y with $CBest$ given by $Best_3$ and $CBestVals$ given by $BestVals_3$. The call is

```
bnb(1, [2,1], [b(u,2), b(2,u)], Best₂, BestVals₂).
```

The goal

```
F < 1, bounded_problem(Vs, [b(u,2), b(2,u)], F)
```

fails and therefore the minimization goal also fails. Thus $Best_2$ becomes 1 and $BestVals_2$ becomes [2,1].

The remaining part of the computation is the second half of the split on X with $CBest$ given by $Best_2$ and $CBestVals$ given by $BestVals_2$. The call is

```
bnb(1, [2,1], [b(3,u), b(u,u)], Best₁, BestVals₁).
```

The minimization goal returns solution $X = 3 \wedge Y = 2$, and $Best_1$ becomes 2 and $BestVals_1$ becomes $[3, 2]$. This is the answer returned for the original goal.

Example 9.2

Consider the integer optimization problem for the smuggler's knapsack defined in Example 3.7 in which we wish to maximize $15W + 10P + 7C$ subject to

$$4W + 3P + 2C \leq 9 \wedge 15W + 10P + 7 \geq 30 \wedge CW \geq 0 \wedge P \geq 0 \wedge C \geq 0.$$

```
problem([W,P,C], -Profit) :-
    4 * W + 3 * P + 2 * C ≤ 9,
    W ≥ 0, P ≥ 0, C ≥ 0,
    Profit = 15 * W + 10 * P + 7 * C, Profit ≥ 30.
```

The goal

```
bnb(_, _, [b(u,u),b(u,u),b(u,u)], Best, BestVals).
```

returns the answer

$$Best = -32 \wedge BestVals = [1, 1, 1].$$

indicating that the most profit of 32 (minimum loss) is obtained by taking one of each item.

9.3.2 Optimistic Partitioning

The above program illustrates how to define a minimization function over a new constraint domain by leveraging from the underlying minimization predicate provided by the CLP system. However, even if the CLP system provides a minimization operator over the constraint domain of interest, it is sometimes possible for the CLP programmer to write a problem-specific minimization predicate which is more efficient than that provided by the CLP system by utilizing knowledge about the structure of a problem's solution space.

In Section 8.5 we used the built-in search predicate `minimize` to find an optimal solution to the original code of the simple scheduling program (appearing on page 273) using the goal:

```
minimize((schedule(problem, End, Joblist), indomain(End)), End).
```

where *problem* is the simple problem illustrated in Figure 8.3.

The typical implementation of `minimize` works by repeatedly finding a solution to the goal which is better than the current minimum. This process is similar to that employed in the backtracking integer optimizer back_int_opt. For this example, evaluation proceeds by finding the first answer

$$TS_1 = 8 \wedge TS_2 = 0 \wedge TS_3 = 24 \wedge TS_4 = 18 \wedge TS_5 = 15 \wedge TS_6 = 11$$

with $End = 32$. The minimizing routine continues by adding $End \leq 31$ as a constraint, and finding an answer to this new problem. The answer found is

$$TS_1 = 8 \wedge TS_2 = 0 \wedge TS_3 = 20 \wedge TS_4 = 14 \wedge TS_5 = 11 \wedge TS_6 = 20$$

with $End = 28$. Computation continues searching with $End \leq 27$. Solutions are found for $End = 26$, $End = 22$, $End = 20$ and finally the optimum in which $End = 19$. The minimization routine continues to search for a solution with

$End \leq 18$ but this fails.

This example illustrates that for this problem the search for an optimal solution involves computing a long sequence of answers, each slightly better than the last, until the optimal solution is eventually reached. In a sense, the default minimization routine performs a linear search through the solution space in which solutions are ordered by the best value of End they allow. Better search strategies are possible.

One alternative search strategy is optimistic partitioning. This works as follows. Given an upper bound, Max, and lower bound, Min, for the value of the objective function, End, we may hope to reduce the number of solutions considered by performing a binary search through the solution space in a way analogous to domain splitting. We first search for a solution in the lower half of the range. If this is found we then look for a better solution in the lower half of the remaining range. If there is no solution in the lower half of the range, we search in the upper half of the range. At each step in the search we keep track of the minimum and maximum values that End can take. The program below implements this search strategy for minimization.

```
split_min(Data, Min, Max, Joblist0, Joblist) :-
    Mid = (Min + Max) div 2,
    (End ≤ Mid, End ≥ Min,
     schedule(Data, End, Joblist1), indomain(End) ->
        NewMax = End - 1,
        split_min(Data, Min, NewMax, Joblist1, Joblist)
    ; (End ≤ Max, End ≥ Mid + 1,
     schedule(Data, End, Joblist1), indomain(End) ->
        NewMin = Mid + 1, NewMax = End - 1,
        split_min(Data, NewMin, NewMax, Joblist1, Joblist)
    ; Joblist = Joblist0
    )).
```

Given a current minimum, Min, and maximum, Max, on the objective function, as well as a current best solution, $Joblist0$, (encoded as a joblist), split_min determines the midpoint of the current range, Mid, and tries to find a solution in the lower half first. If this succeeds and finds a new solution, $Joblist1$, (implicitly the if-then-else only finds a single solution) we continue by updating the maximum to be less than the new solution and updating the current best solution to $Joblist1$. If this fails, we search for a solution in the upper half of the range, and, if we find one, continue as above. If no solution is found in both ranges then the current best solution is returned since it is still the best solution found so far.

For the project described by *problem* we can reason as follows. For each machine, the sum of the durations of tasks that require this machine is a lower bound for the total time. So, in this case 19 and 13 are lower bounds on the total time. The sum of the durations of all tasks is clearly an upper bound, in this case 32. Therefore, we ask the initial goal

$$\text{split\_min}(\textit{problem},\ 19,\ 32,\ \texttt{[]},\ \text{Joblist}).$$

The goal executes as follows: Mid is calculated to be 25 and execution searches for a schedule with End time between 19 and 25. A solution, sol_1, is found with $End = 22$. Next the call

$$\text{split\_min}(\textit{problem},\ 19,\ 21,\ sol_1,\ \text{Joblist})$$

is evaluated. Mid is calculated to be 20 and a solution, sol_2, is found with $End = 20$. In turn, the call

$$\text{split\_min}(\textit{problem},\ 19,\ 19,\ sol_2,\ \text{Joblist})$$

is executed. Now a solution, sol_3, is found at $End = 19$ (the optimal) and the call

$$\text{split\_min}(\textit{problem},\ 19,\ 18,\ sol_3,\ \text{Joblist})$$

is executed, which immediately sets $Joblist$ to sol_3.

The ability to define and program specific optimization strategies, such as optimistic partitioning, is a major strength of constraint logic programming. For this example problem, the cost of continually resolving the scheduling problem outweighs the advantage of finding less solutions before the the optimal solution is reached, so optimistic partitioning is not worthwhile. However, optimistic partitioning is advantageous if the search space of the goal to be minimized when given an upper and lower bound, that is to say, $l \leq$ F, F $\leq u$, goal(F), is substantially smaller than the search space for goal(F). The strategy will find an optimal solution after discovering a chain of solutions of length at most logarithmic in the size of the initial range $Max - Min$.

9.4 Higher-order Predicates

Most CLP predicates take expressions constructed from variables and the functions and constants of the underlying constraint domain. We have, however, also met built-in predicates which take a goal as an argument, for example, minimize, once and if-then-else literals. Since they take a constraint or goal as an argument, such predicates are said to be *higher-order*.

Higher-order predicates are not only provided by the library of the CLP system. The constraint programmer is also free to define their own. This is surprisingly easy. Goals and constraints which are passed as arguments to a higher-order predicate are simply treated as if they were terms in which predicate symbols and the literal conjunction operator "," are treated as tree constructors.

For example, consider the call

```
once( (member(X,L1), X = Y, member(Y,L2)) )
```

which determines if lists $L1$ and $L2$ share a common element. The extra parenthesis are required to ensure the goal

```
member(X,L1), X = Y, member(Y,L2).
```

is not treated as three arguments.

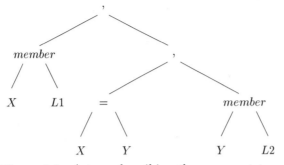

Figure 9.3   A term describing the argument to `once`.

The argument to `once` is treated as the term shown in Figure 9.3. Note how "," in the argument to `once` (but not inside the `member` literals) is treated as a binary tree constructor with the goals it conjoins as its arguments.

This means that programming with higher-order arguments is essentially like programming with trees. The only difference is, sometimes, we wish to evaluate a goal or literal which has been passed as an argument. This may be done by using `call`, the most fundamental higher-order built-in. The predicate `call` takes a goal as its single argument and returns the result of evaluating the goal. If evaluation of the goal finitely fails, the call to `call` finitely fails. In other words, the goal G behaves identically to the literal `call(G)`.

When using `call`, the programmer must be careful to ensure that, at the time of evaluation, its argument is constrained to be a term with the syntax of a goal. Otherwise evaluation will cause a *run-time* error because the system has no idea of how to evaluate it. Thus, the goals `call(Y)` and `call((p(X),Y))` will cause run-time errors since the variable Y is not instantiated to a literal or a goal. On the other hand, the goal `X=p(Y), call(X)` will return the answers to the literal `p(Y)`.

As a simple example of higher-order programming, imagine that our CLP system does not provide `once` but does provide if-then-else. It is simple to define `once` in terms of if-then-else:

```
once(G) :- (call(G) -> true; fail).
```

Here, for the first time in a program, we use the built-in literal `fail`. The fail literal, `fail`, is equivalent to an unsatisfiable constraint, say $0 = 1$. It causes failure when it is rewritten. It is used here to ensure failure when the once goal has no solutions.

This definition of `once` will have exactly the same behaviour as the usual built-in. It first uses `call` to evaluate the goal G. If evaluation of G succeeds, it returns this answer, otherwise, it finitely fails. On backtracking it will not consider other answers to G.

In a well designed CLP system there is little need for the programmer to define higher-order predicates as almost any predicate needed will be provided as a built-in. However, occasionally it is useful, and a knowledge of higher-order programming allows the programmer to implement built-ins missing from their system.

9.5   Negation

One important construct missing from the discussion of modelling with CLP languages is negation. If the constraint domain is rich enough, the negation of every primitive constraint is also a constraint. This holds for the finite domain constraints since we have $=$ and $\neq$ which are clearly the negation of each other, and $\leq$ has as its negation $>$.

Using complementary primitive constraints it is often possible for the programmer to explicitly define the negation of a user-defined constraint. For instance, recall the user-defined constraint `member(X, L)` which holds if X is a member of the list L. We can define its negation using $\neq$ as follows:

```
not_member(_X,[]).
not_member(X,[Y|L]) :- X ≠ Y, not_member(X,L).
```

Indeed, we already saw this user-defined constraint in Section 6.2.

However, writing such user-defined constraints is tedious and sometimes difficult, especially if the underlying solver does not provide the negation of all primitive constraints. For this reason most CLP languages provide a generic form of negation, by means of the higher-order built-in `not`, which can be applied to any goal G to give its negation `not(G)`. The drawback of `not` is that it only behaves correctly for some modes of usage. With other modes, its behaviour may be counter-intuitive, so the programmer needs to be aware of the way in which it will be called.

Definition 9.1
A *negative literal* is of the form $not(G)$ where G is a goal called the *negative subgoal*.

Evaluation of a negative literal is reasonably intuitive: when the literal `not(G)` is encountered, G is run to see if it finitely fails. If G finitely fails, then the negation of G holds so `not(G)` succeeds. Conversely, if G succeeds then, for some solution to the current store, the negation of G is not true, so `not(G)` fails. We extend the standard CLP evaluation mechanism by adding the following derivation step to process negative literals.

Definition 9.2
A *negation derivation step* is a derivation step $\langle G_1 \,|\, C_1 \rangle \Rightarrow \langle G_2 \,|\, C_2 \rangle$, in which a negative literal is rewritten as follows:
Let G_0 be the sequence of literals

$$L_1, L_2, \ldots, L_m$$

and let L_1 be of the form $not(G)$. There are two cases.

1. If the state $\langle G \,|\, C_1 \rangle$ finitely fails, then C_2 is C_1 and G_2 is $L_2, \ldots, L_m$.

2. Otherwise, if evaluation of the state $\langle G \,|\, C_1 \rangle$ finds a successful derivation, then C_2 is *false* and G_2 is the empty goal ($\blacksquare$).

We explore the implementation of **not** further in Chapter 10.

One use of negative literals is to extend the power of the underlying constraint solver. Imagine that our underlying constraint solver supports equations but does not support disequations. We can use a negative literal to define disequality:

```
ne(X,Y)   :-  not(X=Y).
```

Consider the goal

```
    X = 2, Y = 3, ne(X,Y).
```

Evaluation proceeds as follows. First `X = 2` and `Y = 3` are processed, giving the state

$$\langle ne(X,Y) \mid X = 2 \wedge Y = 3\rangle.$$

The **ne** literal is rewritten to obtain the simplified state

$$\langle not(X = Y) \mid X = 2 \wedge Y = 3\rangle.$$

Now the negative literal $not(X = Y)$ is processed. This spawns a sub-computation to evaluate the state $\langle X = Y \mid X = 2 \wedge Y = 3\rangle$. This sub-computation finitely fails since the constraint $X = 2 \wedge Y = 3 \wedge X = Y$ is unsatisfiable. Thus the negative literal $not(X = Y)$ succeeds and so $\langle not(X = Y) \mid X = 2 \wedge Y = 3\rangle$ is rewritten to $\langle \Box \mid X = 2 \wedge Y = 3\rangle$. Thus the initial goal succeeds with the single answer $X = 2 \wedge Y = 3$.

Consider the goal

```
    X = 2, Y = 2, ne(X,Y).
```

Evaluation proceeds similarly to before, arriving at the state

$$\langle not(X = Y) \mid X = 2 \wedge Y = 2\rangle.$$

The sub-computation to evaluate the state $\langle X = Y \mid X = 2 \wedge Y = 2\rangle$ succeeds with answer $\langle \Box \mid X = 2 \wedge Y = 2 \wedge X = Y\rangle$. Thus the negative literal $not(X = Y)$ fails and the state $\langle not(X = Y) \mid X = 2 \wedge Y = 2\rangle$ is rewritten to $\langle \blacksquare \mid false\rangle$.

Unfortunately, because of the limitations of **not**, this predicate is only correct for the mode of usage in which both arguments have fixed values when it is called. For instance, the goal

```
    X = 2, Y = 3, ne(X,Y).
```

will correctly succeed while the goal

```
    ne(X,Y), X = 2, Y = 3.
```

will incorrectly fail. The state $\langle not(X = Y), X = 2, Y = 3 \mid true\rangle$ is reached. The sub-computation for the state $\langle X = Y \mid true\rangle$ clearly succeeds, and hence the whole derivation fails. Nonetheless, it does allow the programmer to use disequations, although in a very restricted fashion. In the next section we shall see how to implement ne in a more general fashion.

Negative literals can only be guaranteed to act as one would expect when all the variables in the literal are determined by the constraint solver to take fixed values. This means that, when using an incomplete solver, the programmer must check that the solver is strong enough to infer the arguments to the negative literal are determined. For instance, the $CLP(\mathcal{R})$ system will finitely fail with the goal

    Y * Y = 4, Y ≥ 0, not (Y ≥ 1).

A related problem with negative literals and incomplete solvers is that the solver may not be powerful enough to determine that the sub-computation spawned by the negative literal should finitely fail. The problem is that if the negative subgoal has a derivation in which the solver determines the satisfiability of the final constraint store is *unknown*, while the constraint is actually unsatisfiable, then the subgoal does not finitely fail, and so the negative literal will, erroneously, fail.

Consider the goal

    X ≤ 0, Y ≥ 1, Z ≥ 2, not(X = Y * Z).

The goal fails because rewriting of literal not(X = Y * Z) requires the evaluation of the state

$$\langle X = Y \times Z \mid X \leq 0 \wedge Y \geq 1 \wedge Z \geq 2 \rangle.$$

This succeeds (in one step) with state

$$\langle \square \mid X \leq 0 \wedge Y \geq 1 \wedge Z \geq 2 \wedge X = Y \times Z \rangle,$$

since the constraint solver is incomplete for nonlinear constraints and cannot determine that this constraint is, in fact, unsatisfiable. Thus, even though there is an answer, the negative literal fails and so does the original goal.

Because of these problems, negative literals are rarely used in CLP programs for modelling the negation of user-defined constraints. Rather, as we saw earlier for not_member, the programmer must explicitly write a definition for the negation of the constraint. variables. are

There are, however, a number of situations in which negative literals are useful. The first situation is for data structure manipulation. Often when data structures are manipulated they have fixed values, meaning that they can safely be used as arguments to negative literals. For instance, if we were manipulating a fixed property list and wished to determine if an item with a fixed key was not in the list, then we could use a negative literal.

The second situation in which negative literals are useful is to test whether a constraint is compatible with the current store without actually adding the constraint to the store. Consider the user-defined higher-order predicate

    is_compatible(G) :- not(not(G)).

Evaluation of is_compatible(G) will succeed if not(G) finitely fails. This occurs precisely when the subgoal G is compatible with the current constraint. However, since successful evaluation of a negative literal does not modify the constraint store, evaluation of is_compatible(G) will not change the store.

The constraint is_compatible is particularly useful when we wish to test whether a non-deterministic user-defined constraint is compatible with the store but do not want to commit to some choice in the definition of the user-defined constraint.

Example 9.3

Suppose we have a complicated problem, in which, midway through the evaluation, we wish to test whether variable X can still take a value whose absolute value is at least 4, because if it cannot, we know there is no solution. We might program this as

```
goal1(X, Y), Z ≥ 4, abs(X,Z), goal2(X, Y).
```

where

```
abs(X,X) :- X ≥ 0.
abs(X,-X) :- X < 0.
```

The disadvantage of this approach is that by using the abs goal the derivation will choose one possibility: either $X \geq 4$ or $X \leq -4$. Suppose that eventually in the evaluation of goal2(X, Y), X is forced to be smaller than 4, then the execution will have to backtrack all the way to the second choice for abs. This may double the size of the derivation tree.

Instead we can use the goal

```
goal1(X, Y), is_compatible((Z ≥ 4, abs(X,Z))), goal2(X, Y).
```

This checks whether X can take a value whose absolute value is 4 or more without adding any constraints or setting up a choice point.

For simplicity, suppose that the subgoals are defined as follows.

```
goal1(X, Y) :- Y ≥ 1, X + Y = 6.
goal2(_X, Y) :- member(Y, [-21,-18,-10,-2,10,16,21,25]).
```

Note that given $X + Y = 6$, then goal2 can only succeed if the absolute value of X is greater than 4. Now consider the leftmost successful derivation for the above goal, skipping some derivation steps. Note that we use $\Rightarrow^*$ to indicate several (collapsed) derivation steps.

$$\langle goal1(X,Y), is\_compatible(Z \geq 4, abs(X,Z)), goal2(X,Y) \mathrel{\text{I}} true \rangle$$

$$\Downarrow_*$$

$$\langle not(not(Z \geq 4, abs(X,Z))), goal2(X,Y) \mathrel{\text{I}} Y \geq 1 \wedge X + Y = 6 \rangle$$

$$\Downarrow_*$$

$$\langle goal2(X,Y) \mathrel{\text{I}} Y \geq 1 \wedge X + Y = 6 \rangle$$

$$\Downarrow_*$$

$$\langle \square \mathrel{\text{I}} Y \geq 1 \wedge X + Y = 6 \wedge Y = 10 \rangle$$

The sub-derivation for the state $\langle not(Z \geq 4, abs(X,Z)) \mathrel{\text{I}} Y \geq 1 \wedge X + Y = 6 \rangle$ is

$$\langle not(Z \geq 4, abs(X,Z)) \mathrel{\text{I}} Y \geq 1 \wedge X + Y = 6 \rangle$$

$$\Downarrow_*$$

$$\langle \blacksquare \mathrel{\text{I}} false \rangle$$

The sub-derivation for the state $\langle Z \geq 4, abs(X,Z) \mathrel{\text{I}} Y \geq 1 \wedge X + Y = 6 \rangle$ is

$$\langle Z \geq 4, abs(X,Z) \mathrel{\text{I}} Y \geq 1 \wedge X + Y = 6 \rangle$$

$$\Downarrow_*$$

$$\langle \square \mathrel{\text{I}} Y \geq 1 \wedge X + Y = 6 \wedge Z \geq 4 \wedge X = Z \rangle$$

The first answer for the original goal is found after the `member` literal tries setting Y to -21, -18, -10, and -2.

Now suppose the original goal was

```
goal1(X, Y), Z ≥ 4, abs(X,Z), goal2(X, Y).
```

The first answer to intermediate goal `Z ≥ 4, abs(X,Z)` adds constraint $Z \geq 4 \wedge X = Z$. Each of the possibilities for the `member` literal fails, and execution eventually searches the derivation corresponding to the second solution to the intermediate goal $Z \geq 4 \wedge X = -Z$ and finds the first solution to the entire goal in which $Y = 10$. In this case the size of the derivation tree explored has more than doubled.

9.6   CLP Languages with Dynamic Scheduling

We have only considered CLP systems which process the literals in a goal in a left to right manner. However, a fixed order of processing restricts the modes of usage for which a user-defined constraint can be used efficiently or correctly. To allow user-defined constraints to be used in multiple ways it would be useful to be able to "delay" evaluation of the constraint until its arguments were sufficiently constrained. That is to say, instead of using a literal processing order which is fixed at compile time, we would like the system to employ a "dynamic" literal selection strategy which takes into account the current constraint store when choosing the literal.

For this reason, many recent CLP systems allow the programmer to annotate predicates with a "delay condition" which tells the system that the literals for the annotated predicate should not be evaluated until the current constraint store satisfies the delay condition.

For instance, recall the predicate from above which implements arithmetic disequality:

```
ne(X,Y)   :-   not(X=Y).
```

This predicate is only correct for the mode of usage in which both arguments are fixed when it is called. In a CLP system with delay, we can annotate the rules for `ne(X,Y)` with the condition that X and Y must be "ground" that is, take fixed values, before it can be evaluated:

```
:- delay_until(ground(X) and ground(Y), ne(X,Y)).
ne(X,Y) :- not(X=Y).
```

When evaluating goals involving the **ne** predicate, the CLP system will use a literal processing order which is basically left-to-right but which is safe in the sense that `ne(X,Y)` will not be rewritten until its delay condition is satisfied. Consider the goal

```
ne(X,Y), X=2, Y=3.
```

Using standard CLP evaluation it finitely fails which is incorrect. Using dynamic scheduling the goal has the single successful derivation (where the processed literal is underlined):

$$\langle ne(X,Y), \underline{X=2}, Y=3 \mid true \rangle$$
$$\Downarrow$$
$$\langle ne(X,Y), \underline{Y=3} \mid X=2 \rangle$$
$$\Downarrow$$
$$\langle \underline{ne(X,Y)} \mid X=2 \wedge Y=3 \rangle$$
$$\Downarrow$$
$$\langle \underline{not(X=Y)} \mid X=2 \wedge Y=3 \rangle$$
$$\Downarrow$$
$$\langle \Box \mid X=2 \wedge Y=3 \rangle.$$

Note that `ne(X,Y)` is not rewritten until the first state in which its delay condition holds.

We now examine the evaluation mechanism behind this example in more detail. In a CLP language with dynamic scheduling the programmer is able to provide declarations that delay the execution of a literal or goal until a particular delay condition holds. A *delay condition, Cond*, simply takes a constraint and returns *true* or *false*, indicating if evaluation can proceed or should be delayed. Typical *primitive delay conditions* are ground(X), which holds if X is constrained to take a fixed value, and nonvar(X), which holds if X cannot take all possible domain values. More complex conditions include Y are identical ask(c) which holds if the constraint c is implied by the store and exists a.X $\leq$ a which holds if X is bounded above by some constant. Of course, as the preceding example shows, delay conditions may be constraint domain specific.

Primitive delay conditions can be combined to create more complex delay conditions. They can be conjoined, written $(Cond_1$ *and* $Cond_2)$, or disjoined, written $(Cond_1$ *or* $Cond_2)$.

Definition 9.3

A *delaying literal* is of the form *delay_until(Cond, G)* where *Cond* is a delay condition and *G* is a goal.

Evaluation of *G* will be delayed until *Cond* holds for the current constraint store. We say that a constraint *C enables* the delaying literal *delay_until(Cond, Goal)* if *C* satisfies *Cond*.

For instance, the constraint $X = 2 \wedge Y = 3$ enables

$$delay\_until(ground(X)\ and\ ground(Y), ne(X, Y)),$$

while the constraint $X = Y$ does not. The enabling of a delay condition depends upon the solver. For example, the constraint $X \times X = 4 \wedge X \geq 0 \wedge Y = 1$ may not enable the above delaying literal if the solver is incomplete for nonlinears.

In CLP languages with dynamic scheduling there are two approaches for specifying the delay information:

■ *Predicate-based*: In this case, the delaying literal appears as a declaration before the definition of the predicate and has the form

```
:- delay_until(Cond,p(X_1,...,X_n)).
```

where $X_1, \ldots, X_n$ are distinct variables and *Cond* is a delay condition over a subset of those variables. Each user-defined constraint for the predicate p inherits the delay condition of the predicate.

■ *Goal-based*: the delay condition is associated with a particular goal. In this case, the delaying literal delay_until(*Cond, Goal*) appears as a literal in the body of the goal or rule body and *Cond* is defined over the variables of that goal or rule body.

It is straightforward to use predicate-based declarations to imitate goal-based declarations, and vice versa. For example,

```
:- delay_until(ground(X) and ground(Y), ne(X,Y)).
ne(X,Y) :- not(X=Y).
```

and

```
ne(X,Y) :- delay_until(ground(X) and ground(Y), ne1(X,Y)).
ne1(X,Y) :- not(X=Y).
```

are equivalent although the first program uses predicate-based declarations while the second uses goal-based declarations. For simplicity, in this chapter we will only use predicate-based declarations.

We now describe how the standard evaluation mechanism given in Chapter 4 can be extended to handle delaying literals. Evaluation with dynamic scheduling means that literals are not necessarily processed in left-to-right order. We define a *literal selection strategy* to be a function that chooses which literal in a state is to be rewritten. We simply require that whenever a literal with a delay declaration is selected, the delay condition is enabled.

Definition 9.4

A literal selection strategy is *safe* if, whenever a literal L of the form $p(t_1, \ldots t_n)$ is selected in state $\langle G_0 \mid C_0 \rangle$ and there exists a delay declaration for p of the form $delay\_until(Cond, p(x_1, \ldots, x_n))$, then $C_0 \wedge x_1 = t_1 \wedge \cdots \wedge x_n = t_n$ enables $Cond$. Note that enabling is solver dependent.

A (selection) derivation is *safe* if it employs a safe literal selection strategy.

Since the evaluation mechanism is required to use a safe literal selection strategy, it may happen that execution arrives at a state containing only delaying literals which are not enabled. We must generalize the definition of successful derivation and answer to cater for this case.

Definition 9.5

A state $\langle G \mid C \rangle$ is said to have *floundered* if G is a non-empty sequence of literals, none of whose delay conditions is enabled by C.

A safe derivation

$$\langle G_0 \mid C_0 \rangle \Rightarrow \cdots \Rightarrow \langle G_n \mid C_n \rangle$$

is *successful* if $solv(C_n) \not\equiv false$ and either $\langle G_n \mid C_n \rangle$ is floundered or G_n is the empty goal. The goal $G_n \wedge simplify(C_n, vars(\langle G_0 \mid C_0 \rangle) \cup vars(G_n))$ is a *qualified answer* to the state $\langle G_0 \mid C_0 \rangle$.

For example, the goal ne(X,Y), X=2 has the single successful derivation

$$\langle ne(X, Y), \underline{X = 2} \mid true \rangle$$
$$\Downarrow$$
$$\langle ne(X, Y) \mid X = 2 \rangle$$

which gives the qualified answer $ne(X, Y) \wedge X = 2$.

We have already seen how we can use dynamic scheduling to robustly handle disequations. As another simple example, consider how we can improve the constraint

$$\langle \underline{not\_empty(L2)}, concat([L1, L2], L), L = [] \mid true \rangle$$
$$\Downarrow$$
$$\langle \underline{concat([L1, L2], L)}, L = [] \mid L2 = [\_|\_] \rangle$$
$$\Downarrow$$
$$\langle append(L1, T, L), \underline{concat([L2], T)}, L = [] \mid L2 = [\_|\_] \rangle$$
$$\Downarrow$$
$$\langle append(L1, T, L), \underline{L = []} \mid L2 = [\_|\_] \wedge T = L2 \rangle$$
$$\Downarrow$$
$$\langle \underline{append(L1, T, L)} \mid L2 = [\_|\_] \wedge T = L2 \wedge L = [] \rangle$$
$$\Downarrow$$
$$\langle \blacksquare \mid false \rangle$$

Figure 9.4 Simplified derivation for concatenation with delay.

solver for sequences given in Section 9.1. We can modify the definition of `append` so that it delays until either the first or third argument is not a variable.

```
:- delay_until(nonvar(X) or nonvar(Z), append(X,Y,Z)).
append([], Y, Y).
append([A|X], Y, [A|Z]) :- append(X,Y,Z).
```

One safe (simplified) derivation for the goal

```
        not_empty(L2), concat([L1,L2], L), L=[].
```

is illustrated in Figure 9.4. The derivation proceeds left-to-right until the third state. It is not safe to select the leftmost literal, $append(L1, T, L)$, in this state since both $L1$ and L are free. However, it is safe to select the next literal, $concat([L2], T)$. In the next state it is still not safe to select $append(L1, T, L)$ so the next literal $L = []$ is selected. Now $append(L1, T, L)$ can be selected since L is no longer free. Rewriting with either rule immediately leads to failure. Therefore, with dynamic scheduling, the goal now behaves as desired and finitely fails.

One of the most important benefits of dynamic scheduling is that it facilitates the construction of simple, yet robust, constraint solvers in the CLP language itself. In particular, it makes it easy to write local propagation based solvers. For example, here is a simple local propagation solver for the Boolean constraints, negation (`bnot`) and conjunction (`and`), implemented using dynamic scheduling.

```
:- delay_until((ground(X) and ground(Y)) or
               (ground(X) and ground(Z)) or
               (ground(Y) and ground(Z)), and(X,Y,Z)).
and(0,0,0).
and(0,1,0).
and(1,0,0).
and(1,1,1).
```

```
:- delay_until(ground(X) or ground(Y), bnot(X,Y)).
bnot(0,1).
bnot(1,0).
```

The program works by delaying the selection of Boolean constraint literals until all but one argument is fixed. In this case the definitions are deterministic (except in two cases).

Compare execution of the program with and without delay declarations for the goal:

$$\text{and(X, Y, Z), and(Y, Z, T), bnot(Y, 0), bnot(T, 0).}$$

Using the delay declarations, every time a literal is selected there is only one rule which can succeed. First bnot(Y,0) is selected, which constrains Y to be 1, then bnot(T,0) is selected, which constrains T to be 1. Now the delay condition for and(Y, Z, T) is enabled. Rewriting this literal constrains Z to be 1. Finally, the literal and(X, Y, Z) is selected and rewriting constrains X to be 1. The simplified derivation tree contains 13 states and it is deterministic. Without delay declarations there are four answers to the first literal, and each of these answers leads to an answer to the second literal. Overall, the simplified derivation tree has 31 states.

Unfortunately, the **and** predicate is not deterministic for all modes of usage possible under the delay declarations. Consider the states $\langle and(X,Y,Z) \mid X = 0 \wedge Z = 0 \rangle$ and $\langle and(X,Y,Z) \mid Y = 0 \wedge Z = 0 \rangle$. For each state there are two possibilities for the remaining variable X or Y. But either possibility satisfies the constraint so we can simply ignore the constraint in these circumstances. Therefore we can rewrite the definition of **and** so as to make it deterministic as follows:

```
:- delay_until((ground(X) and ground(Y)) or
               (ground(X) and ground(Z)) or
               (ground(Y) and ground(Z)), and(X,Y,Z)).
and(X,Y,Z) :-
    (ground(Z), Z = 0 ->
        (ground(X), X = 0 -> true
        ; (ground(Y), Y = 0 -> true
        ; and2(X,Y,Z)
        ))
    ; and2(X,Y,Z)
    ).

and2(0,0,0).
and2(0,1,0).
and2(1,0,0).
and2(1,1,1).
```

If Z is fixed and zero and either X is fixed and zero, or Y is fixed and zero, then the constraint holds and nothing more need be done. In the other cases we just use the previous definition. The definition makes use of the built-in ground as part of the tests in the if-then-else literals. This tests to see if its argument has a fixed value. Since it is not part of a delay condition, evaluation does not delay if the argument is not fixed, instead it fails.

We can see from these examples that dynamic scheduling allows us to write user-defined constraints which are more "robust" and which behave as if they are being evaluated by a well-behaved solver. Indeed, barring non-termination, standard evaluation of user-defined constraints is complete—either the system finds a solution or else it finitely fails. Dynamic scheduling allows the evaluation mechanism to return an "unknown" answer indicating that the evaluation mechanism will not further evaluate a goal it has created because the delay declarations indicate that this will be too expensive or may not terminate

In starred Section 4.8, we saw that the answers to a goal are independent of the literal selection strategy. It is this key property which makes programming with dynamic scheduling feasible, since the programmer knows that, regardless of the precise order of selection chosen with dynamic scheduling, evaluation will still give the same answers. Fortunately, independence from the literal selection strategy continues to hold for dynamic scheduling as long as the delay conditions are reasonably behaved. The key requirement is that the delay conditions must be *downwards closed*, that is once the delay condition is satisfied, it will continue to hold for the remainder of the forward computation. More exactly, delay condition *Cond* is downwards closed if for any two constraints C_1 and C_2 such that $C_2 \rightarrow C_1$, whenever *Cond* holds for C_1, it also holds for C_2. Other requirements are that the delay condition should not take variable names into account and that its behaviour cannot depend on variables which are not mentioned in the condition.

Delay conditions in most CLP languages with dynamic scheduling satisfy these properties. This allows the underlying implementation to use a fixed literal selection strategy, for example, always selecting the leftmost literal which is enabled.

Since Chapter 4, we have introduced constructs, such as once and if-then-else that can destroy the independence from literal processing order. When we make use of them with dynamic scheduling, we need to take care that they are used in a manner in which the answer does not depend on the order in which literals are evaluated. For example, in the deterministic definition for **and** above, the tests in the if-then-else's either succeed or fail, for all possible modes of usage under which the literal can be selected, but never constrain a non-fixed variable. Hence they are independent of the order in which literals are processed.

9.7   (*) Meta Programming

One interesting application of higher-order programming is for meta-programming. *Meta-programs* are programs which manipulate other programs as data. For example, they may analyse, compile, transform or execute other programs. Because programs can easily be represented by tree data structures, CLP languages are well suited for writing meta-programs.

One simple example of a meta-program is an interpreter for $CLP(Tree)$. This is a program that, given a program and goal, imitates the execution of the $CLP(Tree)$ system. This may not sound very useful, but once we have written this program we can modify it to change the standard CLP evaluation mechanism.

The first consideration when writing a meta-program is how to represent the program which will be manipulated by the meta-program. Like goals and literals, CLP programs may be represented by terms and manipulated by means of tree constraints. For instance, the rule

```
traverse(node(T1,I,T2), L) :-
    traverse(T1, L1),
    traverse(T2, L2),
    append(L1, [I|L2], L).
```

can be represented by the term

```
:-(traverse(node(T1,I,T2), L),
    ','(traverse(T1, L1),
    ','(traverse(T2, L2),
    append(L1, [I|L2], L))))
```

illustrated in Figure 9.5. Recall that $[I|L2]$ is notation for $.(I, L2)$.

Representing goals using the comma "," notation is ugly and it also causes difficulty when we wish to build and decompose goals. Instead we will represent the body of a rule as a list of literals, and represent a rule by a two argument predicate `lrule` whose first argument is the head and whose second argument is the body. For example the `traverse` rule above is represented by the fact

```
lrule(traverse(node(T1,I,T2),L),
    [traverse(T1,L1),
     traverse(T2,L2),
     append(L1,[I|L2],L)]).
```

Our meta-interpreter, `derive`, takes a goal, *Goal*, as its sole argument. It selects a literal *Lit* from *Goal*, breaking the rest of the goal into the parts before, *Pre*, and after, *Post*, the selected literal. The replacement, *Rep*, of the literal in the goal part is then inserted between *Pre* and *Post* to form the new goal, that is to say, $NewGoal = Pre :: Rep :: Post$.

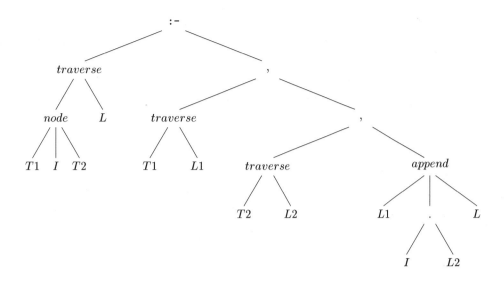

Figure 9.5 A term describing the rule for `traverse`.

If the literal is a tree constraint, the interpreter simply uses `call` to add the equation to the store and the replacement is the empty list. Otherwise `lrule` is used to replace a user-defined constraint by the body of a matching rule. The renaming of the rule and the constraints equating the selected literal and the head of the rule are handled implicitly by the underlying CLP system.

```
derive([]).
derive(Goal) :-
    select(Goal, Lit, Pre, Post),
    replace(Lit, Rep),
    append(Pre, Rep, Tmp),
    append(Tmp, Post, NewGoal),
    derive(NewGoal).

replace(Lit, Rep) :-
    (constraint(Lit) ->
        call(Lit), Rep = []
    ;
        lrule(Lit, Rep)
    ).

constraint(_ = _).
```

The standard evaluation mechanism is simply to take the first literal in the goal

```
select([Lit|Rest], Lit, [], Rest).
```

Consider the `append` program. It is represented by

```
lrule(append([], Y, Y), []).
lrule(append([A|X], Y, [A|Z]), [append(X, Y, Z)]).
```

The simplified successful derivation for the goal

```
derive([append([a,b], [c,d], T)]).
```

is as follows, where we only show the states in which `derive` literals are selected.

$$\langle derive([append([a,b],[c,d],T)]) \mid true \rangle$$
$$\Downarrow_*$$
$$\langle derive([append([b],[c,d],T1)]) \mid T = [a|T1] \rangle$$
$$\Downarrow_*$$
$$\langle derive([append([],[c,d],T2)]) \mid T = [a,b|T2] \rangle$$
$$\Downarrow_*$$
$$\langle derive([]) \mid T = [a,b,c,d] \rangle$$
$$\Downarrow_*$$
$$\langle \square \mid T = [a,b,c,d] \rangle$$

Now that we have written a meta-interpreter we can modify it to, for example, select literals in a different way. Consider the constraint solver for sequences defined in Section 9.1. The goal

```
not_empty(L2), concat([L1,L2],L), L=[].
```

ran forever because there are an infinite number of answers to the first `append` literal that appears in the derivation. We have seen how, using dynamic scheduling, we can control the derivation so that the goal will determine an answer. We now modify our meta-interpreter to mimic dynamic scheduling.

There are only a finite number of answers to any call to `append` if either the first or third argument has fixed length. Since the left-to-right selection rule is explicitly programmed into the meta-interpreter, we can modify the meta-interpreter so that it only selects `append` literals when either the first or third argument is not a variable. We need only change `select` to:

```
select([Lit0 | Rest], Lit, Pre, Post) :-
    (Lit0 = append(X,Y,Z) ->
        (one_nonvar(X,Z) ->
            Lit = append(X,Y,Z), Pre = [], Post = Rest
    ;
            Pre = [Lit0 | Pre1],
            select(Rest, Lit, Pre1, Post)
        )
    ;
        Lit = Lit0, Pre = [], Post = Rest ).
```

```
one_nonvar(X,_) :- nonvar(X).
one_nonvar(_,Z) :- nonvar(Z).
```

The `one_nonvar(X,Z)` literal checks whether one of X and Z is not a variable. It makes use of the library function `nonvar` which succeeds unless its argument is a variable that can take any value.

An example (simplified) derivation of the goal

```
derive([not_empty(L2), concat([L1,L2],L), L=[]]).
```

is shown below, where the literal selected by the meta-interpreter is underlined.

$$\langle derive([\underline{not\_empty(L2)}, concat([L1, L2], L), L = [\,]]) \mid true \rangle$$

$$\Downarrow_*$$

$$\langle derive([\underline{concat([L1, L2], L)}, L = [\,]]) \mid L2 = [\_|\_] \rangle$$

$$\Downarrow_*$$

$$\langle derive([append(L1, T, L), \underline{concat([L2], T)}, L = [\,]]) \mid L2 = [\_|\_] \rangle$$

$$\Downarrow_*$$

$$\langle derive([append(L1, T, L), \underline{L = [\,]}]) \mid L2 = [\_|\_] \wedge T = [\_|\_] \rangle$$

$$\Downarrow_*$$

$$\langle derive([\underline{append(L1, T, L)}]) \mid L2 = [\_|\_] \wedge \ \wedge T = [\_|\_] \wedge L = [\,] \rangle$$

$$\Downarrow_*$$

$$\langle \blacksquare \mid false \rangle$$

In the third and fourth states the first `append` literal cannot be selected since both $L1$ and L can take any value. Thus, the `concat` literal is selected in the third state and the $L = [\,]$ constraint in the fourth state. Finally, the `append` literal can be selected since L is now constrained to be the empty list. Rewriting with either of the rules in `append` leads to failure since T is a non-empty list. Therefore, the system has determined that there is no answer to the goal.

The meta-interpreter described above, in effect, implements a dynamic scheduling literal selection rule. Indeed the above derivation corresponds to that shown in Figure 9.4 which was obtained by using dynamic scheduling. One advantage of meta-programming over dynamic scheduling is that we can program arbitrary selection rules using the CLP language, rather than relying only on the delay conditions provided by the CLP system. Meta-interpretation, however, is much more expensive than using built-in dynamic scheduling facilities. Generally, if dynamic scheduling facilities are available, these should be used in preference to meta-programming.

9.8 (*) **Library Predicates**

Throughout this book we have seen numerous examples of library predicates, often called *built-ins*, provided by our fictional CLP system. Unfortunately, there is, as yet, no agreed upon standard library of built-ins. Each system provides different built-in predicates. Indeed, since many of the built-ins are constraint domain specific, it is not possible for every system to provide all of them.

There is, however, rough consensus on the functionality that should be provided by many of the built-ins. Broadly speaking, the most useful built-ins can be grouped into the following six classes: program consultation and inspection; input and output; debugging; examination of the constraints on a variable and its type; database programming; and higher-order predicates. Built-ins in these classes are largely constraint domain independent and, although the syntax may differ, most CLP systems provide essentially the same functionality.

In the practical exercises we have already seen how to consult, reconsult and list a CLP program. We have also briefly discussed the most common higher-order built-ins in Section 9.4. In this section, we briefly describe the built-ins in each of the other classes. We base our discussion loosely on the built-ins of SICStus Prolog and $CLP(\mathcal{R})$, but other systems provide corresponding library predicates. At least a cursory knowledge of these built-ins is necessary for more advanced programming with CLP.

Unlike user-defined constraints and primitive constraints, understanding the behaviour of most of these built-ins relies on knowledge of the order of literal evaluation and the content of the constraint store at the time the built-in is evaluated. For this reason, programming with built-ins is often quite subtle and may lead to unexpected errors—we advise the programmer to use them carefully and sparingly.

9.8.1 **Input and Output**

Any practical programming language must provide facilities for input and output. In CLP systems the built-in `read` is used to read the next expression from the input stream. Usually the input stream is the sequence of characters typed on the key board, but the user may also direct the input-stream to be the characters in a file. Evaluation of the literal `read(t)` essentially adds the constraint $t = t'$ to the current goal where t' is the next expression on the input stream. A full-stop (or period) "." is used to terminate an input expression.

For example, evaluation of the $CLP(\mathcal{R})$ goal

```
read(X), read(Y).
```

during which the user types

```
1.01.  2.
```

gives the single answer $X = 1.01 \land Y = 2$. Some CLP systems restrict the argument to read to be a variable.

If the input stream is finished, that is if the input file has been fully read, a special expression indicating end of file is returned. The value of this expression is system dependent.

The built-in write is used to write the value of an expression to the output stream. Usually the output stream is to a terminal, but the user may also direct output to a file. Evaluation of the literal write(t) writes the value of t as implied by the current constraint to the output stream. Generally, if t has no fixed value then a representation of a variable is printed, although for tree constraints the solved form of t will be printed.

Evaluation of a write literal does not affect the constraint store. The predicate write can also be called with a string as an argument. In this case the string will be written to standard output. The built-in nl writes the new-line character to standard output.

For example, evaluation of the $CLP(\mathcal{R})$ goal

```
X=2, Y=3, write("X + Y is: "), write(X+Y), nl.
```

outputs the following

```
X + Y is: 5
```

Evaluation of

```
X=2, write("X + Y is: "), write(X+Y), nl.
```

will output the following

```
X + Y is: _t3
```

The _t3 indicates an arithmetic variable.

The write command, although provided in most CLP systems is an historical relic, and does not really fit with the constraint paradigm. Some systems provide a facility for writing the constraints affecting a set of chosen variables. For example the dump facility in $CLP(\mathcal{R})$ does this. The literal dump($[V_1, \ldots, V_n]$) writes the constraints in $simpl(\{V_1, \ldots, V_n\}, C)$ where C is the current constraint store. The built-in dump allows interactive programs to provide information about variables of interest.

For example, evaluation of the goal

```
X < 2, Z=X+Y, Y < 3, dump([Z]).
```

writes the following

```
Z < 5
```

If the literal dump is replaced by write(Z) the output of the goal is merely _t3.

As a more detailed example of the use of these built-ins, consider the `deriv` program from Section 9.2. The following goal when executed prompts the user to enter an arithmetic function f in terms of variable x and a value for x and will write out the value of f and the slope of the function, for this value of x.

```
write("Input function: "), read(F),
write("Input x value: "), read(X),
deriv(F,DF), evaln(F,X,FX), evaln(DF,X,DFX),
write("The value of function "), write(F), nl,
write("when x = "), write(X), write(" is "), write(FX), nl,
write("and the slope is "), write(DFX), nl.
```

If the goal above is executed, the following session occurs (where user input is given in *emphasized text*)

```
Input function: mult(sine(x),plus(x,2)).
Input x value: 1.
The value of function mult(sine(x), plus(x, 2))
when x = 1 is 2.52441
and the slope is 2.46238
```

9.8.2 Variable Examination

Apart from built-ins for input/output, typical CLP systems provide a number of built-ins so that the programmer can determine the "type" of a variable, that is what kind of constraints it has been involved in, and how "constrained" the variable is. Typical built-ins are:

`atom(X)`: This succeeds if the current constraint store contains tree constraints constraining X to be a tree which is a constant.

`compound(X)`: This succeeds if the current constraint store contains tree constraints constraining X to be a tree which is not a constant.

`arithmetic(X)`: This succeeds if the current constraint store contains arithmetic constraints which the solver can determine constrain X to take a fixed arithmetic value.

`integer(X)`: This succeeds if the current constraint store contains arithmetic constraints which the solver can determine constrain X to take a fixed integer value.

`ground(X)`: This succeeds if the constraint solver can determine that the current store implies that X has a fixed value.

`nonvar(X)`: This succeeds if the constraint solver can determine that the current constraint store implies that X is not free. That is to say, it cannot take all values in the constraint domain. Unfortunately, this behaviour is only guaranteed when the variable has only been involved in tree constraints or the solver can determine that X must take a fixed value.

var(X): This succeeds if the constraint solver can determine that X is free, that is, it can take all values in the constraint domain. Again, this behaviour is only guaranteed when the variable has only been involved in tree constraints. It is guaranteed to fail if the solver can determine that X has a fixed value.

We have previously seen the built-in arithmetic in Section 9.2 and the built-in ground in Section 9.6. The built-in ground(X), as opposed to the delay condition ground(X), does not *delay* until X is fixed, it just performs a check, failing if the argument is not fixed. The built-in nonvar(X) is similar. Other built-ins described above act analogously to arithmetic(X).

For instance, the goal

        X = a, atom(X).

will succeed while the goals

        X = f(Y,a), atom(X).

and

        X > Y, atom(X).

will fail. The goal

        X = f(Y,b), ground(X), Y = a.

will fail, while

        X = f(Y,b), Y = a, ground(X).

will succeed. The goal

        X = f(a,Y), var(X).

will fail, the goal

        X = Y, var(X).

will succeed as will the goal

        X = f(Y), nonvar(X).

For CLP systems that support finite domain constraints, there are a number of built-ins for accessing the current domain of a variable. We have already met these in Chapter 8.

mindomain(X,M): Sets M to be the minimum value of the domain of the variable X in the current constraint store. At the time of evaluation, M should be free.

maxdomain(X,M): Sets M to be the maximum value of the domain of the variable X in the current constraint store. Again, at the time of evaluation, M should be free.

`dom(X,L)`: Sets L to the list of all values in the domain of the variable X in the current constraint store. At the time of evaluation, L should be free.

For example, the goal

          `X :: [0..8], X ≥ 4, mindomain(X,Min), maxdomain(X, Max).`

constrains Min to be 4 and Max to be 8. The goal

          `X :: [0..8], X ≥ 3, X ≠ 5, dom(X,L).`

constrains L to be $[3, 4, 5, 6, 7, 8]$ if disequations are handled by bounds consistency, or $[3, 4, 6, 7, 8]$ if disequations are handled by arc consistency.

There are also three useful built-ins for manipulating terms: `functor`, `arg` and `=...` These allow the programmer to build or access terms when the arity and name of the tree constructor is unknown.

The literal `functor(T,F,N)` succeeds if T is a term constructed from the tree constructor F with N children. At the time of evaluation either T must be constrained to be a non-variable term or F and N must be fixed, otherwise a runtime error occurs. For instance, the goal

          `X = record(3,Y), functor(X,F,N).`

succeeds with answer

$$X = record(3, Y) \wedge F = record \wedge N = 2,$$

while the goal

          `F = record, N = 2, functor(X,F,N).`

succeeds with answer

$$X = record(\_Y, \_Z) \wedge F = record \wedge N = 2.$$

The literal `arg(N,T,A)` succeeds if the term T has term A as its Nth argument. At the time of evaluation T must be constrained to be a non-variable term and N must be fixed, otherwise a runtime error occurs. For instance, the goal

          `X = record(3,Y), arg(1,X,A).`

succeeds with answer $X = record(3, Y) \wedge A = 3$, while `arg(N,record(3,Y),A)` gives a runtime error.

The literal `T =.. L` provides similar functionality to `functor` and `arg`.[1] At the time of evaluation either T must be constrained to be a non-variable term or L must be constrained to be a fixed length list whose first argument is a tree constructor. If T is constrained to be a term, then L is constrained to be a list $[F|As]$ where

---

1. Yes, it really is "`=..`" which is pronounced "univ".

F is a constant with the same name as the tree constructor and As is a list of the children of T. If L is a fixed length list with first element constant F and remainder As then T is constrained to be a term with tree constructor F and children As.

We can use `functor` and `arg` to give an alternate definition of vectors in CLP languages.

```
init(N, Vec) :- functor(Vec, vec, N).
access(Vec, I, E) :- arg(I, Vec, E).
```

A vector $\langle v_1, \ldots v_n \rangle$ with n elements is represented by a tree with n children. The literal `init(N, Vec)` initializes Vec to be a term with N children each of which is a distinct variable. The literal `access(Vec, I, E)` equates E with the Ith element v_I of the vector Vec. The advantage of this representation over the list representation used earlier is that access to a particular element in the vector takes only constant time.

The following program for predicate `variables` illustrates many of these built-ins. The predicate `variables(T,L)` succeeds if L is the list of variables occurring in term T. The program makes use of an accumulator. The auxiliary predicate `variables_acc(T,L1,L2)` succeeds if list $L2$ is the result of appending the variables in T to the list of variables $L1$. The list $L1$ acts as an accumulator. The auxiliary predicate has three rules in its definition. The first rule is for the case when T is a variable. It is simply concatenated to $L1$ to give the new list $L2$. The second rule is for when T is a constant. In this case $L1$ simply equals $L2$. The final case is when T is a more complex term with arguments. The predicate `variables_in_args` iterates through the arguments in T appending the variables in each to the list by recursively calling `variables_acc`.

```
variables(T,L) :- variables_acc(T,[],L).

variables_acc(X, L, [X|L]) :- var(X).
variables_acc(X, L, L) :- atom(X).
variables_acc(T, L, L1) :-
    compound(T),
    functor(T,_,A),
    variables_in_args(T, A, L ,L1).

variables_in_args(_T, 0, L, L).
variables_in_args(T, A, L, L2) :-
    A > 0,
    arg(A, T, TArg),
    variables_acc(TArg, L, L1),
    variables_in_args(T, A-1, L1, L2).
```

As an example, the goal `variables(f(X,g(a,Y,X)),L)` returns the answer $L = [X, Y, X]$. It is important to realise that this predicate computes the variables in a term in the context of the current constraint store. Thus, the goal

```
        T = harald, variables(T,L).
```

returns the answer $L = [\,]$, not $[T]$ as the reader may have expected.

As another example, we can use the term manipulation built-ins together with dynamic scheduling to build a more complete constraint solver for disequations if the system does not provide this capability.

```
ne(X,Y) :- neq(X,Y,V,true,false).
```

```
:- delay_until((nonvar(X) and nonvar(Y)) or ground(V),neq(X,Y,V,_,_)).
neq(X,Y,V,Pr,Nx) :-
    (ground(V) -> true
    ;   functor(X, F, N), functor(Y, G, M),
        (F = G, N = M ->
            X =.. [_|Xs], Y =.. [_|Ys],
            neqs(Xs, Ys, V, Pr, Nx)
        ;   V = true )
    ).
```

```
neqs([], [] , V, Pr, Pr).
neqs([X|LX],[Y|LY],V, Pr, Nx) :-
    neq(X,Y,V,Pr,In),
    neqs(LX,LY,V,In,Nx).
```

The literal **ne** does not wait until its arguments are fully ground. Instead it recursively processes the corresponding subterms of its arguments, determining if the current store implies the subterms must be unequal or, if it cannot do this, sets up delayed calls on subterms that might be found to be unequal in the future. Evaluation leads to calls of the form **neq(X,Y,V,Pr,Nx)** where X and Y are corresponding subterms. Such a call sets V to *true* if X and Y cannot be equal, and sets Pr equal to Nx if X and Y must be equal. The literal delays until both X and Y are not variables or V is fixed. V is a communication variable shared between all of these calls to **neq**. If it becomes ground, it causes all the delayed literals to wake up and succeed. V is set to *true* whenever a literal **neq(X,Y,V,Pr,Nx)** is found in which X and Y must be different. The remaining arguments Pr and Nx chain these **neq** literals together. When X and Y are both non-variables then the literal **neq(X,Y,V,Pr,Nx)** is replaced by **neq** literals among their arguments which chain the Pr and Nx variables. Whenever X and Y are found to be identical, Pr and Nx are equated. If all of the X and Y arguments in the **neq** literals are eventually found to be equal, the two values *true* and *false* given as the initial chain values are equated and failure results.

Consider evaluation of the goal

```
    ne(X, Y), X = f(a, U), Y = f(T, b), U = b, T = a.
```

The simplified derivation (with some states omitted) has the form illustrated in Figure 9.6 where the rewritten literal(s) is underlined.

$$\langle \underline{ne(X,Y)}, X = f(a,U), Y = f(T,b), U = b, T = a \mid true \rangle$$
$$\Downarrow$$
$$\langle neq(X,Y,V,true,false), \underline{X = f(a,U)}, Y = f(T,b), U = b, T = a \mid true \rangle$$
$$\Downarrow_*$$
$$\langle \underline{neq(f(a,U), f(T,b), V, true, false)}, U = b, T = a \mid X = f(a,U) \wedge Y = f(T,b) \rangle$$
$$\Downarrow_*$$
$$\langle \underline{neqs([a,U],[T,b], V, true, false)}, U = b, T = a \mid X = f(a,U) \wedge Y = f(T,b) \rangle$$
$$\Downarrow_*$$
$$\langle neq(a,T,V,true,In), neq(U,b,V,In,false), \underline{U = b}, T = a \mid X = f(a,U) \wedge Y = f(T,b) \rangle$$
$$\Downarrow$$
$$\langle neq(a,T,V,true,In), \underline{neq(b,b,V,In,false)}, T = a \mid X = f(a,b) \wedge Y = f(T,b) \wedge U = b \rangle$$
$$\Downarrow_*$$
$$\langle neq(a,T,V,true,In), \underline{neqs([],[],V,In,false)}, T = a \mid X = f(a,b) \wedge Y = f(T,b) \wedge U = b \rangle$$
$$\Downarrow_*$$
$$\langle neq(a,T,V,true,false), \underline{T = a} \mid X = f(a,b) \wedge Y = f(T,b) \wedge U = b \rangle$$
$$\Downarrow$$
$$\langle \underline{neq(a,a,V,true,false)} \mid X = f(a,b) \wedge Y = f(a,b) \wedge U = b \wedge T = a \rangle$$
$$\Downarrow_*$$
$$\langle \underline{neqs([],[],V,true,false)} \mid X = f(a,b) \wedge Y = f(a,b) \wedge U = b \wedge T = a \rangle$$
$$\Downarrow_*$$
$$\langle \blacksquare \mid false \rangle$$

Figure 9.6 Simplified derivation for more complete **ne**.

In the third state, when X and Y are both non-variable, the **neq** literal is selected. Since they have the same tree constructor and number of children, the corresponding children are constrained by **neq** literals, in the chain

```
neq(a,T,V,true,In), neq(U,b,V,In,false).
```

The intermediate variable In allows one of these **neq** literals to equate the last two arguments, but not both. In the sixth state, the second **neq** literal is selected. Since the two terms b and b are identical and have no arguments, the call to **neqs([],[],V,In,false)** sets In to *false*. In the ninth state the remaining **neq** literal is selected. Since the tree constructors are identical and have no children, the call to **neqs([],[],V,true,false)** attempts to equate *true* and *false* and fails. Since all corresponding subterms of the initial two variables X and Y are shown to be identical the disequation is false.

As another example, consider evaluation of the goal

```
ne(X, Y), X = f(a, U), Y = f(T, b), U = a.
```

The simplified derivation proceeds similarly to that above until it reaches the following state:

$$\langle neq(a,T,V,true,In), neq(U,b,V,In,false), \underline{U = a} \mid X = f(a,U) \wedge Y = f(T,b)\rangle$$

$$\Downarrow$$

$$\langle neq(a,T,V,true,In), \underline{neq(a,b,V,In,false)} \mid X = f(a,a) \wedge Y = f(T,b) \wedge U = a\rangle$$

$$\Downarrow_*$$

$$\langle neq(a,T,V,true,In), \underline{V = true} \mid X = f(a,a) \wedge Y = f(T,b) \wedge U = a\rangle$$

$$\Downarrow$$

$$\langle \underline{neq(a,T,true,true,In)} \mid X = f(a,a) \wedge Y = f(T,b) \wedge U = a\rangle$$

$$\Downarrow_*$$

$$\langle \square \mid X = f(a,a) \wedge Y = f(T,b) \wedge U = a\rangle$$

In the second state the **neq** literal is replaced by $V = true$ since the tree constructors of the first two arguments are not the same. Therefore the original terms cannot be identical. When V is set to true, the remaining **neq** literal is selected and replaced with $true$. The goal succeeds since X is constrained to be $f(a,a)$ and Y is constrained to be $f(T,b)$ which cannot be equal.

9.8.3   Database Built-ins

Most CLP languages provide built-ins which allow the programmer to add, examine or remove the rules in a program while the program is executing. Needless to say, the use of such built-ins is fraught with peril since they allow the programmer to write complex self-modifying code. CLP programmers rarely use these built-ins—they are primarily intended for implementation of the other built-ins.

The three main database built-ins are:

clause: This returns the rules in a program.

assert: This adds a rule to a program.

retract: This removes a rule from a program.

The literal **clause(H, B)** succeeds if the rule H :- B occurs in the program. At the time of the call the head, H, must be constrained to be a non-variable term. A fact is represented by a rule with the body $true$. A call to **clause** will backtrack through all rules matching the arguments.

The literal **assert(H)** adds the fact H while **assert((H :- B))** adds the rule H :- B to the program. The extra parentheses in the second call are necessary because of the precedence of the ":-" operator. At the time of the call, the head H, and body B, if present, must be constrained to have the syntax of a user-defined constraint and a goal respectively. Upon backtracking, a call to **assert** will fail, leaving the rule in the program.

The final database built-in is `retract`. The call `retract(H)` removes the fact H while `retract((H :- B))` removes a rule H `:-` B from the program. As for `assert`, at the time of the call H and B, if present, must be constrained to have the syntax of a user-defined constraint and a goal respectively. Upon backtracking a call to `retract` will remove another fact or rule matching the arguments. Those rules previously removed from the program by the call remain removed. If no rules match the arguments then it will fail.

In general, good CLP programming style is to use `assert` and `retract` only to add or delete facts from the program. Furthermore, at the time they are asserted, all variables in the facts should have fixed values. Adding or deleting complex rules containing variables is error-prone and best left to the CLP system implementor. Adding or deleting rules with arithmetically constrained variables (that are not fixed by the solver) is not fully supported by many CLP systems.

One use of database predicates is to define global variables, that is variables that can be accessed from any part of the program. Imagine we wish to profile the use of `member` within the intersection program from Example 7.1. Recall the definition of `intersect`. It succeeds if its two arguments are lists which have a common element.

```
intersect(L1, L2) :- member(X, L1), member(X, L2).

member(X, [X|_]).
member(X, [_|R]) :- member(X, R).
```

We wish to add a flag to `member` which will turn profiling on or off. If the flag is set to 1, we wish to print the solved form of the arguments whenever a call to `member` is evaluated and whenever an answer is found to the call. If the flag is not set to 1, evaluation of `member` should work silently.

We could add an extra argument to `member` and `intersect` and pass the flag's value in to the call through this argument. This has the disadvantage that we also have to modify `intersect`. Instead we can use the database to store the flag value v, using a fact of the form `flag(v)`. This can be accessed in `member` as follows and does not require us to modify the code for `intersect`.

```
member(X,Y) :-
    (clause(flag(1),true) ->
        write("Call: "), write(member(X,Y)), nl
    ; true),
    member1(X,Y),
    (clause(flag(1),true) ->
        write("Exit: "), write(member(X,Y)), nl
    ; true).
member1(X, [X|_]).
member1(X, [_|R]) :- member(X, R).
```

The simplified derivation tree for the goal `intersect([1,2], [0,2,4])` is illustrated in Figure 9.7.

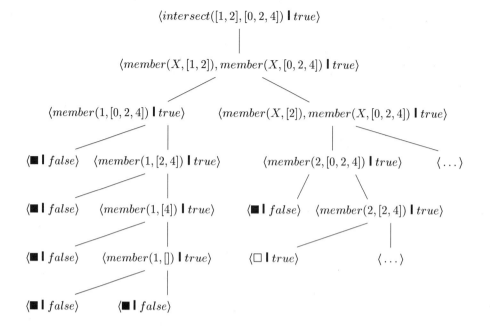

Figure 9.7 Simplified derivation tree for `intersect`.

Evaluation of the goal

```
assert(flag(1)), intersect([1,2], [0,2,4]).
```

Results in the answer *true* and the output

```
Call: member(X, [1, 2])
Exit: member(1, [1, 2])
Call: member(1, [0, 2, 4])
Call: member(1, [2, 4])
Call: member(1, [4])
Call: member(1, [])
Call: member(X, [2])
Exit: member(2, [2])
Exit: member(2, [1, 2])
Call: member(2, [0, 2, 4])
Call: member(2, [2, 4])
Exit: member(2, [2, 4])
Exit: member(2, [0, 2, 4])
```

A call to `member` occurs in the derivation tree whenever the first literal in the state has the predicate name `member`. An exits from that call, indicating that an answer has been found, occurs just before the next literal, in the state in which the original call occurs, is rewritten. For example, the first exit corresponds to the first answer to the first `member` literal.

The goal

```
assert(flag(0)), intersect([1,2], [0,2,4]).
```

simply returns the answer *true* and does not print anything.

For the intersection program, it may seem easier to add the extra argument. However, for larger programs using a global flag in the database is more convenient since it means we only have to modify the definition of member rather than that of all the predicates which indirectly call member.

Another use of database predicates is for communicating information from one branch in a derivation tree to another. For example, we can define facilities for counting using the database predicates as follows:

```
init :- assert(counter(0)).
inc :- once(retract(counter(X)), X1 = X + 1, assert(counter(X1))).
result(X) :- retract(counter(X)).
```

The predicate init initializes the counter to value 0, inc increments the counter, and result(X) removes the counter and returns the value in X. The once in the definition of inc is important since otherwise, if a literal after inc fails, backtracking will cause the retract to remove the already incremented counter value, and assert a new counter value of one more.

Suppose we wish to count the number of answers to a goal. First we shall illustrate this using a very simple goal $X \geq 2$, member(X, [0,3,7]). We need to initialize the counter, execute the goal and, whenever we find an answer, increment the counter. To force the execution to find all answers we fail and look for another answer. After all answers have been found, the value in the counter records the number of answers found. The following program encodes this:

```
simple_count(_) :- init, X ≥ 2, member(X, [0,3,7]), inc, fail.
simple_count(N) :- result(N).
```

Note the use of the built-in fail to force the body of the first rule to fail. A simplified derivation tree for the goal simple_count(N) is shown in Figure 9.8. Derivation steps evaluating the predicates init, inc and result are omitted, but the resulting changes to the database are marked alongside of the derivation step. The annotation $+fact$ indicates that $fact$ is asserted into the database, while $-fact$ indicates that $fact$ is retracted.

We can write a higher-order predicate that counts the number of answers to an arbitrary goal as follows:

```
count_answers(G,_) :- init, call(G), inc, fail.
count_answers(_,N) :- result(N).
```

The goal count_answers(G,N) returns in N the number of answers to the goal G.

Although the (self-imposed) restriction that assert is only used in a mode in which all of the variables in it are fixed means that arbitrary constraints cannot be communicated across different branches in a derivation tree, it still allows the CLP

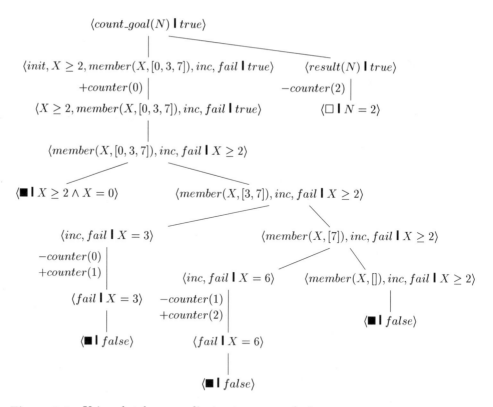

Figure 9.8 Using database predicates to count solutions.

programmer to modify the default search strategy and to program built-ins such as `minimize` for goals.

As a more complex example, consider how one might implement the higher-order built-in `minimize(G,E)`. The first part of the evaluation is to find the minimum value M of the expression E to be minimized. Then G is called to find any answer in which E has this value. The most difficult part is to determine the minimum value, since we do not want to look at all answers but, rather, wish to use the current bound to prune those answers to G which cannot tighten this bound. The following program does this by repeatedly solving the goal G after the bound on E has been tightened. Thus it is very similar to retry_int_opt defined in Section 3.6. Communication of the new bound between different calls to G is by means of the predicate `apply_new_bound(E)` which removes the current bound on B from the database and constrains $E < B$ so as to find a better bound, and the predicate `record_better_bound(E)` which takes the new value of E and posts this to the database. We assume that any answer to G fixes the value of E.

```
minimize(G, E) :-
    get_min_value(G, E, M),
    E = M,
    call(G).
```

```
get_min_value(G, E, _) :-
    apply_new_bound(E),
    once(G),
    record_better_bound(E),
    fail.
get_min_value(_, _, M) :- retract(bestbound(M)).

apply_new_bound(_).
apply_new_bound(E) :-
    retract(currentbound(B)),
    assert(bestbound(B)),
    E < B,
    apply_new_bound(E).

record_better_bound(E) :-
    (retract(bestbound(_)) -> true ; true),
    assert(currentbound(E)).
```

As an example of this program's execution consider the program

```
p(a, 10).
p(b, 5).
p(c, 8).
```

The most interesting part of the derivation tree for goal `minimize(p(X,Y), Y)` is the evaluation of the call `get_min_value(p(X,Y),Y, M)` which calculates the minimal value, M, for Y. The derivation tree for this call is shown in Figure 9.9. For brevity `get_min_value` is shortened to *gmv*, `apply_new_bound` to *anb*, `record_better_bound` to *rbb*, `currentbound` to *cbnd* and `bestbound` to *bbnd*. Derivation steps for database predicates and primitive constraints are omitted, but the effect of the database predicates is indicated next to the derivation step.

The key points in the exploration of the derivation tree are as follows. At the state, s_1,

$$\langle anb(Y), once(p(X,Y)), rbb(Y), fail \mathbin{\vert} true \rangle$$

using the first rule for *anb* leads to the left branch and the state

$$\langle once(p(X,Y)), rbb(Y), fail \mathbin{\vert} true \rangle.$$

The first answer found for the goal `p(X,Y)` is $X = a \land Y = 10$. Next `rbb(Y)` tries to retract a `bestbound` fact (there is none) and asserts the `currentbound(10)` fact. The derivation now fails and backtracks to try the second rule for *anb* in the state s_1. This retracts `currentbound(10)` and asserts `bestbound(10)`, as well as adding the constraint $Y < 10$. For the child state, s_2,

$$\langle anb(Y), once(p(X,Y)), rbb(Y), fail \mathbin{\vert} Y < 10 \rangle$$

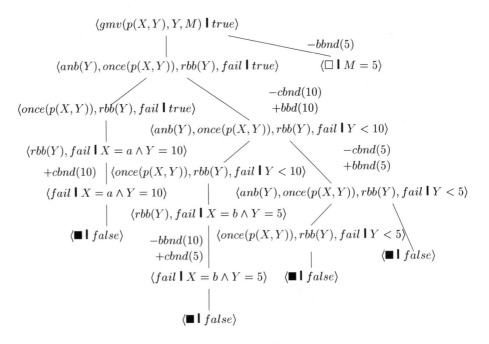

Figure 9.9   Using database predicates for minimize.

the first rule for *anb* leads to the state $\langle once(p(X,Y)), rbb(Y), fail \mid Y < 10\rangle$. The derivation from here acts as before except that the first answer for p(X,Y) is now $X = b \wedge Y = 5$ because of the constraint $Y < 10$, so bestbound(10) is retracted and currentbound(5) is asserted and the derivation fails. The second choice for state s_2 retracts the currentbound fact and asserts it as a bestbound, and adds constraint $Y < 5$. At the state, s_3,

$$\langle anb(Y), once(p(X,Y)), rbb(Y), fail \mid Y < 5\rangle$$

the first rule for *anb* leads to $\langle once(p(X,Y)), rbb(Y), fail \mid Y < 5\rangle$, which immediately fails, since there are no answers for $\langle p(X,Y) \mid Y < 5\rangle$. The second rule fails, because there is no currentbound fact in the database. Finally, the second rule for *gmv* is tried, which retracts the bestbound(5) fact, and constrains the minimal solution value M to 5.

9.8.4   Debugging Tools

No matter how high level the programming language, there comes a time when a seemingly correct program does not give the right answer and so must be debugged. Most CLP systems provide rather primitive debugging facilities based on the "Byrd Box" model of standard Prolog execution. In this model, program execution is understood in terms of predicate definitions. The programmer can specify which predicates they are interested in, and the debugger will provide information about the evaluation of these predicates. The programmer can either specify that all predicates are of interest by commanding that the program should be *traced* or they can specify that a particular predicate is of interest by placing a *spypoint* on the predicate.

The debugger prints out information about a predicate of interest whenever one of the following four events occurs. The first event, *call*, occurs when the predicate is initially called. The debugger prints out the name of the predicate, the level that the call occurs at and some information about the current constraint store simplified in terms of the variables in the call. If the predicate is user-defined, the debugger will now detail when each rule in the definition is tried. If the call to the predicate succeeds, an *exit* event occurs. If the call to the predicate does not succeed, a *fail* event occurs. The remaining event occurs when, after an initial success, subsequent failure causes the predicate to be backtracked to. This causes a *redo* event which is treated very much like the initial call. Again the debugger will detail when different rules in the predicate are being tried. If another answer is found, another exit event occurs. If no other answer is found, a fail event occurs.

We illustrate the library functions of SICStus Prolog. Similar functions are defined and act in more or less the same way in other CLP systems. We advise readers to refer to the user's manual of their CLP system. The most important library functions for debugging are:

trace: Turns debugging on and indicates that all predicates are of interest and so their execution should be traced.

notrace: Turns the debugger and tracing off.

debug: Turns debugging on but does not place spypoints on any predicates.

nodebug: Turns the debugger off.

spy(P): Places a spypoint on predicate P. Debugging should already be on.

nospy(P): Removes a spypoint previously placed on predicate P.

nospyall: Removes all spypoints.

We demonstrate the debugging predicates on the simple goal

```
intersect([1,2], [0,2,4]).
```

where the user-defined constraint `intersect` succeeds if its two arguments are lists which have a common element. The code for `intersect` is given on page 333. The simplified derivation tree for the above goal is illustrated in Figure 9.7.

When using the debugging facilities, each time an event occurs in the execution a line is printed and the user is given the opportunity to modify the execution. The main options are: Enter/Return or "c", continues execution until the next event (regardless of whether the predicate has a spypoint); "l" which leaps to the next event for a predicate with a spypoint; "s" which skips all events until an *exit* or *fail* event for the current literal; "n" which continues the rest of the execution without debugging; "f" which causes an immediate failure for this literal; "r" which causes the literal to be re-executed; and "a" which aborts execution. Tracing evaluation of the goal `intersect([1,2], [0,2,4])` produces the following session in which the user has typed Enter/Return at each prompt.

```
Call: intersect([1,2], [0,2,4]) ?
Call: member(X, [1, 2]) ?
Exit: member(1, [1, 2]) ?
Call: member(1, [0, 2, 4]) ?
Call: member(1, [2, 4]) ?
Call: member(1, [4]) ?
Call: member(1, []) ?
Fail: member(1, []) ?
Fail: member(1, [4]) ?
Fail: member(1, [2, 4]) ?
Fail: member(1, [0, 2, 4]) ?
Redo: member(1, [1, 2]) ?
Call: member(X, [2]) ?
Exit: member(2, [2]) ?
Exit: member(2, [1, 2]) ?
Call: member(2, [0, 2, 4]) ?
Call: member(2, [2, 4]) ?
Exit: member(2, [2, 4]) ?
Exit: member(2, [0, 2, 4]) ?
Exit: intersect([1,2], [0,2,4]) ?
```

Each line in the trace is related to a state in the derivation tree whose first literal corresponds to the printed literal. Different lines detail how this state is visited during the depth-first left-to-right traversal of the derivation tree. A line of the form `Call:` L details the first time the state with first literal L is visited. The line `Exit:` `member(1, [1,2])` indicates that the (first) answer $X = 1$ to the literal `member(X, [1, 2])` has been found. Now the second `member` literal is called. Each `Fail:` L line corresponds to moving back up the derivation tree after discovering that the derivation tree under the state in which literal L was rewritten is finitely failed. The `Redo: member(1, [1,2])` line corresponds to looking for a new answer to the literal `member(X, [1, 2])`, after already finding one, so this begins the traversal down the right branch from the second state. Ideally, the redo goal should be printed as `Redo: member(X, [1,2])` since the previous answer in which $X = 1$ is irrelevant for the purposes of finding the next answer. This behaviour occurs because it is easier to implement than is the idealized behaviour. The `Exit: member(2, [2])` line indicates that evaluation has found an answer, $X = 2$, to the call `member(X, [2])`. This is then returned as the second answer to the call `member(X, [1, 2])`. This leads to the call to the second member literal `Call: member(2, [0, 2, 4])`. Finding an answer to this literal leads to an answer to the overall goal.

As another example suppose the user types the goal

        spy(intersect), debug, intersect([1,2], [0,2,4]).

One possible interaction is as follows:

```
Call: intersect([1,2], [0,2,4]) ? c
Call: member(X, [1, 2]) ? c
Exit: member(1, [1, 2]) ? c
Call: member(1, [0, 2, 4]) ? s
Fail: member(1, [0, 2, 4]) ? c
Redo: member(1, [1, 2]) ? s
Exit: member(2, [1, 2]) ? l
Exit: intersect([1,2], [0,2,4]) c ?
```

Because the intersect predicate is spied upon the user is notified of calls to this predicate. By creeping ("c") the next three events are reported even though member has no spypoints. The *fail* event is generated after skipping ("s") events from the event Call: member(1, [0, 2, 4]). Creeping gives the next event and skipping gives its (next) answer. Finally leaping ("l") skips events until a predicate with a spypoint is reached.

Debugging may be implemented using a source-to-source translation. For example, a version of member which outputs trace information if the fact spy(member) is in the database is:

```
member(X,L) :-
    (clause(spy(member),true) ->
        write("Call: "), write(member(X,L)), nl
    ; true),
    member1(X,L),
    (clause(spy(member),true) ->
        write("Exit: "), write(member(X,L)), nl
    ; true),
    (clause(spy(member),true) ->
        retry_member(X,L)
    ; true).
member(X,L) :-
    (clause(spy(member),true) ->
        write("Fail: "), write(member(X,L)), nl
    ; true),
    fail.

retry_member(_X,_L).
retry_member(X,L) :- write("Redo: "), write(member(X,L)), nl, fail.

member1(X, [X|_]).
member1(X, [_|R]) :- member(X,R).
```

If the fact spy(member) is in the database, the "Call" line is printed when member is first called, and the "Exit" line is printed when an answer is found. The auxiliary predicate retry_member succeeds the first time, doing nothing but leaving a choicepoint. This choicepoint is reached just before execution returns to a choicepoint for the member1 call. The second rule for retry_member prints the "Redo" line and then fails so execution then returns to the choicepoint for the member1 call. Because retry_member is called after member1, it misleadingly prints the literal with the previous answer. Finally, when there are no more answers to member1, the second rule for member prints the "Fail" line before failing.

9.9 Summary

In this chapter we have given examples of advanced programming techniques. The primary aim of these programming techniques is to allow the programmer to modify the underlying CLP system, either by extending the constraint solver or by specializing the standard CLP built-ins such as those for optimization. The ability to do this distinguishes CLP from constraint solving packages. CLP systems provide a programming language and environment in which it is possible, at least in theory, to implement any algorithm.

Extending the constraint solver to handle constraints for a different constraint domain, or new kinds of primitive constraints is a reasonably frequent activity in constraint programming. Unfortunately, if these new constraints are only defined using "vanilla" CLP, as described in Chapter 4, their allowed mode of usage is often quite restrictive. Fortunately, techniques such as dynamic scheduling and meta-programming allow the definition of robust and safe constraints that work correctly, though perhaps incompletely, for all modes of usage.

Dynamic scheduling allows the programmer to control selection of literals at runtime. This makes it easier to assure termination of goals.

Meta-programming is reasonably straightforward in constraint logic programming because terms can be used to represent programs, and the underlying execution method is simple. The advantage of meta-programming is complete control over the search strategy. Meta-programming thus provides an easy way to experiment with different search strategies which the user may implement later using more efficient built-ins such as those for dynamic scheduling.

Just as it is possible to extend the constraint solver, new optimization routines can be programmed. We gave two examples, one in which the program implemented a well-known optimization technique, and an example in which a different kind of optimization search strategy was defined.

Clearly negation is useful in modelling. Unfortunately, the kind of negation provided by CLP systems is limited in usefulness, because it only truly models "logical" negation when the negated goal has all of its variables fixed. However, one use of negation is to test the satisfiability of constraints without adding the constraint to the store.

9.10 Practical Exercises

The floor $\lfloor t \rfloor$ and ceiling $\lceil t \rceil$ functions are provided in SICStus Prolog as `floor(X)` and `ceiling(X)`. They are not provided directly in $CLP(\mathcal{R})$. The $CLP(\mathcal{R})$ built-in `floor`(t, f) holds if f is the integer floor of the fixed number t. One can define ceiling in terms of `floor`. The predicate `integer` can also be defined in terms of `floor`.

The real arithmetic constraint solvers for SICStus Prolog provide a built in branch and bound minimization solver. The built-in `bb_inf`(*Ints*, *Expr*, *Inf*) computes the infimum *Inf* of expression *Expr* given that all the variables in the list *Ints* must take integer values. So, for example, the problem of Example 9.1 could be solved using the goal:

```
problem([X,Y], L), bb_inf([X,Y], L, Best).
```

Both ECLiPSe and SICStus Prolog include facilities for dynamic scheduling. ECLiPSe provides a goal based delay construct `delay`(*Term*, *Goal*) which is similar to

$$\text{delay\_until(nonvar}(X_1) \text{ or } \ldots \text{ or nonvar}(X_n), \; Goal)$$

where X_1 to X_n are the variables in the solved form of *Term* when the literal is selected. It also provides a predicate based delay construct. For instance, the declaration

```
delay append(X,Y,Z) if var(X), var(Z).
```

will delay calls to `append` if both the first and third arguments are variables. Declarations delay the execution of any literal which matches the declaration and where the body of the declaration (after `if`) succeeds. The user can write multiple delay declarations for one literal. For more details see the ECLiPSe User Manual.

SICStus Prolog provides the goal based delay construct `when`(*Cond*, *Goal*) which acts like `delay_until`. The condition can be `nonvar(X)`, which delays until X cannot take all possible values, `ground(X)` which delays until X is fixed, and `?=(X,Y)` which delays until X and Y are either definitely identical or cannot be equal. Conjunctions of delay conditions are written "*Cond*$_1$, *Cond*$_2$" and disjunctions as "*Cond*$_1$; *Cond*$_2$." For example, the not equals predicate can be defined by

```
ne(X,Y) :- when((ground(X),ground(Y)), not(X = Y)).
```

A better implementation of disequations is possible using the `?=(X,Y)` delay condition:

```
ne(X,Y) :- when(?=(X,Y), not(X = Y)).
```

SICStus Prolog also provides a (much more efficiently implemented) predicate based delay construct. The declaration

```
:- block append(-,?,-).
```

uses the pattern (-,?,-) to block the selection of append literals unless either the first or third argument is non-variable. Multiple patterns for the same predicate can be included in one declaration, and the declaration blocks if any evaluate to true. See the SICStus Prolog Users Manual for more information.

$CLP(\mathcal{R})$, SICStus Prolog and ECLiPSe support the debugging facilities described in Subsection 9.8.4, as well as others. For details refer to the appropriate User Manual.

P9.1. Write code for the predicates vs_mult, element and dotprod.

P9.2. Use solve_nr to determine three values x (each further apart than 1) such that $x^3 - 2x^2 - 8x + 1$ is between -0.0001 and 0.0001.

P9.3. Write a program defining predicate bisect(E, L, U, X) to find a zero X of a nonlinear function f on a single variable (defined by predicate f(X, F) using the bisection method. That is given a range $[L..U]$ for which $f(L) \times f(U) < 0$, determine the value of $f(\frac{L+U}{2})$ and replace either the lower or upper bound with $\frac{L+U}{2}$ so that the condition continues to hold. The program should terminate when $U - L < E$. Use this program to check your answers to the above problem.

P9.4. (*) Build a better constraint solver for sequence constraints by incorporating reasoning about lengths. We can represent a sequence as a pair $s(list, length)$ where $list$ is a list representing the sequence and $length$ is its length. The sequence constraint $S3 = S1 :: S2$ can be translated as:

```
N1 ≥ 0, N2 ≥ 0, N3 = N1 + N2, seq_append(L1, L2, L3, N1).
```

where Si is the pair $s(Li, Ni)$, $1 \le i \le 3$ and the seq_append predicate is defined below

```
seq_append([], L2, L2, 0).
seq_append([A|L1], L2, [A|L3], N) :-
     N = N0+1, N0 ≥ 0, seq_append(L1, L2, L3, N0).
```

Determine translations for $S \ne \epsilon$ and $S = nil$.

Try the goal corresponding to the sequence constraint $S2 \ne \epsilon \wedge U = nil \wedge T = S1 :: S2 \wedge U = T :: S3$.

P9.5. Reexamine the problem of Exercise P5.2. Given the river flows at 2 m/s during the flooding of the wet season, and the traveller rows at 1.5 m/s across a 12 m wide river and has to end up exactly 20 m downstream from the setting off position, find the angle θ at which she must row.

The built-in nonlinear constraint solver is not powerful enough to solve these constraints. Convert the problem into an expression e in terms of θ which is zero if the constraints hold. Use the Newton-Raphson method and symbolic differentiation to determine for what value of θ the constraints hold.

What happens if the river is 24 m wide?

P9.6. Write a program for `not_append(X,Y,Z)` which holds if Z is not the list obtained by appending X and Y. Assume each of X, Y and Z is a list.

P9.7. Write a program for `simplify(E0,E)` which simplifies an arithmetic expression $E0$ to another E (both represented as trees). For example the expression $(X - X) \times Y + Z - (2Z + -T)$ might be simplified to $-Z + T$.

P9.8. Extend the delay based solver for the Boolean constraints `bnot(X,Y)` and `and(X,Y,Z)` to handle `or(X,Y,Z)`, `xor(X,Y,Z)`, `if(X,Y,Z)`, and `iff(X,Y,Z)`. Ensure that the predicates are deterministic whenever their delay conditions are enabled.

P9.9. Using dynamic scheduling, write a definition for the user-defined constraint `length(L,N)` which holds if N is the length of list L. Ensure that, with this definition, none of the following goals has an infinite derivation:

(a) `length(L,N)`, `L = [1,2]`, `fail`

(b) `length(L,N)`, `N = 3`, `fail`

(c) `length(L,N)`, `N ≤ 3`, `append([1,2,3,4|_], A, L)`

(d) `length(L1,N1)`, `length(L2,N2)`, `N1+N2≤2`, `append(L1,L2,[1,2,3])`.

P9.10. (*) Using dynamic scheduling and negation, extend the constraint solver to handle the constraint `sqr(X,Y)` which holds when $Y = X^2$. Attempt to make the handling deterministic but as complete as possible, so that the following goals all succeed:

(a) `sqr(X,Y)`, `X = 1`, `Y = 1`

(b) `Y = -3`, `not(sqr(X,Y))`

(c) `sqr(X,Y)`, `var(X)`, `X = 1`, `arithmetic(Y)`

(d) `sqr(X,Y)`, `Y = 4`, `var(X)`

(e) `sqr(X,Y)`, `X ≥ 1`, `Y = 4`, `arithmetic(X)`

(f) `sqr(X,Y)`, `X ≤ 1`, `Y = 4`, `nonvar(X)`.

P9.11. (*) Use the meta-interpreter of Section 9.7 which handles `append` specially to execute the goal `derive([append(X,Y,Z), append(Y,X,Z)])`. Explain the result.

P9.12. (*) The `is` built-in of Prolog provides arithmetic calculation. The literal t_1 `is` t_2 will execute only if t_2 is a ground arithmetic expression, in which case it will evaluate the expression (obtaining n) and attempt to equate t_1 to n. For example, the goal `Y = 3, X is Y * Y + 4` succeeds with $Y = 3 \land X = 13$. We can use this to implement a limited form of arithmetic solving.

Modify the meta-interpreter of Section 9.7 to handle the constraint $Z = X + Y$, represented as `plus(X, Y, Z)` using local propagation. For example, if X and Z are fixed, then Y can be calculated by $Y = Z - X$ using the rule:

```
plus(X, Y, Z) :- ground(X), ground(Z), Y is Z - X.
```

Execute the goal

```
derive([plus(X,Y,Z), plus(Z,Y,U), plus(V,3,U), Z = 3, Z = 1]).
```

Extend the meta-interpreter to handle `mult(X,Y,Z)`.

P9.13. Write a higher-order predicate `solutions(G, X, L)` which collects as a list L all the values of X occurring in answers of the goal G. You will need to use `call` as well as the database built-ins to do so.

P9.14. (*) Consider the blocks world example of Section 1.5.3. We can represent the different blocks in the example world $[yc, gc, rs, gp, rp]$ using integers $[1, 2, 3, 4, 5]$. We can represent a value for a variable in the blocks world obj_1 *on* obj_2 using the number $obj_1 + 5 \times obj_2$ where if obj_2 is the *floor* then its value is 0. Write a $CLP(FD)$ program to define predicates for the constraints `on(X,Y)`, `floor(X)`, `equal(X, Y)`, `not_equal(X, Y)`, `red(X)`, `yellow(X)`, `not_green(X)` and `pyramid(X)`. Use it to find answers to the sample constraints given in Section 1.5.3 and Exercise 1.8.

9.11   Notes

Newton-Raphson is a well known method for finding the roots of differentiable functions. The branch and bound method for integer linear programming is due to Dakin. For more detailed descriptions of branch and bound see, for example, Papadimitriou and Steiglitz [101] or Schrijver [116]. Optimistic partitioning is amenable to straightforward parallelization. Some experiments making use of it are described in [103].

Negation in CLP is inherited from Prolog. This form of negation, negation by finite failure [28], is quite unsuited to constraint logic programming, since, in a typical CLP program, it is unlikely that negative goals only have fixed arguments. Furthermore, this form of negation interacts badly with incomplete constraint solvers. More suitable forms of negation are known for constraint logic programming, so called "constructive negation" [25, 128], but efficient implementation of these ideas is not straightforward so current systems do not support them.

The limitations of a fixed literal selection strategy were recognised early in the development of logic programming languages. Absys1 [47] a precursor to Prolog provided dynamic scheduling as did the logic programming languages IC-Prolog [30], Prolog-II [33] and MU-Prolog [96]. For example predicate based delay is provided by `wait` declarations for MU-Prolog, `when` declarations for NU-Prolog, and `block` declarations for SICStus Prolog. Goal based delay declarations are provided by `freeze` subgoals in Prolog-II, and `freeze`, and `when` subgoals in SICStus Prolog. The use of dynamic scheduling for writing constraint solvers appears in the paper of Kawamura et al [78]. Now most logic programming languages and constraint logic programming languages provide dynamic scheduling. However, the dynamic scheduling delay conditions provided in CLP systems are inherited from Prolog and, therefore, may not provide all of the functionality a constraint programmer desires.

Meta-programming in CLP is inherited from Prolog. Hence some of the meta-programming facilities for CLP are clumsy and unnatural. For a discussion of meta-programming in Prolog see [125, 1], while various approaches to meta-programming in CLP are discussed in [63, 88, 87].

Library functions for CLP languages are inherited from Prolog. Many of them are somewhat ill-defined for constraint domains other than tree constraints. The definition of the `variables` predicate is based on a program given in the SICStus Prolog User's Manual [58].

Debugging constraint programs can be a difficult task since the affect of the constraint solver may be hard to determine. Debugging facilities for CLP are inherited from Prolog and are less than adequate for constraint domains other than the tree constraint domain. Specific extensions for other constraint domains are not standardized at present. The reader is referred to the survey by Ducassé and Noyé of debugging for Prolog-like languages [45]. A source-to-source transformation for tracing is described in this.

10   CLP Systems

In previous chapters we have introduced CLP languages and studied how to program with them. In this chapter we examine CLP languages from a different perspective: their implementation. This is not only of interest in its own right, but also allows the constraint programmer to gain a better understanding of the underlying efficiency issues.

We give a simple backtracking function for goal evaluation and then extend and refine its definition. One of the main implementation issues we will consider is the use of an incremental constraint solver to reduce the cost of constraint solving. We also show how to extend our evaluation mechanism to support the constructs for optimization, if-then-else, finding the first solution and negation introduced in Chapters 5, 7 and 9. The constructs for if-then-else, finding a first solution and negation are implemented in terms of a single primitive, the *cut*, while we give two possible implementations of the optimization construct.

10.1   Simple Backtracking Goal Evaluation

Previously we have understood goal evaluation to be a depth-first left-to-right search through the goal's derivation tree. The following algorithm performs such a search and provides a simplified view of the goal evaluation algorithm used in a CLP system. The function $defn_P(L)$ returns a sequence of rules defining the literal L in order of their occurrence in the program P. Each rule is renamed away from all previously seen variables. The algorithm is a variant of the backtracking algorithm for solving CSPs (Algorithm 3.1). It returns the first answer it finds to the goal, but can easily be modified to find all of the answers to the goal. It is parametric in the choice of solver *solv* and simplifier *simpl*.

The algorithm first identifies the variables of interest, W, then calls the function simple_backtrack to find an answer, C, to the goal, and finally returns the answer simplified in terms of the variables of interest. Most of the work takes place in simple_backtrack which calls itself recursively to find the first answer to a state. If simple_backtrack is called with a state whose goal is empty, it returns the constraint store as the answer. If the goal is non-empty, simple_backtrack processes the first literal in the goal and then calls itself with the new state. If the literal is a primitive constraint it is added to the current constraint and the resulting constraint is

---

G and G_1 are goals;
P is a program;
C and C_1 are constraints;
$L, L_1, \ldots, L_k$ are literals;
and $s_1, \ldots, s_n, t_1, \ldots, t_n$ are expressions.

simple_solve_goal(G)
   $W := vars(G)$
   $C :=$ simple_backtrack($\langle G \mid true \rangle$)
   return $simpl(W, C)$

simple_backtrack($\langle G \mid C \rangle$)
   if G is the empty goal **then return** C **endif**
   let G be of form L, G_1
   cases
   L is a primitive constraint:
      if $solv(C \wedge L) \not\equiv false$ **then**
         return simple_backtrack($\langle G_1 \mid C \wedge L \rangle$)
      else return $false$ **endif**
   L is a user-defined constraint:
      let L be of form $p(s_1, \ldots, s_n)$
      for each $(p(t_1, \ldots, t_n) \; :- \; L_1, \ldots, L_k) \in defn_P(L)$ **do**
         $C_1 :=$ simple_backtrack($\langle s_1 = t_1, \ldots, s_n = t_n, L_1, \ldots, L_k, G_1 \mid C \rangle$)
         if $C_1 \not\equiv false$ **then return** C_1 **endif**
      endfor
      return $false$
   endcases

Figure 10.1   Simple backtracking goal solver.

checked for satisfiability by the solver. If the literal is a user-defined constraint, it is rewritten using a rule from its definition. When evaluating a user-defined constraint, the rules are considered one by one, in the order returned by $defn_P$. This encodes a depth-first search.

Algorithm 10.1: Simple backtracking solver for goals
INPUT: A goal G and a program P.
OUTPUT: An answer to G for P.
METHOD: The algorithm is given in Figure 10.1. $\square$

Example 10.1
As an example of how the simple backtracking solver works, consider the following CLP program to sum the numbers from 1 to N introduced in Section 7.2:

```
sum(0, 0).
sum(N, N + S) :- sum(N-1, S).
```

Consider evaluation of the goal sum(1,S). The initial call to simple_solve_goal sets the variables of interest, W, to $\{S\}$ and then calls simple_backtrack to evaluate the state $\langle sum(1, S) \mathbin{|} true \rangle$. The goal $sum(1, S)$ is treated as being of the form "$sum(1, S), \square$" where $\square$ is the empty goal. Thus L is set to $sum(1, S)$ and G_1 to $\square$. As L is a user-defined constraint, the second case statement is evaluated. The first rule defining L is the fact `sum(0,0)`. This is shorthand for the rule

```
sum(0,0)  :- □.
```

Thus, simple_backtrack is called recursively to evaluate the state

$$\langle 1 = 0, S = 0 \mathbin{|} true \rangle.$$

In this call L is set to $1 = 0$ and G_1 to $S = 0$. As L is a primitive constraint, it is added to the current constraint store, giving $1 = 0$, and this is tested by the constraint solver for satisfiability. The solver returns *false*, so simple_backtrack returns *false* from the call to evaluate $\langle 1 = 0, S = 0 \mathbin{|} true \rangle$. The original call to simple_backtrack now tries the next rule defining $sum(1, S)$, effectively backtracking to the choicepoint associated with $sum(1, S)$ This rule, appropriately renamed, is

```
sum(N', N' + S')   :-   sum(N'-1, S').
```

Rewriting of $sum(1, S)$ with this rule leads to simple_backtrack being called to evaluate the state

$$\langle 1 = N', S = N' + S', sum(N' - 1, S') \mathbin{|} true \rangle.$$

This processes the constraints $1 = N'$ and $S = N' + S'$ by adding them to the current constraint, and then calls simple_backtrack to evaluate

$$\langle sum(N' - 1, S') \mathbin{|} 1 = N' \wedge S = N' + S' \rangle.$$

Evaluation of this call sets L to $sum(N' - 1, S')$ and G_1 to $\square$. The first rule defining $sum(N' - 1, S')$ is `sum(0,0)`. This leads to a call to simple_backtrack to evaluate

$$\langle N' - 1 = 0, S' = 0 \mathbin{|} 1 = N' \wedge S = N' + S' \rangle.$$

Subsequent calls to simple_backtrack will process the constraints $N' - 1 = 0$ and $S' = 0$, adding them to the store. This leads to simple_backtrack being called to evaluate

$$\langle \square \mathbin{|} 1 = N' \wedge S = N' + S' \wedge N' - 1 = 0 \wedge S' = 0 \rangle.$$

This simply returns the current constraint store, namely

$$1 = N' \wedge S = N' + S' \wedge N' - 1 = 0 \wedge S' = 0.$$

This constraint is returned from each of the nested calls to simple_backtrack, until finally it is returned from the original call. The function simple_solve_goal now returns $simpl(\{S\}, 1 = N' \wedge S = N' + S' \wedge N' - 1 = 0 \wedge S' = 0)$, which is simply $S = 1$, as we might hope.

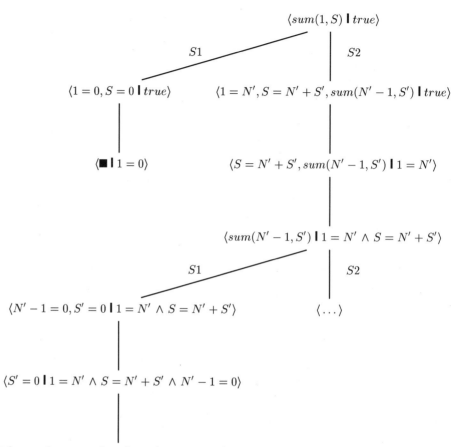

Figure 10.2   Derivation tree for `sum(1,S)`.

We can understand the simple backtracking solver better if we examine Figure 10.2 which shows part of the derivation tree for `sum(1,S)`. We can see that the solver is performing a depth-first traversal of this tree, stopping when it reaches the first success state.

10.2   Incremental Constraint Solving

Unfortunately, the simple backtracking goal solver described above is inefficient. To see why, let us reconsider Example 10.1 and the evaluation of the goal `sum(1,S)`. When evaluating this goal, the constraint solver will be called on to determine satisfiability of each of the constraints in the following sequence:

$$1 = 0,$$
$$1 = N',$$
$$1 = N' \wedge S = N' + S',$$
$$1 = N' \wedge S = N' + S' \wedge N' - 1 = 0,$$
$$1 = N' \wedge S = N' + S' \wedge N' - 1 = 0 \wedge S' = 0.$$

Using the constraint solver to iteratively solve a sequence of constraints like this is not a very good idea, since each time the solver is called with one of the constraints it solves the problem from the beginning, even though it may be repeating work done when solving the previous constraint.

For this reason it is common in CLP systems to keep the current constraint in some sort of "partially solved form." This makes subsequent tests for satisfiability easier and primitive constraints are added to this as they are encountered during execution. Such a solver is said to be *incremental*, since it answers satisfiability questions incrementally by adding one more primitive constraint to an already satisfiable constraint.

Definition 10.1

An *incremental constraint solver*, *isolv*, for a constraint domain $\mathcal{D}$, takes as input a primitive constraint c in $\mathcal{D}$ and returns *true*, *false* or *unknown*. There is an implicit global *constraint store*, S, which is manipulated by *isolv*. Whenever $isolv(c)$ returns *true*, constraint $S \wedge c$ must be satisfiable and whenever $isolv(c)$ returns *false*, the constraint $S \wedge c$ must be unsatisfiable. Additionally, whenever $isolv(c)$ returns *true* or *unknown*, the global constraint store must be updated to be equivalent to $S \wedge c$.

It is quite easy to modify many of the constraint solvers that we have met in Part 1 so that they become incremental. Consider the Gauss-Jordan constraint solver. As this already maintains a solved form S and processes the primitive constraints one at a time, it is straightforward to give an incremental version. The algorithm is given below. The only trick is that we must remember to eliminate the non-parametric variables of S from the new equality c, before processing c.

Algorithm 10.2: Incremental Gauss-Jordan solver
INPUT: A linear arithmetic equality c.
GLOBALS: S is a conjunction of linear arithmetic equations in solved form.
OUTPUT: Returns *true* or *false* indicating whether $S \wedge c$ is satisfiable or not. Updates the global constraint store S.
METHOD: The algorithm is given in Figure 10.3. □

Example 10.2

Consider applying the incremental solver to the following equations which would be encountered when traversing the successful derivation in Example 10.1.

$$1 = N', \quad S = N' + S', \quad N' - 1 = 0, \quad S' = 0.$$

---

c is a linear arithmetic equation;
S is the global constraint store;
C is a conjunction of linear equations;
$e, e_1, \ldots, e_n$ are linear arithmetic expressions;
$x, x_1, \ldots, x_n$ are real variables;
and r is a real number.

inc_gauss_jordan_solve(c)
   $c :=$ eliminate(c, S)
   if c can be written in form without variables **then**
      return eval(c)
   else
      write c in the form $x = e$ where e does not involve x
      $S :=$ eliminate($S, x = e$) $\wedge\, x = e$
      return *true*
   endif

eliminate(C, S)
   let S be of form $x_1 = e_1 \wedge \cdots \wedge x_n = e_n$
   for each x_i **do**
      replace x_i by e_i throughout C
   endfor
   return C

eval(c)
   if c can be written in the form $0 = r$ where $r \neq 0$ **then**
      return *false*
   else
      return *true*
   endif

Figure 10.3   Incremental Gauss-Jordan solver.

Initially the global constraint store S is *true*. First inc_gauss_jordan_solve is called with $1 = N'$. This is processed by first using *true* to eliminate variables from $1 = N'$. This simply gives $1 = N'$. As this contains variables, it is rewritten to $N' = 1$ and the constraint store becomes the result of using $N' = 1$ to eliminate variables from the old constraint store, *true*, and conjoining $N' = 1$. This is simply $N' = 1$. The call to the solver returns *true*, indicating that the store remains satisfiable when $1 = N'$ is added to it.

The second call is with the constraint $S = N' + S'$. The first step is to eliminate variables from $S = N' + S'$ using the current store $N' = 1$. This gives $S = 1 + S'$. As $S = 1 + S'$ contains variables, it is rewritten to $S = 1 + S'$ and the constraint store is updated by using $S = 1 + S'$ to eliminate variables from it and conjoining it with $S = 1 + S'$, giving $N' = 1 \wedge S = 1 + S'$. Note that we could also have chosen to rewrite the constraint to $S' = S - 1$. Finally, *true* is returned, indicating that the constraint store remains satisfiable when $S = N' + S'$ is added to it.

The next call is with $N' - 1 = 0$. First the current store is used to eliminate variables from it, giving $1 - 1 = 0$. As $1 - 1 = 0$ does not contain variables, it is evaluated to see if it is equivalent to *true*. As it is, *true* is returned and the constraint store remains unchanged. This is the expected behaviour since $N'-1=0$ was redundant with respect to the store.

The last call to the incremental solver is with $S' = 0$. Eliminating variables from $S' = 0$ using the current store leaves the constraint unchanged. Now $S' = 0$ is used to eliminate S' from the store and conjoined, setting the constraint store to $N' = 1 \wedge S = 1 + 0 \wedge S' = 0$. The value *true* is returned from the call to the solver indicating the store remains satisfiable.

Therefore the incremental Gauss-Jordan algorithm has efficiently determined that the following constraints

$$1 = N',$$
$$1 = N' \wedge S = N' + S',$$
$$1 = N' \wedge S = N' + S' \wedge N' - 1 = 0,$$
$$1 = N' \wedge S = N' + S' \wedge N' - 1 = 0 \wedge S' = 0$$

are satisfiable. To appreciate the importance of incremental constraint solving, the reader is encouraged to solve each of these constraints in turn with the non-incremental Gauss-Jordan algorithm and compare the amount of work involved.

The following algorithm captures the goal evaluation algorithm used in a CLP system which uses an incremental solver *isolv* that works on a global constraint store. The evaluation function inc_backtrack is similar to simple_backtrack. However, since the constraint component of the state being evaluated is now implicitly available in the global constraint store, it only takes a goal as an argument. Also, since the answer is in the global constraint store, it simply returns *true* or *false* to indicate whether an answer has been found or not. The main difference is that inc_backtrack must now explicitly restore the global constraint store to its previous value when a new rule is tried in the rewriting of a user-defined constraint. The function initialize_store is used to initialize the store so that it represents *true*, the function get_store returns the constraint represented by the global constraint store and the functions save_store and restore_store, respectively, save the current configuration of the store and then restore it.

Algorithm 10.3: Incremental backtracking solver for goals
INPUT: A goal G.
GLOBALS: A constraint store S and a program P.
OUTPUT: An answer to G for P or *false* if none exist.
METHOD: The algorithm is given in Figure 10.4. □

The easiest way to implement save_store and restore_store is by means of a global stack called the *backtrack stack*. The function save_store simply pushes the current configuration of the store on to the stack, while restore_store pops the old

G and G_1 are goals;
P is a program;
$L, L_1, \ldots, L_k$ are literals;
$s_1, \ldots, s_n, t_1, \ldots, t_n$ are expressions;
and W is a set of variables.

inc_solve_goal(G)
   $W := vars(G)$
   initialize_store()
   if inc_backtrack(G) **then**
      return $simpl(W, $ get_store$())$
   else
      return $false$
   endif

inc_backtrack(G)
   if G is the empty goal **then return** $true$ **endif**
   let G be of form L, G_1
   cases
   L is a primitive constraint:
      if $isolv(L) \not\equiv false$ **then**
         return inc_backtrack(G_1)
      else return $false$ **endif**
   L is a user-defined constraint:
      let L be of form $p(s_1, \ldots, s_n)$
      for each $(p(t_1, \ldots, t_n) :- L_1, \ldots, L_k) \in defn_P(L)$ **do**
         save_store()
         if inc_backtrack$((s_1 = t_1, \ldots, s_n = t_n, L_1, \ldots, L_k, G_1))$ **then**
            return $true$
         endif
         restore_store()
      endfor
      return $false$
   endcases

Figure 10.4   Incremental backtracking goal solver.

configuration from the top of the stack. We shall explore better implementation techniques in the next section.

Example 10.3

As an example of the way in which the incremental backtracking goal solver works, consider its operation on the goal and program from Example 10.1. We shall use the incremental Gauss-Jordan algorithm for constraint solving.

The call to evaluate the goal `sum(1,S)` initializes the global constraint store to *true*, sets the variables of interest, W, to $\{S\}$ and then calls inc_backtrack to evaluate $sum(1, S)$ in the context of the global constraint store. As before, L is set to $sum(1, S)$ and the second case is used. The first rule defining $sum(1, S)$ is `sum(0,0)`. The current store is saved on to the initially empty backtrack stack giving the stack:

$$\boxed{true}$$

Now the goal "$1 = 0, S = 0$" is evaluated using inc_backtrack. L is set to $1 = 0$ and G_1 to $S = 0$. As L is a primitive constraint, the incremental solver is called to add $1 = 0$ to the constraint store. This returns $false$, so the call to evaluate "$1 = 0, S = 0$" returns $false$. This means that inc_backtrack must backtrack to the last choicepoint. This is done by calling restore_store, which pops the constraint $true$ from the backtrack stack and sets the global constraint store to $true$.

Evaluation of $sum(1, S)$ now tries the next rule defining $sum(1, S)$. This is

```
sum(N', N' + S')   :-   sum(N' - 1, S').
```

First the current store is saved, giving the backtrack stack:

$$\boxed{true}$$

Next the goal "$1 = N', S = N' + S', sum(N' - 1, S')$" is evaluated using inc_backtrack. This uses the incremental solver to process the constraint $1 = N'$ and then calls itself recursively to evaluate the goal "$S = N' + S', sum(N' - 1, S')$." Similarly, this call uses the incremental solver to process $S = N' + S'$ and then calls itself recursively to evaluate $sum(N' - 1, S')$. At this stage, the current store is $N' = 1 \wedge S = 1 + S'$ and the backtrack stack has not been affected. The first rule defining $sum(N' - 1, S')$ is $sum(0, 0)$. The constraint store is now saved, giving the stack

$N' = 1 \wedge S = 1 + S'$
$true$

and the goal "$N' - 1 = 0, S' = 0$" is now evaluated.

The procedure inc_backtrack processes the constraints $N' - 1 = 0$ and $S' = 0$ in turn, as detailed in Example 10.2, setting the global constraint store to

$$N' = 1 \wedge S = 1 + 0 \wedge S' = 0.$$

The backtrack stack is not affected. As all literals have been processed, the call finishes and simply returns $true$. In turn, $true$ is returned from each of the nested calls, until the original call to evaluate sum(1,S) returns. Finally, inc_solve_goal simplifies the constraint store in terms of the variables of interest and returns the result $S = 1$.

10.3   Efficient Saving and Restoring of the Constraint Store

One consequence of using an incremental solver is the need to explicitly save the constraint store when a choicepoint is reached and then to restore the store when backtracking to that choicepoint. Doing this efficiently is an important issue in the implementation of CLP languages and has implications for the design of the incremental solver.

Naively saving and restoring the entire constraint store by pushing and popping it to and from a stack is expensive in both space and time. Fortunately, it is not really necessary to do this. Instead, we need only save enough information to allow re-computation of the old constraint store from the current constraint store. Imagine that we are at a choicepoint and wish to save the current store C. Now we add the primitive constraints $c_1, \ldots, c_n$ to C, giving an unsatisfiable store C'. We must backtrack to the choicepoint and restore C. It is not necessary to have stored C, rather we need only to have kept sufficient information, δ, such that we can compute C from C' and δ. That is, δ needs to contain enough information to "undo" the effect of adding $c_1, \ldots, c_n$ to C. Exactly what information needs to be kept in δ depends on the particular constraint solver.

We now briefly discuss two choices of δ and the corresponding methods for restoring the store that are used in constraint logic programming systems.

10.3.1   Trailing

One simple technique for restoring the store is to associate an index with each constraint as it is added, in effect *time stamping* the constraint. At a choicepoint we can store the current time stamp and, on backtracking, remove all constraints with a larger time stamp since they must have been added after the choicepoint. However, this does not take into account the fact that adding new constraints may change the form of the old constraints, as, for instance, when the new constraint causes a variable to be eliminated. To handle this we can, whenever an old constraint is modified, save the old value of that part of the constraint which has been modified and restore this on backtracking. This is called *trailing*. Note that, if part of a constraint is repeatedly modified, we need only save the old value once for each choicepoint.

To clarify this discussion, consider the incremental Gauss-Jordan solver. To allow constraints to be easily time stamped, primitive constraints are kept in an indexed sequence. Whenever a constraint is added to the solver it is added to the end of the sequence. When a choicepoint is set up, the index of the last constraint in the store, *last*, is placed on the backtrack stack and the trail associated with that element is initialised. Whenever a primitive constraint is added to the store it may cause earlier constraints to be modified. Constraints may be modified either by changing the coefficient, a, of a variable x to a', say, or by changing the constant, b, to b', say. Whenever constraint i is modified, if $i \leq last$, an entry of the form $\langle i, x, a \rangle$

or $\langle i, constant, b \rangle$ is added to the trail associated with the last choicepoint on the backtrack stack. However, if there is already an entry on the trail for that position, there is no need to add another entry as the value to be restored is already on the trail.

Recall the sum program from Example 10.3 and consider evaluation of the goal

```
sum(1,S), S=2.
```

Initially, both the backtrack stack and store are empty. The first choicepoint occurs when deciding with which rule to rewrite $sum(1, S)$. The first rule tried is sum(0,0). At this stage the current constraint store is empty, that is *true*, so the index of the last constraint in the store is 0. The call to save_store will push this on to the backtrack stack, together with an initially empty trail ([]), giving

$$\boxed{0 \mid []}$$

Next we process $1 = 0$. This returns *false*, causing evaluation to backtrack. The call to restore_store pops 0 and the associated empty trail from the backtrack stack. It then removes all constraints with index greater than 0 from the constraint store, leaving the empty store, *true*. As the trail is empty, the store has been restored.

We now try the next rule defining sum(1,S). This rule is

```
sum(N', N' + S')   :-   sum(N' - 1, S').
```

Again the current store is saved, giving the backtrack stack:

$$\boxed{0 \mid []}$$

Now the constraints $1 = N'$ and $S = N' + S'$ are processed by adding them to the constraint store. Next $sum(N' - 1, S')$ is evaluated. The first rule defining $sum(N' - 1, S')$ is sum(0,0). We must save the constraint store. This pushes the index of the last constraint in the store, 2, on to the backtrack stack. The backtrack stack and constraint store are now:

1: $N' = 1 \ \wedge$
2: $S = 1 + S'$

Note that we have explicitly written the index of the constraints in the store on the left.

Now the constraints $N' - 1 = 0$ and $S' = 0$ are processed. Processing $N' - 1 = 0$ does not change the store. Adding $S' = 0$ changes the store to

$$N' = 1 \wedge S = 1 \wedge S' = 0.$$

The constraint $S = 1 + S'$ has been modified to $S = 1$. Since the index of this constraint is 2, which is less than or equal to the index of the top entry on the backtrack stack, the associated trail must be modified to remember the old coefficient of S'. The backtrack stack and constraint store become

2	$[\langle 2, S', 1 \rangle]$
0	$[]$

1:   $N' = 1 \wedge$
2:   $S = 1 \wedge$
3:   $S' = 0.$

At this point, the call $sum(1, S)$ has been evaluated. Now the constraint $S = 2$ is added to the store. This causes evaluation to backtrack. The call to restore_store first pops the index 2 and the associated trail $\langle 2, S', 1 \rangle$ from the backtrack stack. Then all constraints with index greater than 2 are removed from the constraint store, leaving $N' = 1 \wedge S = 1$. Finally, the entries on the trail are traversed. In this case, the single entry is used to change the coefficient of S' from 0 back to 1 in the constraint with index 2. Thus, the backtrack stack and constraint store become:

0	$[]$

1:   $N' = 1 \wedge$
2:   $S = 1 + S'$

Subsequent evaluation will rewrite $sum(N' - 1, S')$ with the second rule and lead to an infinite derivation.

10.3.2   Semantic Backtracking

The combination of time stamping and trailing is a general technique for saving and restoring the constraint store. However, for particular constraint domains it may be possible to use approaches which do not explicitly store the changes made to the constraint store but, rather, store the high-level operations which have been performed on the store and undo these operations. Such approaches to backtracking are said to be *semantic*.

As an example of semantic backtracking, consider the incremental Gauss-Jordan algorithm yet again. When a new constraint is added, the only way the old constraints in the store can be affected is if the new constraint is used to eliminate a variable, x, say. We can undo the effect of this elimination if we remember the old coefficient of x in each of these constraints.

For instance, imagine that the constraint store, C, is:

$$1:   X = Y + 2Z + 4 \wedge$$
$$2:   U = 3Y + Z - 1 \wedge$$
$$3:   V = 3.$$

And suppose that we add the constraint $Y + 2V + X = 2$.

After we eliminate variables from the new constraint we obtain $2Y + 2Z = -8$. Now imagine that we use this constraint to eliminate Y. This results in the constraint store, C',

$$1: \quad X = Z \ \land$$
$$2: \quad U = -2Z - 13 \ \land$$
$$3: \quad V = 3 \ \land$$
$$4: \quad Y = -Z - 4.$$

To make it possible to undo the effect of eliminating Y from the old constraint C, we must remember the old coefficient of Y in each primitive constraint in C. This can be stored in a list of tuples consisting of the constraint index and the coefficient. For efficiency, constraints with a 0 coefficient are not placed in the list. Thus we must remember the list

$$[\langle 1, 1 \rangle, \langle 2, 3 \rangle].$$

Now imagine that we wish to undo the effect of adding $Y + 2V + X = 2$ to the store. We first undo the effect of using $Y = -Z - 4$ to eliminate Y from each of the old constraints. This is achieved by multiplying $Y + Z + 4$ by the original coefficient of Y and adding it to the right hand side of the equation. That is, the first equation becomes $X = Z + 1 \times (Y + Z + 4)$ which is $X = Y + 2Z + 4$, the second equation becomes $U = -2Z - 13 + 3 \times (Y + Z + 4)$ which is $U = 3Y + Z - 1$ and the third equation remains unchanged since the coefficient is 0. Finally, we remove the last constraint, $Y = -Z - 4$, from the store giving C as before:

$$1: \quad X = Y + 2Z + 4 \ \land$$
$$2: \quad U = 3Y + Z - 1 \ \land$$
$$3: \quad V = 3.$$

Thus, using only the coefficient list, we have been able to recompute C from C'.

From this example we can see that we can undo the effect of adding a primitive constraint c to a store C by remembering the coefficients of the variable c is used to eliminate. If c is redundant or leads to *false* we do not need to remember a coefficient list, as the old constraint remains unchanged.

The advantage of this particular semantic backtracking technique over trailing is that the size of the coefficient list is usually quite small and often requires less space than using a trail. The disadvantage is that restoring the store requires more computation, essentially performing an elimination in reverse, so restoration of the store using a trail is faster.

10.4 Implementing If-Then-Else, Once and Negation

So far we have restricted ourselves to "pure" constraint logic programs as introduced in Chapter 4. However in Chapters 7 and 9 we introduced three additional programming constructs for if-then-else, finding the first solution and negation. We now investigate how these are implemented in a CLP system.

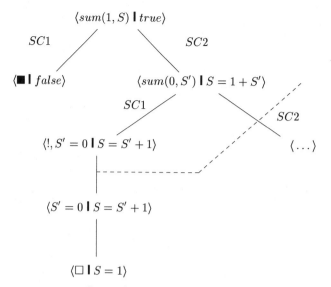

Figure 10.5 Simplified derivation tree for `sum(1,S)`.

In fact all three are implemented by using a single new language construct the *cut*, written !. The cut is used to prune derivations from the derivation tree and works by directing the system to remove previously set-up choicepoints. Cuts are very powerful, but should be used sparingly. We did not introduce them directly since in almost all cases the cut can be replaced by appropriate if-then-else, once or negative literals. In these cases it is preferable to use the appropriate high-level construct rather than the cut.

Example 10.4

Consider the improved `sum` program from Chapter 7.

```
sum(0,0).                                    (S7)
sum(N, N + S)   :-   N ≥ 1, sum(N - 1,S).   (S8)
```

For the mode of usage in which the first argument is fixed, we can rewrite the program using an if-then-else literal to:

```
sum(N, SS) :-
    (N = 0 ->
        SS = 0
    ;
        N ≥ 1, SS = N + S, sum(N - 1,S) ).
```

This program is equivalent to the following program which uses the cut.

```
sum(N, SS).   :-   N = 0, !, SS = 0              (SC1)
sum(N, SS)    :-   N ≥ 1, SS = N + S, sum(N - 1,S).   (SC2)
```

L is a user-defined constraint:
> **let** L be of form $p(s_1, \ldots, s_n)$
> **for** each $(p(t_1, \ldots, t_n) :\!- L_1, \ldots, L_k) \in defn_P(L)$ **do**
>> $i := \mathsf{save\_store}()$
>> **if** for some $1 \le j \le n$, $L_j \equiv\ !$ **then**
>>> **if** $\mathsf{inc\_backtrack}(s_1 = t_1, \ldots, s_n = t_n, L_1, \ldots, L_{j-1})$ **then**
>>>> $\mathsf{remove\_choicepoints}(i)$
>>>> **return** $\mathsf{inc\_backtrack}(L_{j+1}, \ldots, L_k, G_1)$
>>>
>>> **endif**
>>
>> **elseif** $\mathsf{inc\_backtrack}(s_1 = t_1, \ldots, s_n = t_n, L_1, \ldots, L_k, G_1) \equiv true$ **then**
>>> **return** $true$
>>
>> **endif**
>> $\mathsf{restore\_store}()$
>
> **endfor**
> **return** $false$

Figure 10.6 Modification of incremental goal solver for cut.

The cut indicates that, once it has been reached, there is no need to consider the other rule in the definition of sum. For the mode of usage we are interested in this is correct since the rules are *mutually exclusive*. That is, a fixed value of N cannot simultaneously satisfy the constraint $N = 0$ and the constraint $N \ge 1$. Thus, once we know that a particular value of N does satisfy $N = 0$, we know the second rule will fail with this value of N and, so, we can remove the choicepoint set up for sum.

Examining the derivation tree for the goal sum(1, S) shown in Figure 10.5 we can see the effect of the cut. When the cut literal is selected, every branch remaining to the right, up to the state just before the cut was introduced is pruned. These branches will never be explored in the evaluation. For this example, the second rule $SC2$ is never used to rewrite the state $\langle sum(0, S') \mathbin{|} S = S' + 1 \rangle$ because of the cut.

A cut commits the system to all choices which have been made since the parent goal was rewritten with the rule in which the cut appears. To understand the precise definition of the cut, consider the following program fragment.

> A   :- L_1, L_2, ... , L_i, !, L_{i+2}, ... , L_n.

Imagine that this rule has been used to rewrite the literal A_{call} in the current goal and that the literals L_1 to L_i have subsequently been successfully evaluated, perhaps with some backtracking local to their evaluation. When the cut is evaluated, the system commits to rewriting A_{call} with the rule in which the cut appears. That is to say, the choicepoint associated with the rewriting of A_{call} is removed and the remaining rules in the definition of A_{call} will not be considered. Furthermore, all choicepoints placed when evaluating L_1 to L_i are removed. If, on subsequent evaluation the derivation fails, the system will backtrack to choicepoints constructed before A_{call} was rewritten.

It is quite simple to extend the incremental backtracking goal solver of Figure 10.4 to handle cuts. The modification to the case for evaluating a user-defined constraint is shown in Figure 10.6. For simplicity, we assume there is, at most, one cut in a rule.

Since we need to remove choicepoints when a cut is encountered, we must modify save_store so that it returns an index i and provide a function remove_choicepoints(i) which removes all stores on the backtrack stack that have index i or greater.

Example 10.5

Consider the execution of the goal h(X) using the program:

h(X)	:- X $\geq$ 0, p(X), q(X).	(*H*1)
h(4).		(*H*2)
p(X)	:- X $\leq$ 4, r(X), !.	(*P*1)
p(3).		(*P*2)
r(1).		(*R*1)
r(2).		(*R*2)
q(2).		(*Q*1)
q(3).		(*Q*2)

The simplified derivation tree is shown in Figure 10.7. Execution proceeds by calling inc_backtrack to evaluate $h(X)$. This saves the store *true* with index 1. After collecting the constraint $X \geq 0$, inc_backtrack is called to evaluate "$p(X), q(X)$." The store $X \geq 0$ is saved with index 2. Since the rule $P1$ includes a cut, the literals before the cut "$X \leq 4, r(X)$" are evaluated first. The constraint $X \leq 4$ is collected and subsequent evaluation of $r(X)$ saves the store $X \geq 0 \wedge X \leq 4$ on the stack with index 3. The rule $R1$ succeeds, so the store becomes $X \geq 0 \wedge X \leq 4 \wedge X = 1$, which is simplified to $X = 1$ in the figure. Thus, the call to inc_backtrack to evaluate $r(X)$ returns *true* and so in turn, the call to evaluate "$X \leq 4, r(X)$" returns *true*. Since the cut has been reached, remove_choicepoints(2) is called. This pops those stores with index greater than or equal to 2 off the backtrack stack. Thus the stack will be left with only one item, the store *true* with index 1. Now the remainder of the goal, the literal $q(X)$, is evaluated. This saves the store $X = 1$ with index 2, and then fails using rule $Q1$. Evaluation restores the store to $X = 1$ and tries rule $Q2$ which also fails. Hence, the call to inc_backtrack to evaluate $q(X)$ returns *false*, and so the call to evaluate "$X \geq 0, p(X), q(X)$" returns *false*. The store is restored to *true* (since we are within the call to inc_backtrack to evaluate $h(X)$) and the second rule for h is tried which gives the answer $X = 4$. Note that, because of the cut, the rules $P2$ and $R2$ were not tried.

Using meta-level programming, it is straightforward to define negation, if-then-else and once in terms of cut. The simplest is the definition of once. It is

```
once(G) :- call(G), !.
```

The effect is as follows. The goal G is evaluated and if an answer is found, this answer is committed to.

The definition of not is also reasonably simple:

```
not(G) :- call(G), !, fail.
not(G).
```

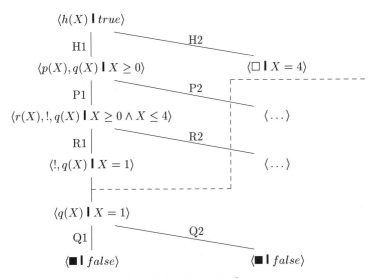

Figure 10.7   Simplified derivation tree for `h(X)`.

The effect is as follows. The goal G will be executed and, if an answer is found, the first rule will be committed to and then it will fail. If G finitely fails, the second rule, which always succeeds, will be used.

Example 10.6

Consider evaluation of the goal `not(a=b)`. Evaluation of the negative literal uses the first rule, calling the goal `a=b`. This fails, so the second rule for `not` is tried, which will succeed.

Now consider evaluation of the goal `not(a=a)`. Evaluation of the negative literal initially tries the first rule, calling the goal `a=a`. This succeeds, so evaluation of the cut removes the choicepoint corresponding to the call `not(a=a)`, in effect committing to the first rule. Now the literal `fail` is evaluated. Thus the first rule fails, and, since the cut has been evaluated, the second rule is not tried. Thus, evaluation of `not(a=a)` fails.

The definition of if-then-else is slightly more complex, but still reasonably intuitive.

```
(G1 -> G2 ; G3) :- call(G1), !, call(G2).
(G1 -> G2 ; G3) :- call(G3).
```

The effect is, if $G1$ has a solution, then the first rule and this particular solution to $G1$ are committed to and $G2$ is executed. Otherwise, if $G1$ finitely fails, the second rule is tried and $G3$ is executed.

The reader is encouraged to verify that these definitions, together with the incremental backtracking goal solver augmented to handle cuts, produce the same behaviour as the conceptual definition of the if-then-else, once and negation constructs given earlier.

10.5   Optimization

Another important language construct provided by most CLP languages is optimization. The idealized optimization construct we have used in this text is `minimize(G, E)`. Like other optimization constructs, `minimize` can be implemented in a number of different ways, no one of which is uniformly more efficient. For this reason many CLP systems provide more than one minimization construct, with different constructs corresponding to different implementation techniques. Here we will discuss two of the simplest methods for implementing `minimize`.

Consider the evaluation of `minimize(G, E)` in the context of constraint store C. Implementation of `minimize` can be split into three parts.

The first part is a domain specific optimization procedure, minimize_store(E). This minimizes the value of the expression E with respect to the current constraint store. For real linear constraints a natural choice is to use the simplex algorithm for optimization and to give a run-time error if the expression to be minimized is not linear. For finite constraint domains the expression is usually required to be fixed by the store, so no "real" optimization is necessary.

The second part of the implementation is an algorithm to search through the derivation tree of the state $\langle G \mid C \rangle$ in order to find the minimum value, m, of the expression E. This part makes use of minimize_store(E) whenever an "interesting" answer to $\langle G \mid C \rangle$ is found.

The final part of the implementation generates the answers to `minimize(G, E)` given that the minimum value, m, of E is known. This may be done by simply returning the answers to the state $\langle E = m, G \mid C \rangle$.

Different approaches to minimization primarily differ in the way in which they search through the derivation tree to find the minimum value. Here we will give two of the simplest approaches. Each corresponds to one of the approaches to finding the optimal solution to an arithmetic CSP integer which were discussed in Section 3.6.

The simplest approach is analogous to retry_int_opt. The idea is to search for an answer, C_1, to the state $\langle G \mid C \rangle$ and then use the domain specific optimization procedure to find the minimal value m of E with respect to C_1. Now we search for an answer to the state $\langle G \mid C \wedge E < m \rangle$. If an answer is found, we update the value of m and repeat the process. If there is no answer, then the minimum value has been found.

It is straightforward to modify the incremental goal solver of Figure 10.4 so as to handle minimization literals using this "retrying" technique. We simply add another case to the case statement for minimization literals. The code for this is shown in Figure 10.8.

Recall the program for the butterfly combination of call options given in Section 5.2. Let us examine how the goal

```
minimize( butterfly(S,P), -P).
```

is evaluated. The simplified derivation tree for the goal `butterfly(S, P)` is shown

> L is a minimization literal:
>   **let** L be of form $minimize(G, E)$
> $i :=$ save_store()
> $m := +\infty$
>   **while** inc_backtrack($E < m, G$) $\not\equiv false$ **do**
> $m :=$ minimize_store(E)
>   remove_choicepoints($i + 1$)
>   restore_store()
> $i :=$ save_store()
>   **endwhile**
>   restore_store()
>   **return** inc_backtrack($(E = m, G, G_1)$)

Figure 10.8 Modification of incremental goal solver for retry optimization.

in Figure 10.9. For brevity the goals G_1, G_2 and G_3 are defined to be

$$G_1 = call\_option(1, 100, 500, S, P1), call\_option(-1, 200, 300, S, P2),$$
$$call\_option(1, 400, 100, S, P3)$$
$$G_2 = call\_option(-1, 200, 300, S, P2), call\_option(1, 400, 100, S, P3)$$
$$G_3 = call\_option(1, 400, 100, S, P3).$$

Execution of the goal `minimize(butterfly(S,P), -P)` begins by calling inc_backtrack($-P < +\infty, butterfly(S, P)$). This discovers the first answer,

$$-P < +\infty \wedge P = -100 \wedge 0 \le S \le 1.$$

Minimizing $-P$ with respect to this store gives $m = 100$. The store is restored to the state it was before evaluating "$-P < +\infty, butterfly(S, P)$" and inc_backtrack is called to evaluate "$-P < 100, butterfly(S, P).$" The first answer found (corresponding to the second answer in the derivation tree for `butterfly(S, P)`) is

$$-P < 100 \wedge P = 100S - 200 \wedge 1 \le S \le 3.$$

Calling minimize_store to minimize $-P$ with respect to this store gives $m = -100$. Again the store is restored and now "$-P < -100, butterfly(S, P)$" is evaluated. This fails. Hence, $m = -100$ is the minimum value for $-P$. Execution proceeds by calling inc_backtrack($-P = -100, butterfly(S, P)$). This returns the first answer $P = 100 \wedge S = 3$ (corresponding to the derivation in Figure 10.9 with answer $P = 100S - 200 \wedge 1 \le S \le 3$). A second identical answer (corresponding to the derivation in Figure 10.9 with answer $P = -100S + 400 \wedge 3 \le S \le 5$) also exists.

Notice that, in calculating the minimal value for $-P$, we repeatedly (in effect), searched the derivation tree for `butterfly(S,P)`. Overall the execution visited states corresponding to those shown in the tree in Figure 10.9 approximately 25 times.

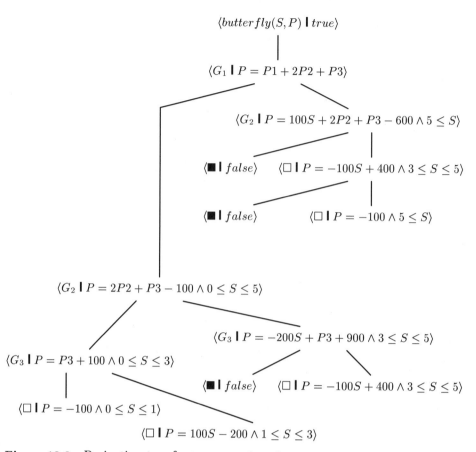

Figure 10.9   Derivation tree for `butterfly(S, P)`.

The second approach to searching through the derivation tree for G in order to find the minimal value of E is analogous to the approach used in backtrack_int_opt. Only a single backtracking search of the derivation tree for G is made, and the minimal value for E found so far is stored in m. Whenever we find a new solution we test whether it is better than the previous one and, if so, update m.

The modification to the incremental goal solver of Figure 10.4 to handle minimization by backtracking is shown in Figure 10.10. It adds two cases to the case statement, one to handle minimization subgoals and one to handle *catch* subgoals. The case for minimization subgoals initializes m and sets up a dummy subgoal $catch(m, E)$ which is reached after a solution to G is found. The case for *catch* subgoals always fails, but updates m to hold the minimum value found so far.[1]

---

1. Unfortunately this program will not work for nested minimization subgoals since m is being used as a global variable. To fix this problem we could use a stack of ms.

L is a minimization subgoal:
    let L be of the form $minimize(G, E)$
    $i :=$ save_store()
    $m := +\infty$
    inc_backtrack$(G, catch(m, E))$
    restore_store(i)
    return inc_backtrack$((E = m, G, G'))$
L is a catch subgoal:
    let L be of the form $catch(m, E)$
    if $isolv(E < m) \not\equiv false$ **then**
        $m :=$ minimize_store(E)
    endif
    return $false$

Figure 10.10 Modification of incremental goal solver for backtracking optimization.

Execution of the goal `minimize( butterfly(S,P), -P)` begins by storing the solver state, initializing m to $+\infty$ and calling inc_backtrack to evaluate "$butterfly(S, P), catch(m, -P)$". Evaluation traverses the leftmost branch finding the answer $P = -100 \wedge 0 \leq S \leq 1$ to `butterfly(S,P)`. Now the *catch* subgoal is evaluated. This adds the constraint $-P < +\infty$ which succeeds and so m is set to 100. Execution continues by backtracking to find the next answer. This is $P = 100S - 200 \wedge 1 \leq S \leq 3$. Again the *catch* subgoal is reached. Adding the constraint $-P < 100$ succeeds so m is set to -100. The next time the *catch* subgoal is reached the store is $P = -100S + 400 \wedge 3 \leq S \leq 5$. Adding the constraint $-P < -100$ fails, so m is not updated. Similar behaviour occurs with the next answer found, $P = -100 \wedge S \geq 5$. After the entire derivation tree for `butterfly(S,P)` has been explored, m has been calculated to be -100. Execution proceeds as before using inc_backtrack$(-P = -100, butterfly(S, P))$. In this case only 13 visits are made to states corresponding to those shown in Figure 10.9, as opposed to retry optimization which made 25 visits.

An even better method for finding the minimum value of the expression E, is to modify the above approach so that it adds the constraint $E < m$ to the constraint store whenever a call to restore_store occurs in the execution of the call inc_backtrack$(G, catch(m, E))$. For simplicity, we omit this definition.

10.6   Other Incremental Constraint Solvers

In Section 10.2 we saw the importance of incremental constraint solving in the case of linear arithmetic equations. The same arguments hold for any constraint solver used within a CLP system. In this section we show how the tree constraint solver, tree_solve, of Section 1.4 and the bounds consistency solver, bounds_solve, of Section 3.4 can be made incremental.

10.6.1   Incremental Tree Constraint Solving

We first look at how to define an incremental solver for tree constraints. As for the incremental Gauss-Jordan solver, the key is to use a solved form representation of the primitive constraints encountered so far. Recall that execution of the tree constraint solver algorithm, unify, from Section 1.4 returns either *false* or a tree constraint in solved form

$$x_1 = t_1 \wedge \ldots \wedge x_n = t_n,$$

where each x_i is a distinct variable not occurring in any of the t_i.

Given the solved form $x_1 = t_1 \wedge \ldots \wedge x_n = t_n$, we can use the function eliminate defined in Figure 10.3 to simplify another tree constraint C by eliminating the variables $x_1, \ldots, x_n$ from C. Although eliminate was originally defined for eliminating real variables using linear equations, the same process can be used for term equations in solved form. The function eliminate replaces every occurrence of a variable x_i in C by the term t_i. For instance, if S is the solved form $X = f(V) \wedge Y = V$ and C is $f(W) = f(X) \wedge X = f(a)$, then eliminate$(C, S)$ is

$$f(W) = f(f(V)) \wedge f(V) = f(a).$$

Elimination allows us to compute the solved form incrementally. Imagine that we first encounter the equation c_0 which is $g(X, Y) = g(f(V), V)$. We compute the solved form, S_0, of c_0 which is $X = f(V) \wedge Y = V$. Suppose we now encounter the constraint c_1, $g(W, X) = g(X, f(a))$. To compute the solved form of $c_0 \wedge c_1$, we first use S_0 to eliminate X and Y from c_1. That is, we compute eliminate(c_1, S_0). This gives c_2 which is $g(W, f(V)) = g(f(V), f(a))$. We now compute the solved form, S_1, of c_2 which is $W = f(a) \wedge V = a$. We can use S_1 to eliminate V from S_0, giving S_2 which is $X = f(a) \wedge Y = a$. The solved form of $c_0 \wedge c_1$ is therefore simply $S_2 \wedge S_1$.

We can see that this is correct by understanding the whole process in terms of how unify operates on the constraint

$$g(X, Y) = g(f(V), V) \wedge g(W, X) = g(X, f(a)).$$

Essentially, what is happening is that we are choosing to process all of the equations originating from c_0 before processing the equation c_1. We are also delaying the elimination of variables in c_1 until we start processing c_1.

The following incremental tree constraint solving algorithm is based on this idea. We first use the current solved form S to eliminate variables from the new primitive constraint c. Then we compute the solved form S_1 of c. If c is unsatisfiable, the whole system is unsatisfiable, otherwise the new solved form is the result of conjoining S_1 with S after using S_1 to eliminate the new non-parametric variables from S.

> S is a global variable containing the solved form of the current tree constraint;
> c is a term equation;
> and S_1 is a solved form term constraint.
>
>
> inc_tree_solve(c)
> $c := \text{eliminate}(c, S)$
> $S_1 := \text{unify}(c)$
>   **if** $S_1 \equiv false$ **then return** *false* **endif**
> $S := \text{eliminate}(S, S_1) \wedge S_1$
>   **return** *true*

Figure 10.11   Incremental tree solving algorithm.

Algorithm 10.4: Incremental tree constraint solver
INPUT: A term equation c.
GLOBALS: S is a solved form tree constraint.
OUTPUT: Returns *true* or *false* indicating whether $S \wedge c$ is satisfiable or not. Updates the global constraint store S.
METHOD: The algorithm is given in Figure 10.11. $\square$

Example 10.7
Let us re-examine the successful derivation for the goal `append([a],[b,c],L)` shown in Figure 6.4 in Section 6.2. The constraints that are collected in this derivation are

$$[a] = [F|R], \quad [b,c] = Y, \quad L = [F|Z], \quad R = [], \quad Y = Y', \quad Z = Y'.$$

After collecting the first two constraints, the constraint store, S, is

$$F = a \wedge R = [] \wedge Y = [b,c].$$

The next constraint encountered, c, is $L = [F|Z]$. A call to inc_tree_solve(c) is made. First, the variables from the current constraint store S are eliminated from c, giving $L = [a|Z]$. The call to unify returns S_1, the solved form of this constraint. This is simply $L = [a|Z]$ since it was already in solved form. Finally, S_1 is used to eliminate the non-parametric variables in S_1 from S (but there are no occurrences) and S is updated by conjoining it with S_1. This gives the new store

$$F = a \wedge R = [] \wedge Y = [b,c] \wedge L = [a|Z].$$

After processing $R = []$ and $Y = Y'$, the constraint store is

$$F = a \wedge R = [] \wedge Y = [b,c] \wedge L = [a|Z] \wedge Y' = [b,c].$$

The last constraint added to the store is $Z = Y'$. After eliminating variables using the current constraint store we obtain $Z = [b,c]$. This is already in solved form. It is now used to eliminate occurrences of Z from the constraint store and then conjoined with the store, giving

$$F = a \wedge R = [\,] \wedge Y = [b, c] \wedge L = [a, b, c] \wedge Y' = [b, c] \wedge Z = [b, c].$$

The incremental tree constraint solvers used in CLP systems do not really manipulate equations and compute solved forms as we have described here. Instead terms are represented by dynamic data structures. Variables are represented by a single memory cell which is a pointer. An unconstrained variable is represented by a self-pointer. If the variable is equated to some tree (in solved form), the variable cell is set to point to the memory cell of the root of the tree. Trees with n children are represented by $n + 1$ contiguous memory cells. The first cell contains the tree constructor and the number of children, n, while the remaining cells hold pointers to the n child trees. A common optimization is to store a sub-tree with no children in the cell rather than to use a pointer to the sub-tree.

For instance, imagine we encounter the term equation $f(a, W) = f(a, V)$. The terms $f(a, W)$ and $f(a, V)$ are represented by:

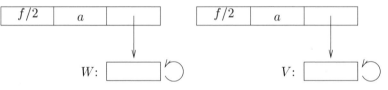

Representing terms and variables dynamically with pointers allows elimination of a variable to be very efficient, since it requires only one pointer change. When we solve $f(a, W) = f(a, V)$, the tree solving algorithm checks that the topmost tree constructors are the same and have the same number of children, and then iteratively unifies the arguments of the two terms. The two first arguments are already identical so no change happens. To equate the second arguments, the algorithm points the cell for V at W, in effect replacing V by W everywhere it occurs. Note that the solving algorithm could just as well have chosen to point W at V. This gives

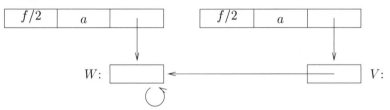

which represents the solved form $V = W$. Imagine we now encounter the equation $g(g(a)) = g(V)$. We first add the cell representation of the terms $g(g(a))$ and $g(V)$. This gives:

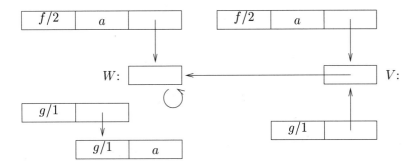

Note that, since V has only a single node representing it, elimination of V from $g(V)$ has been done automatically. That is because, whenever we access the node for V, we will follow the link to W. If we now solve $g(g(a)) = g(V)$, after checking that the top most tree constructors are the same, we try to equate $g(a)$ and V. Following the link from V to W, we set this to point at $g(a)$, giving

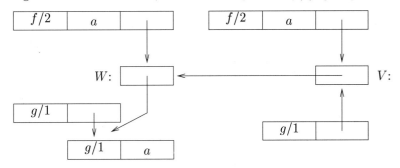

This represents the solved form $V = g(a) \wedge W = g(a)$.

Many real-world CLP systems employ an incorrect solver. The reason is that when a constraint of the form $x = t$ is encountered in the tree solver, where x is a variable, it is costly to test whether x occurs in t. Even using the pointer representation, the simple tree solving algorithm is still quadratic. For this reason CLP solvers usually omit this *occurs check*. This is, in effect, omitting case (5) in the algorithm for unify shown in Figure 1.7. This means, using the pointer representation, the solver has linear time complexity. Even more important, the most common form of unification, in which a new variable is equated to a term, requires only a single pointer to change.

Unfortunately, simplification employed in CLP systems typically removes all hints that a missing occurs check may have caused a problem. For example, in a typical system the goal p with program

```
p    :-   Y = g(Y).
```

will execute by first building the structure shown on the left below and unification will erroneously succeed with the cells in the state shown on the right.

The system will return the answer *true*. Worse still, if the solver is applied to structures which include loops, the solver may execute forever. For example, this is likely to happen with the goal q and program

```
q  :-  Y = g(Y), Z = g(Z), Z = Y.
```

In practice however, few programs require the occurs check to execute correctly and therefore incorrectness of the constraint solver is rarely an issue.

10.6.2   Incremental Consistency Based Solvers

In Chapter 3 we examined constraint solving methods based on repeatedly using constraints to remove inconsistent values from a variable's domain and propagating these new domains to other constraints until no new inconsistent values in the domains are found. We now examine how we can make such consistency based solvers incremental. Thankfully, this is quite simple because propagation is essentially an incremental process

We give an incremental solver based on bounds consistency. It is a straightforward task to modify it to handle other forms of consistency methods.

Algorithm 10.5: Incremental bounds consistency solver
INPUT: A primitive integer constraint c.
GLOBALS: An integer constraint S, together with a range domain D assigning ranges to the variables in S and c.
OUTPUT: Returns *true*, *false* or *unknown* depending on the satisfiability of $S \wedge c$ and updates the global variables.
METHOD: The algorithm is shown in Figure 10.12. $\square$

Essentially, the incremental solver is a copy of the bounds consistency algorithm of Figure 3.13. The only difference is that when we add a new primitive constraint c this is the only element of the active set C_0. The process begins by first applying the consistency rules of c, and then continuing propagation in the normal manner. Note that, if c causes no propagation of information, that is, applying the propagation rules for c does not change the domain of any variable, the solver terminates immediately after adding c. Similar incremental consistency based solvers are employed in most CLP systems that solve finite domain constraints.

One slight complication when using an incremental consistency based solver, is the need to incrementally collect domain information. As new variables are encountered during a derivation, we need to define and collect their initial domain information. For instance, evaluation of the domain declaration X :: [4..8] will

$c, c_1, \ldots, c_n$ are primitive constraints;
S is a global variable holding the current constraint store;
D is a global variable holding the current domain;
D_1 is a domain;
C_0 is a set of primitive constraints;
and x is a variable.

inc_bounds_solv(c)
   $S := S \wedge c$
   let S be of form $c_1 \wedge \cdots \wedge c_n$
   $C_0 := \{c\}$
   while $C_0 \not\equiv \emptyset$ **do**
      choose $c \in C_0$
      $C_0 := C_0 \setminus \{c\}$
      $D_1 := $ bounds_consistent_primitive(c, D)
      if D_1 is a false domain **then return** *false* **endif**
      for $i := 1$ to n **do**
         if there exists $x \in vars(c_i)$ such that $D_1(x) \neq D(x)$ **then**
            $C_0 := C_0 \cup \{c_i\}$
         endif
      endfor
      $D := D_1$
   endwhile
   if D is a valuation domain **then**
      return $satisfiable(S, D)$
   else return *unknown*

Figure 10.12   An incremental finite domain propagation-based solver.

set the initial range for variable X. In effect, it must extend the domain D to map X to the set of values $D(X) = [4..8]$. If $D(X)$ is already defined, the declaration is equivalent to the constraint $4 \leq X \wedge X \leq 8$. If a variable is encountered in a finite domain constraint before it has had a domain declared, it is given a default (usually large) integer domain.

For example, executing the goal

```
X :: [4..8], Y :: [0..3], Z :: [2..2], X = Y + Z, Y ≠ Z.
```

first processes the domain declarations. By the time the first equation is processed, the global constraint store S is still *true* and the global domain D is given by

$$D(X) = [4..8], \quad D(Y) = [0..3], \quad D(Z) = [2..2].$$

Execution of the call to inc_bounds_solv to add $X = Y + Z$ proceeds as follows. S becomes $X = Y + Z$, and C_0 becomes $\{X = Y + Z\}$. $X = Y + Z$ is removed from C_0 and the procedure bounds_consistent_primitive evaluates the propagation rules for it, updating the global domain to

$$D(X) = [4..5], \quad D(Y) = [2..3], \quad D(Z) = [2..2].$$

Because the variable X has changed its range, the constraint $X = Y + Z$ is added to C_0. Again $X = Y + Z$ is removed from C_0, but, this time, its propagation rules cause no change in the domain. Since C_0 is empty, the **while** loop finishes and *unknown* is returned by the solver.

Next inc_bounds_solv$(Y \neq Z)$ is called. S becomes $X = Y + Z \wedge Y \neq Z$ and C_0 is $\{Y \neq Z\}$. $Y \neq Z$ is removed from C_0 and its propagation rules determine the new domain

$$D(X) = [4..5], \quad D(Y) = [3..3], \quad D(Z) = [2..2].$$

Since the range of Y has changed, both $X = Y + Z$ and $Y \neq Z$ are added to C_0. Removing $X = Y + Z$ from C_0 and applying its propagation rules modifies the domain to

$$D(X) = [5..5], \quad D(Y) = [3..3], \quad D(Z) = [2..2].$$

Since the domain of X has changed, $X = Y + Z$ is put back into C_0. In the remainder of the computation, $X = Y + Z$ and $Y \neq Z$ are re-examined but this does not change the domain. The call terminates with answer *true*, since the domain is a valuation domain which satisfies the constraints.

Note that, although it is possible to build an incremental *complete* consistency based solver, this is unlikely to be worthwhile. This is because the backtracking search that is part of the complete consistency based solver, effectively sets each variable to a single value. Any new constraint that does not agree with this assignment can potentially cause the undoing of this search. Since the backtracking search is usually the dominant part of the computation time for the complete consistency based solver there is little incrementality, since at every step most of the work may need to be redone. Rather, as we have seen, in the CLP paradigm it is the role of the programmer to explicitly invoke a complete backtracking search at the end of computation by calling a labelling predicate.

10.7   (*) Incremental Real Arithmetic Solving

We conclude the chapter by investigating how to build an incremental solver for arbitrary arithmetic constraints. This algorithm incorporates techniques from Gauss-Jordan elimination, the simplex algorithm and local propagation to give an efficient incremental constraint solver for arbitrary real arithmetic constraints. This algorithm, or closely related variants, is the basis for arithmetic constraint solving in many current CLP systems.

Our first step is to develop an incremental solver for linear inequalities. A key feature of the Gauss-Jordan algorithm which allowed it to be a easily modified into an incremental algorithm, is that it processes the constraints one at a time, transforming them into a solved form by using each constraint to eliminate a variable. The simplex satisfaction algorithm also uses variable elimination to transform constraints into a solved form, namely basic feasible solved form. This suggests that the simplex satisfaction algorithm might be a good basis for an incremental solver for arithmetic inequalities. As we shall see, this is correct—it is straightforward to modify the simplex algorithm to give an incremental solver for linear inequalities.

For the moment, we shall assume that the linear inequality c has been rewritten into an equality by adding a slack variable and that all variables are constrained to be non-negative. The constraint is to be added to the constraint store S, which is in basic feasible solved form. The first step is to use S to eliminate basic variables from c. We handle the case when all variables are eliminated in the obvious way.[2]

In the case when there are variables left, processing continues by adding an artificial variable, z, to c and then using the simplex algorithm to minimize z. If minimization results in an objective function with associated constant b_1 equal to 0, then the optimum value for z is 0 and so the store remains solvable after adding the constraint. The chief difficulty is removing the artificial variable from the basic feasible solved form, S_1, returned from the simplex algorithm. There are two cases. The first case is when z is a parameter. In this case we need only remove all occurrences of z. The second case is when z is a basic variable. That is, it occurs in an equation of the form $z = \sum_{j=1}^{m} a_j x_j + b$. Now, because the objective function is equal to z and has value 0 at the corresponding basic feasible solution, the constant b must also be 0. Therefore, we can choose any variable, x_J say, with a non-zero coefficient a_J and pivot on this constraint to make x_J basic and make z a parameter. Since b is 0, the resulting constraint will still be in basic feasible solved form. We can then eliminate z from this solved form. In essence the algorithm does this, though pivoting and elimination are performed in a single step. Note that, since the original constraint viewed as an equality was not redundant, some a_j must be non-zero.

Algorithm 10.6: Incremental simplex solver
INPUT: A linear arithmetic inequality c.
GLOBALS: A global linear arithmetic constraint S in basic feasible solved form.
OUTPUT: Returns *true* or *false* indicating whether $S \wedge c$ is satisfiable or not and updates the global variable S.
METHOD: The algorithm is given in Figure 10.13. All variables are implicitly restricted to be non-negative. $\square$

---

2. Note that if we only add equations which have been obtained from inequalities by adding distinct new slack variables, then variable elimination will always leave at least one variable—the new slack variable. However, it will prove useful to allow arbitrary equations.

c is a linear inequality written as an equality by means of a slack variable;
S is the global constraint store in basic feasible solved form;
$y, x_1, \dots, x_m, z$ are non-negative real variables;
$b, b_1, a_1, \dots, a_m, d_0, \dots, d_m$ are real constants;
e, f and f_1 are linear expressions;
c_1 and c_2 are linear equations;
and S_1 is a constraint in basic feasible solved form.

```
inc_simplex(c)
    c := eliminate(c, S)
    if c can be written in a form without variables then
        return eval(c)
    endif
    let c be of form b = ∑_{j=1}^m a_j x_j where b ≥ 0
    f := b − ∑_{j=1}^m a_j x_j
    c_1 := (z = b − ∑_{j=1}^m a_j x_j)
    ⟨Flag, S_1, f_1⟩ := simplex_opt(S ∧ c_1, f)
    let f_1 be of form b_1 + d_0 z + ∑_{j=1}^n d_j x_j
    if b_1 > 0 then return false endif
    if d_0 ≠ 0 then
        % artificial variable z is a parameter
        remove z from S_1
        S := S_1
    else
        % artificial variable z is not a parameter
        let c_2 be the constraint in S_1 in which z is basic
        let c_2 be of form z = ∑_{j=1}^m a'_j x_j
        remove c_2 from S_1
        choose J ∈ {1, …, m} such that a'_J ≠ 0
        e := ∑_{j=1, j≠J}^m (a'_j / a'_J) x_j
        S := eliminate(S_1, x_J = −e) ∧ x_J = −e
    endif
    return true
```

Figure 10.13   Incremental simplex.

Example 10.8

To understand how the incremental simplex algorithm works consider the constraints from problem $(P1)$ on page 65:

$$
\begin{array}{ccccccccc}
X & + & Y & & & & & = & 3 & \wedge \\
-X & - & 3Y & + & 2Z & + & T & = & 1 & \wedge
\end{array}
$$
$$
X \geq 0 \wedge Y \geq 0 \wedge Z \geq 0 \wedge T \geq 0.
$$

Initially the global constraint store, S, is set to *true*. The first call to inc_simplex adds the constraint $X + Y = 3$. This sets c_1 to $A = 3 - X - Y$ and f to $3 - X - Y$ where A is the name of the artificial variable. The function simplex_opt is called to solve the problem

minimize $3 - X - Y$ subject to

$$A = 3 - X - Y \land$$
$$X \geq 0 \land Y \geq 0 \land A \geq 0.$$

Either X or Y can be chosen as the entry variable since both have negative coefficients in the objective function. Suppose that X is chosen, then the exit variable must be A. After pivoting we obtain

minimize A subject to

$$X = 3 - A - Y \land$$
$$X \geq 0 \land Y \geq 0 \land A \geq 0.$$

As no variable in the objective function has a negative coefficient, we have reached the optimal solution. On return from simplex_opt, S_1 will be $X = 3 - A - Y$ and f_1 will be A. Rewriting f_1 to the form $0 + 0 \times X + 0 \times Y + 1 \times A$, it is clear that b_1 is 0 and d_0 is 1. Thus, all occurrences of A are removed from S_1, giving $X = 3 - Y$, and the global constraint store, S, is set to this value. The value *true* is returned indicating the store remains satisfiable.

Next inc_simplex is called with $-X - 3Y + 2Z + T = 1$. First, c is set to the result of using the constraint store, $X = 3 - Y$, to eliminate variables from the input constraint. Thus, c becomes $-2Y + 2Z + T = 4$. Now c_1 is set to $A = 4 + 2Y - 2Z - T$ and f to $4 + 2Y - 2Z - T$. The function simplex_opt is called to solve the problem

minimize $4 + 2Y - 2Z - T$ subject to

$$X = 3 - Y \qquad\qquad\qquad \land$$
$$A = 4 + 2Y - 2Z - T \quad \land$$
$$X \geq 0 \land Y \geq 0 \land Z \geq 0 \land T \geq 0 \land A \geq 0.$$

Either Z or T can be chosen as the entry variable since both have negative coefficients in the objective function. Suppose that T is chosen. The exit variable must be A. After pivoting we obtain

minimize A subject to

$$X = 3 - Y \qquad\qquad\qquad \land$$
$$T = 4 + 2Y - 2Z - A \quad \land$$
$$X \geq 0 \land Y \geq 0 \land Z \geq 0 \land T \geq 0 \land A \geq 0.$$

Since no variable in the objective function has a negative coefficient, simplex_opt terminates as the optimum has been reached. On return, S_1 is

$$X = 3 - Y \land T = 4 + 2Y - 2Z - A$$

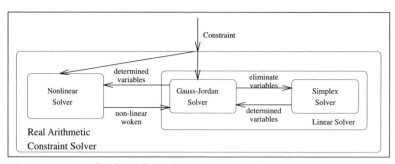

Figure 10.14   Real arithmetic constraint solver.

and f_1 will be A. Again, b_1 is 0 and d_0 is 1. Thus, all occurrences of A are removed from S_1, giving $X = 3 - Y \wedge T = 4 + 2Y - 2Z$, and the global constraint store, S, is set to this value. Finally, *true* is returned, indicating that the store remains satisfiable.

We are now in a position to build an incremental constraint solver for arbitrary arithmetic constraints. In essence, the constraint solver has three different sub-solvers: a variant of the incremental Gauss-Jordan solver for handling linear equalities, the incremental simplex algorithm for linear inequalities and a simple incomplete solver for handling nonlinears. The solver architecture is shown in Figure 10.14.

One difficulty when constructing the solver from the component solvers is that the incremental simplex algorithm cannot directly handle arbitrary linear inequalities, but only linear equations in which each variable is implicitly restricted to be non-negative. In our setting, all of the original variables appearing in the constraint have unrestricted range, it is only the slack variables introduced to change inequalities into equations which are implicitly restricted to take non-negative values.

To overcome this difficulty, the solver processes linear equations and inequalities as follows. First, if the constraint to be added, c, is a linear inequality, it is rewritten into linear equality by adding a slack variable. Next the solved form, S_{GJ}, associated with the incremental Gauss-Jordan solver is used to eliminate variables from c. Now if c contains only slack variables, and so all variables in c are implicitly restricted to be non-negative, it is sent to the incremental simplex solver. Otherwise, one of the non-slack variables in c is chosen for elimination which is performed as in the incremental Gauss-Jordan solver.

What this means is that, at any point in time, the constraint

$$\mathsf{eliminate}(S_{GJ}, S_{sim}) \wedge S_{sim}$$

is essentially in basic feasible solved form where S_{sim} is the solved form associated with the incremental simplex solver. The only difference to basic feasible solved form is, if a non-slack variable x is basic, the constant in the equation in which x is basic may not be non-negative. This is allowed since x is not restricted in the values it can take.

When a primitive constraint is first sent to the solver, it is classified as linear or nonlinear and sent to the appropriate sub-solver. Linear constraints are essentially handled as described above. Nonlinear constraints are handled very simply. Each nonlinear primitive constraint, c, is assumed to be satisfiable until sufficient variables in c are determined by S_{GJ} to make c linear. In this case, the now linear primitive constraint is passed to the linear equality solver. Thus the solver is complete for linear equalities and inequalities, but incomplete for nonlinear constraints.

To process nonlinear constraints efficiently we use a global variable S_{det} which contains the determined solved form (see Section 1.7) associated with the fixed variables of S_{GJ}. Whenever a new nonlinear primitive constraint is encountered, first the variables in S_{det} are eliminated. Then the primitive constraint is tested to see if it is "really" nonlinear. If it has become linear after elimination, it is processed as a linear constraint. Otherwise it is added to the set of nonlinear constraints C_{nl}. Whenever a constraint is added to S_{GJ} or S_{sim}, S_{det} is updated and C_{nl} is checked to see if any primitive constraints have become linear. An invariant of the solver is that all variables in S_{det} have been eliminated from C_{nl}, meaning that when S_{det} is changed we need only eliminate the new variables in S_{det} to C_{nl}. Thus in the algorithm we determine S_δ, the new equalities added to S_{det} because of the addition of the constraint. Then S_δ is added to S_{det} and variables in S_δ are eliminated from the nonlinear constraints. Those constraints that become linear are sent to the linear constraint solver. In a sense, local propagation is used to handle nonlinear constraints.

Algorithm 10.7: Incremental arithmetic constraint solver
INPUT: An arithmetic constraint c.
GLOBALS: A global constraint store S of form $S_{GJ} \land S_{sim} \land C_{nl}$ where S_{GJ} is the solved form of the linear equalities associated with the incremental Gauss-Jordan algorithm, S_{sim} is the solved form of the linear equalities with all slack variables and C_{nl} is the set of nonlinear constraints. In addition, there is a global variable S_{det} which is the determined solved form associated with the fixed variables of S_{GJ}.
OUTPUT: Returns *true*, *false* or *unknown* indicating whether c conjoined with the global constraint store S is satisfiable or not and updates the global variables.
METHOD: The algorithm is given in Figures 10.15 and 10.16. □

Example 10.9
To understand the operation of the incremental arithmetic constraint solver, consider the factorial program first introduced in Section 4.2:

```
fac(0, 1).
fac(N, N * F)  :-  N ≥ 1, fac(N - 1, F).
```

When evaluating the goal N ≥ 1, fac(N,F) the following constraints are added to the solver when constructing the first successful derivation:

$$N \geq 1, \quad N = N', \quad F = N' \times F', \quad N' \geq 1, \quad N' - 1 = 0, \quad F' = 1.$$

S_{GJ} and S_{sim} are conjunctions of linear equations;
C_{nl} is the set of nonlinear primitive constraints;
c is a primitive constraint;
x is a real variable;
e is an arithmetic expression;
and S_{det} and S_δ are determined solved forms.

inc_arith_solve(c)
    if c is an inequality **then**
        rewrite c into an equality by adding a new slack variable
    endif
    cases
    c is linear:
        if not add_linear(c) **then**
            return *false*
        endif
    c is not linear:
        if not add_nonlinear(c) **then**
            return *false*
        endif
    endcases
    if $C_{nl} \equiv \emptyset$ **then**
        return *true*
    else
        return *unknown*
    endif

add_linear(c)
    $c := $ eliminate(c,S_{GJ})
    if $vars(c) \equiv \emptyset$ **then**
        return eval(c)
    else if there is some $x \in vars(c)$
        which is not a slack variable **then**
        write c in the form $x = e$ where e does not involve x
        $S_{GJ} := $ eliminate($S_{GJ}, x = e$) $\land x = e$
    else % c contains only slack variables
        if not inc_simplex(c) **then**
            return *false*
        else
            $S_\delta := $ new_determined_sf(S_{sim})
            $S_{GJ} := $ eliminate(S_{GJ}, S_δ)
        endif
    endif
    $S_\delta := $ new_determined_sf(S_{GJ})
    $S_{det} := S_\delta \land S_{det}$
    return check_nonlinears(S_δ)

Figure 10.15 Incremental arithmetic constraint solving algorithm (part 1).

C_{nl} is the set of nonlinear primitive constraints;
c is a primitive constraint;
$x_1, \ldots, x_n$ are real variables;
$e_1, \ldots, e_n$ are arithmetic expressions;
S, S_{det} and S_δ are determined solved forms;
and N_{tmp} and W are sets of nonlinear primitive constraints.

add_nonlinear(c)
    $c := $ eliminate(c, S_{det})
    if c is not linear **then**
        $C_{nl} := C_{nl} \cup \{c\}$
        return *true*
    else
        return add_linear(c)
    endif

new_determined_sf(S)
    $S_\delta := true$
    let S be of the form $x_1 = e_1 \wedge \cdots \wedge x_n = e_n$
    for $i := 1$ to n **do**
        if $vars(e_i) \equiv \emptyset$ and $(x_i = e_i)$ not in S_{det} **then**
            $S_\delta := S_\delta \wedge x_i = e_i$
        endif
    endfor
    return S_δ

check_nonlinears(S_δ)
    $N_{tmp} := \emptyset$
    $W := \emptyset$
    for each $c \in C_{nl}$ **do**
        $c := $ eliminate(c, S_δ)
        if c is linear **then**
            $W := W \cup \{c\}$
        else
            $N_{tmp} := N_{tmp} \cup \{c\}$
        endif
    endfor
    $C_{nl} := N_{tmp}$
    for each $c \in W$ **do**
        if not add_linear(c) **then**
            return *false*
        endif
    endfor
    return *true*

Figure 10.16 Incremental arithmetic constraint solving algorithm (part 2).

We now describe how the incremental arithmetic constraint solver will process these constraints. Initially S_{GJ}, S_{sim} and S_{det} are each set to *true* and C_{nl} is set to $\emptyset$. When $N \geq 1$ is added, it is first rewritten to $N - S_1 = 1$ where S_1 is a slack variable. As this equation is linear, it is processed with add_linear. Since S_{GJ} is *true*, eliminating variables from it using S_{GJ} does not change it. As $N - S_1 = 1$ has a non-slack variable in it, namely N, it is processed by eliminating this variable. This sets S_{GJ} to $N = 1 + S_1$. Next new_determined_sf is called. Since there are no fixed variables, S_δ is set to *true*. Finally, check_nonlinears is called. This does very little since there are no fixed variables and no nonlinear constraints. The constraint solver returns *true*.

Now $N = N'$ is added. Again, since this equation is linear, it is processed with add_linear. Eliminating variables from it using S_{GJ} gives $1 + S_1 = N'$. As $1 + S_1 = N'$ has a non-slack variable in it, namely N', it is processed by eliminating this variable. This sets S_{GJ} to $N = 1 + S_1 \wedge N' = 1 + S_1$. Finally, new_determined_sf and check_nonlinears are called. Again, they do very little since there are no fixed variables and no nonlinear constraints. The constraint solver returns *true*.

Next $F = N' \times F'$ is encountered. This is nonlinear, so add_nonlinear is called. Eliminating variables in S_{det}, since S_{det} is *true*, does not make $F = N' \times F'$ linear, and so the constraint is added to C_{nl}. This time, the constraint solver returns *unknown* as there are now nonlinears.

Now $N' \geq 1$ is added. It is first rewritten to $N' - S_2 = 1$ where S_2 is a slack variable. As this equation is linear, it is processed with add_linear. Eliminating variables from it using S_{GJ} gives $1 + S_1 - S_2 = 1$. Since all variables in this equation are slack, it is processed by calling inc_simplex. After some computation this will set S_{sim} to $S_1 = S_2$. Finally, new_determined_sf and check_nonlinears are called. They do very little since there are no fixed variables in either S_{sim} or S_{GJ}. Again the constraint solver returns *unknown*.

Next $N' - 1 = 0$ is added. As it is linear, it is processed with add_linear. Eliminating variables from it using S_{GJ} gives $S_1 = 0$. This involves only slack variables so inc_simplex is called. This sets S_{sim} to $S_1 = 0 \wedge S_2 = 0$. Next new_determined_sf(S_{sim}) is called, returning $S_1 = 0 \wedge S_2 = 0$. Using this to eliminate variables from S_{GJ} gives $N = 1 \wedge N' = 1$. Now new_determined_sf(S_{GJ}) is called, returning $N = 1 \wedge N' = 1$. Both S_{det} and S_δ are set to $N = 1 \wedge N' = 1$ and check_nonlinears is called. Using S_δ to eliminate variables from $F = N' \times F'$ gives the linear constraint $F = 1 \times F'$, so the constraint is removed from C_{nl} and processed with a recursive call to add_linear. It is unchanged by eliminating variables from it using S_{GJ}. As it has non-slack variables, namely F and F', one of these is arbitrarily chosen for elimination, say F. This sets S_{GJ} to $N = 1 \wedge N' = 1 \wedge F = F'$. Now, new_determined_sf and check_nonlinears are called. This time they change nothing since there are no new fixed variables and no nonlinear constraints. After returning from the nested calls, the constraint solver will return *true* as now there are no nonlinears.

Note how, after adding the constraint $S_1 = 0$ to S_{sim}, we needed to eliminate S_1 and S_2 from S_{GJ} to discover that N and N' are now fixed.

Finally the constraint $F' = 1$ is added. This proceeds in the obvious way. As it is linear, it is processed by add_linear. Elimination leaves it unchanged, and the non-slack variable F' is chosen for elimination. This sets S_{GJ} to

$$N = 1 \wedge N' = 1 \wedge F = 1 \wedge F' = 1.$$

Now new_determined_sf is called, setting S_δ to $F = 1 \wedge F' = 1$. Then S_{det} is set to $N = 1 \wedge N' = 1 \wedge F = 1 \wedge F' = 1$ and check_nonlinears is called. As there are no nonlinear constraints this has no effect. The constraint solver returns *true*.

10.8 Summary

In this chapter we have considered the implementation of CLP languages. This can be viewed as a variant of the backtracking algorithm given in Chapter 3 for solving CSPs and essentially performs a depth-first search through a goal's derivation tree.

One of the keys to the efficient implementation of CLP languages is the use of incremental constraint solvers. Incremental constraint solvers efficiently answer the sequence of satisfaction problems that arise in a CLP derivation. We gave incremental algorithms for Gauss-Jordan elimination, tree constraint solving and bounds consistency.

A consequence of incremental constraint solving is the need to save a global constraint store at a choicepoint and to restore it when backtracking to that choicepoint. This can be done efficiently by using time stamping and trailing. Another technique is semantic backtracking.

Constraint logic programs may also contain constructs for minimization, if-then-else, finding the first solution and negation. We showed how the last three of these constructs can be implemented using the cut, a low level search construct which prunes branches from the derivation tree. Minimization can be implemented in a number of ways. We gave two possible extensions to the backtracking goal solver for supporting minimization.

10.9 Exercises

10.1. Execute the goal delete([a,b], X, R) using simple_backtrack and inc_backtrack to find the first solution. Compare the number of steps in the **while** loop of unify. Recall that the predicate delete is defined by

```
delete([X | Xs], X, Xs).
delete([X | Xs], Y, [X | R]) :- delete(Xs, Y, R).
```

10.2. (*) Give an incremental algorithm for local propagation.

10.3. Given the program

```
p(N, P, P) :- N = 0.
p(N, P, Q) :- p(N-1, 2*P + Q, Q - P).
```

find the first answer to the goal p(2,X,Y) using inc_backtrack and trailing. When choosing a variable to eliminate from an equation, always select the oldest, that is to say, the variable first introduced into the store.

Repeat this evaluation but now use semantic backtracking. Compare the amount of information placed on the backtrack stack.

Perform the comparison again, but this time choose to eliminate the youngest variable from each equation.

10.4. Give an algorithm for semantic backtracking based on the example in Section 10.3. Illustrate its use with the program from Example 10.3 and the goal sum(1,S), S=2.

10.5. Execute the goals max(4, 3, M) and max(3, 4, M) using inc_backtrack and the program:

```
max(X, Y, X) :- X ≥ Y, !.
max(X, Y, Y).
```

The predicate max(X,Y,Z) is meant to hold if Z is the maximum of X and Y. Now try the goal max(4, 3, 3). Is this the answer you expected? Modify the program (without using if-then-else) so that the expected answer occurs.

10.6. (*) Evaluate the execution of the goal

```
L = dl([a,b|T], T), dl_append(L, L, R)
```

for the program

```
dl_append(dl(H1,T1), dl(H2,T2), dl(H3,T3)) :-
    H3 = T3, T1 = H1, T3 = T2.
```

with and without the occurs check.

10.7. Give an example showing that the tree constraint solver without the *occurs check* is not well-behaved.

10.8. (*) Does the incremental arithmetic solver find all fixed variables? [Hint: consider what happens if the constraints $X \geq 2$ and $X \leq 2$ are added to the solver. Consider how the incremental simplex algorithm could be modified to find more fixed variables.]

10.9. (*) Extend the incremental arithmetic solver to handle disequations, that is arithmetic constraints of the form $s \neq t$, by delaying evaluation of such constraints until all variables in s and t are fixed. Explain how you can now handle strict inequalities, that is arithmetic constraints of the form $s < t$ and $s > t$. Is the solver complete? [Hint: consider your answer to the above question.]

10.10 Notes

Implementation techniques for CLP languages are based on those for Prolog. In particular, most Prolog systems use the same basic evaluation strategy and trail information to allow backtracking. The constraint solving algorithm in Prolog is an incremental tree constraint solver. The efficient implementation using pointers was first used in the WAM [142, 5].

The incremental arithmetic constraint solving algorithm given here is a variant of the algorithm used in one of the earliest CLP languages, $CLP(\mathcal{R})$ [75]. Similar algorithms are used in other CLP languages and constraint solving toolkits. The earliest CLP languages used time stamping and trailing to efficient implement backtracking, see for example $CLP(\mathcal{R})$ [75]. The term *semantic backtracking* is due to Van Hentenryck and Ramachandran who use it in an implementation of $CLP(\Re_{Lin})$ [137]. They also compare it to time stamping and trailing. Recent CLP systems use a revised simplex method and semantic backtracking to implement a backtrackable incremental linear arithmetic solver (see for example [110]).

One important issue arising in the implementation of linear arithmetic constraint solvers is representation of numbers. Two common approaches are infinite precision rationals and (double-precision) floating point numbers. The advantage of rationals is that there is no possibility of numerical inaccuracy. Since decisions about constraint satisfiability may be in error because of inaccuracies caused by floating point roundoff, the problem of precision is important, as it may be completely invisible to the user if the solver erroneously answers *false* for a satisfiable constraint.

Unfortunately, rational numbers are difficult to implement efficiently and can become too large for efficient computation even for small programs and goals. Nor do they allow the use of trigonometric functions without introducing the possibility of inaccuracy in representation. This means that rational number based systems cannot handle some kinds of programs (for example, the mortgage program of Section 5.3). An alternative approach is to use finite domains with floating point boundaries to represent ranges of real numbers. This was suggested by Cleary [31] and Hyvönen [67]. For more discussion see the notes at the end of Chapter 3. Its first use in CLP languages was in BNR Prolog discussed in [98, 99]. There is also some overhead in this method, but it has the advantage of being safe and reasonably efficient.

In this book we defined the constructs for negation, if-then-else and once directly, and then showed how they can be implemented using the cut. Usually the cut is introduced first and these constructs are defined in terms of it. However, almost all uses of the cut can be replaced by one of these three constructs, and since they are conceptually simpler than the cut, we chose to introduce them first. The cut was included in the first Prolog implementation and gets its name from first-order resolution.

III   Other Constraint Programming Languages

11 Constraint Databases

In this chapter we investigate another way of viewing constraint logic programs. Databases allow users to store data, such as names and addresses, and then find data which satisfies a query, for example, finding all of the people living in a particular suburb. We can also think of a constraint logic program as a kind of database, called a *constraint database*.

However, the evaluation mechanism for CLP is not well suited to database applications. Usually when querying a database, the user wishes to find *all* answers to the query at once, rather than laboriously backtracking through each answer and asking for another. For this reason, viewing constraint logic programs as constraint databases leads to a different execution strategy, so called *bottom-up* evaluation, which is closer to standard database evaluation techniques.

Constraint databases are very powerful. They extend relational, deductive and spatial databases and have several advantages over these more traditional types of databases. Throughout this book we have seen how we can use constraints to build simple models of even quite complex relations. In the same way constraints allow complex data to be modelled succinctly using constraint databases. Another advantage of constraints is that different types of data, for example, spatial, temporal and relational data, can all be manipulated using the same uniform mechanism—constraints.

11.1 Modelling with Constraint Databases

In this section we illustrate how simple CLP programs, called *constraint databases*, can be used to model applications which are traditionally handled using databases.

In Section 5.2 we saw how to model a genealogical database using CLP.

Example 11.1
The database contains two relations. The father(X, Y) predicate holds when X is the father of Y and similarly the mother(X, Y) predicate holds when X is the mother of Y. The database consists of the facts:

```
father(jim,edward).              mother(maggy,fi).
father(jim,maggy).               mother(fi,lillian).
father(edward,peter).
father(edward,helen).
father(edward,kitty).
father(bill,fi).
```

Using rules it was simple to express a variety of queries. For instance, the following rules defined the constraint parent(X,Y) to hold when X is a parent of Y.

```
parent(X,Y) :- father(X,Y).
parent(X,Y) :- mother(X,Y).
```

We will now look at two rather more interesting applications. Constraint databases allow the natural expression of spatial information using arithmetic constraints to model shapes.

Example 11.2

George and Rosemary have recently purchased a potential gold mine site. It is shown on the map in Figure 11.1. The areas delineated by the continuous lines show the expected location of the gold ore seams under the ground. The circles detail the sites which are suitable for drilling shafts to reach the gold. The origin $(0,0)$ of the map is represented by two vectors each of unit length. They wish to model their gold mine site using a constraint database and use this to determine the best place to install a mine shaft. How can they do this?

Notice that the shapes of the gold ore seams are not necessarily convex. (A shape is *convex* if a line drawn between any two points within the shape stays entirely within the shape). Non-convex objects are difficult, if not impossible, to represent with only a single constraint, so, instead of representing each gold seam by a single data item, we will model it by breaking it into convex polygons of roughly equal size. These polygons will approximately follow the seam's boundaries and can be represented using a linear arithmetic constraint which holds whenever a point lies within the polygon.

For example, the point (X, Y) is in region a of the leftmost gold seam whenever the constraint

$$X + Y \geq 2 \wedge X \geq Y \wedge X \leq 2$$

holds. Using this approach we can model the gold seams by using the predicate ore. It has multiple rules, one for each convex region. Each rule details the name of the region and its shape. For instance, region a is modelled by the rule

```
ore(N, X, Y) :- N = a, X + Y ≥ 2, X ≥ Y, X ≤ 2.
```

This is a good example of the utility of constraints for representing heterogeneous data—constraints are used to model both the name of the region and its shape.

Suitable drilling sites can be represented as a point together with a name. The predicate shaft details the possible drilling sites with a rule for each site. For

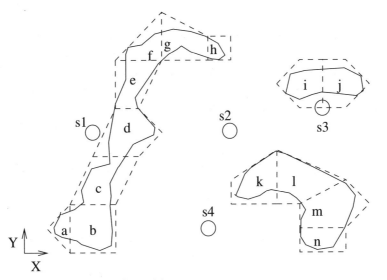

Figure 11.1   Map of a gold mine site.

instance, shaft site *s2* is modelled by the rule

```
shaft(N, X, Y) :- N = s2, X = 9, Y = 5.
```

In order to choose where to drill the shaft we might be interested in finding the regions of ore, O, that are within a certain radius, D, of a proposed shaft site, S. We can model this query using the rule

```
within(S, D, O) :-
    (XO - XS)² + (YO - YS)² ≤ D²,
    shaft(S, XS, YS),
    ore(O, XO, YO).
```

For instance, the goal `within(s2, 4, O)` gives the answers

$$O = d, \quad O = g, \quad O = h,$$
$$O = i, \quad O = k, \quad O = l.$$

Constraint databases also allow natural modelling of temporal data. That is to say, data which changes over time. We can model time by integer values, so time $t + 1$ is the next time instant after time t (if desired, we could also model time using real numbers). Arithmetic constraints over integers allow us to reason about time very naturally. We shall reserve the first argument of every rule to specify the interval of time for which the data in the rule is valid.

Example 11.3

Consider the employment records of CLP Inc. As time progresses the positions of people change in the company—new employees arrive, old employees leave and the management structure of the company changes. We can represent this data using two predicates. The first, job(T, Name, Posn, Dept), details the position *Posn* and department *Dept* of employee *Name* at time T. The second predicate, manager_of(T, Dept, Name), shows the manager of department *Dept* at time T.

Rather than storing individual tuples for each different time we can use constraints to define time intervals. For example, if *bart* is the manager of the *sales* department from 1980–1992 and the manager of *marketing* from 1993–1996, while *maria* is the manager of *sales* in 1996 we can represent this by

```
manager_of(T, sales, bart) :- 1980 ≤ T, T ≤ 1992.
manager_of(T, marketing, bart) :- 1993 ≤ T, T ≤ 1996.
manager_of(T, sales, maria) :- T = 1996.
```

We will assume that the job relation is defined by

```
job(T, peter, salesperson, sales) :- 1985 ≤ T, T ≤ 1987.
job(T, peter, consultant, sales) :- T = 1988.
job(T, peter, analyst, support) :- 1989 ≤ T, T ≤ 1996.
job(T, kim, salesperson, sales) :- 1994 ≤ T, T ≤ 1995.
job(T, maria, salesperson, sales) :- 1988 ≤ T, T ≤ 1991.
job(T, maria, consultant, support) :- 1992 ≤ T, T ≤ 1995.
job(T, maria, manager, management) :- T = 1996.
job(T, bart, manager, management) :- 1980 ≤ T, T ≤ 1996.
```

If we were to store the same data in a traditional relational database then for each of the above facts we would require one tuple for each value that T could take. Representing the above facts would require over 50 tuples. Clearly if time is broken down into smaller periods (for example days) storing individual tuples for each time period becomes impractical. For this reason, databases which allow concise modelling of time varying data are of considerable interest.

We can use this database to answer a number of simple queries in a straightforward way. For instance, we might wish to find all of the people P who have ever been managed by manager M. This is accomplished by using the rule

```
ever_managed(M, P) :- manager_of(T, D, M), job(T, P, _, D).
```

The goal ever_managed(M, P) with respect to the temporal database defined above has answers:

$$M = bart \land P = peter \qquad \text{and} \qquad M = bart \land P = maria.$$

We might also be interested in finding the "long term" employees of CLP Inc. We can define long term employees as those who have worked for CLP Inc for more than 10 years. They are found using the rule

```
long_term(P) :- job(T0, P, _, _), job(T1, P, _, _), T1 - T0 ≥ 10.
```

The goal long_term(P) has the answers $P = peter$ and $P = bart$.

11.2 Bottom Up Evaluation

The preceding examples demonstrate that CLP programs provide a powerful mechanism for modelling many database applications. Unfortunately, the backtracking evaluation mechanism for CLP we have previously described is not well suited to this type of application. There are two main reasons. First, in most database applications we are interested in finding *all* of the answers to a query at once, rather than laboriously backtracking through each and asking for another. Second, the standard evaluation mechanism may not terminate even when there are only a finite number of answers to a query.

Example 11.4
To illustrate these issues, consider the following constraint database which describes the flights offered by a new Australian airline, Oz-air Inc. Each fact `flight(Num,From,To)` details the number of the flight *Num*, its start city *From*, and its destination *To*.

```
flight(300, melbourne, sydney).
flight(301, sydney, melbourne).
flight(500, sydney, brisbane).
flight(501, brisbane, sydney).
```

A reasonable query is: "between which cities can you fly with Oz-air Inc, possibly via other cities?" The following predicate, `connects`, attempts to answer this. It captures the reasoning that you can use Oz-air to fly between two cities if there is a direct flight between the cities or a connecting flight via another city:

```
direct_flight(From, To) :- flight(_, From, To).
connects(From, To) :- direct_flight(From, To).
connects(From, To) :- direct_flight(From, Via), connects(Via, To).
```

If we evaluate the goal `connects(melbourne,T)` using the standard CLP evaluation mechanism, we will obtain the infinite sequence of answers:

$$T = sydney \quad T = melbourne \quad T = brisbane$$
$$T = sydney \quad T = melbourne \quad T = brisbane$$
$$T = sydney \quad T = melbourne \quad T = brisbane$$
$$\vdots \qquad\qquad \vdots \qquad\qquad \vdots$$

The problem is that the flight relationship has cycles which are followed in the derivation. The standard evaluation mechanism is not intelligent enough to realise that it has already "visited" that city and does a large (infinite) amount of work finding the same answers again and again.

For this reason we will give another evaluation mechanism for CLP programs which is based on relational and deductive database evaluation techniques. This mechanism works on a set of answers at a time and works from the "bottom-up."

Consider the flight database again. We can evaluate the `connects(melbourne,T)` by first finding all of the answers to the goal `connects(F,T)` and then selecting those answers for which $F = melbourne$.

A rather natural way to find all of the answers to `connects(F,T)` is as follows. We first find all of the answers to the goal `flight(N,F,T)`. These are

$$N = 300 \wedge F = melbourne \wedge T = sydney,$$
$$N = 301 \wedge F = sydney \wedge T = melbourne,$$
$$N = 500 \wedge F = sydney \wedge T = brisbane,$$
$$N = 501 \wedge F = brisbane \wedge T = sydney.$$

They can be more conveniently represented by the set of facts, S_1,

```
flight(300, melbourne, sydney),   flight(301, sydney, melbourne),
flight(500, sydney, brisbane),    flight(501, brisbane, sydney).
```

Using these we can now find all of the answers to the goal `direct_flight(F, T)`. In essence, we use the program containing the rule defining `direct_flight` together with the above facts. This gives rise to the answers

$$F = melbourne \wedge T = sydney,$$
$$F = sydney \wedge T = melbourne,$$
$$F = sydney \wedge T = brisbane,$$
$$F = brisbane \wedge T = sydney.$$

Again we can conveniently represent these as a set of facts, say S_2:

```
direct_flight(melbourne, sydney),   direct_flight(sydney, melbourne),
direct_flight(sydney, brisbane),    direct_flight(brisbane, sydney).
```

Now we are in a position to compute all of the answers to `connects(F,T)`. This is an iterative process. We start by evaluating the goal `connects(F,T)` with respect to the program containing the facts in S_1 and S_2 and the first rule defining `connects`. This gives the answers,

$$F = melbourne \wedge T = sydney,$$
$$F = sydney \wedge T = melbourne,$$
$$F = sydney \wedge T = brisbane,$$
$$F = brisbane \wedge T = sydney.$$

We now evaluate the goal using the second rule defining `connects` and the facts in S_1 and S_2. This gives no answers since no facts match the `connects` literal at the end of the rule. We represent the answers found in this iteration by the facts, S_3,

```
connects(melbourne, sydney),    connects(sydney, melbourne),
connects(sydney, brisbane),     connects(brisbane, sydney).
```

Since the second rule for `connects` is recursive we continue this process to find more facts. We now find the answers to `connects(F,T)` using a single application of the second rule in the definition together with the facts in S_1, S_2 and S_3. This gives rise to the answers

$$F = melbourne \wedge T = melbourne,$$
$$F = sydney \wedge T = sydney,$$
$$F = brisbane \wedge T = brisbane,$$
$$F = melbourne \wedge T = brisbane,$$
$$F = brisbane \wedge T = melbourne.$$

We represent these using the facts, S_4,

```
connects(melbourne, melbourne),    connects(sydney, sydney),
connects(brisbane, brisbane),      connects(brisbane, melbourne),
connects(melbourne, brisbane).
```

We repeat the above process and find the answers to `connects(F,T)` using a single application of the second rule in the definition together with the facts in S_1, S_2, S_3 and now S_4. This gives the answers

$$F = melbourne \wedge T = sydney,$$
$$F = sydney \wedge T = melbourne,$$
$$F = sydney \wedge T = brisbane,$$
$$F = brisbane \wedge T = sydney,$$
$$F = melbourne \wedge T = melbourne,$$
$$F = sydney \wedge T = sydney,$$
$$F = brisbane \wedge T = brisbane,$$
$$F = melbourne \wedge T = brisbane,$$
$$F = brisbane \wedge T = melbourne.$$

All of these answers have been found in a previous iteration. Thus, we can stop the process since we have now found all of the answers to `connects(F,T)`.

Finally we use the facts we have generated in S_1, S_2, S_3 and S_4 to answer the original goal `connects(melbourne,T)`. This gives the answers

$$T = melbourne, \quad T = sydney, \quad T = brisbane.$$

We call this evaluation mechanism *bottom-up evaluation* and refer to the standard evaluation mechanism for CLP programs as *top-down evaluation*. The advantage of using bottom-up evaluation to answer this goal is clear: the computation finishes because it does not repeat work by cycling through the same cities again and again. We will now explore bottom-up evaluation in more detail.

At each step in a bottom-up computation, we have a set of facts for each predicate. These facts represent the answers which have been found so far for that predicate. In the above example, the facts consisted of a user-defined constraint with fixed arguments, however one of the strengths of constraint databases is that the facts can also contain constrained variables. For instance, consider the employment records of CLP Inc. discussed in Example 11.3. The answers to the goal `manager_of(T, S, P)` are represented by facts of the form

```
manager_of(T, sales, bart) :- 1980 ≤ T, T ≤ 1992,
manager_of(T, marketing, bart) :- 1993 ≤ T, T ≤ 1996,
manager_of(T, sales, maria) :- T = 1996.
```

We can extend our earlier definition of a fact to cover this case.

Definition 11.1
A *fact* is a rule of the form

$$A \;:\!\text{-}\; c_1, \ldots, c_n$$

where A is a user-defined constraint and $c_1, \ldots, c_n$ are primitive constraints.

We will continue to write facts of the form $A \;:\!\text{-}\; \Box$ simply as A.

When evaluating a program bottom-up, it is useful to simplify the facts as they are generated. This reduces the size of the facts and can also help to determine if a fact has been encountered before. Simplification of facts is closely related to constraint simplification.

But what does it mean for two facts to be equivalent? For instance, the facts

```
connects(melbourne, sydney),
connects(F, T) :- F = melbourne, T = sydney,
connects(T, F) :- T = melbourne, F = sydney,
```

are all equivalent since the names of the variables in the head of the fact do not matter—after all the fact will be renamed when it is used to answer a goal— and variables can be equated to arguments without changing the behaviour. When discussing equivalence, it will prove useful to first rewrite a fact into a "head normal form" in which the arguments in the head are distinct new variables.

Definition 11.2
The *head normal form* of the fact

$$p(t_1, \ldots, t_n) \;:\!\text{-}\; C$$

is the fact

$$p(X_1^{\#}, \ldots, X_n^{\#}) \;:\!\text{-}\; X_1^{\#} = t_1, \ldots, X_n^{\#} = t_n, C$$

where the variables $X_1^\#, \ldots, X_n^\#, \ldots$ are fixed distinct variables which do not appear in the body of any fact which is not head normalized.

The head normal form of the three facts

```
connects(melbourne, sydney),
connects(F, T) :- F = melbourne, T = sydney,
connects(T, F) :- T = melbourne, F = sydney
```

is

```
connects(X₁#, X₂#) :- X₁# = melbourne, X₂# = sydney,
connects(X₁#, X₂#) :- X₁# = F, X₂# = T, F = melbourne, T = sydney,
connects(X₁#, X₂#) :- X₁# = T, X₂# = F, T = melbourne, F = sydney.
```

Note that for any predicate, the head normal form of any fact defining that predicate has the same head.

By rewriting the above facts in head normal form it is now apparent that they are equivalent since the constraints in the body of each fact

$$X_1^\# = melbourne \wedge X_2^\# = sydney,$$
$$X_1^\# = F \wedge X_2^\# = T \wedge F = melbourne \wedge T = sydney,$$
$$X_1^\# = T \wedge X_2^\# = F \wedge T = melbourne \wedge F = sydney,$$

are equivalent with respect to the variables in the head of the fact, $X_1^\#$ and $X_2^\#$.

Head normal form provides a general mechanism by which we can define equivalence of facts.

Definition 11.3

Let fact F_1 have head normal form

$$A \text{ :- } c_1, \ldots, c_m$$

and fact F_2 have head normal form

$$A' \text{ :- } c_1', \ldots, c_n'.$$

F_1 and F_2 are *equivalent* if A and A' are identical and $c_1 \wedge \cdots \wedge c_m$ is equivalent to $c_1' \wedge \cdots \wedge c_n'$ with respect to the variables in A.

Analogously to constraint simplification, a fact simplifier takes a fact and returns a fact which is "equivalent" but, in some sense, simpler. Details of the simplification process depend on the constraint domain.

Definition 11.4

A *fact simplifier*, $fsimpl$, for constraint domain $\mathcal{D}$ takes a fact F_1 and returns a fact F_2 such that F_1 and F_2 are equivalent.

Exactly how constraints are simplified is constraint domain and implementation specific. In our examples we will use the following two rules to simplify the facts. The rules are repeatedly applied until neither is applicable.

The first rule simplifies the fact $A \; :\!\!- \; c_1, \ldots, c_n$ to

$$A \; :\!\!- \; c_1', \ldots, c_m'.$$

where $c_1' \wedge \cdots \wedge c_m'$ is $simpl(c_1 \wedge \cdots \wedge c_n, vars(A))$. The two facts are equivalent since the variables in the head $vars(A)$ are the only variables of interest.

The second rule is used to simplify the fact $A \; :\!\!- \; c_1, \ldots, c_n$ when some c_i is of the form $X = t$ where X does not appear in t or elsewhere in the body. The resulting simplified fact is

$$A' \; :\!\!- \; c_1, \ldots, c_{i-1}, c_{i+1}, \ldots, c_n.$$

where A' is obtained from A by replacing every occurrence of X by t.

As an example of simplification, consider the fact

```
connects(X₁#, X₂#) :- X₁# = F, X₂# = T, F = melbourne, T = sydney.
```

Application of the first rule gives the fact

```
connects(X₁#, X₂#) :- X₁# = melbourne, X₂# = sydney.
```

since

$$\mathsf{tree\_simplify}(X_1^{\#} = F \wedge X_2^{\#} = T \wedge F = melbourne \wedge T = sydney, \{X_1^{\#}, X_2^{\#}\})$$

is

$$X_1^{\#} = melbourne \wedge X_2^{\#} = sydney.$$

Applying the second rule twice gives the fact

```
connects(melbourne, sydney).
```

This is the final simplified form since now neither of the simplification rules can be applied.

The basic mechanism in bottom-up evaluation is to use the current set of facts to find the answers to a goal or to find the answers to the body of a rule.

Definition 11.5

The set of answers to a goal G *generated* from the set of facts S, written $\mathsf{gen\_ans}(G, S)$, is the set of constraints C for which there is a successful derivation

$$\langle G \mid true \rangle \Rightarrow \cdots \Rightarrow \langle \Box \mid C \rangle$$

using the facts in S as the program.

For instance, the set of answers to the body of the second rule defining `connects`, namely

```
direct_flight(From, Via), connects(Via, To).
```

generated from the facts in S_1, S_2 and S_3 defined above is the set

$$\{ \quad From = melbourne \land Via = sydney \land To = melbourne,$$
$$From = sydney \land Via = melbourne \land To = sydney,$$
$$From = sydney \land Via = brisbane \land To = sydney,$$
$$From = brisbane \land Via = sydney \land To = brisbane,$$
$$From = melbourne \land Via = sydney \land To = brisbane,$$
$$From = brisbane \land Via = sydney \land To = melbourne \quad \}.$$

We are now in a position to give the bottom-up evaluation algorithm. At each stage in the derivation there is a current set of facts S which represent the answers found so far to the program. Initially this is the empty set. We repeatedly iterate through each rule R in the program using gen_facts to find the new set of facts generated from that rule using the facts in S. After each iteration the set of new facts, S_{new}, is compared to S. If they are the same, evaluation has finished and the set of answers for the goal, generated using the final set of facts, is returned.

The call gen_facts(R, S) finds the set of answers to the body of rule R generated from the set of facts S. For each answer it builds the corresponding generated fact and then simplifies it.

The function same determines if the two sets of facts S and S_{new} contain equivalent facts. It uses new to check if there is some fact F in S_{new} which is not equivalent to any fact in S.

Algorithm 11.1: Bottom-up evaluation
INPUT: A program P and a goal G.
OUTPUT: A set of answers to G.
METHOD: The algorithm is shown in Figure 11.2. $\square$

The facts in S_{new} generated from the old set of facts S are called the *immediate consequences* of S while those in the final set of facts produced in bottom-up evaluation are called the *program consequences*.

Example 11.5
Consider the following program P which defines the predicates `voltage_divider`, `cell`, `resistor`, `buildable_vd`, and `goal_vd` (the last predicate finds a buildable voltage divider cell that satisfies the goal from Section 4.2):

```
voltage_divider(V,I,R1,R2,VD,ID) :-
    V1 = I * R1, VD = I2 * R2,
    V = V1 + VD, I = I2 + ID.
cell(9).
resistor(5).
resistor(9).
```

P is a program;
G is a goal;
S, S_{new} and S_R are sets of facts;
R is a rule;
C is a constraint;
$c_1, \ldots, c_n$ are primitive constraints;
F and F_1 are facts.

bottom_up(P,G)
    $S_{new} := \emptyset$
    repeat
        $S := S_{new}$
        $S_{new} := \emptyset$
        for each rule R in P **do**
            $S_{new} := S_{new} \cup \text{gen\_facts}(R, S)$
        endfor
    until same(S, S_{new})
    return gen_ans(G, S)

gen_facts(R, S)
    let R be of form H :- B
    $S_R := \emptyset$
    for each $C \in$ gen_ans(B, S) **do**
        let C be of form $c_1 \wedge \cdots \wedge c_n$
        $S_R := S_R \cup \{fsimpl(H$:- $c_1, \ldots, c_n)\}$
    endfor
    return S_R

same(S, S_{new})
    for each $F \in S_{new}$ **do**
        if new(F, S) **then return** *false* **endif**
    endfor
    return *true*

new(F, S)
    for each $F_1 \in S$ **do**
        if F and F_1 are equivalent **then return** *false* **endif**
    endfor
    return *true*

Figure 11.2 Bottom-up evaluation of a program P.

```
buildable_vd(V,I,R1,R2,VD,ID) :-
    voltage_divider(V,I,R1,R2,VD,ID), cell(V),
    resistor(R1), resistor(R2).
goal_vd(V, R1, R2) :-
    buildable_vd(V,I,R1,R2,VD,ID),
    ID = 0.1, 5.4 ≤ VD, VD ≤ 5.5.
```

$$\langle voltage\_divider(V, I, R1, R2, VD, ID), cell(V), resistor(R1), resistor(R2) \mathbin{|} true\rangle$$
$$\Downarrow$$
$$\langle cell(V), resistor(R1), resistor(R2) \mathbin{|} V = I * R1 + VD \wedge I = I2 + ID \wedge VD = I2 * R2\rangle$$
$$\Downarrow$$
$$\langle resistor(R1), resistor(R2) \mathbin{|} V = I * R1 + VD \wedge I = I2 + ID \wedge VD = I2 * R2 \wedge V = 9\rangle$$
$$\Downarrow$$
$$\langle resistor(R2) \mathbin{|} 9 = 5 * I1 + VD \wedge I = I2 + ID \wedge VD = I2 * RD \wedge V = 9 \wedge R1 = 5\rangle$$
$$\Downarrow$$
$$\langle \square \mathbin{|} 9 = 5 * I + VD \wedge I = I2 + ID \wedge VD = 5 * I2 \wedge V = 9 \wedge R1 = 5 \wedge R2 = 5\rangle$$

Figure 11.3   Derivation for the body of the rule for `buildable_vd`.

Bottom-up evaluation of this program to solve the goal `goal_vd(V, R1, R2)` proceeds as follows. Initially S and S_{new} are set to the empty set of facts. The first four rules will generate the immediate consequences

```
voltage_divider(I*R1+VD,I2+ID,R1,R2,I2*R2,ID),
cell(9),
resistor(5),
resistor(9).
```

Since S_{new} is empty, the remaining rules do not generate any facts since they contain user-defined constraints in their body. Thus at the end of the first iteration, S_{new} is the set containing the above four facts. As S_{new} is not the same as S, iteration of the main loop continues.

In the second iteration, S is set to the old value of S_{new} and S_{new} is set to the empty set. Again evaluation of the first four rules will give rise to the facts

```
voltage_divider(I*R1+VD,I2+ID,R1,R2,I2*R2,ID),
cell(9),
resistor(5),
resistor(9).
```

This time the rule for `buildable_vd` allows us to find another immediate consequence of S. This is because, using the facts in S, there are successful derivations for the body of the rule for `buildable_vd`

```
voltage_divider(V,I,R1,R2,VD,ID), cell(V), resistor(R1), resistor(R2).
```

One successful simplified derivation is illustrated in Figure 11.3.

Simplifying the answer on to the variables $\{V, I, R1, R2, VD, ID\}$ gives

$$VD = -5 * I + 9 \wedge ID = 2 * I - 1.8 \wedge V = 9 \wedge R1 = 5 \wedge R2 = 5.$$

This derivation gives rise to the simplified fact:

```
buildable_vd(9, I, 5, 5, -5*I + 9, 2*I - 1.8).
```

The total set of simplified facts produced for `buildable_vd` is:

```
buildable_vd(9, I, 5, 5, -5*I + 9, 2*I - 1.8),
buildable_vd(9, I, 5, 9, -5*I + 9, 14/9*I - 1),
buildable_vd(9, I, 9, 5, -9*I + 9, 2.8*I - 1.8),
buildable_vd(9, I, 9, 9, -9*I + 9, 2*I - 1).
```

These correspond to the four choices of pairs of values for the resistors. The final rule in the program, that defining `goal_vd`, does not give rise to any immediate consequences since S does not contain any facts defining the predicate `buildable_vd`. Thus at the end of the iteration, S_{new} contains the facts

```
voltage_divider(I*R1+VD,I2+ID,R1,R2,I2*R2,ID),
cell(9),
resistor(5),
resistor(9),
buildable_vd(9, I, 5, 5, -5*I + 9, 2*I - 1.8),
buildable_vd(9, I, 5, 9, -5*I + 9, 14/9*I - 1),
buildable_vd(9, I, 9, 5, -9*I + 9, 2.8*I - 1.8),
buildable_vd(9, I, 9, 9, -9*I + 9, 2*I - 1).
```

Since this is not the same as the facts in S, the main loop is executed again.

In this iteration, S is set to the above facts. Execution proceeds as in the last iteration except that the rule defining `goal_vd` now gives rise to the immediate consequence:

```
goal_vd(9, 5, 9).
```

Thus, by the end of the iteration S_{new} contains the facts

```
voltage_divider(I*R1+VD,I2+ID,R1,R2,I2*R2,ID),
cell(9),
resistor(5),
resistor(9),
buildable_vd(9, I, 5, 5, -5*I + 9, 2*I - 1.8),
buildable_vd(9, I, 5, 9, -5*I + 9, 14/9*I - 1),
buildable_vd(9, I, 9, 5, -9*I + 9, 2.8*I - 1.8),
buildable_vd(9, I, 9, 9, -9*I + 9, 2*I - 1),
goal_vd(9, 5, 9).
```

Since this is not the same as the facts in S, the main loop is executed again.

This time no new immediate consequences are found, so the main loop terminates as S and S_{new} contain the same facts. Finally, `gen_ans`, is called with the final set of facts to answer the initial goal `goal_vd(V, R1, R2)`. This gives the single answer

$$V = 9 \wedge R1 = 5 \wedge R2 = 9.$$

11.3 Bottom-Up versus Top-Down

Both of the evaluation methods, bottom-up and top-down, have advantages and disadvantages. If they both terminate, they give rise to an equivalent set of answers. This was demonstrated in the preceding example when the answer found for goal_vd(V, R1, R2) using bottom-up evaluation was the same as that found using top-down evaluation (see Section 4.2). This equivalence also carries over to "failure." That is, if both methods terminate for a goal and one method gives no answers, then the other method will also give no answers.

For the user, the main difference between bottom-up and top-down evaluation is their termination behaviour. Bottom-up may not terminate when top-down does or vice versa.

Bottom-up evaluation is sometimes able to terminate when top-down evaluation runs forever. An example of this behaviour was shown in Example 11.4: with the flight database, the goal connects(melbourne,T) did not terminate using top-down evaluation. However, as we have seen, bottom-up evaluation terminates finding the three answers.

Bottom-up evaluation will terminate as long as the set of program consequences is finite. However, even if the set of program consequences is finite, top-down evaluation may still not terminate since it can find the same answer again and again.

On the other hand, because top-down evaluation is goal-directed it may terminate even when the set of program consequences is infinite. This occurs when all answers to the initial goal can be found by only exploring a finite subset of the program consequences. Thus top-down evaluation will sometimes terminate while bottom-up evaluation does not.

Example 11.6

Recall the factorial program from Section 4.2:

```
fac(0,1).                          (F1)
fac(N, N*F) :- N ≥ 1, fac(N-1,F). (F2)
```

The goal fac(2, X) has the derivation tree shown in Figure 11.4. Thus, top-down evaluation of the goal will terminate after finding the single answer $X = 2$.

Now consider bottom-up evaluation of this goal. After the first iteration the set of facts S_{new} contains the fact

```
fac(0, 1).
```

After the second iteration it contains the facts

```
fac(0, 1), fac(1, 1).
```

After the third iteration it contains

```
fac(0, 1), fac(1, 1), fac(2, 2),
```

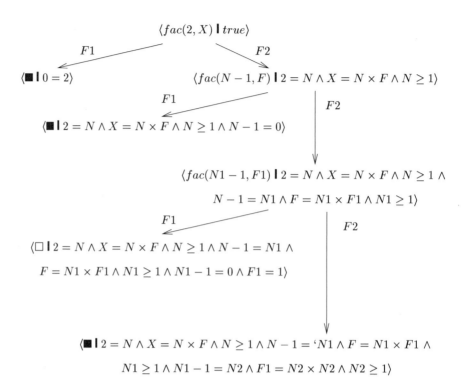

Figure 11.4 Derivation tree for goal `fac(2,X)`.

and after the fourth,

`fac(0, 1), fac(1, 1), fac(2, 2), fac(3, 6).`

Every iteration will produce another fact, so evaluation will not terminate. The reason is that the set of program consequences is infinite.

Because of the different termination behaviour, bottom-up evaluation may fail to terminate while top-down evaluation finitely fails and vice versa.

Example 11.7
Consider the factorial program of Example 11.6. The simplified derivation tree for the goal `fac(2,4)` is shown in Figure 11.5. Since all derivations in the tree are failed, the goal finitely fails. However, bottom-up evaluation of this goal will not terminate since the set of program consequences is infinite.

Example 11.8
Consider the flight database from Example 11.4. Using top-down evaluation the goal `connects(melbourne,darwin)` will not finitely fail since the derivation tree is infinite. With bottom-up evaluation, however, the goal `connects(melbourne,darwin)` will fail since it is not part of the program consequences.

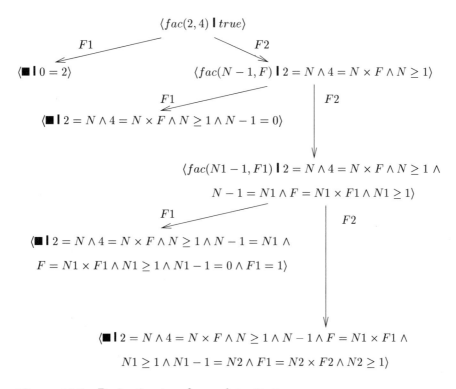

Figure 11.5 Derivation tree for goal `fac(2,4)`.

11.4 Mimicking Top-Down Evaluation Bottom-Up

We have seen that each of the evaluation methods has advantages and disadvantages. Bottom-up evaluation has the advantage of always terminating if the set of program consequences is finite and of recognizing repeated answers. The advantage of top-down evaluation is that it is goal-directed. Evaluation is directed by the initial goal and the goals that are subsequently derived from it. If we are only interested in the answer to a single goal, rather than all of the program consequences, top-down derivation will often be more efficient since it does not bother to determine extraneous information.

To combine the efficiency of both methods, a number of approaches have been suggested for modifying bottom-up evaluation so that it becomes goal-directed. Given a program P and goal G, the key idea is to transform P into *a new program* that, when evaluated bottom-up, will mimic the top-down evaluation of G with the original program.

Example 11.9
We shall first look at how this works for the goal `fac(2, X)` with the factorial program from Example 11.6. Top-down evaluation of the goal gives the derivation tree shown in Figure 11.4.

By examining this derivation tree we can determine the set of calls made to each predicate. We call these the set of *relevant queries*. More exactly, for each state $\langle A, B \mid c \rangle$ in the simplified derivation tree, where A is the rewritten user-defined constraint and B is the remainder of the goal, we collect the state $\langle A \mid C \rangle$ which details that user-defined constraint A has been called with constraint store C. These are the queries that top-down evaluation has needed to answer in order to answer the original goal. In this case they are

$$\langle fac(2, X) \mid true \rangle$$
$$\langle fac(N - 1, F) \mid 2 = N \wedge X = N \times F \wedge N \geq 1 \rangle$$
$$\langle fac(N1 - 1, F1) \mid 2 = N \wedge X = N \times F \wedge N \geq 1 \wedge$$
$$N - 1 = N1 \wedge F = N1 \times F1 \wedge N1 \geq 1 \rangle$$

These are the only queries on which the original goal depends. The idea is to transform the factorial program into a new program whose program consequences only contain facts relevant to one of these queries.

To do this we add a filter literal `query_fac` to each rule for `fac` and add rules to construct the relevant queries as facts for the filter predicate. The original factorial program is

```
fac(0, 1).
fac(N, N * F) :- N ≥ 1, fac(N-1, F).
```

The result of adding the filter literals is the program QP

```
fac(0, 1) :- query_fac(0, 1).
fac(N, N * F) :- query_fac(N, N * F), N ≥ 1, fac(N-1, F).
query_fac(N-1, F) :- query_fac(N, N * F), N ≥ 1.
query_fac(2, X).
```

To understand the transformation, consider how bottom-up evaluation of QP proceeds. To clarify the relationship with top-down evaluation we will not simplify the facts. After the first iteration, S contains the single fact

```
query_fac(2, X).
```

This corresponds to the original goal in the top-down derivation. The next iteration finds the new fact

```
query_fac(N-1, F) :- 2 = N, X = N * F, N ≥ 1.
```

This corresponds to the second goal in the top-down derivation. The third iteration includes the new fact

```
query_fac(N1-1, F1) :-
    N1 = N-1, N1 * F1 = F,
    2 = N, X = N * F,
    N ≥ 1, N1 ≥ 1.
```

which corresponds to the third goal in the top-down derivation. The fourth iteration produces the fact

```
fac(0, 1) :-
      0 = N1-1, 1 = F1,
      N1 = N-1, N1 * F1 = F,
      2 = N, X = N * F,
      N ≥ 1, N1 ≥ 1.
```

This fact can be simplified to `fac(0,1)`. It may be understood as an answer to the state

$$\langle fac(N1 - 1, F1) \mid 2 = N \wedge X = N \times F \wedge N \geq 1 \wedge$$
$$N - 1 = N1 \wedge F = N1 \times F1 \wedge N1 \geq 1 \rangle.$$

Once the answer is computed for this state it can be used to generate an answer to the state

$$\langle fac(N - 1, F) \mid 2 = N \wedge X = N \times F \wedge N \geq 1 \rangle$$

since both a `query_fac` and `fac` fact are available.

Subsequent iterations create the answers to the second and first states. The total set of (simplified) facts produced is shown below, where the BUi label indicates that this fact was first generated in the ith iteration of the main loop.

```
query_fac(2, X),     (BU1)
query_fac(1, F),     (BU2)
query_fac(0, F1),    (BU3)
fac(0, 1),           (BU4)
fac(1, 1),           (BU5)
fac(2, 2).           (BU6)
```

Note that the set of program consequences for the transformed program is finite. Evaluation of the original goal `fac(2, X)` with this set of facts gives the single answer $X = 2$.

In general we can make bottom-up evaluation goal-directed by adding a new predicate $query\_p$ to the program for each of the original predicates p. The new predicate, $query\_p$, generates the calls made to p during the top-down evaluation of the goal G. The query predicates act as filters, preventing bottom-up evaluation from computing facts which are not *relevant* to the queries. The general transformation is defined as follows.

Algorithm 11.2: Query transformation

INPUT: A program P and goal G of form $c_1, \ldots, c_n, q(r_1, \ldots, r_m)$ where each c_i is a primitive constraint and $q(r_1, \ldots, r_m)$ is a user-defined constraint.

OUTPUT: A program QP which, when evaluated bottom-up, mimics the top-down evaluation of G using P.

METHOD: Initially, QP is an empty program.

1. For each predicate p in P, create a new predicate *query_p* with the same arity as p.

2. For each rule in P, add the *modified version* of the rule to QP. If a rule has head $p(s_1, \ldots, s_m)$, the modified version of this rule is obtained by adding the literal *query_p*$(s_1, \ldots, s_m)$ to the front of the body.

3. Create a *seed rule*, *query_q*$(r_1, \ldots, r_m)$:- $c_1, \ldots, c_n$, and add this to QP.

4. For each rule R in P of the form

$$p(s_1, \ldots, s_m) \text{ :- } L_1, \ldots, L_k$$

and for each literal L_i, $1 \leq i \leq k$ which is a user-defined constraint, add a *query rule* to QP of the form

$$query\_p_i(t_1, \ldots, t_m) \text{ :- } query\_p(s_1, \ldots, s_m), L_1, \ldots, L_{i-1}.$$

where L_i has form $p_i(t_1, \ldots, t_m)$.

☐

The transformation rules can be understood as follows. The modified rules restrict the original rules so that they only produce facts that are relevant to the query. That is to say, they have a corresponding query fact. Calculation of the relevant queries is initiated from the seed rule which states that the goal is a relevant query. The remaining relevant queries are deduced by mimicking the top-down computation. There is a relevant query for p_i the ith literal in a rule for p if there is a relevant query for p and answers to all the preceding literals $L_1, \ldots, L_{i-1}$.

Example 11.10

Consider Ackermann's function

$$ack(m, n) = \begin{cases} n + 1, & \text{if } m = 0; \\ ack(m - 1, 1), & \text{if } m \geq 1, n = 0; \\ ack(m - 1, ack(m, n - 1)), & \text{otherwise.} \end{cases}$$

The following program is a natural translation of this function with the predicate `ack(M,N,A)` holding whenever $A = ack(M, N)$.

```
ack(M, N, A) :- M = 0, A = N + 1.
ack(M, N, A) :- M ≥ 1, N = 0, ack(M-1, 1, A).
ack(M, N, A) :- M ≥ 1, N ≥ 1, ack(M, N-1, A1), ack(M-1, A1, A).
```

Given this program and the goal `ack(2,1,A)`, application of the query translation algorithm gives rise to the following program

```
ack(M,N,A) :-
    query_ack(M,N,A),
    M = 0, A = N + 1.
ack(M,N,A) :-
    query_ack(M,N,A),
    M ≥ 1, N = 0, ack(M-1,1,A).
ack(M,N,A) :-
    query_ack(M,N,A),
    M ≥ 1, N ≥ 1, ack(M,N-1,A1), ack(M-1,A1,A).

query_ack(2,1,A).
query_ack(M-1,1,A) :-
    query_ack(M,N,A),
    M ≥ 1, N = 0.
query_ack(M,N-1,A1) :-
    query_ack(M,N,A),
    M ≥ 1, N ≥ 1.
query_ack(M-1,A1,A) :-
    query_ack(M,N,A),
    M ≥ 1, N ≥ 1, ack(M,N-1,A1).
```

The advantage of applying the query transformation is that the bottom-up evaluation of the resulting program will compute only those facts that are relevant to the original query. This may improve termination behaviour since, even if the original program does not terminate, the transformed program may. The factorial program gives an example of this behaviour.

In general, since the query transformed program mimics top-down evaluation, it will always terminate when top-down evaluation will terminate (after finding all answers). However, sometimes it will terminate even when top-down evaluation does not. This is because repeated answers are detected. For instance, bottom-up evaluation of the transformed flight database from Example 11.4 with goal `connects(melbourne,T)` will terminate, even though top-down evaluation of this goal will not.

In most cases, application of the query transformation is worthwhile. It improves efficiency by substantially reducing the number of facts that need to be computed and often improves termination behaviour. However, the query transformation is not always beneficial. First, the resulting program is more complex than the original and so may take longer to evaluate if all facts are relevant. Second, very occasionally, bottom-up evaluation of the resulting program may not terminate even though bottom-up evaluation of the original program does.

Example 11.11

Consider the following simple program:

```
stupid(X) :- stupid(X+1).
```

Top-down evaluation for the goal `stupid(4)` never halts. Bottom-up evaluation halts after a single iteration since there are no facts. For the goal `stupid(4)`, the query-transformed program is:

```
stupid(X) :- query_stupid(X), stupid(X+1).
query_stupid(4).
query_stupid(X+1) :- query_stupid(X).
```

Bottom-up evaluation of this program will not terminate since an infinite number of query facts will be generated.

11.5   (*) Improving Termination

The bottom-up evaluation algorithm employs the function new(F,S) to determine if information in the fact F already occurs in the old set of facts S or is new. Evaluation terminates when information from all of the "new" facts S_{new} already occurs in S. We now examine two refinements of new which improve the termination behaviour of bottom-up evaluation, although with greater cost in a call to new.

The definition of new given in Figure 11.2 tests whether fact F is equivalent to some fact F_1 in S. If a *canonical form simplifier* (introduced in Section 2.6) is available for the constraint domain of interest, it is simple to implement new using this simplifier. This is because a canonical form simplifier ensures that equivalent constraints are simplified to exactly the same form. To determine if two facts are equivalent, we can, therefore, convert the facts to head normal form and use the canonical simplifier to simplify the body of each in terms of the variables in the head of the fact. If the resulting facts are syntactically identical, then the original facts are equivalent. Otherwise, they are not.

If a canonical form simplifier is not available for our constraint domain we can use an *equivalence tester* (see Section 2.7) to determine equivalence.

However, the definition of new can be improved, so that even if the new facts are not equivalent to the old facts, bottom-up evaluation terminates. This is because the new facts, even though they are not equivalent to old facts, may hold no new information.

Example 11.12

The following simple program over the domain of real numbers computes successively smaller boxes centred on the origin.

```
box(X, Y) :- X ≥ -4, X ≤ 4, Y ≥ -4, Y ≤ 4.
box(X, Y) :- X = X1/2, Y = Y1/2, box(X1, Y1).
```

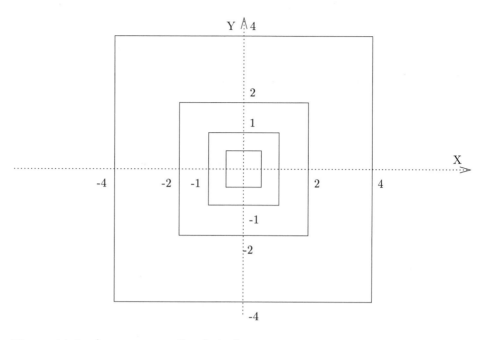

Figure 11.6   Areas representing facts for box.

Bottom-up computation produces the facts

```
box(X, Y)   :-   X ≥ -4, X ≤ 4, Y ≥ -4, Y ≤ 4,
box(X, Y)   :-   X ≥ -2, X ≤ 2, Y ≥ -2, Y ≤ 2,
box(X, Y)   :-   X ≥ -1, X ≤ 1, Y ≥ -1, Y ≤ 1,
box(X, Y)   :-   X ≥ -0.5, X ≤ 0.5, Y ≥ -0.5, Y ≤ 0.5,
              ⋮
```

in this order. A diagram of the areas described by the facts is given in Figure 11.6.

The set of program consequences is infinite since it contains arbitrarily small boxes centred at the origin and none of the facts in this set are equivalent. However, all of the "information" in this set is captured in the first fact

```
box(X, Y) :- X ≥ -4, X ≤ 4, Y ≥ -4, Y ≤ 4
```

since each of the other facts is *subsumed* by this fact in the sense that every solution to another fact is also a solution of this fact. Thus bottom-up computation could stop, with no loss of information, after producing the first fact.

To overcome this problem we can use a modified version of bottom-up evaluation. In this modification, a fact is considered new only if it is not redundant with respect to any earlier fact. To make this precise, we need to generalize our earlier notion of constraint implication from Chapter 2 to take into account the variables of interest.

Definition 11.6

Constraint C_1 *implies* constraint C_2 with respect to the set of variables $\{x_1, \ldots, x_n\}$ if for each solution $\{x_1 \mapsto d_1, \ldots, x_n \mapsto d_n, \ldots\}$ of C_1, $\{x_1 \mapsto d_1, \ldots, x_n \mapsto d_n\}$ is a partial solution of C_2.

Definition 11.7

Let fact F_1 have head normal form

$$A :\text{-} c_1, \ldots, c_m$$

and fact F_2 have head normal form

$$A' :\text{-} c'_1, \ldots, c'_n.$$

F_1 is *subsumed* by F_2 if A and A' are identical and $c_1 \wedge \cdots \wedge c_m$ implies $c'_1 \wedge \cdots \wedge c'_n$ with respect to the variables in A.

We can replace the call in **new** to test if two constraints are equivalent by a call to test if one subsumes the other. This gives the definition

new(F, S)
    for each $F_1 \in S$ **do**
        if F is subsumed by F_1 **then return** *false* **endif**
    endfor
    return *true*

We call the resulting variant of bottom-up evaluation, bottom-up evaluation *with subsumption testing*.

Example 11.13

Bottom-up evaluation with subsumption testing of the program of Example 11.12 and goal box(X,Y) proceeds as follows. The first iteration produces the fact

box(X, Y) :- X $\geq$ -4, X $\leq$ 4, Y $\geq$ -4, Y $\leq$ 4.

In the next iteration S is equal to the singleton set containing the above fact and S_{new} is computed to be the set containing this fact as well as the fact

box(X, Y) :- X $\geq$ -2, X $\leq$ 2, Y $\geq$ -2, Y $\leq$ 2

which was produced from the second rule. Evaluation of same(S, S_{new}) returns *true* since each fact in S_{new} is subsumed by the single fact in S. Thus the main loop terminates and the algorithm returns the single answer

$$X \geq -4 \wedge X \leq 4 \wedge Y \geq -4 \wedge Y \leq 4.$$

By now the reader might hope that we have conquered all problems with termination. Unfortunately, this is not the case, because seemingly new facts may not be subsumed by a single old fact, but only by a number of old facts considered together.

Example 11.14

The following simple program produces rectangles and quarter-planes over the domain of real numbers.

```
rect(X, Y) :- X ≤ 0, Y ≥ 0.
rect(X, Y) :- X ≤ 0, Y ≤ 0.
rect(X, Y) :- X ≥ 1, X ≤ 2, Y ≥ -1, Y ≤ 1.
rect(X, Y) :- X = X1 + 2, rect(X1, Y).
```

The first iteration produces the facts, S_1

```
rect(X, Y) :- X ≤ 0, Y ≥ 0,
rect(X, Y) :- X ≤ 0, Y ≤ 0,
rect(X, Y) :- X ≥ 1, X ≤ 2, Y ≥ -1, Y ≤ 1.
```

These define two half-planes that together include all of the non-positive values of X, and a rectangle of size 1×2 that is centred around the X axis and starts at X coordinate 1. The next iteration produces in addition to the facts in S_1 the new facts,

```
rect(X, Y) :- X ≤ -2, Y ≥ 0.
rect(X, Y) :- X ≤ -2, Y ≤ 0.
rect(X, Y) :- X ≥ -1, X ≤ 0, Y ≥ -1, Y ≤ 1.
```

The first two facts are subsumed by one of the half planes in S_1. However, although the third fact is not subsumed by any single fact in S_1, it is redundant with respect to the first two facts in S_1. If this redundancy is not detected evaluation will continue, producing the facts

```
rect(X, Y)   :-   X ≥ -3, X ≤ -2, Y ≥ -1, Y ≤ 1,
rect(X, Y)   :-   X ≥ -5, X ≤ -4, Y ≥ -1, Y ≤ 1,
        ⋮
```

and will not terminate.

A diagram of the areas described by the facts is given in Figure 11.7. The shaded areas correspond to the first two facts in S_1, while the rectangles correspond to the third fact in S_1 and the facts produced later which are not subsumed by a single fact.

We can avoid the type of behaviour exhibited in the above example by extending the subsumption check so that it succeeds if a new fact is subsumed by the set of old facts considered together. We leave the definition of the new version of new as an exercise. Unfortunately, such multi-fact subsumption testing is usually very expensive—and thus impractical.

However, in some constraint domains, multi-fact subsumption testing is no harder than testing if a fact is subsumed by a single fact. This is because in such domains, the solutions to a constraint C are covered by the solutions to a number of

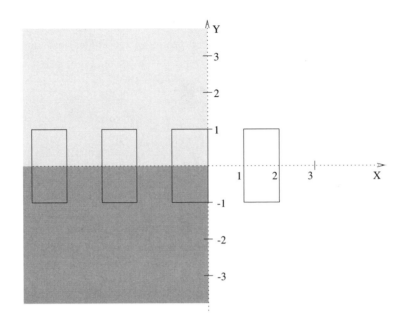

Figure 11.7   Areas representing facts for `rect`.

constraints $C_1, \ldots, C_n$ only if C is subsumed by one of the C_i. Such domains are said to have *independence of negative constraints*. For instance, the tree constraint domain has independence of negative constraints, while, as the above example demonstrated, linear arithmetic constraints do not have independence of negative constraints.

11.6   (*) Relationship with Relational Databases

The relational data model is currently the most popular form of database, in part because its high level nature frees the user from decisions about how queries are to be answered. A constraint database is, arguably, even more high level. In this section we use examples to show that constraint databases are a natural generalization of relational databases.

We assume the reader has some basic understanding of (relational) databases, but shall give the basic definitions to clarify our notation and terminology.

Definition 11.8

A *relational domain* is a set of values. The *Cartesian product* of (not necessarily disjoint) relational domains $D_1, \ldots, D_k$, written $D_1 \times \cdots \times D_k$, is the set of all k-tuples $(d_1, \ldots, d_k)$ where $d_i \in D_i$ for each $1 \leq i \leq k$. A k-ary *relation* is a subset of $D_1 \times D_2 \times \cdots \times D_k$. We may associate with a k-ary relation a k-tuple of *attributes* which uniquely names each argument of the relation.

Relational databases store, update and manipulate relations. A *relational database* can be viewed as a (time-varying) collection of relations. Since the database relations are stored and used in computation we assume that they are finite in size.

Example 11.15

Consider a simple database storing information about the teaching operations of a computer science department. Some appropriate relational domains are: courses, teachers, days of the week, times, rooms and integers. We can model our data using two relations. The first is a relation lecture with six attributes which gives information about lectures. It details the course name, lecturer, day, start and finish times and room of each lecture. It is described by the following table in which the attribute names are given at the top of each column in the table.

	Course_Name	Lecturer	Day	Start_Time	Finish_Time	Room
lecture	logic	harald	mon	1000	1230	theatre2
	theory	harald	tue	1100	1200	theatre2
	theory	harald	thu	1100	1200	theatre2
	constraints	peter	mon	1215	1315	theatre1
	constraints	peter	fri	1515	1615	theatre1

The second is a binary relation enrol which gives the number of students in each course. It is detailed in the following table. Again the table details the attribute names.

	Course_Name	Enrolment
enrol	logic	46
	theory	27
	constraints	142

Queries are made to relations in the database by constructing a relational algebra expression. This defines a new relation in terms of the given relations, and the answer to the query is the tuples of this relation. There are many different possible operations over relations. Here we restrict ourselves to the five most fundamental.

Union: If r_1 and r_2 are two k-ary relations then the *union* of r_1 and r_2, written $r_1 \cup r_2$, is the relation

$$\{(d_1, \dots, d_k) \mid (d_1, \dots, d_k) \in r_1 \text{ or } (d_1, \dots, d_k) \in r_2\}.$$

Projection: If r is a k-ary relation and V is the tuple of attribute identifiers $(\$v_1, \dots, \$v_n)$ where $v_1, \dots v_n$ are numbers from the range 1 to k, the *projection* of r on to V, written $\pi_V r$, is the relation

$$\{(d_{v_1}, \dots, d_{v_n}) \mid (d_1, \dots, d_k) \in r\}.$$

Selection: If r is a k-ary relation and c is a primitive constraint (from some constraint domain) over the attribute identifiers $\$1, \ldots, \$k$, the *selection* of r using c, written $\sigma_c r$, is the relation

$$\{(d_1, \ldots, d_k) \in r \mid \{\$1 \mapsto d_1, \ldots, \$k \mapsto d_k\} \text{ is a solution of } c\}.$$

Product: If r_1 is a k-ary relation and r_2 is an n-ary relation then the *product* of r_1 and r_2, written $r_1 \times r_2$, is the relation

$$\{(d_1, \ldots, d_k, e_1, \ldots, e_n) \mid (d_1, \ldots, d_k) \in r_1, (e_1, \ldots, e_n) \in r_2\}.$$

Natural join: Let r_1 be a k-ary relation and r_2 an n-ary relation. The *natural join* of r_1 and r_2, written $r_1 \bowtie r_2$, is rather complex to define. We give the definition for the case in which r_1 and r_2 have no attribute names in common and the case when they have a single attribute name in common. The generalization to two or more attribute names in common is straightforward but tedious to formalize.
In the case that r_1 and r_2 have no attribute names in common, $r_1 \bowtie r_2$ is simply the product $r_1 \times r_2$.
In the case that r_1 and r_2 have a single attribute name in common, say attribute i of r_1 and attribute j of r_2 have the same name, then $r_1 \bowtie r_2$ is

$$\{(d_1, \ldots, d_k, e_1, \ldots, e_{j-1}, e_{j+1}, \ldots, e_n) \mid (d_1, \ldots, d_k) \in r_1, (e_1, \ldots, e_n) \in r_2, d_i = e_j\}.$$

If a k-ary relation r has an associated list of attribute names $(a_1, \ldots a_k)$ we may also use a_i to represent $\$i$ in projections and selections.

Definition 11.9
A relation name is a *relational expression*. Furthermore, if R_1 and R_2 are relational expressions then so are $R_1 \cup R_2$, $\pi_V R_1$, $\sigma_c R_1$, $R_1 \times R_2$ and $R_1 \bowtie R_2$. A *query* on a database D is a relational expression involving only relation names from D.
The evaluation of a query Q on database D is the relation given by the relational expression Q where D gives the meaning of the named relations in Q.

Using relational operations it is simple to ask various questions about the sample database from Example 11.15.
For instance, using the query $\pi_{\$1, \$2}(\mathsf{lecture})$ we can ask for the names of the lecturers teaching a course. Alternately, instead of using a numerical identifier to refer to the attributes, we can use the attribute names. This gives rise to the equivalent query $\pi_{Course\_Name, Lecturer}(\mathsf{lecture})$. Evaluation of either query gives the relation

Course_Name	Lecturer
logic	harald
theory	harald
constraints	peter

Using the query $\sigma_{\$2 \geq 100}(\mathsf{enrol})$ we can determine which classes have more than 100 students. In this case the corresponding query using attribute names is simply $\sigma_{Enrolment \geq 100}(\mathsf{enrol})$. Evaluation of either query results in the relation

Course_Name	Enrolment
constraints	142

A slightly more complex query is to ask for the classes which are non-standard in size. That is to say, they are large with 100 or more students or small with 30 or less students. The query

$$\sigma_{\$2 \geq 100}(\mathsf{enrol}) \ \cup \ \sigma_{\$2 \leq 30}(\mathsf{enrol})$$

will find such classes. Evaluation will return the relation

Course_Name	Enrolment
theory	27
constraints	142

An even more complex query is to ask for the names of lecturers that teach large classes. This requires us to use the natural join to concatenate tuples in the two relations which refer to the same course. The answer can be found by evaluating

$$\pi_{\$4}((\sigma_{\$2 \geq 100}(\mathsf{enrol})) \bowtie (\pi_{\$1,\$2}(\mathsf{lecture})))$$

or, alternately using attribute names, by evaluating

$$\pi_{Lecturer}((\sigma_{Enrolment \geq 100}(\mathsf{enrol})) \bowtie (\pi_{Course\_name, Lecturer}(\mathsf{lecture}))).$$

The result is the relation consisting of a single tuple (*peter*).

It is not too hard to show that any relational database and query can be translated into a constraint database program and goal. We demonstrate this translation by means of several examples.

In a relational database a relation is simply a finite set of tuples. We can naturally represent each relation by a predicate with one argument for each attribute and represent each tuple by a fact in the definition of the predicate.

Consider the database of Example 11.15. It can be represented by the constraint logic program:

```
lecture(logic, harald, mon, 1000, 1230, theatre2).
lecture(theory, harald, tue, 1100, 1200, theatre2).
lecture(theory, harald, thu, 1100, 1200, theatre2).
lecture(constraints, peter, mon, 1215, 1315, theatre1).
lecture(constraints, peter, fri, 1515, 1615, theatre1).

enrol(logic, 46).
enrol(theory, 27).
enrol(constraints, 142).
```

Each of the relational operations—union, selection, projection, product and join—can be naturally modelled using constraint programs. Consider our example queries to the above database.

Projection corresponds to "forgetting" the value of local variables. For instance, the query asking for the names of the lecturers teaching a course, $\pi_{Course\_name,Lecturer}(\mathsf{lecture})$ is modelled by the rule

```
teaches(C, L) :- lecture(C, L, D, S, F, R).
```

Answers to the goal `teaches(C, L)` correspond exactly to the tuples in the answer to the original query. If we evaluate the goal `teaches(C, L)` with the above definition of `lecture` we will obtain the three answers

$$C = logic \wedge L = harald,$$
$$C = theory \wedge L = harald,$$
$$C = constraints \wedge L = peter,$$

which correspond to the three tuples resulting from the original query to the database.

Selection is easy to implement using constraints. The query asking for those classes which have more than 100 students, $\sigma_{Enrolment \geq 100}(\mathsf{enrol})$, is modelled by the rule

```
large_class(C, E) :- enrol(C, E), E ≥ 100.
```

The answers to the goal `large_class(C, E)` correspond to the answers of the original query.

Union is modelled using multiple rules in the definition of a relation. For instance, the query

$$\sigma_{\$2 \geq 100}(\mathsf{enrol}) \ \cup \ \sigma_{\$2 \leq 30}(\mathsf{enrol})$$

is modelled by

```
non_standard_class(C, E) :- enrol(C, E), E ≥ 100.
non_standard_class(C, E) :- enrol(C, E), E ≤ 30.
```

Natural join is modelled by two user-defined constraints in a body with shared attributes having the same variable as their argument. Consider the query asking for the names of lecturers that teach large classes,

$$\pi_{Lecturer}((\sigma_{Enrolment \geq 100}(\mathsf{enrol})) \bowtie (\pi_{Course\_name,Lecturer}(\mathsf{lecture}))).$$

Using the above definitions this is modelled by the program

```
teaches(C, L) :- lecture(C, L, D, S, F, R).
large_class(C, E) :- enrol(C, E), E ≥ 100.
teaches_large_class(L) :- large_class(C, E), teaches(C, L).
```

The last rule models the natural join between `large_class` and `teaches` projected on to the attribute *Lecturer*. The goal `teaches_large_class(L)` has a single answer $L = peter$ corresponding to the single tuple in the answer to the query.

Product is modelled similarly to natural join. We simply define a new predicate which has all of the arguments of each of the relations.

It should be apparent from these examples that constraint databases are as powerful as relational databases: any data or query which can be expressed using a relational database can also be expressed using a constraint database. In fact, constraint databases are more powerful than traditional relational databases. There are two reasons. First, constraint databases provide *deduction*. This is provided by recursive rules such as those defining the `connects` relation in Example 11.4. Expressing such a recursive relation is not possible using relational algebra. Second, in applications such as those involving temporal and spatial data, they allow many tuples to be succinctly described by a single constraint.

11.7 Summary

Constraint databases are a distinctive new type of database. The use of constraints provides a uniform framework which generalizes other types of databases such as relational databases, deductive databases and spatial databases.

Here we have viewed constraint databases simply as constraint logic programs. However, one important difference is that, in constraint logic programming, we are usually interested in obtaining only one answer to our goal, while in constraint databases we usually want all of the answers. For this reason we have introduced a new kind of evaluation mechanism for constraint logic programs, called bottom-up evaluation, which iteratively computes a set of facts called the program consequences.

Bottom-up evaluation has advantages and disadvantages when compared with the standard top-down evaluation of CLP programs. The main advantage of top-down evaluation is that it is goal-directed. To combine the advantages of bottom-up with that of top-down, we have detailed a transformation that, when applied to a program and goal, gives a new program whose bottom-up evaluation is goal-directed and mimics the top-down evaluation of the original program.

One advantage bottom-up evaluation has over top-down evaluation is that it can include sophisticated checks for termination. We have discussed various possibilities including equivalence, subsumption testing and multi-fact subsumption testing.

Our presentation has ignored many interesting issues in constraint databases. The bottom-up evaluation strategy we have defined is quite simplistic, repeatedly evaluating the entire program in each iteration. More efficient evaluation methods which do not repeat computation unnecessarily are usually used for evaluating recursive constraint database queries. We have also ignored many important database operations, such as negation and aggregation, on constraint databases and concentrated only on constraint logic programs as a database language.

11.8   Exercises

11.1. Show the bottom-up evaluation of the program in Example 11.3.

11.2. Give the query transformation of the `mortgage` program of Section 5.3 for the goal `mortgage(2000, 2, 10, R, 0)`. Show the bottom-up evaluation of the resulting program.

11.3. Using the genealogical database and rules defining `parent` from Example 11.1 and the additional rules

```
sibling(X, Y) :- parent(Z, X), parent(Z, Y), X ≠ Y.
cousin(X, Y) :- parent(Z, X), sibling(Z, T), parent(T, Y).
```

show the bottom-up evaluation of the query `cousin(peter, X)`. Perform the query transformation for this query and re-evaluate. Compare the number of facts in the program consequences for each evaluation.

11.4. Perform the query transformation for the program below with the goal `p(3)` and then with `X ≤ 4, p(X)`.

```
p(0).
p(X) :- X ≥ 1, p(X-1).
```

Determine which form of the routine `new` is required to ensure the termination of bottom-up evaluation of each of the resulting programs.

11.5. (*) Give a relational expression that finds pairs of courses whose lectures overlap in time. Give a corresponding constraint program.

11.9   Practical Exercises

P11.1. Write a query to determine the times when two lecturers $L1$ and $L2$ are teaching at the same time. Test it with the data for the lecture relation.

P11.2. Write a CLP program which will terminate using top-down evaluation and which defines the `connects(X,Y)` predicate for Example 11.4. [Hint: use an extra argument which keeps the list of cities already visited and checks that each new city has not been previously visited.]

P11.3. (*) Write a program to perform bottom-up evaluation of CLP($Tree$) programs as described in Algorithm 11.1. Make the `new` routine as complete as possible.

P11.4. (*) Write a program to perform the query transformation to a program P and goal G. Use the `lrule` representation of programs described in Section 9.7. Check that the resulting program QP gives the same answers as the original program P for goal G.

11.10 Notes

The bottom-up evaluation viewpoint of constraint logic programs is implicit in the original paper on constraint logic programming [69]. Kanellakis, Kuper and Revesz [77] were the first to formally define a *constraint database* in terms of "generalized tuples" (corresponding to facts in this presentation) and proposed a framework for constraint databases using this approach.

Although phrased somewhat differently, equivalence between bottom-up and top-down evaluation is shown in Jaffar and Lassez [69]. The query transformation is a simplified version of the Magic Templates transformation of Ramakhrishnan [108], which is a generalization of the Magic Sets transformation [7].

Bottom-up evaluation is more efficient if performed in a differential or semi-naive method [6] in which in each iteration a rule is only used to produce more facts if a new fact for a literal in its body was created in the previous iteration.

Currently, constraint databases implementations are rare. This is because it is a new field and, since it requires much of the machinery of relational and deductive databases, implementation of constraint databases is time-consuming. The best example is perhaps the C^3 system [18]. This constraint database is built in C++ using the object oriented database ObjectStore to manage persistent storage of constraint relations and the linear programming package CPlex as a constraint solver. The database provides an SQL-like language for querying the constraint relations. The query language does not allow recursive queries but instead provides a powerful notion of iterators that can be used to define very complex forms of queries without recursion. This has the advantage that termination is guaranteed without special checks.

12 Other Constraint Programming Languages

In the previous chapter we examined constraint databases which we viewed as CLP programs but with a different evaluation mechanism. However, constraint logic programming languages are not the only approach to constraint programming. In this chapter we will investigate other constraint programming languages and paradigms and compare them with the CLP paradigm.

We first look at concurrent constraint programming languages which extend CLP languages by providing asynchronous communication between "agents" by using constraint entailment. We also look at constraint handling rules which are a useful variant of concurrent constraint programming languages specifically designed for writing constraint solvers. Next we look at various attempts to combine constraints with other programming paradigms. This research is motivated by the view that CLP is "constraints + logic programming" and so we have "constraints + functional programming", "constraints + term rewriting" and "constraints + imperative programming." Then we examine "constraint solving toolkits" which are libraries for traditional programming languages that provide many of the features of CLP. Finally, we look at mathematical languages that make use of constraints—modelling languages for operations research and symbolic algebra packages.

We shall see that many of the other approaches extend or are based on the CLP paradigm. This is not surprising since, in a very real sense, CLP languages are the archetypal constraint programming language. One reason is historical—they were one of the first true constraint programming languages, so have had great influence on the design and implementation of subsequent languages. A second reason is that the constraint logic programming paradigm is at the heart of any other constraint programming language because, in essence, constraint programs are simply user-defined constraints and any reasonable constraint programming language will provide user-defined constraints.

12.1 The CLP Paradigm

Before we examine the other approaches to constraint programming, it is worthwhile summarizing the key features of the CLP paradigm, since this will be the yardstick with which we shall compare the other approaches.

As we saw in Part 2, CLP programs consist of rules which define user-defined constraints or predicates. Rules may be recursive and there may be multiple rules in the definition of a predicate. Multiple rules allow the programmer to express choice and mean that a goal may have more than answer. The default behaviour of the CLP system is to find answers, one at a time, to the given goal. However, the programmer may also specify that they want the answer which minimizes a given objective function.

Programs are parametric in the choice of the underlying constraint domain, solver and simplifier. Different CLP languages and systems result from different choices. However, they all share the same underlying evaluation mechanism—a depth-first left-to-right search through the goal's derivation tree. In this book we have examined three CLP languages in some detail: $CLP(Tree)$ which provides tree constraints and may be considered the core of the logic programming language Prolog, $CLP(\mathcal{R})$ which extends $CLP(Tree)$ by providing arithmetic constraints over the real numbers and $CLP(FD)$ which extends $CLP(Tree)$ by providing constraints over finite domains.

CLP languages can be understood from two complementary viewpoints. The first is that they are modelling languages. From this viewpoint, the job of the CLP programmer is to process the constraints which model the problem at hand into a form which is suitable for the underlying constraint solver. Term constraints and recursion mean that the modelling language is very powerful, allowing the model to make use of complex data structures and iteration.

The second viewpoint is that they are programming languages. Because of tree constraints and recursion they are computationally adequate, so in principle they can be used to implement any desired algorithm. This viewpoint better describes more advanced CLP programming activities, such as extending the underlying constraint solver or programming different types of search, for instance, by developing a problem specific labelling predicate.

CLP languages are, of course, quite different to traditional programming languages. One major difference is that search is built into the CLP evaluation mechanism. The system tries each rule until it finds an answer—a priori it doesn't know which rule to use, so must try all of them. This is often called *don't know non-determinism*.

Apart from search, however, evaluation of a CLP program is similar to the evaluation of a program written in a procedural language. Predicates behave much like procedures—procedures are executed by evaluating the statements in the procedure definition in order, while predicates are evaluated by evaluating the literals in their definition proceeding left-to-right. If the literal is a constraint, it is added to the constraint store, and, if it is a call to a predicate, the call is evaluated.

12.2 Concurrent Constraint Programming Languages

We now examine other approaches to constraint programming. We shall start with concurrent constraint programming, since this is firmly based on the CLP paradigm.

Extending constraint logic programming with dynamic scheduling, as discussed in Section 9.6, not only allows us to write programs which work in a variety of modes of usage. It also allows a completely different style of programming in which we have "processes" or "agents" which execute concurrently and which communicate through the global constraint store.

Example 12.1

Consider the following program. The first two rules define a producer `prod` which produces a list of `a`'s and the remaining rules define a consumer `con` which consumes the list of `a`'s as they are produced. Note that the consumer predicate `con` delays until the list it is operating upon is constructed.

```
prod([]).                  (P1)
prod([a|L]) :- prod(L).    (P2)

:- delay_until(nonvar(L),con(L)).
con([]).                   (C1)
con([a|L]) :- con(L).      (C2)
```

The goal `con(L), prod(L)` has an infinite number of successful derivations since `prod(L)` produces lists of arbitrary length. If the leftmost enabled literal is always selected for rewriting, each derivation has essentially the same form. As soon as a rule for a `prod` literal is used to build more of the list L, the consumer `con` will "consume" the new element. Thus there is a form of synchronisation between the consumer and producer. An example simplified derivation is

$$\langle con(L), \underline{prod(L)} \mathbin{|} true \rangle$$
$$\Downarrow P2$$
$$\langle \underline{con(L)}, prod(L') \mathbin{|} L = [a|L'] \rangle$$
$$\Downarrow C2$$
$$\langle con(L'), \underline{prod(L')} \mathbin{|} L = [a|L'] \rangle$$
$$\Downarrow P1$$
$$\langle \underline{con(L')} \mathbin{|} L = [a] \wedge L' = [] \rangle$$
$$\Downarrow C1$$
$$\langle \Box \mathbin{|} L = [a] \rangle.$$

The answer is $L = [a]$, but the important feature of the derivation is how the consumer only executes after each part of the list is produced.

Concurrent constraint programming (CCP) languages are based on this "process" reading of CLP rules in which a user-defined constraint is viewed as a *process* and a state is regarded as a network of processes linked through shared variables by means of the store. Processes communicate by adding constraints to the store and synchronize by waiting for the store to enable a delay condition.

Rules in a CCP language have the following form

$$p(X_1, \ldots, X_m) :\text{-} G \mid L_1, \ldots, L_n$$

where the literal $p(X_1, \ldots, X_m)$ is the process defined by the rule, the literals $L_1, \ldots, L_n$ form the *body* of the rule and G is the *guard* which is a delay condition that must be enabled for the rule to be used. The syntax we use follows that of early CCP languages—modern CCP languages usually use a process notation which although semantically equivalent to the early notation, obscures the strong relationship with CLP languages.

Thus the above program might be written as the CCP program:

```
prod(X) :- true | X=[].
prod(X) :- true | X = [a|L], prod(L).

con(Y) :- emptylist(Y) | true.
con(Y) :- nonemptylist(Y) | Y=[a|L], con(L).
```

where the delay condition `emptylist(Y)` is enabled when the constraint $Y = []$ is implied by the current constraint store and the delay condition `nonemptylist(Y)` is enabled when Y is constrained to be a non-empty list by the current constraint store.

Both these delay conditions are a type of *ask* delay condition. An ask delay condition has the form $ask(C)$ and is enabled when the constraint store implies the constraint C. For instance, `emptylist(Y)` is equivalent to $ask(Y = [])$. Ask conditions may also involve local variables. These are indicated by existentially quantified ($\exists$) variables in the constraint C. The delay condition `nonemptylist(Y)` is equivalent to $ask(\exists E \ \exists L \ Y = [E|L])$, since this is enabled whenever there exists values for E and L such that the constraint store implies $Y = [E|L]$.

Apart from the ask-based delay conditions, another delay condition widely used in CCP languages is the *tell* condition. This is written $tell(C)$ and is enabled if constraint C is consistent with the global store. If the guard is enabled, another effect of $tell(C)$ is to add C to the constraint store. A typical guard consists of an ask and tell condition.

A major difference between CCP and CLP languages is how multiple rules defining the same predicate are handled. CLP languages, employ don't know non-determinism, trying each rule until an answer is found. In CCP languages, on the other hand, the evaluation mechanism delays choosing which rule to use until at least one of the guards is enabled. If more than one rule has its guard enabled, the evaluation mechanism arbitrarily chooses one of those rules to rewrite the literal with. Regardless of what happens in the future, it never goes back to try the other rules whose guard is enabled or those rules whose guard is still not enabled. It is the programmer's responsibility to provide each rule with a guard that ensures that once it is enabled, then this is the correct rule to choose. Thus CCP languages provide *don't care non-determinism*—if more than one guard is enabled we don't care which of the corresponding rules are used since any will be correct.

Example 12.2
The following program to merge two lists into a third list is a good example of the use of don't care non-determinism. The first rule is enabled whenever there is an element in the first list, and places this element on the merged list. The second rule is enabled when the first list is empty. In this case, the merged list is set to the second list. The third and fourth rule are analogous, except that they apply to the second list rather than the first.

```
merge(XL,YL,ZL) :- nonemptylist(XL) |
    XL=[X|XL1], ZL=[X|ZL1], merge(XL1,YL,ZL1). (M1)
merge(XL,YL,ZL) :- emptylist(XL) | ZL=YL.          (M2)
merge(XL,YL,ZL) :- nonemptylist(YL) |
    YL=[Y|YL1], ZL=[Y|ZL1], merge(XL,YL1,ZL1). (M3)
merge(XL,YL,ZL) :- emptylist(YL) | ZL=XL.          (M4)
```

If more than one rule is enabled, then we do not mind which one is chosen. For example, if the constraint store contains

$$XL = [a] \land YL = [b]$$

then the user-defined constraint merge(XL,YL,ZL) may be rewritten with either the first or third rule. Two possible successful simplified derivations are:

$$\langle merge(XL, YL, ZL) \mid XL = [a] \land YL = [b]\rangle$$
$$\Downarrow M1$$
$$\langle merge([\,], YL, ZL1) \mid XL = [a] \land YL = [b] \land ZL = [a|ZL1]\rangle$$
$$\Downarrow M2$$
$$\langle \square \mid XL = [a] \land YL = [b] \land ZL = [a, b]\rangle$$

and

$$\langle merge(XL, YL, ZL) \mid XL = [a] \land YL = [b]\rangle$$
$$\Downarrow M3$$
$$\langle merge(XL, [\,], ZL1) \mid XL = [a] \land YL = [b] \land ZL = [b|ZL1]\rangle$$
$$\Downarrow M1$$
$$\langle merge([\,], [\,], ZL2) \mid XL = [a] \land YL = [b] \land ZL = [b, a|ZL2]\rangle$$
$$\Downarrow M4$$
$$\langle \square \mid XL = [a] \land YL = [b] \land ZL = [b, a]\rangle$$

The two answers are different, but equivalent if we *don't care* about the order of elements occurring in ZL.

The CCP paradigm is not well suited for solving combinatorial search and optimization problems, since it does not directly provide don't know non-determinism. Some recent constraint programming languages, such as Oz, provide both don't know and don't care non-determinism as well as guards, effectively combining the CLP and CCP paradigms. We shall discuss Oz further in Section 12.4.

We also note that, as long as the delay conditions and run-time tests are sufficiently expressive, it is possible to translate CCP programs into CLP programs which use delay conditions to mimic the guards and use the cut to implement don't care non-determinism.

The CCP paradigm arose from the concurrent logic programming paradigm whose major application area was the implementation of "reactive" programs and systems. Conventional programs are designed to take an input and to compute some output. On the other hand a program which behaves reactively is not required to compute a final result but rather interacts with its environment. Reactive programs are employed in operating systems, database and transaction handling systems, for example.

The CCP paradigm is thus designed for building reactive programs. In particular, this means it is suitable for building incremental constraint solvers since these are a good example of a reactive system. After all, the role of an incremental constraint solver is simply to react to constraints sent by the CLP system, its "environment."

12.3 Constraint Handling Rules

Constraint handling rules (CHR) are closely related to the CCP paradigm. They are specifically designed for writing constraint solvers and consist of multi-headed guarded rules which repeatedly rewrite the constraint store until it is in a solved form, that is to say, when further rewriting does not change the store.

For example, the following CHRs define a partial order constraint $\leq$.

```
reflexivity @ X ≤ Y          <=> X = Y | true.
antisymmetry @ X ≤ Y, Y ≤ X <=> true | X = Y.
transitivity @ X ≤ Y, Y ≤ Z ==> true | X ≤ Z.
```

The first rule (named `reflexivity`) states that if the store implies that $X = Y$, then $X \leq Y$ can be simplified to true. The second rule enforces antisymmetry, that is, if both $X \leq Y$ and $Y \leq X$ appear in the store, they can be replaced by $X = Y$. The third rule implements transitivity, if both $X \leq Y$ and $Y \leq Z$ appear in the store then we add $X \leq Z$. The first two rules are used to simplify the constraint store, while the third rule adds the logical consequences of constraints in the store. This is similar to propagation.

Constraint handling rules manipulate a constraint store which is treated as a set of primitive constraints. The evaluation mechanism finds primitive constraints in the store which match the pattern on the left hand side of the rule and whose guard (the constraint to the left of the "|") is implied by the constraint store.

$$\underline{\{A \leq B, B \leq C, C \leq A\}}$$
$$\downarrow transitivity$$
$$\{A \leq B, B \leq C, \underline{C \leq A, A \leq C}\}$$
$$\downarrow antisymmetry$$
$$\underline{\{A \leq B, B \leq C, C = A\}}$$
$$\downarrow antisymmetry$$
$$\{A = B, C = A\}$$

Figure 12.1 CHR evaluation of partial order constraints.

Rewriting takes into account equality constraints for the purposes of matching and implication. For example, it can determine that $A \leq B, B \leq C$ matches the pattern for antisymmetry when $C = A$ is present. A simplification rule (`<=>`) replaces the matching primitive constraints with the constraint on the right hand side. A propagation rule adds the constraint on the right hand side to the constraint store.

The constraint store $\{A \leq B, B \leq C, C \leq A\}$ is rewritten as illustrated in Figure 12.1.

Constraint handling rules, when combined with a programming language, provide a very straightforward way of defining constraint solvers. Solvers based on a normal form can be implemented straightforwardly using CHRs to place constraints in normal form. Incomplete constraint solvers for complex forms of constraints can be implemented by just giving cases where the solver writer can determine that information can be propagated. CHRs have been used to implement a number of solvers for a wide variety of constraint domains. The ease of writing allows the solver to be highly specialized for the form of constraints expected in an application.

The programmer can use CHRs within a CLP system to provide sophisticated constraint solving behaviour. For example, in Section 8.5.1 we added redundant constraints to the program for scheduling in order to reduce the search space. We know that if tasks with start times $TS_1, \ldots, TS_n$ all require the same machine and have durations $D_1, \ldots, D_n$ and each must finish before the task with start time TS can start, then we can add the constraint

$$TS \geq D_1 + \cdots + D_n + \text{minimum}\{TS_1, \ldots, TS_n\}.$$

CHRs are ideal for implementing these redundant constraints and keeping them updated whenever we make choices about the relative order of tasks on the same machine.

We represent precedence relations using a CHR constraint `pred` as follows. `pred(TS`$_1$`, D`$_1$`, M`$_1$`, TS`$_2$`)` represents that task t_1, with start time TS_1, duration D_1 and machine M_1, must be completed before task t_2 with start time TS_2. The redundant constraints are generated in the form `machpred(MinT, ToTD, M, TS)` indicating that there are tasks with minimum start time $MinT$ and total duration $TotD$ all requiring machine M which must be completed before a task with start time TS.

By replacing the inequalities generated in `prectask` and `exclude` by precedence constraints of the form `pred(TS₁, D₁, M₁, TS₂)` the following CHRs can be used to add the precedence and redundant constraints.

```
transitivity @ pred(TS1,D1,M1,TS2), pred(TS2,_,_,TS3) ==> true |
      pred(TS1, D1, M1, TS3).
machine @ pred(TS1,D1,M1,TS2) ==> true | machpred(TS1,D1,M1,TS2).

constraint @ machpred(MinTS,TotD,_,TS) ==> true | TS >= MinTS + TotD.
join @ machpred(Min1,Tot1,M,TS), machpred(Min2,Tot2,M,TS) <=> true |
      Min3 = minimum(Min1,Min2),
      Tot3 = Tot1 + Tot2,
      machpred(Min3,Tot3,M,TS).
```

The first CHR transitively builds the precedence relation between tasks. The second CHR creates a `machpred` constraint for each precedence constraint. The third CHR adds the constraint on the times, namely that the start time TS must be greater than the minimum of the start times plus the total duration. Note that it also has the effect of adding the constraints from each precedence relation because of the rewriting

$$pred(TS1, D1, M1, TS2) \rightarrow machpred(TS1, D1, M1, TS2) \rightarrow TS2 \geq TS1 + D1.$$

The final CHR combines two `machpred` constraints for the same machine and final task, and creates a new one which sums the durations and takes the minimum of the start times. It replaces two `machpred` literals by one.

For the example problem of Section 8.5, the `precedences` user-defined constraints creates the following `pred` literals:

$$\{pred(TS_1, 3, m1, TS_5), pred(TS_1, 3, m1, TS_6),$$
$$pred(TS_4, 6, m2, TS_3), pred(TS_5, 3, m2, TS_3)\}$$

The first CHR uses the first and last literal to create $pred(TS_1, 3, m1, TS_3)$ because, from transitivity, task $j1$ must be before task $j3$ (through $j5$). The second CHR creates `machpred` literals for each of these `pred` literals. The fourth CHR performs one simplification, the literals $machpred(TS_4, 6, m2, TS_3)$ and $machpred(TS_5, 3, m2, TS_3)$ are replaced by $machpred(T, 9, m2, TS_3)$ where T is constrained to be the minimum of TS_5 and TS_4. The third CHR creates inequalities over the times corresponding to the `machpred` literals:

$$TS_1 + 3 \leq TS_5 \wedge TS_1 + 3 \leq TS_6 \wedge TS_4 + 6 \leq TS_3 \wedge TS_5 + 3 \leq TS_3 \wedge$$
$$T = minimum(TS_5, TS_4) \wedge T + 9 \leq TS_3.$$

We assume that the third rule is always used before the fourth rule replaces a `machpred` literal. The propagation solver obtains the range domain

$$D(TS_1) = [0..6], \quad D(TS_2) = [0..12], \quad D(TS_3) = [9..12],$$
$$D(TS_4) = [0..6], \quad D(TS_5) = [3..9], \quad D(TS_6) = [3..16].$$

The information about TS_3 is better than that obtained without adding the redundant information.

The machine exclusion constraints add further `pred` literals which cause new inequalities on start times to be added and the `machpred` literals to be further collected. For this small example, this causes no further difference in behaviour.

This approach using CHRs automatically maintains the predecessors of a task, given the current choice of ordering of tasks on the same machine, and adds the redundant information about predecessors on the same machine after each choice is made. It illustrates how CHRs, when used in conjunction with CLP, can be a very powerful tool for the constraint programmer. With little programming effort powerful redundant constraints can be added to the model which are maintained throughout the evaluation.

12.4   Functional Languages

We now look at how constraint programming has been integrated into a number of other paradigms. Like logic programming languages, functional languages are declarative—that is to say, the programmer specifies what to compute, not how to compute it. Given that constraints are declarative, and that the marriage of constraints and logic programming has been so successful, it is natural to ask whether constraints and functional languages can be combined. This has been an area of active research, and there are currently three main approaches.

The first, and one of the simplest approaches, is to embed primitive constraints and user-defined constraints into a functional language by viewing them as a function which returns a list or set of answers. As the set may be infinite, a lazy functional language is needed. The problem with this approach is that it loses much of the appeal of the constraint programming paradigm, since the programmer must explicitly program constraint solving and search using functions. Furthermore, there are difficulties dealing with variables in the answers.

The dual approach in which functions are embedded into constraint logic programming has also been tried. We note that CLP languages do provide functions—namely functions such as "+" in the underlying constraint domain. However, for many problems it is natural to want user-defined functions, such as a function *append* to concatenate two lists. At first this seems easy enough, after all, an *n*-ary function can always be thought of as a relation with an extra argument representing the result of the function. Ideally, the user should be able to define at least first order functions using syntactic sugar. For example, the functional definition of how to concatenate two lists,

```
append([],L)        =  L
append([X|LX], L)   =  [X| append(LX,L)]
```

can be straightforwardly translated into the standard append relation,

```
append([],L, Ans)        :-  Ans = L
append([X|LX], L, Ans)   :-  Ans = [X|Ans1], append(LX,L,Ans1).
```

Unfortunately there are difficulties with this approach. First, one would like constraint solving over user-defined functions to be as powerful as that over the pre-defined functions. For instance, you might write the constraint

$$X = [1], append(Y, X) = Y.$$

Unfortunately no straightforward evaluation mechanism is going to detect failure. The problem is that the function definition is operationally efficient for one mode of usage but probably not for all. A related problem is that of non-determinism—what should the evaluation mechanism do to answer the constraint

$$append(X, Y) = [1, 2, 3, 4, 5]?$$

One approach has been to extend the evaluation mechanism by providing term-rewriting for user-defined functions. Another approach has been to delay function evaluation until enough input arguments are fixed.

There is yet a third approach to combining constraints and functions. The third approach is designed to be an equal marriage of constraints and functions, unlike the previous two approaches in which constraints are built on top of a functional language, or functions are built on top of a CLP language. The key idea is to extend the lambda calculus, the rewrite system providing the evaluation mechanism for functional languages, by including a global constraint store. Function application may now add constraints to the store. The chief difficulty is determining how the the contents of the constraint store can be used to control program evaluation.

One method, known as *constrained lambda calculus*, uses the store to determine the values of variables. If the store determines a variable has a fixed value then it replaces the variable by its value throughout the lambda expression. The problem with this approach is that the constraint store is rather passive—it cannot be actively queried to guide the search.

Another approach is based on the CCP paradigm. The idea is that lambda expressions may have a guard associated with them. They may only be evaluated if the constraint store enables the guard. Variables may range over lambda expressions, and in particular procedure definitions. Thus, in this approach, as well as a constraint store there is a *procedure store* which holds the definition of procedures and their binding to "procedure variables". Not surprisingly, evaluation of a procedure is delayed until its definition is known.

This approach was pioneered in the language Oz. Oz includes constraint solvers for tree constraints and finite domain constraints, and supports the addition of new constraint solvers through its object oriented nature. An example of an Oz program for the send-more-money problem described in Section 8.1 is given below:

```
proc {SendMoreMoney Sol}
    [S E N D M O R Y] = !Sol
    in
    Sol ::: 0#9
    {FD.alldifferent Sol}

    M \=: 0   S \=: 0
    1000*S + 100*E + 10*N + D +
    1000*M + 100*D + 10*R + E
    =: 10000*M + 1000*O + 100*N + 10*E + Y
    {Forall Sol FD.enum}
end
```

The definition in effect defines the procedure variable *SendMoreMoney* which takes a single argument *Sol*. *Sol* is made up of a list $[S, E, N, D, M, O, R, Y]$ of local variables which are all digits, and constrained to be all different using the **alldifferent** method of the module *FD* (for finite domains). The arithmetic constraints are straightforward. The final statement is analogous to a **labelling** step. It adds an enumerator *FD.enum* to each variable. Notice the similarity in form to the CLP program given in Section 8.1.

Search in Oz is implemented quite differently from that in CLP languages. Search is programmable rather than being by default left-to-right depth-first. A search procedure must be used to explore the search tree. This is achieved by setting the query of the *Search* object and asking it for a next solution. For example,

```
{Search query(SendMoreMoney)}
{Search next}
```

The *Search* object encodes a search strategy. By elaborating the computation of *SendMoreMoney*, it finds a suspended choice corresponding to the enumeration routine. The search procedure can then choose how to explore this suspended choice. This approach relies on the ability to create named local computation spaces and pass them as arguments to procedures.

Oz generalizes the CLP and CCP paradigms and provides a very flexible approach to constraint programming by allowing the use of arbitrary search strategies. Unfortunately, since the search strategy is arbitrary, the techniques discussed in Chapter 10 for efficient incremental backtracking with constraint solving are not always applicable. Hence, the price of this flexibility may be a significant performance overhead if the constraint store needs to be copied during search.

12.5   Term Rewriting

Constraint programming has also been integrated into another declarative paradigm, term rewriting. Term rewriting uses pattern matching to apply *rewrite rules* to simplify terms. For example the following rewrite rules

$$
\begin{aligned}
\neg\neg X &\rightarrow X \\
\neg(X \vee Y) &\rightarrow (\neg X) \wedge (\neg Y) \\
\neg(X \wedge Y) &\rightarrow (\neg X) \vee (\neg Y) \\
Z \vee (X \wedge Y) &\rightarrow (Z \vee X) \wedge (Z \vee Y) \\
(X \wedge Y) \vee Z &\rightarrow (X \vee Z) \wedge (Y \vee Z)
\end{aligned}
$$

can be used to rewrite a Boolean formula into its conjunctive normal form. For instance, consider the Boolean formula $\neg(X \vee (Y \wedge \neg Z))$. This can be rewritten as follows where the subexpression which is rewritten is underlined.

$$
\underline{\neg(X \vee (Y \wedge \neg Z))}
$$
$$
\downarrow
$$
$$
(\neg X) \wedge \underline{\neg(Y \wedge \neg Z)}
$$
$$
\downarrow
$$
$$
(\neg X) \wedge ((\neg Y) \vee \underline{\neg(\neg Z)})
$$
$$
\downarrow
$$
$$
(\neg X) \wedge ((\neg Y) \vee Z)
$$

Note that in term rewriting, rewrite rules may be applied in any order and at any position they match in the term. A major concern is, therefore, that whichever rules are chosen and in whatever order they are used, the same result is obtained.

Term rewriting have been widely used to encode decision procedures for determining if equations hold under certain axioms. The idea is that both sides of the equation are rewritten using the rewrite rules, and they are equal if they are both rewritten to the same term. As an example, the above rules provide a partial axiomatization of Boolean algebras. They can determine that two Boolean expressions are equal whenever they can be rewritten into the same conjunctive normal form. Term rewriting has also been used for specification of abstract data types and as the basis for programming languages.

There have been two main approaches to combining term rewriting and constraints. The first approach, called *augmented term rewriting*, has many similarities to CLP. Like CLP, the programmer provides user-defined constraints, specified by rewrite rules, and execution proceeds by rewriting these rules. However, unlike CLP languages, there is no underlying constraint solver—the constraint solver is written in the same formalism.

Augmented term rewriting extends standard term rewriting in two main ways. The first extension is to allow non-local substitution. This is provided by the special expression X *is* e which is processed by being rewritten to *true* and by replacing X by e throughout the term being rewritten. For instance, the expression,

$$X \; is \; Y + 5 \wedge X = 2 \times Y$$

can be rewritten to

$$true \wedge Y + 5 = 2 \times Y.$$

Substitution is provided because it allows the easy definition of solvers, such as Gauss-Jordan, which are based on variable elimination. The second extension is to allow new local variables to be introduced in the right hand side of the rewrite rules. This is important because it allows user-defined constraints to be specified in a natural manner.

The following example, taken from [86], illustrates augmented term rewriting.[1] The program specifies how to append two lists. Note that append is used as an infix operator.

```
[] append L        →   L
[X|L1] append L2   →   [X|(L1 append L2)].
```

The programmer must also specify how constraint solving works for lists. The following rewrite rules define list equality:

```
[] = []            →   true
[X|L1] = [Y|L2]    →   X=Y  ∧  L1=L2.
```

The equality relationship for the integers is built in, but is conceptually defined by

```
1 = 1   →   true
2 = 2   →   true
3 = 3   →   true
          ⋮
```

The conjunction operator "∧" has the following rewrite rule

```
true ∧ X   →   X.
```

Now consider the expression $([1,2] \; append \; x) = [1,2,3,4,5]$. This will be rewritten as illustrated in Figure 12.2 We can also solve for x in the expression $([1,2] \; append \; [3,4,5]) = x$.

However, the expression $(x \; append \; y) = [1,2,3,4,5]$ cannot be rewritten. There is no mechanism to solve queries of this form as the operational semantics does

---

1. The syntax is slightly modified to fit that of rewrite systems

$$\underline{([1,2] \ append \ x)} = [1,2,3,4,5]$$
$$\downarrow$$
$$\underline{[1|([2] \ append \ x)]} = [1,2,3,4,5]$$
$$\downarrow$$
$$\underline{(1=1)} \ \wedge \ ([2] \ append \ x) = [2,3,4,5]$$
$$\downarrow$$
$$\underline{true \ \wedge \ ([2] \ append \ x)} = [2,3,4,5]$$
$$\downarrow$$
$$\underline{([2] \ append \ x)} = [2,3,4,5]$$
$$\downarrow$$
$$\underline{[2|([] \ append \ x)]} = [2,3,4,5]$$
$$\downarrow$$
$$\underline{(2=2)} \ \wedge \ ([] \ append \ x) = [3,4,5]$$
$$\downarrow$$
$$\underline{true \ \wedge \ ([] \ append \ x)} = [3,4,5]$$
$$\downarrow$$
$$\underline{([] \ append \ x)} = [3,4,5]$$
$$\downarrow$$
$$x = [3,4,5]$$

Figure 12.2 Rewriting $([1,2] \ append \ x) = [1,2,3,4,5]$.

not include search since the operational mechanism employs "don't care non-determinism." This is one of the main drawbacks of augmented term rewriting and means that it is not suitable for solving combinatorial problems.

On the other hand, a nice feature of augmented term rewriting is that term rewriting provides a uniform mechanism for both constraint solving and evaluation.

The other approach to combining constraints with term rewriting is *constrained term rewriting*. The idea here is to add constraints to rewrite rules which specify when they may be used for rewriting. As a simple example, consider the rewrite rule for commutativity of "+,"

$$X + Y \rightarrow Y + X.$$

Unfortunately, such a rule leads to non-termination since it can be applied an infinite number of times. However, if we use the constrained rewrite rule

$$X + Y \rightarrow Y + X \ || \ X \succ Y$$

then we no longer have this problem. We have added a condition $X \succ Y$ that ensures we can only apply this rule when X is greater than Y where $\succ$ is some fixed total ordering on the expressions. At each step in rewriting some underlying constraint solver is used to verify that the constraint associated with the rule is satisfied by the expressions mapped to the variables in the rule.

Constrained term rewriting is primarily intended for implementing automatic theorem provers. Apart from the application area, the main differences to CLP are that: (1) there is no global constraint store, (2) matching is used when applying rules rather than equating arguments, (3) it rewrites expressions, rather than goals, and (4) rules are applied using a "don't care non-determinism." Because of (4) and because (2) can be implemented by using delay condition on rule application, constrained term rewriting is more closely related to CCP languages than to CLP languages.

12.6   Imperative Programming Languages

One interesting area of research is to integrate constraints into traditional imperative programming languages, in particular object oriented languages. The motivation for doing so is clear. Constraints allow the programmer to declaratively specify what they want, allowing simple concise programs. This is particularly useful in incremental contexts where repeated changes to one variable must be communicated to other variables. Conversely, the imperative paradigm allows the programmer to write code which is guaranteed to behave efficiently and which can be easily integrated into existing applications. However, the integration of the two paradigms is not easy. In contrast to the constraint paradigm, the imperative paradigm allows a variable to have different values at different times in the program execution. It also requires that a variable has a fixed value when it is used.

An interesting approach is used in the *Kaleidoscope* family of languages which generalize both the constraint and imperative paradigms. In this paradigm there is a single global constraint store. As in the imperative paradigm, at different times during the execution of a program, the same variable may appear to have different values. Of course, giving a variable more than one value is anathema to the constraint paradigm. However, the Kaleidoscope family of languages circumvent this problem by regarding a program variable as a sequence of logical variables. At different points in time, the program variable stands for different logical variables, essentially subscripted by the time of execution. Thus the assignment

```
X  :=  X+1;
```

is really understood as representing the constraint

$$X_{t+1} = X_t + 1.$$

In the Kaleidoscope paradigm, every variable has a fixed value at all points in the execution. This is achieved by using a hierarchy of constraints in which, each constraint has an associated weight. Constraints weighted with `always` must be satisfied at all time points, this is the strongest requirement. While for constraints with other weights, those with heavier weights are satisfied in preference to those with lighter weights. There is a weak default constraint which ensures that variables remain the same over time whenever reasonable, that is $X_{t+1} = X_t$.

As a simple example, consider the following Kaleidoscope'90 program:

```
always: X = Y;
X := 10;
while mouse.down do
  X := mouse.posn.x;
end;
print Y;
```

The program specifies a global constraint $X = Y$ and then assigns values to X. This will automatically update the value of Y so as to maintain the constraint.

The Kaleidescope approach to the integration of constraints and the imperative programming language relies much on the CLP paradigm. Like CLP there is a global constraint store and incremental constraint solving algorithms must be employed. However, the Kaleidescope approach deliberately eschews search and backtracking, in order to remain deterministic. This makes it suitable for incremental applications such as graphical user interface building, but not suitable for solving combinatorial search or optimization problems.

12.7   Constraint Solving Toolkits

Constraint solving toolkits provide another approach for integrating constraints into a traditional programming language. Although not an equal marriage between constraints and imperative programming like the Kaleidescope approach, the integration provided by these toolkits is quite natural. This is possible because of the object oriented nature of the implementation languages which allow constraints, (logical) variables and solvers to be first class entities. However, the toolkits do not provide a single unified paradigm like constraint logic programming. Rather the integration embeds constraint programming into a host imperative programming language in a simple way.

These toolkits are an offshoot of the CLP paradigm and employ incremental constraint solving algorithms similar to those used in CLP systems. Many of the solvers also employ the same model of computation as CLP in which there is a single global store to which constraints are added and non-deterministic search is used to find solutions to a given goal.

Current toolkits tend to be problem domain focused, for instance on graphical applications or scheduling applications. We shall look at two example toolkits, in order to give some feel for their power and use.

Our first example is the ILOG SOLVER toolkit which is designed for solving finite domain problems. The following C++ program from [107] employs the ILOG SOLVER toolkit to solve the N-queens problem (described in Example 3.2).

```
#include <ilsolver/ilcint.h>

void main() {
  IlcInit();
  int i, nqueen = 1000;
  IlcIntVarArray x(nqueen,0,nqueen-1),
                 x1(nqueen), x2(nqueen);
  for (i=0; i<nqueen; i++) {
    x1[i] = x[i] + i;
    x2[i] = x[i] - i;
  }
  IlcTell(IlcAllDiff(x));
  IlcTell(IlcAllDiff(x1));
  IlcTell(IlcAllDiff(x2));
  IlcSolve(IlcGenerate(x, IlcChooseMinSize));
  cout << x << endl; //prints
  IlcEnd();
}
```

The initial call to `IlcInit()` initializes the internal data used by the constraint
solver and evaluation mechanism while the call to `IlcEnd` releases the memory
used. The call to `IlcIntVarArray` declares x, x1 and x2 to be arrays of size *nqueen*
of constrained integer variables or expressions. The additional arguments for the
declaration of x specify the domain of the variables to be $0, \ldots, nqueen - 1$. The **for**
loop constructs expressions which are placed in the arrays x1 and x2. Note the use of
overloading of the standard arithmetic operators. The call to `IlcAllDiff` creates
a constraint which specifies that all expressions in the input array are different,
that is no two expressions are equal. The `IlcTell` function adds a constraint to
the global store. Finally, the function `IlcSolve` searches for one solution to a goal
while `IlcGenerate` is a goal which is evaluated using standard labelling techniques.
The argument `IlcChooseMinSize` is the name of a strategy to be employed by
`IlcGenerate` when choosing which variable to label. In this case, the strategy is to
choose the variable with smallest domain.

This program is rather typical of the way in which the ILOG SOLVER toolkit
is used. First, the constraints are built using overloading and the control facilities
of C++, then they are placed in the store, and finally non-deterministic search is
used to find the a solution or minimum to the constraints in the store.

This indicates one difference between the toolkit approach and CLP. In the CLP
paradigm user-defined constraints are used to collect the primitive constraints which
are added to the constraint store. In a toolkit this is done by using the control and
abstraction facilities of the host language. A consequence of this is that it is difficult
to dynamically control the addition of the constraints in the same way that you
can in a CLP system. Another, consequence is that debugging and optimization is
at the level of the host language rather than at the level of the constraints being

used to model the problem.

On the other hand, the toolkit approach has at least two advantages over earlier CLP systems. First, some toolkits allow the programmer to define new primitive constraints by extending the solver and search mechanism to handle these constraints. This provides considerable flexibility and potential efficiency gains for the programmer. Second, code developed using a toolkit can be more easily integrated into a large application.

However, it is worth reemphasizing that these object oriented toolkits are based on the CLP paradigm and most of the modelling and programming techniques we have described for CLP can be employed when using a toolkit. These toolkits are therefore very different in nature from the traditional mathematical software libraries of numerical algorithms provided in such languages as C or FORTRAN. In mathematical software libraries, constraints, variables and search strategies are not explicit in the program but rather implicitly represented in the implementation by, for example, an array of coefficients. Thus mathematical software libraries require the programmer to work at a very different level. Of course, it is possible to take an existing mathematical software library and encapsulate it using a high level interface.

The second major application area of constraint solving toolkits is for graphical applications. Typical graphical applications have three important requirements which are not met in the usual CLP paradigm. First, they require arbitrary removal of constraints since the user can select any graphic object and delete it, thus requiring its associated constraints to be removed. Second, rather than just testing for satisfiability, graphical applications require a solution to be found to the current constraint store, as this solution determines how the graphics will be displayed on the screen. However, not just any solution will do, since it is unsatisfactory if objects unnecessarily move all over the screen whenever a constraint is added. Various techniques, including finding the solution as close as possible to the old solution and the use of hierarchical constraint systems in which some constraints are optional (similar to that described for Kaleidoscope), have been used. Third, the toolkits must support very fast direct manipulation. Typically this is done by looking at the current constraints, determining dependencies between them and then "compiling" a function which can quickly compute the changes to the last solution if the values for the fixed (small) set of variables being manipulated are modified.

QOCA is an example of C++ toolkit for graphical applications. The following C++ program makes use of QOCA to perform the same task as the example Kaleidoscope'90 program from the previous section.

```
CFloatHandle x,y;
LinEqSolver solver;
LinConstraint eqxy = (1.0*x - 1.0*y == 0.0);
```

```
solver.AddConstraint(eqxy);
x.SetValue(10.0);
solver.AddEditVar(x);
while (mouse.down) {
   x.SetDesValue(mouse.posn.x);
   solver.Resolve();
   }
solver.ClearVarsOfInterest();
cout << y.GetValue() << endl;
```

The call to `solver.AddConstraint` adds the linear constraint `eqxy` which constrains the values of the variables `x` and `y`. The call `solver.AddEditVar` indicates that variable `x` will be the subject of direct manipulation. The first call to `solver.Resolve` generates data structures which are used in subsequent calls to `solver.Resolve` to solve the constraints for different values of `x`.

Toolkits for graphical applications are more closely related to the Kaleidescope paradigm than to the CLP paradigm. In particular, they do not provide search and variables always have a fixed value which may change over time.

12.8 Mathematical Languages

Finally, we shall look at mathematical languages. We use this term to cover two types of language for specifying and dealing with constraints: *mathematical modelling languages* and *symbolic algebra packages*. Mathematical modelling languages provide a way of specifying large conjunctions of primitive constraints, in CLP terms a user-defined constraint, in a way that is natural and easy for the modeller to express, and which can be automatically translated into a form that can be handled by an underlying constraint solver. Symbolic algebra packages support symbolic manipulation of mathematical expressions, such as constraint solving, integration, differentiation, and usually provide numerical manipulations, such as numeric constraint solving, and graphical display of functions.

12.8.1 Modelling Languages

The process of modelling can be thought of as providing an abstract system of primitive constraints that represent the general form of the problem to be solved. Questions are then asked by specifying data for a particular problem instance. The model and data are converted to a solver digestible form and fed to the solver to find the answer.

There are a number of popular modelling languages used in the operations research and mathematics community. One example language is AMPL, a language for specifying linear arithmetic optimization problems in a convenient human readable form.

One of the most pleasing features of mathematical modelling languages are their broad facilities for handling sets and variables that are indexed by sets, that is arrays. This is a core aspect of these languages, designed to make it simple to specify large numbers of linear constraints succinctly. The languages themselves are usually designed so that constraints are specified in a syntax which is close to mathematical notation.

Another feature of mathematical modelling language is that data for different problem instances can be input separately from the model and different optimization functions can be specified for the same constraints, so a single model can be used to specify many different problems.

As an example, consider the following AMPL model of the problem discussed in Example 6.4 of determining temperatures in a finite element description of a metal plate described using $W \times H$ elements, in which the top edge is set to one temperature and the remaining edges to another.

```
param W > 2; # width of plate
param H > 2; # height of plate

param toptemp; # temperature at top of plate
param edgetemp; # temperature on other edges

var Temp {1..W, 1..H} # temperature at positions of the plate

subject to topedge {c in 1..W}: Temp[1,c] = toptemp;
subject to leftedge {r in 2..H}: Temp[r,1] = edgetemp;
subject to rightedge {r in 2..H}: Temp[r,W] = edgetemp;
subject to bottomedge {c in 1..W}: Temp[H,c] = edgetemp;

subject to dirichlet {r in 2..H-1, c in 2..W-1}:
4*Temp[r,c] = Temp[r-1,c] + Temp[r,c-1] +
        Temp[r,c+1] + Temp[r+1,c];

minimize totaltemp: sum {c in 1..W, r in 1..H} Temp[c,r];
```

Although the original problem is a satisfiability problem we are forced to add a dummy minimization goal so that it can be solved by AMPL. The 6×7 instance of the problem illustrated in Figure 6.1 can be specified by the data file

```
param W = 7;
param H = 6;
param toptemp = 100;
param edgetemp = 0;
```

Mathematical modelling languages are excellent for solving the problems that fit within the class they are designed to model. One advantage of modelling languages is that they can usually be used with a variety of linear arithmetic optimization packages, for example MINOS and CPlex. As we have discussed, another advantage is that they neatly differentiate the model of a problem from the constraints that describe the data for a particular instance of the problem.

The restrictions of mathematical modelling languages arise from the underlying solver capabilities. These languages can usually only be used to specify a conjunction of linear constraints together with a linear optimization function. Although these constraints can be built in a number of flexible and intuitive ways the lack of nonlinear constraint handling means that, for example, the `mortgage` program cannot be defined.

While mathematical modelling languages provide excellent facilities for handling sets and arrays, they are more difficult to use with other types of data. For example, even though all the arithmetic constraints produced in the tree layout program of Section 6.6 are linear, and so it is a linear optimization problem, it is difficult to see how to use a mathematical modelling language such as AMPL to construct these constraints from the initial tree description, since it is not a general purpose programming language.

Because mathematical modelling languages merely specify a conjunction of constraints and an optimization function, and then send them to a remote solver there is no way to specify search strategies within them. Choices need to be converted to a conjunctive form using methods analogous to those discussed in Section 8.7 and Exercise P8.16. If the underlying constraint solver uses search to solve such constraints then it is largely beyond the control of the modeller.

We foresee CLP languages becoming the mathematical modelling languages of the future because of their greater flexibility (they are full programming languages) and their ability to specify search within the same language. However for this to happen, CLP languages will need to incorporate the excellent handling of sets and arrays of current mathematical modelling languages and provide the ability to interface with other solvers.

12.8.2 Symbolic Algebra Packages

As their name suggests, symbolic algebra packages are designed to perform symbolic algebra manipulation automatically. Their main use is as a toolkit for mathematicians and scientists who are interested in solving algebraic problems. Many of the facilities in a symbolic algebra package are constraint operations. Algebraic expressions can be constructed, rewritten and simplified. Arithmetic constraints can be specified, and solved by the package. Such packages usually include sophisticated handling of nonlinear constraints.

Mathematica is an example of a symbolic algebra package which also includes a completely general programming language. It allows programming using functional, procedural and term rewriting paradigms. An example of a Mathematica program to solve problems about mortgages (when the number of time periods is fixed) is:

```
mortgage[p_, t_Integer?Positive, i_, r_] :=
    mortgage[p * (1 + i) - r, (t-1), i, r];
mortgage[p_, 0, i_, r_] := p;
```

The program defines a function `mortgage[p, t, i, r]` which returns the balance at the end of a mortgage for principle p for length t periods with interest rate i and repayment r. It works by constructing a mathematical expression of the balance in terms of the inputs. The expression can then be used to build a constraint which can be passed to the solver. For example the command

```
Solve[mortgage[p, 10, 10/1200, r] == b]
```

asks for the relationship between principal, repayment and balance for a 10 month mortgage at 10% per annum. The answer is

$$\left\{\left\{\ b \to \frac{672749994932560009201\ p}{619173642240000000000} - \frac{53576352692560009201\ r}{5159780352000000000}\ \right\}\right\}.$$

This is the exact rational answer, a floating point representation is determined by

```
N[Solve[mortgage[p, 10, 10/1200, r] == b]]
```

which gives the answer

```
{{ b -> 1.08653 p - 10.3835 r }}.
```

Because Mathematica provides very sophisticated nonlinear constraint solving and simplification, it can be used to answer some difficult questions. For example "What is the interest rate for a mortgage of 3 periods for $1000 with repayment $500 to end up with balance 0?" can be expressed as:

```
N[Solve[mortgage[1000, 3, i, 500] == 0]].
```

Mathematica determines three exact answers (two complex values for i) which are large and complicated expressions. Since we asked for the numeric values we obtain only one

```
{{ i -> 0.233752 }}.
```

Symbolic algebra packages allow very powerful reasoning about arithmetic constraints, particularly nonlinear constraints. They are designed as a support tool for mathematicians. They are not really designed for specifying and solving large systems of constraints. Because symbolic constraint packages like Mathematica include general purpose programming facilities, it is possible to do so, but it is not straightforward. Since there is no implicit constraint store or search mechanism, both must be programmed using the facilities of the language. The constraint solving facilities are not designed for incremental constraint solving and so they can be very slow, especially when solving problems which involve search. Symbolic algebra packages do, however, provide many useful facilities, such as nonlinear constraint solving and simplification, so they are sometimes used within other constraint languages.

12.9 Notes

Clark and Gregory introduced committed choice and don't care non-determinism into Prolog [29]. For more information about concurrent logic languages see the survey by Shapiro [117]. Maher generalized concurrent logic languages to the constraint setting by recognizing that the synchronization operator used in concurrent logic languages can be thought of as constraint entailment [90]. The formal properties of concurrent constraint programming languages [59, 139] have been widely studied since then. In particular, Saraswat has provided elegant theoretical semantics for these languages [115] and was responsible for the term "concurrent constraint programming."

Constraint handling rules were introduced by Frühwirth [51] and are described more fully in [52]. An implementation of constraint handling rules is included in the ECLiPSe system. It also contains many constraint solvers built using constraint handling rules including solvers for Booleans constraints, set constraints, equation solving over real or rational numbers, temporal reasoning and geometric reasoning about rectangles. A number of applications of constraint handling rules are described in [52]. Mark Wallace suggested their use for adding redundant constraints in the scheduling example.

Before the advent of constraint logic programming there was considerable interest in combining the logic and functional programming paradigms—indeed to some extent the generalization of logic programming to allow functions naturally paved the way to the theory of constraint logic programs. See for example the collection of papers in [40]. The first approach to the integration of constraints into functional languages is due to Darlington *et al* and described in [39]. The paper of Crossley *et al* [36] describes the constrained lambda calculus approach in which only definite values can be communicated from the constraint store. The Oz programming language has been developed by Smolka. In addition to incorporating functional and concurrent constraint programming, it also provides objects. It is introduced in [121, 120]. Oz can be obtained via the Web from `http://www.ps.uni-sb.de/oz/`

Augmented term rewriting was introduced by Leler in [86]. Constrained term rewriting generalizes ordered rewriting systems. An introduction is given by Kirchnir [79].

Combining constraint with imperative programming languages has not been investigated very fully. Kaleidoscope [49] developed by Borning and others, is one of the few examples of such languages. The Kaleidoscope approach seems less successful than the constraint toolkit approach in combining the two paradigms, in part because of the conflict between the imperative programmer's desire to fully know the state of every variable during execution and the constraint programming view of complex flow of information. In the toolkit approach the programmer is limited in their handling of constraints and constrained variables by the abstract data type provided by the toolkit.

CHARME [100] and ILOG SOLVER [106] are commercial constraint-solving toolkits for finite domain constraints. They are both offshoots of the CLP language CHIP developed at ECRC and use similar propagation based constraint solving techniques. An object oriented Lisp based toolkit called PECOS [105] was the precursor to ILOG SOLVER.

The use of constraints in computer graphics dates from Sutherland's system SKETCHPAD [133]. Since that time this has been a fertile research area with applications in CAD, simulation, user interfaces and modelling of dynamic physical objects. Two toolkits especially designed for such applications and which employ incremental arithmetic constraint solving techniques developed for CLP are QOCA [64, 16], which is a C++ toolkit providing linear arithmetic constraints, and Ultraviolet [15], which is a Smalltalk toolkit providing local propagation and linear equality solvers.

Mathematical modelling languages were first introduced in the 1970's, replacing matrix generators as the way of specifying large linear programs. The majority of mathematical modelling languages are designed for real linear arithmetic constraints with real linear optimization functions, since these are the constraints supported by the underlying solvers used by the modelling languages. Mixed integer constraints are supported by later modelling languages. AMPL [46] fits in this category and also provides additional forms of modelling such as facilities for modelling graphs. ALICE [83] is a somewhat different mathematical modelling language designed for integer optimization problems. It allows models to be written using abstract functions which may be injective, bijective, etc. Constraint solving is handled by consistency methods such as those discussed in Chapter 3 as well as by reasoning about abstract functions.

The first widely available symbolic algebra packages were MACSYMA [57] and REDUCE [109] developed in the late 1960s. Even these early systems provided a wide range of facilities and were extensible and modifiable. Modern symbolic algebra packages such as Mathematica [143] and MAPLE V [26] enhance earlier packages by including extensive facilities for programming and graphical display of functions.

References

1. H. Abramson and M. Rogers, editors. *Meta-programming in Logic Programming*. MIT Press, 1988.

2. A. Aggoun and N. Beldiceanu. Extending CHIP in order to solve complex scheduling and placement problems. *Journal of Mathematical and Computer Modelling*, 17(7):57–73, 1993.

3. A. Aggoun and N. Beldiceanu. Overview of the CHIP compiler system. In F. Benhamou and A. Colmerauer, editors, *Constraint Logic Programming: Selected Research*, pages 421–435. MIT Press, 1993.

4. A. Aggoun, M. Dincbas, A. Herold, H. Simonis, and P. Van Hentenryck. The CHIP System. Technical Report TR-LP-24, European Computer Industry Research Centre (ECRC), Munich, Germany, June 1987.

5. H. Aït-Kaci. *Warren's Abstract Machine: A Tutorial Reconstruction*. MIT Press, 1991.

6. F. Bancilhon. Naive evaluation of recursively defined relations. In Brodie and Mylopoulos, editors, *On Knowledge Base Management Systems—Integrating Database and AI Systems*, pages 165–178. Springer Verlag, 1985.

7. F. Bancilhon, D. Maier, Y. Sagiv, and J. Ullman. Magic sets and other strange ways to implement logic programs. In *Proceedings of the ACM Symposium on Principles of Database Systems*, pages 1–15, Cambridge, Massachusetts, March 1986.

8. G. Di Battisa, P. Eades, R. Tamassia, and I. Tollis. Algorithms for drawing graphs: an annotated bibliography. *Computational Geometry: Theory and Applications*, 4:235–282, 1994.

9. F. Benhamou and A. Colmerauer, editors. *Constraint Logic Programming: Selected Research*. MIT Press, 1993.

10. F. Berthier. A financial model using qualitative and quantitative knowledge. In F. Gardin, editor, *Proceedings of the International Symposium on Computational Intelligence 89*, pages 1–9, Milano, Italy, September 1989.

11. F. Berthier. Solving Financial Decision Problems with CHIP. In J.-L. Le Moigne and P. Bourgine, editors, *Proceedings of the 2nd Conference on Economics and Artificial Intelligence*, pages 233–238, Paris, France, June 1990.

12. R. Bland. New finite pivoting rules for the simplex method. *Mathematics of Operations Research*, 2:103–107, 1977.

13. G. Boole. *An Investigation of the Laws of Thought*. Walton, London, 1847.

14. A. Borning. The programming language aspects of ThingLab, a constraint – oriented simulation laboratory. *ACM Transactions on Programming Languages and Systems*, 3(4):252–387, October 1981.

15. A. Borning and B. Freeman-Benson. The OTI constraint solver: A constraint library for constructing interactive graphical user interfaces. In U. Montanari and F. Rossi, editors, *Constraint Programming: Proceedings of the 1st International Conference*, volume 976 of *LNCS*, pages 624–628, Cassis, France, 1995. Springer Verlag.

16. A. Borning, K. Marriott, P. Stuckey, and Y. Xiao. Solving linear arithmetic constraints for user interface applications. In *Proceedings of ACM 10th Symposium on User Interface Software and Technology (UIST)*, pages 87–96. ACM Press, 1997.

17. R. Boyer and J. Moore. A fast string searching algorithm. *Communications of the ACM*, 20(10):62–72, 1977.

18. A. Brodsky and V. Segal. The C^3 constraint object-oriented database system: An overview. In *Proc. CDB'97 and CP'96 Workshop on Constraint Databases and their Application*, volume 1191 of *LNCS*, pages 134–159. Springer–Verlag, 1997.

19. J. Broek and H. Daniels. Application of constraint logic programming to asset and liability management in banks. *Computer Science in Economics and Management*, 4(2):107–116, May 1991.

20. F. Brown. *Boolean Reasoning: The logic of Boolean equations*. Kluwer Academic, 1990.

21. R. Bryant. Symbolic Boolean manipulation with ordered binary-decision diagrams. *ACM Computing Surveys*, 24:293–318, 1992.

22. W. Büttner and H. Simonis. Embedding Boolean expressions into logic programming. *Journal of Symbolic Computation*, 4:191–205, 1987.

23. Y. Caseau and F. Laburthe. Improving CLP scheduling with task intervals. In P. Van Hentenryck, editor, *Logic Programming: Proceedings of the 11th International Conference*, pages 369–383, Santa Margherita, Italy, June 1994. MIT Press.

24. Y. Caseau and F. Laburthe. Cumulative scheduling with task intervals. In M. Maher, editor, *Logic Programming: Proceedings of the 1996 Joint International Conference and Symposium*, pages 363–377, Bonn, Germany, September 1996. MIT Press.

25. D. Chan. Constructive negation based on the completed database. In R. Kowalski and K. Bowen, editors, *Logic Programming: Proceedings of the 1988 Joint International Conference and Symposium*, pages 111–125, Seattle, Washington, August 1988. MIT Press.

26. B. Char, K. Geddes, G. Gonnet, B. Leong, M. Monaghan, and S. Watt. *Maple V Language Reference Manual*. Springer Verlag, 1991.

27. B. Cheung, J. Lee, and J. Wu. Speeding up constraint propagation by redundant modeling. In *Constraint Programming: Proceedings of the 2nd International Conference*, pages 91–103, Cambridge, Massachusetts, August 1996. Springer-Verlag.

28. K. Clark. Negation as failure. In H. Gallaire and J. Minker, editors, *Logic and Databases*, pages 293–322. Plenum Press, 1978.

29. K. Clark and S. Gregory. A relational language for parallel programming. In *Proc. ACM Conference on Functional Languages and Computer Architecture*, pages 171–178. ACM Press, 1981.

30. K. Clark and F. McCabe. IC-Prolog - language features. In K. Clark and S. Tarnlund, editors, *Logic Programming*, pages 122–149. Academic Press, 1982.

31. J. Cleary. Logical arithmetic. *Future Computing Systems*, 2(2):125–149, 1987.

32. J. Cohen. Constraint logic programming languages. *Communications of the ACM*, 33(7):52–68, July 1990.

33. A. Colmerauer. PROLOG II reference manual and theoretical model. Technical report, Groupe Intelligence Artificielle, Université Aix – Marseille II, October 1982.

34. A. Colmerauer. Opening the PROLOG-III universe. *BYTE Magazine*, 12(9), August 1987.

35. A. Colmerauer. An introduction to PROLOG-III. *Communications of the ACM*, 33(7):69–90, July 1990.

36. J. Crossley, L. Mandel, and M. Wirsing. First-order constrained lambda calculus. In F. Baader and K. U. Schulz, editors, *Frontiers of Combining Systems 96—First International Workshop*, pages 339–356. Kluwer, 1996.

37. G. Dantzig. Maximization of a linear function of variables subject to linear inequalities. In T. Koopmans, editor, *Activity Analysis of Production and Allocation*, pages 359–373. John Wiley & Sons, 1951.

38. G. Dantzig and W. Orchard-Hays. The product form of the inverse in the simplex method. *Mathematical Tables and Other Aids to Computation*, 8:64–67, 1954.

39. J. Darlington, Y.-K. Guo, and H. Pull. A new perspective on integrating functional and logic languages. In *Fifth Generation Computer Systems*, pages 682–693, Tokyo, Japan, 1992.

40. D. DeGroot and G. Lindstrom, editors. *Logic Programming: Relations, Functions, and Equations*. Prentice-Hall, 1985.

41. D. Diaz and P. Codognet. A minimal extension of the WAM for clp(FD). In D.S. Warren, editor, *Logic Programming: Proceedings of the 10th International Conference*, pages 774–792, Budapest, Hungary, June 1993. MIT Press.

42. M. Dincbas, H. Simonis, and P. Van Hentenryck. Solving a Cutting-Stock Problem in Constraint Logic Programming. In R. Kowalski and K. Bowen, editors, *Logic Programming: Proceedings of the 1988 Joint International Conference and Symposium*, pages 42–58, Seattle, WA, August 1988. MIT Press.

43. M. Dincbas, H. Simonis, and P. Van Hentenryck. Solving Large Scheduling Problems in Logic Programming. In *EURO-TIMS Joint International Conference on Operations Research and Management Science*, Paris, France, July 1988.

44. M. Dincbas, P. Van Hentenryck, H. Simonis, A. Aggoun, T. Graf, and F. Berthier. The Constraint Logic Programming Language CHIP. In *Proceedings of the International Conference on Fifth Generation Computer Systems*, pages 693–702, Tokyo, Japan, December 1988.

45. M. Ducassé and J. Noyé. Logic programming environments: Dynamic program analysis and debugging. *Journal of Logic Programming*, 19/20:351–384, 1994.

46. R. Fourer et al. *AMPL : a modeling language for mathematical programming*. Boyd & Fraser Publishing, 1993.

47. A. Foster and E. Elcock. Absys1: An incremental compiler for assertions: An introduction. In B. Melzer and D. Mitchie, editors, *Machine Intelligence 4*. Edinburgh University Press, 1969.

48. J. Fourier. Analyse des travaux de l'Académie Royale des Sciences, pendant l'année 1824; partie mathématique. In *Histoire de l'Académie Royale des Sciences de France* **7**, *xlvii–lv*. 1827. English translation (partially) in D. Kohler, Translation of a report by Fourier on his work on linear inequalities, *Opsearch* **10**: 38–42, 1973.

49. B. Freeman-Benson and A. Borning. The design and implementation of Kaleidoscope'90: A constraint imperative programming language. In *Proc. IEEE Int. Conf.*

Computer Languages, pages 174–180. IEEE Computer Soc. Press, 1992.

50. E. Freuder and A. Mackworth, editors. *Constraint-Based Reasoning*. MIT Press, 1994.

51. T. Frühwirth. Constraint simplification rules. In A. Podelski, editor, *Constraint Programming: Basics and Trends*, volume 910 of *LNCS*. Springer-Verlag, 1995.

52. T. Frühwirth. A declarative language for constraint systems: theory and practice of constraint handling rules. *Journal of Logic Programming*, to appear.

53. M. Garey and D. Johnson. *Computers and Intractability*. W. Freeman and Company, New York, 1979.

54. C. Gauss. Beiträge zur Theorie der algebraischen Gleichungen. In *Werke, Vol. 3*, pages 71–102. K. Gesellschaft Wissenschaft, Göttingen, Germany, 1876.

55. M. Gorlick, C. Kesselman, D. Marotta, and D. Stott Parker. Mockingbird: A logical methodology for testing. *Journal of Logic Programming*, 8(1/2):95–119, 1990.

56. T. Graf, P. Van Hentenryck, C. Pradelles, and L. Zimmer. Simulation of hybrid circuits in constraint logic programming. In *Proceedings of the Eleventh International Joint Conference on Artificial Intelligence*, pages 72–77, Detroit, 1989.

57. MATHLAB Group. *Macsyma Reference Manual*. MIT Press, 1977.

58. Programming Systems Group. *SICStus Prolog User's Manual*, release 3#5 edition, 1996.

59. D. Gudeman, K. De Bosschere, and S. Debray. jc: An efficient and portable implementation of Janus. In K. Apt, editor, *Logic Programming: Proceedings of the 1992 Joint International Conference and Symposium*, pages 399–413, Washington, November 1992. MIT Press.

60. R. M. Haralick and G. L. Elliot. Increasing tree search efficiency for constraint satisfaction problems. *Artificial Intelligence*, 14:263–313, 1980.

61. N. Heintze, J. Jaffar, C. Lim, S. Michaylov, P. Stuckey, R. Yap, and C. Yee. The CLP($\mathcal{R}$) programmers manual – version 1. Technical Report 59, Department of Computer Science, Monash University, June 1986.

62. N. Heintze, S. Michaylov, and P. Stuckey. CLP($\mathcal{R}$) and some electrical engineering problems. *Journal of Automated Reasoning*, 9:231–260, 1992.

63. N. Heintze, S. Michaylov, P. Stuckey, and R. Yap. On meta-programming in CLP($\mathcal{R}$). In E. Lusk and R. Overbeek, editors, *Logic Programming: Proceedings of the North American Conference*, pages 52–68, Cleveland, Ohio, October 1989. MIT Press.

64. R. Helm, K. Marriott, T. Huynh, and J. Vlissides. An object-oriented architecture for constraint-based graphical editing. In C. Laffra, E. Blake, V. de Mey, and X. Pintado, editors, *Object-Oriented Programming for Graphics*, pages 217–238. Springer-Verlag, New York, 1995.

65. J. Herbrand. *Recherches sur la théorie de la démonstration*. PhD thesis, Université de Paris, France, 1930. English translation of Chapter 5 in J. van Heijenoort, editor, *From Frege to Gödel*, Harvard University Press, 1967.

66. T. Huynh and C. Lassez. An expert decision–support system for option–based investment. *Computer Mathematics with Applications*, 20(9/10):1–14, 1990.

67. E. Hyvönen. Constraint reasoning based on interval arithmetic. In *Proceedings of the Eleventh International Joint Conference on Artificial Intelligence*, pages 193–199, Detroit, 1989.

68. J. Jaffar. Minimal and complete word unification. *Journal of the ACM*, 37(1):47–85, 1990.

69. J. Jaffar and J.-L. Lassez. Constraint logic programming. In *Proceedings of the 14th ACM Symposium on Principles of Programming Languages*, pages 111–119, Munich, Germany, January 1987. ACM Press.

70. J. Jaffar, J.-L. Lassez, and M. Maher. A logic programming language scheme. In D. DeGroot and G. Lindstrom, editors, *Logic Programming: Relations, Functions and Equations*, pages 441–468. Prentice Hall, 1986.

71. J. Jaffar and M. Maher. Constraint logic programming: A survey. *Journal of Logic Programming*, 19/20:503–582, 1994.

72. J. Jaffar, M. Maher, K. Marriott, and P. Stuckey. The semantics of constraint logic programs. *Journal of Logic Programming*, To appear.

73. J. Jaffar, M. Maher, P. Stuckey, and R. Yap. Projecting CLP($\mathcal{R}$) constraints. *New Generation Computing*, 11:449–469, 1993.

74. J. Jaffar and S. Michaylov. Methodology and implementation of a CLP system. In J.-L. Lassez, editor, *Logic Programming: Proceedings of the 4th International Conference*, pages 196–218, Melbourne, Australia, May 1987. MIT Press.

75. J. Jaffar, S. Michaylov, P. Stuckey, and R. Yap. The CLP($\mathcal{R}$) language and system. *ACM Transactions on Programming Languages and Systems*, 14(3):339–395, July 1992.

76. J. Jaffar and P. Stuckey. Semantics of infinite tree logic programming. *Theoretical Computer Science*, 42(4):141–158, 1986.

77. P. Kanellakis, G. Kuper, and P. Revesz. Constraint query languages. *Journal of Computer and System Science*, 51(1):26–52, 1995.

78. T. Kawamura, H. Ohwada, and F. Mizoguchi. CS-Prolog: A generalized unification based constraint solver. In K. Furukawa et al, editor, *Sixth Japanese Logic Programming Conference*, volume 319 of *LNCS*, pages 19–39. Springer Verlag, 1987.

79. H. Kirchner. Some extensions of rewriting. In H. Comon and J.-P. Jouannaud, editors, *Term Rewriting*, volume 909 of *LNCS*, pages 54–73. Springer Verlag, 1994.

80. D. E. Knuth, J. H. Morris, and V. R. Pratt. Fast pattern matching in strings. *SIAM Journal of Computing*, 6(2):323–350, 1977.

81. S. Lakmazaheri and W. Rasdorf. Constraint logic programming for the analysis and partial synthesis of truss structures. *Artificial Intelligence for Engineering Design, Analysis, and Manufacturing*, 3(3):157–173, 1989.

82. C. Lassez, K. McAloon, and R. Yap. Constraint logic programming and options trading. *IEEE Expert, Special Issue on Financial Software*, 2(3):42–50, 1987.

83. J.-L. Laurière. A language and a program for stating and solving combinatorial problems. *Artificial Intelligence*, 10:29–127, 1978.

84. J. Lee, H. Leung, P. Stuckey, V. Tam, and H. Won. Using stochastic methods to guide search in CLP: a preliminary report. In J. Jaffar and R. Yap, editors, *Second Asian Computing Science Conference*, number 1179 in LNCS, pages 43–52, Singapore, 1996.

85. J. Lee, H. Leung, and H. Won. Extending GENET for non-binary CSPs. In *Proceedings of the Seventh IEEE International Conference on Tools with Artificial Intelligence*, pages 338–343, 1995.

86. W. Leler. *Constraint Programming Languages: Their Specification and Generation.*

Addison–Wesley, 1988.

87. P. Lim and J. Schimpf. A conservative approach to meta-programming in constraint logic programming. In *Proceedings of the International Conference on Programming Language Implementation and Logic Programming*, number 714 in LNCS, pages 44–59. Springer Verlag, 1990.

88. P. Lim and P. Stuckey. Meta programming as constraint programming. In S. Debray and M. Hermenegildo, editors, *Logic Programming: Proceedings of the North American Conference*, pages 416–430, Austin, Texas, October 1990. MIT Press.

89. C. Lucas, G. Mitra, S. Moody, and E. Hadjiconstantinou. Tools for reformulating logical forms into zero-one mixed integer programs. Technical Report TR/03/92, Brunel, The University of West London, 1992. To appear in EJOR.

90. M. Maher. Logic semantics for a class of committed-choice programs. In J.-L. Lassez, editor, *Logic Programming: Proceedings of the 4th International Conference*, pages 858–876, Melbourne, Australia, May 1987. MIT Press.

91. G. Makanin. The problem of solvability of equations on a free semi-group. *Math. USSR Sbornik*, 32(2), 1977 (English translation AMS 1979).

92. K. Marriott and P. Stuckey. The 3 R's of optimizing constraint logic programs: Refinement, removal and reordering. In *Proc. ACM SIGPLAN Symposium on Principles of Programming Languages*, pages 334–344, Charleston, North Carolina, January 1993. ACM Press.

93. U. Martin and T. Nipkov. Boolean unification—the story so far. In C. Kirchner, editor, *Unification*. Academic Press, 1990.

94. U. Montanari. Networks of constraints: Fundamental properties and applications to picture processing. *Information Science*, 7(2):95–132, 1974.

95. I. Mozetič and C. Holzbaur. Integrating numerical and qualitative models within constraint logic programming. In V. Saraswat and K. Ueda, editors, *Logic Programming: Proceedings of the 1991 International Symposium*, pages 678–693, San Diego, California, October 1991. MIT Press.

96. L. Naish. The MU-PROLOG 3.2db reference manual. Technical report, Department of Computer Science, University of Melbourne, Victoria, Australia, 1985.

97. L. Naish. *Negation and Control in Prolog*, volume 238 of *LNCS*. Springer-Verlag, 1985.

98. W. Older and A. Vellino. Extending Prolog with constraint arithmetic on real intervals. In *Proceedings of the Canadian Conference on Electrical and Computer Engineering*, pages 14.1.1–14.1.4, 1990.

99. W. Older and A. Vellino. Constraint arithmetic on real intervals. In F. Benhamou and A. Colmerauer, editors, *Constraint Logic Programming: Selected Research*, pages 175–195. MIT Press, 1993.

100. A. Oplobedu, J. Marcovitch, and Y. Tourbier. Charme: Un langage industriel de programmation par contraintes, illustré par une application chez renault. In *Ninth International Workshop on Expert Systems and their Applications: General Conference, Volume 1*, pages 55–70, Avignon, May 1989. EC2.

101. C. Papadimitriou and K. Steiglitz. *Combinatorial Optimization: Algorithms and Complexity*. Prentice-Hall, 1982.

102. A. Podelski and P. Van Roy. The beauty and the beast algorithm: Quasi-linear incremental tests of entailment and disentailment over trees. In M. Bruynooghe,

editor, *Logic Programming: Proceedings of the 1994 International Symposium*, pages 359–376. MIT Press, 1994.

103. S. Prestwich and S. Mudambi. Improved branch and bound in constraint logic programming. In U. Montanari and F. Rossi, editors, *Constraint Programming: Proceedings of the 1st International Conference*, volume 976 of *LNCS*, pages 533–548. Springer Verlag, 1995.

104. T. Le Provost and M. Wallace. Domain-independent propagation. *Journal of Logic Programming*, 16(3/4):319–359, 1993.

105. J.-F. Puget. PECOS: A High Level Constraint Programming Language. In *Proceedings of SPICIS'92*, Singapore, September 1992.

106. J.-F. Puget. A C++ Implementation of CLP. In *Proceedings of SPICIS'94*, Singapore, November 1994.

107. J.-F. Puget and M. Leconte. Beyond the black box: Constraints as objects. In J. Lloyd, editor, *Logic Programming: Proceedings of the 1995 International Symposium*, pages 513–527. MIT Press, 1995.

108. R. Ramakhrishnan. Magic templates: a spellbinding approach to logic programs. In R. Kowalski and K. Bowen, editors, *Logic Programming: Proceedings of the 1988 Joint International Conference and Symposium*, pages 140–159, Seattle, WA, 1988. MIT Press.

109. G. Rayna. *Reduce: Software for Algebraic Computation*. Springer–Verlag, New York, 1987.

110. P. Refalo and P. Van Hentenryck. $CLP(\Re_{Lin})$ revised. In M. Maher, editor, *Logic Programming: Proceedings of the 1996 Joint International Conference and Symposium*, pages 22–36. MIT Press, 1996.

111. J. Regin. A filtering algorithm for constraints of difference in CSPs. In *Proceedings of the National Conference on Artificial Intelligence*, pages 362–367, 1994.

112. J. Robinson. A machine-oriented logic based on the resolution principle. *Journal of the ACM*, 12:23–41, 1965.

113. J. Roth. Diagnosis of automata failure: A calculus and a method. *IBM Journal of Research and Development*, 10:278–291, 1966.

114. E. Sacerdoti. *A Structure for Plans and Behaviour*. Elsevier, 1977.

115. V. Saraswat. *Concurrent Constraint Programming*. ACM Distinguished Dissertation Series. MIT Press, 1993.

116. A. Schrijver. *Theory of Linear and Integer Programming*. Wiley and Sons, 1986.

117. E. Shapiro. The family of concurrent logic programming languages. *ACM Computing Surveys*, 21(3):412–510, 1989.

118. H. Simonis and M. Dincbas. Using an extended prolog for digital circuit design. In *IEEE International Workshop on AI Applications to CAD Systems for Electronics*, pages 165–188, Munich, Germany, October 1987.

119. H. Simonis, H. Nguyen, and M. Dincbas. Verification of digital circuits using CHIP. In G. Milne, editor, *Proceedings of the IFIP WG 10.2 International Working Conference on the Fusion of Hardware Design and Verification*, Glasgow, Scotland, July 1988. IFIP, North-Holland.

120. G. Smolka. An Oz primer. Technical report, Programming Systems Lab. DFKI, Available at `http://www.ps.uni-sb.de/oz/`, 1995.

121. G. Smolka. The Oz programming model. In J. van Leeuwen, editor, *Computer Science Today*, Lecture Notes in Computer Science, vol. 1000, pages 324–343. Springer-Verlag, Berlin, 1995.

122. Z. Somogyi, F. Henderson, and T. Conway. Mercury: an efficient purely declarative logic programming language. In *Proceedings of the Australian Computer Science Conference*, pages 499–512, Glenelg, Australia, February 1995.

123. G. Steele. *The Definition and Implementation of a Computer Programming Language Based on Constraints*. PhD thesis, Dept. of Electrical Engineering and Computer Science, M.I.T., August 1980. Available as technical report MIT-AI TR 595.

124. M. Stefik. Planning with constraints (MOLGEN: Part 1). *Artificial Intelligence*, 16:111–139, 1981.

125. L. Sterling and E. Shapiro. *The Art of Prolog*. MIT Press, 1986.

126. T. Sthanusubramonian. A transformational approach to configuration design. Master's thesis, Engineering Design Research Center, Carnegie Mellon University, 1991.

127. D. Struik. *A Concise History of Mathematics*. Dover Publications, 1948.

128. P. Stuckey. Negation and constraint logic programming. *Information and Computation*, 118(1):12–33, 1995.

129. P. Stuckey and V. Tam. Models for using stochastic constraint solvers in constraint logic programming. In H. Kuchen and S. D. Swierstra, editors, *Proceedings of the International Conference on Programming Language Implementation and Logic Programming*, number 1140 in LNCS, pages 423–437, Aachen, Germany, 1996.

130. D. Subramanian and C.-S. Wang. Kinematic synthesis with configuration spaces. In D. Weld, editor, *Proc. Qualitative Reasoning*, pages 228–239, 1993.

131. K. Supowit and E. Reingold. The complexity of drawing trees nicely. *Acta Informatica*, 18:377–392, 1983.

132. G. Sussman and G. Steele. CONSTRAINTS — a language for expressing almost-hierarchical descriptions. *Artificial Intelligence*, 14(1):1–39, 1980.

133. I. Sutherland. Sketchpad: A man-machine graphical communication system. In *Proceedings of the Spring Joint Computer Conference*, pages 329–346. IFIPS, 1963.

134. E. Tsang. *Foundations of Constraint Satisfaction*. Academic Press, 1993.

135. P. Van Hentenryck. *Constraint Satisfaction in Logic Programming*. MIT Press, 1989.

136. P. Van Hentenryck and Y. Deville. The cardinality operator: A new logical connective for constraint logic programming. In F. Benhamou and A. Colmerauer, editors, *Constraint Logic Programming: Selected Research*, pages 383–403. MIT Press, 1993.

137. P. Van Hentenryck and R. Ramachandran. Backtracking without trailing in $CLP(\Re_{Lin})$. *ACM Transactions on Programming Languages and Systems*, 17(4):635–671, July 1995.

138. P. Van Hentenryck, V. Saraswat, and Y. Deville. Constraint processing in cc(FD). Technical report, unpublished manuscript, 1992.

139. P. Van Hentenryck, V. Saraswat, and Y. Deville. Design, implementation and evaluation of the constraint language `cc(fd)`. In A. Podelski, editor, *Constraint Programming: Basics and Trends*, number 910 in LNCS. Springer-Verlag, 1995.

140. M. Wallace. Practical applications of constraint programming. *Constraints*, 1:139–

168, September 1996.

141. D. Waltz. Generating semantic descriptions from drawings of scenes with shadows. In P. H. Winston, editor, *The Psychology of Computer Vision.* McGraw Hill, 1975.

142. D. H. D. Warren. An Abstract Prolog Instruction Set. Technical report, SRI International, Artificial Intelligence Center, October 1983.

143. S. Wolfram. *Mathematica: A System of Doing Mathematics by Computer.* Addison-Wesley, 1991.

144. S. Wright. *Primal-Dual Interior-Point Methods.* SIAM Press, 1996.

145. L. Wu and C. Tang. Solving the satisfiability problem by using randomized approach. *Information Processing Letters,* 41(4):187–190, 1992.

146. R. Yap. A constraint logic programming framework for constructing DNA restriction maps. *Artificial Intelligence in Medicine,* 5:447–464, 1993.

Index

Bold face page numbers are used to indicate pages with important information about the entry, e.g. the precise definition of the term or user-defined predicate, while page numbers in normal type indicate a textual reference.

!, 362–365
::, 32
$[X|Y]$, 188
[], 188
■, 144
□, 135, 141
⇒, 141
⇒*, 313
≡, 21
⌈ ⌉, 118, 303, 343
↔, 14
⌊ ⌋, 101, 118, 303, 343
≠, 102
∧, 13
| |, 60
(-> ;), 230, 365
=.., **328**
%, 216
_, 12, 134, 188

accumulator, 197, 210, 329
Ackermann's function, 410
addkey, 194, 200
alldifferent, **110**, 190, 256, 268, 269, 271
alldifferent_neq, **190**, 254
anonymous variable (_), 188
answer, 141, **142**, 147
        generated, 400

qualified, 316
answer redundant, 223, 225, 229
append, **189**, 317
arc consistency, **92**, 92–96
arc_consistent, **94**
arc_consistent_primitive, **94**, 110
arc_solv, **95**
arg, **328**
arithmetic, 299, **326**
arithmetic constraint solver
        Gauss-Jordan, 20
        incremental, 376
        incremental Gauss-Jordan, 353
        simplex, 71
arithmetic CSP, 98
artificial variable, 69
ask delay condition, 315, 428
assert, **332**
assignment problem, 266–269
association list, 193–198, 200, 204, 238, 274
        accessing a record, 193
        deleting a record, 194
        empty, 194
        inserting a record, 194
        modifying a record, 195
atom, **326**
attribute (of relation), 416

back_arc_solv, **96**
back_int_opt, **117**, 305
backtrack stack, 355
backtrack_solve, **90**
backtracking
        chronological, 89
        in evaluation, 147
        semantic, 360

backtracking goal solver, 350
    for cut, 364
    for minimization
        backtracking, 368
        retry, 366
    incremental, 355
backtracking integer optimizer, 305
base (in nucleotide), 31
basic feasible solution, **65**
basic feasible solved form, **65**, 377
basic variable, **65**
bb_int_opt, **119**
binary CSP, 88
binary search tree, 199, 200
    finding an item (find), 199
    inserting an item (insert_bst),
        200
binary tree, 198–201, 203
    layout, 203–207
    search, *see* binary search tree
    traversal (traverse), 198
Bland's anti-cycling rule, 72
blocks world, 32–33, 61
body of rule, *see* rule
bool_solve, **30**, 35
Boolean
    constraint, 27–30
    solver, **30**, 317
bottom-up, **402**
bottom-up evaluation, 395–404
    mimicking top-down, 407–412
    termination, 412–416
    with equivalence, 401
    with subsumption testing, 414
bounds consistency, **98**, 97–109
bounds propagation, 97–109
bounds_consistent, **106**
bounds_consistent_addition, **100**
bounds_consistent_inequality, **101**
bounds_consistent_primitive, 110
branch and bound, 119, 301–305
building a house, **17**, 62, 195, 196
built-ins, 179, 230, 234, 303, 308, 309,
    324–342

database, 332–338, 341
    debugging, 338–342
    examining variables, 326–332
    input/output, 324–326
butterfly, *see* options trading

c_add, **186**, 294
c_mult, **186**, 294
call, **308**, 321
call option, *see* options trading
canonical form, **73**
canonical form simplifier, 77, 412
cardinality (| |), 60
Cartesian product, 416
CCP, 427
ceiling (⌈ ⌉), 118, 303, 343
children of a tree, 22
choice, 169–174
choicepoint, **143**, 358, 362
CHR, 430
chronological backtracking, 89
clause, **332**
CLP scheme, **151**, 425
$CLP(FD)$, **152**, 251
$CLP(Tree)$, **151**
$CLP(\mathcal{R})$, **152**, 167
CNF, *see* conjunctive normal form
combining models, 270
comment (%), 216
complete solver, *see* solver
complex number, 186, 294
compound, **326**
concat, **294**, 295, 322
concatenation (::), 32, 189, 294
concurrent constraint programming,
    427
conjunction (∧), **13**, 34
conjunctive normal form, 30, 79, 436
cons, 22, 188
consistency, 91, 92
    arc, **92**, 92–96
    bounds, **98**
    generalized, 109–114
    hyper-arc, **97**, 283

node, **92**, 92–96
constant, 22
constrain and generate, 253, 275
constrained lambda calculus, 434
constraint, **13**, 11–15
    Boolean, 27–30
    complex, 110, 256–258
    disjunctive, 138
    equivalent, **14**
    primitive, **12**, 38
    projection, **54**, 53–60
    redundancy-free, **52**
    redundant, **52**, 223, 276, 278, 431
      answer redundant, 223, 225, 229
      in rule, 223
      solver redundant, 225, 226, 239
    reified, 284
    satisfaction, 18–21
    satisfiable, **14**
    sequence, 31–32, 294
    solved form, 20
    solver, *see* solver
    store, *see* constraint store
    tree, **24**, 22–27
    unsatisfiable, **14**
    user-defined, **134**, 133–137
      deterministic, 221
constraint based graphics, 442
constraint database, 391, 393
constraint domain, 12
    Real, 12
    Tree, 22
    blocks world, 32
    Boolean, 27
    sequences, 31
constraint handling rules, 430
constraint logic program, *see* program
constraint satisfaction problem, *see* CSP
constraint solver, *see* solver
constraint solving toolkits, 440
constraint store, **141**, 353, 355, 366
    saving and restoring, 358–361

contig, 31
crypto-arithmetic problem, 254, 287
CSP, **86**, 86–88, 275
    arc consistent, **92**
    arithmetic, 98
    binary, 88
    bounds consistent, **98**
    false domain, **92**
    hyper-arc consistent, **97**
    node consistent, **92**
    valuation domain, **92**
`cumulative`, **112**, 256, 278
cut (!), 362–365

data structures, 185–207
    association list, *see* association list
    list, *see* list
    record, *see* record
    tree, *see* binary tree
database
    constraint, 391, 393
    relational, *see* relational database
    spatial, 392
    temporal, 393
`debug`, **339**
debugging, 338–342
definition of a predicate, 135
delay condition, 315, 430
    ask, 315, 428
    tell, 428
`delay_until`, **315**
delaying literal, **315**
`deleteff`, **260**
`deleteffc`, 261
`delkey`, 194
`deriv`, **299**
derivation, **141**
    failed, **143**, 146
    infinite, 146, 149
    safe, **316**
      successful, 316
    selection, **154**
    simplified, **150**

step, *see* derivation step
successful, **142**, 146
derivation step, **141**
if-then-else, **230**
minimization, **180**
negative, **309**
once, **234**
selection, **154**
derivation tree, **143**, 143–151, 213
simplified, **150**, 217
determined solved form, **37**
determined variable, **36**, 37
determines, **38**, 39
deterministic, 221, 222, 230, 318
difference list, 210
disequation ($\neq$), 102, 267
solver, 310, 315, 330
DNA mapping, 31
dom, 259, 261, **327**
domain, **86**, 252
false, **92**
for relational database, 416
range, **98**
valuation, **92**
domain splitting, 264, 306
don't care non-determinism, 429, 430, 438
don't know non-determinism, 426, 428
dump, 80, 325
dynamic scheduling, 157, 313–319, 330, 343
goal-based, 315
predicate-based, 315

electric circuit, 15, 202
RLC, 201, 202
element, **114**, 256, 268–271
eliminate, **354**, 370
empty goal ($\square$), **135**, 141
$\blacksquare$, 144
empty list ([]), 188
empty_alist, **194**, 200
emptylist, 428

enabled literal, 315
entry variable, 66
equiv, **77**
equivalence ($\leftrightarrow$), **14**, 75–78
fact, **399**
projected, **58**
tester, **77**, 412
eval, **354**
evaln, **299**
evaluation, 140–143 **147**, 349–352
algorithm, 350, 355
backtracking, 147
bottom-up, 395–404
bottom-up vs top-down, 405–406
incremental solver, 352–357
top-down, 140–143
exit variable, 66

fac, **139**, 141, 143, 144, 148, 150, 154, 160, 164
fact, **135**, 398
equivalence, **399**
head normal form, **398**
simplification rules, 400
simplifier, **399**
subsumed, **414**
fail, **308**, 335, 365
failed derivation, **143**
false, **13**, 34, 141, 151, 154
false domain, **92**
find, **199**
finite failure, **146**
finite tree, **23**
first fail principle, 261, 263, 281, 291
first phase problem, 69
fixed variable, 214
floor ($\lfloor \; \rfloor$), 101, 118, 303, 343
floundered, 316
Fourier elimination, 55, 56, 60
fourier_eliminate, **57**
fourier_simplify, **57**, 60, 63
free variable, 214
fsimpl, **399**
functional languages, 433

functor, **328**

Gauss-Jordan elimination, 20, 353
gauss_jordan, **21**, 27
gauss_jordan_simplify, 73, **74**, 78
gauss_jordan_solve, **21**, 35, 159
gen_ans, **400**
gen_facts, **402**
generate and test, 256
goal, **135**
    answer to, *see* answer
    empty (□), **135**, 141
    rewriting of, **136**
goal evaluation, *see* evaluation
ground, 315, **326**
guard, 428, 430

head normal form, **398**
head of rule, *see* rule
height of tree, **23**
hierarchical constraints, 439, 442
hierarchical modelling, 201–203
higher-order predicate, 307
hyper-arc consistency, **97**, 283

if-then-else, **230**, 362, 365
iff, 271
immediate consequences, 401
imperative languages, 439
impl, **76**
implication (→), 52, 75–78
    projected, **414**
    tester, **76**
inc_arith_solve, **382**
inc_bounds_solv, **375**
inc_gauss_jordan_solve, **354**
inc_simplex, **378**
inc_solve_goal, **356**
inc_tree_solve, **371**
incomplete solver, **35**
incremental arithmetic solver, 381
incremental Gauss-Jordan solver, 353
incremental solver, **353**
    arithmetic, 381
    bounds consistency, 374

Gauss-Jordan, 353, 358, 360
    simplex, 377
    tree constraints, 371
independence of negative constraints,
    416
indomain, 259
infinite tree, **23**
insert_bst, **200**
integer, 303, **326**, 343
intended mode of usage, **215**
intersect, **333**, 339
is_compatible, **311**
isolv, **353**, 355
iteration, 174–179

Kaleidoscope, 439
Kirchhoff's Laws, 15

labeling, 253
labelling, 258–266, 271, 280
    domain splitting, 264
    value order, 259, 261
    variable order, 259, 261
labellingff, **260**
length, **261**, 262
less_than, 199, 200
library predicates, *see* built-ins
linear constraint, 19
linear expression, 19
linear inequality, 19
list, 188–193
    notation, 188
list_append, **196**
literal, **135**
    delaying, **315**
    enabled, 315
    if-then-else, **230**
    minimization, **179**
    negative, **309**
    once, **234**
literal ordering, 220
literal selection
    fair, 157
    independence, 153–157

right-to-left, 154
strategy, **316**
safe, **316**
local propagation, 35–41, 317
local_propagation_solve, **39**
lookup, 194, 200, 205, 277

map colouring problem, 86
matrix, 191
max_D, **98**
maxdomain, 259, 264, **327**
maximal bipartite matching, 112
member, **193**, 199, 259, 263, 312, 333
meta-program, 320
meta-programming, 320–323
metal plate problem, 185, 191, 444
min_D, **98**
mindomain, 259, 264, **327**
minimization, *see* optimization
minimize, **179**, 180, 204, 227, 276,
        336, 366
mode of usage, **214**, 220, 222, 227,
        232, 314
    intended, **215**
    satisfies, **214**
modelling, 15–18, 86–88, 167–180
    a function, 173
    a graph, 195
        adjacency list, 195
    choice, 169–174
    combining models, 270
    different models for a problem,
        114, 266–272
        comparing models, 269
    electric circuit, 15, 202
    hierarchical, 201–203
    iteration, 174–179
    list, *see* list
    matrix, 191
    negation, 309–313
    optimization, 179–180
    record, *see* record
    relation, 252
    symmetry, 289

vector, 294, 329
modelling language, 426
    mathematical, 443–445
modkey, 195
monotonic solver, **35**, 156
mortgage, 175, 178

N-queens problem, 86, 262
natural join, 418
ne, 310, 314, 315, 330, 343
negation, 309–313
negative subgoal, **309**
new, **402**, **414**
Newton-Raphson method, 297, 300
nil, 22, 188
nl, **325**
node, 23, 198
node consistency, **92**, 92–96
node_arc_consistent, **95**
node_consistent, **94**
node_consistent_primitive, **94**, 110
nodebug, **339**
non-parameter, 20
nonemptylist, 428
nonvar, 315, 323, **326**
normalising solver, 20
nospy, **339**
nospyall, **339**
not, **309**, 364
not_empty, **294**, 322
not_member, **190**, 309
notrace, **339**
NP-complete, 29
null, 23, 198

objective function, **61**
occurs check, 373
Ohm's Law, 15
old-fashioned marriage problem, 87,
        252, 283
once, **234**, 274, 335, 364
optimal solution, **61**
optimization, 61–72, 114–120, 179–
        180, 204, 227, 301–307, 445

implementation, 336, 366–369
integer, 114–120
   backtracking, **117**, 368
   branch and bound, **119**, 301–305
   retry, **115**, 366
optimistic partitioning, 306
problem, **61**, 64, 179
simplex, **67**
options trading, 170–174, 210
   butterfly, 172, 174, 180
   call option, 170
   put option, 170
   straddle, 180
Oz, 434

`parallel_resistors`, **134**, 135, 136
parameter, 20, 65
partial solution, **54**, 134
pivoting, 66
`predecessors`, **196**, 234, 277
predicate, **134**
   definition of, 135
   higher-order, 307
preferred valuation, **61**
primitive constraint, **12**, 38
primitives, **15**, 34, 35
principle of least commitment, 264
probabilistic algorithm, 30
problem
   NP-complete, 29
   optimization, *see* optimization
   satisfaction, **18**
   solution, **18**
process view of CLP, 427
product, 418
program, **135**
program consequences, 401
projected equivalence, **58**
projected implication, **414**
projecting simplifier, **60**
projection, **54**, 53–60
   for relational databases, 417
   of constraint, **54**

propagation
   bounds, 97–109
   local, 35–41
propagation rules, 99–105
   for minimum, 102
   for addition, 99
   for disequations, 102
   for multiplication, 103, 104
put option, *see* options trading

qualified answer, 316
query
   on database, 418
query transformation, 410

range, for finite domains, **98**
`read`, **324**
Real, 12, 152
`real_opt`, 118
record, 186–188, 202
recursion, 139, 175, 189, 206, 220
redundancy, **52**
redundancy-free simplifier, **60**
reified constraint, 284
relation, 169–170, 416
relational database, 170, 416–421
   attribute, 416
   domain, 416
   natural join, 418
   product, 418
   projection, 417
   query, 418
   relation, 416
   relational expression, 418
   selection, 418
   union, 417
relational expression, 418
renaming, **34**, 136, 141, 154
   application of, 34, 136
`retract`, **333**
retry integer optimization, **115**
`retry_int_opt`, **115**, 366
rewrite rules, *see* term rewriting
rewriting of goal, *see* goal, 141, 154

river crossing problem, 168
rule, 133, 134, **135**, 137–140
    body of, **135**
    head of, **135**
    recursive, 139, 198
rule ordering, 220

same, **402**
SAT, 29
satisfaction problem, **18**
satisfiable, **14**
satisfiable, **38**, 39, 89, 92
scheduling, 251, 272–281, 431–433
search space, **146**
seesaw problem, 257, 265, 289
selected literal, **154**
selection, 418
selection derivation, 316
semantic backtracking, 360
sequence constraint, 31–32, 294
set based solver, **35**, 154
shadow of space, 55
simpl, **58**, 142, 149, 150
simple_solve_goal, **350**
simplex algorithm, **67**, 63–72, 376
    artificial variable, 69
    basic feasible solution, **65**
    basic feasible solved form, **65**
    basic variable, **65**
    Bland's rule, 72
    entry variable, 66
    exit variable, 66
    first phase problem, 69
    form of constraints, **64**
    incremental, 377
    pivoting, 66
    slack variable, 65
    solver, **71**, 377
simplex_opt, **68**
simplex_solve, **72**
simplification, 51–60
simplified derivation, **150**
simplified derivation tree, **150**, 217
simplified state, **150**

simplifier, **58**, 57–60, 151
    canonical form, **73**, 72–74, 77, 412
    properties, 60
        projecting, **60**, 152
        redundancy-free, **60**
        weakly projecting, **60**, 152
slack variable, 65
smm, **4**, **254**, 260
smuggler's knapsack problem, 101, 108, 114, 115, 117, 252, 304
solution, **14**
    basic feasible, 65
    of state or goal, **180**
    optimal, **61**
    partial, **54**, 134
    problem, **18**
solv, **34**, 141, 154
solved form, **20**
    basic feasible, **65**
    determined, 37
solver, 18, **34**, 33–35, 151
    arc consistency, 281
    backtracking, 89, 96
    Boolean, 30, 317
    bounds consistency, 281, 374
        complete, 108
        incomplete, 107
    branch and bound, 267
    complete, **35**, 89, 96, 253
    finite domain, 267
        backtracking, 89
        bounds consistency, 107, 108
        node and arc consistency, 95, 96
    Gauss-Jordan, 21, 353
    incomplete, 30, **35**, 95, 225, 252, 381
    incremental, *see* incremental solver
    local propagation, **38**, 317
    node and arc consistency
        complete, 96
        incomplete, 95
    normalising, 20, 53

properties, 33–35
   monotonic, **35**, 156
   set based, **35**, 154
   variable name independent, **35**, 152
  simplex, **71**
  tree constraints, 25, 371
  well-behaved, **35**, 141, 152
solver redundant, 225, 226, 239
spatial database, 392
spy, **339**
spypoint, 339
state, **141**
  critical, **150**
  fail, **142**, 144
  success, **142**, 144
store, *see* constraint store
straddle, *see* options trading
subsumed
  fact, **414**
successful derivation, **142**, 146
symbolic algebra package, 445–446
syntactic identity ($\equiv$), 21
syntactic object, 136

tell delay condition, 428
temporal database, 393
term, **24**
term equation, **24**
term rewriting, 436
  augmented, 436
  constrained, 438
time stamping, 358
top-down evaluation, 397
trace, **339**
trailing, 358
traverse, **198**, 205
Tree, 22, 151, 152
tree, **22**
  binary, *see* binary tree
  children of, **22**
  constraint, 22, **24**
  constructor, **22**, 188
  finite, 23

  height, **23**
  infinite, 23
tree_simplify, 59, **59**, 60, 73, 151
tree_solve, **26**, 35, 151
true, **13**, 34
true, **232**

underscore (_), 12, 134, 188
unify, **26**, 27, 53, 59, 370
union, 417
unknown, 30, **34**, 252
unsatisfiable, **14**
user-defined constraint, *see* constraint

valuation, **14**, 33
  extension, **54**
  preferred, **61**
valuation domain, **92**
var, **326**
variable, 11
  anonymous, 188
  artificial, 69
  basic, 65
  Boolean, 267
  determined, **36**, 37
  fixed, 214
  free, 214
  non-parameter, 20
  parameter, 20, 65
  procedural, 177
  slack, 65
variable name independent solver, **35**, 152
variant, **34**, 35, 136
vars, **14**
vector, 294, 296

weakly projecting simplifier, **60**
well-behaved solver, **35**, 141, 152
write, **325**